Life in
Black
and
White

Life in
Black AND White

*Family and
Community in the
Slave South*

Brenda E. Stevenson

New York   Oxford

OXFORD UNIVERSITY PRESS

1996

Oxford University Press

Oxford   New York
Athens   Auckland   Bangkok   Bombay
Calcutta   Cape Town   Dar es Salaam   Delhi
Florence   Hong Kong   Istanbul   Karachi
Kuala Lumpur   Madras   Madrid   Melbourne
Mexico City   Nairobi   Paris   Singapore
Taipei   Tokyo   Toronto

and associated companies in
Berlin   Ibadan

Copyright © 1996 by Brenda E. Stevenson

Published by Oxford University Press, Inc.,
198 Madison Avenue, New York, New York 10016

Oxford is a registered trademark of Oxford University Press

Library of Congress Cataloging-in-Publication Data
Stevenson, Brenda E.
Life in black and white : family and community
in the slave South / Brenda E. Stevenson.
p. cm.   Includes bibliographical references and index.
ISBN 0-19-509536-7
1. Loudoun Country (Va.)—Social conditions.
2. Family—Virginia—Loudoun County—History—19th century.
3. Slavery—Virginia—Loudoun County—History—19th century.
I. Title.
HN79.V82L687   1996
306.8'09755'28—dc20   95-17359

9 8 7 6 5 4 3 2 1

Printed in the United States of America
on acid-free paper

This book is dedicated to
the first historian of the southern family I had the honor of
knowing and loving,

Emma Gerald Stevenson, 1926–1990

PREFACE

We are getting on here, in all respects, very much as usual. You will find, when you come back, but little change, except in the natural progress of man and events—death—marriages—their consequences—and the intermediate steps.

Robert Y. Conrad, 1851

Writing to his son Powell in 1851, Robert Conrad quickly addressed the subject of domestic activity within their family and neighborhood, moving briskly on to more pressing issues. Powell was a new student at the University of Virginia and his father had many instructions. Mr. Conrad lectured his son on what subjects to take, how to impress his professors, which friendships to and not to pursue, what clothing to buy, and proper health habits. Despite his brief survey of family matters in this particular letter, however, Robert Conrad—the quintessential southern public personae in the shape of planter, lawyer, state assemblyman and slaveholder—was, above all else, a family man—a husband and a father. Indeed, it was Conrad's dedication to his private life, to his wife Betty and their nine children, that was the central motivating force of his adult life.[1]

Twenty-two years earlier in December 1829, Robert Conrad, then an ambitious young lawyer with powerful political connections, married Elizabeth Whiting Powell, the youngest daughter of Major Burr Powell, a cornerstone of the local gentry. The large wedding, held at the bride's home, was a festive event that brought together friends and family members in a celebration that lasted several days. The year had been an important one for the Powell and Conrad families and the wedding was an especially joyous event for both. The private lives of other Loudoun folk in 1829 too were marked with milestones, but they had not been such happy ones.[2]

At about the same time that Betty and Robert were marrying in Middleburg, several members of another family in Leesburg also were preparing for a new life. Jesse Lucas, his wife Amelia, and their four children, along with three other adult members of the Lucas clan, left their Loudoun home in December 1829 to travel to the seaport town of Norfolk. There the Lucases and forty other free people of color boarded a ship on their way to Monrovia on the west coast of Africa. With growing white antagonism toward free blacks, hundreds, like members of the Lucas family, left Virginia for Liberia. Thousands more relocated elsewhere in the United States. The southern community which had been so proud and celebratory of the Powell and Conrad families eagerly discarded the Lucases amid claims of black racial inferiority and degeneracy. Free blacks hoped that their migration to Africa would give them a chance to live prosperous, free lives in the foreign communities that they created; communities full of opportunities for their families not only to survive, but to thrive in ways that were impossible even to anticipate in the South.[3]

George Shover, his wife Susannah, and their children also left Loudoun in 1829. Like so many Virginia yeomen, the Shovers looked to the West for the promise of a new and successful life. Their eighteenth-century ancestors had helped to establish the German community of Lovettsville in Loudoun. There, they prospered and passed on their property and their dreams to their children. During the early 1820s, George Shover too had been determined to make a comfortable life for his family. But a sagging local economy soured his investment choices. Emigration must have seemed their most reasonable choice as they solemnly faced bankruptcy. The Shovers eventually settled in a frontier German community in Ohio, perhaps with some of the same excited anticipation that their ancestors had held almost a century earlier when they first arrived in Loudoun.[4]

The black slaves who left the county in 1829 as part of the domestic slave trade had no say as to their final destinations or the fate of their marriages and families. Unlike whites and free people of color, county slaves did not leave Loudoun in order to secure their family's prosperity or to find more welcoming communities. Their legacy of involuntary exodus was overwhelmingly destructive to their marriages, kin groups, and communities. On October 30, 1829, for example, William Kish shipped ten slaves he had purchased in Loudoun to New Orleans aboard the *United States*; all were male and all were at least seventeen years old. The constant withdrawal of men from slave families had a decided effect on slave marriage and family life. Yet men were not the only slaves sold away from their kin. An 1829 letter from a concerned county resident to the *Genius of Universal Emancipation* described some of the tragic consequences of the sale of local slaves to the Deep South. The anonymous author described an incident involving the sale of Hillsboro slaves to a long-distance trader: although two of the men eventually escaped, one woman in the group committed suicide rather than face permanent separation from her Loudoun family and friends. By 1829, and increasingly so in the decades which followed, females like this Hillsboro slave woman were a vital part of the intra- and interstate slave trade. Their growing absence eroded one of the last vestiges of slave family stability—operative matrifocal kin groups.[5]

This study begins in and sometimes returns briefly to the colonial era, but is centered on Virginians who lived during the decades between the American Revolution and Civil War. It describes many of the familial and communal ideals, relations, and experiences of the white elite, their slaves, free blacks, and, to a lesser extent, yeoman farmers and other middling and poorer folk in the Upper South. While *Life in Black and White* is not organized strictly as a comparative study, there is enough comparable information to allow some broad conclusions about important similarities and differences and the origins of both in the southern familial experience.

The residents of Loudoun County, located in the northern piedmont region of Virginia, are the central characters. Sharing as they did kinship, economic ties, cultural propensities, and political quarrels with residents of neighboring counties, this study draws broadly on informational sources descriptive of their extended families, friends, and peers who lived nearby, but not necessarily in Loudoun. In this sense, *Life in Black and White* is regional in orientation, with Loudoun as its principal focus.[6]

Loudoun County is both an exceptional and typical Upper South site. Within its borders lived important branches of some of the South's most illustrious and influential families, including the Carters, Byrds, Harrisons, Janneys, Lees, Masons, Mercers, Peytons, and Powells. Their presence alone guaranteed Loudoun's role in important state and national events. During the War of 1812, for example, President James Madison and his Secretary of State, James Monroe, fearful that the British would gain control of the nation's capital, temporarily moved to Loudoun. They brought with them important state documents, including the Declaration of Independence and the Constitution, which they hid first at the courthouse in Leesburg and then at the Bentley's "Rokeby" estate. It was also at Monroe's Loudoun's plantation, "Oak Hill," that he wrote his famous "Doctrine" of 1823 and entertained the Marquis de Lafayette in 1825.[7] There also were more controversial episodes in Loudoun's history which both lent it national attention and suggested its strong ties with regional concerns.

Pre-Civil War Loudoun was a slave society. From its inception, slavery had been a vital part of the county's economy, society, and culture. As such, the institution of slavery was at the center of countywide political debates that mirrored heated national conflicts. Loudoun, for example, was the birthplace of the celebrated fugitive slave Daniel Dangerfield who escaped to freedom in 1853, placing the county in the middle of the national controversy about fugitive slave legislation. The county's northern boundary also was only a stone's throw away from Harpers Ferry, the site of John Brown's infamous 1859 raid. It was, in fact, the locally prominent jurist and legislator Robert Conrad to whom Brown first appealed for legal counsel. Finally, it was a Loudouner, John Janney, who served as chairman of the Virginia state convention that voted for secession from the Union in April 1861.[8]

It is not just the exceptional and illustrious in Loudoun's history, however, that makes it a practical research site for this kind of study. Loudoun's diverse population was derived from various African, European, and Native American groups of numerous religious beliefs, political ideals, social customs, and other distinguishing cultural traits. They also represented decided "tidewater" and "upcountry" factions. This variety of peoples and cultures—some competing, others complementary—both complicated racial and class allegiances and provided a panorama of familial and community perspectives that was not unusual in the pre-Civil War South. Beneath the cumbersome image of the "Solid South," there is the real challenge of the region's great diversity apparent even in discrete, rural counties like Loudoun.

Topics explored in *Life in Black and White* are not new to southern history or the history of southern slave societies. The general excellence of the work of Ann Malone, Herbert Gutman, John Blassingame, Eugene Genovese, Cheryll Ann Cody, Allan Kulikoff, and Deborah White on the slave family; that of Suzanne Lebsock, James Roark, Michael Johnson, Loren Schweringer, and Reginald Butler descriptive of the domestic relationships of southern free blacks; the contributions of Anne Scott, Catherine Clinton, Jean Friedman, Elizabeth Fox-Genovese, Victoria Bynum, and Stephanie McCurry on women and family in the antebellum South; and the achievements of scholars like Daniel Blake Smith, Jane Turner Censer, Bertram Wyatt-Brown, and Orville Burton, who have written imaginatively on various aspects of the southern family of the past, signified a coming of age of southern social history during the 1970s and 1980s.[9] The investigation of family and community in the Upper South presented here both supplements and challenges these impressive traditions.

Building on central ideals and experiences which scholars have established as common ground, the study refines some older theses, while arguing the legitimacy of more original conclusions. The overriding theme of the book, summarized in its title, is that in a slave society in which one's race virtually defined one's status as slave or free, family and community differed profoundly for black and white people. So too did their perceptions of each other's lives. Blacks and whites in the old South rarely understood the contours of the other's life— even the significance of some of the most profoundly important aspects of one's existence eluded the comprehension of the other. This expansive cultural gap, and the oppressive social system which held it in place, was a constant source of suspicion, disappointment, and dismissal of the one by the other.

This, of course, is the primary lesson in southern history—race has always defined and differentiated southern life in fundamental ways. Simply put, easily accepted. Yet the exact junctures of similarity and difference, of acceptance and rejection, between black and white life have proven to be more elusive. This study explores these junctures, and consequently the truism exploited in the book's title, by examining in intricate detail the numerous spheres of eighteenth- and nineteenth-century southern community and family life for African—and European—Americans.

The study emerges, not surprisingly, from two fronts. Part I is an analysis of white courtship, marriage, childrearing, and divorce, linking these social phenomena to issues of class, ethnicity, property, honor, and community control. Part II considers slave and free black life as it suggests a provocative reassessment of African American family structure and relations. Of particular concern are black residency patterns, diverse marriage arrangements, the practical and cultural origins of familial structure and expression, external pressures on their private lives, and significant internal conflicts.

Several significant issues both underlie and direct *Life in Black and White*. Slavery, of course, is an essential topic in any discussion of a slave society. Throughout it receives much critical attention, both as a separate phenomenon and particularly as part and parcel of the construction and exploitation of racial difference. The study, however, turns on the issue of race.

The race of slaves, free blacks, planters, and yeomen influenced their choices of social and domestic organization and fostered important differences between them. Race, in fact, was such an important dimension of one's life and identity in the slave South that other significant social variables like class, culture, ethnicity, and gender were as much embedded in "race" as they were distinctive operatives. Monogamous marriage, patriarchal privilege, and a nuclear-core household clearly composed the foundation of southern white families across class, cultural, and ethnic lines. The racial and, therefore, cultural and situational differences of free people of color and slaves, however, produced a vastly different picture of family life. The most important characteristics of their families and domestic households were the overarching importance of the extended family and the constancy of variety—variety in household composition, marital relationship, longevity, and leadership. Poverty, legally sanctioned instability, and growing white hostility meant that free men and women who were black continuously had to rely on alternative familial and marital styles. Despite the tendency among the upwardly mobile of their community to embrace monogamous marriage and patriarchy, diverse domestic styles, the extended family, and a growing number of matrifocal families were the southern free person of color's most common familial experiences.

Blacks who were slaves endured similar, albeit more harsh, domestic lives. The sale and rental of men, and increasingly women and children, without family members that was so prominent in the Upper South had lasting and profound effect. So too did the labor concerns of owners who, throughout the eighteenth and nineteenth centuries, often separated slave families among various farms or other properties, creating a tremendous number of "abroad" marriages and physically "absent" fathers and husbands even among "monogamous" marriages and "nuclear" families. Enslaved blacks' cultural concerns also could have had great impact on their marital styles and living arrangements. Contrary to the assertions of Herbert Gutman, Eugene Genovese, John Blassingame, Jacqueline Jones, Deborah White, and, most recently, Ann Malone, most slave children in Virginia did not grow up in two-parent homes; the slave man's roles as father and husband were much diminished; and slaves indicated their desire for a variety of marital and domestic styles, not just a nuclear family structure. Clearly, race and its affiliated cultural considerations had tremendous differentiating influence on southern community and family life.

So too did gender and class, variables which, both individually and as a part of one's racial distinctiveness, reveal much of the South's social complexity. Companionability increasingly influenced one's choice for a spouse in European American marriages and probably those of free people of color. But such a factor is much less clear among slaves. Moreover, class and cultural compatibility remained significant factors among both races and across gender lines. Likewise, neither one's class nor gender translated into different ideals of gendered behavioral patterns in the white community, although ethnicity and religion may have; and one's class certainly affected the gap between ideal and actual gendered behavior. Among African Americans, class, culture, and legal status informed both ideals and realities of male and female spheres of activity. But amidst all this diversity and conditions, there were some general rules of thumb. In free nuclear families, most women provided domestic labor, but existed as the dependents of men. Free white men routinely were their families' breadwinners. Relatedly, in most families, regardless of class, race, or condition, men who had physical or emotional access to their families wielded some manner of control even if they did not provide much financial attention or other kinds of traditional patriarchal "protection."

The personal histories of the Powells, Lucases, Shovers, local slaves and others portrayed in *Life in Black and White,* therefore, not only depict the haunting differences that their race, culture, class, and gender imposed on them. They also are a testament to their connection and commonality as southerners. One important bond across these tightly drawn lines of difference was a profound belief that a good family life was vital to one's identity, survival, and happiness. Family, they all agreed, lent organization and structure to their lives and resources; it implied comfort and peace in a southern world that, more often than not, could be harsh, unpredictable, or even violent. Thus Robert Conrad's succinct definition of family, that it was the arena where the most natural "progress" of man and womankind—birth, life, and death—took on a legitimacy that guaranteed one's humanity, is an appropriate one for any southerner. Men and women of the South of all shades and status constantly sought and vigilantly protected the most crucial source of their humanity, their families.

Family may have been at the center of one's connection to humanity, but community regularly competed for that privileged place. Community in the Old South regulated group behavior and determined one's social position. Thus the primacy of the community in the face of individual, spousal, and familial concerns is argued throughout *Life in Black and White*.

The larger southern community was hierarchical. Several variables explored here, including race, class, gender, and culture, formed the basis of the South's stratification and traditionally placed planter status (Caucasian, wealthy, male) at its pinnacle. As such, planter hegemony was not just a political or economic phenomenon in the slave South. It also held a strong grasp on the region's social ideology and practice. For one's family to develop outside the context and confines of the southern patriarchy, therefore, problematized and diversified that development. Thus while everyone agreed that family was precious, societal inequities linked to the community's stratification dictated that a family's resources often were limited. Likewise, the hierarchy of the larger southern community assigned differentiating value to one's family according to their racial, cultural, or class affiliation. Thus while *Life in Black and White* overwhelmingly affirms that "family" was a social concept of great significance to southerners, it also substantiates that community could threaten family, particularly when it came into conflict with the South's community ethos or hierarchy.

I especially would like to thank and recognize the years of dedicated mentorship of John W. Blassingame and Nancy F. Cott.

The completion of this work would not have been possible without the generous support of several funding institutions, mentors, and associates. Prominent among the institutions which supported research and writing efforts are: the Yale Bush Center in Child Development and Public Policy; the Yale Graduate School; the Mellon Foundation; the University of Texas at Austin; the Chancellor's Office at the University of California, Los Angeles; the Chancellor's Office at the University of California, Berkeley; and in particular the Association of American University Women and the Virginia Foundation for the Humanities and Public Policy.

I extend a heartfelt thanks to James H. Cones III, Beverly J. Stevenson-Harris, James W. Stevenson, Sheldon Meyer, Mary Ryan, Leon Litwack, Nell Painter, Jacqueline Jones, Ellen DuBois, Regina Morantz-Sánchez, Darlene Clark Hine, Catherine Clinton, Barry Gaspar, Rosalyn Terborg-Penn, Marie-Josée Cerol, Lersie Marrero, the late Sylvia Boone, the late José Vigo, and Alice Jackson Stuart for their guidance, kind words, and support. I also would like to thank Daina L. Ramey, Rosia Ivey, Joan Johnson, Natalia Molina, Carla Harris, and Erika Harris for their research assistance and especially the staff of the Virginia Historical Society for their invaluable service rendered during the fifteen months spent conducting research in their facility.

CONTENTS

I

Marriage, Family,
and the Loudoun
White Community

Introduction

William Yonson was not alone when he crept into his bedroom that late December night in 1847. Accompanied by four of his Leesburg neighbors and armed against the darkness with just a dim lantern, he soon discovered the answers to questions that he had agonized over for weeks. There, lying in bed with his wife Eliza Jane, was her lover William Smith.[1]

The presence of four "witnesses," representatives of the local patriarchy, must have made the moment particularly embarrassing. But their inclusion at the scene was necessary for later they would swear to all they had seen that night, making it possible for William to receive a divorce.

Yonson, an inventor and manufacturer of wheat threshing machines, did not have the kind of prestige or power that the county's landed gentry had been able to cultivate over the generations. But he did have certain rights as a man and as a husband. He especially had the right to his wife's sexual loyalty. He knew it and so did the other men. That he chose to defend those rights through a legal procedure that ended in divorce, rather than the honorable duel so romanticized in southern lore,[2] was a sign of changing times, especially definitions of civility and the state's role in private affairs. It was not, however, a sign of changing values.

The themes which emerge from the Yonson divorce case are not novel ones, but they remain significant to any discussion of pre-Civil War southern family and community. Honor, patriarchal rights, and female sexual purity and exclusivity were all weighty topics that southern men and women wrestled with most of their lives. They all embodied issues which helped to define the sociocultural ideology of white southerners living in a slave society.

William Yonson acted out of many concerns that evening, not the least of which was his determination to retain male honor within his white community. Indeed, his willingness to publicly disclose and admonish Eliza Jane's adultery was a good first step in demonstrating his southern manhood. It proved that he could still *act*—a vital tenet of white masculinity—and that he could *act honorably*. Rumor and innuendo, his wife's brazen infidelity—they all threatened to undermine his attempts to embody the traits of manliness that were so vital to his status and identity as a white man in the slave South.

While there were many levels to southern slave societies, race defined the most fundamental divisions. White men, even poor white men, had control of their domestic lives and the people in them. That control set them apart, profoundly, from black men who legally and customarily had little command over any aspect of their public or private lives. Likewise, southern white women's experiences differed from those of black women. White women exercised at least nominal control of their sexual organs and desires, a control that marital duty bound them to relinquish to their husbands. Black women on the other hand, especially slave women, were thought to have no sexual discipline and, as property, no dominion over their sexual organs. They had no rights of sexual exclusivity to retain or to yield to their husbands.

Taken together, the designs of white manhood and womanhood, expressed through acts of male sexual dominion over (white and black) female sexual expression and exclusivity, undergirded much of the racial boundary between family and community life in the slave South. The adultery of Eliza Jane Yonson and William Smith challenged this racialist iconography. Is it little wonder then that the Yonsons' white community took extreme interest in their marital relationship?

The male "witnesses" agreed to go with Yonson that night partly out of a titillated curiosity, but also out of their responsibility as respectable members of the local patriarchy to enforce standards of white community morality. It was their duty to expose the dishonor of William Smith and Eliza Jane Yonson in order to restore honor to Mr. Yonson and their community. After a reasonable period of time, the young inventor could obtain a new wife who would exemplify community-sanctioned feminine virtues of sexual discipline and duty—a wife who would allow him to regain the kind of partriarchal control of his home that was expected of white men.

But there was more to the witnesses' behavior than just protecting community codes of sexual morality and allowing Mr. Yonson to regain his personal honor. If left unaddressed, William Smith's decision to "take" another man's wife, in the husband's bed no less, could have undermined longstanding oaths of white male solidarity and loyalty that were part of their patriarchal ethos of public accountability and honor. Smith's behavior was unforgivable, even given the double sexual standards of the day, because through his compromise of his neighbor's rights as a husband and as a member of the patriarchy, he had compromised all of them and the concept of patriarchal rights itself.[3]

The price that Eliza Jane paid for her infidelity, not surprisingly, surpassed the temporary disgrace her lover bore. A scorned woman, she experienced public shaming, banishment (she made a hasty retreat to her family in Pennsylvania) and the loss of her only child, a daughter whom she was forced to leave with her husband. Without husband, child, or reputation, there was little left for her in the small southern community. In their eyes, her immorality had profoundly impaired her worth as a white woman. But her worth had not been lost in vain. Mrs. Yonson's public punishment and the cooperation the other men in the community offered her husband revitalized community-sanctioned marital and sexual mores while bolstering male solidarity and patriarchy. This patriarchy, symbolized so well in the roles that Yonson, his male neighbors, and the state legislature played in this unfortunate domestic episode, stood steadfast as a righteous guardian of white marriage, family, and community (to say nothing of the patriarchy itself) in the slave South. Here, as elsewhere in the public record of the era, the women—Mrs. Yonson and the wives and female kin of the other men—remain silent, absent from the documents descriptive of this event. Their silence and invisibility in the face of patriarchal authority sum up much about their public lives and private power in this community.[4]

Cognizant that marriage and family wove together the disparate threads of their individual and communal existence, white southerners (in the form of a righteous, hierarchial community) collectively imposed certain ideals of family life on one another, severely chastising those whose actions betrayed a disregard for these values. In these mostly rural, interdependent farming communities, family business often meant community business. Family, friends, and neighbors, like those of William and Eliza Jane Yonson, rarely hesitated to interfere in someone's personal affairs when communal values seemed at risk.

Loudouners' ideal of public accountability as members of families and communities did not vary much from those of other white southerners. Neither did their social credo that everyone should marry and bear and rear children; nor their ideal that duty, compatibility, honesty, and sometimes love bred honor in a marriage. Everyone was aware of the negative stigma of the unattached adult. Authors of popular, didactic literature were only part of the societal influence which emphasized the importance of marriage. Poems and brief essays ridiculing or pitying elderly bachelors and spinsters drove home the point. The first issue of Richmond's *American Gleaner and Virginia Magazine* in 1807, for example, included a typical poem which described elderly bachelors as unattractive, lonely men who lived by themselves with only pets to offer them solace in their old age. "What sullen old mortal is that," the author queried, "Who sits in his hut all alone,/Excepting his dog and his cat,/That grey with their master have grown." Spinsters received like literary treatment for their "misfortunes." They only could expect, experts warned, being "severed from the rest of the human race" with just the "feline family" to offer them "treacherous endearments or candid scratches."[5]

With few exceptions, white southerners of every class and culture relied on notions of God-ordained or "natural" and distinctive traits of the sexes—weak and strong; dependent and aggressive; intelligent and emotional; selfless and pragmatic—to prescribe "complementary" gendered roles in one's marriage, family, and community. These ideals were easier for the South's middle and upper classes to affect, but surprisingly few pitched alternative ideals. The majority of yeoman, artisans, and the poor felt subtle pressure to accept, or at least mimic, the marital and familial structures and behavior that their "betters" emulated. But these institutions and attitudes also were important standards in their cultures and communities. Not even a white southerner's ethnic or religious distinction seemed to make much difference; and parents painstakingly reared their children to respect these conventions.

The nuances of the region's economy had as much affect on, or was as much affected by, the traditional roles that southern society prescribed for free men and women within their families and communities as any other sphere of the society. It was nearly impossible, for example, for white women not to be financially dependent on men since Loudoun, like most of the South, held virtually no economic avenues for women. Females held the class status of their fathers or husbands and could actively change it only through marriage or remarriage. The lack of occupational opportunities meant that working women were the poorest of Loudoun's white community, especially single working mothers. But even upper-class married women usually did not have domestic power independent from what their husbands bestowed on them. Popular notions of "separate" spheres where males and females reigned according to their "natural" abilities did not suggest any kind of gender equality. Men routinely held dominion over woman's "domain" because they controlled its purse.

Holding economic power within one's household, however, did not guarantee marital bliss, as William Yonson and many of his male contemporaries discovered. Men may have controlled the household budget and all that that implied, but women like Eliza Jane still had the power to withdraw from a man sexually and emotionally. What many men and women soon came to understand was that marriage and family were challenging commitments with sometimes devastating consequences. Even in the happiest of marriages, a husband occasionally felt pressure to be both emotionally and physically attentive to his family while his financial duties robbed him of the time or affinity to do so. Likewise, most brides soon learned that the physical and emotional demands on "good" wives and mothers, particularly in the face of being treated like childish dependents, left much to be desired. The financial pressures middling and poorer husbands and wives faced predictably worsened their situation. It is amazing that most remained loyal to and relatively pleased with the instititution.

That most couples remained united suggests the homogeneity of marital and familial ideals, but not necessarily experiences, that whites shared across a heterogenous community fractured by cultural and socioecomic differences. The elite, touting distinguished family names such as Mason, Carter, Lee, Powell, Mercer, Fitzhugh, and Tayloe, were landed slaveholders who usually had estates in the eastern and southern portions of the county. The lifestyle that they created, symbolized by the beauty and majesty of their mansion homes, was the stuff that inspired as much the myth of southern grandeur as the reality of a powerful patriarchy set atop the South's social hierarchy.

Their wealth, superior education, and leadership in the Church of England guaranteed them economic power, social prominence, and political advantage anywhere in Virginia. They vied for positions of community leadership which the colonial government provided in the way of appointments to key legislative, judicial, law-enforcement, and church offices. They likewise had tremendous influence on the county's economy since they owned most of the land and the labor needed to develop it. Yet the planter class faced continuous challenges, culturally and politically, from a much larger group of persons who did not wholeheartedly accept their social vision or political leadership.

To the west and north of the county's plantation district, men and women of more modest means and diverse ethnicity and culture created yeoman farmer and artisan communities. From the 1730s on through the Revolution, a flow of Quakers, Germans, Scotch-Irish, Irish, and Welsh settled in Loudoun. Most came in families and sometimes clusters of families, working hard to develop interdependent communities of family farms and workshops and to safeguard their cultural difference. Many preferred to reach out across broad geographic distances to other communities of like culture or ethnicity rather than to succumb to the assimilative process akin to building a white homogeneous community in Loudoun.

Clearly to be "white" meant something in a society where to be black meant to be enslaved. The significance of that identity deepened over time as abolitionist rhetoricians and proto southern nationalists both vied to create the image of a solid, proslavery South. But the racial polarity endemic to the slave South was only one part of the formula. It also meant something to be German or Irish or Quaker. It meant as much to be a small farmer or mechanic struggling against the power and prestige of the privileged planter. These kinds of ethnic, religious, and class identities colored the reality of "whiteness" and continuously challenged white solidarity. The seeds of division came to fruition soon enough. After years of political bickering between planters and ethnically diverse yeoman, the state divided Loudoun in 1798. Many members of the planter elite, centered in the county's southeast, were pleased to find themselves no longer residents of Loudoun, but of neighboring Fairfax, a county where the landed gentry traditionally held overriding political power.

This literal territorial division was profoundly symbolic of the kind of conflict and difference that Loudoun's white community embodied. What homogeneity of domestic culture and familial ideology among whites of various ethnicity, class, and culture that actually did exist was in part responsible for the limited white solidarity that was operative. Their shared attitudes and actions as family men and women helped to link together the landed gentry and the landless poor, the Quaker antislavery activist and the Anglican proslavery advocate, the German artisan and the Scotch-Irish farmer. Yet Loudoun never could boast that it was truly a "solid" white society.

I

The White Community:
Patterns of Settlement,
Development, and Conflict

Europeans first began to settle the northern Virginia wilderness that was to become Loudoun County during the 1720s and 1730s. Coming over the hills from the east and the north, most probably were not especially struck by the primeval beauty of the Virginia piedmont. After all, much of Virginia and the other colonies still were untouched by the kind of "civilization" and its costs that Europeans and their slaves would bring in the next generations. Still the place must have been beautiful. Covered with crisp, dark forests of pine, oak, sugar maple, walnut, and sycamore, dotted by grasslands and rolling hills, it was crisscrossed by numerous rivers and streams overrun with fish, swans and other waterfowl, fur-bearing otters and beavers. So plentiful were the wild geese on the Potomac River above the falls that indigenous peoples traded in goose feathers and named the waterway Cohongaroton—or Goose River—and the name stuck. Four hill ranges, including the breathtaking Blue Ridge Mountains, encased numerous valleys. Magnificent birds passed through the skies. Buffalo grazed the grasslands. Deer and elk darted in and out; bears and wolves were in abundance.

The sounds and smells of the forest were everywhere, seemingly little disturbed by the earliest dwellers who had been present since the Paleolithic era. Among the most populous were the Algonquin, who built stationary farming communities; the Manahoacs or Piedmonts, who had a semi-nomadic lifestyle they supported by hunting, fishing, and gathering; and the Susquehannocks, a people who early Englishmen, struck by their large size, physical beauty, and obvious ability as warriors, described as "the most noble and heroic nation . . . that dwelt upon the confines of America."[1]

The earliest European settlers complained bitterly of the "Indian menace," but local native peoples hardly provided a unified threat. Throughout the seventeenth century, war parties from the powerful Five Nations of Iroquois passed through this part of Virginia in their attempt to establish sovereignty all along the eastern seaboard They eventually forced the most populous of the local people, the Piedmonts, to leave, creating a vast hunting reserve for themselves. They also finally subdued the Susquehannocks. And while representatives of other Indian groups undoubtedly traveled the region, few dared to linger long in territory that the Iroquois claimed. A small group of Piscataway (of Algonquin stock) did manage to survive, moving southward in about 1699 to settle on Conoy, a small island in the Potomac River. Some Susquehhanock also remained, but posed no longstanding threat. As warfare and especially disease took their toll on the once populous bands, they scattered westward.[2]

Finally in 1722 after years of negotiations, Virginia's Lieutenant Governor Alexander Spotswood, along with the governors of New York and Pennsylvania, met with Iroquois representatives and finalized the Treaty of Albany—an agreement which essentially forbade a native presence in the land south of the Potomac and east of the Blue Ridge Mountains on threat of their death or enslavement in the West Indies. Yet the treaty was not the complete end of the Indian presence in Loudoun. Some married local folk, especially blacks. Others traveled through or worked in the area. Bit by bit these decimated and exiled populations reasserted themselves in local history, mythology, and material culture, even though evidence of what lasting cultural influence they had on regional community and family life remains largely unearthed.[3]

The old Iroquois, Algonquin, and Susquehannock territory from which Loudoun County was carved was part of a six-million-acre grant that England's Charles II gave in 1649 to seven loyalist associates—Ralph Lord Hopton, John Lord Culpeper, Sir John Berkeley, Sir William Morton, Sir Dudley Wyatt, Thomas Culpeper, and Henry Lord Jermyn. His gift, all the land that lay between the Potomac and Rappahannock rivers from the Chesapeake Bay in the east to an unspecified western frontier, was meant to be both a grand gesture of gratitude to those who had proven especially loyal to him during the English Civil War and a potential place of refuge for his followers. Terms of the grant stipulated that the Proprietors only had to give the Crown one-tenth of all the silver and one-fifth of all the gold found and an annual nominal rent of six pounds, thirteen shillings, and four pence.[4]

The six-million-acre gift was a magnificent reward, even if its absentee owners could not immediately take advantage of it and had little intention of ever moving permanently to Virginia. But what were the implications of this kind of act for the thousands of immigrants and creoles who eventually would come to settle the area? Clearly Charles's bequest set the stage for almost immediate western expansion from the lower tidewater counties and expansive land development. Yet placing this huge quantity of property in the hands of such a few Englishmen, especially at a time when land was the key to one's financial success in Virginia, also encouraged a kind of acute class stratification that early on came to characterize the locale's history.[5]

For those privileged seven, the Northern Neck proprietary was a portentous bequest, even by royal standards. It also was a controversial one. Under normal circumstances money secured from renting the vast acreage alone would have provided richly for its new owners. But they were not operating under normal circumstances. Their benefactor was an exiled Stuart king who hardly had the power to enforce his pledges at home or abroad. It is not even certain that creditable information about the proprietorship even reached Virginia before Charles regained his thrown in 1660. In the meanwhile, settlement of the Northern Neck began in his "absence." In fact, land speculators, many of whom were among the colony's elite, while actively creating Virginia's first real land boom, acquired much of the area's finest land before the Restoration ever occurred. They bought huge parcels and began selling them off in smaller sections at inflated prices almost immediately. There also were squatters to contend with, poorer folk who had carved out small farms on some of the more isolated tracts.[6]

When faced with the terms of the original patent after Charles regained his throne, many in both classes refused to honor them. Likewise, the death of four original proprietors during the interim and the continued "absenteeism" of the remainder destroyed the likelihood that any of the King's "honored" would ever gain control of all the land that he initially promised them. This early scenario of potential class conflict over land and the kind of power and prestige its ownership guaranteed would become a recurring, divisive theme in the political economy of the white community.[7]

Governor William Berkeley, fearful of consequent political and economic unrest, sent Colonel Francis Moryson to negotiate a compromise. The King eventually recognized the ownership of lands settled during Cromwell's rule, but not those patents acquired after his restoration. Colony emissaries traveled again to England, this time with directives to purchase the entire Northern Neck property. Meanwhile Charles further confused the situation by issuing another large grant in 1673 which included some of the original Northern Neck proprietary lands. This time he showered his generosity on the Earl of Arlington and the 2nd Lord Culpeper.[8]

According to one contemporary, there was "unspeakable grief and Astonishment" when news of this new "Arlington Charter" reached the colony. But before the Crown could respond to protests, Bacon's Rebellion erupted. At the end of these difficulties, the original Northern Neck proprietors and their heirs were more than ready to settle their claims. All except one sold their land to Lord Culpeper, and the huge Proprietary passed down the Culpeper line to the Fairfax family.[9]

Loudoun became one of thirteen counties that the Virginia government eventually carved out of the Northern Neck. Land that originally was part of the expansive Stafford County formed parts of Prince William County in 1664 and Fairfax County in 1742. Loudoun was formed in 1757 from the southern and western lands of Fairfax County. It initially consisted of only Cameron parish. In 1770, however, a rapidly growing population successfully petitioned the colonial government to have Shelburne parish formed from land in the western region of Cameron.[10]

Land purchases began in the early eighteenth century when Loudoun was still part of Stafford County. Virginia's tidewater gentry were Loudoun's earliest large property holders, many representing families that would dominate Loudoun's economy and define its upper class for generations. Some used part of their large holdings as an investment in land speculation; others acquired "western" lands to expand their eastern agricultural operations and their heirs' fortunes. Until the middle of the eighteenth century, members of the Culpeper-Fairfax family remained in England, hiring prominent colony men to act as their land agents and/or surveyors.[11]

While agents provided a valuable service to their employers, it was not unusual for these men, including such illustrious colonial figures as Robert "King" Carter, Thomas Lee, Edmund Jennings, John Warner, Amos Janney, and George Washington, to exploit their positions and act more as land speculators for themselves than as representatives of absentee English landlords. The result was an early monopoly of the best lands in the hands of a few men and women. Their families' wealth and local resources created the foundation for a consistently powerful landed gentry and planter class, while poorer whites were relegated to the status of yeoman owner or renter. Consider, for example, the brief financial and family histories of two of Loudoun's earliest landholders, Daniel McCarthy and John McIlhany.[12]

Captain Daniel McCarthy of Westmoreland County was the first to officially acquire Loudoun land, setting in many ways a standard for those planters who followed. According to land records, McCarthy purchased a tract of 2,993 acres "above the falls of the Potowmack River" in 1709. Within the next few years, he began to import slaves to work his tobacco farms that were scattered throughout Northern Neck counties. By midcentury, McCarthy probably quartered the largest number of blacks on any Loudoun estate.[13]

Daniel McCarthy's race, class, and gender typified his landholding peers in numerous ways, although his lineage distinguished him even among Virginia's colonial gentry. He was the grandson of Donough McCarth, Earl of Clancarty and a direct descendant of Carmac, King of Munster in 483 A.D. Daniel's father, Donal, had been an officer in the Irish Army that was defeated by King William III. When the family was exiled, Daniel, who was still a boy, traveled with his parents to Virginia, settling in Westmoreland County. McCarthy began to acquire land in the Loudoun vicinity as a young man. Like many of the early elite immigrants, the McCarthys married within their class, creating a wealth of family resources in land and slaves in the process. Daniel married Ann Lee Fitzhugh, sister of Thomas Lee and widow of Colonel William Fitzhugh. Their eldest son and principal heir, Colonel Dennis McCarthy, married Sarah Ball, first cousin to George Washington's mother. As was customary, the McCarthys invested heavily in large tracts of land for tobacco production, passing on their name, land, slaves, and status to their eldest sons.[14]

John McIlhany's life is equally exemplary. Born in Scotland, McIlhany was about to be married when, in 1745, he joined the forces of the "Young Pretender" in his efforts to capture the British Crown. After defeat at Culloden, McIlhany and his bride fled to Virginia. They arrived at Yorktown later that year, but soon moved on to the Hillsboro area of Loudoun. There he developed "Ithica," the family's plantation, and became involved in local politics, becoming Loudoun's High Sheriff in 1768. Like McCarthy, McIlhany was able to pass his wealth and prestige on to his children.[15]

Yet clearly every immigrant family did not succeed, even among the well-to-do. Gaston De Maussion, for example, was a French soldier who came to the colonies as part of the Marquis de Lafayette's force in 1780. After the war, he sent for his wife and children, and they settled on a plantation that he bought in the Loudoun vicinity. De Maussion stayed on for more than fourteen years, but he never succeeded financially. He and his wife continuously found themselves borrowing money from Gaston's mother and even local friends. In the end, he lost his plantation for debt and returned to France, completely deserting his family. His wife, Chastenay, stayed on for four years, hoping to hear from him. In the meanwhile, she had no other alternative but to take a job as a companion for an elderly woman in New Orleans, leaving her children with a neighbor. An inheritance left to her by her employer allowed her and the children to be reunited and to return to France in 1800. The Maussions' immigration to the Virginia piedmont had ended much differently than that of McCarthy or McIlhany, but not so differently from many others whose dreams of financial success, family, and community often ended in much harsher realities.[16]

Daniel McCarthy and John McIlhany were first-generation immigrants when they purchased Loudoun land and began building their fortunes and families. Other early planters had much longer histories in Virginia. Their role as Loudoun landholders signified not a beginning, but an extension of their plantocracy, or at least its economic influence, from the tidewater reaches of the colony to the west. Many of these planters had less early influence on Loudoun than might be imagined because they remained "east," acting as absentee planters of Loudoun properties. Robert Carter of "Nomini," for example, was a fourth-generation Virginian who was able to acquire, mostly through inheritance, 39,509 acres in Loudoun. He never moved to the county, but did have his overseers and slaves establish a tobacco and grain plantation on a 2000-acre tract and rented out other parcels for a tidy annuity.[17]

Among the wealthiest of the colony's elite, Councillor Carter's family set the highest standard for colonial creole aristocracy. It was a family that included, among others, "King" Carter, the wealthiest and most powerful man in early eighteenth-century Virginia. The Carters were a force to be reckoned with, a family that held in its grasp several hundred thousand acres of Virginia land and thousands of slaves to work it. As such, Robert Carter, King Carter's grandson, was part of a different and elevated class of eighteenth-century planter than McCarthy and McIlhany. Because of his inordinate wealth, extensive landholdings outside of Loudoun, and permanent absentee status, Carter initially cultivated few family or community ties in the area. It would not be until the end of the eighteenth century, when Carter heirs actually began to live in Loudoun and base their considerably smaller fortunes there, that they established local branches of their families and contributed to the community's cultural and institutional development in the way that McCarthy and McIlhaney had done the previous generation.[18]

Early planters, residential and absentee, had tremendous influence on the county's socioeconomic evolution and, consequently, its class stratification. Tobacco was still the premier cash crop when they began to create plantations in Loudoun and slaves were outnumbering white indentured servants, especially on the larger tobacco quarters. Controlling as they did both land and labor resources, it is little wonder that planters had such sway over the county's economy. This kind of power guaranteed their representation in local and colonywide offices of established institutions of authority such as the county court and vestry, House of Burgesses and Governor's Council.[19]

Their power, however, did not extend to all reaches of cultural or community development. Ironically, planter influence may have retarded community growth in some ways, and not just because many initially were absentee. Most harmful were their actions as large landholders. Acting monopolistically and speculatively, the elite kept land prices high and, consequently, white population low. In the southern and southeastern regions of the county where planter holdings were concentrated, white population remained sparse through the era of the American Revolution. An English visitor to Loudoun as late as the 1770s had good cause to comment: "The Land is pretty good, but is monopolized and consequently thinly inhabited."[20] It was not unusual for thousands of acres of uninhabited Loudoun land to circulate in the hands of one wealthy speculator after another, each sale drawing a price more difficult for poorer folk to meet. Eventually an owner would divide a parcel into several moderately sized tracts and sell or rent them to middling folk at a substantial profit. Renting, of course, had the additional advantage to the land's owner of having one's property "developed."[21]

Most leasing contracts stipulated that renters reserve most of its woods,[22] erect a house or outbuildings, plant fruit orchards, and construct fences. When George Johnston, a local lawyer, leased 152 acres to farmer Thomas Champe in 1771 for an annual sum of £4.10, for example, he required that Champe leave untouched a minimum of "twenty five acres of woodland." The renter also had to plant "one hundred and fifty Peach trees and as many good apple Trees . . . and incluse [*sic*] with a good strong sufficient and Lawfull fence" as well as build within five years "a good Dwelling House Twenty feet by sixteen . . . [and] a Barn twenty feet square with shingled Roofs."[23]

Despite these requirements, most settlers leased rather than bought. High land prices (anywhere from £3 to £5 per acre after 1750) and long-term, secure leases were effective incentives. Most who did manage to buy property could afford only moderate sized tracts. In 1769, for example, only forty years after Europeans began to move to the Loudoun vicinity, more than 75 percent of its landholdings were between 100 and 500 acres. It was a pattern that stuck over the generations. From the very beginning of white settlement, therefore, yeomen farmers, located to the north and west of the plantation district, outnumbered most other groups. They tended to cluster in small communities that often had a strong ethnic flavor.[24]

The most populous faction, the Scotch-Irish, began to arrive from Pennsylvania and Virginia's tidewater during the late 1720s. They settled throughout Loudoun as did smaller numbers of British, Scottish, Welsh, Irish, and Cornish emigrants, creating thriving farming hamlets especially along the county's south central border.[25] At about the same time Quakers, also largely from Pennsylvania, began to form somewhat exclusive communities in Loudoun's central, north-central, and western reaches.[26]

"Jacob Janney . . . came from Bucks county, Pa., to Loudoun county, Va about the year 1745, being one of the earliest settlers in that neighborhood where Goose Greek Monthly Meeting was afterwards established," one local Friend wrote of his family's early Loudoun history. Both Jacob and his wife Hannah were elders in their meeting and, as was the custom of the day, had a large family. Samuel Janney, the family's unofficial historian, traced his family's move through Thomas Janney, a Quaker minister who was imprisoned in seventeenth-century England because of his "religious testimony" and who later migrated with his family to Pennsylvania. Two generations later, Jacob and Hannah moved to Loudoun. That there were other Janney kin there when they arrived was no coincidence. Amos and Mary Janney, also from Bucks County, had settled in the area more than a decade earlier. Amos had been a land agent for the Fairfax family and had managed to purchase almost 4000 acres of local land. With this kind of economic and social foothold in the infant Quaker community, it is little wonder that more Janneys and Friends from Bucks County soon made their way to Loudoun.[27]

Clad in the simple-styled garments that symbolized their cultural ethos and distinctiveness, they created communities of mostly nonslaveholding planters, yeoman farmers, ministers, teachers, merchants, professionals, and craftsmen which differed from those of their neighbors in some fundamental ways. Certainly they had social and business contacts with other local folk, but they strove to maintain some psychological and physical distance from those who did not share their religious beliefs. Instead of trying to build a county-wide community with other local whites, Friends established and maintained strong ties with other Quakers in Virginia, Maryland, Pennsylvania, New Jersey, and elsewhere. Their mandates to marry within their ranks and to migrate in family groups, their residential clustering, and their active participation in periodic religious gatherings that drew members from long distances enabled them to be part of a geographically disparate, but philosophically homogeneous, Quaker community. One local Quaker spoke for most when he explained: "Friends prided themselves on being a peculiar people unto the Lord who did not seek converts and were content to draw in upon themselves."[28]

Yet limiting social relations to members of their faith did not preclude class formation within Quaker communities, just as it did not do so among those who shared a common ethnicity or race. Dennis McCarthy was a Scottish Presbyterian and John McIlhany was an Irish Catholic, both proud of their ethnic and cultural heritages, but as colonial land and slaveholders they still represented the upper class in their ethnic communities and in the county at large. Their wealth, education, and consequent status allowed them to have social, political, and economic status that was not largely determined by their ethnicity. Similarly, class based on wealth, education, and status within the Quaker meeting had profound influence on one's "place" in and outside of their towns and hamlets, linking him or her to those outside of their faith in ways that religious difference could not erase. Still intermarriage and, therefore, family formation with non-Friends was strictly avoided among those who, despite their class affiliation, hoped to remain Quakers.

Probably few county whites who were not Quakers challenged their separatist practices. Some expression of religious intolerance, after all, was not unusual in colonial Virginia or Loudoun. Moreover, local whites of other faiths may have kept their distance socially because they were not attracted to the Quakers' emphasis on the inornate and nonrecreational. But while these kinds of differences may seem superficial, some ascertained that there was cause for deeper concern. Quaker church principles could conflict with ideas and practices that others believed fundamental to their way of life. These conflicts severely threatened white community cohesiveness over the generations. Quaker policies, for example, repeatedly challenged local custom and law during times of military or social crises. Quaker religious policy forbidding military participation, for one, caused them to be the focus of great resentment and exclusion during the eras of the American Revolution, the War of 1812, and certainly the American Civil War.[29]

Still many Loudouners had to begrudgingly admit their admiration and respect for county Friends. Their success as farmers, artisans, and businessmen was obvious. Local folk also had to applaud their social vision and activism, particularly their campaign for a literate white South. It was, instead, their views and actions regarding local blacks that most distinguished and alienated them from other whites. For Friends to take on the cause of poor whites was one thing. For them to act as advocates for blacks, slave or free, in a slaveholding county was quite another matter. Over the years, but especially during the antebellum decades, Quakers articulated controversial racial policies that few in Loudoun's largely proslavery white community found acceptable.

Yet it would be misleading to suggest that county Quakers ever unanimously agreed on mounting a vocal and active opposition to slavery. Although the Quaker church condemned the institution of slavery as early as the 1750s, not all members were antislavery. Friend Elisha Hall, for example, had the dubious distinction of being the second largest slaveholder in Loudoun in 1749; he had twenty slaves. When Quakers began to oust slaveholding members from their ranks during the 1780s, not a few left the Society because they refused to relinquish their black property. Yet Friends were by far the single most important group of county whites who acted liberally toward slaves and free people of color.[30]

Their antislavery activism deeply alienated them from mainstream white community life, irrevocably fracturing white solidarity. Not only did local Friends provide free blacks with educational opportunities, they also encouraged residential and economic ties. Perhaps even more important, they helped to maintain an Underground Railroad network, while openly advocating policies of gradual, but universal, emancipation. "There is no part of our religious concerns in which these considerations are more important than in supporting our righteous testimony against slavery. . . . I am fully persuaded that a calm, temperate, and yet decided bearing, will have the most salutary influence in promoting the great cause of universal emancipation," Samuel Janney, Quaker minister, headmaster of Loudoun's Springdale School for Girls, and the county's premier abolitionist wrote typically in 1844.[31]

Quakers were not the only "isolationists" in the county. Loudoun's German settlers also defined their communities exclusively. First arriving in large family groups during the 1720s, most eventually settled north of Quaker strongholds, in and around Lovettsville in the northwestern corner of the county. From the very beginning, they were committed to organizing a self-contained society, separate and independent, composed only of persons of German origin and culture, although evidence of some Swedish influence has surfaced. Retention of their German cultural heritage, particularly their language, was paramount to their plans for community development.[32]

Still there was a large enough regional German community, scattered especially throughout the neighboring piedmont and Shenandoah Valley as well as in Maryland and Pennsylvania, to provide sufficient social and cultural support. Loudoun's Germans benefited from locally and regionally based leadership, schools, newspapers, printing presses, churches, and organized social activities for several generations after their arrival. Large arrivals of German Lutherans (those from the earlier years largely had been of the German Reformed Church) around the mid-eighteenth century, followed by Shenandoah Valley Germans fleeing from the violence of the French and Indian War in the 1750s and '60s, also substantially bolstered support for their otherwise locally isolated community.[33] Persons of European ethnicities of smaller local or regional representation such as the French were much less fortunate. They had to become bicultural and bilingual almost immediately if they hoped to establish any kind of community ties with other whites.[34]

The presence of comparatively large numbers of artisans among the first Germans produced a diversified economy and an important sense of independence that also helped them to sustain their separatist ideology well into the first decades of the nineteenth century. While farming and livestock still were the basis for much of their financial well-being, local carpenters, clock and furniture makers, weavers, shoemakers, millers, masons, tanners, blacksmiths, wheelwrights, and distillers contributed much to the settlement's economic success and continuing cultural focus.[35]

German farmers traditionally leased and bought small tracts of land on which they cultivated grains and raised sheep, cattle, and other livestock. Everyone worked the family farm and German women performed much more field work than their neighbors. Clothed in their short, linsey wool dresses and petticoats, German female laborers undoubtedly drew the comment and criticism of other whites who reserved field work for only the poorest white women or slave females. But like their Quaker neighbors, most Germans were not slaveholders; and those who did own blacks, such as Jonathan Monkhouse or the Shovers and Sanbowers, owned relatively small numbers.[36]

There also is some evidence that there was antislavery sentiment in the county's German community. Klaus Wust asserts, for example, that the Lutheran piedmont hub in Loudoun "became a center of antislavery sentiment." Yet it seems more reasonable to conclude that the choice of some Loudoun Germans not to be slaveholders derived more from their commitment to ethnic and

cultural purity and ideals of free labor and fair competition within the local
agrarian economy than from their concern for blacks or the moral issues surrounding slaveholding. Few, if any, were members of Loudoun's colonization
organizations or publicly supported the antislavery efforts that local Quakers
mounted. All evidence, in fact, suggests that the Lutheran and Reformed
leaders and membership in the area responded leniently to the practice of slaveholding, with several ministers and churches owning slaves outright. Even had
some Loudoun Germans fundamentally and actively disapproved of slavery,
they never were so great in number or commanded enough economic strength
to have the same influence that some local Quakers had and used to support
antislavery.[37]

The Germans' support of military efforts and their noncritical stance on
slavery held them in better stead with other local whites. Their impressive
military record as patriots in the American Revolution especially increased
their local status. Still Germans faced some local white criticism from for other
reasons. Many viewed their cultural differences as a mark of their ethnic and
class inferiority, describing them as crude and brutish, backward and ignorant.
Area Germans seemed to have had a running battle, verbally and physically, in
particular with Irish settlers—each demonstrating and responding to xenopho-
bic ideology incumbent in the Anglo-Saxon and Celtic cultures that they represented.[38]

Early political and cultural differences eventually led to the county's permanent division. Representatives of the southeastern planter element began petitioning the state legislature as early as 1781, requesting a division of county
land along parish lines. The opposition counterpetitioned. Finally in 1798, the
General Assembly allowed adjacent Fairfax County to annex the area between
the two waterways called Difficult Run and Sugarland Run. A large body of
planters concentrated in this district automatically became residents of Fairfax.
Those planters remaining in Loudoun, therefore had even less influence with
which to combat yeoman influence. Time eroded some, but certainly not all, of
the diversity and conflicts of Loudoun's white population, particularly that centered on the slavery issue. Ethnic affiliation, cultural difference, and class stratification also had some lasting impact.

Despite their various backgrounds, all Loudoun whites faced similar challenges during the first difficult generations of settlement. They also lived and
worked alike in many fundamental ways. These common experiences, embedded in their agrarian culture and patriarchal family structure, bound them together as a community of white men and women in important ways that their
differences could not completely undermine.

Settling the wilderness meant universal hardship. When whites began to
arrive in the 1720s and '30s there was little in the way of cultured society,

intellectual resources, or material comfort waiting for them. So desolate was the place that many of the early land grants referred to it as "wasteland."[39] Homesteads and settlements were few and far between. Roads, the few that existed, were badly rutted and nearly impassable during the rainy seasons (fall, winter, and spring). Most lived in rural isolation, rarely seeing those outside of their households except at the occasional religious gathering, barn raising, corn shucking, wedding, baptism, or funeral. Even as late as 1774, a British visitor to Loudoun commented that the county was "almost all woods," and there were very few places of public gathering.[40] There were no public schools, churches, shops, banks, post offices, or the other accoutrements of town life. Many among the slaveholding elite responded to the barrenness simply by remaining "absent" for several years at a time, depending on their overseers and drivers to establish and make their "western" farms prosper.[41] For those who chose or had no choice but to remain, their first priority was to provide shelters for themselves and their families.

Virtually everyone lived in small log or frame houses which usually measured sixteen by twenty feet in size. Each "tenement" usually had a house that was one and a half stories high with two rooms and a loft, with a fence around it, a small orchard of fruit trees, and a few outhouses. There generally was only one entrance to the cabin and a small, multifunctional front room served as bedroom, kitchen, dining room, parlor, and chapel. It was there that poor as well as middling colonial families and their indentured servants and black slaves, ate, slept, labored, laughed, and learned from one another. "In the evening, after the dishes were washed and cleared off the table and the table set back," one Loudoun resident recalled, "the candle stand would be moved out from its proper corner and the whole family gathered around it; some of the men reading a newspaper or a book and the women sewing or knitting, or spinning flax or tow."[42]

Colonial households had to be self-sufficient. Most generated their own food, clothing, furniture, medicines, and entertainment and lived without those items that they could not make for themselves or acquire through local barter. Family and household members produced family gardens, livestock pens, and fruit orchards. While boys and men usually hunted and fished, females raised, butchered, cured, salted, cooked, and picked, pickled, and preserved. This pattern changed little over the years, persisting from the colonial through the antebellum decades.

Eighteenth- and nineteenth-century gendered labor divisions affected almost every activity on a Loudoun family farm. The older boys and men cleared land and constructed buildings, fences, and furniture. Girls and women made domestic commodities like rugs, candles, and soap, and, along with young boys, cleaned the yard and tended to the barn and animal pens. While the nineteenth century offered them the luxury of manufactured clothing, many women continued to spin, weave, and sew clothing, blankets, coverlets, quilts and curtains. Males were the principal agriculturists and artisans in their communities, but only very elite women did not help out in the fields during harvest time. Almost every farmwoman routinely prepared meals and medicine for farm workers as well as provided valuable family income by trading and selling their livestock and dairy products.[43]

Furniture usually was scant and crude. The poor more often than not sat on three-legged stools and wooden blocks, ate out of a few wooden bowls or dried gourds and slept on pallets or homemade mattresses they laid on dirt floors. More fortunate settlers had chairs or benches, sat at a table to have their meals and slept in feather beds. Middling households included a few pewter dishes and spoons, but usually only those considered "well-to-do" possessed iron pots, a kitchen table, china, crockery, featherbeds, and bedsteads.[44]

But these were the very early settlers. Material accumulation over the generations, greater family income, and increased availability of market goods meant more aesthetically attractive homes and furnishings. By the Revolutionary War era, traveling salesmen and local stores allowed most to purchase cups, dishes, coffee pots, jars, jugs, and other kitchen fare. By the 1760s and 1770s, county estate inventories documented even luxury items for middling folk. Mary Janney, for example, a woman of only moderate means, bequeathed to her daughter her two "best" featherbeds and furniture, her three best chairs, a black walnut table, and her silver tablespoons and teaspoons in 1767.[45]

And between the end of the American Revolution and the third decade of the nineteenth century, many of Loudoun's wealthiest landholders began to take up permanent residence in the county, recreating a lavish lifestyle usually restricted to tidewater planters. This part of the Loudoun experience is most readily documented in the exquisite manor homes that they constructed and furnished. Many built on local waterways which supported wharves, mills, and ferry service. Some even had their own private chapels, schools, and hospitals, not to mention the other numerous outhouses, orchards, stables, and barns and wooden, stone, and brick slave quarters.[46]

"Coton," the mansion of Thomas Ludwell Lee and Fanny Carter, was perhaps typical of the grand style taken on by the county's wealthiest. When Thomas Lee inherited the 4700-acre Loudoun estate and "fifty Negroes above the age of ten years" from his father in 1751, all that was on the land were the structural rudiments that had signified one of his father's several outlying tobacco plantations—a stone kitchen, laundry, meat house, and some slave housing. After he married in 1786, Lee began to construct a main house which he later renovated several times. By 1804, additions to the house had increased its size to 24′ by 96′. "Coton" became a county showplace, one of the most beautiful mansions in the region, and the property boasted, in addition to the house and many outhouses, two stone mills, a distillery, and a school. Others followed suit.

Perhaps the most famous of the Loudoun homes was the residence of President James Monroe. "Oak Hill" was a three-storied brick house with porticos and Doric columns, facing a massive formal garden. Thomas Jefferson was its original designer. James Hoban, builder of the White House and architect of the Capitol building, completed its plans. Monroe built the house in 1820 and hired an Englishman, William Benton, to supervise his surrounding plantation, worked by the largest slave force in the county.[47]

Of course few could afford to live like Loudoun's elite. Most estate inventories from the period document much more moderate, but comfortable furnishings—"a cherry bureau in each of two bed rooms, a mirror . . . in the parlor and one in two bed rooms, a dozen 'windsor' chairs, . . . book case and desk . . . with a cherry table in the parlor" for the early nineteenth century Quaker home of John Janney. German farmer Simon Shover had a home that boasted more luxurious items—four tables (two of walnut) and two stoves (six- and ten-plate), a kitchen cupboard and dresser, six common chairs, one corner cupboard, four beds, a walnut desk, a "parcel of old books," and numerous pots, pans, jugs, tubs, barrels, forks, and knives.[48]

Living conditions changed, but they changed slowly for most. Certainly there were more people, larger settlements, and a growing urbanization in a few areas, but farms and farm families remained the norm. Communities grew in number and size, but they did not outgrow the dominating rural landscape. Even most "town folk" of the middling, professional, and upper classes had nearby farmland and invested in agriculture and an agrarian lifestyle. The inelaborate and utilitarian ways of most Loudouners were, by the nineteenth century, a well-honed tradition of which they were proud. To those who stayed over the years, married, raised their families, and committed themselves to their communities, it was a way of life that they had long grown to appreciate.

John Janney described the architectural changes that occurred in his family's Loudoun farm house from the mid-eighteenth century through the 1830s, changes that suggest what both colonial and antebellum homes of middling farm families were like. Although the house grew in size and construction materials varied somewhat, in the end it was not so different. Nor were the generations of Janneys who lived in it. When they "first occupied the farm," John began his narrative, "they lived in a log cabin." But over the years, "they built another which was of hewed logs" that were "'chinked' with bits of wood and then plastered with mortar so that it made a warm and comfortable room." By the end of the eighteenth century, Janney's grandfather was ready to build a more elaborate home for his expansive household which then included two generations of kin, indentured servants, and free black workers. He completed "a six room stone house adjoining the log one," and turned the old house into the family's kitchen. Still, the Janneys insisted on more changes during the early nineteenth century. In 1816, they added a large frame barn; and an uncle who inherited the farm several years later built a stone kitchen to replace the wooden one.[49]

The least sophisticated or adorned of Loudoun homes were those of the German community. Reputed to be unpretentious and frugal, German homes were seldom large and many observers, perhaps betraying their cultural biases, found them comparatively unattractive and uncomfortable. Some even commented that German livestock barns were better constructed and more handsome than German houses. Even neighboring Quakers who esteemed material simplicity sometimes made mention of the German community's lack of aesthetic charm. As late as 1853, for example, Yardley Taylor described Lovettsville as filled with "many old log houses that are barely tolerable." While he admired the German's "economy" and "desire for competence," he thought that they needed to pay more attention to "improvement" and "something of the ornamental."[50]

While many continued to lack material comfort, there was growing opportunity for "spirited" recreation and spiritual richness as the years passed. Indeed, "playing together" often broke down ethnic and class boundaries that praying apart enforced. Ordinaries and churches emerged in the late colonial period as the centers of social activity. The ordinary's heyday in Loudoun was between 1750 and 1830 when men and women operated facilities in private buildings and their homes. Travelers and locals alike came for "ordinary" or regular meals and to talk politics, gossip, drink, and eat. Rates for meals varied over the years—a breakfast or supper cost about 19 cents in 1806, a hot dinner with beer or cider—26 cents; both ale and a cheap bottle of wine cost 36 cents, although good Madeira was 60 cents a bottle while port was 40 cents. Lodging in "clean sheets" was nine cents a night; hay and pasturage were 30 cents.[51]

There also were other recreational avenues. Card playing, cockfights, fist fights and brawls, shooting, wood chopping, tobacco spitting, riding contests, horse shoes, hunting, dancing, and storytelling were typical male "sports." Things sometimes got out of control and ended in violence, especially when where there was a lot of drinking. Court records from the era are replete with accounts of drunken mêleés in which more than heads and furniture were broken. Local ethnic tensions sometimes were at the root. Descendants of area Germans, for example, tell the tale of how several men from their community volunteered to help their neighbor repair his mill dam. As was customary, the men drank as they worked. A quarrel broke out between an Irishman and a German about their home countries. A group brawl ensued and several persons were seriously hurt. The next day the German man died from his wounds. There also was the story of how local Germans angered the Irish by parading a St. Patrick in effigy with a potato necklace around his neck. The following Michelmas, Irish neighbors struck back by posting an archangel with a necklace of sauerkraut up for the entire village to see. Such was good fun for some, but too raucous for others who sought their entertainment at less bawdy community events.[52]

Religious activity was important in southern homes and farming communities, not only because it brought comfort to those who inhabited this unpredictable, often violent or tragic world, but also because it was the center of "respectable" social life. Church meetings, when they were held, could last all day. But when they were over, worshippers conversed with friends and family, exchanged gossip, and even shared a meal. According to county lore, attendance at Quaker meetings was very regular and everyone, even neighborhood dogs, got into the habit of going. On one particular day, the dog's master went outside to hitch his horse so that he could ride to the Waterford service. Suddenly feeling ill, he went back into his house and unexpectedly died. His dog waited briefly for his master to return to the horse. When he did not, the dog trotted off to town, found his usual spot at the meeting under his owner's accustomed bench, and sat out the service.[53]

Initially one's ethnicity almost bespoke one's choice of faith. But for some, one's religious sentiments also prescribed a certain kind of ethnicity. Quakers and their culture, for example, were more distinguishable by the religion and the kind of lifestyle that affiliation demanded than perhaps any other characteristic.[54] Presbyterians dominated the first Scotch-Irish neighborhoods of the 1730s.[55] Most local Irish were Catholic.[56] The first several generations of Germans were almost unanimously members of the German Reformed Church or Lutherans, although Mennonites, Dunkers, Moravians, Separatists, and Inspirationists also were present in small numbers.[57] Many British settlers were members of the Anglican Church.[58] As time wore on, however, some denominational affiliations were shared across ethnic and even racial lines. The forceful entry of the Methodists and Baptists among these communities had much to do with this phenomenon. So too did the county's population growth and natural forces of acculturation.

As early as the 1760s, and certainly by the time of the American Revolution, the Baptists and Methodists were the most prominent denominations in Loudoun. Many of these worshippers were Scotch-Irish and Welsh yeoman farmers, shopkeepers, artisans, and poorer people, although there always were some from among the county's elite and especially free blacks and slaves. Unlike the Episcopalians and Presbyterians, local Methodists and Baptists held numerous camp meetings which served as extensive membership drives. They also were able to attract large numbers of people through special appeals to the "ordinary" man and woman and a ceremonial structure which encouraged an open expression of one's spiritual feelings.[59]

Congregations large enough to attract ministers on any basis suggested a steady increase in the white population. And increase it did, from about 1500 in 1749 to more than 15,000 in 1800.[60] Town development barely kept apace. Predictably, the most important urban spot was Leesburg, the county seat, located near the county's central-eastern boundary.[61] The center of Loudoun's business, intellectual, and political life, residents could boast of several academies, a library, numerous general stores, taverns, hotels, artisan shops, churches representing most of the major denominations, a branch of the Bank of the Valley, professional offices, a regular stage coach stop, and a mail office by the 1830s. Other smaller, but similarly important urban spots, were the southwestern town of Middleburg and the Quaker strongholds of Waterford in north-central Loudoun, Hillsboro to its west, and Lincoln. Aldie, located in the south-central part of the county; Lovettsville, in the German settlement; Snickersville to its south; Hamilton; Purcellville; Arcola; Neersville; Wheatland; and Bloomfield all slowly crept into being, providing a few urban amenities for its residents and those farm families that lived close by.[62] (See Fig. 1.)

By the dawning of the antebellum era, Loudoun was a full-blown society with an admittedly small but comparatively respectably sized population. While there still were some large expanses of forest to be conquered and roads remained bad in most sections, there was a density to the population, neighboring farms, and towns that bespoke of generations-old settlements. Ethnicity, class, and culture, symbolized so well in housing styles, choice of religion, and especially one's occupation and control of resources such as land and slaves, continued to be the most distinguishing characteristics in the county's white society, both dividing and coalescing broad sectors over time.

Almost in the midst of the county's growth and development, however, there were signs of decline. While the second half of the eighteenth century fostered significant population increases among whites, there were initially only slight increases after 1800 and then significant losses during the 1830s. By 1860, fewer whites lived in Loudoun than in 1800. This kind of decline, due mostly to vigorous emigration to the Lower South, Southwest, and West, predictably stalled urban and industrial development, slowed the county's agricultural economy, and drained many communities of younger generations of families and especially young men.[63] (See Table 1.)

The pull for the hundreds and perhaps thousands of white Loudouners who left was the availability of affordable land elsewhere. The push was a county and a state with a sagging agrarian economy that remained dominated by wealthy planters who controlled land and labor resources. Added to this dismal scenario was the consistent fear of slave insurrection, drove home by the bloody Nat Turner rebellion of 1831 (it probably is little coincidence that the largest numbers of white emigrants (more than 3000) left Loudoun that decade). While the local economy demonstrated some diversity, due mostly to a growing urban class of artisans and elite professionals, merchants, and businessmen, most people were either farmers or provided services for the agricultural sector. As late as 1850, farm land still comprised 88 percent of the county's acreage,

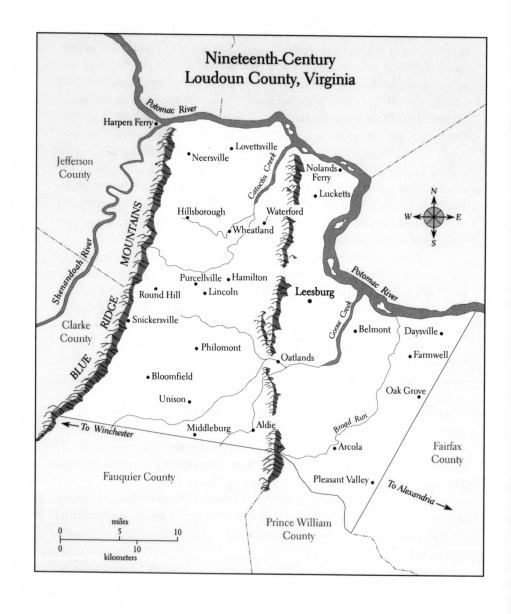

Figure 1. Map of Nineteenth-Century Loudoun County. Source: Maps of Loudoun
County by Yardly Taylor (1853) and The Guide to Loudoun by Eugene M. Scheel (1975)

Table 1   Loudoun County Population, 1800–1860

Year	Total	Whites	Free Blacks	Slaves
1800[a]	20,523	15,210	333	6,078
1810[b]	21,338	15,575	604	5,001
1820[c]	22,702	16,390	829	5,729
1830[d]	22,796	16,374	1,079	5,343
1840[e]	20,431	13,840	1,318	5,273
1850[f]	22,679	15,681	1,357	5,641
1860[g]	21,774	15,021	1,252	5,501

[a] Donald M. Sweig, "Free Negroes in Northern Virginia: An Investigation of the Growth and Status of Free Negroes in the Counties of Alexandria, Fairfax and Loudoun, 1770–1860" (M.A. thesis, George Mason University, 1975), appendix C, 66.

[b] U.S. Department of Commerce, Bureau of the Census, Manuscript Federal Census, 1810, Loudoun County, Virginia, Microfilm Roll 69.

[c] U.S. Department of Commerce, Bureau of the Census, Manuscript Federal Census, 1820, Loudoun County, Virginia, Microfilm Roll 137.

[d] U.S. Department of Commerce, Bureau of the Census, Manuscript Federal Census, 1830, Loudoun County, Virginia, Microfilm Roll 193.

[e] Sweig, "Free Negroes in Northern Virginia," appendix A, 63.

[f] J. D. B. DeBow, *Statistical View of the United States . . . Being a Compendium of the Seventh Census . . . 1850* (Washington, D.C.: A.O.P. Nicholson, 1854), 242, 244, 246, 248, 250, 252, 254, 259.

[g] Joseph G. Kennedy, *Population of the United States in 1860; Compiled from the Original Returns of the Eighth Census* (Washington, D.C.: Government Printing Office, 1864), 517.

and the value of Loudoun's farm land and buildings equaled 92 percent of the total value of the county's real estate. (See Tables 2 and 3.)[64]

Problems with Loudoun's antebellum economy derived from multiple sources. Infertile land was a large part of the dilemma. The story was the same all over. Farmers who invested in tobacco cultivation during the eighteenth century routinely used inefficient or few soil conservation methods, systematically stripping land of its fertility. Only occasionally did they allow a field to lie fallow long enough to replenish its vital nutrients, or routinely use fertilizer. "The value of manure is not known here," Nicholas Cresswell commented in 1777. "If it is, they are too lazy to make use of it. Their method is to clear a piece of land from the woods, generally put it in wheat the first year, Indian corn the next, and so alternately for six or seven years together." After that, farmers would complain that "the strength of the Land is gone . . . it is worn out," and they let it grow into woods again while clearing another tract for cultivation. This kind of negligence carried over to the next generations. Loudoun's nineteenth-century farmers witnessed a steady decline in soil fertility and crop yields as land prices continued to rise sharply.[65]

Table 2   Valuations of Loudoun Farm Land with Improvements, 1850–60

Year	Total value	Average/farm	Average/acre
1850[a]	$8,849,371	$6,648	$28
1860[b]	$10,508,211	$8,706	$35

[a] Compilations from data located in James W. Head, *History of Loudoun County, Virginia* (Leesburg, Va.: Park View Press, 1908), 92.

[b] Ibid.

The county's economy began to recover by 1840, partially because of changing land-use techniques. Two Loudoun farmers, John Alexander Binns and Israel Janney, aggressively addressed the problem of soil infertility. Janney was not unique among local Quakers, for many came to Loudoun in the eighteenth century using the kinds of soil conservation techniques that Binns later introduced to his community. An avid observer, Binns, for one, took notice of the farming practices of Pennsylvania farmers and local Quakers who used land plaster or gypsum and clover as fertilizers. He and his slaves experimented, combining the application of fertilizers with deep ploughing and crop rotation. Binns documented his tremendous success, publishing findings in 1803 that demonstrated that a farm he purchased in 1793 produced triple amounts of corn and wheat after five years of his applied technique.[66]

In the end, a significant number of farmers seemed to have embraced Binns's ideas, if only briefly. Thomas Jefferson, for one, was quite optimistic and sent a copy of Binns's book to friends in England and Europe. Israel Janney also publicized the benefits of gypsum and clover at about the same time. Just how important and long-term was the impact on Loudoun farming is difficult to assess. Yet certainly many county farmers eventually tried lime-based fertilizers, while others used animal manure, and most took up deep plowing.[67]

Table 3   Valuations of Farm Equipment and Livestock in Loudoun, 1850–60

Year	Equipment ($ total)	Equipment ($/farm)	Livestock ($ total)	Livestock ($/farm)	Land, equipment, livestock, ($/farm)
1850[a]	195,794	156	937,592	746	7,550
1860[b]	238,264	197	1,182,355	980	9,883

[a] Head, *History of Loudoun County*, 92–94.

[b] Ibid.

Loudouners interested in agricultural reform also initiated a regional forum. Local farmers formed the Agricultural Society of Loudoun, Fauquier, Prince William and Fairfax in 1825. Several years later, county farmers created the Agricultural Society of Loudoun. The group sponsored, among other educational and social activities, an annual county fair which encouraged farm families to exhibit their products and to take pride in their rural culture. In 1855, Benjamin Hyde Benton and James Gulick opened the Loudoun County Agricultural Academy and Chemical Institute. Located just three miles north of Aldie, the academy was the first locally to provide "instruction in all branches of mathematics and science useful to the farmer and man of Science."[68]

The interest in agricultural practices did not miss the attention of local inventors. Stephen McCormick patented a popular plow and William Yonson invented and manufactured a wheat threshing machine that county planters publicly recommended. Yonson advertised his goods in the local papers, assuring area farmers in 1844 that his factory in Leesburg, staffed by the "most experienced workmen," produced "upon the shortest notice" all orders for "Threshing Machines of every description in use, Wheat Fans, Shellers, Farm and Road Wagons, Ploughs of All Kinds, and especially important to Farmers, the improved Screw Spike portable Threshing Machine."[69]

Life could be difficult for farmers and town dwellers alike who weathered the storms of Loudoun's fickle economy. But most were successful enough to provide a subsistence income for their families. Yet, there always were poor people who needed county welfare. Loudoun's impoverished were of every ethnic group, generational cohort, and gender. They included blacks and whites, single, widowed, and deserted mothers and their children, the elderly, farmers, and mechanics as well as spendthrifts, alcoholics, and criminals. Court records of bankruptcies and debtor suits forcefully document the financial problems of some while accounts from the Overseers of the Poor tell of the incidence of debilitating local poverty.

Overseer records, officially kept since 1800, document that local folk actually did little to help the impoverished, centering their attention on the small numbers of visibly poor urban dwellers and especially families. Not surprisingly, they gave most support to those families without an adult male breadwinner. Every year, county officials assessed a tax on tithables to support the expense of aiding the county's poor. In 1800, for example, tax was 68 cents on each of Loudoun's 4,932 tithables, creating a fund of $3,353 to support the "estimated" "forty to fifty" poor white and black persons in the county that year. The Overseers slowly increased the amount of the tax over the next two decades until it became $1.20. But then in a chilling reversal that may have reflected the county's overall financial decline, they cut the tax back to 65 cents in 1830, 55 cents in 1840, and then even lower.[70]

Part of the loss in tax funds was made up in moneys generated on the county's poor farm which officials purchased in 1822. A small percentage of the poor also had temporary accommodations in Loudoun's poor house, built in 1801. Some 40 to 60 persons, including some free blacks and slaves, resided there for periods that could be as brief as a few nights or as long as several months. The Overseers of the Poor also provided temporary rent, food, clothing, and medical attention. The county generally gave some form of assistance to between 130 and 220 persons per year, of whom 5 to 25 percent were black. Many recipients of public charity were widowed or abandoned wives and their children, as the county stepped in to take the position of the family patriarch when he could not, or refused, do so. When Nancy Turner's husband deserted her and their children in 1810, for example, the county purchased and returned the furnishings that Mr. Turner's creditors had seized.[71]

The paternal and patriarchal role of the Overseers of the Poor in needy families far exceeded their distribution of public charities. More important, they assigned court-approved apprenticeships and indentures to poor children and orphans (fatherless children) whom they deemed had no vital means of support. Virginia law compelled these youngsters to remain apprentices until they became adults, and Overseers decided when, with whom, under what conditions, and precisely how long they lived and worked as such. Ideally, guardians supplied their wards with food, clothing, shelter, and a lucrative skill. The county court ordered on May 10, 1813, for example, that the "Overseers of the Poor bind James Barbour 8 years old on the 14th December last and John Peason 10 years old the 27th Feby last [as] apprentices to Tho[mas] Collins, according to Laws to learn the art and mystery of a stone Mason."[72] Given the lack of educational opportunities for poor children, apprenticeships were appealing to more than a few.[73]

Some who were aware of shrinking public funds tried organizing private charity, particularly that which helped struggling families. Gender-segregated organizations, such as women's church groups, sewing circles, mothers' associations, male lodges, and benevolent societies routinely solicited private moneys for public benefit. The Benevolent Society of Leesburg, organized in 1849, was perhaps the most well known. Its membership included some of Loudoun's most prominent men, including Francis W. Luckett, William A. and John D. Powell, Charles W. Blincoe, and Colonel Robert G. Saunders. Their goals were to provide material relief to the poor, emotional support to the ill, and financial assistance to widows and their children. The Society of Friends and other county churches also helped. Moses Gibson, for example, was a widower Friend with two daughters and a son who asked for and received assistance "in kind" from the Goose Creek Meeting for four consecutive years during the 1820s.[74]

Unfortunately, most of Loudoun's poor never received any kind of sustained or reconstructive assistance, and continued to live on the margins of society.

Often homeless, these individuals and families moved from one part of the county to the next, seeking work, a place to live, and relying on their own wits and sometimes crime for daily survival. Loudoun's middling and upper classes responded by giving reluctantly and meagerly, preferring instead to support oppressive legislation like apprenticeship and child residency laws which mandated their removal from impoverished and father-absent homes.

Poverty, however, was only one social problem which affected family and community life. Alcoholism, illegitimacy, spousal abuse, and desertion were just as common. But these social "ills" were discretely different from poverty. They cut deeply across class lines, often leveling socially and culturally constructed hierarchies that poverty, given its class-specific nature, did not. Alcoholism and the disorderly and sometimes abusive behavior that resulted could have plantation mistresses sounding and acting like overseers' wives or even poorer women as they strove to keep their men in check and their families stable. "Mother says tell Grandmother that Uncle William is getting along very well," Agnes Davisson of Hillsboro wrote to her sister in 1852. "He is perfectly sober and has promised Mother that he will be for the next six months, at least." Early nineteenth-century Friend John Janney recalled the "classless" nature of "drunkards" "in and just outside" of his Lincoln neighborhood. Farmer Samuel Iden, blacksmith Henry Fredt, tanner Samuel Russell, the wealthy German planter Conrad Bitzer, and a man of lesser means, "Suky" Poulson, routinely drank and got drunk together, a habit that both infuriated and amused witnesses. It also threatened to dissolve established ethnic and class distinctions.[75]

Yet drinking was so much a part of recreational culture that it was difficult to control, stigmatize, or even isolate. For southern adolescent boys and men of every distinction, drinking, even excessive drinking, remained one of the fundamental tests of their manhood. But to sit around drinking and boasting with friends was one thing. To allow your drinking to threaten your family life, your commitment as a husband and a father, your status as a patriarch in the society was quite another. The worst case of alcoholism Janney could remember was that of Edmund Carter. Mr. Carter, who had married a respectable widow and become the stepfather to her five girls, would become intoxicated almost daily and then "drive his wife and her daughters out of the house at night, and they would [have to] seek shelter at a neighbors."[76]

In Janney's neighborhood, serious family frays that became public knowledge were community concerns. Residents of the quiet Quaker settlement did not politely ignore grim social problems like drunkenness or domestic violence. To do so would have threatened the moral fabric and cohesiveness of their communities. Nor did they readily seek the aid or intervention of county officials. Neighborhood leaders assessed the situation, decided on a course of action, and then carried it out. Usually the process was informal; but it held the powerful support of the majority and offenders did well to abide by it.

Janney's neighbors quickly tired of Carter's debauchery and decided to take matters into their own hands. Believing that a severe whipping would help him mend his ways, a group of local men went to Edward Carter's where they found him in a drunken stupor. They dragged him out of bed, beat him severely, placed him in a shallow grave, and then proceeded to cover him up with wooden boards.

Hurt, angry, and frightened, Carter lay in his untimely grave most of the night before he finally managed to crawl out. He brought suit against those neighbors he believed were involved in his kidnapping and assault, but was unable to prove his accusations. (Not surprisingly, no one from the community volunteered any evidence on Mr. Carter's behalf.) Not a person to hold a grudge, and keenly aware that he needed his community's support more than they needed his, he found it best to conclude that his mishap "was the work of the Devil." [77]

Unfortunately, Carter's whipping did not have the desired affect. Again his neighbors organized against him. Catching him coming home very drunk, "one of the company stepped in front of him and accosted him. The rest made their appearance on the side of the road." Carter reacted angrily, asking if they intended to beat him again. The posse of local men and boys decided instead to threaten him with a tar and feathering. "The threat proved efficient," Janney concluded, "for [Edward Carter] left the neighborhood soon after." While Janney and his neighbors rid their community of a man they perceived as a threat to its common morality and certainly to the well being of Carter's wife and children, there were no local resources available to aid persons like him who had severe emotional problems or drug or alcohol dependencies.

Although John Janney could not recall any specific "grog" shops in his neighborhood, "tippling" houses, ordinaries that retailed wine and alcohol, and personal stills were numerous. General concern for the growth of alcoholism among county residents in the colonial period provided fertile ground for the creation of antebellum temperance societies. Both men and women participated in the movement to ban public drinking. The Sons of Temperance, established in Leesburg in 1846, for example, was a "temperance, friendly and beneficial society." Male and female members agitated against establishments which sold liquor and encouraged habitual drinking. Others planned and executed activities to publicize and aid their cause. Lively parades and regional conventions "for the purpose of adopting a plan for the legal suppression of the traffic in intoxicating liquids throughout the State" were fairly common. There were also petitions to the state legislature. On February 25, 1858, more than sixty Loudouners, a significant majority of whom were women, petitioned the General Assembly to "no longer . . . permit the retailer of ardent spirits to prosecute under the sanction and authority of the laws of the commonwealth."

They argued that a "large portion of the enebriates [sic]" in Loudoun "acquired a taste for ardent spirits and formed the habit of intemperance at the bar room or the tippling shop." Alcoholism, they asserted, affected every realm of their society, even Loudoun's youth and respectable husbands and fathers. It created "criminals" and "fanatics" out of those who otherwise could make a positive contribution to family and society.[78]

Other social problems also elicited community response. It is clear from the Edward Carter incident that local violence of one sort or another was quite usual. It was both the source of community problems and one of the measures local folk readily relied on to solve personal and group concerns. Court records are full of incidents of interpersonal and group violence, and that was only the tip of the iceberg. During one court session alone, John McGeath was convicted of assaulting Patrick McHolland; Hugh and Adam Barr, and Robert and Moses Wilson, faced charges of beating Weedon Smith "without provocation"; and the Justices found Andrew Smarr, "laborer," guilty of assaulting Matthew Weatherby. A short time later, five other county men were in court facing the charge of "disturbing the quiet repose of Whitson Birdsall, entering his enclosements, annoying his house with horns and bells and firing of guns, [and] insulting his person." Six months earlier, Sarah Sexton and Fielding Brown brought charges against one another, both asking the court to make certain that the other "shall be of good and quiet behavior towards all the good citizens of this commonwealth," especially each other.[79]

Church and county officials also had the authority to punish men and women whose crimes had direct influence on family life—those, for example who parented illegitimate children, adulterers, and those guilty of fornication. Charles Chinn, a member of a prominent but morally unconventional Middleburg family, was one of many men found guilty of illegal cohabitation with local women. And it is little wonder that the court took an inordinate interest in James Whaley, Jr., who was charged with "absenting [himself]" from his wife and taking up with another woman. This other woman, the mother of Mr. Whaley's illegitimate child, was his wife's sister.

The Chinn and Whaley cases notwithstanding, little legislation actually was in place to address numerous and complex social problems. Legislators passed few laws that had any impact on state-wide or local policies concerning divorce, spousal and child abuse, financial support to deserted women and children, or general relief to the poor. Instead, Loudoun's lawmakers, a small elite centered on a few planter-professional families, spent most of their energies on local fiscal concerns and modernization, rarely championing issues that impinged on family or protected it.

Loudoun politics was exciting, sometimes corrupt, or even dangerous business. Early in the county's history, for example, the landed gentry tried to create a distinct county so that they could have political dominance instead of sharing power with the small farmers and artisans. Their efforts failed, but political tensions remained high for this and other reasons.[80]

The right to participate in Loudoun's political arena was a privilege reserved for white men who met specific property qualifications. By the 1840s, poorer men were still trying to obtain the right to vote. Yet despite numerous state-wide petitions, even one from Loudoun in January 1845 which requested that the legislature "consider all the free white male citizens of the Commonwealth as having an unquestionable right to an equal participation in the government under which they live," Virginia did not expand its legal franchise to include propertyless white men until 1852.[81]

The question as to who could and could not vote and the implications for election fraud continually problematized local elections. Misspelt names on voter rolls, changes in property holdings from one election to the next, the presence of a mobile voter population, and a tradition of heavy drinking on election day consistently created confusion and sometimes contested election results. The way in which Virginians structured the polling event did not help. Loudouners held elections at the courthouse in Leesburg. The custom was to have a polling table set up either inside the building or in the adjoining yard. Upon approaching the table, each voter had to announce loudly the candidate of his choice as clerks recorded the choice. The problems that could, and did, result are obvious. Peer pressure and closely monitored choices not only threatened tainted election outcomes but created lifelong hostilities among neighbors and sometimes kin. An election for the House of Representatives in 1818, for example, led to a fatal duel between two of Loudoun's most illustrious citizens—John McCarthy and General Armistead Mason. The two were first cousins who had been raised on adjoining plantations.[82]

The Federalist party was prominent in Loudoun immediately following the American Revolution and remained so well into the second decade of the nineteenth century. Local historians credit Colonel Leven Powell, founder of the town of Middleburg, planter, and Revolutionary War officer, with the Federalists' early popularity. Having created a powerful political hold over the area during the Revolutionary and early republic eras, Leven Powell's descendants and their in-laws dominated regional politics for most of the antebellum years. Indeed, the Powell-Harrison-Conrad-Jones faction was one of the most important political dynasties in nineteenth-century northern Virginia. Leven Powell's son, Burr, served in the Virginia Assembly from 1798 to 1807 and was state senator from 1813 to 1815. Another son, Cuthbert, was elected as senator immediately after his brother's tenure and was a member of the United States Congress.[83]

The Democratic-Republican party had its heyday in Loudoun during the 1820s. By the 1830s, most had become Whigs. They controlled county politics during most of the pre-Civil War period, consistently delivering three-to-one margins for presidential candidates. Locally, Whigs campaigned on platforms which supported government funding for public works such as canals, railroads, and highways—important resources for planters and businessmen who wanted greater access to distant markets. They also organized the powerful Central Clay Club which provided a forum for local political discussions and debates as well as publicized party platform.[84]

Powell men also carried considerable weight in the Whig party. George Powell served as a Whig member of the General Assembly from 1835 to 1836. Cuthbert Burr Powell was Whig assemblyman and representative to Congress from 1841 to 1843. Two of Burr Powell's sons-in-law, Burr Harrison and Robert Conrad, and a son were Whig state legislators. Matthew Harrison represented the fourth generation of Powell politicians. An ambitious young lawyer, Matthew enhanced his wealth and political connections through his marriage to the daughter of General Walter Jones. Harrison was elected, along with his cousin Burr Noland, to the Virginia Assembly in 1861. He also served Loudoun in the Confederate state legislature from 1862 to 1863 and as a Democrat in the General Assembly for one post-Reconstruction term.[85]

By the end of the antebellum era, many had come to deeply resent the hostility and activism of northern abolitionists and the threat it brought to their society. They blamed northern "extremists" for an increase in local fugitive slave activity and especially for the John Brown Raid at Harper's Ferry federal arsenal, located just three miles north of their county line, in 1859. As the issue of disunion took center stage, Loudoun sent Quaker lawyer John Janney and planter John Carter to represent them in the special convention on secession held in Richmond during the week of February 13, 1861. Janney was elected chairman of the convention, and droves of curious, excitable onlookers traveled to Richmond in anticipation of momentous decisions. Loudouner Mason Ellzey attended the convention at the invitation of Janney. Years later Ellzey proudly remembered that he had been present when Jonathan Goode gave his persuasive speech for secession. He also had seen General Lee accept the command of the Virginia forces. But unlike Ellzey, both John Janney and John Carter opposed secession, initially voting against it. The convention eventually concluded that a decision should be made by state-wide referendum. Loudoun held its polling on May 23, 1861. The majority of voters (1,626) supported secession; 726 persons opposed it.[86]

With the onset of Civil War, life changed profoundly for Loudouners. Some communities grew stronger as others faltered in the wake of the devastation military battles like Bull Run and eventual Union occupation brought to the area. Political and other ideological differences which historically had caused divisiveness among county whites exploded. The German town of Lovettsville and the Quaker stronghold of Waterford voted overwhelmingly against secession, the only two districts to do so.[87] This was only the beginning. During wartime, Loudoun divided its allegiance along the lines that the May 23rd vote predicted. The majority of the county supported the Confederate States of America, but those sections which were primarily German and Quaker sided with the Union. The Loudoun Rangers, composed mostly of males from the German community of Lovettsville, was the only organized white Union regiment to come out of Virginia during the Civil War. Loudoun was occupied by both armies during the war at tremendous loss in property and life. In August 1864 General Ulysses S. Grant found cause to order Major General Sheridan: "If you can possibly spare a division of Cavalry, send them through Loudoun County to destroy and carry off the crops, animals, negroes and all men under fifty years of age capable of bearing arms." Two months later, Sheridan carried out his orders. Loudoun was conclusively lost to the Union army.[88]

2

Gender Convention
and Courtship

*I would advise marriage if you could form an advantageous match —
a good girl of good health[,] good temper[,] good habits and good appearance with means to enable you to maintain her for the present
would [add] to yr happiness and success in life. . . . Be careful however in the selection.*

Burr Harrison, 1849

M atthew Harrison was a young lawyer minding the family business when
he received his father's brisk missive. In the last few years Matthew had
taken on tremendous responsibilities for his widowed parent, and the strain was
beginning to show. At first he had been proud that his father had allowed him to
run his law office, to oversee his plantation, and to control household affairs at
stately Morrisworth while the elder Harrison was away in Richmond serving in
the legislature. But Matthew had begun to grow agitated and frustrated tending
to his father's domestic and business affairs. Burr Harrison sensed the change in
his son's attitude, repeatedly assuring him that his stint as surrogate father,
planter, and businessman was both appreciated and near its end. In the meanwhile, he hoped to brighten his son's outlook by suggesting that he entertain the
idea of marriage. After all, Matthew was in his late twenties, from a prestigious
family, was well educated and on his way to having a lucrative law career—
there was even the hint of political talent. Certainly, his father mused openly, his
son soon would be in the position to "form an advantageous match."[1]

Mr. Harrison also had distinct ideas about the "advantage" he wanted
Matthew to acquire through marriage. He knew just the kind of woman that
would suit Matthew, or so he believed. And as he had done so often in the past
when he believed that this son or one of his other children needed his guidance,

Burr Harrison did not hesitate to advise Matthew on "the selection" of his bride. His son, however, had many more sources of counsel than the traditional founts of parental opinion.

Single men and women like Matthew and his siblings, who hoped to be or even find the perfect spouse, were an important audience for a growing number of professional writers. These were scholars, ministers, philosophers, moralists, and physicians who took it upon themselves to try to shape nineteenth-century society by offering their readers guidelines for ideal adult behavior. While the early literature pointed to aiding the new Republic through shaping the personal behavior of the individual citizen, it was an idea that had growing appeal.

As southerners like the well-to-do Harrisons began to envision their region as distinctive—culturally, economically, and politically—they followed suit, popularizing a social ideology congruent with their evolving vision of "southern nationhood." These national and southern traditions shared common ground and consequences, particularly their upper- and middle-class audiences and their focus on gender-specific differences and societal roles. Loudoun and other southern communities became righteous harbingers of these ideas, rewarding those who complied, punishing those who did not. They expected Burr Harrison and other parents to act similarly—to make certain that their sons and daughters exhibited the appropriate personal philosophy and behavior and that they chose spouses who did so as well.

By the 1820s, popular social architects envisioned spheres of human activity which, philosophically and practically, separated the public from the private. They also envisioned a separation of the sexes, placing man in the public domain of the world and woman in the privacy of the home. In their ideal scenario the "home" was the natural, idyllic "sphere" of woman where she provided her family with a "haven" from the corrupt, competitive public sphere of men.[2]

Notions of appropriate gender convention in the South as throughout the nation, therefore, were class-distinctive. Outside the middle and upper classes, women and men were less likely to be expected to inhabit separate domains, or to exert influence over either since working women in urban or rural environments could ill afford the luxury of remaining at home. Neither did they nor their husbands typically have the kind of control over their labor, compensation, or, consequently, their home environment that writers typically presupposed. The inability of poor folk to embrace values and behavior that were becoming more and more mainstream, in turn, continuously undermined their attempts to improve their status in their community's hierarchy.

The character traits professional advisors applauded in men and women were profoundly different but linked to their distinct spheres of activity. Women were to be meek, pliant, submissive, and dependent; men should demonstrate aggressiveness, courage, physical strength, and leadership. "It will generally devolve on man to provide the means of subsistence, and to wield the arm of civil power. Woman," on the other hand, "must never forget that *home* is the very *center* of her sphere." It only was through this gendered division of spheres that nineteenth-century social "experts" could even begin to articulate an equality of purpose between men and women. The woman in the home, the author added, " may irradiate that spot with so fair a light that its beams may penetrate far into the world around. . . . And, perhaps, when the real good of society is concerned, the influence of the one is worth as much as that of the other."[3]

But despite fleeting references to equal "worth," popular ideals about women's roles, or men's, for that matter, were solidly grounded in sexist ideology and practice. On the one hand, articulate experts burdened women with unwieldy emotional and physical tasks in the name of female domesticity; while, on the other, they advocated female powerlessness in the name of feminine virtue. Women's most important duty, they argued, was to relinquish control to men; men's most significant act was to maintain control of his "dependents." Experts took for granted that women should center their lives on addressing men's needs, and that men should provide them with support and protection in return. As such, the home was women's sphere, but man's dominion. "Oh, young and lovely bride, watch well the first moments when your will conflicts with his, to whom God and society have given the control. Reverence his *wishes* even when you do not his *opinions*," writers typically advised. The wife's role was to obey and guide, sacrificing herself in order to be the living "example of patience, of discretion, of candor, kindness and sincerity" which would elevate her husband's performance in the "world." "In whatsoever age, station or country, we view the condition of man," the author of "Female Influence" offered, "we must be struck with the remarkable fact that the admiration, the love, or the approbation of woman has excited him to the accomplishments of undertakings which no other cause could prompt him to commence." Through meekness and pliancy, a woman had the power to "soften," "refine," and "elevate," her spouse. A man's duty was to provide his wife with the material wherewithal and social status to keep her "soft," "refined," and "elevated."[4]

The responsibilities of the adult woman fell completely within the confines of her self-sacrifice and submission; while manhood impinged on one's self-determination and control. But if the first lessons of appropriate female behavior centered on submission and self-sacrifice, the importance of female piety came quickly thereafter. "The duties of the female sex all concur in enjoining the cultivation of a pious and devotional spirit," they explained. Self-sacrifice, submission, and piety, of course, were female virtues extolled in the Judeo-Christian tradition, a point which ministers did not hesitate to hail and exploit in their sermons about woman's roles in their families and communities.[5]

The Reverend Dr. Bishop's remarks were exemplary. According to his article "A Good Wife," a woman had six essential traits—"common sense," "self-command," industry, piety, prudence, and discretion. These served well what he believed were a woman's three fundamental roles within her family: devoted wife, affectionate mother, and skilled housekeeper. Others provided even more detailed instructions and included lists of mandatory housewifery skills like embroidery, sewing, knitting, spinning, cooking, baking, table service, and, of course, childrearing.[6] Command of all these tasks, one author concluded in 1833, not only made a family's home pleasant, but had the added advantage of keeping a wife trim and fit—a benefit both to herself and her husband.[7]

Literate Loudouners and other Virginians could find these opinions expressed in a number of periodicals. Even some agricultural, political, and literary journals contained stories, poems, essays, and debates which explored popular notions of gender convention. Magazines directed at female audiences and those which focused on moral and religious issues consistently gave the most extensive coverage. Ever popular and available were Virginia publications like the *Southern Literary Messenger* and *The Southern Planter* as well as short-run local offerings like the Winchester *Monthly Magazine and Literary Journal* and Harper's Ferry's *Ladies Garland*. Sarah Hale's *Ladies Magazine and Literary Gazette* (later *Godeys Lady's Book*) attracted many readers throughout the region and the hearty endorsement of the local press. "[It] is the most elegant magazine in the country, and no Ladies centre table should be considered complete without it," advised the editor of the *Loudoun Chronicle* in 1849.[8]

Some nationally circulated journals included articles specific to their southern readership. Hale's *Ladies Magazine*, for example, ran a series of stories entitled "Domestic Sketches from a Southern Pen." Not surprisingly, the target audience was the elite—slaveholding women. Most of the articles varied little thematically from other selections, but did focus more on the issue of slavery and its impact on slave mistresses' unique domestic role. Writers advised planter women to be able to perform their own household labor as to do so was the mark of a "well-born" "well-bred" female. Others counseled kindness and benevolence to slaves, but also the importance of gaining control of them.[9]

Although proponents of female gentility, piety, and domesticity argued that these traits came naturally to women, few believed that those born poor were meant to be "ladies" or even ideal wives and mothers. "But remember, such taste is the offspring of refinement and gentility, a common person would never have dreamt of such things," one voiced clearly. Even those who did acknowledge poor women never really considered their different lifestyles, offering only the same advice they gave the more privileged. The closest any advisor came to addressing the needs of poor farm women is suggested in a depiction of two southern ladies who had been reduced to poverty. The article's basic theme centered on their ability to rise psychologically above their new station in the community's hierarchy; to, in effect, affect a wealthy demeanor. The conclusion was predictable even in its absurdity: "'Once a lady, always a lady.'"[10]

Or so the saying went. Yet the "lady" hardly was suited to farm life, even genteel farm life. Rural southern families and communities needed hardworking women who were willing to labor in the privacy of their homes and in the semi-public domain of their farms. Certainly many who were part of an agrarian culture or whose religion forbade them to take on a "fancy," fashionable lifestyle could not and did not wholeheartedly embrace the concept of "the lady," southern or no. The men in their families rejected the image as well. Rural-based fathers, even members of the gentry, writing to daughters who had gone to urban settings to study or on vacation, for example, cautioned them not to emulate the behavior of "city belles." These same fathers advised their sons to marry "country" girls.[11]

Practical notions of southern womanhood, therefore, rarely excluded the importance of female productivity, particularly after marriage. Women's labor was much too important to their husbands, families, and communities to ignore its significance. Prescriptive literature authors may have promoted the image of the southern single "belle" as frivolous and idle, but even they realized that the ideal southern matron was a productive, selfless, submissive wife and mother. Indeed, southern parents often promoted frivolity in their adolescent "belles" because they realized it was short-lived, ending abruptly when a daughter married and especially after her first child was born. The differences in acceptable images of southern female behavior, therefore, did not separate just along class lines. They also responded to other conditions, including a woman's age, whether or not she was reared in an urban or rural location, and her marital status.[12]

Beyond the day-to-day practicality of acceptable gender convention, however, was the importance of southern womanhood and manhood as symbols of southern moral superiority. Popularized images of the southern lady and the southern gentleman flew in the face of abolitionists' accusations of a corrupt slaveholding class and society. As southerners strove for the moral, civilized high ground, wives and mothers tried to imitate romanticized versions of their lives. Likewise, men felt moved to protect, defend, and support the southern woman.[13]

But to what end? As dependents on men for financial support and protection, southern women had limited volition and status in their community's hierarchy. While they certainly had a kind of privilege derived from their race that fundamentally held them above the status of black slaves, and especially black slave women, dependency linked the two. For dependency seemed to imply an infantilization some attributed to white women as quickly as to black slaves. In his classic treatise *Sociology for the South, or the Failure of Free Society*, for example, Virginia's foremost proslavery philosopher George Fitzhugh was quick to liken the innate intellectual and emotional failings of women to those of children and the enslaved. "We do not set children and women free because they are not capable of taking care of themselves, not equal to the constant struggle of society," he assured his devoted proslavery audience. "To set them free would be to give the lamb to the wolf to take care of. Society would quickly devour them. If the children of ten years of age were remitted to all the rights of person and property which men enjoy, all can perceive how ruin and penury would overtake them. But half of mankind are but grown-up children, and liberty is as fatal to them as it would be to children. . . ."[14]

Incapable, like slaves, of caring for themselves, Fitzhugh suggests that women should love, respect, and obey their male guardians. To do otherwise would be to suggest ingratitude and rebellion, attitudes that would undermine those peculiarly feminine qualities that attracted men. "A man loves his children because they are weak, helpless and dependent," Fitzhugh explained. "He loves his wife for similar reasons. When his children grow up and assert their independence, he is apt to transfer his affection to his grandchildren." In other words, when women demanded control and independence, they were acting more like men than women. A husband, he concluded, "ceases to love his wife when she becomes masculine or rebellious. . . ."[15]

Fitzhugh's analogy was not the only tie proslavery supporters made between white southern womanhood and slavery. They also manipulated models of southern femininity in order to justify slave ownership. In order for a woman to secure male protection, they argued, she "was endowed with the capacity to create a magic spell over any man in her vicinity." In short, she was "the most fascinating being in creation . . . the delight and charm of every circle she move[d] in."[16] And why was the southern white woman so gifted and privileged? She was, according to Virginian Thomas R. Dew, because of the effects of slavery. "We behold," he asserted, "the marked efficiency of slavery on the conditions of woman—we find her at once elevated, clothed with all her charms, mingling with and directing the society to which she belongs, no longer the slave, but the equal and the idol of man." It was slavery, Dew and others argued, which shielded the white woman from the status of the slave woman. Slavery was the constant cultural reference, the negative incentive which both defined white womanhood and manhood and kept both in the proslavery camp. Without the enslavement of some well-defined "different" group, they all felt the threat of the perpetual debasement that was the slave's fate.[17]

It is little wonder then that southern white men were not the only proponents of female domestic spheres and submission to male authority. Women often proposed the same kinds of female behavior, and not for reasons different from those of their husbands. Julia Gardiner Tyler, wife of President John

Tyler, was clear in her famous response to abolitionist criticism. Tyler wrote at length and passionately about the southern woman's exalted position in her community. "Her circle is," she noted, "that of the family, and such she is content that it shall be. Within that circle her influence is felt over the relations of life, as wife, mother, mistress-and as she discharges the duty of one or all of these relations, so is she respected or otherwise." She also wrote of the community's response to southern women moving outside of her "circle," particularly their possible participation in political debates such as those centered on slavery. This kind of activity, Tyler assured her critics, was well beyond the southern woman's domain. Domesticity reigned supreme. "Such is emphatically the case with the women of the Southern states," she reiterated. "Do you wish to see them, you must visit their homes."[18]

This ideology permeated southern communities and fueled their attempts to censor or denigrate alternative views. Anxious parents took these considerations to heart and passed them on to their children. Gendered patterns of behavior appropriate to a southern patriarchal context, therefore, were central criteria for choosing the right husband or wife.

Racial, cultural, or ethnic and social compatibility were essential concerns that almost everyone shared. This compatibility, after all, undergirded the racial hierarchy of southern communities. State laws absolutely forbade marriages across racial lines; while customs made it difficult for those of various class, ethnicities, and even religions to intermarry.[19] Yet a few interracial "married" couples always lived openly in the county even if the white community completely shunned them. Loudoun census records from 1830, for example, document that free blacks David Smallwood, Douglass Gayle, Henry Newman, and his three brothers all were "married" to white women. Many more couples undoubtedly existed but, given the society's pervasive hostility, felt compelled to live more clandestinely. Society was easier on interethnic couples, but not always. Members of Loudoun's German community continued to demand that their children marry among the ranks of their cultural community. Middling- and upper-class folk wanted their children to marry within or above their class. Some even choose to protect their privileged status and their family's property holdings by marrying close family relations. Many prominent family trees, like those of the Powells and Harrisons, for example, were replete with first- and second-cousin marriages, especially among their wealthiest branches. Nancy Conrad responded typically when she noticed that her young cousins, James and Frederica, were *casting sheeps eyes* at each other: "They would suit [each other] admirably."[20]

The specter of interracial marriage was so rare and strong prohibitions against interethnic couples restricted to such a small number of people that compatibility for many hinged on comparable class status. Class, of course, affected gender-specific behavior within the context of their families' economy.

Middling-class and poorer wives, for example, earned income by selling the live-stock that they raised. They also helped their families' budget by raising food-stuffs and making clothes and household furnishings. Wealthy women usually brought substantial dowries into their marriages, that is, property and cash which their husbands could use for the family's future support. Yet men still had the special burden of primary breadwinner. That duty, in fact, was in many ways synonymous with manhood. To be unable to support one's wife and chil-dren not only denied a man his personal and public honor, it emasculated him.

The financial pressures of marriage were so substantial for men that it effec-tively extended the age at which they first married. Records indicate, for ex-ample, that European American men in Loudoun married late, on average at 25 or 26. Many, like Matthew Harrison, married even later. Their choice of oc-cupation had much to do with their lengthy bachelorhood. Most young men, for example, became farmers. Yet land and labor prices made it difficult for them to get the proper "start" before they reached their mid-twenties. Most could not afford to purchase farm land outright, so they spent much of their early twenties working as farm hands, overseers, or apprentices, saving what they could to be able to rent or eventually buy. Some fathers allowed their sons to farm the land that they eventually would inherit. But farmers were not the oldest cohort to marry; planter/professional men were. By the time they fin-ished college, completed their medical or legal training, set up their practice, and began to earn enough money to support a wife, most were at least 25. It was not unusual for some to be in their early thirties by the time they wed.[21]

Many fathers could not afford to subsidize the income of their married sons after having invested in their education and helping them to establish a profes-sional office. "When your education is completed you will have to depend wholly upon yourself" was a typical decision. Of course, very wealthy fathers could afford to act otherwise, and some did. Robert Carter, for example, gave his sons George and John fully stocked Loudoun plantations when they were in their early twenties. Yet even those fathers who had the means to help their sons to gain early financial independence sometimes did not, reasoning that to let them find their own way would strengthen their masculine character. Of course, all the reasoning in the world had little sway with the fathers of poten-tial brides.[22]

Burr Powell was quite explicit about the question of a husband's financial duty when he discussed the possible marriage of his youngest daughter with her suitor, Robert Conrad. Powell was one of Loudoun's most prestigious leaders and when he married Catherine Brooke, the attractive, educated, wealthy daughter of Colonel Humphrey Brooke and Elizabeth Braxton of Fauquier County, in 1794, it was a "pleasing" match to both families and com-munities. Catherine brought a sizable dowry to her marriage and received a healthy estate from her father when he died. Burr Powell also inherited a considerable amount of land and slaves when his father died. As a young man and throughout their marriage, he worked tirelessly to give his family a comfortable lifestyle on their "Chestnut Hill" plantation. Major Powell was determined that his daughters' status not change when they married.[23]

As a responsible father, Burr Powell studied the future "prospects" of his children carefully. He made certain, for example, that they all had fine educations. He also tried to insure that they marry the "right" person. He especially wanted his daughters to marry promising men of equal class status. Powell did not demand that their suitors have large fortunes, but they at least had to possess moderate-sized estates and the character, ability, health, and willingness to earn enough income to support his daughters in comfort. When Robert Conrad asked for Betty's hand in marriage, therefore, Mr. Powell did not hesitate to make clear that his "daughters had not the strength of constitution to make good wives to men who were too poor to keep them from hard labor." Withholding his final decision, Powell told the anxious young man that his answer hinged on Betty's feelings and evidence of Conrad's ability to support her.[24]

All in all, Powell was pleased when Robert indicated interest in marrying Betty. He appeared to be a young man destined to make his mark—with his West Point education and national political connections, the risk of his failure seemed small. Powell also liked Robert's strong allegiance to the region's planter/professional elite—his father had been a highly esteemed doctor/planter in Winchester. At the time that Robert proposed to Betty, he and his widowed mother occupied the family's spacious Georgian mansion and they owned a moderate-sized plantation. Still, Burr Powell was willing to take little for granted when it came to his daughter's future.[25]

Robert Conrad had to consider these very same issues a generation later as his nine children neared maturity. His attitude was not very much different from that of his father-in-law. "Berta you know is married; and from what I heard of General Brown, is married well," he wrote to his wife regarding the recent wedding of a young cousin. Upon hearing that his eldest son Daniel, who was just about to enter medical school, had "fallen in love with some young lady," Conrad responded rather nonchalantly. "[W]ho it is I did not hear, nor is it a matter of consequence, as a love affair so far in advance of his being able to support a wife, is pretty certain to be succeeded by a good many more." Robert knew that few fathers would let their daughters marry someone who was not yet able to support a family. He also knew that his son realized that he had no intention of assuming the support of a daughter-in-law and would never consent to Daniel entertaining the notion of marriage before he was financially independent.[26]

Brides had some financial responsibilities too, for a woman's dowry was important to a young couple's financial survival. When Betsy Settle married Lewis Edmonds, for example, her dowry included the beautiful plantation estate of "Belle Grove." In Burr Harrison's note to his son Matthew about the possibility of marriage, he listed a woman's "means" to "enable" her husband to "maintain her for the present" as a fundamental selection criteria, certainly one that he had considered important when he married. Burr Harrison and Robert Conrad were married to sisters, the second and third daughters of Burr Powell. Both Harrison and Conrad benefited from the generous dowries of slaves and household furnishings that Powell gave them when his daughters married. Powell himself had gained substantial property through his wife's dowry. By the time that Burr Harrison came to counsel his son some fifty years later about the necessity of marrying a woman with a substantial dowry, the practice had become a prized family tradition.[27]

Harrison promised to give Matthew $5000 in property and bonds along with a house in Leesburg when he married, but the issue of a sizable dowry remained important. "A good estate is ever desirable," he wrote in 1849, "one to enable you to get on till yr professional profits was sufficient would perhaps be almost indispensable. . . ." Two years later, at the age of thirty, Matthew married Anne Jones, the wealthy daughter of Anne Lee and the politically powerful General Walter Jones. Young Harrison's marriage to Anne was not only financially lucrative, but strengthened his status among the elite and was a tremendous boost to his legal and political careers. Needless to say, Matthew's family, and particularly his father, were pleased with his choice.[28]

Although social climbing through marriage was a well-honed tradition among some, virtually no one wanted a poor man or woman to improve his or her status by marrying into their family. Society was especially suspicious of men of unfortunate means who sought the affections of wealthy single or widowed women. Hortensia Hay made a habit of identifying potential fortune hunters. Commenting on the courtship of one of her less favorite cousins, the granddaughter of President Monroe smirked: "I am glad to hear Mr. Lynch is so taken with Miss [Frances] Monroe for I think it would be a good match, I mean in joint of figure for in anything [else] I do not think it would suit either. . . . [for] Jays purse is too light for him to think of being a follower of the venus Celeste, and I do not imagine Frances could bloom long upon sentiment and crackers as he contrives to do with so much effect." "Poor Jay," she added sympathetically, "I believe he has a good heart and some head—indeed I give him credit for a good many qualities but he is very poor and he acts only right in looking out for a rich woman as a remedy for all his misfortune. . . ."[29]

Race and class, therefore, were considered the most important signs of marital compatibility, but not the only ones. Religious beliefs and practices, often at the heart of one's family history and community identity, also were significant. The Society of Friends, for one, was adamant that their members marry within their faith on threat of being dismissed from their Meeting and disowned by their families. Unfortunately, the demands of such communities were often difficult to meet, especially when a small population meant limited choices. The results were predictable—older ages at first marriage and a healthy number of cousin marriages, cross-sibling couplings, and out-of-faith matches.[30]

An analysis of Quaker marriages among members of Loudoun's Goose Creek Meeting, for example, indicates that between 1800 and 1860, the Society of Friends excluded 21 percent of those persons for whom they retained marriage records, because they chose non-Quaker spouses. Eli Janney's case was typical. When he wanted to marry a woman who was not a Quaker, the Goose Creek Meeting expelled him. Janney could have rejoined his local meeting when, several years later, as a widower he married a Quaker woman. Yet he refused to do so, probably because he still resented the kind of tremendous influence his community tried to have on his personal life. Defiance of this kind undoubtedly contributed to the large numbers of out-of-faith marriages. So too did emigration patterns. Quaker men were among the most numerous Loudoun emigrants during the end of the eighteenth century and the first decades of the nineteenth. Thus while both Quaker men and women married out of faith, females were slightly more apt to do so and more likely to do so during those clusters of years when the numbers of male emigrants were highest.[31]

Members of other denominations tended to be less squeamish about interfaith marriages, but still wanted their kin to worship as was their family's tradition. If there was a "mixed" marriage, most expected wives to defer to their husbands' preferences. "Our neighbor Miss Baldwin is to be married very soon to Mr. John Atkinson," Robert Conrad informed one of his daughters. "[T]hey are to married by his brother the Episcopal clergyman in Balt[imore] which some of our strictest Presbyterians seem to think may be ominous to his going over to the bride's church, instead of taking her to his."[32]

Scrutiny of a potential spouse's ethnic or racial background, class affiliations and religious practices was only part of the screening process. One's general lifestyle also came into question. Whether someone was raised in the city or the country, for example, was of importance. Loudoun farmers, artisans, planters and even planter/professionals, most of whom were born and raised in the countryside, believed that the kinds of morals and lifestyles they attributed to a "country" upbringing were both superior to and incompatible with those of city "belles" and "gentleman." Burr Powell, for example, found more than one occasion to instruct his daughter Betty to remember that she was the daughter of a "country gentleman" and not a "city belle," and to act accordingly. Twenty years later, Burr Harrison advised his son Matthew that a "country girl" would be a "better companion" than any he might meet in a city like Richmond. Farmers had the most practical objections to "city belles." Few wanted their sons to marry women who were not accustomed to the rigors of female farmwork.[33]

Family and community alike believed that a couple's compatibility was foundation for a sound companionate marriage. Definitions of "companionate" varied with each couple, but most instinctively believed that if women and men lived up to community-sanctioned ideals of gender-differentiated behavior they would be good companions for almost anyone. Women who were nice, of even temper, honest, intelligent, hardworking, pious, and modest were the best companions. "An agreable [*sic*] intelligent companion with good temper etc. . . . is eminently qualified to smooth the rugged path of life and promotes a mans standing and improvement and business here," one father wrote to his son in 1849. "Gentle, amiable, and intelligent," Robert Conrad advised his daughter were the traits which endeared a woman to her husband and family. When Alfred Powell wrote to congratulate his brother on his marriage during the 1820s, he predicted that the young couple would have a wonderful life together because the bride demonstrated so many admirable qualities, including intelligence, an amiable disposition, and "every trait of character that can adorn and enoble [*sic*] her sex." While writing of his marriage, Quaker Samuel Janney noted that his wife's most important contribution had been her consistent role as a "sympathizing companion and a helpmeet stedfast [*sic*] in love and devotion." And when Louise Harrison Love described her uncle's bride to her sister-in-law, she centered her comments on the woman's "companionate" qualities, noting that she "appear[ed] to possess a very amiable disposition, indeed, one would think that she was never out of temper in her life. . . ."[34]

Good male companions had to have some of the same personality traits as women. They had to be kind, even tempered, and devoted to family. One young woman found that men most worthy of the love of any "girl" " were those who had "a good, affectionate, susceptible heart." Others emphasized good moral fiber, a quality that most believed was more "natural" to women than men.[35] Burr Powell, for example, especially was fond of one of his daughter's beaus because he had a "standing for a good moral character." Robert Conrad believed that the best men, husband or not, were those of "excellent judgment, of warm and kindly sympathies, . . . great public spirit" and who demonstrated a "universal and sincere regard" for not just their wives and families, but for everyone in their acquaintance. They were men whose families and friends "could always know where to find [them] and could confidently rely upon [their] friendly offices." Enlightened members of other local communities were in full accord. Paul Henkel, area minister and poet, dedicated some of his prescriptive lyrics to problem marriages among his fellow German Americans. One such poem, descriptively entitled "Heathenish Housekeeping," was a critique of lazy husbands and sons who took advantage of the selfless wife and mother:

> While sons and fathers hug the fire
> And winds each window rattle,
> The mother trudges to the byre,

To tend the horse and cattle.
The lazy louts their places hold,
Nor budge an inch, though chilled with cold,
In comes the faithful mother.[36]

Paul Henkel despised indolent male farmers who insisted that their wives do the kind of harsh labor usually reserved for slave women. He had even fewer kind words for local "dandies" who threatened a woman's virtue and purse. He warned young "maidens" to take "special care" when choosing a husband lest they be charmed by "worthless rascals" "whose talk is false and flattering jest."

Henkel wrote for a specific ethnic audience, but almost everyone believed that a dishonest or dishonorable man was the worst kind of male companion. "I feel so sorry for her and I dislike Dr. Turner more than ever," Rose Davisson wrote of her aunt's fiancé in 1857. "I do not think him *strictly honourable*." Ms. Davisson had heard from a reliable source that Turner had pursued other women after becoming betrothed to her aunt. She believed his action betrayed a character flaw that had all kinds of negative implications for their future life together. "How I wish she could discard him," she wrote bitterly some time later. "If I were placed in her position and the gentleman were to treat me as *he* her, I would discard him in one moment, and it *should not* make me unhappy either."[37]

Some feared that a woman's attraction to a ne'er-do-well's charm or physical beauty might blind her to other important flaws. Yet a prospective bride usually saw more in a physically attractive man than a winning smile or handsome physique. Physical attractiveness often was conflated with good health, and no woman savored the idea of marrying a man who did not have the physical fortitude to support her. Would-be grooms were equally interested in the health of their romantic interests. A woman without a strong constitution could not sustain the many years of childbearing that most married Loudoun females experienced, and that many men depended on as sources of additional farm or workshop labor. Nor could a sickly woman take on the typical workload of a rural housewife. "It is important *to get good health and good constitution* (I mean free of any hereditary traits) . . . mind-manner-temper-health and good looks (not beauty) make the companion. They last[,] and as long as they do affection and esteem and love continue to grow," one widowed father advised his son. Certainly few men wanted to marry a woman whose health problems meant constant financial and emotional costs or an ineffectual partner.[38]

Although parents discouraged their children from placing too much emphasis on beauty, physical and sexual appeal always were important. Some men valued beauty basics like healthy teeth, a clear complexion, an average weight, form, and height, rather than transitory, picture-perfect prettiness. But what young woman did not want her beau to think that she was the most beautiful woman in the world?

Despite Quaker prescriptions of simple and plain dress, beauty and fashion were especially important to many young women. They constantly commented on their looks and those of others. Competition for male attention only fueled their interests. When Betty Powell's parents finally relented and let her go to the balls at Bath one season, for example, she had hardly finished thanking them for this extravagance when she began to ask for new clothing and jewelry to wear. "I feel very much pleased with my intended trip and very grateful to my parents for such indulgence," she admitted.

As she already had her mother's "pretty cambric dress and two handsome black silks," the young woman did not feel that she needed another "frock." She would have a seamstress make "two white bodices" and purchase "some little articles such as gloves, ribbons, etc." What Betty really wanted was some new jewelry—a gold chain and heart, pearl earrings, and a pin set with amethyst. "I am afraid you think my wants and wishes will never end—but such things as these are more necessary at Bath than a great variety of dresses and they are always useful and never out of fashion," she explained. "Will you if you please beg papa a little and let me hear the result by the next mail."[39]

Betty Powell's youthful vanity kept her and her parents in the fashionable shops. "I do not need another frock yet," she wrote to her mother in May 1829, "but I expect by August I shall and then I should like to have a silk and take my crape for a winter frock." She also needed "stuff shoes" (with toes stuffed) that she wanted "figured" (embroidered), as was the style at the time. As a young woman in boarding school, Ann Maund made similar requests of her guardian and uncle, George Carter. "Miss Henning would thank you to send me in addition to the things mentioned in the last letter, five yards of white figured cambric, and two yards of lace to make me tuckers such as the ladies wear in Baltimore," she wrote to him in 1805. By the 1850s, Mrs. Betty Powell Conrad and her husband were purchasing their adolescent daughter Kate the "New York finery" she desired.[40]

Some fashion statements were more amusing than complimentary. "I never saw the ladies dressed in better taste or beaming with more animation," the recently married Robert Conrad reported to his wife in February 1830. One woman especially caught his attention. "Mrs. Newton, formerly Miss Mary McCaudless," he chuckled, was "dressed in the latest New York, ultrafashionable costume—a la morgue—. . . a very scanty frock and large white pantaloons." The following morning, Conrad spotted the clothes horse again, " in the street with *blue cloth gaiters*."[41]

Even local newspapers encouraged female beauty and fashion. In articles like "Woman" which appeared in the *Loudoun Chronicle* in 1849, writers crooned:

"When we see a neat, pretty girl, with a free but innocent air, with cheeks which we can hardly help kissing, and with a pair of heavenly blue eyes, which seem to repose in perfect security beneath their silken lashes, how can we help loving her." How indeed! Certainly young women and men were influenced by this kind of popularized connection between beauty and love. It was as if one who possessed the former innately deserved the later. Such messages pressured women to be as physically appealing to men as possible.[42]

But women also could turn the tables on their beaus, pushing aside those who did not meet their exact standards of attractiveness and fashion, and praising those who did. "I assure you upon the strength of a new brown coat; pale yellow cravat[,] white pantaloons[,] and silk stockings," Hortensia Hay wrote to one of her friends about a love interest, "the fascinating Cane . . . is well worth receiving a message from." Of course, a man's personal style was also part of what made him attractive. "In addition to the above improvement," Miss Hay added, "he has an interesting languor in his air that I think would touch even you."[43]

Beauty and, to a lesser extent, fashion obviously were important to would-be husbands. Still most men wanted wives who not only were attractive, but also excelled in domestic skills. While the upper class, represented by the Powells, Conrads, Carters, Lees, Hays, and Harrisons, could rely on domestic servants to provide a comfortable home for their families, others depended on the domestic labor of wives. Even women in the upper class had to learn at least the most basic domestic skills, such as sewing, cooking, and child care. As time passed, this kind of emphasis deepened. By the 1840s, elite parents, like their poorer neighbors and relations, also insisted that their single daughters know how to conduct themselves in the kitchen, garden, sewing room, nursery, and sick room before their marriages.[44]

Of course, these kinds of concerns presupposed that daughters would marry, and most did. Yet the inevitability of marriage did not erase the long, sometimes circuitous, process known as courtship that led to it. There were several distinct elements to the courtship ritual that had to transpire before a wedding took placed. One of the most important components was the initial introduction.

Young women and men who eventually married met under all kinds of circumstances, although the formal debut has come to represent elite southern courtship. It was there that well-to-do young women were introduced to the most eligible single men at lavish, properly chaperoned social events. The debut usually took place after a girl finished her education. Proud fathers introduced their single daughters, dressed in the finest clothing their parents could afford, to the social world of the southern gentry. A young woman's "season" was supposed to be the happiest and most exciting time of her life. "Cousin Lucy spent a week at Llangollen and says Uncle John is full of Jennie's grand debut and intends giving her a large dancing party," Ann Maria Harrison wrote to her younger sisters in the 1850s. "There was a large company—about 20 ladies when I got there and several had already gone home," one pleased observer reported of a typical ball. "Miss Mary Lee was upon the floor-having come around to the opinion I expressed to her (*before I was married*) that she was too young & too pretty to turn devotee. Several ladies were in from the country."[45]

It was the responsibility of relatives and friends to make certain that belles were introduced to anyone they considered eligible. Some parents from local rural areas even sponsored debut parties in Richmond, so that their daughters would have a proper introduction to Virginia's upper-crust. Robert Conrad, for example, attended the Richmond "debut" of Anna Mason, a daughter of old friends. Anna, he noted, was the "belle" of the party scene in Richmond, "imparting great pleasure or pain" to "numerous and ardent" "beaus." Conrad arrived early at one of these events in order to make sure that Anna was having a good time and was meeting people. But "seeing plainly that she required no service from me," he decided not to "venture to another." Of course many of the young men and women who met at these parties had known each other most of their lives; many were cousins or neighbors, had gone to church together, played together, or even attended the same grammar schools. But the debut was meant to wash away images of childhood play, unveiling an adult ready to take on adult roles.[46]

Since introductions and initial encounters were so important to the courtship ritual, both men and women strove to make favorable impressions. Young men had to play the aggressor, but still relied on family members, friends, employers, ministers, and chaperones to guarantee their good character and promising futures. This kind of highly stylized courtship provided amusing scenes for curious onlookers. Agnes Davisson recalled her older sister's "romantic" evening strolls with potential suitors. Writing to another sibling, she laughed:

We were all going to church the other night. Sister was walking with Button Turner and just as she got to the parsonage, she fell flat on the ground. She was very much mortified, of course. But was very glad I reckon that it was not the night before when Cousin Li was walking with her. It was exactly in the same place, you recollect, at which she got a fall once when she was in company with the gentleman with the "perfectly Grecian face."[47]

Ms. Davisson does not refer to her sister's chaperone on these occasions, but these "attendants," preferably older adolescent or adult relations, were important fixtures in the lives of Loudoun's white women. Parents constructed elaborate plans to insure the "safe" arrival of their daughters from one destination to another.[48] But young men and women still found ways to circumvent the best laid plans.

When Robert Conrad, for example, agreed to accompany a friend's daughter to a ball and make certain that she was back home by midnight, he had no idea of the lengths to which Sarah Jane, the young woman, would go to undermine his efforts. "I thought (good soul [that I am]) that she really desired my protection," he began his explanation to his wife, "and, of course (though I did not intend to go to the ball) was bound to give it cheerfully." But Sarah Jane had schemed to use him only as a decoy. "Well—I sallied up there to night and after tea, led her out to the carriage. As soon as we got out of the gate a student, in whiskers and white pantaloons, sprung from the shade of the wall, where he had been lying in wait, and they were both in the carriage before I could uncover from the surprize." Conrad "deliberated a moment about kicking him out, or taking her back to her father—but gave it up as too troublesome." "So it was," he concluded, "she entered the Ball room upon the students [*sic*] arm; and I put my hand in my pockets and winded home." When Robert returned at 12 o'clock to take Sarah Jane home, he had to wait two hours before she would consent to leave. Amused by the young woman's antics, he only had two other things to note about the incident: Sarah Jane's "student" was so hairy that Robert could not tell if he was a "man or a monkey"; and he felt absolutely certain that he was "cured" of the "dancing mania for the balance of [his] life."[49]

Sarah Jane seemed to have been serious about her "student" beau, but few early dates actually led to a real courtship. Men and women indulged in mindless flirtations sometimes for years before they were ready to think soberly about marriage. Francis Powell, for example, wrote to his sister that he was having a very busy spring in Leesburg—studying medicine, working in his brother's store, and seeking the attentions of the Miss Warrens, three lovely and "very rich" sisters. Needless to say, Frank's intentions were far from sincere—his "courting" was little more than a fantastical diversion from his studies.[50]

While Frank genuinely enjoyed his social world and the young women he romanced, some single men had some difficulty appreciating the maze of frivolity and meaningless encounters that sometimes characterized a formal courtship. Shy, unassuming Levi White, for example, complained that he had been unable to find a wife in his farming community. Writing to a cousin in 1804, Levi declared: "You would wish to know whether I am likely to get a wife yet or not. Maby [*sic*], but I am hardly able to inform you . . . for there is a Plenty of wiming [*sic*] to be had but I am afeard [*sic*] but a few Wifes amongst them."[51]

Snobbish John Scott Peyton was much more cynical. Corresponding to his younger brother in 1829, John depicted the local "reigning belles" as a frivolous, vain lot, with little to offer. He was happy to prove his point by caricaturizing the women at a wedding he had attended. He began with a cousin. "First[,] Maria Scott (who has turned out as it is called since you left here), she has no desire to be distinguished for her learning, she wishes to know merely enough of books to fit her for the light conversation of the drawing room." "Her highest ambition is to be called the fascinating little creature, to be more attended to than any other young lady in the room. To have admirers not lovers is her aim. She takes no interest in a sighing dying scion." But Maria had some stiff competition. She feared that "she might be eclipsed by a Miss Bland from Maryland who had been making a great noise in the county." "Next," he continued, "Lucy Kinker[:] she is in one respect quite the reversal of Maria Scott[.] [S]he wishes it to be said that she had been courted by this, that and the other gentleman. In company she assumes a modest, innocent retiring aim and endeavors to secure a Conquest." Finally, there was another cousin, Christian Scott. "She is a little coquettish too but particularly values herself for repartie." In the end, the young lawyer did have to admit that he found the gathering "very pleasant." As for the young ladies and their particular concerns, he added parenthetically: "A single glance at Miss Bland convinced Maria that she had nothing to fear and her vanity was flattered by assiduous attention from the most genteel beau." "As for Lucy Kinker," John added with a dash of pride, "she cast so many sweet looks at me, that I suspect that she has marked me out for her victim. I escaped however with a slight wound."[52]

Mr. Peyton's remarks said much about an "indelicate" reality of courtship ritual. The pressure to woo, and win, a marriage partner publicly—at weddings, parties, and church bazaars—could retard a process already flawed by rigid rules and unrealistic standards of success. Public courting, while fascinating and amusing, often created scenes of silly chatter and fierce matches between women for male attention. One also risked the embarrassment of public rejection. But women were not the only ones affected. The men too had to do their best to be dashing and charming. And they, like the women, sometimes failed.

Dreams filled with romantic expectation often proved elusive. Amanda Edmonds, for example, wrote poignantly on her twentieth birthday about her desire for romance. Like so many of her friends, she hoped that her "young and blooming heart may yet be caught by a true, noble, generous soul that may ever beat responsive" to hers. But her active social life hardly satisfied her fantasies. "O! Romance! Romance!, companion of my dreams—why does the realization leave my soul so restless?" she lamented seven months later. No one she had met during the throng of church socials, parties, balls, and weddings had caught her fancy, none she had met were "present of right heart, character or fascinating eye, or the rich mellow voice of the soul." "Better expressed," she confided to her journal, her "ideal was not there."[53]

The ritual of mate selection, as artificial and pretentious as it may have been for many, occurred within the confines of a culture that supported one's participation and rewarded one's success. One's family and community celebrated tirelessly once a "successful" match was made. Still, it could be a hollow experience for many. Some simply were unlucky in love, constantly choosing some-one who later proved to be lacking some essential trait or not particularly inter-ested in a romantic relationship or permanent commitment. Others had extremely high standards that one person hardly could meet. Combine such standards with a much stronger desire for romance than a realistic relationship offered and one can begin to understand why women like Amanda Edmonds continually turned away suitors. Yet few could afford to wait forever.

Spinsterhood was not an honorable status. Women who reached maturity during the 1840s and 1850s, however, faced a dwindling pool of marriageable males as large numbers of young men of every class left Loudoun for places west and south. The onslaught of the Civil War made the situation even more desperate. Yet women still faced ridicule and sometimes even cruel alienation if they did not marry. Amanda Edmonds was only twenty when her "friends" began teasing her about not having a special beau. One sent her a valentine with a picture of a "hideous old maid" "pitched up on a fork," like a devil. "What a delight," Amanda responded sarcastically, for a "young blooming lass" to be so quickly "shifted to old maidenhood!"[54]

Because most single women could not support themselves, "spinsters" lived with their parents or married siblings. They were a good source of domestic labor, but received little reward for their work; and spinsterhood could be an unbearable, lonely fate. Some single women chose to pursue "careers," be-coming teachers, midwives, weavers, shopkeepers, or taking in boarders, thus providing for their own support. Sophie Davisson, for one, became a teacher, moving away from Loudoun and its disapproving community. A few single women like Sarah Ellzey with landed property and slaves became planters in their own right, usually employing an overseer to run the day-to-day activities of their plantations. Yet few survived as well as Ellzey. Sophie Davisson's fate was one that mature single women and their families constantly feared. A few years after she left Loudoun, she died a single, childless woman away from her family and friends in the distant county where she worked.[55]

Most meaningful encounters between single men and women who married did not occur in the ballroom or some equally ornate setting. They happened, rather, in the parlors of parents' homes and on their front porches, after church meetings, at Sunday socials, during barn raisings and corn huskings, riding to-gether, and walking and talking along forested paths and other clandestine spots that would-be lovers of every class grew to know one another.

While courting Betty Powell, for example, Robert Conrad left little to chance. Since Miss Powell's relatives and Mr. Conrad's mother were social ac-quaintances and often attended the same events, the young couple could see each other frequently. Eventually Betty became a close, young friend to the wid-owed Mrs. Conrad, and often accepted her invitations to visit her home. Still Robert wanted to spend more intimate time with Betty, and arranged to do so by inviting her to the Sulphur Springs where he was vacationing with friends. Betty was excited about the plan, but needed her father's permission. In her letter of request she avoided the issue of her intended rendezvous, only saying that she wanted to visit the popular watering hole with two female friends. Her father reluctantly agreed, but cautioned that he was "not sure it . . . [would] be exactly proper" for her to be there without "some lady married *or old enough to be married* to take care of" her. If Mr. Powell had known of Robert's plans, he never would have allowed her to go. Once there, Conrad made certain that they spent some romantic time together, sending one note that asked if the "purless [*sic*] ladies upon the hill [would] choose to repair to the fountain of health . . . called the Sulphur Spring—this afternoon upon horseback?" If Betty and her friends agreed to come, he promised to have three horses as "fleet as the clouds—beautiful as doves—smooth as the sheaves" waiting for them and two of his closest associates to entertain her friends.[56]

As the father of a restless young woman some twenty-five years later, Robert Conrad found himself in the same predicament Burr Powell once faced. By 1852, Robert and Betty had been married for thirty-two years, and their sixteen-year-old daughter Kate was determined to vacation at the Springs that summer. Undoubtedly remembering his own romantic encounters there, Conrad allowed Kate to go only if she had a male chaperone and promised to visit only during the day. "It will not do to mingle in any way the life of a school girl with that of a belle," he lectured. "And I do not think any young lady should be at a watering place, even after she is grown up, without the protection of her *mother*."[57]

Church activities such as picnics, circuit preachings, revivals, and holiday pageants were perhaps the most frequent sources of social interaction for young men and women. And worshippers were not the only ones looking for love. Single ministers were quite popular among female parishioners. Perhaps fewer parents would have striven to center their daughters' social lives on church activities if they had known the kind of romantic fantasies ministers sometimes inspired in adoring young worshippers. Many pastors wed women in their congregations, often clinching a position among the elite by marrying a wealthy daughter. Rose Davisson, for example, fell in love with and married a Methodist minister whom she met at a church function. Amanda Edmonds also lost her heart to a young clergyman, but was not as fortunate as Rose. Her "beloved Brother George" was moved to a church in Maryland and later married a young woman there. The news came as a hard blow to the girlish romantic. "I am writing till tears have dimmed my eyes and what for?" she wrote. "Over the happiness of another one whom my heart has learned to love, now to relinquish for the affections of a brighter star."[58]

Amanda kept her romantic feelings and fantasies private, concealing them in her diaries. Others sent their written thoughts on to would-be lovers. For the literate, letter writing could be the perfect vehicle to express and receive such sentiment. The resourceful bachelor used letters to convey emotion, to let his "sweetheart" know about upcoming social events, and to prevail on mutual friends to arrange communications and meetings. While George C., a member of the Army Medical Corps, was stationed in San Antonio, Texas, for example, he tried to attract Rose Davisson's attention by sending her messages via Dr. J. W. Taylor, Rose's future brother-in-law. Taylor wrote that George intended courting her if her "affections" were not "irrevocably engaged" by the time that he returned to Loudoun. Mr. Taylor promised another Davisson sister that he would see one of her suitors in New Orleans and would "attend to any private communications he may communicate . . . on her account."[59]

Letters were especially important in long-distance relationships. There was, as ever, an art and system—a decorum—that had to be maintained in romantic letter writing. It not only protected the young couple from parental reprisals should they happen to read the letters, but also protected authors from outright rejection. Yet many couples still used this medium to express feelings that they were too shy to convey verbally. Robert Conrad, for example, thanked Betty for allowing him to write to her: "There is one advantage," he explained, " . . . in this mode of correspondence with you, my sweet life, which strikes me very forcibly; . . . I should be rather more at my ease, here, in my office, with pen, ink and paper—than if we were full face to face; and . . . I can hold freer converse with you in this way, than in another."[60]

Robert Taylor Scott's written pursuit of Fanny Carter was relentless. "Fanny, sometimes when I tell you how much I love you, and how often I think of you, you give an incredulous smile and tell me it is 'all talk,'" he complained in one letter. "Indeed you are mistaken . . . I hope henceforth and forever you will cease to allege it against me and give me credit for what I profess, *devoted attachment to you.*" Six weeks later, his language was openly passionate. "I cannot express, dearest Fanny, the pleasure I experienced from my *last* visit, . . . I love you *more than ever.*"[61]

According to Robert's letters, there was no end to his desire for Fanny. Nothing, he assured her, "could induce me to defer one day the time that is to make you *mine.* To hasten that day dear Fanny my every energy shall and is exerted." Despite his open professions, however, Miss Carter proved to be much more reluctant to commit her feelings to paper. "When away from you, don't you think you could *promise* to write occasionally?" he implored.[62]

Letter writing was so important to Rose Davisson and her fiancé, who lived some 100 miles away in Petersburg, that they often discussed in detail what was, and what was not, appropriate for them to write to one another. The Reverend Poulton feared that he was being too forward in his first epistles, but complained that Rose did not express herself explicitly enough. Miss Davisson reassured him that she did not consider his letters "rather presuming and extravagant" and asked him to please let her know if he understood "*every-thing*" that she wrote. After several more months, Rose finally dared to be a little less formal, ending one letter with "Good-bye dear Frank," followed by a playful query: "have you any objection to that?"[63]

Romantic letters were diverse in style and content, necessarily reflecting the individuality of each couple. Some, like those of Miss Davisson and John Poulton, emphasized the religious and intellectual interests of the couple, but also included discussions of home life, school, work, local gossip, and private thoughts about their relationship. Others, such as those from Robert Conrad to Elizabeth Powell, were filled with Byronic metaphors, treatises on Betty's infinite beauty, and discussions of past and future social events. Those of Robert Scott to Fanny Carter were passionate, but also friendly and funny with many stories about their families and mutual friends. Whatever the content or style, however, there was one overarching purpose: to provide some means of communication between a couple which permitted a deeper acquaintance while bolstering feelings of romance and intimacy.[64]

For those young couples who lived close to one another, courting was easier to maneuver. But it also meant parents had to be more vigilant about a couple's sexual behavior. A single woman's virtue was her greatest asset; to lose it, even through rumor, was disastrous. Unfortunately, vicious gossip was a favorite pastime. "Well don't you [know] Miss Annie withdrew from our church a month before her marriage but that is not the worst of it," Rose Davisson wrote her fiancé. "The morning she was married she took the cars and went to Alexandria *by herself*. There Mr. Lockwood and Mr. Morgan met her and they went to Washington, and were married, and what do you think of that?" "I am perfectly amazed," she wrote with relish, "and think her having a northern minister the smallest part of it, although *under the circumstances that was bad enough*."[65]

Despite the emphasis on female purity, county court and church records related to cases of illegitimacy were frequent enough to suggest that a significant minority of young Loudouners willingly indulged in premarital sex. Many more probably experienced, if not the actual act of sexual intercourse, then some sexual contact with persons whom they were dating or to whom they were engaged.[66]

Premarital conception often forced reluctant parents to accept an otherwise unacceptable son- or daughter-in-law. When Arthur Rogers initially asked William Nichols for permission to marry his daughter Hannah, for example, Mr. Nichols said "no." Arthur had been courting Hannah for almost a year, but the Nichols were devout Quakers and Rogers refused to convert. For both men the issue was not just one of conversion to the Quaker faith, but Rogers's adoption of a distinct way of life that would force him into a new community and limit access to his old one. It also was a matter of control; that is, which of these men would have the last say as to Hannah's fate. Society dictated that Hannah accept the authority of her father until she marry. Dutifully, she stopped seeing Rogers, although the separation caused her great anguish, anguish over their separation and Hannah's secret pregnancy. In the end, her father decided that the shame of having an illegitimate child was greater than marrying out of faith. Mr. Nichols finally relented, allowing the couple to marry one month before the birth.[67]

The kind of embarrassment and loss of honor that a premarital pregnancy caused a family only underscored parents' doubts about the young man or woman whom their children wanted to marry. Some parent-child conflict over courtship was inevitable. Most usually resolved the problem amicably, but an impasse was not uncommon. Determined lovers sometimes eloped. To do so may have seemed like the only solution, but the act had a devastating effect on the families involved. It not only signaled desperation and a lack of discipline, but also deeply compromised parental authority. For one to elope was to rebel against a system of control and prerogative that was fundamental to the southern patriarchy. The event could be particularly heart-wrenching for the parents of the female involved, since a woman's challenge to patriarchal authority threatened the foundation of familial stability and male governance. To do so upset the gendered hierarchy that was fundamental to the white community. Even if the family patriarch wanted to accept the situation for the sake of domestic harmony, he risked community criticism and a public loss of personal power if he did so.

Ann Powell, for example, eloped in 1814 with her childhood sweetheart, Lloyd Noland. It is not certain why the couple eloped. Certainly on the face of it Lloyd was an acceptable candidate for son-in-law. Like Ann, he was a member of the local gentry and the two families had been close business and social associates for generations. But Ann was only fifteen years old when she married, barely finished with her schooling. She also might have been pregnant, for closely kept genealogical records conveniently omit the birthdate of the couple's first child. Whatever the reason, the elopement came as a hard blow to the powerful Powell clan. Burr Powell just recently had been elected to the state legislature and was spending most of his time in Richmond trying to build a political career. His wife Catherine was at home with the couple's children, including two impressionable younger daughters. As ugly gossip and speculation spread, they felt they had to cut all ties with their eldest daughter. Relations also must have been strained between them and the Nolands, who offered the young couple shelter. Even after Mr. and Mrs. Powell welcomed Ann back into the fold some years later, relations between the Powell and Noland families were never the same.[68]

Sally Ringgold eloped in 1829, also causing quite a local sensation. Community elites were quick to condemn her actions, labeling them signs of uncontrolled passion and dysfunctional familial relations. Hortensia Hay, who heard of Sally's elopement while vacationing at Saratoga Springs, immediately contacted her good friend Mary Custis for "an account of the whole affair." Calling Sally's behavior sheer "stupidity," Hortensia was typically unsympathetic: "I confess I was amazed, I always thought she had not much character, but I had no idea she would break her solemn promise never to run off which she gave her family." She then asked the inevitable: "Why did her parents continue to oppose her choice when it was clear that she was determined to marry him?" The best solution, she surmised, would be for the Ringgolds to "send for them and forgive and forget as fast as they can," for "all regrets and recriminations will now be useless." And the longer the family remained at odds, she concluded, the greater the harm to familial relations, the couple, and, of course, the community's opinion of both.[69]

Yet despite the pressure to maintain family peace and honor, it was difficult for parents, who usually exercised so much control over their children, not to interfere with their adult decisions. It was even more difficult for them to accept a child's outright rejection of their advice. A son or daughter's marriage, after all, was one of the most important events that a family experienced. Flirtations, dating, even courting were one thing; engagement and marriage were entirely different and much more serious matters.

When a man decided that he wanted to marry, he usually proposed first, and then sought her father's permission. "Mindful" daughters were suppose to defer to their father's decision. When Robert Conrad proposed to Betty Powell in 1828, she told him that she "could neither approve nor disapprove of [his] suit," until she discussed the matter with her father. Mr. Powell was duly "gratified" at his daughter's "course." He rewarded her deference to his authority by assuring her that he would "remonstrate" only if he thought that she was "erring very much in judgment." In the meanwhile, he suggested that she withhold her answer until she got to know Mr. Conrad better, was certain of her "heart," and "appeal[ed] to [God] for counsel and direction."[70]

The length of a couple's engagement varied substantially. It could be as brief as a few weeks or longer than a year. Some even lasted for several years. Families who expected to hold elaborate weddings usually did not make public announcements until the event was near at hand. Inquisitive neighbors, casual friends, and other suitors insisted on gossiping. "Who to?" asked one nosy friend when John Poulton told him that he was going to marry soon. "I enquired of Col Wright—he only spoke from the Authority of Madam Rumor." Rose Davisson, like her fiancé, was quite secretive about her engagement. Yet word of her impeding wedding soon spread, and she found herself in the uncomfortable position of defending her choice to another suitor. "[H]e asked me if my mind was fully made up upon that subject and if the gentleman he saw here the evening before was the person, and I replied in the affirmative to both questions most emphatically," she reassured John.[71]

Betty Powell did as her father suggested. She took some time, several months in fact, to decided whether or not she wanted to marry Robert. Once she officially accepted the proposal, her family began to plan her wedding. It was a full seventeen months later before the couple married. Thomas Peake informed Sally Adams in the spring of 1820 that he had written to her father "on the important subject," and should be "so Happy as to obtain his approbation." The Loudoun bachelor also expressed his hope that once Mr. Adams gave his approval that Sally would not keep him in suspense about her feelings, but would "equally participate" with him in "the desire of Consumating [sic]" his "Earthly Bliss." The two married several months later. Hugh Sidwell and Thomasin Haines had a much longer courtship. After Hugh met Thomasin, a deep friendship eventually developed, and then a "warmer attachment." Yet it was still another "eight or nine years" before the two wed.[72]

Courtship and engagement in the Quaker community differed significantly from those of the Powells, Davissons, and Peakes, who were respectively Presbyterian, Methodist, and Episcopalian. Proof that one was in good standing with his or her local meeting was as important as parental approval. It was only then that an appointed member of their Society notified both the men's and women's business meetings of the couple's intention to marry. The Meeting subsequently elected a committee of two persons from each business meeting "to make inquiry concerning the clearness of the parties in regard to any other marriage engagements." Once they completed their investigation, the couple and their families could plan the wedding.[73]

Parents promoted long engagements so that the couple might get to know each other better before the wedding, but also so that they might become better acquainted with the prospective spouse and his or her family. Familial interaction and acceptance on both sides was important and could insure a smooth transition from being single to being married. Elizabeth Davisson nurtured a very close personal relationship with her daughter's fiancé for several months before the wedding. So too did Rebecca Conrad. Since many brides moved into their in-laws' home, it was important that they try to establish amicable relations before doing so.[74]

Parents understood how important these relationships were and often made overt efforts to establish friendly ties among themselves. Burr Powell was determined to form good relations with his daughter Betty's prospective mother-in-law. Accordingly, he wrote to Mrs. Conrad about two months before the scheduled wedding and invited her to stay in his home during the week of celebration. He also took the opportunity to solicit her future help and to inadvertently assure her that Betty's presence would not undermine the elderly woman's status in her home. Powell used the couple's inexperience with domestic matters to further endear Mrs. Conrad to his daughter. He confided in her that he was "relying" on her "prudence" and "influence to prevent their conforming . . . too much to the prevailing customs of the times and running into wasteful and unnecessary expenditures." "My daughter gives up, in a measure, the protection of a father and the counsel of a mother," he added, "but I am happy in assuring you, that there is no young man of my acquaintance, to whom I could more confidently resign my charge, . . . [and] there is no lady . . . better qualified, or better disposed than yourself to supply to her a mothers [*sic*] place."[75]

As the wedding day approached, brides and grooms readied themselves for their new stations in life. It was an anxious, even frightening time, tempered by feelings of hope, romance, and passion. For Rose Davisson and so many others like her it was the true beginning of her life as a responsible adult in her southern community. Writing to her fiancé just a few days before their marriage, her words captured typical sentiments as the formality of the courtship ritual finally gave way to the passion of sanctioned love.

> Dear Mr. Poulton:
>
> I cannot realize that this is my last letter to you, and yet it is. It really seems so strange. . . I felt like writing my last letter here by my window where I have so often sat and written to you, sometimes with an aching heart, but most frequently light-hearted and happy. Well can it be possible that we shall so soon meet and under such circumstances. I can scarcely believe it. . . . And now goodbye. May God bless my own Frank.
>
> Yours only,
> Rose[76]

3

Marriage, for Better
or for Worse

Man is not born to be alone. He is not born alone. He is above as
below human nature — Life has no pleasure without a companion.
It is hardly life.—
Burr Harrison, 1849

Burr Harrison was speaking from bittersweet experience. Twenty-seven years earlier he had married a wonderful young woman, settled in at the family estate just south of Leesburg, and the two had begun their life together. Less than a year later, their first child—Matthew—was born. Burr had had many happy years with his wife Sarah and their eight children, and when she died in 1845, he felt in some ways that his life had ended too. Reflecting back on his twenty-three years of marriage, Harrison easily remembered the happy times—the delight of seeing his children grow and accomplish, the joy his wife's companionship had given him, the comfort of their home life together. But if he was to be honest, he also had to remember other times. The financial difficulties he had had as a young man trying to support a wife and growing family. The endless days and evenings that his work as an attorney, planter, and politician had taken him away from his family. The illnesses his wife endured as she grew sickly and prematurely old with incessant childbirth and responsibility. Her untimely death and the subsequent unraveling of close family ties. These tragedies colored Burr Harrison's memory of his marriage, of his life with his "companion." Yet he still believed in the institution; in fact he highly recommended it. He had learned, as his children would come to learn, that marriage was much more than that suggested by the pleasured smiles of young couples and the ritualistic beauty and revelry of local weddings. Marriage meant a coming of age in the eyes of one's family and community; it meant adulthood and its attendant responsibilities.

Southerners like Burr and Sarah Harrison took seriously the duties that their community dictated were appropriate for men and women of their race, class, and time. In so doing they accepted both the rewards and costs of life as southern patriarchs and mistresses. The private pressures of marital duty that they confronted were part and parcel of the many constraints to personal happiness that society proffered. As husband and wife they learned full well that the domestic responsibilities of married women and the financial cares of husbands often played to a physically and emotionally depleting standard. The southern bride certainly had her work cut out for her as lover, mother, laborer, friend, hostess, and counselor.[1] Likewise, husbands soon found out that marital bliss often was compromised by their responsibilities as provider and protector, by their need to succeed simultaneously as breadwinners, attentive husbands, and responsible fathers. "You enquire of my intentions for the future," William Fulton wrote to a Loudoun friend. "I shall move to Leesburg the first of July, visit the west in April or May in company with my wife and youngest boy. Purchase some land for *my* rising 'responsibilities,'—return home to live in old Loudoun, perhaps the balance of my days," he replied resolutely.[2]

Fulton, a local teacher and small-time politician who liked to contemplate "the human condition," undoubtedly spent many hours attending and commenting on Loudoun's premier social events—weddings. Perhaps he and Burr Harrison met at such a celebration. Southern weddings had a way of bringing people together, if just briefly, since they were not only meant to solemnize intimate bonds between two people but also to strengthen community ties. It was at weddings that persons of different classes, generations, and cultures celebrated and serenaded the couple, met and mingled among themselves, each maintaining their "place" but nonetheless finding commonality in their respect for a commitment that lay at the foundation of shared community values.

Loudoun weddings usually took place in the bride's home or at a local church. As the host family readied themselves, selecting and making special clothes and food and priming their home for guests, they relied on extended kin and close friends to help them prepare and celebrate. "We are to have a great wedding, to judge from the preparations, in which Betty has involved herself. . . ," Robert Conrad commented on his wife's participation in a neighbor's marriage plans. Indeed, it was so customary for weddings to have a communal face that the uninvited often felt socially rejected. "There is no way that I can so readily get over my disappointment of not receiving an invitation," one disgruntled friend found occasion to write.[3] Rose Davisson was in an even more uncomfortable situation. She tried to face the implications of her extended family's refusal to attend her wedding bravely, but it was an obvious signal of their disapproval. Hoping to reassure her intended that her family's absence would not distress her in the least, she tried to center his attention on the large number of their mutual friends she expected would come.[4]

It was customary for the bride's family to incur all wedding expenses, except the honeymoon trip. Poorer folk had a small affair at the bride's home. There usually were one or two attendants, a potpourri of neighbors and kin, a reception of simple, but delicious, refreshments, and a celebratory dance. Local elites were expected to be much more generous and had to provide well wishers with an elaborate reception, including a formal dinner, wedding cake, and plenty of fruit, cookies, cakes, sweet meats, drinks, and entertainment. Extravagant nuptials not only included the sumptuous wedding dinner but also several days of pre- and post-wedding parties and fêtes.[5]

Quakers celebrated a marriage somewhat differently and with different implications for community-wide cohesiveness. Their wedding ceremonies usually took place at their mid-week meetings, and while they were open to all members, they usually did not include non-Friends. Their weddings were procedurally simple—the head of the Meeting announced the couple's intention to marry after the service. At the appropriate time, the bride and groom stood up, joined their right hands and promised "in the presence of the Lord" and before their peers to be "loving" and "faithful" to each other until "death should separate them." A dinner at the bride's followed the ceremony, and the next day there was a "home coming" at the groom's. "The dinner was always the best that could be furnished," but there was no music, dancing, or any other kind of "unbecoming behavior" allowed.[6]

Bridal gowns varied in style, color, texture, and expense. Designs changed over time to reflect the latest fashions, but some traditional characteristics remained popular. Floor-length gowns that were light-colored silk, wool, or cotton, with lace trimming around the neck and sleeves were typical. Female attendants wore less ornate but similar dresses. Elaborate weddings boasted large wedding parties with both bridesmaids and male waiters. Grooms and waiters wore dark formal suits. Agnes Davisson's description of a cousin's wedding is typical of what and whom one might expect to see at a Loudoun wedding. "[E]verything was carried on in grand style," she recalled. Her cousin married at night, in a white beige gown that was "surplus to the waist, with a thule sham." Several relatives and friends acted as attendants. Bad weather prevented the wedding from taking place in the local church, and was held in the bride's home instead. A lavish reception followed.[7]

But even the "grand style" of Agnes's cousin's wedding paled in comparison to that of Eleanor Love Selden. Selden, daughter to one of Loudoun's wealthiest planters, married John Augustine Washington in 1842 at "Exeter." According to one of the hundreds of guests in attendance, the Selden family supplied abundant amounts of "wines, game, fruit and confectionery" that they ordered from Philadelphia. The wedding supper, a veritable feast, "was served on long tables decorated with pyramids of iced cakes and with baskets of nougat filled with colored flowers filled with sugar." They served all kinds of meats, breads, seafood, all "washed down with imported wines." Many stayed on to celebrate for days.[8]

Most weddings were much less elaborate. Likewise, most couples could not afford the kinds of wedding trips that the elite took. Instead, they found romantic solace in the private room of a parent's or other family member's home, especially cleaned and decorated for the occasion. Others reserved rooms at local taverns or hotels located in the closest city. Washington, New York, Philadelphia, and Niagara Falls were the most popular honeymoon sites for those who could afford such an extravagance; the very elite went to Europe or other equally distant places. When Professor Thomas Dew of the College of William and Mary married Miss Latilia Hay of neighboring Clarke County in 1846, for example, they honeymooned in Europe. Armistead Filler and his bride had one of the most unique wedding trips. Filler was a Lovettsville cattle dealer of considerable wealth who traveled to western territories in order to purchase livestock. A businessman at heart, he decided to combine one of his cattle purchasing trips with his honeymoon, taking his bride west by stagecoach. Quaker Samuel Janney happily recalled his wedding trip: "Soon after our marriage we went on a tour to the Falls of Niagara, thence to Montreal and Quebec, returning by way of Lake Champlain and through several of the New England states. It was a season of unalloyed enjoyment." Somewhat of a romantic, Janney celebrated his love and the natural beauty that he enjoyed on his trip with self-styled poetry: ". . . long will my heart hold dear/ The bright remembrance of the hours passed here; /Where love's bright flame and friendship's genial ray/ . . . gave a lovelier form and brighter hue/ To every scene that met my wondering view." It was, he admitted, the beginning of a "union that I regard as the greatest of all my temporal blessings."[9]

Sometimes family members and friends went along with the bride and groom, extending family and community participation in new marriages past the actual events of the wedding, reception, and after-parties. Having loved ones along on the first day or so of the honeymoon sometimes brought added comfort to anxious grooms and nervous brides. Rose Davisson, for one, was pleased to know that some of her friends and her sister planned to accompany her on part of her honeymoon. She warned her fiancé just a few days before their marriage: "I expect *some* of our attendants will go to Harpers Ferry with us and perhaps Sophie will go to Washington. I have been begging her to go but she won't tell me." But Rose's reaction probably was exceptional. Parents placed so much emphasis on chaperones during courtship that some couples undoubtedly were nervous at the thought of finally being left alone with one another, but most still welcomed their new privacy. Indeed, honeymoons sometimes were the only really private time newlyweds had, since many of them began their married lives residing with one or the other's parents.[10]

When Armistead Filler and his bride finally returned after their honeymoon, they moved into his imposing, two-story mansion. Filler's "Linden Hall" boasted 22 rooms, a spacious ballroom, and several outhouses, including a school building. When George Carter finally married at the age of sixty, his wife moved to "Oatlands." The huge estate included the county's most exquisite mansion filled with furnishings Carter purchased in Baltimore, New York, and Europe, one of the state's largest private libraries, an expansive formal garden, and a permanent staff of twenty or so slaves. Both Armistead Filler and George Carter married late in life and had had the kinds of opportunities to establish themselves financially that most young men only dreamed about by the time they married. Still even only the most successful of men of Filler and Carter's cohort could live as they did. While some families lived in small stone dwellings and a few invested in brick homes, most Loudouners lived their entire lives in two- to four-room log cabins.[11]

Many newlyweds could not afford to establish a separate residence and often went to live at the husband's parental home. This was so even among middling and wealthier folk. When Burr Harrison and his brother-in-laws Robert Conrad and Lloyd Noland married during the 1810s and 1820s, for example, they all moved their brides into their parents' homes. It was customary then for young married couples to live temporarily with older kin who could give them financial assistance and help them to "adjust" to married life. But this custom began to change over time, especially among the more well-to-do.[12]

When Matthew Harrison began to contemplate marriage during the late 1840s, for example, his father Burr offered to let him use one of his town houses in Leesburg, rather than insist that he move in with him. This important shift in newlywed lifestyle was due in part to an increasing effort by parents to give their sons a greater sense of independence and self-assurance. Most began before their child reached the age of marriage, teaching them as young adults how to administer, finance, and care for a household of their own. But this formative trend had other bases. It was part of a growing emphasis on single-family households and privatization among the South's upper and middle classes, particularly the urban elite. Town residences, such as the one that Burr Harrison offered his son Matthew, seemed especially suited for young couples moving away from the predominant agrarian lifestyle. Matthew was a lawyer with political ambitions. Moreover, a town house required much less upkeep than rural homes like his father's estate. The "town" also had the added advantage of access to social networks and resources outside immediate and extended families. Urban life obviously agreed with the Harrison couple. In 1858, Matthew, who was by then well established in his career, hired Charles Haskins, a Washington, D.C., architect, to build his family a home in Leesburg.

The contract stipulated an expansive two-story brick house at a cost of $4300. It was to be completed by 1861, the same year that Harrison was elected to the Virginia House of Delegates.[13]

Parents' generosity did not end with offers of temporary or permanent shelter. Relatives routinely gave young couples a variety of gifts that they hoped would help them settle comfortably into their new lives. Even those who were moving into parental homes still received linen, dishes, furnishings, and other houseware. Others gave income-producing presents—livestock, money, real estate, and slaves remained popular. Burr Powell, for example, had several pieces of furniture, including a bureau with glass knobs and a head and foot board, made for his daughter Betty when she moved into her mother-in-law's home. He also gave the couple several of his valuable field and domestic slaves. John Custis and his wife not only provided their daughter and son-in-law with several slaves, but also luxurious furnishings for their new home. Writing soon after her daughter's marriage to Robert E. Lee, Mrs. Custis assured the bride that she was about to send carpets and other furnishings, and promised to provide her "everything else" she needed to make her house comfortable.[14]

Often parents extended other kinds of financial assistance as well. Although they did not want to feel that they had to support the newlyweds fully, most knew how difficult it was for a young man to assume the support of a wife. Burr Powell, for example, willingly passed on some of his lucrative legal business to his son-in-law, Burr Harrison, during Harrison's first few years of marriage to Powell's daughter Sarah. If Harrison's father had been alive at the time, he probably would have offered to help Burr. Instead, the young husband gratefully accepted the kind aid of Powell, who not only was his father-in-law, but his maternal uncle and a paternal second cousin.[15]

When Harrison's younger brother, Thomas Jefferson Harrison, married a few years later, he wrote to his older sibling requesting money to help him organize his new home. Burr still was not in any position to lend Thomas money, but he did promise to expedite the young man's inheritance so that he might use it to get settled. Likewise, Simon Shover of Lovettsville repeatedly made financial opportunities available to his son George after he married. The elder Shover leased him farm land and helped him to establish a wool-carding business. Even after Simon died, George's paternal uncles and aunts continued to provide him with financial assistance. George's wife Susan also had some additional security. Instead of giving her a hearty dowry, her father converted her inheritance into a separate estate to which her husband, or his creditors, could not gain access.[16]

Regardless of the various kinds of support that parents and the community extended, however, marriage was a difficult emotional and physical transition. The marital experiences of Sarah Powell, her younger sister Elizabeth, and their husbands, Burr Harrison and Robert Conrad, as well as those of the Jan-neys, Shovers, Davissons, Fultons, and Poultons, constitute revealing examples. The Powell and Harrison families represented the elite in Loudoun, while the Shovers, Janneys, and Poultons were of lesser means. What all their experiences disclose is that the pressure to perform as ideal husbands and wives was not re-stricted to one class, but felt throughout society. So too were the kinds of emo-tional responses they had to the other challenges marriage proposed.

Elizabeth Powell Conrad, known fondly as Betty, married in 1829. The details of her marriage are much more accessible than those of her sister Sarah because of the large extant body of Conrad family correspondence. One of the most certain lessons gleaned from this rich source is that the kinds of fears and anxieties that wives experienced differed profoundly from those of their husbands. More than a few women had difficulty adjusting to their new do-mestic responsibilities. For many middle- and upper-class women who had lived a life of relative leisure until their marriages, their domestic duties after marriage seemed physically debilitating and their overall lifestyle psychologi-cally frustrating.

Betty and her mother, Catherine Powell, typified upper-class belles and ma-trons. Miss Powell married when she was nineteen, just a few months after completing her formal education. Up until that time, she had had few domestic duties. Whether in school, at home, or visiting a friend or relation, slaves and their mistresses took care of most household needs. Her father, for example, employed almost twenty of his slaves as full-time domestics in their home. Her mother, as mistress of "The Hill," managed the slaves and did what other household work that was necessary. Neither Betty nor her sister Sarah did much in the way of domestic labor when they were growing up—perhaps some sewing, knitting, embroidering, or nursing when they had the time or inclina-tion to do so. Betty's life may have been even more leisured than her sister's, for as the youngest daughter, her parents and siblings probably spoiled her. With no domestic responsibilities and a regular allowance, Betty as a single young woman led the good single life—attending private schools, visiting adoring relatives, frequenting parties, vacationing at the local Springs, and shopping and socializing with equally privileged young women and men.

Marriage was a rude awakening. Only two weeks after she became Mrs. Conrad, Betty was so homesick and weary of her new commitments that she confided to her father: "[I am] quite as happy and contented as I could expect to be in so novel a station[;] but I have such a variety of employments that it makes the hours appear twice as long as they did when I had nothing to do (or rather when *I did nothing*) at home."[17]

A few weeks later, feelings of inadequacy surfaced. Writing to her mother, she openly told of her fears of trying to manage a household alone. "I feel quite alarmed at the prospect," she sighed. "I expect to take many a hearty cry from vexation of spirit—now we get on very well—while mother [in-law] is here to advise with us to what we shall eat and what we shall drink. . . ." Betty did not know how she would fare once her in-law went on holiday.[18]

Betty's appreciation for Mother Conrad's guidance was an important acknowledgment of the crucial role that older women, that is, sisters, mothers, aunts, in-laws, and favorite female slaves, played in the apprenticeship of brides. Bound to the same responsibilities all of their married lives, these women formed deep bonds with each other as they shared their skills, advice, and support with struggling novices. Betty was fortunate to have had ample opportunity to meet and build a strong relationship with her mother-in-law before she married. By the time that Betty and Robert married, Rebecca Conrad cared deeply for her new daughter-in-law and seemed anxious to help her adjust. She did so not only because it was customary, and as a favor to the young woman and her son, but also because it was her household that Betty was learning to administer.[19]

Regardless of the aid available to brides from family, friends, and loyal slaves, however, the time finally came when these young women had to function independently. That time came for Betty when her mother-in-law went on a planned visit to Martinsburg. Betty sorely missed her advisor. Only a few days had passed before she asked her to return. Writing that she was "quite disappointed" that she had not heard from her and that she had felt "very solitary and lonely, . . . the day [Rebecca Conrad] left . . . ," Betty whined sweetly: "Indeed dear mother, we want to see you very much[.] [Y]ou have no idea how very desolate your room looks." Robert and I, she confided, will get into "great trouble" if you do not return "shortly."[20]

Less privileged women, and even those from wealthy families of later generations, were more comfortable with the domestic responsibilities of marriage. Years later, for example, Betty Conrad made certain that her daughters performed household tasks as children and teens, tasks that prepared them to one day take over their own households. Middling and poorer girls or those who grew up without mothers usually learned how to care for children and a home by the time they reached puberty.

Betty Powell Conrad's privileged class and generation afforded her no such skills. In fact, her fears of impending "trouble" during her mother-in-law's absence probably were well founded. Determined to plunge head-first into her domestic duties, Betty decided to clean and polish Rebecca Conrad's expensive silver service. Sylvia, the Conrad "Mammy," feeling no particular affection for this new mistress and taking advantage of her owner's absence to escape additional labor, offered Betty no assistance. Upon finishing, Betty turned to Sylvia for her opinion. The slave woman replied quite coolly that she believed Betty had "nearly ruined" the family treasure. Justifiably panicked, the new bride scrubbed and rinsed the silver until it regained its original look. Young Mrs. Conrad clearly had as much to learn about "handling" her slaves as she did about domestic labor.[21]

Faced with numerous mistakes, uncooperative servants, and an absent husband, Betty soon found it all too much to bear. Instead of persisting, she made a temporary escape, writing to her own mother: "You may expect to see me in Loudoun the second week in next month unless it is *morally impossible.*" "Indeed I cannot endure it any longer[.] I *must* go home[.] I think it will be more delightful to me than ever."[22]

In the meanwhile, the discontented bride tried to amuse herself by attending a round of local parties, in effect living a public lifestyle that resembled her days as a "belle." Her ambiguity about her new status did not go unnoticed. It irritated her own mother immensely, prompting her to write on at least three occasions to chastise Betty for spending so much time outside of her home. Now that she was married, Mrs. Powell expected her daughter to act like a respectable "matron." Betty, ever so politely, resisted. "Indeed my dear mother," she wrote reassuringly, "I do not think you need fear my becoming too much accustomed to visiting and fashion and gaiety." Mrs. Powell, however, probably feared more Betty's inability to become "accustomed" to the loneliness and drudgery inherent in her new status as wife and mistress.[23]

Betty wanted her mother's approval, but beneath her polite responses and her mother's heated insistence were the workings of a power struggle that many recently married adults waged with their parents. No matter her need for continued maternal care and guidance, Betty wanted to make it perfectly clear that, as a married woman, her mother no longer had the kind of control over her daughter's life that she had had when she was single. Mrs. Conrad tactfully responded to her mother's criticism: "I think from what I have seen of the society of this place that I shall generally prefer my own fireside to the ballroom or the crowded drawing room." Although she seemed to acquiesce, Betty coyly insisted that it was her "preference" and not her mother's that was key.[24]

Both Betty and her mother had difficulty adjusting to her marital status. Mothers were not eager to relinquish the reins of control and it was emotionally imperative to them that their girls continue to need, love, and hold them in high esteem, even after they married. Mrs. Powell wanted her daughters to succeed as wives, but had no intention of letting them forget their responsibilities to their family of birth. Several months after Betty's wedding, when perhaps the newlywed was feeling more comfortable as a wife, she began to correspond less frequently with her mother. Mrs. Powell, quite sensitive to her "loss," was not pleased. Are you "so busy" with your new duties, she inquired, that you do not have time to write to your own mother? Betty had little patience with her mother's insecurity. Perhaps it was only as a mother herself that she began to fathom some of what Mrs. Powell had experienced when she married and left home.[25]

Childbirth changed a woman's life forever and fundamentally shaped her marital experience. Most Loudoun women began to have children soon after they married and usually had several more before they reached menopause. Indeed, it was not unusual for these women, who had little access to birth control information, to have eight, ten, and sometimes even more children. Children and a household to run were immense, oftentimes overwhelming, responsibilities. All evidence suggests that Sarah Powell Harrison, for example, was deeply devoted to her roles as wife and mother of eight. She took great pride in knowing that she excelled at them even if it cost her dearly. Yet she also realized how much she suffered from the physical and emotional strain of childbirth and her other domestic responsibilities. Over the years, Sarah's health slowly deteriorated as she lost her strength and eyesight, to say nothing of her youthful beauty. Because of her husband's busy professional schedule, she often was left alone to care for their growing family. Her domestic schedule was a hectic one—she served as her children's primary caregiver (along with her slave nurses of course), supervised the work of her house servants, helped to care for her aging parents, and attended to the needs of her husband, all on a household budget that she often complained was stretched beyond practical utility. Still Sarah continued to aspire to be the kind of wife and mother that she believed her husband and children needed and deserved. This, she undoubtedly assured herself over and over again, was her duty as a Christian woman, particularly as an elite Christian woman. A kinswoman's note during the 1830s suggested a kind of physical pathos that was both consequential and characteristic of married women's lives: "[My health] seems quite restored tho of course my condition will never be strong again. . . . I feel well, and my complexion is healthy, but you would be shocked to see how old I look with one of my front teeth gone."[26]

Despite help from domestic slaves and other household women, many of Loudoun's well-to-do women, and certainly their poorer peers, found precious little time for themselves. "I have had a scolding letter from Ann Williams for not writing her but have indeed found no time as yet to defend myself," Sarah wrote to her sister Betty on one occasion. When she did find time to write, she could not help but complain about her busy routine, failing health, and lack of funds. "For such a length of time," she confessed, "you cant conceive the quantity of work that could not be put off that is constantly pressing in on me[;] and now that I do make the attempt to write[,] my mind is so harassed that I sometimes forget before I finish a sentence what I designed to say."[27]

Rising early that morning, Sarah wrote of her duties: she had managed to get one daughter off to boarding school, helped care for her other seven youngsters, picked several bushels of apples, and patched a worn bedroom carpet. Just as she was about to finish the rug, an aunt arrived to assist with the confinement of another relative. She came unexpectedly, bringing with her a small nephew who was subject to epileptic "seizures." A few hours later, another carriage surprised the exhausted mistress—two other unexpected guests had come to visit for a few days.

To be sure, Sarah Harrison had an enviable seat compared with most Loudoun women. When one compares the details of her married life with those of someone like Nancy Turner, married to an abusive drunkard who refused to work and who made a habit of beating her until she gave him her wages, or Susan Moore, the woman whose husband tried to win a divorce by publicly accusing her of having deformed genitalia, or even the typical lives of most rural southern women, one has little sympathy for Sarah. The wife of a wealthy planter, lawyer, and politician, Sarah lived in one of the most attractive homes in Loudoun. She obviously had many more educational and social opportunities than poorer white and free black women, to say nothing of her female slaves. She had had several children but, unlike most of her peers, had lost only one. Although she had a busy work routine, she did not perform the heavy, dirty, and tedious work that poorer women had to do daily; her slaves did that. Female kin living in her home also helped. In a very real sense then, Sarah Powell Harrison lived the good life. Yet her letters portray a woman who often felt physically and emotionally drained.[28]

Challenged daily by the limitless demands of her children, a husband who believed in firm obedience from all of his dependents, and the elusive wall of resistance that her house slaves formed, Mrs. Harrison often felt she exerted little control in her life. Although she was a privileged white woman who lived during an era and in a place where one's socioeconomic and racial status determined the most basic elements of the quality of one's life, Sarah's gender sealed upon her an uncomfortable fate.[29]

It was not just the exhausting house and yard work, childbearing and child-rearing, or the lingering duties to parents and other kin. It also was the reality of male domination, a difficult submission for many. Young wives often realized that their husbands were just as inexperienced and naive about married life as they were. Yet they were compelled by law, religion, and community custom to trust their lives to these men. Dr. Alfred Harrison Powell stated the popular attitude quite succinctly. A migrant from Loudoun who had gone to live in Tennessee, Dr. Powell wrote his brother John to congratulate him on his recent marriage and to invite him to move to Tennessee with his bride. There, he promised the groom, he would have a "brilliant mercantile business." Dr. Powell also gave John some instructions for future success, among which was a formula he believed would be useful in subduing his wife's will. "If Maria says *nay*, stop her mouth with the best of the scripture maxims: "Wife obey your Husband in all things." Yet even this confirmed bachelor was uncertain that his argument was effective. He added wisely: "[I]f it is rather in violation of some of the specifications in your article of agreement before marriage—make necessity your plea an unanswerable one."[30]

Sarah and Betty Powell's married lives were strikingly similar. Both (just as their mother) were married to lawyer/planters involved in state politics. Both had moved into their husbands' homes after marrying, and had become mistresses of these homes when their mothers-in-law died. Both Mr. Harrison and Mr. Conrad, because of the nature of their work, often were absent from home. Both had very particular ideas about home and family. Robert Conrad, for example, wrote constantly to his wife with instructions about the many domestic activities that he felt she should undertake as well as her general behavior as a wife and mother. A survey of his comments provides much information about how men perceived both their wives' roles and their own roles as husbands.[31]

Mr. Conrad did not communicate with his wife in a confrontational tone— to have done so would have been ungentlemanly. Instead, he cultivated an air of polite condescension. Robert liked to address Betty as if he were an older advisor, gently prodding his well-meaning, but incompetent, wife to behave properly. Underneath it all was the reassurance that he loved her and wanted only the best for her and their children. Certainly, Robert did love Betty deeply and she knew it. His insensitivity to her needs was part and parcel of his role and privilege as family patriarch, a tradition she must have watched the older women in her family endure and that she struggled, as a wife, to come to terms with. When Betty refused to accept his advice, Robert predictably changed his tone—he chided her for her insensitivity to his needs.

Robert seemed to know little about his wife's busy work schedule, its cyclical quality, or even its periodic fluctuations. Despite whatever else might be going on in their household, he insisted that she contact him regularly with news of herself, the children, or any other information he might find interesting. Writing to her just four months after the birth of their first child, Conrad whined: "You cannot tell my Dear, how I was disappointed at not receiving an answer yesterday to the long letter I sent you by Ann Elizers. This is only to ask the reason." Frustrated by her silence, and apparently unaware of the emotional and physical strain that a new mother experienced, Robert closed his brief note with a snapping question: "And the boy. Do you think I have no interest in him? Let me hear from you by all means on tomorrow. Can he walk or talk, or does he only cry?"[32]

Mr. Conrad's personal designs were clear. He knew what he needed to be comfortable in his home, made his needs clear to his wife, and expected her to accommodate him. To his credit, Robert did secure several house slaves to help Betty. But once he had done that, his attention to domestic labor was limited to that of critic, consumer, and, not unoccasionally, appreciative onlooker. Betty, however, still had the onerous task of training and then constantly administering her household staff. Even after handling slave property for several years, many mistresses still felt the need to watch and supervise their work and behavior. Moreover, Betty had to do much more than just maintain a comfortable and clean home. She also had to act the role of consummate hostess to any of a number of family members and friends who visited regularly, to say nothing of the throng of business and political associates of her husband who often appeared at *his* invitation. Robert did not hesitate to call on his wife to entertain for him while he was away. Writing from his legislative post in Richmond in February 1841, for example, Conrad asked Betty, who was now the mother of five young children, to "give a party to those young ladies from Staunton," because his "friend Wm Peyton, the Senator from that district" had "several times alluded to their visit." Accordingly, the dutiful Mrs. Conrad interrupted her busy winter schedule, invited the young women to stay in her home, and hosted a reception for them.[33]

The opportunity to entertain undoubtedly brought much needed variety and stimulation to women like Betty. Yet it still must have been unnerving for them to have their husbands impose these additional responsibilities with little regard for their other commitments. Mr. Conrad often asked his wife to perform several such tasks within the space of a few days. That same month that Betty busied herself entertaining the young women from Staunton, for example, her husband offered his home and his wife's hospitality to Tudor Tucker, the adolescent son of one of his prestigious associates in the Virginia Assembly. Again he extended the invitation before he even consulted Betty on the matter. Conrad later explained to his wife that the Tuckers were having trouble with Tudor, who was opposed to his father's recent remarriage. The new Mrs. Tucker had decided to resolve her problem by enrolling her stepson in a "country school." Robert had offered an alternative—to let Tudor stay in his home and go to school with his sons. When he finally did write to Betty to inform her of his plans, he cheerfully assured her that Tudor was "a fine boy—[who] would be of service to [their eldest son] Dan, and no trouble" to her. He also added that he had taken the liberty to promise Mrs. Tucker that Betty and "her flock" would spend some of their summer vacation with the Tuckers. These plans, Robert noted, he negotiated "in lieu of [Mrs. Tucker's] scheme for [Betty] to spend next winter" in Richmond.[34]

Unfortunately, Betty Conrad remains conspicuously silent on these subjects, as she does on most, since few of her letters remain. Yet one can imagine what her response might have been. Not only did Robert tell her that he had arranged, without her knowledge, for her to take on the responsibility of rearing another child for several months, but Tudor obviously had emotional problems and resented authority. But that was not all. Robert then went on to undermine a long conceived plan of Mrs. Conrad to move with her young children to Richmond for the next congressional session so that the family could be together. Fortunately, Judge Tucker and his wife decided to send Tudor to a school in Williamsburg, much to Mr. Conrad's disappointment and probably his wife's relief. Betty, however, never did get to spend a season in Richmond with her husband, although Mr. Conrad remained a member of the state legislature for the next four years.[35]

What was perhaps even more frustrating for Betty than her husband's constant absenteeism and denial of her needs was his insistence that she had no right to be unhappy about any aspect of her life, including their marriage. In one of his lengthy lectures, Mr. Conrad informed his wife in no uncertain terms: "There is nothing in my situation or yours of which we have the least right to complain." "It is mere folly to be *unhappy*. . . . Diseases of the mind are more under our control than those of the body. . . . The man who permits himself to be melancholy as a permanent State is as much of a fool as one who should continually pick a wound to prevent it from healing."[36]

Robert practically ordered Betty to be content with her life. Perhaps he hoped that a "reasonable" explaining away of her depression, coupled with his insistence that she not be depressed, would end her melancholia. His counsel certainly was related to his personal determination not to give in to his own depression, which resulted from his constant absence from home. He also did not want the additional emotional burden of worrying about a sick wife while he was away. Yet there was much more at stake for Robert. It was necessary for him to dismiss his wife's depression as unreasonable because of his need to feel that he was providing a happy and satisfactory lifestyle for her and their children. Her unhappiness suggested that he had failed as a husband. Betty had to feel comfortable and happy in her roles as his wife and the mother of his children so that he could feel that he was fulfilling his roles as a husband and a father. "So my love let us find you healthy and happy when I get home; and then I will do my best to keep you so," he concluded optimistically.[37]

But Mr. Conrad's refusal to acknowledge the legitimacy of his wife's emotional stress, regardless of his reasons, may have even deepened the psychological distance between the two. Betty came to understand that she could not rely on her husband for emotional support during difficult times, but instead had to turn to her mother or other female relatives. When Mrs. Conrad's father suffered a stroke in 1831, for example, she could not visit him because of her postpartum confinement. Physically weak and psychologically drained from the recent birth, Betty found her father's illness a great emotional blow, for the two were very close. Mr. Conrad, who was then on a trip to the area, went to check on his father-in-law's condition. He reported home immediately that he did not believe that Mr. Powell's stroke was as severe as everyone first thought and insisted that Betty stop worrying about it. "Your mother is well and cheerful under the affliction," he added, "you ought to imitate her example." Moving on to other topics of interest to him, Conrad concluded his correspondence with a reminder to Betty to take care of his "hot bed plants" for he feared that they had "sufferd with the cold weather."[38]

Meanwhile, Betty's mother was not at all "well and cheerful." Mrs. Powell was devastated by her husband's illness and fearful that he would not recover. Forever cognizant of her role as wife and mother, however, Catherine put on a brave face for her son-in-law and the rest of the visitors. It was only to her female kin and friends that she felt she could reveal her deepest fears, for it was from them, not her male relations, that she expected and received support and sympathy. A few weeks later, Mrs. Powell wrote to Betty with news about Mr. Powell's health. It was then that she readily admitted that she was physically and emotionally drained by it all. "I wish it was over and all quiet," she confessed, "but I fear rest is not for me in this world."[39]

Catherine Powell's constant examples of self-sacrifice and control in the face of adversity were important lessons for her daughters. She knew that regardless of her own personal pain, it was her duty to be available at all times to comfort and care for her family. It had not been easy. But these were responsibilities and attitudes that wives had to learn to accept. A woman's honor, after all, partly lay in her dedication and service to her husband and family.[40]

It was also a wife's obligation to do everything within her power to remain healthy so that she could continue to serve her family. Accordingly, husbands often counseled their wives on such. Robert Conrad, for example, routinely sent Betty advice about her health, as well as that of their children. He stressed proper exercise, diet, clothing, and, above all, one's determination to be healthy. "Do take care of yourself my dear," he wrote in 1844. "The worst habit . . . which any one can contract is the habit of being sick; and the first duty of every one, at least so far as the world is concerned, is to take care of their own health."[41]

Although husbands expected their wives to confine themselves to the domestic sphere, women sometimes could step outside of it, if to do so provided their families with necessary income or relieved a busy spouse of some trivial business matters. Betty, like her mother and sisters, often attended to small errands for her husband while he was away. Delivering messages, shipping forgotten items, and addressing plantation overseers were a few of the tasks that these women took on during their husbands' absence and when there was no other male to do so. Most women received little credit for this additional labor and as well the additional insult of being shut out from involvement in their husband's more serious affairs. Robert Conrad's determination to exclude his wife from his professional life caused obvious strain in their relationship. In an attempt to help him with a client, for example, Betty forwarded one of Robert's business letters to one of his peers. "It was entirely unnecessary to send my letters to any one and I left no such Direction," Mr. Conrad snapped, furious at her presumption. "Keep them until I get back. . . . Send no more letters unless you send them to me."[42]

Both the tone and meaning of Robert's letters to Betty point to the manner in which he, and many other husbands, perceived the differential abilities, "natural" and acquired, of men and women. Many believed their wives incapable of maintaining a fixed and efficient work schedule. Southern males, especially those like Conrad whose professional or skilled occupations placed them in a developing capitalistic economy, found this "female trait" particularly frustrating. Despite his obvious affection for his wife, Conrad also doubted her ability to "act" promptly, efficiently, or at all, especially when it came to matters outside their home. His attitude was not unique. Since the privileged position of free males clearly rested on the assumption that women could not function in the "world," a woman who did so challenged a basic premise of patriarchal power.[43]

Some women found this kind of treatment humiliating, especially those who had lucrative skills, formal training, or generally were competent to participate in a variety of public activities. Moreover, community attitudes about women's abilities often undermined their confidence to act otherwise for many eventually came to doubt even their performance as mothers and wives. Betty's skill with children, her household staff and duties, for example, obviously grew over time, but her husband still made all the important decisions that influenced their lives. And most women were completely left out of financial matters. Husbands even arranged for a male relative or family friend to give their wives a few dollars when they were away from home. Others sent checks for small sums—five or ten dollars—so that they would have money for trivial expenses. "Enclosed is $5.00 to give to [your brother] Cuthbert, if you want any more, he will supply you" were typical instructions.[44]

Some well-to-do women like Octavia Balls or even those of middling means like Susannah Shover had their own incomes, generated from the separate estates that their parents arranged before they married. A woman's separate estate, however, could bring on marital discord even if it did lend a measure of security to her life. Men often balked when their wives refused to turn these assets over to them. When Caroline Balls refused to assign her separate estate to her husband's control, for example, he began to argue constantly with her about it and to steal her furniture and other property. He finally abandoned her.[45] Caroline retained her property, but her private life was in shambles when she petitioned for divorce in 1850. Some women emerged from these kinds of disputes with even less. Consider, for example, the experience of Julia Carter, sister to Loudoun planter George Carter.

When Julia married Dr. Robert Berkeley in 1804, she was a wealthy woman, with at least $40,000 in land and slaves. Dr. Berkeley's financial resources at the time of their marriage were considerably less. Her family was not overly concerned, however, because Julia's father had had the wherewithal to place his daughter's assets in a separate estate. Moreover, he had given Julia a substantial dowry when she married—500 acres of land, ten slaves, and a large quantity of livestock valued in excess of $10,000, to say nothing of luxurious household furnishings, linens, and tableware. The couple also occupied one of Julia's several plantations. Altogether a handsome deal for her beloved, or so the family believed. Despite her father's precautions, however, Julia's husband still managed to gain control of all her property within the space of a few years.[46]

By common law, the husband obtained outright ownership of a wife's "worldly" goods, earnings, and inheritance when they married, unless a marriage contract or provisions attached to inheritances stipulated otherwise. Although marriage contracts were not the rule in Loudoun, some did exercise that right. Issued by the county court, a woman's prenuptial agreement created a "separate estate" and was one of the ways in which parents and guardians, such as Robert Carter, established some secure means of economic support for their married daughters. Separate estates also existed as separation agreements that couples could have drawn up after they married. They also often were included as stipulations in wills, deeds, gifts, or deeds of sale. These agreements essentially set aside property to be administered by a trustee who was responsible for keeping it for the separate support of the stipulated spouse. Trustees were men or unmarried women who managed all of the business related to the property and determined the amount of control, if any, the actual owner had. The trustee could choose to retain complete control, share it with the owner, or transfer complete power to her. Husbands also sometimes created separate estates in the name of their wives in order to shelter property from creditors. Yet a woman's separate estate usually meant complete exclusion of her husband's control.[47]

By the time that Dr. Berkeley met his untimely death at the hands of his wife's slaves in 1818, Julia had given him most of her property and other financial holdings. Approximately one year after their marriage, she legally conveyed to him all of her "separate" assets through her executor, John Richards. Her family knew nothing of her actions. Since she took no measure to insure that she would get her property back if her husband died before she did, he felt free to leave most of his estate to his eldest son, not to her. When she finally called on brother George to help her figure out the mess, it was too late.[48]

Julia's brother was appalled at the situation. What could she have been thinking, he mused, when she signed her property over to her husband? How could she have let the man take such advantage? Julia, he concluded, had acted immaturely; her husband had acted roguish. "Julia . . . thinks correctly upon most questions," he confided to another sister, "but upon the subject of giving up the absolute control of her landed estate to her Husband—she has unquestionably acted a peruile [*sic*] part." Carter was "pleased to see a woman love her husband," but she still had to protect herself. "It shews but a small mark of regard in a Husband," wrote the confirmed bachelor, "who has won the affections of his wife, to make use of that affection as an Engine to influence her to convey all her estate to him for the purpose of aggrandizing either himself or a particular child." Overcome with emotion, George rashly predicted that Dr. Berkeley's actions had made Julia a "*forlorn beggar.*"[49]

Mr. Carter was speaking in relative and exaggerated terms when he suggested Julia's impending poverty. But his outrage at his sister's situation does some shed some light on upper-class views about a woman's financial independence. Many elite fathers and guardians would rather their female kin live without the "protection" of a husband, if this "protection" was only a pretense bought at the expense of their daughters' emotional, physical, or material well-being. Marriage was an important duty for all, but none relished the idea of a son-in-law wasting—or, even worse, stealing—their child's property. Upper-class families could afford the kind of criticism the community unleashed on spinsters—women as wealthy as the Carters hardly needed a man's status, support, or protection. George Carter, for one, concluded, that it would have been better for his sisters to live as wealthy, independent spinsters than to marry foolishly. "*I hope you will never agree to make any pauper rich by intermarriage,*" he wrote another sister, "*—for Sheer love convey him your Birthright. . . .* Keep your 'honourable fee simple' as the 'paladium' of [your] 'Liberty.'"[50]

It was a "liberty" that some women, especially widows, could exercise as long as they were independently wealthy and the men in their lives allowed them to do so. Mr. Carter's complaints about his sister's predicament notwithstanding, a significant number of widows did have at least moderate control of their lives. These women mostly appear in official county records as heads of households. In 1830, for example, women comprise almost 18 percent of the heads of white Loudoun households. While their representation in this census year is relatively large (they usually were closer to 12 percent of household heads), the majority stood relatively in good stead financially. As the widows of farmers, planters, artisans and mechanics, many owned property. Slightly over 50 percent of the female heads of households in 1830, for example, owned slaves; and a majority of these owned more than five. These descriptive statistics hold true for 1810 and 1850 as well. While most had sons or other male kin and sometimes overseers who controlled much of their financial investments, as women of means and as household heads, they still enjoyed a particular kind of "liberty" that poorer women, regardless of their marital status, did not.[51]

Of course, they jeopardized this status if they ever remarried, particularly if there ever developed a financial crisis. Under such circumstances, wives with even small separate estates were expected to lend a helping hand. When Samuel Janney's factory failed in Occoquan during the 1830s, for example, it was his wife's assets that went to pay off his debts and help him begin a new financial venture. Wives usually did not have enough money to really make a difference during times of great financial duress, but some did manage to put aside a few dollars of the cash they raised by selling eggs and the livestock. John Janney, for example, recalled that most of the married women in his neighborhood raised and sold poultry and eggs to local hawkers. Even slaveholding women like Betty Conrad sometimes raised a few head of cattle, chickens, or other fowl for sale. Loudoun's wives who resided in urban areas sometimes took in boarders, while others like Nancy Turner worked as weavers or seamstresses. A few poor white women also were domestics and midwives, providing essential income for their families.[52]

But their husbands or some male household head still decided how their earnings should be spent. As such, both wealthy and poorer women experienced the frustration of having their husbands dictate their household budget. Indeed, many elite women, who had to keep up the appearance of leisure and luxury, often felt the pinch. Sarah Harrison, for example, wrote to her sister in November 1843 that she could not understand how the "girls of modern days" were able to get along with the "limited means" that their husbands provided. She certainly was not. "I can scarcely manage to keep up my establishment decently," she admitted, "although I work like a dray horse rising early and settling late and eating the bread of carefulness."[53] Many husbands refused to believe that their wives needed as much money as they requested, often accusing them of waste and extravagance.

This kind of constant scrutiny and implied doubt took a devastating emotional toll. Many wives were unable or reluctant to identify the source of their sorrows, while others sought some relief by its mere articulation. Elizabeth Davisson, for example, the wife of a prominent Loudoun physician, found ample cause to write to a young friend about her feelings of inadequacy and uselessness. "It really distresses me to think of" my inability to live up to my duty of "Christian usefulness," she confessed. Elizabeth prayed that before she died she would be able to "do some little good, if it is only" for my family. "I awfully fear that even there I have been very difficult. Oh! the responsibility of a mother, of a mistress, of a wife."[54]

Depression among southern wives was a consistent complaint, one not limited to a particular period of their married lives, but which reappeared throughout the duration of their marriages. It was not unusual, therefore, for at least two, or even three, generations of women of the same family to suffer from depression concurrently. Betty Conrad, her sister Sarah, their mother Catherine Powell, and many of their female relations, for example, all suffered from prolonged "melancholia." A frequent witness to his wife's troubled feelings, Robert Conrad had little problem identifying the symptoms. Writing to Mrs. Conrad about her aunt's health in 1832, he commented in part: "Cuthbert's wife is at her father's where she has been for a week or more confined—don't be alarmed—by the mind." Cuthbert Powell's daughter, who happened to be married to Mrs. Conrad's brother, suffered from depression as well. Four years after reporting on her mother's uneasy mental state, Robert noted that Ann Powell's spirits were lower than he had "ever seen them." Another female relation, he added, "looks thinner, and is depressed in spirits." So common was melancholia among women that they usually discussed it openly in letters. "Mary is at Shirley we think as she left E. View on Monday last," Mary Lee Custis wrote to her daughter. "Her health and spirits are better now, but she is still in a very anxious state of mind respecting Her husband and children's spiritual welfare." "Catherine has been in Aldie for more than a week. Her spirits have improved very much lately," Marietta Powell wrote reassuringly to a sister-in-law in 1844.[55]

Many personal and complex reasons contributed to female depression, a phenomenon that cut across class lines. The reality of their dependency, however, clearly was paramount. Unable, and unwilling, to break away from this female tradition, women unwittingly helped to sustain this painful legacy as they passed their "ideals" of gendered behavior onto their children, teaching that silent acquiescence to a husband's will was the appropriate response for a wife. Feelings of loneliness, a fear of failure as wives and mothers, a sense of worthlessness, and a lack of control were other contributing factors. Many like Elizabeth Davisson were not convinced that woman's work was important to society. They also recognized the profound lack of control that they had over their lives and the people and events which shaped them, deeply resenting their small share of power in their homes as well as in their communities.

Women typically began to feel "blue" in the fall, following the gay round of spring and summer visits with friends and relatives. Their recreation during the warm months was more than just lighthearted entertainment. It gave them an opportunity to be with extended family and other female friends with whom they could discuss their problems, gain some legitimation for their roles in society, and reaffirm their sense of worth. The Loudoun women who entered into these kinds of bonds with one another, particularly those which had the added weight of kinship, treasured them and were reluctant to let them go. "[W]hy cant you avail yourself . . . to pay me a visit—. . . if you with your large family and [me] with mine wait for all things to suit [us] we shall never meet at all in this world," Sarah Harrison wrote to her dear younger sister.[56]

Women bemoaned the approach of cold weather and the end to their active social lives. Their physical confinement, children's school schedules, poor country roads, and the seasonal design of their domestic routines, did not allow them much fall or winter recreational diversion. Most of the year, they remained at home day in and day out, contemplating what many sometimes believed was the monotonous, menial state of their lives. Men too got depressed, but for different reasons.

New husbands usually described the first period of their married lives as happy ones. Two months after his marriage to Elizabeth Powell, for example, Robert Conrad had to leave home to attend to court business in Leesburg. "This little separation," he wrote his bride, "would convince me more (if it were possible to be more convinced than I am) how necessary your presence is to my happiness. It requires an effort—here in my old room, all alone, with my batchellor [*sic*] 'appliances' to satisfy myself that I have just not awoke . . . from a pleasant dream and found things as they were before I slept; and that I have, in good truth, a sweet wife, who is thinking about me, and could be glad to see me." Two weeks later, Conrad wrote his wife again. This time she was away from home, visiting her parents. Complaining of the lack of correspondence from her, the lonely newlywed insisted that they "never be separated so long again if it can be avoided." "I have this day been three months married and everyday becoming more pleased with it," Thomas Harrison wrote to his brother Burr. Harrison explained that he was so happy with his present "situation" that he now felt, "I must keep myself as much at home as possible to get along and live as I wish with my love."[57]

Yet like most new husbands, Thomas Harrison felt intensely the strain of his new financial responsibilities. It was an awesome burden for young men, even those who had promising careers, to find themselves accountable for the material needs and wants of another adult. As an officer in the Army stationed at Fort Jefferson in St. Louis, Thomas found it difficult for him and his wife to live comfortably on his salary. He confided in his brother that "all I wish is that I had some situation unconnected with the army, on the salary of which I could live tolerably comfortable. . . ." Harrison still had to admit, however, that he had discovered that "a man can live (at least I can) much cheaper married than single and a thousand times more to his satisfaction." A younger brother who recently had migrated from Loudoun to Alabama concurred. He wrote dismally back to his family that he could not live long on the frontier "without a wife."[58]

Still the expense of setting up housekeeping or even providing for the food, clothing, medical attention, travel, and entertainment of a wife were frightening commitments, particularly during the first few years of their marriages. One might, like Robert Conrad, also feel a continual pull between his duties as a breadwinner, which often took him some distance from his home, and his need and desire to be with his loved ones. In the end, most chose to focus on their roles as sole financial supporter, leaving their wives to keep the home warm and welcoming.

Well-to-do men also felt the tug of public duty, often dedicating some of their time and energy to matters of the state and nation. They met their fiscal and public responsibilities by working late hours outside of their homes, taking business risks, making prolonged business trips, and gaining political office—experiences that many wives, left home to their dull domestic routines, may have secretly coveted or misunderstood. Again, the strain related to gender convention passed from one generation to the next.

Having grown up in sex-segregated cultures, Loudouners often were unable to understand the needs, priorities, and perspectives of their spouses. Each viewed the other with some envy, often believing that their husband or wife lived more comfortably than they did, and at their expense. Loudoun wives, it seems, were no more sympathetic to their husbands' doubts and disappointments, than their husbands were to theirs. Absentee husbands of the middle and upper classes lived what must have appeared to their wives as glamorous lives—staying in hotels or boarding houses with other well-educated, interesting gentlemen and the women who were free to accompany them, attending all-night card parties and other social events, enjoying their power to shape society, seemingly at will. Indeed, free men of any class had the "right" to go when and where they pleased, an advantage that only began to spell out the kind of "freedom" that their wives believed they had. Men, they surmised, were the power brokers in their communities with active and stimulating social lives. While this was the common perception, men, even wealthy ones, rarely articulated this same view.

Perhaps they were trying to appease envious spouses, but many of the letters husbands sent home rang true when they spoke of the tedium of their lives in Richmond, on the court circuit, in the countryside attending to business, or even in Washington and other cities. Most envisioned their homes as *the* desirable spot, not their stressful work world, and were uncomfortable taking long trips alone. While away they found themselves waiting impatiently for letters from their wives with details about life at home and their children, complaining bitterly when they did not receive them. If they could afford to give up the work which demanded their absence from home, most insisted, they would do so. In the meanwhile, they struggled with their loneliness.

The correspondence of three generations of men in the Powell family identify the conflicts between business and domestic responsibilities that husbands confronted over the years. Leven Powell (1737–1810), his son Burr (1768–1838), and Robert Conrad (1804–75), son-in-law to Burr Powell, all complained of financial pressures and public responsibilities that mandated their long absence from home. Their wives' consequent resentment was another source of bitter frustration. The Powell men repeatedly lamented their lack of a home life, and the need they felt to be close to their wives and children. "Another disappointment in not hearing from you today," Robert Conrad wrote to his wife from the Leesburg court in 1835. "I wish you would make it a point to write every mail. . . . You have no idea (and I sometimes fear, no care) how much it disturbs me especially during court, when my nerves are stretched like fiddle strings, and when it is so important they should not give way, but keep in tune." As the years passed, Mrs. Conrad did not become more willing to accommodate her husband's requests for frequent contact. "You cannot be half as impatient, my dear," he wrote home from the state legislature in 1842, "as I am myself; and the feeling is increasing so much that it is with the strongest effort only can I refrain from throwing up my budget of public duties and leaving here without notice."[59]

No matter how much Mr. Conrad complained about the lack of letters, however, his wife refused to write more frequently. Her refusal to do so was a subtle, but decided, attempt at protest and control. Undoubtedly angry with her husband for leaving her and their children alone so often, Betty Conrad refused to ease her husband's mind about what was occurring in the family. Robert obviously understood Betty's motive for silence, but still was affected by it. Writing again from Richmond in 1842, he remarked: "No letter from you or news from home for more than a fortnight. Have you forgotten me, or grown careless, or is it intended to punish me for being here. . . . Write anything—as little as you please—as much as you please, so that you write at all. This going to the post office day after day and turning back disappointed, anxious and apprehensive of all sorts of evil," he had to admit, "is more than I can bear and yet it cannot hasten my return home—for my time and services until the first of March or thereabouts are *sold* and beyond my control." Outwardly, Betty was not moved by her husband's obvious need for communication, or his excuses for being away. He continued to write to her faithfully, hoping in vain that she would be more responsive. She rarely wrote back.[60]

Husbands, moreover, were not the only spouses who sometimes were separated from their families. Elite women, like Mrs. Conrad, often were absent during the summer months when they went visiting. Poorer women also found occasion to visit their friends and families, escaping for a few hours or days while they assisted an ailing relative, helped a friend with her new baby, or attended a church meeting or sewing bee. Many undoubtedly relished the idea of leaving their husbands at home to take on the responsibilities of the domestic sphere. When Robert Conrad returned home from the state legislature in the late spring, for example, his wife usually would be ready to begin her schedule of summer activities away from home. Again, he would find himself compelled to ask his wife to write to him and even to return home.

In June 1839, Conrad wrote Betty an amusing, light-hearted commentary on life at home without her. Conrad's playful, tongue-in-cheek attitude exemplifies the tone husbands and wives sometimes adopted in order to deal with the potentially explosive issue of absenteeism. "Do not flatter yourself . . . that I am so completely miserable," he begins, "for although it is rather dull by one-self," the slaves unreliable, and housekeeping troublesome, "my mode of life is not without its compensations." With his wife gone, Conrad teased, he could "sleep cool of nights" and "long of mornings," he did not get "dispeptic" from her pies, no one scolded him, he could walk around in his "morning gown" as long as he liked, and drank in the evening without interference. "If you will give me a few weeks more I think I can aim to get on very well without you."[61]

Betty Conrad probably learned such techniques of subtle control from her own mother. Catherine Powell behaved similarly when her husband was a member of the Virginia state legislature some thirty years earlier. Mrs. Powell not only managed to be away most of the summer months her husband was at home, but also often refused to write to him when he was away. "I have rec'd but one letter from you since I came here," Mr. Powell wrote to his wife in 1814. "I have a thousand things to think of at home and greatly desire to be with you."[62]

The deliberate withholding of information from husbands about family and home was a tool that Loudoun wives used with limited success. So too were outright demands that husbands return home. Burr Powell's mother, for example, tried to get her husband, Colonel Leven Powell, to give up his responsibilities as an officer in the patriot army and to return home during the military crisis. A man with a remarkable sense of duty to his country and family, Colonel Powell probably was absent from his home more than any of his male descendants. He not only served as an officer in the Continental Army, but also was a Virginia assemblyman for several terms and was a member of the National Congress from 1799 to 1802. It was as an officer in the Virginia forces during the American Revolution, however, that he most keenly felt the conflict between his responsibility to his society and his family.[63]

Camped with his troops in Fredericksburg, Colonel Powell sat waiting for military action, while afraid that British forces or sympathizers might threaten the safety of his wife and children in Loudoun. Powell relieved himself of some of his guilt and fear by sending his brother to stay with his family. Yet he still regretted his absence as much as his wife resented it. The letter that he wrote to her from his camp on December 5, 1775, is a telling example of the pressure that his beloved Sarah placed on him and his well tempered response. "You request my coming home before I march further. I am not at my own disposal but belong to my Country," he replied to her earlier correspondence. Powell explained that he would return home "with pleasure" if he could be "spared," "but cannot you be sensible of the variety of affairs which commands my direction." He assured his wife that he deeply lamented not being with her at such frightening times, but he had great responsibilities at his camp and he had to set the proper example for the other men who had left their wives and families too. "The first duty of a man in temporal matters," he lectured, "is to exert his utmost abilities in the defense of the Just rights of his country. . . . the first

Legacy I could wish to Bequest to . . .[our children] is Freedom[,] or at least such as we have hitherto enjoy it."[64]

Leven Powell's attitude concerning one's family stake in one's public service undoubtedly impressed his sons. As adults, they too would use similar reasoning to justify prolonged absences from their families. "I have given information to the members of Loudoun and Fauquier that I shall not be a candidate for the Senate at the next election and if I am permitted to rejoin my home once more, it will be my settled purpose never again to leave i[t] for so long a time, during the remainder of m[y] life, with my own consent," Leven's son Burr wrote with a sigh of relief to his wife in 1814. After years of her complaints about his being away from home, he finally was giving up politics. "You would have me leave my business, and my court, on which we must depend for living comfortably together, for the momentary gratification of seeing you and returning—this would be selfish on my part and no proof of a proper affection for you," Robert Conrad found occasion to write to his wife (Leven Powell's granddaughter) in 1830. Conrad's treatise on the importance of his work was only one of many to come in the next two decades. He eventually became a Virginia legislator and spent much of the 1830s and 1840s in Richmond away from his growing family.[65]

Obviously the demands of "man's work" sometimes clashed loudly with the needs of their wives to have them as active participants in their families. Moreover, husband absenteeism was not just a phenomenon among the elite. Divorce records from Loudoun indicate that lonely wives were just as common among the middling and lower classes as among the gentry.[66] Southern men who worked away from their families felt compelled to do so as principal breadwinners. Respectable and honorable men did not let their wives work, and were able to supply their families at least their basic material needs. Those men who were unable to provide adequately for their families were subject to community and familial criticism or—even worse—ridicule and pity. Yet "lean" years and bankruptcy were not uncommon experiences for Loudoun's yeoman farmers and the working class, as the records of the county's Overseers of the Poor and court orders of estate sales, instigated by local officials in order to satisfy debtors, document.[67]

So many variables could contribute to the financial ruin of a man who did not have substantial financial resources. A farmer could not survive without adequate land and labor resources. Sometimes even then, weather, infestation, disease, equipment, market prices, or just plain bad luck could mean a farm family's financial ruin. Even the wealthy sometimes found it difficult to maintain economic independence, particularly over several generations. When serious financial problems did occur, it was a devastating experience for a married couple. Often the husband experienced a loss of self-esteem and feelings of emasculation; his wife felt disappointed, angry, and sometimes betrayed.

First came the threats of legal action for debts and neighborhood gossip, followed by lawsuits and costly judgments. Then came notices in local newspapers and other public locales of impending property seizures for sale at auction. The first items up for bid were those which constituted the husband's sphere—his means of livelihood and symbols of previous financial accomplishment such as his land, house, slaves, farm tools, crops, and livestock.

If the first sale did not net enough income, local authorities continued to hold these auctions until either all of the property was gone or the debts resolved. Finally up for sale were the household items—beds, pots, pans, wash buckets, chairs—everything that symbolized the wife's domain. As one reviews the remaining documents from these kinds of private disasters that were played out in the public eye, it is possible to feel the creeping confusion, anger, panic, and final resolution of those Loudoun families who experienced bankruptcy. Take, for example, the declining financial status that characterized the Shover family during the late 1820s.

George and Susannah Sanbower Shover were cousins and both heirs of modestly successful families of German descent. Susannah's father had been fortunate enough as a farmer to leave each of his children and his wife some land when he died. Also, he had had the forethought to set aside Susannah's inheritance in a separate estate—an ominous sign of hard times to come. George Shover's father, Simon, was even more successful than Sanbower—he owned land as well as eighteen slaves at the time of his death, and had other profitable business interests within the county.[68]

The Shover family had the utmost confidence that George would succeed. His father named him sole executor of his estate. He was well educated and had served in the Virginia militia as a lieutenant. As a young man, George also was involved in a number of potentially lucrative business ventures.

Receipts from George Shover's customers detail his enterprising plots—he carded wool for local people, manufactured whiskey and brandy, milled wheat, rented out rooms, sold straw, operated a saw mill, and managed three farms—all at the same time. Despite his extended family's assistance, much of Shover's financial fate depended on Major Robert Braden, a much wealthier and older planter, businessman, and politician who supplied the young man with many of the materials that he needed to initiate his many business ventures. In April 1821, for example, Braden rented Shover his grist mill, saw mill, and carding machine together with the house at the saw mill, the garden, and use of the meadow for an annual payment of $200. Shover also rented stills from Braden and in 1822 contracted to pay a hefty annual fee of $400 to use another of Braden's farms along with the mills and machines on that property. Braden knew that George's father had died recently and that he was due to inherit land and slaves. He had to be aware of the possibility of Shover's failure, and perhaps was anxious to capitalize on it for he stipulated that George post a $5000 bond to seal the 1822 agreement.[69]

George Shover had other business interests as well. In 1819, for example, he purchased one-half interest in a wool carding machine from John Webb for $200. The following year he rented another carding machine from John Janney. Shover hoped to earn enough money from his various investments to pay the rent on his farms and to purchase slaves. In 1817, for example, he paid $300 for a male slave who had been part of his paternal uncle's estate. He also entered into a farming partnership with his brother-in-law, Michael Sanbower, in 1823, and that same year rented a tract of land from another cousin, Simon Michel. Shover apparently was adept at manipulating blood lines for his financial benefit. Not only did he borrow money from them, bought their slaves at wholesale prices, rented their land and entered into various agreements with them that he believed would be lucrative, but he also hired some to work for him at very low wages.[70]

George Shover was, without a doubt, a man on the move in the early 1820s. He was trying to acquire as many resources—labor, land, and technological— as quickly and as inexpensively as he could. He did so by calling on kin, friends, and willing businessmen for assistance. Shover was not satisfied with just renting; he also invested his few initial earnings in purchasing resources. In 1824, for example, he bought two small parcels of land totaling 62 acres from two of his relatives. Determined to succeed quickly, he was not a man to move slowly, carefully, or compassionately. He did not hesitate, for example, to divide and sell slave families for a profit. Nor was he reluctant to charge family members for his services, collecting, for instance, money from the Widow Shover for carding her wool. He also charged his family for the care of the insane aunt he kept in his home from 1821 to 1834. Indeed, there was no doubting George Shover's desire to prosper financially.[71]

Yet the timing of Shover's business ventures was ill-advised. Loudouners witnessed a decided decline in the county's economy during the 1820s, symbolized by the large numbers of white migrants who left for Ohio and points farther west and south during that decade. It was difficult to obtain land, and that which was available was either infertile or too expensive for most to buy. Slave labor also was expensive and many poor whites who could have provided county residents with a cheap labor pool chose to emigrate instead. Moreover, Mr. Shover hoped to make a profit by offering his neighbors a number of services that he could not furnish adequately, given his lack of capital and labor. By stretching his financial resources so thinly over a number of unrelated projects, he was unable to organize and support any of his business ventures efficiently or profitably. Also, the services that he offered were not unique ones, particularly in his German community which had a disproportionately high number of skilled artisans. His potential customers had many other local options that represented more firmly established service enterprises than those which he operated. Add to Shover's impulsive, often misguided, business sense his penchant for domestic and personal luxury and one begins to understand his rapid financial decline.[72]

By 1825, with his local credit options exhausted and no liquid assets with which to make payments on his substantial rents and loans, George Shover's bout with financial disaster became public knowledge. In March 1825, the court in neighboring Frederick County issued a warrant against Shover, his wife, and a business associate for nonpayment of debts. In January 1826, Robert Braden sued Shover for nonpayment of a $100 debt. By mid-1826, numerous creditors were calling for payments and threatening to sue if they did not receive them. "You will please to meet me [or] it will be the means of putting you to some trouble," read a typical note. Later that year, the Loudoun sheriff posted notification of the sale of George Shover's horses, cattle, hogs, wagons, household and kitchen furniture, and other miscellaneous items to satisfy legal judgments against him. Local authorities held several such sales of the Shovers' property between 1826 and 1827. One of the first auctions occurred in January 1826. The first items sold were George Shover's crops and farming equipment.[73]

Throughout his trials, George's kin remained his allies—they still genuinely liked him and there was, after all, the family's reputation to consider. George's brother Adam remained a faithful supporter throughout it all, volunteering to administer his affairs in 1826 and lending him $150 in 1827. As time wore on, however, some family members began to feel betrayed and acted to protect their own interests. In 1826, for example, George Shover became so desperate for money that he spent the $300 that he owed his cousin Catherine Sanbower. A year later, the Loudoun court awarded Miss Sanbower the 21 remaining acres of Shover's land in order to settle his debt to her. By 1828, all that was left to be sold of the Shover household items was one clock, the family's beds, a table, and a few other kitchen utensils. The sheriff soon auctioned them off, however, in order to satisfy the "rents and costs" that George Shover owed to Charlotte Shorts and the uncle for whom he was named, George Shover Senior.[74]

In the meanwhile, Susannah Shover had become more frustrated and angry as her family's financial situation deteriorated. A proud woman with a strong middling-class background that emphasized the duty of a husband to support his wife, her disappointment in George's inability to do so must have been apparent. Moreover, since her husband's financial impropriety had had an adverse effect on some of her family as well, relations between her and her husband undoubtedly were strained. Her loss of face in her community and within her own family weighed heavily on Susannah and must have caused her many moments of private torment. Yet she was not one to accept defeat easily.

Mrs. Shover remained with her husband throughout his financial demise. She also fought off those creditors who wrongfully tried to gain access to the property that she held in a separate estate. One can just imagine her explosive reaction when she learned that a local businessman, Joseph Waltman, was cutting timber on her land because her husband owed him money. Susannah threatened to sue Waltman in county court if he continued "cutting[,] waisting [*sic*] and carrying timber of [f] the land" that she had inherited from her father." In coming forward to defend her property against her husband's creditors, Susannah temporarily relieved her spouse of his duty as her protector and provider. Her aggressive behavior probably eroded even more Mr. Shover's lagging sense of self-esteem and his claim as family patriarch. The tone and content of her letter suggests that this dispossessed mistress was none too satisfied with her husband's attempts to rescue the family from complete financial ruin. "[I]f you have been so fortunate as to get my Husbands life Estate," she concluded in her note to Waltman, "for little or Nothing, you have not mine." Persist in your actions, Mrs. Shover offered as final threat, and "I shall Prosecute a suit against you to the utmost of my Power."[75]

Yet Mrs. Shover's attempts at financial survival were in vain. By the end of the 1820s, they were completely bankrupt. Like so many Loudoun families of ill-fortune, they opted not to remain in the county, but instead moved west. They went first to Ohio where other extended family members had settled. There George tried his hand at teaching. Unable to prosper, they moved on to Missouri and Mr. Shover took on the questionable occupation of selling tonics and other kinds of medicines. The last trace of evidence of George Shover's family comes from their residence in Clayton County, Iowa. Their trek west did not hold for them the promise that they had envisioned when they left Loudoun. The family never prospered.[76]

George and Susannah Shover were only one of many Loudoun couples who suffered substantial financial losses sometime during their marriage. Fortunately, these crises sometimes brought husbands and wives closer together and strengthened their commitment to one another. Samuel Janney and his wife, for example, also experienced the pain and humiliation of bankruptcy when his cotton factory in Occoquan failed during the 1830s. For almost a decade, Janney unsuccessfully tried to sell his factory. Finally in 1842, he succeeded. Yet even before that he had received the strong support and counsel of friends, relatives, and especially his wife.[77]

Elizabeth Janney had a substantial separate estate which she used to pay off some of Samuel's debts. The couple then invested the remainder of her assets, and her small inheritance from another relative, to establish the Springdale School for Girls in 1842. Still, it took them twenty years to recover completely from their losses.[78] During that time, Janney never doubted his responsibility to support his family and pay his debts.

As a man of strong religious convictions, Samuel Janney also believed that the financial trials he endured would result in even more "divine blessings" for him in the future. Throughout it all, he relied on his wife for emotional and financial support. He especially was thankful for her continued emotional aid. Thinking back on his honeymoon at some point during the crisis, Janney noted that he could not help "contrasting" the "high spirits and . . . bright prospect" that he and Elizabeth faced when they first married and the reality of their lives then. "[B]ut I have much consolation in knowing that the divine favor is not withdrawn from me and that those best earthly blessing[s] still remainst and that our love for each other is even stronger now than then," he concluded contentedly.[79]

But despite Samuel Janney's eventual triumph, the inability to support one's family, even for a short period of time, was a disheartening experience. Some men, like Alexander Turner, deserted their wives and children rather than face the ongoing humiliation. Not a few women, like Eleanor Bagent, left their husbands to live with other men who could provide them with a more comfortable lifestyle. Many more like Hannah Barr stayed on in a bad situation that only turned worse. Constantly pregnant, she became the bane of her husband, who routinely beat her.[80]

Men who were unable to support their families often had to withstand the criticism of their community and of their wives and children, as well as their own personal shame. Joseph Caldwell, for example, remembered that much of his impoverished childhood was spent on a small farm which his father administered poorly. "My Father managed all of his affairs badly and was always involved and embarassed [sic]," Caldwell confessed in his autobiography. "We lived exceedingly low, sassafras tea and bread was our common food for all the day and often we had no bread; and we considered that we got along quite well if we had a good supply of potatoes." Joseph explained that his father lamented his inability to provide for his wife and family, but could not find any way to rectify the situation. Mrs. Caldwell did not work, so that her husband's efforts, aided only by the labor of their young sons and an elderly slave couple, were all the family could rely on for income.[81]

Still, the Caldwell family survived better than many others. They owned land, two slaves, and Mrs. Caldwell did not work outside her home. Moreover, Joseph eventually did have an opportunity to get some formal education. Through the eyes of a child, however, the family's situation seemed grim. Although young Caldwell understood his father's dilemma, he never was able to forgive his parents for their poor lifestyle and the few opportunities they provided for his future. Joseph Caldwell never ceased believing that his father's life was a failure because he was a poor breadwinner.[82]

E. P. Buck of Leesburg was an adult when her father faced economic difficulties, but the situation still proved trying to her. Writing to a nephew in October 1848, for example, she began excitedly: "You have no doubt heard of Papa's desperate circumstances. He is *insolvent*." While Miss Buck's age and gender perhaps made her more sympathetic to her father's dilemma than Joseph Caldwell had been to his parent's financial woes, she too felt threatened personally by her father's financial insecurity.[83]

Given such expectations from one's loved ones, it is not surprising that few men were willing to compromise economic opportunities, even when it temporarily took them away from their families. Absenteeism for many was an easier pill to swallow than loss of one's family's esteem and respect because they failed as providers.

Despite the problems that Loudoun's married couples faced at various times during their sojourn together, however, many were content in their marital relationships. The few petitions for divorce which emerged from the county were not only a result of restrictive laws and peer pressure to remain married, but also an indication that these lifelong commitments were an agreeable form of interaction and intimacy for many of the men and women who entered into them. Isaac Fouch, a Loudoun millwright, stated openly that he still was "much attached" to his wife Elizabeth after six years of marriage and had since the time of their wedding "cherished the most ardent, tender, affectionate Love and Regard for her." Hortensia Rogers made little secret of the fact that she missed her husband terribly whenever he was away from her. Rose Poulton of Hillsboro too remained quite happy in her relationship with her husband through the years. Writing to him in 1862, she lamented their separation, noting, "I shall wait patiently (if I can) and I know I shall be so happy and enjoy your visit so very much." She went on to tell her "precious darling" that she especially enjoyed his letters, for their tone was "so sweet," so expressive of the pure feelings of his "noble heart," that she read them "over and over."[84]

Elizabeth Janney also expressed loving feelings for her absent husband over the years. "I was rejoiced when Uncle Jasper handed me a letter last third day to find the superscription that it was from my beloved Samuel," the Quaker school teacher wrote in 1825. Although Mr. Janney often was away from home on business trips or pursuing his interests in religion, abolition, and other reform efforts, he and his wife were able to retain a close, loving relationship. Like Rose and John Poulton, their compatibility helped them to maintain their intimate emotional and intellectual ties even after weeks of separation. So too did Mr. Janney's liberal support of a woman's right and ability to contribute equally within and outside of her home. The respect and admiration that they held for one another, along with their deep abiding romantic love, helped them to forge a strong marital bond. While away from home, for example, it was not unusual for Mr. Janney to create fantasies about their life together from loving memories. "How often do I find myself drawing a picture of domestic happiness *at our own fireside* . . . ," he wrote from New York in 1825. " Me thinks I see thee sitting by the stand either conversing with me, or sewing while I read to thee. . . . Dost thou ever indulge in such fancies?" he asked. "If so let us hasten to realize the picture which I am sure will exceed the pleasure of antici-pation." He closed his letter familiarly: "With unabated love, I remain my dear girl, Forever thine."[85]

Robert and Betty Conrad probably had more problems than some. They cer-tainly seemed not as compatible a couple as the Poultons and Janneys. Yet they did have strong ties, initially wrought by their physical and emotional attrac-tion for one another, common social class and priorities, and the many friends and social activities that they shared. As the years passed, their relationship became stronger with their combined efforts to be good parents and to weather the many problems, crises, and good times that all couples faced as they created memories together.

Although their relations became strained at times, Robert and Betty re-mained lovingly close. Indeed, most of their complaining about one another came from missing each other, not because of any genuine feelings of dislike or disregard. And Mr. Conrad did not hesitate to reassure his wife repeatedly of his love and admiration. Trying to clear up a disagreement which came about as a result of his being linked to another woman in a newspaper article, for ex-ample, Robert responded compassionately: "There must be no quarrel between you and I my love. . . . To say nothing of my duty and pleasure to love and cherish you, I do assure you, there is not one person in this world for whom I have as great a respect."[86]

Aware of the tension that his high-powered political career and his own per-sonal designs sometimes brought to bear on his marriage, Robert Conrad was willing to make some sacrifices. Likewise, while Betty might have complained long and hard about his frequent absence from home, she ultimately did accept that much of it was due to his desire to provide a comfortable lifestyle for her and their children. Writing from Richmond in 1851, Robert made sure to thank Betty for the surprise present she had placed in his trunk—an amusing novel that she hoped he would enjoy reading while away from home.[87]

As a marriage aged, therefore, most couples came to recognize and learned how to cope with the many challenges of the institution and the community ideals which shaped it. The duties incumbent in being the kind of wife or hus-band that white southern society deemed ideal or even adequate mostly were shared across class and cultural lines; so too were the difficulties of living up to such commitments. In the end, most of those who had long-lasting, reasonably satisfying marriages must have come to respect what their kin and community had stressed during their courtships—the importance of compatibility and companionability within a marriage expected to endure one's lifetime.

4

Parenting

Tomorrow is yr birthday — I thank my God upon many remember-
ances of you my child.

                                        Elizabeth Conrad to Kate Conrad, 1856

W ithout a doubt, parenting was a couple's most important commitment to their families and their communities, and it could be a rewarding one.[1] The benefits of a "good" child were both emotional and pragmatic.
Elizabeth Conrad believed that her daughter was a tremendous blessing to her
and her family. Over the years, Mr. and Mrs. Conrad had taken care of her,
loved and guided her. Kate, in turn, had grown up to be a loving, mostly obedient, intelligent daughter who brought her parents much comfort through her
affection, loyalty, and dedicated service. In their estimation, the covenant between parent and child had been fulfilled, the circle completed.[2]

Given the importance of the parent-child relationship, it comes as little surprise that nineteenth-century editors and authors, concerned with social development and control, dedicated much of their attention to parental duty and
child socialization. Along with this onslaught of advice manuals came some
significant changes in the ideas about the "nature" of childhood and "adolescence." Seventeenth- and even some early eighteenth-century writers often focused on innate flaws evident in a child's early nature. "Above all other"
dangers, John Robinson wrote in 1628, "how great and many are their spiritual
dangers, . . . for nourishing and increasing the corruption which they bring into
the world with them." This harsh reality called for harsh measures. "And

surely there is in all children . . . a stubbornness, and stoutness of mind arising from natural pride, which must, in the first place, be broken and beaten down; that . . . other virtues may, in their time be built thereon." Many believed that "He, who spares his rod, hurts his son."[3]

Influenced by Jean-Jacques Rousseau's theories of childhood innocence, John Locke's analogy of children as "blank slates," and others who considered issues of child physiology, psychology, and morality in the eighteenth and early nineteenth centuries, antebellum "experts" were more likely to characterize children as moral "innocents" and the hope of the future. Parents, they explained, had a perfect opportunity to rear useful, righteous citizens if they took the task seriously. "In other words," Horace Bushnell concluded, "the aim, effort, and expectation should be, not, as is commonly assumed, that the child is to grow up in sin, to be converted after he comes to a mature age." It is "that he is open on the world as one that is spiritually renewed . . . seeming rather to have loved what is good from his earliest years."[4]

While some popularized their ideas in book-length works like William Buchan's *Advice to Mothers on the Subject of Their Own Health; and on the Means of Promoting the Health, Strength, and Beauty of Their Offspring*, Lydia Maria Child's *The Mother's Book*, and William Alcott's *The Young Mother*, others began publishing in specialized periodicals like the *Mother's Magazine*, *Mother's Journal and Family Visitant*, *The Mother's Assistant*, and *Parent's Magazine*.[5] They also appeared in serialized columns in "ladies" journals. Each edition of *The Ladies Magazine and Literary Gazette*, for example, included "Letters from a Mother" with detailed advice on almost every aspect of childrearing. In literary periodicals as well as religious magazines, and even occasionally in the latest agricultural publications, readers found instructive, often moving, lines dedicated to parental duty. Maternal associations cropped up and women just as frequently discussed the topic in their church organizations and literary groups.[6]

Although perspectives varied, nineteenth-century specialists did establish some common ground. All agreed, for example, that the role of the mother in early child development—physical, emotional, moral, and intellectual—was paramount. Mothers, they lectured, functioned as their children's first teachers of every major lesson in life. As such, children viewed the world through their mother's eyes and incorporated their attitudes, ideals, and practical knowledge. Experts lectured that no force, even those of the church, school, or state, had as much influence on a child's development as his or her mother. "And as the mother is the guardian and guide of the early years of life, from her goes the most powerful influence in the formation of the character of man," John Abbott wrote in *The Mother at Home* in 1833. "[M]ore than all, [woman] was born to train the sons and daughters of men for this world, and for the world to come; a few to act as master spirits in the management of that inheritance which one age transmits to another," another typical author wrote.[7]

Certainly the non-economic responsibilities of colonial parenting weighed heaviest on the mother and other women in the household. During the early nineteenth century, however, child care experts and enthusiasts more broadly defined the mother's role, trying to convince women that they could and should do more than just feed, clothe, bathe, heal, and nurture their children. Mothers also learned that they should know how to resolve early problems of child development such as teething, weaning, and masturbation. It was their duty as well to teach their sons and daughters early survival and social skills, to provide moral instruction and example, to initiate their formal education, and even to act as disciplinarian.[8]

Thus the early nineteenth century witnessed an evolution of parental roles in which childrearing duties were expressly those of the mother, while the father's prescribed role shrank. Yet even the most "mother-centered" expert had to concede that male parents provided early examples of "masculinity" to their sons that were vitally important. Likewise, fathers regained much of their status as principal childrearers as youngsters matured into adolescents.[9]

Some authors, heaping prestige on the additional labor that they assigned women, labeled them "Republican mothers" and extolled their contribution to the future success of the nation.[10] Proponents of female education manipulated this new emphasis on the importance of the mother to assert the need for more and better intellectual opportunities for females. Not surprisingly, they were not opportunities which challenged woman's domestic-bound lifestyle. "The importance of female education, as connected with the general happiness of the community," one author of the series "Letters from Mothers" asserted, "will be readily admitted, if we advert to that powerful moral influence, which women hold over their children at the periods of infancy and childhood, and which is continued with their female children almost to the age of maturity." Another wrote similarly: "Now if a mother have no education, or, what is as bad, one that was merely superficial and showy, ... her children will inherit the deficiencies of her character, and will prove either incumbrances or positive evils to the community."[11]

While many emphasized the important role mothers played in their children's early emotional and intellectual development, others focused on their influence on youngsters' physical well-being. A large body of childrearing literature, for example, revolved solely around the issue of infant feeding. Antebellum writers advocated that the mother breastfeed her babies and cautioned against using wet nurses. In so doing, they hoped to avoid the consequences of a child developing a strong emotional attachment to a woman other than his or her mother, the questionable health of these nurses, and the permanent negative influence that these women, generally thought to be morally inferior because of their poverty and ethnic or racial difference, might have on the character formation of innocent babies.[12]

Southern elite women undoubtedly took notice of this advice, for evidence indicates that by the 1820s many did not use slave women to nurse their children. Others did. Harriet Newby, a slave in the Loudoun vicinity, for example, had occasion to write her husband in 1859 that her mistress had had a baby girl and that she had to "nurse her day and night." Some, however, used bottles if their poor health precluded their breastfeeding. Experts also advised mothers how and when to wean—the consensus was that they should do so over a one- to two-week period when the child was between eight and twelve months old.[13]

Parenting obviously garnered tremendous interest among intellectuals and social architects of the age. Yet the impact that this flourishing of literature and dialogue actually had on southern childrearing generally, or even specifically, is difficult to gauge. Two things are certain. First, this discourse was meant to influence the activities and decisions of middling and wealthier folk, those people social experts believed had most influence on their society's traditions. It was not meant for poor southerners. Second, self-styled childrearing experts hardly took into account the importance of non-nuclear kin in the lives of almost all southern children.

Childrearing advisors assumed several characteristics of the families that they targeted: that they had a strong, nuclear base; that fathers were the principal breadwinners; and that mothers had no other occupation except those of wife and parent. For them, these kinds of conditions formed the basis for the only "legitimate" family in their society, that is, the patriarchal, nuclear family. "Leading" members of most southern locales like Loudoun agreed. But their general disdain for persons whose lives veered far from this scenario only worsened the harsh realities of that substantial number of southern families and their children who found themselves in structurally or functionally different kin groups. Consider, for example, the plight of illegitimate children and their parents.

Court records routinely listed numerous cases of bastardy among the county's poor. The legal system, to say nothing of public opinion, stipulated tough penalties for everyone involved. Both the father and mother either had to enter a bond with the county court or serve a lengthy indenture in order to guarantee the support of their youngster's first few years of life. After that, their child became the ward of the county Overseers of the Poor and was directed by the county court to serve a mandatory apprenticeship until he or she reached adulthood. A typical case was that of Jesse Smith, Anna Bealle, and their son heard in the Loudoun court in August 1807. Records document that "on hearing the complaint of the Overseers of the Poor, against Jesse Smith and the testimony of Anna Bealle," the court decided that Smith was the father of Bealle's "male bastard child" and ordered him to pay $20 every quarter for seven years as a matter of financial support. At the age of seven, if neither parent was able (and willing) to provide further support, the boy would enter a court-assigned apprenticeship until he was twenty-one.[14]

It probably was the hope of the court and the Overseers that these apprenticeships as, for example, joiner, cabinetmaker, tanner, wheelwright, and miller, would allow young county men who had had tenuous familial beginnings the kind of occupational stability necessary to begin their own marriages and family under more "acceptable" circumstances. But at what price? Undoubtedly, illegitimate children, their parents, and other kin suffered tremendously at the hands of these kinds of social policies. Consciously or not, the actions of the Overseers and the court undermined the hope of a patriarchal, nuclear family for these people. Their judgments, after all, denied the father patriarchal control and removed the child from the mother's care, sometimes permanently. Their children, therefore, grew up outside the example of the "ideal" and thus had no first-hand experience with this kind of familial experience. This was only part of the problem. One's public reputation and honor also were irreparably damaged.

Public opinion especially was hard on single women with children. Despite some criticism of the father and the county's determination to make him partly responsible for the child's early support, a double standard of sexual behavior was fully operational in small southern towns and counties like Loudoun. The mother not only faced the burden of providing some financial support for her child when he was young as well as the pain of loss due to their eventual separation, she also often endured a kind of threefold rejection—from her lover, her family, and her community—that could be psychologically devastating. Rare newspaper reports of children abandoned by their mothers only begin to point to the enormous desperation and hopelessness of those impoverished women who "voluntarily" gave up their children. These accounts just as readily attest to the hostile response of local folk who believed that these acts of child abandonment were so foreign to maternal instinct as to suggest the monstrous.

The Leesburg *Washingtonian* reported in July 1846, for example, that Washington officials arrested a Loudoun woman named Mary Calvert after they discovered that she had left her "newly born male white child" in a local coal house. When questioned by authorities, Calvert confessed that she had left the baby "hoping it would be taken care of." Mary faced imprisonment not only for "inhumanely abandoning her own offspring," but also because he died of starvation soon after authorities found him. The court justices who interviewed Calvert—all undoubtedly upstanding, well-to-do men—could express little sympathy for the bereaved mother. They did make it clear, however, that Calvert's "betrayal" of her sacred maternal duty offended them deeply—they did not know whether to characterize her as "wretched," "inhumane," or "insane." In the end, they decided that she was not insane, but rather a "wretched" (poor, white) woman whose "criminal" actions caused her son's death. They judged Mary Calvert's intrinsic challenge to prescribed conventions of southern white motherhood inexcusable, even if those who defined these conventions never meant for them to be embraced by single, poor women.[15]

Most poverty-stricken mothers did not give their children away; the county court usually took them away. Still, even those poor single, widowed, estranged, or divorced women who struggled to hold on to their children and to give them some semblance of a stable family life received little applause, or even help, from mainstream society. Few Loudoun communities had the wherewithal—financially, psychologically, or morally—to extend a compassionate hand to those whose principal shame was their poverty and lack of a breadwinner husband. Even those who worked in the few "respectable" jobs available to poor women—as domestics, seamstresses, hotel and tavern servants, store clerks, weavers, midwives, and nurses—could not expect their society's full acceptance. Instead, many thought of them as "poor white trash," a stigma difficult for impoverished adults, much less their children, to ever lose. Society considered them inferior, not just socially and economically, but culturally as well. Their children, unlike those of the middling and upper classes, had uncertain futures at best. Poor Loudouners, therefore, faced immense challenges, not the least of which was a pervasive social ideology that rejected those not rooted in a patriarchal reality. For those families, public disdain, social invisibility, poverty, and separation were common experiences.

Nineteenth-century childrearing experts not only ignored the social circumstances poverty imposed on families. They also rarely considered the importance of "other" or extended kin so important in the southern childrearing experience. In fact, they focused so much attention on the role of the mother in the young child's life that all other persons traditionally and actively involved, including fathers, older siblings, and single female kin, almost disappear altogether from the scenario. From the time that a child's conception became family news (or gossip), however, both nuclear and "other" kin also became involved, reassuring the mother, congratulating the father (or vice versa), helping to make plans, extending suggestions for names, promising hand-me-down clothes, and all kinds of other help. And that was only the beginning. Over the years, they acted to insure that family events always would be more public and expansive than private and exclusive in nature. If one ever doubts the importance of non-nuclear kin in the lives of southern children one need only refer to an accurate genealogical chart and make note of the repetition of first and family names across and within generations to begin to comprehend the intricate and complex levels of southern family ties that were operational. While "other" kin did not challenge the basic nuclear structure of Loudoun's European American families in any fundamental way, they did assure southern youth a richly textured kinship. They also helped, over the generations, to convey important notions of duty and accountability, beginning, of course, with the commitment to have children.

Many women faced pregnancy and motherhood with ambivalence and fear, largely because of the health risks involved. They had legitimate fears. The state of medical science, particularly pre- and postnatal care, gynecology, and obstetrics, hardly could permit physicians, midwives, husbands, or female kin and friends to offer any guarantee that an expectant mother would have a trouble-free pregnancy, birthing, or recovery. Even after gynecology and obstetrics became pioneering "sciences" (rather than "mysteries"), through institutionalization in medical school curriculum in the early 1800s, practitioners still had much ground to break.

Miscarriage, still births, pre- and postnatal infections were frequent occurrences among all early nineteenth-century southern women despite the generation in which they lived or their class. Family papers that span the decades sufficiently document these private tragedies and scares. "Her fever came on . . . Saturday and has continued since, accompanied with pain & throbbing in the head. Her milk is very abundant and may be the cause of the fever and headache," Robert Conrad noted in his description of his wife's first birthing ordeal. Conrad's agitation grew as his wife's condition lingered. "She had a very bad night," he wrote to his mother-in law the next morning. "The Doctor . . . says that the fever proceeds from the irritation peculiar to her situation, and he is in hopes that by keeping her quiet it will wear off. I feel uneasy and anxious of course." Mrs. Conrad, who eventually recovered and lived to have eight other children, was hardly the only woman in her upper-class family to suffer during childbirth. Younger generations of her kin as well as those of her own and older generations faced similar ordeals. Twenty years later, for example, her husband again had occasion to write concerning the complications of a kinswoman's pregnancy. Mrs. Conrad's expectant niece, Rebecca Noland, had undergone an attack of convulsions, considered "a very dangerous symptom in her situation." Instead of a pregnancy filled with loving anticipation and hope, then, many women, even privileged ones, could not help ruminating over memories of women like themselves—beloved mothers, aunts, cousins, and friends—who died trying to fulfill this "sacred" female duty.[16]

Pregnant women and their unborn children suffered not just because of local practitioners' primitive obstetrical knowledge. Even if they had known more, there were too few to serve the local communities and most people could not afford them. By the turn of the nineteenth century, their availability had increased, but their clientele still usually were only the well-to-do. It is clear from Mr. Conrad's remarks, for example, that male physicians were available to treat middling and wealthy women in Loudoun and its vicinity. The well-educated, sophisticated son of a prominent Winchester physician, Conrad might have been more comfortable during the 1830s with a male obstetrician than some of his less worldly peers. Advertisements in local papers and the receipts of physicians, such as that of Dr. John Richards, who had studied "physic, surgery and midwivery" at the University of Glasgow and Edinburgh or Dr. T. Floyd, who had studied midwifery in London and listed his expertise as "diseases of women and children," however, suggest that they were gaining popularity even during the first decade of the nineteenth century.[17]

Yet female midwives continued to be the mainstay of poorer Loudoun women and those who lived in isolated areas. Sometimes a family would request a physician if complications arose, but it often was difficult to predict problems before they occurred. And when they did occur, it might be too late to reach a doctor or even a more experienced nurse or midwife. On other occasions, but less so as the era progressed, slave midwives serviced their mistresses or their owners hired them out to other women for a fee. Mildred Graves recalled, for example, that "whenever any o' de white folks . . . was goin' to have babies dey always got word to Mr. Tinsley dat dey want to hire me fer dat time. Sho' he let me go—twas money fer him, you know." She, like other female practitioners, white and black, however, faced mounting competition and opposition from male "specialists." Graves complained, for example, that the doctors who lived in her neighborhood had little respect for her skills, calling it "witch doctor or hoodoo stuff." Still, local women asked for her help when they had trouble. Remembering one case in particular, Mildred added with pride that after successfully delivering the baby of a woman no one believed would survive, "even de doctors dat had call me bad names said many praise fer me."[18]

Expectant mothers, especially poor women, suffered from a host of medical problems, including gynecological and venereal infections that went undetected before and during their pregnancies, unsanitary delivery conditions, poor prenatal diets, emotional strain, and physical exhaustion. The majority of Loudoun women did not routinely have domestic help except that of other females and older children who lived in their homes. Rural poor women, particularly those of the German tradition, not only worked in their homes, gardens, livestock pens, and barns, but also did field work. They rarely could be spared unless it was absolutely necessary. Even pregnant wealthy women usually had to attend to their major domestic and childrearing tasks. Writing retrospectively to her daughter on the occasion of her birthday, for example, Elizabeth Conrad remembered that at the time of her daughter's birth, her overriding concern had been the health of her two-year-old son, not the impending delivery. "This night 23 years [ago] was a time of great suffering in mind and body to me," she noted. "So great was my anxiety about Powell that I took but little note of other suffering. You were here about 7 in the morning[,] I left Powell about two hours before[;] the crisis had passed and he was better."[19]

The type of emotional strain that Mrs. Conrad admitted she sustained during the night of her daughter's birth hardly suggests some of the psychological torture some pregnant women withstood for months. Fear and anxiety for their own condition heaped on top of a host of other domestic concerns that was "women's work," combined with the physical discomfort and emotional highs and lows of any pregnancy sometimes were too much to bear. Tragic, for example, is the story of Mrs. John Kyle, born a member of the county's prestigious Ball family and mistress of the beautiful "Foxcroft" estate. According to county legend, Mrs. Kyle had a psychological collapse after the birth of one of her children. No other details of her condition, or the events that precipitated it, remain for public scrutiny. What is known, however, is that her family, ashamed of and bewildered by her insanity, hid her away in the Foxcroft garret for several years. Left unattended one day, Mrs. Kyle managed to escape, falling down the stairs to her death.[20]

It is uncertain how Mr. Kyle responded to his wife's pregnancy or the problems that emerged after it. The brief account of her tragic life that remains part of the county's female lore poses more questions than answers. Some local husbands, however, did assume much of the responsibility for caring for their confined wives, expressing their delight for their new babies and their wives' "sacrifice" by waiting on both infant and mother. "Ann we hope is mending," Burr Powell wrote of his daughter-in-law's postnatal recovery. "She says he [her husband] is the best nurse in the whole world and I believe that his presence is to her better than friend or Physic."[21] Mr. Powell was openly pleased at his son's show of affection and dedication to his wife.

Most women depended more on their female friends and relations to get them through the ordeal than their husbands, even well-meaning ones. Having babies, after all, lay at the heart of female culture and was an important bonding ritual. Besides, few men could afford to take time off from their work for more than a few days. New fathers, as much as new mothers, depended on the aid of female kin. Mothers and mothers-in-law especially were solicitous of the needs of their pregnant daughters.

Writing earlier that year about the birth of another grandchild, for example, Burr Powell commented humorously about his wife's resolution to attend the birthing. Mrs. Powell, traveling alone against her husband's wishes, left her home in Middleburg to visit her daughter Anne in nearby Warrenton. "Mr. Williams came over on the morning to let her know that Catherine [Williams] would accompany her in the carriage if she would put off the journey one day," Powell explained, but Mrs. Powell refused to wait. Her husband could not resist comparing her aggressive determination to that of a man. "But she was like Patrick Ceruts when about to see his friend Col. Byrd, who was lying very ill," Powell added. "[A friend] sent word to him [Ceruts] to wait a short time and he would go with him[.] He returned for answer that when Patrick Ceruts was ready he waited for no man."[22]

Well aware of potential problems, and feeling a special obligation to this daughter with whom she and her husband only recently had restored amicable relations, Catherine was determined not to miss the birth. Anne had eloped as a young teenager with Lloyd Noland, causing her parents to end familial contact. Mrs. Powell's appearance at "Noland Mansion" that day undoubtedly helped to reunite Anne to her family of birth and to strengthen bonds between the two families.[23]

A mother's confinement after the birth of a child usually lasted from one month to six weeks, and women considered it a blessing to be able to resume some semblance of a normal life after shorter periods of time. "I got a note from Harriet yesterday," Marietta Powell informed a sister-in-law. "Her child is just three weeks old [and] she has been downstairs. Is not she a fortunate woman?" Some kin and friends stayed only a few days; others lingered for weeks to help the mother get through a reasonable period of recuperation. Catherine Powell stayed with her daughter Anne for several days. The birth had not been an easy one, and she was recovering slowly. Her concerned, but sedate father, reported to a younger daughter that the new mother was "doing as well as could be expected with her weak frame and a great strapping boy to nurse." Repeating his wife's report dryly, he added that baby Noland was, "when born, the largest child she ever saw."[24]

Burr Powell, as family patriarch, remained coolly removed from the details of this "women's work," but he was not a disinterested party. While his wife was busy helping their daughter, he busied himself informing interested kin of Anne's and the baby's progress. Both he and Mrs. Powell's handiwork helped to strengthen existing kinship bonds, initiating a broad family network for the newborn in the process.

The efforts of Burr and Catherine Powell to reconnect the Powell and Noland families seem largely to have succeeded. Anne and her husband Lloyd also did their part to mend the rift—naming one of their sons Burr Powell Noland. A generation later, another birth to a Noland woman commanded the loving concern of many of the Powell clan. Twenty-two years after Mrs. Powell's trek to the Nolands', her daughter Anne was performing the same duty for her daughter Rebecca—traveling all the way to Cumberland in order to attend to the mother-to-be for six weeks. Mrs. Noland's stay was unusually long, but Rebecca was ill throughout her pregnancy and her family feared that her life and that of the child were in jeopardy. Soon after the birth, watchful kin sighed in relief. This time it was one of Burr Powell's sons-in-law who conveyed the happy news to other family members. Writing to his own daughter in 1852, he noted that Rebecca was doing quite well and her "baby thriving."[25]

Expectant mothers, therefore, were not the only ones who drew concern. Many feared, and rightfully so, for the health of infants and small children. Relatives inquiring about the outcome of a delivery were quick to ask about the health of the mother and the child. Family and friends celebrated the birth of a healthy child with cheers, toasts, and praises to God. Signaling a tentative sigh of relief, Quaker Samuel Janney wrote to his wife that "Sister Hannah had been confined five days before and had another daughter[.] Both she and the child appeared to be doing well." Writing to a sister-in-law after the birth of her fourth child, one woman asked worriedly: "How is your health[?] Holmes told me you did not look well, but you had hardly recover'd from your confinement then[.] I am glad to hear you[r] Baby is a strong healthy fellow, for it is a great blessing."[26]

Indeed it was. Worry about the mother and her infant was even greater when there were unusual circumstances to consider. When Loudouner Betsy White had twins in 1806, for example, her mother and father were happy to report the good news to their family in Tennessee. "[T]he Thirtieth of may *Betsy* brought forth a (daughter and a son) and they are both alive and well and She calls them *Elizabeth* and *Joseph*." "[T]he garl is the oldest . . . but she (Elizabeth) had like to died. I think that six days out of seven I went to the doctor for her but she is a getting about again and Seems to be Reasonable Harty."[27]

An end to a child's infancy, however, did not mean an end to threatening health problems. Indeed, some scholars liberally estimate that the mortality for white youngsters under the age of ten was 40 percent and could be as high as 60 percent during years of widespread epidemic for those younger than sixteen. "I must inform you that our country has been afflicted more with sickness this last summer and fall than ever," Levi White wrote typically in 1804. "[T]here has been many hundreds taken off by the fever since last harvest.[28] Children and teens alike suffered from a number of ailments, especially pulmonary tract infections like tuberculosis, whopping cough, diphtheria, flus, colds, and pneumonia. There also were the standard childhood diseases such as chicken pox and measles; and other maladies, sometimes in epidemic form, like yellow fever, dysentery, smallpox, typhus, and cholera. Severe cases of worm infestation, as a result of eating poorly cooked meat and habitual bare feet of all children during warm weather, also was a common problem that could be very serious. Loudoun youth also had to contend with the kinds of infections and complications that came from numerous scrapes, breaks, bites, burns, and accidents that were virtually the way of life on a farm. As ever, the poor suffered most of all since they were the least well nourished and often did not have safe and sanitary housing, adequate clothing, or reliable medical attention. Those who could not find shelter at the county farm or poor house suffered tremendously during what could be bitterly cold, wet winters in their shanty-like housing. The effects of poor sanitation, particularly during the summer months, as well as their close living conditions meant they sometimes were the victims of devastating epidemics.[29]

Fear and skepticism underlay simple preventive methods. One of the easiest solutions was to avoid contact with illness. Once a town or neighborhood learned that a family was suffering from a particularly virulent illness, most stayed away until they believed it was safe to visit again. "Our overseer, Mr. Hodgson, has had three of his children . . . with scarlet fever at once," Robert Conrad wrote to one of his sons in 1852. "The neighbors are in such dread of it that not one came near the house during the time." The Hodgson family's health was improving, he added, and two of Conrad's youngsters, Dan and Kate, were "just recovering from the effects of their attacks." Mr. Conrad was expecting that visits to his home from friends and neighbors would begin again as soon as word reached town that the fever had passed.[30]

Most felt that prevention was the surest measure since they routinely did not have "much confidence in phisic [*sic*]" or their drugs.[31] Instead, they relied on time-tested prescriptions. Cleanliness, exercise, proper diet, rest, and relaxation, along with medical and dental care when necessary summarized the advice that they hoped would keep their youth healthy. Keeping clean and bathing in cold water were perhaps the most readily prescribed recommendations. "I would advise careful attention to personal cleanliness," Robert Conrad wrote to his namesake in 1855. "Not to satisfy yourself with the mere appearance, but to be always scrupulously clean, whether it can be seen or not." He added detailed instructions: "[W]ash yourself all over every few days—Keep your feet as clean as your face—and change your under clothing oftener than your outer. A man may have fine cloathes [*sic*] outside; but cannot feel like a gentleman if he is conscious that his skin is foul or his linen dirty." "These may strike you at first as trifling, but depend upon it that your health, comfort and self respect cannot be preserved without strict regard to these matters. I speak from experience—and, you know, only for your good."[32]

Whatever the details of health advice, the principle lesson was simple enough: one's physical and mental health were the key to happiness. Nothing warranted a threat to either. "Your plans for study and exercise are very good—shew your courage by preserving them," a father wrote to an overzealous son eager to make good grades. "But do not task yourself so far as to affect your health. [W]henever you find that threatened, relax your efforts until exercise and diet has [*sic*] restored it."[33]

Family correspondence from the era is replete with either alarming or calming news about the health of young and older children. They dutifully wrote details of children's health to other kin, reinforcing the ties between non-nuclear relatives and their children as they did so. Often a single correspondence between friends and relations chronicled both the birth and death of small children in one family. Louise Love wrote to her sister Sally in 1825, for example, that:

> I suppose you have heard that Aunt Peggy has a fine son; it has a red head[,] pin[k] eyes and white eyelashes exactly like its Father—they talk of calling it Wm Hale[.] Uncle Henry was so unfortunate as to loose his youngest son; it was about 3 months old—let me congratulate you my dear Sally on the birth of your little daughter[.] I suppose she is very sensible[,] interesting and beautiful—what do you call her[?]³⁴

"Brother . . . writes and never says a word about the children more than 'all are well' which is not very satisfactory," Betty Conrad complained to her sister. While Mrs. Conrad sent her wishes that her nieces and nephews were healthy, her fears about her own children's welfare also were on her mind. "I wish [my] Charles would run a few weeks with [your Charles Henry] this summer at Morrisworth. I am sure it would make him stouter. . . Cuthbert promises to be much more robust though he has been suffering with disordered bowells"[*sic*].³⁵

Despite Betty's complaint about her brother-in-law's silence, many men betrayed an anxiousness about their children's health equal to that of their wives. Writing to his wife in 1820, for example, Thomas Peake admitted that he could not "rest contented at so great a distance" from his wife and children. Peake was particularly disturbed by the report that "poor Drummer," his little boy, "was bit by a snake." He feared that it had poisoned him. Unable to return right away, he trusted "in the bountiful mercies of [the] blessed redeemer . . . to protect . . . and support" him and his family through all their "trials and difficulties." A child's health and welfare were subjects on which both men and women found enormous common ground to build companionable relationships. Sharing concern for their children, therefore, not only bound family women together, but also couples and other kin.³⁶

During most of his adulthood, for example, Robert Conrad was consumed with concern for his children's health and well-being. It was a paternal concern that elicited tremendous respect and admiration from his wife. Conrad's record of paternal devotion began with the birth of their first child, Daniel, in 1831. After excitedly writing his in-laws the details of the birth, he continued to closely monitor and communicate his son's development. When he had to be away from home on business, he wrote often to Mrs. Conrad with questions about the children and rarely failed to return without marbles, dolls, or some other kind of toy or gift. Likewise, it was not unusual for him to call on older, more experienced female kin for childrearing advice, especially his mother, mother-in-law, aunts, and other women in his community, sometimes even using them as a sounding board when he and Betty disagreed about child care.

"I was just summoned home in great haste," he wrote to his mother in 1831. "Betty had let the child fall on the hearth. I found her almost [hysterical] as she thought the skull was punctured." According to Conrad, Daniel had "sprung out of [his mother's] lap" during his bath. Betty, in a panic, had sent a slave to get him, the doctor, and a nearby aunt. Fortunately, little Daniel was more frightened than hurt, and was soon laughing "as merrily as ever." Mr. Conrad eventually went back to his office, but only after Mrs. Chilton, Betty's aunt, had arrived to restore order.[37]

Conrad became so competent at caring for his children (or so he believed) that his wife sometimes left him in charge. Domestic slaves assisted him, of course, as well as the family's domestic overseer, a poor white woman whom Conrad worried was not spending enough time with her own children. Fathers also sometimes asked other family men to get involved. William Ellzey, for example, wrote to his nephew in 1828, requesting him to check on his children while he was away. "I wish you would call and see the girls now and then and inquire how they are going on," he asked.[38]

It was the duty of mothers and fathers to attend to the many needs of their children and especially to safeguard their well-being. Not a few parents, however, part of families that were dysfunctional in some way or another, failed miserably to do so. Some note has been made of the problems poor people had providing material support and the consequent multifaceted instability of their families. There also were examples of child abuse, battery, and neglect. On September 1, 1757, for example, in one of the first domestic criminal cases that Loudoun justices heard, the county court accused Robert Colcough of raping his daughter Charity. The court terminated the case before the justices could make a decision however, because Colcough died. A few years later, the county court summoned James Coleman and his wife to appear in order to answer the charge of "incestuous copulation" with their children. These two cases of child sexual molestation and incest give only a slight hint of the range and frequency of child neglect and abuse that were endemic to almost any community. The presence of an abusive family member often meant layers of abuse and multiple offenders and victims. Nancy Turner, a local weaver, for example, was hardly the only Loudoun woman married to a man who habitually got drunk and battered and sexually assaulted her in the presence of their children. Even while she was "confined" after the birth of twins, he beat her and refused to provide food, adequate housing, clothing, or even firewood for their family. Turner also verbally and physically abused their children before he abandoned the family entirely. Hannah Barr's husband Hugh beat her so often and brutally that a kinsman reporting the abuse in 1810 called him the worst batterer in the county. Both Barr and Turner beat their wives while they were pregnant.[39]

Those families not struck by outright physical abuse still had children who had to cope with emotional battery and sometimes the many problems derived from alcohol or some other kind of drug addiction. Samuel Janney had occasion to write his wife, for example, that upon visiting his cousin Israel and his family he found Israel's wife to "be a precious woman," but Israel, "poor fellow" was "in the broad road to ruins, being addicted to intemperance." Edward Carter was another local alcoholic who would drink almost every day and then return home to "drive his wife and daughters" out of their home. His drinking and depression made him suicidal and an obvious threat to his children's psychological and physical well-being. He later abandoned his family. Unfortunately, there seemed to be little county officials could do to protect the Turner or Carter children from this kind of abuse.[40]

Other health, developmental, moral, and social issues drew more general concern and comment. All children, for example, had to learn basic physical, motor, and social skills—how to sit up, crawl, walk, talk, master their bowel and bladder functions, and how, what, and when to eat—usually before their second birthday.[41] Teaching them was as difficult for caretaker mothers, female kin, and slaves as it was for the children. Lessons were time consuming, required tedious repetition, and sometimes took much longer than either anticipated. Persistent example, deliberate personal instruction, careful reasoning, and a reward and punishment system were basic techniques. But realistically, it was difficult, if not impossible, for busy mothers to devote this kind of time and energy, especially if they had more than one child.

Even those who had slave help hardly could rely on black women and children to give devoted attention consistently. A local slave woman, Nancy Williams, provided some sense of the danger attendant to using busy domestics who had no strong emotional ties to the white babies in their care: ". . . his ole 'oman tol me to min' de baby, give it some toas' [toast]; wash dem dishes an' git dem 'tatoes peeled for cookin' dinner. . . ," she complained of her heavy work schedule. "Soon's I git to wuk dat baby start cryin.' I run to see what de matter." The baby, left to eat without supervision, had choked on the toast.[42]

One of a young mother's most important and difficult chores was to wean her child. They often had to be both unyielding and creative before reaching the desired results. John Jay Janney, for example, recalled how attached he was to his mother's breast and the length she went to wean him. "I was the first and only child and my mother allowed me to use her breast late," he recalled. "I remember one day worrying her for my dinner, at a time when she was trying to wean me. Finally, she called me to her, and upon baring her breast, I saw she had covered her nipples with soot from the back wall of the fire place."[43] Janney had to admit that this antic was immediately successful. Some determined mothers arranged to take an extended trip so that their children had no alternative but to wean themselves. Others gradually combined a diet of mother's milk with increasing amounts of table food. A few transferred their toddlers from the breast to the bottle, using rubber nipples that became available by the late 1830s.[44]

Weaning was one of a child's first significant lessons in self-control. By the early nineteenth century, parents were trying to be more patient and encouraging of a youngster's emotional expression, but still placed emphasis on obedience and discipline. Many had begun to rely on "the power of love" and "consistent example" in their instruction. Some also preferred to "reason" with children about disciplinary issues, rather than always respond with harsh words or corporal punishment. "My father . . . adopted a mode of parental government less rigorous than that of his father, and he was enabled, through the power of love and the influence of consistent example, to educate all his children . . . in the principles and practice of virtue," Samuel Janney, for example, explained.[45] Previous generations had believed that more forceful measures were necessary. Janney noted of his grandfather, for example, that "in the education of his large family of children, . . . he was careful to maintain obedience by strict discipline."

Despite some changes, however, guardians still demanded that their children obey them. Specialists agreed that children never were too young to learn how to mind their parents. Experts also counseled to guard against too much severity." "Fear is a useful and a necessary principle in family government," they concluded. "But it is ruinous to the disposition of a child, exclusively to control him by this motive."[46]

Antebellum parents may have moved away from habitual whippings, but the practice never became extinct. When Sarah Ann Abbott, for example, discovered that her little boy had thoughtlessly hurt his slave companion, she did not hesitate to beat him. "She got holt Marse Tom an' give him a good whuppin'," the ex-slave recalled. "How I knowed dat was cause I heard him cryin'. White folks never whupped white chillun in front of niggers, no matter what dey do." Just how public or private were family whippings is uncertain. Parents did allow teachers to publicly discipline their children. "One special qualification for a teacher was the ability to whip any boy in school, and a week rarely passed without the switch being used," one Loudoun resident remembered. "The boys were not punished after school and privately, but before the whole school, some of the boys laughing and some of the girls crying."[47]

John Janney's cousin and contemporary, Samuel, did not forget his early lessons about child discipline. He and his wife became the guardians of an orphan girl during the 1840s and eventually had much to say about their role in her character development. "On the first extension of parental care," he noted, "we found it difficult to bring her mind to right obedience, for her will was strong and the illness of her mother had prevented her from pursuit of that temperate and steady course which encurs [*sic*] from a child the highest amount of obedience and respect." Over the next several months, however, Samuel and Elizabeth Janney spent much of their time successfully trying to influence Julia's conduct and expression: "The calm and firm conduct of my wife, guided by warm attachment . . . and a sense of duty, and urged at times with needed severity, soon subdued . . . and Julia became one of [the] most submissive, lively and affectionate children."[48]

The Janneys were Quakers but their use of the rod and the Bible to discipline and teach their children the difference between right and wrong were common practices. Early on parents introduced their youngsters to religious concepts and instruction they believed would guide them to daily righteous behavior and prepare them for the "other world." "My care hath been for my sons, that they may be kept in the fear of God. I have been a good example to them; I have a care upon me that they may be kept humble while they are young; that they may bend their necks under the yoke of Christ" was Thomas Janney's feelings on the matter during the eighteenth century. Loudoun folk of later generations may not have viewed their children's spiritual conversion as a "bent neck under the yoke," but most wholeheartedly believed that religious influence in a child's life was especially important.[49]

"I have had my boys Christened," Sarah Harrison wrote proudly to her sister in 1834. "I begged Mr. Harrison to have them baptized in Sunday school that evening and after a good deal of *quiet* persuasion he consented." Mrs. Harrison's request was an impromptu one that came before they had made a final decision about the children's names or godparents, thus her husband's initial hesitation. He too cared deeply about the disposition of their sons' souls. The Church, kin, and "experts," however, expected mothers to provide their children with their early religious education—to teach them how to pray, tell them Bible stories, and send them to Sunday school (which was popular in antebellum Loudoun) and other church services to make certain that they knew the fundamentals of Christianity. "If you would be the happy mother of a happy child," one specialist typically lectured, "give your attention, and your efforts, and your prayers, to the great duty of training him up for God and heaven."[50]

Since Loudoun residents centered much of their social life and educational resources in local religious institutions, most children grew up with the church as part of their lives. From the colonial era on, parochial schools sponsored by almost every denomination were some of the most available educational institutions. Mothers also combined early literacy lessons with Bible study, encouraging their children to use their reading skills for religious instruction.[51]

Church was available to Loudoners of all status, but class, as ever, had the potential to have tremendous influence on a child's character development. Poor children more often than not were drawn into or at least aware of the underside of county life. Many were exposed to extralegal, survival strategies like prostitution and theft, or became caught up in an adult's violence or abusive behavior. Some, like James Mobberly, grew up with feelings of shame and personal degradation. The illegitimate son of a poor woman whose morality had become the subject of public ridicule, the boy felt alienated from local white society, alienated enough to accept a job from a local free black. By the time Mobberly had become a young man, he had gained a reputation for being vicious and sometimes violent. Although poor, Jacob Bagent had managed to secure a job and a home for his family in Loudoun. He undoubtedly hoped that he and his wife, through their own good example, would have a positive influence on their sons' character. It was only after Mrs. Bagent moved into her lover's home with their boys that he began to fear that their future would be permanently tainted by her promiscuity and the family's shame. Yet the poor families hardly had a monopoly on local social ills. Slavery, for example, undoubtedly had some negative impact on the moral integrity of middling- and upper-class youngsters.[52]

Southern slavery exposed slaveholders' children to much more than the "respectful," "kind" black faces they were so fond of recalling during the postbellum era.[53] Planter children, like their parents, could not escape the institution's violent, oppressive, or dehumanizing nature. Instead they learned how to perpetuate it. An ex-slave named Henrietta, for example, had quite different memories of her childhood than Henrietta Dangerfield, who remembered her Mammy's "tender" and "loving arms."[54]

The slave child was a domestic who worked cleaning up her owner's home. One day her mistress caught her stealing a piece of peppermint candy. In a fit of rage she not only beat the child brutally, but called on her own daughter to help her. In the end, the slaveholding woman and her child caused Henrietta to be physically deformed for life—they had placed Henrietta's head under the rocker of a chair and rocked forward on it in order to hold her in place while they whipped her. Because Henrietta was still young, her jaw bones were soft enough for the force of the rocker to meld them together. She never was able to open her mouth completely again or to eat solid food. Over the years her mistress had a local doctor visit the slave child regularly. When that failed to improve Henrietta's condition, she tried to hide her cruelty by giving the slave to a cousin. One can only imagine, however, how this experience might have affected the conscience and character of the planter youth whose mother forced her to participate in this kind of violence against another child.[55] Henrietta's whipping was a particularly savage one, yet it was not unusual for planter children to witness these brutal acts and sometimes be drawn in as collaborators.

It is little wonder then that some slaveholding parents did not allow their children to form "friendships" with slave youngsters. Those who allowed these kinds of relationships made certain that their children learned that their black playmates were their inferiors and their servants. "Me and young marser Tom was a caution," Fannie Berry recalled. "He was my real marser too. . . . Us used to play together all de time." Although Fannie and Tom played together almost every day that he was not in school, Fannie called him "marser"; he had the right to command her; and his mother made certain that Fannie never saw

Tom's authority as a white male challenged. By the time that Tom was old enough to play without adult supervision, he knew that he was Fannie's owner and would not let her breech that bond. Others came more slowly to that realization.

Parents who feared that their children would not learn to adhere to their society's racial hierarchy constructed forceful, violent lessons. Robert Ellett, for one, had some fond memories of the childhood he shared with his two masters. "I grew up with the young masters," he explained. "I played with them, ate with them and sometimes slept with them. We were pals." That all changed, however, when the boys grew older and their father wanted them to behave as masters and demanded that Ellett act the part of the slave. "One day the old master carried me in the barn and tied me up and whipped me 'cause I wouldn't call my young masters, 'masters,'" Robert confessed. "He beat me till the blood run down," but Robert refused to call his former playmates "master." Needless to say, the boys' childhood friendship ended that day. Ellett's two young masters seemed to have learned their lesson. As soon as their father stopped whipping Robert, he and the sons began to fight—again because he refused to address them "properly."[57] The problems that black and white youth struggled with as their society forced them to define themselves publically as either master or slave usually surfaced as they approached adolescence. It was only the beginning of finding one's "place" in the southern hierarchy.[58]

Most children growing up in the Old South were part of a way of life that was changing rapidly; so too were some of the basic assumptions of their parents' world. Traditional avenues to success like land and slaves were becoming more difficult to acquire. Education, on the other hand, was becoming more valued as a resource for future success and, thus, more expensive. William B. Lynch, editor of the Leesburg *Washingtonian*, was one of a few civic leaders who lent a welcome voice of optimism. His 1852 editorial, "Our Youthful Days," was a reminder to white, male youth of the promises of American society to those who applied themselves: "Boys, do not misspend your time," he lectured, "but improve every moment as it flies and you will reap your reward." A local father echoed Lynch's motto: "There is no ground for fear about your prospects—good habits—good education—and good principles are sure warrants to success."[59]

Access to individual success, however, was only one of many concerns of parents trying to prepare their teens for the challenges of adult life. Emigration to the West and the Lower South altered, destroyed, and created white families and communities. Tobacco's decline, the rise of cotton beyond all expectation, and the lingering importance of grain in counties like Loudoun affected the destiny of many local folk. The closing of the international slave trade, the explosive growth of the domestic slave market, free black colonization, abolition, home-grown southern rights, and the inroads of the Underground Railroad inevitably signaled the closing of more than an era, but a way of life that many would risk everything, even home and hearth, to forestall. There were of course some changes that even the most traditional southerner might accept. But those founding principles of antebellum southern culture—agrarianism, slavery, planter hegemony, honor, and family—were sacred. Parents felt that it was their duty to pass on this legacy and their reverence for it to their youngsters as they emerged into adolescence.

With an end to childhood,[60] therefore, antebellum southern youngsters, perhaps more so than those of earlier generations, faced growing responsibilities that not only meant marriage and family, but centered on loyalty to their society. Not only homes, but regional academies, boarding schools, churches, newspapers, and even recreational literature and activities supported the political, economic, and cultural designs that characterized so much about life in the pre-Civil War South. As this way of life sustained mounting attacks from "outsiders"—social and economic reformers, political analysts, and the nation's intelligentsia—the push was on among Southern citizens not only to embrace, but to establish and support, those institutions that, in turn, would help to sustain and enhance what they believed was their unique civilization.

When Mason Ellzey, Hunter McGuire, and Edward Luckett of Loudoun, who had been students at the Jefferson Medical School in Philadelphia, therefore, left to enroll in the Medical College of Virginia in 1860, it was no surprise that folks at home applauded them. This one act had tremendous symbolic potential, for it was an expression of their coming of age both as men and southerners. They had left Philadelphia in order to protest the "riotous" reaction of city abolitionists to John Brown's execution.[61] "Here and there, a man frankly approved our movement," Ellzey recalled some years later, "and declared we had done entirely right, and that in any event, our home institutions ought to be patronized by the young men of the South." Virginians did more than that. Governor Henry Wise greeted them in Richmond and the students and faculty at the Medical College gave them a "joyous" banquet at the elite Columbia Hotel.[62]

Virginia's educational facilities, like the fledgling Medical College, increasingly became bastions of southern rights ideology. While national church organizations split with southern branches over the issue of slavery, schools and teachers too faced increasing scrutiny. Concerned parents, heavily invested in the traditional order of southern society, tried to exclude the influence of "foreign" textbooks, teachers, and administrators from their schools and academies. Colleges also felt the purge, forcing faculty and pupils to act accordingly. Students at the University of Virginia, for example, formed a Southern Rights Association in 1850 that, among other things, urged their fellow students at other southern schools "'to prepare for the contest, for. . . our rights and liberties can only be preserved by firm, decisive, and united action.'"[63] Regional educational leaders and advocates openly defended slavery as a symbol of southern civilization.

Thomas R. Dew, one of the South's tireless defenders of slavery and a professor of political economy at the College of William and Mary, was one of the first antebellum Virginia scholars to take on a defense of the South's "peculiarities." As early as 1831, he asserted: "We take it for granted that the right of the owner to his slave is to be respected." Others followed his lead and increasingly so as time passed. In 1856, William A. Smith, then president of Virginia's Randolph-Macon College, published a long proslavery defense in which he urged abolitionist "'poison . . . be distilled from college textbooks.'" The following year, Albert T. Bledsoe of the University of Virginia published an "Essay on Liberty and Slavery," defending the morality of the southern institution.[64]

For scholars, professors, or students to assert otherwise at a time when proslavery and abolitionist rhetoric threatened to destroy national unity would have been inexcusable. Since there essentially was little or no tolerance of abolitionist thought among Loudoun county whites except among Quakers and some persons of German descent, parents were adamant that their children act accordingly. When Burr Harrison learned that his son Matthew had thought of speaking openly in support of Congress's right, through the Missouri Compromise, to regulate the territorial expansion of slavery, the elder responded swiftly. "Advocate no extreme proposition," he warned. "It is an exceedingly difficult matter to manage. I would advise [you to] let it alone. . . You may impair your usefulness by an indiscreet move."[65]

Harrison's lecture to Matthew touched on an important issue of family governance. One of the compelling conflicts parents faced was their children's growing need for autonomy. As teenaged boys began to leave their homes as students, apprentices, or paid laborers, their independence influenced their relationships with their adult kin. Girls too felt some need to claim, if not some independence, then certainly some individuality and choice in their lives. Subtle and sometimes confrontational struggles arising from these changes often were the source of family tension. These contests of will also became the proving ground for the parent-child bond as both were forced to come to terms with the shifting power dynamic within their domestic world.

Parental distress came not just from an adolescent's sometime effective challenge for control, but also from the parent's emotional need to remain a central force in a child's life. It especially was exacting for fathers who, despite their desire for control, realized that they had to prepare their boys to become society's decision makers. Likewise, adolescent boys and young men must have found it increasingly difficult to learn how to accept the great responsibilities of manhood when their parents continued to make all the important decisions for them.

Robert Conrad constantly felt "obliged" to write and advise his adolescent sons on virtually every aspect of their private and public lives. His vigilance, he explained, was because the boys were "left pretty much to their own responsibility" in their "public" schools, a strategy that academy and college officials hoped would build male independence, initiative, and leadership. Since southern parents did not have to concern themselves with preparing their girls to live as autonomous adults, they rarely considered allowing them the same kind of independence or choices that their sons could have had while away at work or school. A father's attention to his sons' education, apprenticeship, or career choices and sense of family and community obligation, therefore, was substantial.[66]

They also made the most important decisions in their daughters' lives, including the kind and amount, if any, of formal education they should receive; if and under what circumstances they could work outside their homes; who and when they should marry; and what disciplinary measures the fathers themselves or their wives should take if their girls disobeyed. Yet mothers were much more involved with their maturing daughters' day-to-day activities, serving as health expert, fashion consultant, advisor for their love lives, and a host of other roles. In so doing, female parents carefully structured their adolescent daughters' socialization and deliberately drew them into women's familial, social, and religious networks. Mothers, aunts, grandmothers, female cousins, teachers, and close family friends all helped to guide, nurture, and govern these young women's emerging femininity and womanhood.

Loudoun parents probably believed that young women were "innately" more governable than young men. Popular notions of female passivity, submissiveness, and passionlessness would suggest that society accepted that women succumbed to authority easier than men and, therefore, needed less constant governance. Still specialists pointed to the onset of puberty as a disquieting or rebellious period of a girl's life. The greatest parental concern, of course, was possible sexual misconduct.[67]

A young woman's indiscretion could have a profound effect on her family, threatening their honor and resources, to say nothing of ruining her chances for a "useful" life as someone's respectable wife. Premarital sexual activity, however, was not unusual. Court and church records document that illegitimate births were frequent enough to suggest that at least a significant minority indulged in premarital sex. The limited information found among the records of the local Quaker Goose Creek Meeting, for example, indicates that at least nine of their female Friends who married during the antebellum era were pregnant when they did so, and there were many other citations for "fornication" in these and other local church records, enough certainly to dispel the notion that sexual misconduct was class-bound.[68]

A daughter's sexual rebellion was a parent's greatest fear, yet adolescent girls could find as many ways to resist parental authority as their brothers. Personal style, clothing, social and romantic relationships, and the ways in which they spent their money were just a few of the other avenues to points of contention. Isaac Nichols, for one, had quite a time trying to persuade his daughter to live by the social mores of Quakers. According to a local Quaker historian Mary loved all kinds of music, singing, dancing, laughter, and beautiful clothing. Her father disapproved of it all. He even forbade her growing flowers. After spending several years trying to force Mary to conform, Nichols finally disinherited her. Fortunately, a local woman minister intervened. Although they eventually developed a tenuous peace between themselves, Mr. Nichols undoubtedly was happy when Mary married a well-to-do local man and moved out of his home.[69]

Isaac Nichols hardly was the last Loudoun parent to have trouble controlling a daughter. Teenager Betty Harrison hoped that her father's persistent absence would give her an opportunity to exert some control over her own life. Her father reacted predictably when he found out that she had broken two cardinal rules of young female social life—she had gone out without permission and without an escort. "I am very sorry to hear of her doing anything of this kind without consulting her sister and I do not wish her sister to indulge her with much insisting at any rate," he snapped. It would be best, he advised, that she not go out without being accompanied by one of her older siblings and only then to visit one of her aunts.[70]

While daughters, like sons, routinely challenged parental governance, there were some predictable differences linked to the nature of their gendered culture. Girls rarely had a chance to rebel publicly or violently. Mostly confined as they were to their homes, schools, and churches, early nineteenth-century girls had less opportunity to display public misconduct than young men who, from the time that they were ten or eleven, could have some kind of public presence. Likewise, because they were not part of the militant and militarized subculture of southern males that allowed them to carry and use firearms, girls had much less opportunity to express their rebelliousness violently. And since there were so few opportunities for females to earn a living, comparatively few had the chance to run away or leave their homes, even temporarily, without their parents' permission. Realizing the vulnerable position of women in their society also made it easier for teenaged girls to resist the authority of women.

It was much easier for Kate Conrad, for example, to mount a rebellion against her female school mistress than it was for her to stand her ground with a patriarchal figure. Several days after her arrival at boarding school in 1851, it became clear that Kate was not getting along with the head mistress, and the two openly disagreed over what courses she should take. But there was more to Kate's complaints. Usually bound to the female ideal of submission, her first real stay away from her parents proved liberating. Academy instructors and proprietors, however, expected otherwise. Since Kate's parents willingly shared their authority with the school's proprietress, Kate's rebellion against her was tantamount to her rebelling against her mother or, worse still, her father. When Mr. Conrad learned of her behavior, he demanded her immediate compliance. You should, he instructed, "submit" yourself "entirely."[71]

Clearly, few children could please their parents or guardians all the time, even when they earnestly tried to "submit" to their authority. Late eighteenth-century parents like Isaac Nichols may have found it nearly impossible to accept a child's inability to obey parental orders, oftentimes concluding that a disobedient child was innately wicked or inappropriately strong-willed. By the mid-nineteenth century, however, some were beginning to understand that children had differing personality types. Juvenile individuality was becoming more recognizable even if parents were uncertain how it should affect their notions of adolescent maturation and success or socialization. Robert Conrad, for one, deduced that while some of his children might perform well in a very disciplined environment, others could not, because of what he termed their distinct "characters." He asserted this point repeatedly when faced with his son Holmes's failure at the Virginia Military Institute.[72]

As all institutions based on military discipline, administrators at VMI expected students to obey orders without question, to put aside their pride for the good of the group, and to let one's "superiors" define honor. Some Loudoun youth like Mason Ellzey flourished under this system. Others, like William Harrison, managed to squeak through despite some brushes with the school's superintendent. More than a few failed miserably. Ellzey, Harrison, and Holmes Conrad were all cousins attending VMI during the 1850s. Mason and William both graduated, but young Conrad was expelled. His father recollected that Holmes began to encounter difficulty soon after becoming a cadet in 1854.[73]

"It seems next to impossible for him to observe all the minutiae of their regulations," Robert reported to his wife in June 1855. General Smith, the institute's superintendent, had informed him that Holmes seemed incapable of maintaining the discipline required of cadets. Sometimes he would be "very careful," Smith explained, but then he would seem "to lose all thought about the matter, and [would get] a whole volley of demerits, all at once." Conrad, of course, was very upset when he learned of Holmes's problems. His elder sons had both finished college successfully, and initially Holmes had been determined to do likewise. Instead of confronting his son accusatorily, however, he reasoned that Holmes had a distinct personality that caused him to inevitably clash with the VMI regimen. "Their system is a 'bed of Procuster' and makes no provision for such a mercurial character as Holmes," the father concluded. "It certainly is desirable for Holmes to remain, but as the Colonel expressly acquits him of any serious fault, and says they [the demerits] all arise from thoughtlessness—why, I should not regard his withdrawal, for such reasons, as any serious calamity."[74]

Like a growing number of parents at the end of the antebellum era, Mr. Conrad clearly was disposed to believe that his son's inability to achieve in a chosen field was not because he was disobedient or dishonorable. Holmes, he offered defensively, was a victim of his own personality quirks and an institution whose administration refused to acknowledge their students' individuality.

Not every parent, however, was as understanding.[75] William Harrison, for one, had much greater difficulty persuading his father that his problems at VMI were not due to his own inappropriate behavior. This is not surprising given that Burr Harrison and Robert Conrad differed significantly in the way that they approached childrearing—Harrison, who was older and had more ties to Loudoun's agrarian traditions, generally was more stern.

Conrad believed his children needed continuous parental guidance and he acted forcefully when necessary. But he also seemed to place more trust in their good intentions and eventual success than his brother-in-law. Robert derived immense pleasure from their presence, routinely viewing their individual accomplishments as great triumphs and their failures as problematic, but not earth-shattering disasters. Burr Harrison, on the other hand, was more aloof and less openly affectionate. Perhaps the death of his wife and two of his children had caused him to be more cautious. He preferred an orderly, warm, peaceful home life, perhaps at the emotional expense of other family members.[76]

Despite their different parenting styles, Burr Harrison and Robert Conrad probably both would have characterized all of their boys as generally obedient and dutiful. Yet adolescent boys and young men often resented lingering parental control. Popular models of manhood, after all, called for a show of aggressive independence. Likewise, most Loudoun whites did not rear their sons to be passive men. They taught them to respect their patriarchal elders, but they also taught them that a "man" acted reasonably when confronted with authority, he did not necessarily bow to it. Since a father's ability to control members of his household, including his sons, also was a measure of his own masculine power, however, there was much room for confrontation. Few fathers were willing to yield much. Burr Powell, for example, responded typically in 1830 when a son complained about the college he had chosen for him. "I have now written him . . . [leaving] it to his own choce [*sic*] to persue [*sic*] the plan I had proposed or return directly home at the close of the first session."[77] George Carter was less certain how to handle his five nephews a generation earlier. His father had raised him to be loyal, respectful, obedient, and devoted, traits he seemed unable to instill in his widowed sister's sons.[78]

Born to the elite world of the Carter family, Tom, George, Robert, John, and Henry Maund had high expectations. After their grandfather moved permanently to Baltimore, their mother had taken over the family's luxurious "Nomini" mansion. But this wonderful bequest was not a sure sign of things to come. The boys' father, the illustrious legislator John James Maund, died without leaving them adequate funds to maintain their privileged lifestyle. Their mother, Harriot, called on her brother George to provide her boys with an education and some behavioral guidance as they entered adolescence; to be, in essence, a surrogate father. From the beginning, however, problems with their governance abounded. Four circumstances were early deterrents: George

Carter was young and inexperienced; the boys lived with their mother some distance away from him; Carter had little time, and perhaps little inclination, to be a father figure; and he was stingy with his time and his fortune.

Initially, Carter decided to take a somewhat stern, no-nonsense approach to the youngsters' upbringing. He wanted to make certain that they grew up to be independent, useful young men, but he feared that their mother was spoiling them. One of his first decisions, therefore, was to spend little money on their behalf. The Maund boys were not wealthy in their own right, and he did not intend to indulge them. They would have to learn how to make their own way in the world. Instead of providing them with tutors and a college education, George placed them in apprenticeships in Philadelphia after a few years of formal schooling.[79]

Apprenticeship was an uncertain investment at best. Poor treatment and even poorer training sometimes rendered the process completely useless, if not outright harmful. In Carter's case, his nephews barely gave it a chance. Of the five, three ran away from their masters. Their uncle took it as a breach of family honor and absolute rebellion against his authority.[80]

None of George Carter's nephews bore up well under their apprenticeship contracts. More important, they openly resisted the more fundamental contract between themselves and their uncle, a contract that many parents, sometimes openly, sometimes only subconsciously, established with their children. George Carter was an excellent businessman who relied on contracts and honor and, those failing, the courts to protect his investments. His business style, in fact, influenced his parental governance style. Carter proposed, for example, to provide more than minimal financial support for his nephews and at least the opportunity for them to gain lucrative skills. He hoped that they would reward him with cooperation, respect, and perhaps affection. If these initial investments proved to be worthwhile, he had some unspecified plans to sponsor further formal education or perhaps provide them with financial backing for some profession or other. When his nephews refused to cooperate or demonstrate the kind of initiative and honor that would have convinced him that his investment was worthwhile, he refused to do more. While parenting styles changed over the years, as did the ways in which parents perceived their children's "nature," the basic contractual agreement remained fundamental to the parent-child relationship and notions of governance.[81]

One tactic which parents relied on over the years to gain control of their teens and budding adults was religious instruction. They began teaching them the tenements of Christianity when they were small children, but intensified their efforts as they reached adolescence. Even local academies and popular colleges included classes in Christian thought and Bible study. Headmaster Enos Newton and the owners of the Middleburg Academy, for example, expanded the school's course listings in the 1820s to include, among other things, "Recitations in the Scriptures, Catechism, and evidences of Christianity." Parents expected their sons and daughters to take religious study as seriously as their other academic work. Burr Harrison, for example, rebuffed his son William when one of the teen's teachers accused him of not believing in the Bible.[82]

Mothers had a softer approach. Betty Conrad, for one, was happy that her daughter Kate had joined a local Presbyterian Church, but she still could not rest until all of her children were converted. She repeatedly wrote to her son Holmes, trying to persuade him to become a church member. "What joy it would give me to know that with the beginning of a new year of yr life—you began to live a Christian life," she included in a birthday note to him. "To live and serve the great and glorious God—is a noble, an exalted privilege." It had been of some comfort to Mrs. Conrad that another son, Robert Jr., had declared his faith before his untimely death. Knowing how much Holmes loved his brother, she played on his emotions: [M]y beloved son—let it not be an eternal separation—Can you bear the thought of never seeing him again."[83]

Girls and young women seemed most susceptible to the call to church membership and service. Many parents probably would argue that it was easier to persuade their daughters to develop an interest in and devotion to religion because of a woman's distinctively pious nature. Their female children might suggest otherwise. The church, as the center of a rural woman's extrafamilial social, educational, and political life, was her best hope for having some impact on community values and issues. It was one of the few places where women could "act," as teachers (in Sunday schools), organizers of local charity efforts (through sewing, collecting, and donating for the poor), and leaders (against such social ills as intemperance). The church also was a place where females had some say as to their community's social life—it was the women who planned and prepared church picnics, fairs, and dances. Among local Friends, Quaker meetings traditionally had been a haven for strong-minded women with leadership qualities. Two of the first Quaker ministers in eighteenth-century Loudoun, for example, had been female; and women elders and lecturers were not unusual during the nineteenth century. Moreover, the equitable educational opportunities that Quaker schools afforded Loudoun girls prepared and encouraged their young women, more than those of any other denomination, for paid labor and fulfilled lives outside their homes.[84]

Parents believed that creating early habits of Christian fellowship and righteousness would help them to produce the kind of obedient, honorable, loving children they all wanted. "We brought little Eliza with us to see her Aunt Mary," Hortensia Hay began her description of a cousin. "She is indeed a lovely child not only in appearance but in mind . . . the children are all I think uncommonly fine ones being affectionate and guileless." Her "deportment was affectionate and attentive to all with whom she associated," Samuel Janney wrote in loving memory of his young ward Rebecca Headley. "Selfishness was a failing she scarcely knew the existence of. . . . By this kind and judicious conduct, my intercourse with our dear child was rendered one of affection and gentleness scarcely interrupted by a single severe expression."[85]

"Affectionate," "guileless," and "attentive" were traits which post-Revolutionary southern parents adored in their children. These characteristics, along with a child's strong sense of love and duty and overall family loyalty, were all important. Yet it often was difficult to have close family ties when large families typically meant a tremendous age span among siblings. It was not unusual for older children to have married or left their parental home before younger siblings were even born or old enough to remember them. Levi White, for example, wrote somewhat typically to one of his relations in August 1830 that both his daughter and his wife had given birth in the last several months. Likewise, the emigration of young men, a continual pull on family cohesiveness, made it even more difficult for kin to remain emotionally intimate.[86]

Parents faced with this dilemma agreed that it was necessary for the older children to make a concerted effort to stay in contact with younger siblings. George Harrison, for instance, made certain that he wrote his family regularly and visited occasionally so that he could maintain strong ties. His sister was one of his favorites. "We count on having a good deal of your company next winter & it is my intention, unless I am tempted to linger too long in the northern city, to spend a week in Frederick towards the end of September so that you . . . may exchange a good many loving looks yet before I encounter the perils of the ocean," the navy man wrote to her in 1820. A generation later, Daniel Conrad's father asked him to write detailed letters to his young brothers while away on a naval tour: "The little boys have been entirely unable to realize how long it will be before they see you again, and are asking about you everyday. Unless you can keep up their impressions of you by your letters (which we will always read to them) three years of time . . . will erase from their minds almost all recollection of you."[87]

Burr Harrison was just as adamant about keeping his children involved and interested in each other's lives. After his wife died in 1845, he especially feared that his family's closeness might suffer. When his eldest daughter Ann Maria went off to boarding school in 1846, he demanded that she write regularly to her little brother Willy. Ann had served as something of a surrogate mother to little Willy after Mrs. Harrison's death. When Willy wrote to Ann, Mr. Harrison attached a note commanding his daughter to respond appropriately. "I dare say more elegant specimens of epistolary efforts have been seen but I venture to say that few have been the offspring of more genuine affection and good feeling. You must therefore avail yourself of the earliest leisure moment to acknowledge the receipt of it and to reply directly addressed to him."[88] Parents also typically asked teachers to insist that their students write home, at least occasionally.

Beyond the confines of the family and the church, southerners regarded educational institutions as the most important force that could shape their children's culture, character, ideals, and, most important, their future utility. The middle classes always viewed education practically, as a means for their sons to gain professional opportunities and to make their daughters more attractive to suitors. The landed gentry viewed education pragmatically as well, but also appreciated its "enlightenment" value.

During the late eighteenth century, the well-to-do usually hired professors to teach writing, reading, mathematics, history, science, and sometimes elementary Latin and French. Boarding academies or colleges then followed. Leven Powell, like his father, provided private tutors for his sons until they were teens and then sent them to the College of William and Mary. Ann Mason sponsored her son Thomson's legal education in England as did Thomas Lee for his two sons. All these young men eventually returned to Loudoun to become planters and planter/professionals. By the middle of the antebellum era, however, some things were beginning to change.[89]

Expensive land and labor prices meant that fewer men would become planters, or at least Virginia planters. Some fathers even began using funds that, in the past, traditionally would have been spent on land instead on expensive college and professional school tuition and to set their sons up in businesses. Robert Conrad's father, for example, had provided him with private tutors, study at West Point and the College of William and Mary, along with an inheritance of land and slaves. He had to explain to his sons, however, that he was very willing to provide them with the best possible education, but would have little money left for their benefit after so doing. He wanted his sons to become doctors, lawyers, and engineers, not especially planters, not even part-time planters. It was not that Conrad or his peers believed that the plantation system would cease to exist—indeed, those who could afford to do so continued to bequeath or purchase land and slaves for their adult sons. But upon considering the rising cost of education not only for their sons, but for their daughters too, and faced with the reality of Loudoun's land shortage, they clearly were taking precautions.[90]

By the 1830s there were some "infant" schools for small children, but the real increase in educational institutions were those for older youth. In Virginia alone, there were twelve colleges, many with fine intellectual reputations by 1850. There also were a tremendous growth in the number of academies. Still, the amount and quality of the education that a Loudoun boy or girl received could vary substantially.[91]

Most early nineteenth-century academies and seminaries had curriculums that stressed the classics, modern languages, mathematics, science, history, and geography. As time passed, many added new courses to both accommodate the growing number of female students and to take advantage of the changes in the philosophy of education. With a growing interest in education for middling folk, the utilitarian value of scholarship took hold. New courses in bookkeeping, geography, agricultural, and military science changed drastically some curriculums and were the founding principles of other academies. In December 1855, Benjamin Benton and James Gulick, for example, petitioned the state legislature for incorporation of the Loudoun Agricultural Institute, the first school established for vocational training in the county. Loudoun Agricultural included not only a school building but also an experimental farm for practical experience. Girls also gradually acquired the opportunity to study more math, science, and history.[92]

Loudoun had several academies. The Waterford School, founded in 1761, offered both elementary and advanced courses and eventually admitted females. Local leaders created the Leesburg Academy in 1799. It remained all-male, as did Middleburg, founded in 1803.[93] These three schools continued to operate throughout the era, but there were others of shorter duration and lesser prestige, such as the Flint Hill Academy in Hughesville, coeducational Hillsborough, and the Reverend Ben Bridges's school in Sterling.[94]

Hillsborough was probably typical. Students could either board or not. Most completed the "Elementary branches," but boys also could take Latin and Greek, while girls could study the piano or voice. Middleborough offered a more rigorous and diverse curriculum. Early owners boasted that their academy really was three schools in one—English, mathematical, and grammar—each more academically advanced than the other. When administrators admitted females in the early 1820s, they placed painting, drawing, music, and poetry on their list of course selections. As the years passed, courses in chemistry, logic and ethics, bookkeeping, rhetoric, elocution, natural philosophy, and religious history were added. The educational focus at Middleburg Academy shifted again in 1826, when school owners hoped to benefit from the growing attraction to military academies by including male courses in fencing, drills, and rules of military conduct.[95]

Prominent folk usually sent their sons to Virginia colleges. The University of Virginia eventually became a favorite because of its geographic proximity. VMI, the first state-supported military college in the country, was extremely popular. Founded at Lexington in 1839, the institute was a welcome alternative since it was virtually impossible to get into West Point. Quaker Samuel Janney enrolled his son John at a teachers' seminary in Philadelphia. Young German-descended men who wanted to become ministers could attend the Reformed Theological Seminary in Carlisle, Pennsylvania, or the Lutheran Theological Seminary in Gettysburg. After 1840, local folk also could send their sons to the Lutheran Collegiate Institute in Roanoke. The University of Virginia held the distinction of being the first college to offer German as a regular course. Those who went on to study law usually clerked in the office of a local attorney, learning the profession first-hand. Later generations enrolled in law courses offered at universities. As time passed, more and more also demanded that their doctors receive formal training, prompting attendance at the Jefferson Medical School in Philadelphia and the Medical College of Virginia, established in 1837.[96]

Although coeducational institutions became more popular over time, many females continued to attend single-sex schools. Of the county's 21 advanced educational institutions in 1835, nine were reserved exclusively for males, five for females, and seven were coeducational.[97] Female academies like Margaret Mercer's prestigious "Belmont" and Samuel Janney's popular "Springdale" were most available during the second half of the era, and then only to relatively few students. The small numbers of female academies sometimes detracted from their overall quality.[98] But "quality" meant more than just curriculum or teaching staff. It also meant the social class and moral reputation of school's proprietors and the students. Parents wanted to be assured that their daughters' character and reputation would not be jeopardized under any circumstances. That probably is why Elise Carter's Middleburg School, founded in 1828, never was popular. Miss Carter unfortunately located her school "opposite Mr. John Boyd's tavern," not a favored location for young ladies.[99]

"We have at last decided upon Kate's school," Robert Conrad told one of his sons in 1851. "The Misses Milligan's in Fauquier. . . . It is highly spoken of as a school of the highest grade." Conrad was pleased that his daughter's best friends and second cousins also were going to enroll. Mrs. Conrad also applauded the choice. But she and her husband had not always agreed on what was the proper educational environment for young Kate. Mrs. Conrad's tastes were more extravagant than her husband's: she proposed that they send Kate to school in Richmond, the state's social hub. Mr. Conrad protested, preferring that his eldest daughter remain closer to home and in more socially familiar surroundings. When they finally settled on the Milligan school, it was a relief to everyone. "I never knew a school I approve of as entirely as Miss Milligan's," Mrs. Conrad wrote to her niece. "They are Christian ladies—appear to have the improvement of their pupils constantly in view. They spare no expense to get the best teacher—. . .—the girls are treated in the kindest manner [and] there is nothing *sectarian* either about the school."[100]

The issue of religion in the school curriculum and activities was an important consideration. One of Kate Conrad's friends, Mary Faulkner had to wait several months before her parents came to some agreement about her future education. In the end, Mr. Faulkner decided to bear tremendous financial expense and place all of his daughters in a convent. William Gray enrolled his daughter Frances in Margaret Mercer's "Belmont" in 1836. The Harrisons also sent one of their daughters there in the 1840s; so too did the Masons. Mercer was known for her religious fervor and fascination with contemporary moral issues, publishing in 1841 her *Popular Lectures on Ethics, or Moral Obligations for the Use of Schools.*[101] While some approved of her approach, others were wary of the deep psychological hold she seemed to have on many of her students. Mary Custis, for one, found reason to comment: "There has appeared to be such a religious influence there that cousin Mary was quite willing to indulge the *Ardent mistress.*"[102]

Parents who did send their girls to "Belmont" paid handsomely for the privilege. "To recommend her present residence is unnecessary," a typical advertisement read in a local paper. "The beautiful mansion, so long the hospitable abode of one of our most distinguished families is well known throughout the country. Its reputation for health and its proximity to the Capitol, are its greatest advantages." Mercer charged $250 per year, a fee which included board, bedding, washing, and instruction in "all the English branches," Latin, Greek, ethics, and mathematics. French, drawing, music, chemistry, and philosophy were extra.[103]

The mere fact that some fathers were willing to pay handsomely for their girls' education suggested more than the status they derived from having an educated daughter. It also implied their genuine interest in their girls' intellectual development. Writing to his daughter Sarah in 1813, for example, Burr Powell warned that he would allow her to continue her schooling only if she applied herself rigorously. "I am always disposed to gratify my children in every reasonable request they make of me. I am pleased indeed, when I discover a disposition in any of them, to improve in mental or personal gratification," he conceded. "But you must make up your mind before you enter another quarter that you are to loose no part of it. Nothing but sickness will be admitted by me as an excuse for not attending every day that is paid for." Another father was just as clear a generation later: "To this end, you must first make yourself contented and cheerful, and upon the best terms with your teachers, tak[ing] your assignments up with courage, industry and perseverance."[104]

Many young women did take their studies very seriously. Samuel Janney's ward, Julia Headley, for example, so dedicated herself to her education that she refused to leave her school when she was ill, insisting that she was "improving fast" and "ought to be at school." Unlike most young women of the time, even those who were Quaker like her, Julia had distinct career plans—she wanted to become a naturalist. Sophie Davisson also wanted a career. Raised in a doctor's family where female intellectual development was encouraged, Sophie first acted as teacher for her younger siblings and then left her Hillsborough home in 1857 to accept a teaching position in another county. Despite Rebecca and Sophie's career interests, however, few young Loudoun women expected that their education would lead to a lucrative career outside of marriage. Most families drew a clear line between female education and a career. Writing to her older sister in 1853, for example, Etta Davisson asked her to return home before she graduated. "I wish they would not put such notions in your head," she lamented. Sophie's life as a teacher in Buckingham County, "so far from home," proved to be sad and lonely, something that came as no surprise to her family.[105]

Still it was a decided privilege for girls to receive any kind of formal education, much less that of a "finishing" school. Female literacy in the county grew slowly compared with that of males, an accurate reflection of available female learning facilities and parental attitudes. While parents in middling and even poorer families struggled to provide their sons with at least a rudimentary formal education, female instruction outside of Quaker communities remained largely an elite experience guided by male parents.

Fathers concerned themselves not only with the entrance of their sons into college, but also with their courses of study. Robert Carter advised his son George at the end of the eighteenth century to expand his intellect by studying Hume, Milton, Dryden, and Pope and reading English journals like the *Spectator, Guardian* and *Tattler* "as the Models of Language." Samuel Janney's uncle, much more so than his father, directed his education during the early 1800s. Janney studied a variety of subjects, but in particular mathematics, French, Latin, surveying, natural philosophy, chemistry, and literature. Robert Conrad typified concerned fathers at the end of the antebellum period who believed that their sons should have a "rigorous" and "useful" intellectual experience. He emphasized the importance of mathematics, sciences, and the classics regardless of career choice.[106]

Fathers also pressured their sons to complete their degrees at the top of their class, a testament not only to their intellect but to other important "male" success traits such as perseverance, discipline, and confidence. "I hope you are making every exertion to keep your standing in your class," John Scott Peyton wrote in 1829 to his brother Richard, a cadet at West Point. "Your friends are just proud of the rank you have attained as a scholar and they would be mortified if you should lose it." Some felt pushed even to the point of physical exhaustion. "Alf[red] Powell is looking badly," a concerned cousin wrote to his family, "he studies too hard and drinks too much—coffee—. . . . He studies sometimes all night."[107]

Others were unable to perform under the stress of competing for top recognition. "The fellows all said I was as pale as I could be and when I commenced to read it was as much as I could do to talk to save my life," William Harrison explained of his response to a French exam.[108] Francis Powell was so worried that he was not going to succeed in medical school that he feared a complete loss of memory at the time of his exams. "I am so eager to grasp every idea of the professors and so fearful lest a word should be lost that might be useful that I sometimes imagine my memory will retain nothing," he wrote his sister. "[T]he time is fast approaching when my fate must be known, when the ordeal must be past, that is to constitute me a respectable member of a learned profession, or stamp me with eternal disgrace. God deliver me from . . . a degradation the idea of which to me is worse than death."[109]

Fathers also counseled their sons about important adult responsibilities and forming habits of dependability, self-sufficiency, and self-discipline that would hold them in good stead not only in their academic work but throughout their adult life. Important lessons included how to make the appropriate choices and to follow through with them. When Powell Conrad asked his parents for permission to leave the university to pay a social call to an uncle for several days, both answered a resounding "No." "What would be said of me if I should, on such a whim, leave one of my courts, or neglect other professional business? What would you have thought of one of your engineer corps leaving the work upon such an errand?" his father replied, emphasizing the importance of a commitment. The following week, he congratulated Powell on his "cheerful" acquiescence to their wishes. Yet it was not the last time that Mr. Conrad found occasion to lecture his son on striking an acceptable balance between labor and leisure. Every lesson about Powell's college life, it seems, became a metaphor for his future life in the adult world. "We are constantly called upon to resist our impulses however natural and proper in themselves," he found occasion to lecture two years later, "because higher duties call up in a different direction:—to sacrifice the agreeable to the useful."[110]

One of life's most important lessons, fathers reiterated, was the necessity of learning how to keep a budget. "Accounts, regularly kept, of all your receipts and expense, will be a gratification to you, prevent any embarrassments in money matters and fix your habits of order" was typical advice. "Order, method and punctuality whether applied to one's finances, studies, recreation or physical needs is necessary for any type of accomplishments or success." George Carter could not agree more. Faced with his nephews' mounting financial demands, he determined to curb their appetite for frivolous spending. Carter explained in a denigrating letter to one of them written in 1817, for example, that he was enclosing fifty dollars that he could spend as he pleased, but he wanted him to know that it was the "last cent" he could expect to receive from him for some time. It was not just that the young man asked so frequently for money. It also was the way that he asked. "The alternate flattery and importuning with which your letters are worded render them disgusting and tiresome beyond description." "Your maxim I believe is not to want a thing if it can be gotten by hard and incipant [sic] begging for, and indeed you do not care how often."[111]

Fathers routinely emphasized George Carter's credo that young people should spend as little as possible. "You ask me how much pocket money I chuse [sic] you shall spend," Burr Powell wrote to one of his daughters studying in Alexandria in 1825. "I answer as little as you can possibly do with. . . ." He also demanded that she "keep a regular account of what" she got and how she "la[id] it out," so that she could be "methodical" and see that she "la[id] it out judiciously." Twenty-five years later, this daughter and her husband were addressing the same issue with their son. "We think you took money enough with you to bear all reasonable expenses and therefore decline to send any more," he wrote. "On your own account too, it is much better that you should learn the lesson that to spend money, to indulge your wants, it is necessary first to earn it." She added in like fashion: "You do not need any more clothes—Yr aunt will have anything washed for you."[112]

While southern parents wanted both their sons and daughters to grow up to be fiscally responsible, they placed much more emphasis on preparing their male children to be so. When parents sent their children away to school, for example, they demanded that both keep a strict account of their expenses and how they resolved them. Fathers typically allowed their sons to pay all of their educational expenses including tuition and board fees, clothing, and other necessary items with money that they gave or sent to them. They gave them a real opportunity to learn how to manage their income.[113]

They took a much more confining approach, however, to their daughters' practical fiscal education. Parents usually gave their female teens only a small monthly allowance for "pocket money," paying all major expenses themselves or directing other male kin to do so. "Pay Ann Maria five dollars if she wants it or any little sum occasionally," Burr Harrison wrote to his son. He did "not want her to be without funds." Although only two years older than his sister, Matthew was in charge of all his father's household accounts while Mr. Harrison was away on business. Even those parents who gave their daughters small allowances also gave them detailed directions as to how to spend it. "I will inclose [sic] you a bank note in this," Robert Conrad wrote to his daughter Kate in 1852. "Pay attention to your Expenses, and confine them to necessaries[.] [E]specially do not buy cakes, candies, or eatables of any kind—They will only spoil your teeth and yr health."[114] Kate's grandmother had lectured her daughter similarly when she was an adolescent. When she was eighteen years old, Elizabeth Powell went to spend a summer with her aunt and uncle. Her parents instructed her that, upon arrival, she was to give all of her money to her relatives so that they might spend it for her. They did not even allow the eighteen-year-old to purchase her own clothing.[115]

Parents even controlled their daughters' earnings. If fathers did not confiscate it as their own, they often arbitrarily placed it aside to use as part of their daughters' dowries. "Father has traded your mare and colt off to cousin Thomas Ellezey and he has killed your cow and she was a very nice beef," William Harrison wrote to his sister Ann Maria. "Father says he owes you about 20 dollars for your cow and 40 for the mare and colt. So that your estate consists now of a small heifer and your calf with your 60 dollars to begin the world with."[116]

Boys grew up to become breadwinners and needed both to learn to be fiscally responsible as well as to choose a lucrative vocation or profession. The most "desirable" male occupations other than that of planter were those which required both academic and professional training. Lawyer, doctor, and engineer were premier antebellum choices for young men who might still have had the option of retiring to the life of the local landed gentry as they grew older. Others joined the military; some became businessmen, bankers, ministers, or teachers. Most well-to-do parents, however, frowned on such "middling" positions because they rarely guaranteed one's financial security. "As to . . . teaching don't think of that," Burr Harrison wrote to his son Matthew. "You have [a] mind for law if you exert it."[117]

The majority became farmers or agriculturists of one sort or another. Most began by helping their fathers to farm, learning both the rudiments and the administrative aspects. As they grew older, they gained more responsibility, perhaps even managing some of their father's fields or a particular crop or herd themselves—land and livestock that one day probably would be theirs. When Jonathan Carter wrote his will in 1849, for example, he bequeathed to his son Benjamin Franklin Carter "two hundred acres of land being a part of a larger tract conveyed by me and my wife to him by deed," a slave male, some oxen, and furniture, "all of which property has been delivered into the possession [*sic*] of my said son. . . ."[118] Many who were not as fortunate as Ben eventually had to rent land. Others acquired property through marriage, while a few were able to buy their own.

Farming, of course, was not just an occupation; it was a way of life for most southerners. But not everyone was cut out for farm life. John Janney, for one, complained bitterly of his parents' demand that he become a farmer. "My mother insisted," he remembered, "but I told her that I never would be, not that I did not like the work, but I wanted to study, and there was then no inducement for a farmer to study. As it was then conducted, it was plow, plant and reap, just as their fathers had done." Janney successfully resisted his mother's plans, opting instead to take a $1500 inheritance and move to Ohio. Looking back on the incident, he had less than kind words for the popular system of family governance that allowed parents to choose their children's occupations: "They too often fail to consult the wishes of their children. It frequently happens that the wish of the boy or girl is in the right direction, needing only proper assistance and guidance."[119] Unfortunately, most Loudoun youth did not have Janney's financial or educational opportunities.

Educational institutions for the poor were practically nonexistent.[120] Some attended parochial schools, particularly local Quakers. Like most Quaker children, John Janney began when he was six years old and continued until his mid-teens. According to him, their education was "plain" and practical, but when completed, it provided a solid background for scholars to enter a post-secondary school.[121]

Other middling-class youth usually only had one or two years of formal schooling, three or four if they were lucky. Receipts from George Shover's educational expenses for the 1820s, for example, indicate that his son attended a local day school about 49 days a year at a cost of about $2.20. John Sanbower knew that he was fortunate to be able to attend school before committing himself to an apprenticeship in Ohio. Writing to his cousins, he eagerly explained: "I am going to school at present in Lovettsville and am very much pleased with it." John's courses included grammar, composition, and geography. He expected that he would continue his education until "after harvest" and then would migrate west. For him, as for so many of Loudoun's young men, obtaining the rudiments of a formal education, gaining lucrative skills, and eventually migrating west or south seemed the best prescription for future "usefulness."[122]

Shover and Sanbower were members of Loudoun's German ethnic community. Although they studied in English, a German-language primary education was available through the 1830s. Lutheran parochial schools, some which were taught in German, operated only a few months per year, but they insured the community high literacy rates. Likewise, Shenandoah Valley printers like Matthias Bartgis, Johannes Weiss, Jacob Dietrick, and Ambrose Henkel, who specialized in German texts, provided many of the students' books as well as children's stories, catechisms, newspapers, sheet music, literature, and agricultural news.[123]

While many parents made certain that their children had adequate formal training, members of the German ethnic community, like other local yeoman farm families, tended to be conservative about higher education. Most believed advanced education a great luxury and that only boys should have the best opportunities. There were, however, a few exclusively German academies in nearby towns like Winchester and New Market or the more distant southwestern county of Wythe. Others attended the English-speaking academies of the Reverend George Schuyler first founded in Leesburg in 1791.[124]

Public school education captured the attention of some of Virginia's most powerful men, but it never became a popular mandate among the majority of its voters. The legislature rejected, for example, Thomas Jefferson's proposed "Bill for the More General Diffusion of Knowledge" that guaranteed a free education of all white male children, but in 1796 did establish an act to allow counties voluntarily to create public schools where white males could learn reading, writing, and arithmetic at the state's expense. It was only fifty years later in 1846, however, that Loudoun established school districts and made provisions for the regular instruction of "indigent" male and female white children. As one might imagine, the system was riddled with problems. Poor, unreliable funding and a small pool of teachers, coupled with the precarious lifestyles of "indigent" students themselves, precluded much of its success.[125]

Only one annual report (1851) of the Board of School Commissioners for Indigent Children of Loudoun is extant, but its contents include substantial information descriptive of county-wide attitudes about public education. Each of Loudoun's twenty-three school districts had a commissioner; collectively they comprised the County Superintendent of Schools. The commissioners provided some school supplies but never gave any serious consideration actually to building schools for Loudoun children. Rather, they paid locally recruited teachers to instruct small numbers of youngsters in "makeshift" schools. Teachers conducted their classes almost anywhere there was room to do so—in vacant buildings or rooms in business establishments, churches, or any other available structure.[126]

The county clearly lacked the commitment to provide efficient service. More important, teachers' salaries were so low that they attracted few able instructors. Wages were four cents per day per student. The 82 teachers employed in 1851, for example, earned an average of only $16.19 each that year and, obviously, could accept these assignments only as part-time work. Regularly employed teachers in private schools at the same time usually earned between $100 and $200 per year.[127]

To make matters worse, the commissioners rarely paid on time, usually because they did not know beforehand exactly how much money the state would allot to them, or when during the year it would arrive. As such, they moved cautiously, typically choosing only a sample of the indigent to instruct. Of the 881 white children eligible for public instruction in 1851, only 498 (286 males and 212 females), or 56 percent, received any that year.[128]

Moreover, those children who actually did benefit from the school fund still received comparatively limited instruction. The curriculum and the quality of the courses offered obviously varied with each teacher. Also, state legislators mandated that the fund was to provide only the basics of education—reading, writing, some elementary math, and perhaps some history or geography; there was to be no classical instruction. And since many poor children did not live in stable home environments, they could not attend school regularly, even when they had the opportunity to do so. Records indicate that the average public funded child attended school only 66 days a year, at a total tuition cost of $2.80, and most did not frequent any school for more than one or two years. Those who patronized private schools, on the other hand, attended class almost three times as frequently.[129]

Apprenticeship often was the avenue to future success for many males who could not afford an education or land. Blacksmiths, coopers, stonemasons, shoemakers, tinsmiths, cabinetmakers, tanners, storekeepers, carpenters, millers, printers, book binders, jewelers, wood carvers, potters, clock makers, and a host of other southern tradesmen offered, formally and informally, to train boys and young men in exchange for their services. Some females also became apprentices, mostly as domestics, although the more fortunate learned midwifery skills or to spin, weave, and sew.

Some masters also promised to educate their charges formally. The Widow Ritcher of Lovettsville, for example, contracted with a Mr. H. Ruse a four-year apprenticeship of her son Solomon beginning in 1826, whose terms included a stipulation that Ruse provide "eleven months schooling." But for most, the appeal was learning a lucrative trade. When Alex McIntyre outlined his plans for his children in his will, for instance, he stipulated that adequate money be set apart to educate them until they reached the age to be "put to such trades as they may make choice of and at that period to be bound out to such Trades until they arrive at the age of twenty one years." While there was no guarantee that they would find work in Loudoun, many did. Some moved from one apprenticeship to the next until they found just the right vocation for them. Joseph Caldwell, for example, started as a farm helper when he was seven or eight and then went on to apprentice with a carpenter and then a cabinet maker before he became a dentist.[130]

Many benefited from apprenticeships, but others found their masters abusive. George Carter's nephews complained bitterly of dishonest masters who put them to "ill use." Hugh Sidwell, who was an apprentice to local tanner David Pusey, concurred. He described his experience as "severe, being deprived of many comforts to which he had been accustomed, and receiving little sympathy of encouragement." Not trusting anyone else to teach his sons a trade, he taught them both farming and tanning.[131]

Apprenticeship also appealed to wealthier folk with a variety of other opportunities. Fathers found the type of mentorship, practical education, and responsibility apprenticeship afforded their sons especially attractive. George Carter fastidiously sought out respectable, well-established artisans and craftsmen to whom his nephews could apprentice—three trained as printers, one as a jeweler, and another as a watchmaker. He believed that the experience would, among other things, strengthen their characters. Robert Conrad also approved of a short "apprenticeship" for his son Powell with a civil engineer corps before he went off to college. Apprenticeships, of a kind, also were prevalent among professionals—almost everyone wanting careers as doctors and lawyers, for example, had to "intern" with an older, experienced practitioner.[132]

But despite the pressure that families could place on children and adolescents to become useful citizens, they still wanted their sons and daughters to enjoy their youth. The first rule of southern sociability was that southerners were very social. The second rule was that play imitated life (or vice versa)—

boys' recreation suggested their budding masculinity, while girls' play often mimicked women's work.

Since Loudoun was overwhelmingly rural, much of young male recreation occurred outdoors and within the context of agrarian culture. John Janney's description of local life for yeomen youth detailed a male social world that spanned generations and sometimes even erased racial barriers. He remembered with delight, for example, the camaraderie of the men, black and white, who worked together harvesting the corn, sharing whiskey and listening to the unmistakable sound of slaves singing their corn songs, playing the banjo, and dancing or patting "jubor." Similar festivities marked barn and house raisings. Shooting matches and turkey shoots also were popular male sport—they too ended with a sharing of the communal whiskey bottle.[133]

These were lively times for ordinary Loudoun folk. Yet Janney's description also betrayed a kind of monotony or boredom that was not unusual. The local stores were a center of social contact at the end of the work week when boys and men alike "would spend the afternoon in gossip; shooting at a mark with squirrel rifles; pitching quoits . . . [and] cents. . . [and] half dollars or dollars." There they also competed athletically, in events like wrestling, foot races, and throwing matches.[134]

Other outdoor sports like swimming, fishing, riding, and hunting also were popular, especially hunting. Boys as young as eight and nine tracked opossum, raccoon, squirrels, deer, fox, and wild fowl with slingshots, guns, and traps as a testament to their marksmanship and their budding masculinity. Family letters often chronicled the hunting escapades of teenaged boys. "This being Saturday[,] all the boys . . . ," Robert Conrad wrote a daughter, "are out with their guns. . . . They keep our breakfast table pretty well supplied with birds—but whether the cost of powder and shot would not buy more birds in market, they would be unwilling to calculate," he added, obviously amused.[135]

Despite its popularity, hunting with rifles proved too dangerous for many. "We had quite a serious accident here on Saturday, a consequence of this mania of the boys for hunting," Conrad also had reason to report. "Young Hugh Lee with Lewis Burwell, . . . and others were together out of town with guns, and Lee in jest, snapped his at his cousin Lewis. . . . The gun went off, and lodged the load of bird shot in the face and forehead of Burwell." No one was certain of the extent of Lewis's injury, but feared that he would be blind in one eye and "much disfigured" for the remainder of his life.[136]

The community's response to the Burwell hunting accident is particularly suggestive of just how important guns and hunting were to southern male culture. This accident was not Burwell's first. Just one year earlier, another young man accidentally shot Lewis while they were hunting. Yet his parents let him continue to hunt with guns. Likewise, Robert Conrad, fully aware of both accidents, still applauded his own sons' use of guns while hunting. Given Loudoun's rural character and the cultural association between hunting, gunmanship, and manhood, it is clear that fathers believed the use of guns was both a necessity and a natural rite/right of white manhood.[137]

Boys also participated in a number of other games that tested their physical strength, coordination, and ability to act both cooperatively and competitively. Several ball games including "town ball" and "cat," which were similar to baseball; "foot ball," which resembled soccer; bandy, or hockey; "corner ball"; and "trap" were popular. Going off to academies and college also meant attending formal balls, informal drinking parties, and a host of other activities. Older single men also frequented the local springs for relaxation and to meet young women. "I have no objection to you taking a trip to Bath or Bedford," Burr Harrison wrote his son Matthew in 1846, but "put it off till the proper season, . . . I mean the Fashionable season." Mr. Harrison was himself writing from Warrenton Springs. "I would not advise you to come here," he added, for "the water has little or no effect . . . and there are only two or three young ladies."[138]

No matter what the activity, parents wanted to insure that their children met the "right sort" of young people, that is, those of the appropriate race, class, and culture. "When will you get home and do you expect a visit this summer from any of yr fellow students," one mother wrote to her son away at college. "W[oul]d like you to make friends among the best and have them visit you." Her husband agreed: "I desire you to go some into society, cultivate the friendship of such of your fellow students as you may find worthy of it," he added.[139]

Robert Conrad made every effort to introduce his boys to powerful friends and relations. His concern was not just that his sons be able to take advantage of the political and economic power of their extended family, but that they also reinforce important kinship lines and bolster family unity. "If you go to Baltimore," he typically instructed one son, "your best course will be to pass once to Washington to 'call on,' among others, Mr. Charles Conrad," a paternal great uncle and an important congressman, and Captain Powell, a maternal great uncle who also had substantial political power and social prestige.[140]

Of course Conrad would never extend to his daughters the opportunity to travel alone. Respectable men and/or women had to accompany them on their public outings. When Kate Conrad traveled to New York and Canada in 1855 as a graduation gift, she was well chaperoned. So too were Hortensia Hay and Mary Selden when they visited Europe. But it was not just a matter of chaperones. While female children participated in numerous activities outside their home—playing with friends, horseback riding, foraging in the woods, picking berries and fruit, for example—their parents confined them more to their homes and yards than their brothers. Many spent much of their childhood playing indoors with dolls and imitating their mother's household work. As their daughters matured, parents confined them even more to their homes where they combined leisure with domestic labor—sewing, quilting, needlework, embroidery, and weaving.[141]

Female networks were their social mainstay. Mothers especially favored close relationships between their teen daughters and their extended female kin. Betty Conrad, for example, was anxious that her daughter Kate form a "sisterhood" with her first cousin, Elizabeth Harrison, Mrs. Conrad's namesake and godchild. "I look forward to the time when I hope to have Kate and yrself as sisters—with me," she wrote her niece in 1853. "Kate will come home next August and you too will leave school—then . . . you must come up and with Joe and Betty McGuinn all of you just the same age—we shall have a *nice* company of *nice* young ladies." She continued to encourage their friendship by arranging for the two to attend the same school and enjoining them to write to each other often.[142]

Aware that too much of a social life could turn a girl's head or mature them too quickly, parents also tried to keep them from rushing into adult situations. "I have often observed that girls who had been allowed to go into fashionable society when too young never seemed to have enjoyment in it," Conrad wrote to his daughter Kate in response to her request to visit a local spring. "At first they can only look on, as at a show, and when old enough to participate[,] the novelty of the thing is gone: the fruit is picked when unripe; and veneer acquires the full natural flavor of maturity."[143] Burr Powell also feared that his teenaged daughter Betty (later Kate's mother) wanted to enjoy the sophisticated world of adults before her time. "The Miss Roberts I take to be fine girls," he began one lecture in 1825, "but you must not expect to be as dressy as town ladies that have quit school and turned out. . . . You must always remember that you are a country girl and the daughter of a country farmer and not attempt all the aires and graces of the City Belles."[144]

Yet parents did want their daughters to be sociable. Burr Harrison worried that his daughter Catherine Cornelia was too shy. "I rather infer that you feel awkward or not at ease in society or that you had anticipated more from it than you enjoyed or received," he wrote to her in 1855. He encouraged Catherine to try to enjoy the company of others. "It is right and proper and natural to cultivate a social feeling," he advised, "to mix with society—the best of course you can get. It is unnatural not to have such a taste. . . ."[145]

Despite the gendered line which often separated Loudoun's young social world, there were many shared experiences. Church picnics and bazaars, holiday celebrations, wedding parties and receptions, corn huskings, and barn raisings all were the playground of teenaged boys and girls. They also shared a love for equestrian events. Local girls grew up riding horses alongside their brothers. While females did not participate in many of the public sporting events, they did watch boys compete in numerous races and tournaments that showcased their equestrian skills, including popular medieval festivals. "Don't loose that spear you [won] . . . in Alex[andria]," Powell Conrad had occasion to write to his brother Holmes. "It is a trophy worth preserving and would grace the walls of our castle well."[146]

But parents were quick to enforce the line between male and female social life when they feared their daughters would be exposed to the less genteel aspects of Loudoun society. They wanted to protect their sons as well, but gambling, drinking, and frequenting houses of ill repute were as much a part of southern male culture as hunting and horses. Mothers who took seriously their duty to prepare their children's souls for the next world especially were ashamed of this kind of revelry. John Janney's mother, for example, demanded that he move back in with his grandparents after his uncle's coarse language persuaded her that he was a bad influence on her son's developing character. Years later Janney had to admit that it was not his uncle, but rather a young woman in his grandfather's home who had tested his moral fiber. "I went back to my grandmother's," he confessed, "which brought me in close contact with a vulgar, lascivious girl whose influence on me has been a curse to me all my life." "Tom Tidball has been very ill but now seems likely to recover," a father wrote as a lesson to one of his sons. "His attack was brought on by dissipated habits, and his poor mother is almost dying from the effects."[147]

Mothers and fathers also worried about the influence of slaves and slavery on their young ones' characters. The *Southern Cultivator* succinctly captured the opinion of those southerners who believed that slavery was a moral and intellectual hindrance to whites. One of its writers explained in 1855, for example, that, although planter children were "fond" of associating with blacks, there were severe consequences to consider, particularly the influence of the slave's "indelicate, vulgar and lascivious manners and conversation." "I never conversed with a cultivated Southerner on the effects of slavery," Frederick Law Olmstead observed, "that he did not express a wish or intention to have his own children educated where they should be free from demoralizing association with slaves." The fear of juvenile ruin at the hand of slavery was so widespread in fact that Loudoun abolitionists like Samuel Janney were able to capitalize on it in their campaign against slavery.[148]

Unfortunately, corruption bred corruption. Some parents caught up in the perversion of it all could not help but taint their children's lives. Some of the most devastating stories to have emerged from slave-era Virginia, for example, are those which chronicle the deliberate passing on of abusive, perverse behavior within the context of slavery from one generation to the next. Recall, for example, the slave mistress who asked her daughter to help her mercilessly whip a slave child whose only offense was lying about eating a piece of peppermint candy. Equally, if not more horrifying was the legacy of slave sexual abuse that passed from one generation of slaveholders to the next. "Bird" Walton, for example, recalled that Ethel Jane, a teenaged "yaller gal," was raped by both her owner and his son. "Marsa br[ought] his son, Levey down to the cabin. They both took her—the father showing the son what it was all about—and she couldn't do nothing 'bout it."[149]

No one can deny that slave girls and women were the victims of sexual abuse, coercion, and experimentation. Those realities of southern slave society are now accepted as fact. Less discussed, however, have been the physical and emotional consequences for the young people involved—the slave girls and slaveholding boys who, as victim and victimizer, became a part of this dehumanizing phenomenon of force and violence. The shame and sense of powerlessness that the slave female experienced followed her through the rest of her life, minimally affecting, if not crippling, her future intimacies. Yet the corrupted sense of power and authority that both originated from and helped to justify female slave rape or sexual coercion also affected the personal lives of slaveholding boys and men.

Many parents, especially mothers and female kin, vehemently opposed their sons' involvement in premarital or extramarital sexual relationships with any female, principally for moral reasons. A slave woman's difference—culturally, physically, and socially—however, made slaveholding women's response to their sons' sexual involvement with such a woman closer to revulsion than moral opposition. Most did not speak openly about this kind of activity, at least not within their own families. Even when they did speak out, it usually was to criticize the women for their promiscuity or their men for their lack of restraint. They rarely constructed a discourse inclusive of the notion of black female powerlessness and rape. And in those instances where coercion was not a principal factor in the relationship, the notion of biracial, heterosexual love simply was beyond the psychological or intellectual responses of most planter women. Instead, it was their obvious inability to prevent their sons and husbands from acting outside the bounds of sexual propriety that was most emotionally engaging for them.[150]

Oftentimes, of course, problems with a child's sexual impropriety arose after he or she married and had begun a life of their own. Yet one's adulthood and eventual marriage did not necessarily mean an end to close relationships with one's family of origin. It usually did, however, mean a profound shift in the parent/child relationship as time shifted the burden of responsibility. As parents aged and loosened the reins of support, nurture, and guidance, male children often assumed stewardship or patriarchal power, while daughters cared for elderly, sometimes ailing, parents and administered their domestic affairs. Referring cautiously to the health of a young relative, W. Staber roundly articulated a common perspective: "I sincerely hope that he may be spared to comfort his parents."[151]

Regardless of the emphasis parents of all classes increasingly placed on their children's individual success, personal growth, and development, therefore, they continued to stress the overriding importance of a child's contribution to the family's survival and comfort. Their most profound lesson to their children, and especially to their adolescents and young adults, was that one should derive one's individual power, whether it be social, political, or economic, largely out of a need to protect and nurture oneself and one's family. That is what married couples ideally committed themselves to when they took on the burden of bearing and rearing children, and that was the duty they strove to pass on to their young loved ones.

Broken Vows and "Notorious" Endings: Divorce

I just commenced preparing a report on the subject of divorces,
which have annoyed us this winter by hundreds.

Robert Conrad, *1841*

Robert Conrad's rather mundane marital problems paled in comparison with those he was charged with sorting through as a member of the state senate's Judiciary Committee. Hundreds of divorce petitions flooded the legislature that season and Conrad and his fellow committee members had the questionable honor of reading and assessing the sorrowful, and sometimes sickening, details of failed marriages. Most southerners, including Conrad, believed divorce an inexpedient, perhaps immoral solution to marital problems. The state's policies echoed their concerns, making it extremely difficult for most to divorce. The only chance of receiving an absolute divorce, or *a veniculo matrimoni*, was by successful petition of the state legislature. But as time passed, divorce laws, again perhaps as a reflection of community attitudes, began to change slightly. Prior to 1848, for example, Virginia laws stipulated that the legislature could grant absolute divorces only in cases of documented sexual impotence, idiocy, or bigamy. New laws passed at the end of the antebellum era still called for a petition to the legislature, but it expanded the criteria for divorce to include adultery and desertion. Yet in the end, stringent laws, a prohibitive application procedure, and unpredictable results deterred most from seeking legislative redress—evidence of only eight Loudoun legislative petitions for divorce submitted between 1800 and 1860 remains.[1]

There were some alternatives measures. Separation agreements allowed a husband and wife to live independently and without claim to each other's property. Yet neither could remarry. In 1827, the state legislature sanctioned another kind of divorce—*a mensa et thora*, or "from bed and board"—which county courts could grant in indisputable cases of adultery, cruelty, or physical abuse. These writs ended marital obligation by either spouse and were obtained more easily but, like separation agreements, prohibited remarriage. Loudoun laborer Jacob Bagent, for example, obtained a divorce "from bed and board" in 1841 on the grounds of his wife's adultery. Three years later, he unsuccessfully petitioned the state legislature for a divorce *a vinculo matrimoni*, stating that he was only thirty-four years old and may want to remarry.[2]

Robert Conrad's tenure on the senate Judiciary Committee coincided with Jacob Bagent's submission of a divorce petition. Perhaps some of Conrad's Loudoun relations had heard of Bagent's predicament. It would be unusual if they had not. Bad news traveled fast through the area's small towns and farming communities. Although Conrad's position in the senate mandated that he remain aloof and impartial when helping to decide the fate of Bagent's marriage, his neighbors and kin gave no such pretense. As far as they were concerned, divorce was serious community business and they had a right to get involved—to speak their mind about something they felt affected them.

Marital problems that became public knowledge were taken as a threat to the moral and cultural fabric of southern white society. Marriage, after all, was a badge of white respectability and morality. To put it crudely but aptly, whites married, blacks copulated. Whites did not just marry, they stayed married. Blacks moved promiscuously from one partner to the next, or so the racialized mythology of the day went. In the American South, therefore, where notions of racial difference shaped social hierarchy and expectations so profoundly, marriage and divorce in European American communities took on incredible significance, privately and publicly.

Anyone who hoped to divorce had to provide public documentation of the events which precipitated the desire to end one's marriage. As such, family members, friends, and neighbors were a vital part of the divorce procedure. Just as a wedding was a public acknowledgment of a couple's commitment, a divorce was an instrument of public confession to the end of that commitment. The public's participation in the ritual of divorce insured that the demise of one marriage did not threaten communal values. But that did not mean that one's community always agitated against divorce. The sworn depositions of the petitioners and their witnesses, for example, verify that kin and neighbors sometimes urged a husband or wife to seek a divorce if the spouse's behavior seriously challenged fundamental local mores.

Like the General Assembly, Loudoun residents had certain criteria by which they determined whether or not a marriage should end. Their "judgments" relied heavily on their community-sanctioned ideals of gendered behavior within the context of marriage and family. Men and women, local folk agreed, had certain roles to play and behaviors to exhibit in a marriage. Those who did not act accordingly should suffer as punishment a loss of the respectability and resources that their marriages held for them. Almost everyone agreed, for example, that female adultery, or "notorious" infidelity, as it was called, severed marital ties. A wife's infidelity was a negation of woman's "natural" piety, purity, and selflessness. Female adultery was a double-edged sword—it flew in the face of idealized white southern womanhood and imperiled southern white manhood. The community was clear on its response: since a woman of infamous morality brought extreme dishonor to her husband, her sex, and her race, it was morally imperative that her husband rid himself of her as soon as possible. Only then could he regain some honor and status within his community. Only through her public shaming and exclusion from her home as a result of her husband and her community's rejection could the community be assured that her debauchery would not be a source of further moral unraveling. Even if a husband might want to "forgive and forget," the community was hardly willing to let him do so. Consider, for example, William Yonson's marital predicament during the winter of 1847–48.

By all accounts, William Yonson was an industrious, ambitious, young man—a maker of wheat-threshing machines who lived in Leesburg. In about 1840, he married Eliza Jane, a young woman from Pennsylvania who had left her family to come and live in Loudoun with her new husband. The couple had one child, a daughter. Filing for divorce in 1848, Mr. Yonson readily admitted to the Virginia legislature that he had been "sincerely attached" to Eliza Jane. Some time in December 1847, however, he had begun to fear that his wife was having "illicit intercourse" with a neighbor, William P. Smith. His suspicions were encouraged by the "admonitions of some neighbors and friends, who had great respect for . . . [the] petitioner and who took an interest in his behalf." Determined not to sit back and let Mrs. Yonson threaten the moral fabric of their community, Yonson's neighbors openly admitted to him their doubts about his wife's infidelity. Yonson was determined to get at the truth, and so devised a plan which, as he described in his sworn deposition, was meant to reveal his wife's innocence or guilt.[3]

Yonson already believed his wife guilty when he put his plan into action, but he needed to gather enough public documentation to win a divorce. As such, he insisted on the help of his "family and friends" as part of his plan to "catch" her. His determination to have his community's participation also would convince them that he sought the truth and acted according to community standards when he had it. Yonson wanted to be certain that his wife's immorality did not intimate something negative about his own values or his manhood. Likewise, the public witnessing of Mrs. Yonson's impropriety would leave no doubt in their mind that Yonson should sever his emotional as well as financial support of her. His neighbors agreed to go along with his plot, provided that Yonson swear not to do bodily harm to either Mr. Smith or Eliza Jane.[4]

Yonson' plot was a clever one. First, he lied to his wife—telling her that he was going to be out of town for several days. After leaving their house he hid at a neighbor's. There, he and several of his friends waited and watched. Yonson also included his male boarder in the plan—he had to stay at the house in order to document exactly when Mr. Smith arrived. Yonson's friends—Messrs. Brayan, Hewitt, Ryan, and Jordan—agreed not only to wait with him but also to sneak up to the house, peek through the bedroom window, and then actually tiptoe through the house in a surprise confrontation with the illicit couple. According to Daniel Hewitt, at about midnight he, Yonson, and two others went to Yonson's to "bear witness" to the discovering of his wife's guilt. Together they "entered the house softly and silently with shoes off" and in Yonson's bedroom "they plainly discovered from the light of a lantern . . . a certain Wm. P. Smith in the bed with the wife of said Yonson.[5]

Surprised, embarrassed, and probably a little afraid when the men burst into the room, Mrs. Yonson and her lover had no recourse but to admit their guilt. Mr. Smith dressed quickly, apologizing clumsily to the jilted husband. Yonson asked Smith if he intended taking Eliza Jane with him, but Smith declined to do so, choosing a hasty retreat instead. Mrs. Yonson left for her family's home in Pennsylvania the next day, leaving behind her seven-year-old daughter.[6]

Undoubtedly the discovery of Mrs. Yonson's infidelity and the manner by which it was detected was one of the most exciting events to rattle their Leesburg community that sleepy winter. The community support that Mr. Yonson received once he decided to reveal his wife's "bad character" and the pressure his "cooperative" neighbors brought to bear on him to investigate the validity of local gossip are obvious from his divorce petition. Through his decisive action, public acknowledgment, and then rejection of his immoral wife, Yonson was able to retain his male honor and respect. His petition to the General Assembly for a divorce was his final public attempt to remove the taint of his wife's dishonor.

Yonson's petition not only included the sworn depositions of several neighbors but also a brief letter of explanation tendered by a local elite, H. M. Janney, who hoped his support would expedite the cause. Cognizant of the difficulty of acquiring a legislative divorce without sponsorship from one's elected representatives from the district, Janney specifically asked that the petition be brought to the attention of Loudoun legislators, noting in part that Yonson was a "worthy good citizen" and that the facts detailed in his petition were "decreed" by "everybody" as true. "Do give your attention to this case," he pleaded.[7]

A recent amendment to the state divorce laws stipulated adultery as a reason for ending a marriage. This change in law, Yonson's overwhelming evidence, and his community's support, signaled the General Assembly's granting of his petition. Even before the laws changed, however, the legislature sometimes could be persuaded to accept adultery as a cause for divorce if the act of infidelity was "notorious," that is if it was an overt assault on communal values and morality. Such was the case of Isaac Fouch, a Loudoun millwright who petitioned for a divorce in December 1808 on the grounds that his wife was "of a Lewd, incontinent, profligate disposition and practice."

Isaac Fouch married Elizabeth Beach in January 1802. At first, the young millwright was proud of his new wife, a young woman he "believed of fair Character and unsullied Reputation," whom he admittedly was "much attached to" and with whom, "from his first acquaintance with . . . cherished the most ardent, tender, affectionate Love and Regard for." Six years later, Fouch still was in love with his wife, but he found himself in a heart-wrenching situation that placed him on the brink of divorce.[8]

Whether or not Elizabeth Fouch ever loved her husband as much as he loved her remains unknown. Regardless of her feelings, she had to have known what her affair with James Watt, a local free black, would mean for her marriage. More than any other act, voluntary biracial sex between a white woman and a black man unquestionably alienated the woman from her community. Mrs. Fouch's adulterous affair with a man of color undoubtedly branded her promiscuous and lewd, far beneath the status of any respectable white woman and not fit for any white man. In the eyes of her peers, Elizabeth's "notorious" adultery deemed her no longer white or female, but some monstrous other. Her husband's acceptance or even forgiveness could only bring him greater dishonor and shame. Still he initially hoped to salvage the marriage.[9]

"Hoping that she might yet be reclaimed," he swore in his deposition, he "heeded her with all that tenderness and respect which the most upright and Virtuous woman ought to expect." After discovering the affair, Mr. Fouch worked diligently to reform his wife, "admonishing her repeatedly of the Wickedness of such a course, of the infamy and disgrace which must result from it, [and] that if persisted in[,] a separation would assuredly take place." Elizabeth, however, remained unmoved by her husband's persistent demonstrations of love, speeches about proper moral behavior, and his threats to leave her. "But alas!" Fouch had to admit, all his efforts had but little effect except to produce "a contrary effect" in her. Twice after pleading with her to give up the relationship, Fouch found Elizabeth in bed with James Watt. She simply refused to end the affair. Disgusted and disgraced, Isaac decided to leave Loudoun so as to avoid further scandal. Unable to persuade his wife to leave Watt and go with him, he packed some of his belongings and took off for the "western country."[10]

Mrs. Fouch also seemed determined to escape the gossip and chagrin of her neighbors, but she was not about to leave Loudoun without her lover. Packing all that her husband left behind, Elizabeth and James planned to make a hasty departure and would have, if her neighbors had not intervened. Residents of the Fouches' community had witnessed Watt's comings and goings and wondered about his business in Isaac's home. Their curiosity no doubt was whetted by the reports of Jane Campbell, the Fouches' white house servant, who readily swore in her deposition that soon after coming to work for the couple she noticed a "particular fondness and intimacy" between the white woman and black man.[11]

Miss Campbell liked Mr. Fouch and felt a certain loyalty to him. She also was outraged that Mrs. Fouch treated her husband so badly, a man who seemed to be "so kind and affectionate" to his wife. The inquisitive servant was, in fact, so loyal to her employer that she took it upon herself to investigate the situation. According to her, every time Mr. Watt arrived at the Fouches', Mrs. Fouch would send her on an errand, usually to milk the cow or get some water from the spring. Jane was not fooled by these diversionary tactics, and instead of going about her tasks, she would stay and peek through a hole in the wall. There, she swore that she observed the biracial lovers "in the very act" numerous times.[12]

Mrs. Fouch detected the woman's suspicions and resorted to fastening the bedroom door and stopping up the holes in her wall. But it was too late. The entire community soon seemed aware of her infidelity and, with Miss Campbell, were determined to protect Mr. Fouch along with their sense of sexual and racial propriety. Accordingly, when they saw Mrs. Fouch driving away in a wagon packed with household goods and Mr. Watt following, they quickly alerted the local sheriff, who stopped the couple and recovered the goods.[13]

What especially is significant about Fouch's divorce petition is his revelation of the public pressure he felt to leave this woman who, despite her transgressions, he still loved. He confided to the state assembly, for example, that he felt that he had no other alternative but to dissolve his marriage, since a reconciliation seemed impossible, and, at any rate, any attempt on his part to reconstitute the marriage "would only insure the contempt and disrespect of the worthy and virtuous part of [Loudoun] Society."[14] The legislature agreed. Their approval of this petition not only meant the legal end to the Fouch marriage, but also was a public stand that state lawmakers took against intimate interracial relations which involved a white woman. When confronted with equally compelling evidence against other women who committed adultery, but within the confines of their own race, for example, they often refused to grant a petition for divorce. The General Assembly had little compassion for Jacob Bagent, for example, when the jilted Loudouner applied for a divorce in 1844, on the grounds that his wife was having an affair with a local white man.[15]

Jacob and Eleanor Bagent married in 1829. Unlike Elizabeth Fouch and Eliza Jane Yonson, however, the vivacious Irish woman had a local reputation for having a "bad character" and for "being too fond of men" before she ever met Jacob. Unfortunately for her husband, rumors about her reputation proved true after they married. Mr. Bagent took his wife to live on the property of John Waters, a farmer who employed Bagent as a laborer and driver to the Harpers Ferry market. For two years, the Bagents lived in a small house about fifty yards from that of Waters and his wife without incident. But then Mrs. Waters became ill and Mrs. Bagent began to spend a great deal more time in the Waters home. At first her husband believed that she was helping his employer and his ill wife with domestic tasks. But when Jacob began to hear from his neighbors that Waters often came to visit Mrs. Bagent in their home while he was away, he became suspicious.[16]

Jealous of the attention his boss was giving his wife, Bagent often quarreled with Eleanor about her personal relationship with Waters. Instead of trying to reassure her husband, Mrs. Bagent took his jealousy in stride, warning him that if he did not stop accusing her of such things she would leave him. In the meanwhile, Mr. Waters's wife died, and he extended an invitation to the Bagent family to move in with him. Jacob would hear nothing of the offer. Mrs. Bagent, however, had hoped to improve her material status through her liaison with Waters. Anxious to be rid of her poor husband, she left Jacob on Christmas day, taking her three children with her. When Bagent asked her to return, she humiliated him by confessing her adulterous relationship with Waters— even telling him that Waters was the father of her last child. She also made it clear that she had no intention of leaving Waters or returning Jacob's two sons.[17]

Eleanor Bagent and John Waters continued to live together well past 1840, when Jacob Bagent filed for a divorce "from bed and board" from the Loudoun Superior Court. The illicit couple were, in fact, still together when Jacob petitioned the Virginia state legislature for an absolute divorce in 1844; and by that time Eleanor had bore Waters two more children. The Loudoun Superior Court deemed that her adultery was adequate grounds to grant her husband a divorce *a mensa et thora* in 1841 as well as custody of their youngsters. When Jacob later submitted a petition for a divorce *a vinculo matrimoni* to the Virginia General Assembly with an explanation that he hoped to remarry in the future, however, they rejected his request. Although his divorce from bed and board removed the dishonor that Eleanor had brought to him and his sons, Jacob Bagent's inability to legally remarry still alienated him from the possibility of establishing a respectable relationship with another woman, to live happily and responsibly as a married man.[18]

The Bagent divorce case is unique among those from Loudoun because it included detailed information about child custody procedures. It is curious, for example, that Mrs. Bagent took custody of her children when she decided to abandon her husband. Jacob initially may have hesitated to accept the responsibility for the day-to-day care of his two young boys because of the time constraints of his occupation and his inability to afford a housekeeper or get a female family member to assist him. It also was imperative that he find a new job and place to live since his position at Waters's had become, at the very least, "uncomfortable." Perhaps he felt that without a wife or a job he did not have much of a home to offer his sons. By the time that he began to legalize the separation, however, he was determined to regain custody.

The county court carefully reviewed each parent's qualifications for legal guardianship . The Bagent boys were old enough by 1841 to care for themselves without their father's constant supervision. Moreover, Jacob now was settled in a new home and was financially secure. It was obvious from his deposition that he had become increasingly concerned about his sons' futures and was certain that neither his wife nor her lover had any intention of preparing them for any worthwhile occupation. Witnesses who had visited the Waters home confirmed Bagent's fears. William Magathy, brother to Mrs. Bagent, for example, testified that he believed that Jacob Bagent or some other responsible person should have custody of the boys. Magathy stated in part: "I think they ought to be taken away from her [Eleanor Bagent], and put where they will be treated better, and prepared to be useful for themselves. . . .—the oldest is nearly ten years old[;] the other is a year or two younger—and they are now living in idleness." The Loudoun justices agreed and granted Jacob Bagent custody.[19]

Virginia divorce law in 1844 did not allow absolute divorce on the grounds of spousal infidelity, and the assemblymen refused to make an exception for Jacob Bagent. Eleanor, after all, had not committed the same kind of egregious crime as Mrs. Yonson—her lover was white, not black. Nor did Mr. Bagent have the kind of social, economic, or political clout necessary to gain an exceptional ruling from elected officials. Since the character and focus of the Virginia state legislature could change with each new election, it was difficult to predict just how conservative or liberal they might be about such issues. Jacob Bagent just happened to apply for a divorce at a time when legislators were bemoaning the large number of divorce petitions and believed that they could dissuade future petitioners by acting in strict accordance with the law. Had the custody of the Bagent children still been at issue when Jacob applied for a divorce, the General Assembly may have acted otherwise. But the Loudoun Court already had granted Jacob custody, and the state legislature saw no reason to act further. Members of the General Assembly, however, sometimes did rule against the grain of the law if they believed that to do so would benefit the dependent children of the petitioner. It was mostly in the interest of Nancy Turner's children, for example, that state law makers decided to grant this Loudoun woman a divorce in 1817.

Nancy Turner's divorce petition especially is illuminating because of its detailed documentation of persistent spousal abuse—physical, verbal, and sexual.

Turner was herself a rare woman, because she was one of the very few Loudoun females who dared to protest publicly the inhumane and abusive treatment of her husband, and to gain the support and participation of her community in so doing. Most of the scant evidence of spousal abuse is found in the personal papers of male kin and friends of the abused woman, rather than in those of females, for few women were willing to speak out openly about this kind of victimization. Even Nancy Turner hesitated to discuss the problems she had with her husband Alexander. But with overwhelming community and kin support, she finally was able to do so. It was not, after all, something that she could hide, since her husband rarely tried to conceal his acts of violence and domination from public view. Both Nancy's sisters, for example, witnessed Alexander's abuse on different occasions. And when forced to flee her home one evening or risk another beating, Nancy had no other recourse but to go to her brother's house, explain her situation, and ask for his protection.[20]

Unlike the other women who petitioned the state legislature for a divorce, Mrs. Turner was neither rich nor socially prominent. She came from a modest family and worked as a weaver in order to support her husband and her growing family. All agreed that her husband was a poor excuse for a man. He was not just a lousy provider, he also was a vicious, mean-spirited alcoholic. It was common knowledge that Turner would disappear for days while on drinking and whoring binges and then return to his wife and small children "a verry [sic] cross and illnatured husband and father." He routinely abused Mrs. Turner physically—usually while trying to force her to give him her meager earnings to support his dissipated lifestyle. He also verbally and sexually molested her in front of their children and her female relations. Holly Phillips, sister to Mrs. Turner, noted in her deposition, for example, that, while she lived with the Turners, Alexander "was in the habit of coming home drunk and cursing, abusing and using her in a most shameful manner."[21]

Indeed, Alexander Turner appeared to reject or resent all of the duties that Loudoun society expected white men to take on once they married. He was neither protective nor physically and emotionally supportive to his wife and children, a self-centered man who seemingly lacked all regard for his family's well-being. Mrs. Turner's brother, Israel Phillips, explained, for example, that while they were married the Turners lived in a house that "was not in a situation to live in" and the children were "in a measure without cloaths [sic] and frequently nothing to eat, [and their home had] no wood except what she carried."[22] Another of Nancy's sisters added that Alexander even had refused to help his wife with her heavy domestic chores or provide her with financial support during her pregnancy and subsequent confinement. Sarah Phillips swore in her deposition that she had found her sister "grating corn to feed herself and her small naked children" while Turner was away at "some Tavern or Still

House." Phillips also stated that two weeks after Nancy had given birth to twins, she went to her home and found the still "confined" mother fetching wood in the rain to make a fire for the family. A frightened Nancy told Sarah that Turner had "threatened to beat her when he returned."[23]

Fearing that her husband would carry out his threat, Mrs. Turner took her children and sought refuge in her brother's home. This kind of ill treatment of a woman who only recently had given birth aptly demonstrated to relatives and friends Turner's "unnatural" and unmanly disregard for Nancy and their children. Although most Loudouners did not believe that a woman should leave her husband, several residents actually encouraged Nancy Turner to do so once they realized the extent of her husband's abuse and neglect.

Soon after Mrs. Turner went to live with her brother, her husband completely abandoned his family, disappearing without any word of his whereabouts or intentions to return. After he had been gone for several years, most believed him dead. Mrs. Turner remained in the county and retained close ties with her family and friends. For a while she was forced to lived on public charity for, soon after her husband's departure, his creditors seized all of her household belongings in order to pay some of his debts. Loudoun's Overseers of the Poor interceded and purchased Mrs. Turner's property at public auction and returned it to her. She continued to support herself and her children with her weaving. When Nancy finally applied for a divorce, she remembered the kindness of the Overseers and called on them to give a statement in her behalf. They obliged her request and swore in an affidavit that she had "much better provided for [her] family *without* the said Alexander Turner than what they were provided for by him."[24]

Seven years passed before Nancy petitioned for a divorce. Obviously, she had hoped that she and her children were rid of the abusive man forever. Imagine her anxiety when a neighbor came back from a trip to Maryland and informed her that not only was Alexander Turner alive, but that he was residing in nearby Baltimore. It seems that some time after Mr. Turner left Loudoun, he joined the army and was stationed at Fort McHenry. It was there that he lived openly with another woman whom he referred to as "his wife."[25]

Once she learned of her husband's whereabouts, Mrs. Turner did not hesitate to act decisively. Gathering together her meager resources and seeking the aid of sympathetic family members and friends, she retained a lawyer who took several sworn depositions on her behalf and instigated the necessary public notification of her intentions to seek divorce. Nancy had completed all the criteria for submission of her petition to the General Assembly only eight months after she learned of her husband's location.

Nancy Turner admitted in her petition that she no longer had any loving feelings for her husband, not only because of his horrendous treatment of herself and their children, but also because of his longstanding desertion and blatant adultery. She added, however, that her primary reason for requesting a divorce was not her ill feelings for the man, but rather her fear that he would return and try to claim her wages, thereby denying her the only source of support she had for her children. She explained to the legislators that she believed "if he does [return] that it would only be to oppress her and to deprive her of her little honest earning which she wishes to apply to the support of her children." The state legislature "judged" Mrs. Turner's petition "reasonable" in January 1818 and ordered that the appropriate bill for divorce be drawn. Undoubtedly, the Assembly awarded Nancy Turner's petition on the legal grounds of bigamy, but her husband's threat to the financial security of their children probably also influenced their decision.

Like Nancy Turner, Ann Peyton Aldricks was able to strengthen her petition for divorce through a plea for her children. Mrs. Aldricks also had the weight of her prestigious family name and the social and political clout that it carried to further her cause. As a Peyton, she was a member of one of Loudoun's and Virginia's most prestigious families. Her status, therefore, was an important condition which undoubtedly caused legislators to look more favorably on her case than the law mandated at the time.

Ann Aldricks had had to support two daughters since her husband deserted them some eleven years prior to her divorce application. Lacking lucrative skills, she relied solely on her family's voluntary financial assistance. Although she had been able to manage caring for her children with the aid of her wealthy kin, Ann realized that as her daughters grew older, their expenses were increasing rapidly. It was now time for her to consider their secondary school costs and soon it would be necessary to amass appropriate dowries. The picture that she and her elite male supporters—referred to as "Gentlemen of the first respectability in the neighboring counties"—painted in her 1808 petition was one of a naive rich girl who married a scoundrel at the age of fifteen, bore him two daughters, and soon thereafter was deserted with no means of support but her charitable family. Mrs. Aldricks did have some financial resources that could be useful—property that her father had left her—but as a "femme couverte," she could not use it without the permission of her husband. "The only provision that fortune has left within her reach is so circumstanced," her male kin wrote in a deposition for her petition, "as only to tantalize with the precarious prospect of ever making it really useful."[26]

It was a scenario with which most of the members of the General Assembly (white, elite fathers) could identify and sympathize. Accordingly, they granted Ann a divorce on the grounds of desertion in 1808. State law, however, did not recognize abandonment as a legitimate reason for divorce at that time. Undoubtedly, Mrs. Aldrick's position in Loudoun's upper class helped her win the legislature's approval.

The sympathy that Virginia legislators held for young, wealthy, supposedly innocent females who married unworthy men also seems to have influenced their decision regarding the divorce petition of Caroline Balls, a Loudoun woman who married for love, only to discover that her husband had married for money. The history of her brief and troubled marriage again documents some of the problems that a woman's separate estate and a husband's greed engendered in a marital relationship.

From the outset of their marriage, Robert Balls seemed anxious to get his hands on Caroline's paternal inheritance, set aside in a separate estate, and openly resented his inability to do so. Balls declared that it was his right, as Caroline's husband, to have access and virtual control of all of her financial assets. He tried unsuccessfully on several occasions to persuade her to cooperate. For her to deny him this power not only foiled his plans to manipulate her wealth for his own financial benefit; Robert also argued that it challenged his patriarchal authority and was an affront to his personal honor.[28]

Caroline refused to waiver. Angry and frustrated, Balls soon began to abuse his wife. He argued with her constantly and habitually left her for several days on end without any explanation of his absence or when he expected to return. As time passed and the relationship deteriorated, Robert began to act even more desperately—stealing some of Caroline's household furnishings and eventually filing for divorce in New York—the couple's temporary place of residence. Failing to obtain a divorce in that state, Balls gave up. He soon disappeared, and this time he left no indication that he would ever return.[29]

Obviously, unresolved conflict regarding the separate estates of married women could bring hostile feelings quickly to the surface. To be sure, Mrs. Balls was hurt when she realized that her husband cared more about her wealth than he did for her. But she eventually recovered. Back in the comfort of her Loudoun home, among family and friends, she petitioned for a divorce. She did so, according to her deposition, in order to have "[restored] to her the unlimited right to dispose of her own property, which she had before marriage." Again the Assembly decided to aid a jilted female member of the elite. On February 27, 1851, they passed an act dissolving the marriage, noting in part that "Caroline Octavia [is] forever divorced from her husband . . . and the power and authority of the said Robert M. over the person and property . . . shall henceforth cease and determine."[30]

Taken as a whole, most of Loudoun's divorce petitioners presented claims which, at least superficially, turned on the threat of male dishonor or the financial ruin of female spouses and their children. Yet the underlying thrust of the petitions and the legislature's response to them was grounded in widespread beliefs about adult gendered responsibility within the confines of the family and its implications for the morality of the white community. Far from presenting any threat to the institution of marriage, the personal, public, and state response to divorce, especially their support of certain cases and denial of others, privileged established rules of behavior operative in a community stratified along race, class, and gender lines.

The "honor" of women, for example, hardly was at issue in any of the petitions, even those which documented flagrant male abuse or infidelity. Women rarely came forth to ask for a divorce on the grounds that their husband's aberrant behavior was a blot on their reputation or offensive to their honor. Indeed, few men in this patriarchal society envisioned women as having honor except as manifest in their chastity or that which their male kin conferred on them. Honor in southern society, men surmised, primarily was a male privilege and priority. Given the few and meager financial opportunities that women had outside of male support, it is not difficult to understand that few women could afford to take their "honor" seriously, particularly when the men whom they relied on for economic survival were the very ones who threatened it. Given all this, Susan Moore's petition to the state legislature in 1849 is particularly enlightening. It was because she wanted to restore her female "honor" that Mrs. Moore counterpetitioned her husband's divorce request. Through her aggressive response to his attack on her "femaleness," Susan Moore composed one of the most socially provocative documents that any Loudoun female ever produced.[31]

Peter Moore hoped to get a divorce by convincing the state legislature that he had been denied his conjugal rights. His wife's sexual organs, he swore, were "unnaturally malformed" and she was "deprived of those members pertaining to all females and necessary to the enjoyment of the married state." Although Mr. Moore lied in his petition, he believed he could win on two fronts. First, state law did allow the legal end to a marital relationship if a spouse could prove that his or her partner was impotent. Clearly, Mr. Moore hoped that the all-male legislature would view a wife's deformed genitalia as tantamount to impotency—if not hers, then a condition forced on him by her deformity. Second, he was certain that his wife's sense of female propriety would keep her from submitting to the vaginal examination she needed in order to counteract his charges. Contrary to Peter Moore's calculation, however, Mrs. Moore had no intention of being manipulated in such a manner.[32]

Hurt and angered by her husband's accusations, Susan particularly was incensed that his claims of her genital deformity had become a source of virulent gossip in their community. Determined to protect her pride in her feminine and sexual attractiveness, she vehemently denied her husband's complaint. In retaliation, she submitted her own petition to the General Assembly denying his allegations. In her defense, Mrs. Moore stated that she had lived with her husband "between two and three years . . . happily together in every connection as husband and wife." She went on to assert in her explicit deposition that "during the whole time [we were married] he did treat me with particular attention and apparently the strongest affection . . . and that he never did complain or even intimate the least dissatisfaction with me in any way. [N]or had he any cause for complaint," she assured her audience.[33]

But Mrs. Moore was willing to go much further to counter her husband's derogatory account of their sex life together. She called his bluff, submitting to physical examinations of her sex organs both from women in her neighborhood and by a respected local physician. Her decision to request an examination by neighboring women not only provided evidence for her legislative petition, but also reestablished her status among her female peers as their equal, physically and sexually. Clearly, the sense of honor that she attached to her sex organs—the physical manifestation of her membership in a "community of women"—was as important to her as the honor that husbands hoped to protect when they divorced adulterous wives. She openly stated in her petition, for example, that it was not her husband's desire to divorce her to which she objected, but rather that he should do so at the expense of her honor as a woman and wife.

Dr. William B. Day examined Mrs. Moore and submitted as part of her petition a notarized statement which supported her assessment of her intimate relationship with her husband. Dr. Day noted that not only were Mrs. Moore's sexual organs formed normally, but that he was "satisfied from the absence of the Hymen and the enlarged state of the Vagina, [that] she has had frequent sexual intercourse with her husband." The only evidence of sexual dissatisfaction in the marriage he added, was Mrs. Moore's small clitoris, which, he explained, had no effect on Mr. Moore, but probably hindered his wife's sexual enjoyment.[34]

The General Assembly considered closely the evidence that Mrs. Moore, her neighbors, and her physician presented. Although most probably were shocked at Susan's decision to allow public scrutiny of her genitalia and sexual history, for her the question of female propriety came second to her identity and pride as a woman and, as part of that role, an adequate sex partner to her husband. Although the Moores no longer lived together as husband and wife, they did remain married.[35]

Susan Moore's petition to the state assembly obviously was exceptional, but it does suggest some of the power that a divorce petition extended to women of all classes. Extant divorce records, for example, indicate that Loudoun females were almost as likely to end a marriage legally as men. Moreover, the legislature, given the appropriate incentive, was as likely to grant the petition of a female as a male. Still, the process and its result often meant something quite different for women than it did for men. A divorced woman, for example, gained the freedom to act as a reasonable adult, that is, to make her own personal choices. Men had this kind of personal freedom, at least comparatively so, even while married. Likewise, men's and women's experiences were not the same in divorce, just as they were not in marriage. The reasons that they petitioned for divorce and the timing of the petition submission, for example, differed substantially.

Women seeking divorce usually acted as a result of long-term desertion and the financial problems which accrued from it. They postponed acting legally to end their marriages for various reasons, but usually because it was so difficult for them to live without their husband's support that they hoped their straying spouses might come back. Also, the legislature demanded irrefutable proof that the husband had no intention of returning and that his absence absolutely threatened the financial survival of the petitioner and her children before they would consider granting the divorce. These kinds of concerns and legal restrictions kept Loudoun wives waiting to petition for divorce sometimes years after their husbands had abandoned them.

Husbands, on the other hand, usually acted quickly, within a few months of first learning of their wives' offenses, to put an end to their marriages. Moreover, since married men retained the right to earn income and own property regardless of the disposition of their wives, they usually did not petition for divorce on financial grounds. Most husbands filed for divorce in order to distance themselves from the public shame of a wife's adultery. The double sexual standard operative in Loudoun, and its implications for white southern manhood and womanhood, demanded that a jilted husband reject his wife but that a scorned woman ignore her husband's philandering. One's gender, therefore, had great influence on one's grounds for divorce, the ways in which the complainants participated in the process, and the results of their actions.

Class and gender together influenced the process even more. Female petitioners tended to be members of the upper class, while male applicants represented middling and poorer folk. Two of the five Loudoun male petitioners—William Yonson and Isaac Fouch, for example—were literate, skilled laborers, a mechanic and a millwright respectively. Jacob Bagent was an illiterate day laborer. Two of the three women, on the other hand, who submitted petitions for divorce—Ann Peyton Aldricks and Caroline Hodgson Balls—owned considerable amounts of land and represented Loudoun's elite.[36]

Surely upper-class men also were vulnerable to marital dispute and discord. Yet elite males may have viewed divorce from a different perspective than wealthy women and poorer men. Most well-to-do husbands had little to gain financially from divorce since most already had complete control of their wives' assets, a control that they would retain as long as they remained married. Issues of wealth consolidation among married couples of the upper class, therefore, were not just an incentive for well-off men to marry well-to-do women, but also a reason to stay married despite problems. Poorer husbands usually had little if anything financial to gain from remaining with their wives.

Elite Loudoun men also must have realized that the public airing of intimate problems through divorce might impugn their moral character or, perhaps more disturbing, undermine their patriarchal leadership within their households and communities. It is of little surprise that none of the men who petitioned for divorce on the grounds of spousal adultery was a member of Loudoun's gentry. They undoubtedly devised more private means to deal with their wives' indiscretions and failings.

Non-elite husbands, on the other hand, seemed to be much less able to control the public's access to their spouse's immoral behavior. They often had little recourse but to confess their wives' sins openly and try to maintain what honor they could through their public rejection symbolized in the ritual of divorce. Social constraints, along with economic and social reprisals of female impropriety, also could be much more binding to women of the upper class, for their status demanded an untainted reputation. A wealthy woman's improper sexual behavior might not get her name on a divorce petition, but any inkling of it in public meant absolute rejection from her social world and long-lasting shame to her family.

Unlike their wives, men with substantial financial resources had extramarital emotional and sexual options. They routinely traveled, for example, throughout the year on business-related trips and during the spring and summer months to spas and other recreational locales. These sojourns away from home allowed them, if they so desired, to establish or sustain intimate relationships with other women. Wealthy men, more so than those of more moderate means, also could afford discreet mistresses. These relationships were a plausible outlet for those with problematic marriages, but who believed divorce an inexpedient or embarrassing solution.

The legislative divorce petitions of Loudoun folk, however, tell us much more than just the distinguishing characteristics of the couples who submitted them. They remain as profound statements descriptive of marriage among county whites, especially unique summaries of marital ideals. The disappointments and frustrations that these men and women testified to suggest that most hoped that marriage would produce a relationship filled with love, loyalty, respect, honor, and honesty, in other words, a companionate marriage. Such was the ideal expressed across class, generational, and gender lines.

Of course it was not always the erosion of the marital relationship that eventually led to a petition for divorce. Many more Loudouners than represented by these eight remaining legislative petitioners undoubtedly had severe marital problems of one kind or another, but never acted legally to end their marriages. Other concerns than just the loss of a companionate marital ideal fueled the efforts behind divorce petitions. Especially important was the public's view of one's marriage and what should be done about it. Few persons were willing to act contrary to the opinion of their community and family, the people from whom they drew their sense of identity and purpose. Moreover, one's "society" of family and friends were those whom one could always depend on—would have to depend on—if one's marriage failed. As Nancy Turner, Ann Peyton Aldricks, and others discovered during the travail of their failing marriages, one's community and kin could be a godsend at a time of marital crisis. They also could be the straw that broke the camel's back.

Isaac Fouch's predicament is the perfect example of how a community's disapproval could mean a troubled marriage's final demise. Fouch openly admitted loving his wife, but he was almost certain that a "reconciliation" could never occur because of his community's insistence that he reject her. Even if there were a chance that their marriage could withstand Mrs. Fouch's indiscretion with a man of color, Mr. Fouch knew that any attempt to reconcile would (and his words bear repeating) "insure the contempt and disrespect of the worthy and virtuous part" of his society.[37] Others surveyed here felt a similar community pressure to divorce. No matter how important the institution of marriage was to the white community, therefore, this same community would absolutely reject a marriage that, in some way or another, threatened fundamental social mores of their white southern world.

II

Black Life,
Family,
and Community

Introduction

I wish you had ordered Daniel to be well whipped by the constable on his return. He is a worthless scoundrel, who deserved it. Tell him that you are authorized to sell him to the New Orleans Purchasers, and that you will do it, for the next offense. The most rigid discipline must be maintained over all the servants, and particularly my slaves, as an example to the others.

President James Monroe, Master of "Oak Hill" Plantation,
Loudoun County, 1819

James Monroe undoubtedly was Loudoun County's most illustrious resident. As Revolutionary War officer, senator, foreign diplomat, governor, Secretary of State and later President, Monroe's role as an agriculturist hardly was his central life work.[1] Yet in addition to his exemplary political and diplomatic career, President Monroe was a planter and slaveholder. His impact on black life, therefore, was in many ways as typical as his own life was extraordinary. As an absentee planter, he was not unlike some of the county's earliest elite who lived elsewhere while developing "satellite" Loudoun plantations.[2] Likewise, Monroe's other financial, personal, and especially civic interests kept him removed from the day-to-day activities of his plantations which he placed in the hands of overseers. Also like other wealthy slaveholders, Monroe did not own just "Oak Hill," but numerous plantations throughout the state. Many of his slaves, therefore, did not find a permanent home in Loudoun but were compelled by Monroe's overseers to move from one farm to the next in accordance with the properties' production and maintenance needs. These concerns, rather than those of the slaves' families or communities, determined their residence and much about the quality of their domestic life.

The size of James Monroe's Loudoun slaveholding, one of the largest in the county in 1830, might suggest slave domestic stability in the form of nuclear families and monogamous marriages. The size of a slaveholding, however, hardly was indicative of this kind of lifestyle, particularly if slaveholdings were large enough, as was Monroe's, to permit frequent changes in slave location, rentals, or sale. President Monroe's slave Daniel, for example, had a proclivity for running away—taking short absences from Monroe's plantation in Albermarle county to visit other properties and locales without his overseer's permission. To do so was typical of slaves trying to maintain a modicum of family stability in the face of their master's disruptive priorities. The reality of nineteenth-century slave life re-emerges in Monroe's description of Daniel's "worthlessness." Even though the slave man lived with large numbers of other blacks, the people Daniel identified as his family and community probably resided elsewhere. As such, the "scoundrel" was willing to risk everything, even the threat of permanent sale to the Deep South, to protect precious bonds that either were invisible or insignificant to his owner and overseer.[3]

Scholars have argued, eloquently and convincingly, about the nature and stability of southern slave families. Most now contend that slave family structure and life were surprisingly stable given the many undermining forces the institution of slavery imposed. Supporters of this conclusion offer a formidable base of evidence—examples of long-term, monogamous marriages and father-inclusive and male-headed families culled from slave testimony, postbellum marriage records, slave lists, and other planter documents. Family stability was possible, they further posited, because of a remarkably even adult sex ratio, the cultural designs and desires of slaves, and the moral and economic incentives of masters.[4]

Still there always were those whose scholarship pointed to other circumstances of slave life and the consequences for black domesticity. Indeed, the revisionists themselves avidly described the "countervailing" forces which easily and often undermined what they believed were "stable" forces in slave family life.[5]

Contrary to popular views of family stability, the familial history of slaves in colonial and antebellum Loudoun and throughout Virginia offers compelling evidence that many slaves did not have a nuclear structure or "core" in their families. There also is very little evidence which suggests that a nuclear family was the slave's sociocultural ideal. Virginia slave families, while demonstrating much diversity in form, essentially were not nuclear and did not derive from long-term, monogamous marriages. The most discernible ideal for their principal kinship organization was a malleable extended family that, when possible, provided its members with nurture, education, socialization, material support, and recreation in the face of the potential social chaos that the slaveholder imposed. Matrifocality, polygamy, single parents, abroad spouses, one-, two-, and three-generation households, all-male domestic residences of blood, marriage, and fictive kin, single- and mixed-gender sibling dwellings—these, along with monogamous marriages and co-residential nuclear families, all comprised the familial experiences of Virginia slaves like James Monroe's Daniel. Beneath this overwhelming record of diversity, however, the extended slave family remained the consistent norm and the most identifiable ideal.

Even when the physical basis for a nuclear family among slaves—the presence of a husband, wife, and their children—existed, as it did for a significant minority, this type of family did not function as it did for free people, whether blacks in precolonial Africa or whites in the American South. Slave family life, in particular, differed radically from those of local whites of every ethnicity or class. There were both institutional and customary bases for these differences. Virginia law, for example, did not recognize, promote, or protect the nuclear slave family or slave patriarchy. In fact, the only legal guideline for slave families did much to undermine these concepts—it determined that black children should take the status of their mothers, and in so doing, the law inadvertently defined slave families as matrilineal and matrifocal. Custom seemed to follow the direction of the law: neither white nor black society demanded that slave men provide the sole or most significant means of financial support for their wives and children. And since "husbands" had no legal claim to their families, they could not legitimately command their economic resources or offer them protection from abuse or exploitation.

The primary role of the slave woman within her family, while more predictable and "stable" than that of the slave man, also was uniquely different from that of free women. She never was able to give the needs of her husband and children great attention, much less first priority. Even though most slave children were part of matrifocal families, the slave woman's most important duty was the labor she performed for her master, not her family. This responsibility claimed so much of her time and energy that childbearing was limited, while childrearing necessarily was a task she shared with a number of other females.

Slave marriages, even monogamous ones, rarely were uncompromised. While slave couples committed to monogamy may have been devoted to one another and able to sustain feelings of love and respect over time, feelings sufficient to lead them to marry legally after emancipation, many did not have the opportunity to express their feelings for more than a few years while enslaved. Across time and space, the frequent and indiscriminate separation of slave spouses, temporarily and permanently, denied them the opportunity to live together, to share the responsibilities of their households and children, and to provide each other with sociosexual outlets.

Free people of color, by law and custom, had more control of their family lives and greater domestic stability than slaves. Their free status guaranteed them at least the possibility of "traditional" monogamous marriages, nuclear families, and other functional familial structures. Their race and its stigma, nonetheless, had incredible impact on every aspect of their communities, and especially their family life.

The growing uneasiness of Loudoun whites to the free black presence was unmistakable. At least by the beginning of the eighteenth century, freedom was conceived as the general condition of whites; slavery as the status of blacks. Only when one understands this kind of brutal social rejection and cultural alienation can one begin to comprehend the difficulties of southern free black family life and community development. How, indeed, does one legitimate the right to exist in a society whose fundamental premises deny one that very right? Ask any Loudoun free black and the answer undoubtedly would include words like "carefully," "secretively," "quietly," and, of course, "tentatively."

Even this kind of ployed invisibility was not enough. The county's racial hierarchy placed the free person of color outside sanctioned boundaries of southern society. Free blacks, even more than slaves, were social pariahs. There seemed to be no limit to the kind of fear, suspicion, and even repulsion that their presence bred. Free people of color's intimate associations with slaves and their political and economic ties with local Quaker activists fueled whites' determination to rid their society completely of their "menace."[6]

Slaves, therefore, were not the only Loudoun blacks displaced. More than a few free blacks responded to white hostility by relocating to the west and north of Virginia. Some went to New York, Ohio, Michigan, Canada, and even Liberia. Often they sought the resources and opportunities of large urban centers like the District of Columbia, Baltimore, and Philadelphia. Unlike slaves, however, most free people of color did not travel alone. Having realized the inestimable value of family and friends, they usually emigrated in family groups and sought out extended kin and friend networks in their new homes.

Yet most chose to remain in Loudoun. The families and communities that they created there, as compromised as they were, still were the backbone of their survival, and what progress they could claim, individually and collectively, usually flowed from the domestic group, not the individual. They were able to progress in some important ways, increasing in size, for example, from a minuscule 333 in 1800 to more than 1200 in 1860.[7] Their growth, in turn, fostered a clustering of homesteads and strong communities that provided various economic, educational, social, and leadership resources. They created core communities in the economically vital towns of Middleburg, Hamilton, and Snickersville, and particularly in the Quaker strongholds of Waterford and Hillsborough, where a variety of job opportunities for skilled and day laborers, domestics and washerwomen existed. Few lived in Leesburg, the center of county slaveholding, because of consistent hostility to their presence. Their communities, culturally diverse repositories of ex-slaves, free-born blacks, mulattos, and their families, had intricate social, cultural, and private ties to those of other local people, creating an expansive, supportive network of free and slave, black and white.[8]

But neither the size of the free black population nor their resources were ever substantial enough to challenge effectively the racist southern patriarchy and oppressive conditions it imposed on their lives. Unlike county slaves who represented as much as 30 percent of the county's population at one time, free people of color remained a tiny, mostly impoverished minority, barely one-fourth the size of Loudoun's slave population.[9] All demographic, economic, social and legal indices pointed to their unenviable "middle" status.

Free black families and households exhibited both differences and similarities to those of southern whites and slaves. The majority were smaller than those of county whites, usually by three or four persons. This was for a number of reasons, but especially the larger number of children that white women bore; the greater likelihood that European American households in the South would include, in addition to family members, slaves, servants, and employees; and because free black households did not include, on the other hand, a substantial number of family members who customarily lived with their employers. Most free people of color, like whites, but unlike slaves, had male household heads. Relatedly, most free black children lived with both their parents. Yet, like many slave families, extended kin networks were vitally important to Loudoun's free people of color because they provided supplemental sources of financial and emotional support.

Free black extended families especially provided significant resources for the growing number of female-headed households and matrifocal families within their communities. Unfortunately, these free women of color, who became increasingly responsible for free black families and children, were the poorest and least powerful of the group. Since very few black women owned property of any kind or had the skills or opportunities to succeed financially, they were, by all measures, financially inferior to free black males. Accordingly, their households were far less stable.

Local free blacks, also like slaves, had a high incidence of intergenerational and multi-surnamed members in their households. These phenomena too were important survival mechanisms for impoverished and embattled free men and women. Like their white and slave neighbors, therefore, free African Americans clung to their families as the symbols, sources, and measures of their survival in the American South.[10]

Taken all together, free and enslaved blacks never constituted more than a third of Loudoun's population; but they were a significant force in the county's society, economy, and history. Thomas R. Dew's eloquent antebellum hyperbole held both sway and significance in the piedmont county: "It is, in truth, the slave labor in Virginia which gives value to her soil and her habitations." Eliminate slavery and "on the day in which it shall be accomplished, . . . the Old Dominion will be a '"waste howling wilderness.'" Blacks, especially slaves, were the most important agricultural laborers in Loudoun's agriculturally driven economy. Probably few of Loudoun's residents felt as keenly the economic necessity of black labor as Professor Dew exclaimed. But county slave masters and renters or employers of free people of color would not deny the importance of this labor to either their livelihood or their accustomed way of life.[11]

While the advantages of black labor were obvious to and extolled by many, others were less than complimentary. Early social commentators on southern life complained that the presence of the African slave made blacks "insolent" and "mischievous," and whites "idle" and "proud" beyond worth. Proslavery ideology encompassed this strained dichotomy which posited blacks as inferior and useless on the one hand and absolutely necessary for the South's financial well-being on the other. (Recall, for example, James Monroe's description of his errant slave man Daniel: in Monroe's eyes he was both "worthless" and valuable property.) As this ideology came to dominate regional, state, and local thought, it affected both black and white life tremendously.

The presence of slaves and free people of color unmistakably created social and political divisiveness among local whites. Since proslavery ideology came to define the mainstream, those whites who did not espouse it became outsiders in the European American community. County historians rightfully credit the institution of slavery as the most divisive phenomenon to affect county cohesiveness during the decades before the Civil War. It certainly divided the county during the war.[12] Yet the controversy surrounding slavery in Loudoun also was a symbol and product of the cultural and economic diversity of county whites, a diversity that even an entrenched racial hierarchy could not fully erase.

From the first years of settlement, class merged with cultural differences to form the roots of persistent white tension. Perhaps the most active dissenters were local Friends. Their resistance was real and provocative as they became more and more identified with a small radical group who openly agitated against slave ownership, supported free black colonization, and actively aided the local Underground Railroad.[13]

Blacks contributed to the growing tension about the slavery issue by mounting a formidable front of resistance. Little evidence suggests that the legal status which separated the slave from the free black divided their racial loyalties. While color, class, and perhaps sometimes culture could be divisive forces in the African American community, there is much evidence of their solidarity against racial oppression which they shared more and more over time. Many free people of color also were bound to local slaves through marriage and culture. Black solidarity translated into an active manipulation of white divisiveness and concerted efforts to forge alliances with those in the Quaker community who could help them. Local blacks, therefore, deliberately and continuously demanded a significant psychological price of those who threatened their families and communities. For them, the end to antebellum life was momentous, and one which they helped to shape, at least locally. When white Loudoun divided over the issue of secession and one faction formed the pro-Union Loudoun Rangers, free black men from the county went off to fight and serve with them.

The Nature of Loudoun Slavery

We went to work at sunrise, and quit work between sundown and dark. Some were sold from my master's farm, and many from the neighborhood. If a man did anything out of the way, he was more in danger of being sold than of being whipped. The slaves were always afraid of being sold South. . . .

George Johnson, Loudoun slave

African and creole blacks came to Loudoun with its first white settlers during the 1720s. At first there were only very few—in 1749, after almost thirty years of settlement, they numbered only about 4 percent of the general population. Yet their arrival, however minuscule, signified the beginning of plantation agriculture in one of the last frontiers of the colony's Northern Neck. Given the history of the early proprietors, and the first Europeans to purchase land in this area, it was no surprise that Africans and tobacco would come to play such a prominent role in Loudoun's eighteenth-century development. While governor of Virginia during the 1670s and 1680s, the Northern Neck's principal proprietor, Lord Thomas Culpeper, received numerous "instructions" from the "Lords of Trade and Plantations" to encourage settlers to patronize the Royal African Company, instructions which he enthusiastically endorsed. Unlike the blacks who came to reside in tidewater Virginia during the time of Governor Culpeper, however, those who came to the northern piedmont were overwhelmingly African in origin—a review of the ports of origins of slaves arriving by ship in the Loudoun vicinity between the years 1729 and 1760, for example, indicates that at least two-thirds came from Africa. Moreover, by the time these Africans began to arrive there was no longer any question as to their status—legally they were slaves.[1]

Although the exact locations in which slavers secured their black cargoes largely are unknown, as are the precise numbers of those who came, most scholars now believe that slaves arriving on the Virginia coast during the eighteenth century originated from a variety of African locations, in addition to the Caribbean and other mainland colonies. They traveled on ships whose manifests noted general places of origin such as "Gambia," "Guinea," the "Coast of Africa," "Old Calabar," and, to a lesser extent, Senegal, Madagascar, and the Gold Coast. These areas represented culturally and linguistically diverse ethnic groups inclusive of the Tiv, Kongo, Mandinga, Yoruba, Ibo, Fon, Ewe, Asante, Ibibio, Fula, Coromantee, and others. There also were Caribbean re-exports, mostly from Barbados, but also from Bermuda, Antigua, Jamaica, St. Christopher, and the Spanish West Indies. They too were of varied African ethnic origins. Domestic trade and planter relocation provided Loudoun with a few slaves from South Carolina, Pennsylvania, and New England. Some also came from Virginia's and Maryland's tidewater. These were a mixed group of unseasoned or "outlandish" Africans, seasoned or "new negroes," and creole blacks who already had begun to develop distinctive African American cultures before being forced to relocate to the Virginia piedmont.[2]

Slaves traveled up the Rappahanock and Potomac rivers by boat where they were sold, many by consignment, to wealthy planters like Robert Carter, John Tayloe, and Daniel McCarty, who then resold them to local farmers for a percentage of the buying price. Inspected, handled, and haggled over, sold, branded on their cheeks and legs and sometimes on their hands, then chained by their feet and wrists or necks, they walked overland through the dense forests to their new homes, the isolated farms and hamlets of the old Northern Neck grant. They mostly were young and male, although African women represented quite a significant portion of the international market by the time slaves began to arrive in Loudoun.[3] The small numbers of female slaves found through the middle of the eighteenth century, therefore, was due not only to the lack of availability, but also to the design of frontier masters who favored male laborers.

The Africans' experience as market "goods" in Virginia was not their first—they were handled similarly in Africa. Nor would it probably be their last, for some were sold repeatedly in the New World. Their status as "slave" also was not novel, at least not the title. Most blacks who came to be enslaved in the Americas were familiar with indigenous African slavery of one sort or another; some had been slaves in Africa. Certainly by the eighteenth century, when the transatlantic slave trade had been flourishing for several generations and across a vast expanse of western and central African, many knew of the possibility of permanent enslavement in a foreign country.[4]

While slave owners designed a general "seasoning" process for "outlandish" Africans aimed to teach them their "place" and function, the slave's response to this process varied tremendously. Even for those Africans who had the benefit of living with numerous other blacks, it was a process that could take anywhere from two years for a slave to master some occupational skills, to four years for an adult to fashion a minimally functional language, or an entire lifetime, perhaps generations, to influence subtle cultural attributes and psychological responses.[5]

"Seasoning" began before many ever reached Virginia—harsh lessons learned during the Middle Passage were not soon forgotten. The process was slow and painful, if not physically threatening. African cargoes seemed particularly susceptible to pneumonia and other pulmonary infections. "Outlandish" and seasoned Africans alike also suffered from a number of other serious illnesses including malaria, small pox, sickle cell anemia, typhus, worm infestation, whooping cough, dysentery, and a host of venereal and gynecological ailments. Exhaustive work routines, nutritionally deficient diets, insufficient clothing and shoes, and poor medical attention worsened their physical condition, particularly that of small children and childbearing-aged women. Despair and depression were additional deterrents to good health.[6]

Once Africans reached Loudoun, masters emphasized labor and discipline. One of their first tasks was to build living quarters. Not surprisingly, some were striking similar to pre-and early colonial west African domestic structures with thatched grass, cylindrical roofs, rounded walls, and hard mud floors. Instructed by white overseers, seasoned black drivers, or their owners, they soon began to do the agricultural work that brought immediate meaning to their slave status. They performed rudimentary field labor—clearing land, fencing it in, cultivating tobacco, wheat, oats, barley and other grains, preparing vegetable gardens, and raising livestock. But there was some time for recreation.

Dance and music—especially singing, drumming, and the use of string instruments like the fiddle—story telling, prayer and other religious ritual, gardening, hunting, and fishing provided some social and cultural context for their otherwise bleak and harsh lives. Nicholas Cresswell, a British visitor to the area during the 1770s, recorded something of slave life that he witnessed. One event was a "Negro Ball" that occurred on a tobacco plantation in May 1774. According to Cresswell, the dance occurred on Sunday, "the only day these poor creatures have to themselves," and consisted of "Dancing to the Banjo." The songs that they sung, Cresswell continued, were "very droll" because "they generally relate the usage they have received from their Masters or Mistresses in a very satirical stile [*sic*] and manner." He was much more critical of their dancing style—it is a "most violent exercise, but so irregular and grotesque. I am not able to describe it." The curious onlooker concluded that they "all appear to be exceedingly happy at these merrymakings"; "they seem as if they had forgot or were not sensible of their miserable condition."[7]

These slaves took what opportunity they had to enjoy themselves and their culture, to celebrate their lives and criticize those who held them captive. Fortunately they found cultural expressions similar enough (in superficial form) to those of their owners to be expressed publicly. But it was difficult for Africans to express more "foreign" aspects of their old lives. The life of Job Ben Solomon, on a tobacco plantation near Annapolis in 1730, was in some ways atypical because of his favored status. Yet it does reveal something important about the "outlandish" African's desire to retain his or her culture and the kind of common opposition he or she often faced, even from unlikely sources.[8]

Job's master first "put him to work in making Tobacco," but the slave man, who had been an Islamic scholar in his home, was not physically able to do this kind of work. His owner then assigned him to tending cattle, unsupervised work which allowed him time to pray. "Job would often leave the Cattle," his biographer noted, "and withdraw into the Woods to pray." Yet he could not conduct his prayers appropriately because "a white Boy frequently watched him, and whilst he was at his Devotion would mock him, and throw Dirt in his face." Frustrated by his cultural and linguistic alienation, Job ran away, "thinking he might possibly be taken up by some Master, who would use him better, or otherwise meet with some lucky Accident, to divert or abate his Grief." He was not alone in his "grief."[9]

Newly arrived Africans in Loudoun with names like Mima, Coombo, Winny, Mingo, Minah, Dakars, Quasheba, and Nanbossey struggled on a number of fronts, but especially to communicate and to comprehend their new lives. The immediate urge was to seek out members of their own ethnic groups or someone who spoke their native language. Those who were unable to do so spent years in silence before they were able to converse fluently in a creole language.[10] Colonial fugitive slave advertisements repeatedly emphasized their various stages of English language acquisition. "RAN away from the Subscriber's Quarter . . . Sambo . . . speaks English so as to be understood; . . . Aaron . . . , can't speak English [and] Berwick . . . can't speak English. . . . They are all new Negro's and went together; they have not been above 8 months in the Country" was a typical notice.[11]

While one cannot emphasize more the lack of community that the first arrivals must have sensed, runaway notices suggest some of the close bonds that some were able to create, particularly with members of their indigenous ethnic groups. They also suggest the kind of bonds they created with creole slaves whom they came to know. "Ran away from the Subscriber, . . . a short likely Madagascar, named Gruff; . . . being imported young speaks very good English" began one 1745 advertisement. Gruff, who was about twenty-six years old and a carpenter, escaped with Tom, "likewise a Madagascar," about thirty-five years old who also spoke "pretty good English" and was a sawyer by trade. Although long since removed from "Madagascar," Gruff and Tom probably formed an intimate relationship because of their common African ethnicity. But they did not travel alone. They took with them a teenage slave named

Spark whom they undoubtedly had come to know and trust. Spark was Virginia-born and had served as a "Waiting-man" on their plantation. His gender and status as a domestic probably had brought him in close contact with the other two men, who were skilled artisans. Since it was usual for single male slaves to reside together, it also is possible that the three shared housing. Perhaps Gruff and Tom, who were considerably older than Spark, developed some kind of paternal feelings for him. Certainly they had some kind of bond that, for them, extended both across generations and cultures. Whatever the basis for their relationship, it was a close one—close enough to share the life-threatening experience of escape.[12]

In some ways, Gruff, Tom, and Spark were fortunate—at least they had been able to establish some companionable, perhaps fictive, kinship ties with each other. So too was Roger, "born at Angola," who was about thirty years old when he ran away with Moll, his Virginia-born slave wife who, at the time of their escape, was "very big with child." The lack of opportunity to create social relationships and networks which might eventually become kin connections was one of the colonial slaves' most devastating experiences. Olaudah Equiano's recollection of his brief sojourn in eighteenth-century Virginia tells of the agony that other slaves without families must have suffered, as do the records of those fugitive slaves like Jumper, "a very Black Mandingo Negro Man," and Dick, "a whitish Mulatto Man Slave, . . . with the Letter R branded on his right Cheek," who sought new lives as free men alone. According to Equiano, it was not the labor which made his life miserable, but rather his utter loneliness and lack of companionship. Because he "had no person to speak to that [he] could understand," he found himself "constantly grieving and pining, and wishing for death rather than anything else."[13]

Slave men and boys probably were more successful at finding "companions," especially same-sex persons, than African women and girls. Their numbers were so small that the first African women in Loudoun no doubt felt keen isolation and loneliness. The owners' policy to not allow slave women to "night walk" only exacerbated the problem, severely limiting their opportunity to create expansive slave communities or cultural networks beyond their own quarters. Not surprisingly, few tried to escape. Who would they run away with? And to whom would they run? In the more than one thousand fugitive slave notices advertised in the *Virginia Gazette* during the period from 1730 to 1790, fewer than 10 percent were for women.[14]

Whatever the European, African, or creole cultural designs that emerged on the eighteenth-century Loudoun frontier, it is clear that men, and their perspectives, dominated them.[15] If the "outlandish" nature of African men must have appeared particularly foreign to white masters and vice versa, that of African women must have seemed even more so. The repression of African women's traditional lifestyles and rituals, therefore, was not just a matter of a slave

owner's desire to control his plantation's cultural environment. It also was because there were so few black women to promote and prolong their traditions.
Since much of their indigenous female cultures and activities were expressed
communally and cooperatively, there was little hope that they would be able to
maintain their distinctive ways of life as long as there were so few of them.[16]

This dynamic changed with population shifts. Bolstered by increasing numbers during the 1750s and '60s, black women influenced local work, social,
and domestic environments. African females, for example, probably were less
dismayed by the kind of agricultural labor they performed than some African males, for in many of their indigenous societies, farm work was women's
work. Many had grown up cultivating gardens, grains, and cotton and caring
for livestock, skills that they brought with them. Their production of domestic
wares, such as textiles, baskets, containers, and buttons, also was drawn on traditional knowledge. Along with African men, women helped to introduce
various West African foods such as millet, groundnut, beans, gourds, "congo"
peas, and yams and were instrumental in maintaining African-influenced religious beliefs, medicinal practices, clothing and hair styles, dancing, and work
songs. They especially were responsible for maintaining some semblance of the
rituals that defined their lives as women—solemnizing and celebrating the
birth and naming of their children, menstruation, courtship, marriage, and
death.[17]

Early syncretization probably weighed more heavily on the African side on
those Loudoun farms and districts where blacks outnumbered whites. Even if
owners had demanded that their slaves assimilate more, there was little that
whites or even creole blacks could do to impose their cultural choices on the
less obvious details of the Africans' indigenous cultures. Names and scarifica-
tion were overt signs of a multitude of more subtle traits that remained. Yet
most masters probably realized that the mere physical survival of their labor
force and a healthy profit were difficult enough to accomplish. Few could
afford to center their attention on cultural traits that did not directly affect the
productive work environment they wanted to maintain.[18]

Intense African acculturation probably continued through the third quarter
of the eighteenth century. It was only then, with the closing of the international
slave trade, that the number of native-born Africans began to subside. That decline, along with increased cultural contact with whites and creole slaves, signaled significant cultural change and a developing creolization shared by most
blacks. So too did the growing incidence of heterosexual marriages and the
consequent birth of a new generation of "African American" slaves.[19]

The early incidence of slave owner absenteeism in Loudoun also was important, not only because it affected the slaves' material, working, and living conditions, but also because it meant an acute absence of European cultural influence on some of Loudoun's most populous plantations. Those slaves in such

quarters resided in physically and culturally isolated environments that probably were more conducive to the reinforcement of common indigenous cultural traits than later generations would experience. All in all, 52 percent of Loudoun's slaves in 1760 lived in quarters with absentee owners; one-seventh of their overseers were black. While the rate of absenteeism had dwindled by about half by the time of the next tithable list, some of the county's largest slaveholdings still had absentee owners.[20]

When a cadre of previously absentee slaveholders finally moved to Loudoun during the last decades of the eighteenth century, the cultural impact was significant. They brought along their kin, indentured servants, artisans, professionals, and tutors, encouraging a growth in both white population density and European-American cultural influence, and also some urban development. Their entourage also included domestic slaves, the most assimilated of the black labor force and the most likely to promote the adoption of creole culture.[21] Their developmental influence in Loudoun slave communities derived not just from their status as domestics, but also because of their gender—many were female and potential marriage partners.

There were few colonial slaveholdings large enough to generate many functional black families or expansive slave communities. In 1749, 138 slaves comprised only 4 percent of the locale's population and were present in only 12 percent of Loudoun households. The majority of slave masters at midcentury owned fewer than ten slaves; only three had more than 15 and no one owned 20 or more. Yet there was some numerical basis at least with which slaves could initiate community—the majority of first blacks did live on farms with at least ten other slaves.[22] (See Table 4.)

When compared with the characteristics of the slave population of other late colonial tidewater and piedmont Virginia counties, however, Loudoun's slave community was numerically thin. Slaves made up at least 30 percent and often 50 or 60 percent of the population in most colonial Virginia locales. Only Loudoun, Bedford, and Pittsylvania counties had fewer. This demographic characteristic, in turn, may have meant that Loudoun had a lesser African cultural impact than other parts of eighteenth-century Virginia; this despite the "clustering" of county slaves in moderate-sized holdings. It also suggests a greater need among Loudoun blacks to establish wide social and cultural networks with slaves in surrounding, more densely black populated, areas.[23]

Early patterns of Loudoun slaveholding persisted and actually intensified as the slave population increased, allowing further speculation about slave acculturation and community formation. By 1760, slaves made up 29 percent of local residents, still lived mostly in holdings of ten or more, and many had absentee owners. Likewise, a small elite continued to control local slave property—35 percent of slaveholders owned 52 percent of all Loudoun slaves in 1760. And a substantial minority of blacks lived on large holdings—25 percent lived on

Table 4   Slaveholding Patterns in Colonial Loudoun[a]

Slaveholding size	1749		1760	
	Number of owners	Number of slaves	Number of holdings[b]	Number of slaves
1–5	6 (37.5%)	24 (17.4%)	73 (55.3%)	244 (22.6%)
6–10	5 (31.25%)	36 (26.1%)	35 (26.5%)	286 (28.8%)
11–15	2 (12.5%)	26 (18.8%)	9 (6.8%)	112 (11.3%)
15–20	3 (18.75%)	52 (37.7%)	8 (6.2%)	134 (13.5%)
20–30	0	–	3 (2.3%)	84 (8.5%)
30–40	0	–	3 (2.3%)	100 (10.1%)
40+	0	–	1 (0.8%)	52 (.75%)

[a] Donald Sweig, "Northern Virginia Slavery: A Statistical and Demographic Investigation," (Ph.D. dissertation, College of William and Mary, 1982), 32, 43.

[b] "Number of Holdings" refers to the actual size of the number of slaves located on a particular agricultural, industrial, or residential unit. It is not a measure of the number of slave owners since several of these persons had the total number of their slaves divided between more than one unit. Sweig, "Northern Virginia Slavery," 43.

farms with more than 20. (See Table 4.)[24] Resident slaveholders continued to own much smaller numbers of blacks than absentee planters. Fully 94 percent of residential slaveholders, for example, held 84 percent of their slaves on farms with fewer than 10 slaves present; no one in this cohort had more than 15 slaves. Absentee owners also persistently employed black overseers, while most local slaveholders did not. Five farms belonging to three absentee owners with a collective slave population of more than 50 persons all had black overseers. These tobacco planters, all members of the powerful Carter clan—Robert Carter, Landon Carter, and Carter Burwell—were some of the colony's wealthiest and most influential men.[25]

One would expect that slaves who lived and worked among large numbers of other blacks, such as the 26 on Thomson Mason's "Raspberry Plain" estate, might have developed a culture distinctive from those on smaller holdings where the ratio of whites to blacks favored the former. This was true to a certain extent. Slaves in smaller quarters, however, also had contact with larger local slave communities and with blacks in neighboring counties. Slaves in Fairfax County, for example, made up almost 60 percent of the population. Since those sections of Loudoun with the most dense slave population bordered on Fairfax County, and some slaveholders, such as William Fitzhugh and Robert Carter, owned and operated farms in both counties simultaneously, it is certain that Loudoun and Fairfax slaves were able to interact with one another frequently. Both fugitive slave notices and travelers' accounts attest to a sprawling comradeship, if not kinship, among Loudoun area slaves and also with those who lived further away.[26]

When Henry Lee composed his 1769 notice for his fugitive slave Tom Salter, for example, he was careful to include a detailed description of the man's relations and their locations. According to Lee, an absentee owner living in Prince William, Tom had worked several years as an under "overseer" on his Richmond County plantation before he transferred him to his Loudoun property. Thirty-eight-year-old Tom was a man of many skills—he was literate, a fiddler, and, generally speaking, an "artful," pleasant fellow. He also was husband to Sebra, a woman who lived in Hanover County. Given Tom's many social ties throughout the colony, Lee was not certain where the runaway might be found, but he thought he might be located in one of the four counties he frequented—a distance of some eighty miles between extreme points.[27]

Tom Salter had inordinate skills and privileges for a slave man of his generation. Henry Lee allowed him to travel long distances, which gave him the opportunity to form a broad social and kin community. Most Loudoun slaves were not as fortunate. Yet those who lived in Cameron Parish certainly had much more of an opportunity to build slave communities than those few blacks who lived in Shelburne Parish. Shelburne, located in the county's northern and western regions, was densely populated by Quakers and Germans, and there were few slaveholders. In the German districts, less than 3 percent had slaves in their households, and those households had very few. There were, however, some larger Shelburne holdings which probably attracted slaves from smaller quarters. Slaves also could work and socialize with nearby kin. But it still must have been difficult, given the general paucity, for blacks in Shelburne to form effective communities.[28]

Once Loudoun's slave population reached a substantial size and density, a vibrant slave social network developed. Interplantation marriages became especially important. Females comprised 40 percent of Loudoun's adult slave population by 1760. With a male/female ratio of 1.46 to 1, there finally was some opportunity for substantial numbers to marry and begin to have children. Yet some planters still favored male slave laborers, particularly on their frontier farms (and much of Loudoun was still frontier at that time). They purposefully kept their quarters overwhelmingly male. Thomson Mason, Loudoun's largest slaveholder in 1760, for example, held 23 adult males but only three females on his estate that year.[29]

Fortunately, Mason purchased or transferred a number of slave women to his Loudoun property over the next few years. He only purchased "Raspberry Plain" in 1760 and was just beginning to amass his labor force there when the population census for that year was taken. His initial group of laborers was weighted toward men because of the need to clear land, create new fields, and construct plantation buildings—work usually done by slave men, not women. But by 1771, he was staying on his Loudoun land; his slaves had cleared and cultivated several fields and had just finished the construction of their master's new house. It is no wonder then that there were many more women living on the estate and working as domestics and agriculturists when the census was taken that year. In fact, the slave women at "Raspberry Plain" then outnumbered the men 1.27 to 1, an unusual statistic for county holdings even at that late date.[30]

Clearly by the eve of the American Revolution, therefore, it was not rare for Loudoun masters to own several slave women domestics and farm workers. Most slaveholders of more than two or three slaves owned at least one woman. Benjamin Edwards, for example, had six adult slaves—Joseph, Tom, George, Joan, Sarah, and Letty. John Lewis quartered four slaves—Jonas, Dublin, Phillis, and Nan; as did John Harryford—Joe, Judy, Cloe, and Moses. There were even a few holdings with just women. James Leith, for example, had only Esther, Hannah, and Luce on his farm, probably all field workers. Those who owned only one or two slave women often used them both in the field and as domestics, and sometimes as concubines or breeding women.[31]

The gradual increase in the number of childbearing slave women had tremendous effect on the slave population's growth. By 1800, there were 6,078 county slaves, the largest number that there would ever be. The increase is even more dramatic when one considers that a substantial portion of Loudoun's slave population (perhaps as much as 20 percent) officially became residents of Fairfax County in 1798 as a result of annexation of part of Loudoun's heaviest slaveholding district. Coincidentally, the increase in the number of slaves occurred as the local domestic slave trade also was becoming important.[32]

Slaveholders in the Upper South always had participated in the domestic slave trade, but the sale of blacks to the Lower South and Southwest was a vital factor affecting Loudoun slavery in the post-Revolutionary and antebellum eras. Four considerations stimulated the trade's growth: the invention and widespread marketing of the short-staple cotton gin, the availability of land in southwestern territories for cotton production, the shift in the Upper South from tobacco culture to large-scale grain production, and the official closing of the international slave trade.[33]

By the turn of the nineteenth century, tobacco production had lost prominence in Virginia's northern piedmont counties. While farmers continued to grow some tobacco, more and more began to focus on the less labor intensive cultivation of marketable grains. This shift occurred against a backdrop of increased slave population through purchase and natural increase. The region also had sustained a significant decline in soil fertility which made it continuously difficult to produce good grades of tobacco. The leap in the size of the slave population coupled with change and decline in the agricultural sector prompted some Loudouners to believe that there was an "excess" of slaves in their society. For those who had switched from tobacco to grain production, the belief was correct. Some consolidated their slave holdings, selling their "surplus." Others took advantage of lenient, late eighteenth-century manumission laws and freed many. Numerous others migrated to more fertile and less expensive lands to the South and West, taking their slaves with them.[34]

The impact of the forced migration of county blacks was felt almost immediately. The numbers of slaves dropped drastically, while white and free black populations increased. Between 1800 and 1810, Loudoun lost more than 1000 slaves primarily through the domestic slave trade. And this was only the beginning.[35] The number exported did decline slightly after 1840, as a result of improved economic conditions and an increase in the white population. Many who might have sold their "excess" slaves in previous decades now rented large numbers to new, small-, and moderate-sized farmers who did not want to invest in lifetime slave ownership. Still Loudoun's slave exportation business never came to a standstill and by 1850, rates were on the rise again. Approximately 1300, or about 19 percent, of the total slave population left the county between 1850 and 1860.[36]

Area newspapers documented the almost daily movement of southernbound slave treks. "A drove of negroes consisting of about one hundred . . . unhappy wretches that included men, women and children pass[ed] through Leesburg on Saturday on their way to a 'southern destination,'" the *Genius of Liberty* reported on September 4, 1821. A local slave named Frank Bell vividly remembered seeing his Uncle Moses "standing there chained up with 40 or 50 other slaves what had been sold along with him" on his way to Mobile, Alabama in the 1850s.[37]

Predictably, changes in the local economy and acceleration of the domestic slave trade eventually fostered some shifts in slave ownership patterns. Having reached a peak in the number of county slaves and slaveholders in 1800, both indices declined rapidly and almost proportionately over the next several years. In 1820, for example, 41 percent of Loudoun's households reportedly included slaves, but by 1850 only 28 percent did. Ten years later, the number of slave-inclusive households had declined to almost half of what it had been forty years earlier.[38]

The size of slaveholdings also changed. Most notably, the proportion of Loudoun slaveholders with a moderate number of slaves (10 to 20) increased over time. Escalating land and slave prices no doubt caused small owners to lose out to those who had more substantial financial resources. Instead of trying to purchase land and slaves, some migrated to less competitive areas of the country while others stayed and rented both resources. In 1820, some 89 percent of Loudoun's slaveowners had small holdings, that is, fewer than 10 slaves. By 1850, only 81 percent fell into that category; and only 77 percent the following decade. At the same time that the number of small holdings was declining, the number of Loudoun slave masters who owned 10 to 20 slaves was increasing. They made up only 7 percent of slaveholders in 1820, but had increased to 15 percent in 1850 and 17 percent in 1860. Likewise, but less dramatically, those

Table 5   Distribution of Moderate and Large Slaveholdings
Among Antebellum Loudoun Households

Slaveholding size	Number of households		
	1810[a]	1830[b]	1850[c]
10–15	48	52	94
15–20	25	20	30
20–30	17	14	24
30–40	7	6	9
40–50	3	0	3
50+	1	2	2

[a] U.S. Department of Commerce, Bureau of the Census, Manuscript Federal Census, 1810, Loudoun County, Virginia, Microfilm Roll 69. The largest slaveholdings that census year belonged to Wilson Seldon (52); Aris Buckner (46); Israel Lacey (42); Samuel Clapham (40); and Bayley Powell (37).

[b] Ibid., 1830, roll 1193. The largest slaveholdings that census year belonged to James Monroe (70); George Carter (61); Landon Carter (37); Reuben Hutchinson (35) and Frances Armistead (35).

[c] Ibid., 1850 Slave Schedule, roll 989. The largest slaveholdings that census year belonged to: Elizabeth Carter (85); Lewis Berkley (58); John P. Dulany (42); Robert Moffitt (45) and George Rust (40).

who owned 20 or more slaves increased—from approximately 3 percent in 1820 to almost 5 percent in 1860. (See Table 5.) Despite these shifts, however, many slaves consistently belonged to men and women who owned larger numbers of blacks: 46 percent of Loudoun slaves were part of holdings of 10 or more slaves in 1820; 45 percent in 1850.[39]

A generation earlier, planters like Robert Carter had controlled many of the African slaves who arrived on Virginia's wharves. The advent of the domestic slave trade as the only supply of slave labor, however, witnessed the rise of professional traders, local and long-distance, who dominated the marketplace. Out-of-state slave traders provided rising competition for local buyers and eventually came to monopolize the business. Loudoun residents, even planters, increasingly had to settle for the "leftovers." Sometimes local gentry authorized their overseers to buy slaves, and it usually was possible to orchestrate a few "swaps" with kin, close friends, and business associates. Most, however, relied on factors who had regular contact with local slave traders, sheriffs, and planters. As George Carter's business and legal advisor, for example, George Whitlock often purchased slaves for him. Carter did not give specific instructions often but, like most of his peers, preferred to buy young males. Their popularity meant exorbitant prices. "We have not met with any Negro boys," Whitlock reported in 1804. "Those are the most difficult of their kind to purchase and it is not certain we shall be able to buy such as you want unless at high prices."[40]

Prospective slaveholders of more modest means had little recourse but to rely on their own wits and personal contacts. They searched local newspapers, contacted area slave dealers, relied on word of mouth, checked for estate sales, attended the usual auctions held in Leesburg on court days, and inquired of sheriffs and constables when fugitive slaves would be sold. Sheriff sales meant bargain prices that even the rich could not resist. Frustrated with his attempts to build his labor force at "Oatlands," George Carter, for example, was beginning to acquiesce to locally inflated prices when his factor advised that he wait. "I think you ought not to be in haste to buy," he warned. "Certainly one may meet with some [slaves] at sh[eri]ffs sales by and by on better terms. . . ."[41]

Professional slave trading eventually became quite a prominent, but not very respectable, occupation. It was one thing for wealthy planters to sell "outlandish" Africans straight off the boat to "civilizing" masters in the eighteenth century; it was quite another to sell "family members" and generations-old acquaintances to the unknown "horrors" of the antebellum Deep South. Despite the stigma, however, several men served the Loudoun area. Charles P. McCabe, William B. Noland, J. M. Saunders, and John Avis were among the best-known, but usually handled short-distance exchanges. Long-distance traders to places like Charleston, Mobile, and New Orleans included local entrepreneur George Kephart, R. C. Ballad of Richmond, James Purvis of Baltimore, Thomas Jones from Easton, Maryland, Alexander Grigsby of Centreville, and especially James Franklin, William Swann, and Joe Bruin of Alexandria. Bruin employed William Noland as his Loudoun agent.[42]

Area newspapers were valuable resources for those who wanted to buy or sell. Readers found weekly advertisements for upcoming slave sales on the last two pages of the *Loudoun Chronicle* and the *Washingtonian*. Notices varied in format and content, but usually included the physical and occupational traits of the slaves to be sold and the location, date, and time of the auction. Some were less informative, including only minimal information. "I will sell to the highest bidder . . . , at public auction on Monday 11 of March next Two Negro Men, Belonging to the estate of Hugh Lacey, dec'd. The said Negroes are now in jail in Leesburg, where the sale will take place," read an ad in the *Loudoun Chronicle* in March 1850. Slave merchants who ran a high volume business and were invested in the long-distance trade also ran local advertisements. P. C. Hansbrough, for one, solicited in the *Washingtonian* in 1836: "The highest cash prices will be given for 30 or 40 LIKELY NEGROES of both sexes, from 12 to 30 years of age," he promised Loudoun masters. "Apply to the subscriber at Sinclair's Hotel."[43]

Slavemasters accepted all kinds of payment, but preferred cash. Burr Harrison, for one, demanded that traders offer fair prices and pay in cash or on "very well secured" credit. Others were more flexible, particularly if the sale was local or within one's family. When Simon Shover and Christian Sanbower sold the slaves of a deceased relative, for example, they allowed their buyers six months' credit if they gave "bonds with goods and approved security and [agreed] not to take the slaves out of the state of Virginia."[44]

The beginning of the year was the time of heaviest trading. "On New Year's day we all were scared, that was the time for selling, buying and trading slaves. We did not know who was to go or come," recalled one ex-slave from the area. Traders and owners alike sold slaves privately and publicly, securing them in the county jail until the auction. It was there that prospective buyers came personally to inspect those for sale, for few trusted slave traders or owners to give an honest assessment of a slave's health, skills, or character. Health was such a serious concern for most that some even brought physicians to examine the slave before bidding. When Robert Conrad told his wife that she could buy a female domestic, for example, he cautioned her to have their family doctor examine the slave before she purchased her. If the woman proved to be in ill health, he stated emphatically, he would "not have her for nothing." "Do not give up your efforts to fix yourself comfortably in this respect," he wrote, "but be very cautious not to have a sickly negro put upon you. I suspect Graham, and believe it very much the practice to trade off such negroes without scruple as in [the] case of horses." A few years earlier when his brother Holmes was "much annoyed for want of servants," Conrad inquired into the matter, and finding what seemed to be an acceptable candidate he promised to see her himself in order to verify the slave's good health.[45]

Most buyers also wanted to know why owners were selling certain slaves, hoping to avoid those who were infertile, rebellious, or lazy. Other than financial reasons, masters most readily sold slaves as punishment or a means of control. "Boys git to cuttin' up on Sundays an' [dis]turbin' ole Marsa," one ex-slave explained. "[He] come . . . down to the quarters. Pick out de fam'ly dat got de most chillun an' say, "Fo' God, nigger, I'm goin' to sell all dem chillun o' your'n lessen you keep 'em quiet.' Dat threat was worsen prospects of alickin'. Ev'ybody sho' keep quiet arter dat." Just as this master threatened, many actually sold blacks whom they believed were guilty of any number of offenses, particularly those who threatened their owners' authority, economic well-being, or plantation discipline. John Fallons, for instance, sold his black driver because of his escape attempts. William Powell sold one of his female domestics because she repeatedly stole from him. His father, Burr Powell, counseled a son-in-law to sell any of his slaves who proved to be "troublesome." George Carter's agent advised him to sell the slave man Sam because he had temporarily escaped and returned with a "sore leg" and unable to work. "I think you ought to sell him," he wrote, "such conduct is [a] dreadful example." George Johnson's master sold a slave who killed an abusive overseer. For Johnson, who grew up in Loudoun near Harpers Ferry, slave sales were ordinary, but fearful, events. "Some were sold from my master's farm, and many from the neighborhood," he explained. "The Southern masters were believed to be much worse than those about us."[46]

Slaves' prices varied according to their age, sex, health, skill, and, for women, their sexual attractiveness and fertility. Young, healthy adolescent and adult males cost between $250 and $450 in the early nineteenth century. William Forbes, another agent working for George Carter, for example, wrote to him in April 1805 that he had "got a valuable negroe fellow" whom he purchased for £100. "His price was $400," Forbes explained, "which John would readily . . . [bring] as he is a very fine Boy—an expert servant. But the ready cash which Newton was much in want tempted him to take my offer for you." A month later, Forbes again wrote to the Loudoun planter, this time explaining that while males continued to be scarce, he had located another slave Carter might be particularly interested in—a "very likely" female slave "—*a virgin*— of about 14 or 15." Skilled male slaves—blacksmiths, carpenters, wheelwrights, and others—commanded the highest prices. Ordinary female, elderly, and young slaves cost considerably less.[47]

In 1817, local slave prices seem to have been only slightly higher than those in 1805: unskilled men cost about $450; single females brought $300; a woman with a small child usually cost approximately $400; and slave boys sold at $100 to $150 each. But these were Loudoun's depression era prices. The growing need for slave labor in the Lower South and Southwest and a gradual economic recovery locally increasingly inflated slave prices. In 1838, for example, Samuel DeButts bought a slave man with no specified skills for $600. Charles Lucas's Leesburg owner tried to sell the blacksmith and journeyman in 1841 for $1500. Prices remained high. By 1858, Loudouners who were selling slaves demanded, and received, $1500 for a blacksmith, $1,590 for a woman and her two small children, and $1,350 for a prime male field worker. Throughout, male slaves generally cost more than females, skilled laborers more than field hands, and the young more than the elderly.[48]

Only "fancy" women commanded higher prices than skilled male slaves. "Marie was pretty, dat's why he took her to Richmond to sell her. You see, you could git a powerful lot of money in dose days for a pretty gal," Carol Anna Randall explained of her sister's sale to the Carolinas. Joe Bruin of the Alexandria firm of Bruin and Hill placed Emily Russell, a beautiful mulatto whom he planned to sell as a prostitute in New Orleans, on the market for $1800. Bruin and Hill realized the profit that could be garnered from the "fancy girl" market and often purchased females in Virginia and Maryland for that purpose. What, after all, could be more valuable than a woman of "white" complexion who could be bought as one's private "sex slave"? James Pennington explained: "It is under the mildest form of slavery, as it exists in Maryland, Virginia and Kentucky, that the finest specimens of coloured females are reared. . . . for the express purpose of supplying the market [to] a class of economical Louisia [sic] and Mississippi gentlemen, who do not wish to incur the expense of rearing legitimate families, they are, nevertheless, on account of their attractions, exposed to the most shameful degradation." Pennington went on to illustrate his claim by presenting the case of slaves Mary Jane and Emily Catherine Edmondson, ages fourteen and sixteen, of Alexandria, whom Bruin and Hill had acquired and offered to sell back to their father for $2,250. They charged such an exorbitant fee, Pennington claimed, because they had intended to sell them as prostitutes in the Deep South.[49]

Potential slaveholders viewed "white-skinned" male slaves somewhat differently. They found it difficult to reconcile their skin color and gender with their slave status. Some pitied them. Asked if he was a slave or not, James Smith responded that he was. "He said I was too white to be a slave," Smith explained further. "It is often the case that these rascals feel for their own blood—they will say to a man of my color, 'It's a pity you're a slave—you're too white to be a slave.'" Other masters found them difficult to be around, perhaps fearing they were more likely to run away or were more attractive to white women. Cornelius Scott, a slave of Henry Brooke, thought that his "fair complexion" was decidedly against him. Although only twenty-three years old and "quite stout," he believed he would sell for only $500 in 1857. It also is possible that traders sold mulatto or lighter complexion males in their teens as prostitutes.[50]

Despite the impact of the "fancy girl" market on the overall price of females, males still were the most valued slaves. The preference for young males was reflected in Loudoun's nineteenth-century slave population. In 1820, males comprised 52 percent of the county's slave population and outnumbered female slaves in every major age cohort except that of children aged zero to fourteen years. The male majority was especially obvious among "prime" slaves.[51] By 1850, women had assumed a slight majority, suggesting the devastating impact of the domestic slave trade on the male slave population and the growing fondness for "breeding women."[52]

While small slave holdings usually boasted a majority of adult females, there were more men than women on moderate- and large-sized plantations. John Carter, for example, master of 32 slaves in 1850, boasted a slave community in which men outnumbered women 2.5 to 1. His neighbor John Dulany owned 44 slaves that year. The men in his quarters whose ages ranged from fifteen to forty-five years made up 76 percent of their cohort. Overall, the male/female ratio for Loudoun slaves of that age group in holdings of 10 or more slaves was 1.6 to 1; in holdings of smaller size, women outnumbered men by more than 2 to 1. Perhaps in an attempt to promote natural procreation, some of Loudoun's largest slaveholders had an almost identical number of male and female slaves within child-bearing cohorts. Elizabeth Carter, widow to George, with 85 slaves at "Oatlands" in 1850, for example, was the county's largest slaveholder that year. Her slave property included 43 males and 42 females, and there was an equal number of men and women between the ages of fifteen and forty-five. Not surprisingly, a healthy minority, 26, were twelve years or younger, representing a new generation of Carter blacks.[53]

It is possible that the slave men and women at "Oatlands" not only produced a "crop" of new slave laborers for the Carters, but witnessed many of their children being sold. The growing demands of the domestic slave trade meant a gradual reduction in the ages of slaves in the market. While it is clear that it remained difficult for Loudoun masters to sell slaves who were past their "prime," it did become easier to sell slave children. Many realized that a slave child's chance of physical survival increased dramatically after he or she passed the age of ten years. This kind of reasoning, bolstered by the demographics of the slave population, provoked the eventual popularity of preadolescent slaves in the market.

Fully 45 percent of Virginia's antebellum slaves were younger than fifteen. Likewise, the large majority of Loudoun's slave population was not older than twenty-five. In 1830, for example, those Loudoun slaves aged below twenty-four years comprised 65 percent of the total slave population. Twenty years later, those aged fourteen and younger represented 47 percent, while slaves twenty-nine years and younger made up fully 75 percent of the county's unfree. These numbers are even more impressive when one considers that most of the thousands of slaves exported from Loudoun were not yet thirty years old at the time that they left.[54]

Owners of slave children usually could not sell them until they reached preadolescence. Potential buyers rightfully feared that the devastating mortality rates of younger slave children, conservatively estimated to have been between 40 and 45 percent, would rob them of any investment they placed in a child purchase. Many who did sell children sold them locally along with their mothers. An 1818 newspaper advertisement for the sale of a "family of Negroes, consisting of a woman and children," for example, stipulated that they were to be sold together, to a "good master" only, and not under any circumstances "to a southern trader." Thirty years later when prices were much better for slave youth, some masters still indicated a desire to sell in family units and to area residents. "A citizen of Loudoun offers for sale a Negro Woman about 27 years old, and her 2 children, one is 4 and the other is about 2 years old," a sale notice read. "She is a good house servant, healthy, honest, of good disposition, and sold without fault. He would prefer selling them in the county of Loudoun." A similar advertisement appeared the following year: "A valuable house servant with 3 healthy children, one male and two females. As they will not be sold for any fault," the owner explained, "it is desirable that the whole be held together, [and sold] to a resident purchaser." Others did not bother to make certain of their final destination. When Charles Peyton Lucas's Leesburg owner sold his brother, his sister, and her two children, for example, they all went to Georgia.[55]

The growing desire for younger slaves was obvious in the attitudes of both buyers and sellers. An interested subscriber advertised in 1829, for example, that he wanted to buy slaves aged between eight and twenty-four years old. Moreover, as the domestic slave trade became more demanding and young children began to command lucrative prices on their own, it became an acceptable practice to sell children and mothers individually. Burr Harrison of Leesburg, for example, wrote to his son Matthew in 1856 about the possible sale of several of his slaves that he "would let the small boys go too—But the prices must be fair." Harrison wanted "about 250 to 325 [dollars] each" for the boys. He stipulated that the buyers had "to live in the county or adjoining county" and "be good masters," but made no provision about selling them with any kin. Local slave Dan Josiah Lockhart confirmed that some slave children were sold without any kin. Recalling his first experience in the market, he noted that his master sold him when he was "five years of age." He did not remember meeting his mother "to know her" until he was an adult with a wife and child of his own.[56]

While youth was a priority for most, others preferred older slaves, especially for domestic service. "There is a woman to be sold at Griffin Taylor's this week between 35 and 40—whom Mrs. Taylor spoke highly of to me," Robert Conrad wrote to his brother in September 1831. The fact that the slave woman was already thirty-five probably pleased Conrad. He assumed that his brother did not want a domestic who might be susceptible to pregnancy-related illness or the cares of her own children. Some slaveholding parents also may have hesitated to buy young female house slaves who might prove sexually appealing to their sons. One ex-slave recalled, for example, the story of Rachel, a "beautiful girl about twenty-four" who was a domestic in her master's household about a year before "one of his sons became attached to her, for no honourable purposes; a fact which was not only well-known among all the slaves, but which became a source of unhappiness to his mothers and sisters." Eventually the owner sold Rachel. Slave masters also may have feared young male domestics might "seduce" their wives or daughters, preferring to retire "older" male slaves to domestic work and keep "prime" men in their fields. Others believed that even after a man passed his "prime," he still could be a good field worker. William Brown, a slave born and raised in the Loudoun vicinity, for example, explained that when his master decided to move to Missouri, his wife's owner offered to buy him for $220. "William is old, and his family are here; his work won't amount to much now," the would-be buyer reasoned. But Brown's master believed he could "get that out of him in Missouri in three years" and refused to sell the slave. William Brown's experience notwithstanding, age, as a general indicator of a slave's health and vitality, remained an important consideration for buyers and traders.[57]

As the antebellum era progressed, increasingly more Loudouners solved their labor problems through slave hiring rather than buying. Each January large numbers of slave owners rented out, usually for the entire year but sometimes for shorter periods, several hundred and sometimes more than one thousand slaves. J.E.S. Hough's advertisement in the *Loudoun Chronicle* was typical: "I have several very valuable SERVANT MEN for hire for the coming year. One is an excellent dining room servant, the rest are good farm hands. Those in want of good, steady and industrious servants, will do well to call early on this subscriber. . . ." The county also rented out slaves, sometimes opting to hire out the services of unclaimed runaways rather than sell them. "Ordered that Negro Jim, a Runaway slave now in the Jail of the County be hired by the Sheriff to the highest bidder for three months and that he be cloathed [sic] and garnished with a blanket and hat and shoes at the expense of the County," read a typical notice. Not surprisingly, local slave rentals increased over time as a thriving domestic slave trade inflated prices beyond the means of many would-be buyers. In 1860 alone, census records indicate that approximately 516 Loudoun residents hired the services of at least 1,037 slaves from local slaveholders. Those rented represented at least 34 percent of the county's adult slaves and almost one-fifth of the entire Loudoun slave population.[58]

A renter paid a hiring fee which could vary substantially. In 1843, Robert Conrad expected to rent out his slave Jesus for $60, John for $50, and Jasper for $20. Slave blacksmiths and other skilled personnel commanded as much as $100 annually, while female domestics usually brought $25 to $40 per year. Some paid in advance, while others paid quarterly or at the end of the year. Contracts stipulated that renters provide the slaves with adequate food, clothing, shelter, and sometimes medical attention. When Samuel Debutts hired a "Negro woman named Fanny" from Townsend McVeigh of Middleburg in January 1839, for example, he promised to pay McVeigh $35 for her services and to supply the slave with the following: "Three shirts, two summer habits, one pair of shoes for summer, one homemade Linsey frock, homemade shoes, stockings for winter, blanket of good size [and a] Bonnet."[59]

Some slaves lived well under the system. Charles Lucas, for example, was hired out in Leesburg as both a blacksmith and journeyman. "I worked out five or six years, and was well fed, well clothed, and well used. I enjoyed life then very well, and had many privileges," he later wrote of the experience. Still hirers had little incentive to protect property that did not belong to them and some worked and punished these slaves severely. Slave owners, wary of damage to their valuable property, often periodically investigated living and working conditions; others warned renters not to beat their property. "Ole Marser Fallons . . . . [always] told the white man who hired his slaves dat if dey didn't do right he was to bring them back an' he wuld handle them, but not to hit any of his property," a local ex-slave explained.[60]

Nancy Williams of nearby Yanceville detailed her abuse at the hands of her "po' white [to]bacy-chewin'" hirer. According to Williams, her renter expected her to do an overwhelming amount of domestic work. Her reminiscences are important not only because she documented her brutal treatment as a hired slave, but also because her statement indicates the kind of contempt that some slaves and planters had for poor whites. "Po white trash gimme dat bundle o' wuck to do!" she began. "Soon's I git to wuk dat baby start cryin'. I run to see what de matter. It was chokin' an' turnin' black all de time! . . . Said Ise de cause o' it. . . . Den dat devil took me an' carry me out do's de col'es' mo'nin in de year, cross my han's tied an' thowd me on de groun' an' whup me wid a leather paddle til I couldn' holler." Once untied, Williams escaped and returned home, anxious to inform her master of her mistreatment. She was delighted with her master's response: he refused to return her to the hirer, threatened to kill the man and embarrassed him in front of the other slaves by telling him to "Get home to yo' lazy wife an' nurse yo own baby. You shan have dis nigger no mo' neither de money for her."[61]

Despite these kinds of rifts in the system, slave rentals were an important boost to the local economy. There was, however, some opposition, particularly if slaves had the discretion to choose their own hirers. Virginia law dated 1805 prohibited "persons permitting their slaves to go at large and hire themselves out, under a promise of paying their masters or owners a certain sum of money in lieu of their services." Yet many openly disregarded it. Citizens in Warrenton organized to write in protest. The practice, "so very much in vogue in many of the towns and villages of the State, of letting slaves hire their own time through a master of their choice," they asserted, "is expressly contrary to law, ruinous to the negro as a slave, and at war with public polity." Their fear was that masters allowing some blacks to hire themselves out would lead to the envy and "dissatisfaction" of other slaves who were not allowed to do so. They also disliked the air of freedom the practice projected. "It is a species of negro emancipation, full and complete," the authors added, but even worse because those "favored" slaves had the privileges, but not the legal restrictions, of free blacks. They implored county authorities to "enforce the statute in such cases . . . to its utmost extent."[62]

Some hired slaves did live comparatively well, especially in urban settings. The infamous fugitive slave Anthony Burns, for example, who lived in Alexandria, had been hired out since a youngster. By the time Burns reached adulthood, he had learned how to manipulate the system in his favor—he was literate, had been trained as a minister, had acquired several other occupational skills, was able to pay his owner a nominal fee and keep the remainder of his earnings for himself. Eventually, he was sent to Richmond where he virtually lived on his own while supervising the labor of four of his master's slaves. This kind of "freedom" was precisely what some local whites resented and feared.

Burns's eventual escape to Boston and the fervor that developed over his recapture and trial were even further proof that a liberal hiring policy "ruined" slaves and fundamentally threatened the institution of slavery.[63]

The protest had little impact on the system, however, probably because slave hiring was lucrative and "easy" for masters and because it was much more widespread than even official records indicated. Not only did masters allow "favored" slaves to rent themselves out for long periods of time; some even let their slaves earn money by working for others on their days off. Field laborers, for example, occasionally worked for other farmers for pay, particularly during harvest time. One local slave, Silas Jackson, recalled that on Saturdays the slaves "were allowed to work for themselves." Overseers issued passes which stipulated their return "by 10:00 P.M. or when cabin inspection was made." "Sometimes we could earn as much as fifty cents a day—which we used to buy cakes, candies or clothes."[64]

Loudoun slaves earned money in other ways as well. Some received small amounts of cash or trading power from selling the corn and other crops that they grew in their assigned garden plots. William Gray of Loudoun's "Locust Hill" plantation annually paid his male slaves in cash and clothing for the corn that they grew and the work that they performed for him on their days off. In 1852, Gray noted in his farm book that he had paid the slave Sam "three dollars and in boots one dollar" for extra work that he did during the harvest season. William's corn brought him an unspecified amount of cash and a new pair of boots. Michael got $3.33 and Daniel made $4 for their crops, but George earned only fifty cents for his half-bushel of corn that year.[65]

The ability to earn some money, regardless of how meager the amount, was important to slaves. The receipt of cash income for their labor was a stimulant to the slaves' self-esteem and enabled them to help their families. A few even were able to save enough to purchase their freedom or finance a successful escape. Verlinda Perry reported in the *Loudoun Chronicle* in August 1849 that her slave Bill Lazenbury left with some "money in his possession" which he probably used to "buy new clothes to aid his escape." Forest Griffith, born a slave in the Quaker town of Hillsboro, eventually earned enough money to purchase himself and to become one of Loudoun's few free black property holders.[66]

Bill and Forest were the exceptions. Most had little "legal" opportunity to earn income. The experience of George Jackson was much more typical—he did both domestic and field work, but "never got any money" for it. Even skilled slaves found it difficult to retain any income for their own personal use or for their families. Local blacksmith Thomas Harper, for example, explained that although his skilled labor netted his owner in excess of $100 per year, he could not keep any of his earnings for himself.[67]

Most slaves, at least 90 percent in Loudoun, were field laborers. As a blacksmith and resident of Alexandria, therefore, Thomas Harper was part of a small elite force of skilled, urban slaves who had unusual privileges.[68] Loudoun's "town" slaves usually were domestics or skilled artisans of one kind or another, especially maids, laundresses, cooks, waiting men and women, gardeners and drivers. Women also worked as weavers, midwives, seamstresses; men in their masters' blacksmith shops, taverns, or hotels, or as carpenters, cobblers, bakers, coopers, boatmen, firemen, porters, tailors, printers, painters, fishers, millers, railroad men, and miners. Most domestic staffs were small, but in Loudoun's county seat a considerable number employed more than ten slaves in their homes.[69]

Field workers traditionally cleared and prepared land and grew, harvested, and readied for market crops like wheat, barley, corn, oats, rye, and some tobacco. They also raised livestock, took care of their masters' vegetable gardens and fruit orchards, and built and repaired fences and farm buildings. Their work was hard and often monotonous, their workdays were long, and their punishments for not meeting assigned work quotas could be brutal. Despite their commonality of experience, however, a slave's age, gender, and occupation could substantially differentiate their work experiences.

Most children began to work when they were about six or sometimes earlier depending on their size and physical maturity. Masters and overseers routinely enforced early gender distinctions. Boys learned how to herd sheep and cattle, while girls helped to take care of small children and worked in the kitchen. As adolescent males and females entered the adult world of "prime" slaves, some of this held. Yet owners rarely spared women from the exhausting field labor that unskilled males routinely performed unless they were specially assigned domestics or particularly talented sewers, weavers, or midwives. Future agricultural laborers began as children by picking up stones and trash. As they grew older, they began to help stack and bind wheat, pull weeds, worm tobacco, and carry water. Additional tasks included caring for livestock and picking fruit, nuts, and berries. Other slave children, delegated as the next generation of domestics, sometimes were companions to young masters and mistresses, but mostly assisted cooks, maids, and baby nurses. Dan Lockhart, reared near Loudoun, remembered that when he was five, his "business" was "to clean knives, forks, candlesticks, etc., until . . . say when I was twelve or thirteen."[70]

Childhood was a time when slaves began to learn not only work routines, but also work discipline and related punishment. Slaveholding women usually were in charge of chastising those slave children who worked in and around their homes. One ex-slave interviewed in 1841 stated that whenever his mistress did not like his work she would hit him with tongs or a shovel, pull his hair, pinch his ears "till they bled," or order him to sit in a corner and eat dry bread "till [he] almost choked." George Jackson recalled that his mistress "scold and beat" him when he was pulling weeds. "I pulled a cabbage 'stead of weed," he confessed. "She would jump me and beat me. I can remember cryin'. She told me she had to learn me to be careful. . . ." Leesburg's Charles Lucas spoke bitterly of his mistress who used to beat him "over the head with a dairy key about as big as a child's fist." Some owners could be even more vicious. An elderly Eliza Little explained that the scars on her arms, hands, and face resulted from her mistress hitting her with a broken plate and a blow from a stick of wood. Once, she added, the woman knocked her "lifeless." "Guess I was a girl 'bout five or six when I was put wid de other chillun pickin' de bugs off de terbaccy leaves," another Virginia ex-slave began. "Gal named Crissy . . . kep' whisperin' to me to pick em all off. Didn' pay no 'tention to her, any dat fell off I jus' let lay dere. Purty soon old Masser come long, dough, an' see dat I done been missin' some of dem terbaccy worms. Picked up a hand full of worms, he did, an' stuffed em inter my mouth. Lordy knows how many of dem shiny things I done swallered, but I sho' picked em off careful arter dat."[71]

One's physical coming of age meant more grueling labor. Most were full-time workers by the time they reached fourteen or fifteen; some even earlier. Henry Banks recalled: "When I was eight years old, I was put to work regularly on the farm, ploughing, hoeing corn and doing farm work generally." Silas Jackson explained that because he "was a large boy" for his age he began his task work at nine. "In Virginia where I was," he added, "they raised tobacco, wheat, corn and farm products. I have had a taste of all the work on the farm, besides . . . digging and clearing up new ground to increase the acreage to the farm." Jackson also described the intense labor schedule that overseers enforced and the beatings they received if they failed to comply: "The slaves were driven at top speed and whipped at the snap of the finger, by the overseers[.] [W]e had four overseers on the farm[;] all hired white men." Henry Banks concurred. "Let daybreak catch me in the house, instead of currying the horses, that was as good for a flogging as any thing else . . . the least of any thing would provoke it. I was whipped once because the overseer said I looked mad."[72]

Working slave children also soon realized that the reward for their labor was meager. Food and clothing allowances offer ample examples. Most masters broadly interpreted advice manuals on slave diet.[73] The staple for children was some bread item, usually hoe cake made from cornmeal that women mixed with milk to produce a "mush." Masters allowed older children to have small portions of meat, primarily pork. Some also let slave families raise their own vegetables and livestock. Silas Jackson remembered that each family was given garden land and raised chickens and that his owner rewarded each "man" who produced his own food $10 at Christmas time. Not all Loudoun slaves, however, had such privileges. George Jackson, for one, recalled that his master's slaves "did not own der own garden." According to him, slaves usually ate "fat pork, corn bread, black molasses and . . . milk" even though they technically could eat vegetables from "de big garden."[74]

Weekly food rations came on Saturday. Silas Jackson's owner allowed adult slaves ten pounds of corn meal, a quart of blackstrap molasses, six pounds of fat porkback, three pounds of flour and some vegetables, "all of which were raised on the farm." Slaves also fished and hunted rabbits and opossum. "These were our choice foods as we did not get anything special from the overseer," Silas added. Some local slaveowners also supplied fish, a high-protein source readily available in the nearby Potomac River. Burr Harrison, for one, was quite explicit about the inclusion of fish in his slaves' diet. One local slave recalled that he ate more herring than pork.[75]

Masters distributed slave clothing twice a year, during the late fall and early summer. Young girls and boys wore loose fitting shifts, or "shirt tails," that usually came down to their knees and were made of homespun cotton or wool or flax for the cold season. Virtually no slaves wore shoes in the summer and most slave children were without winter shoes until they began to work. Sometimes extremely cold winters did convince masters to shoe young slaves. In his December 1846 instructions for his slave property, for example, Burr Harrison mandated that "they all have shoes." Older working children wore the gender-distinctive clothing of adults—males wore pants and shirts; females had skirts and blouses or dresses. Winter adult clothing included shoes, coats, felt hats, and cotton handkerchiefs for women. Straw hats protected men from the summer sun. Undergarments were scarce, but some older girls and women made them out of discarded material, old sacks and cloth bags.[76]

Several factors impacted on the slave's material well-being. Owners' "pets" and children of domestics, skilled laborers, and free fathers usually ate and dressed better than others. Skilled weavers and seamstresses gathered scraps of thread and materials to make additional garments or remake old clothing for themselves and their families. Women used natural dyes to make brightly colored dresses for special occasions. Nancy Williams, for one, could boast that she had a number of pretty party dresses, including a "Junybug silk" dress that had three ruffles which she wore with tasseled slippers. Williams, a favorite of her owner, earned extra money by selling her handmade quilts to local whites for as much as $10 each. Her expertise as a seamstress and her imaginative skills as a designer kept her altering her dresses' designs and colors.[77]

Quilting and sewing were Nancy Williams's hobbies as a young, single woman—work that she did in her "leisure time"; but there was precious little of that. "We went to work at sunrise, and quit work between sundown and dark," one Loudoun ex-slave reported. All full and part "hands" had to complete a daily "task" or labor quota. They usually worked from very early in the morning until almost dark, from Monday through part of the day on Saturday. Austin Steward, born a slave near Loudoun in 1793, described the work schedule as grueling. "It was the rule for the slaves to rise and be ready for their task by sun-rise, on the blowing of a horn or conch-shell," Stewart recalled. They had approximately thirty minutes to get to the fields. A thirty-minute breakfast break came at about nine o'clock. Then they worked until noon, took a long dinner break (about one hour) and returned to work until sunset.[78]

Despite the general "sunrise to sunset" schedule, tobacco and wheat cultivation required very different timing and labor. Tobacco, the premier eighteenth-century "cash" crop in Loudoun, was a particularly labor-intensive, difficult plant to grow. The delicacy of its leaf, insect control, and the intricate technology needed to produce a good "grade" were substantial obstacles. Most tobacco farmers needed a minimum of nine to twelve prime hands.[79]

Every farm had to begin with cleared fields, a task masters usually assigned to slave men. A typical field was fifty acres and was in operation until infertile. Owners then let it lie fallow until it regained some fertility while slaves cleared other "new fields." Although some nineteenth-century tobacco farmers changed the way they rotated their fields and used guano, lime, and other fertilizers, tobacco cultivation techniques remained the same.[80]

First, they prepared seedlings in special beds during the late winter or early spring as they began to ready the fields for planting. Breaking the soil was backbreaking labor. "I useto [*sic*] help my brothers plow," former bondsman George White reported. "Two would get in front of de plow, one on each en' of de single tree an' pull while de others would get behind to hold de plow. We would break up all de land . . . this way." Some women also plowed. "When I got growd up an' start dis cou'tin' dey took me ouder de house an' put me in de fiel to wuck, jes' lak de men, plowin' an' doin'," Nancy Williams recalled. "Lawd, you outer seed me an' dat ole ox. He go slow so I jes' follow long [be]hin[d] him." After the spring rains, both men and women planted seedlings, each planting more than a thousand per day. Some owners insisted on the task system—every tobacco worker had to prepare, plant, and care for several rows of tobacco plants in specially marked sections of the field. Others divided laborers into gangs that were responsible for the care of a predetermined acreage. Nicholas Cresswell witnessed part of the process: "The Land is first hoed into small round hills about the size of Molehills and about 4000 of them in an acre . . . they only make a hole with their fingers or a small stick and put them in, one in each hill. Two Negroes will plant three acres in one day."[81]

Several weeks of planting, weeding, and replanting passed, followed by "topping" the upper portion of the stalk and pulling off suckers that inhibited the tobacco leaves' size. While prime workers were "topping" and "stalking," young, infirm, or elderly slaves were pulling horn worms. "I could generally find the tobacco worms by a hole through the leaf," William Johnson, a local slave, recalled. "But in the heat of the day, they get under a leaf and do not eat: and the hands passing along, breaking off suckers, don't always see them. . . . if [the overseer] finds the worm, the man is called back to kill it, and he gets five or six blows from the hickory or cow-hide." Everyone had to be careful not to damage leaves while pulling suckers, and some overseers even forced females to pull up their dresses so that their skirts would not get entangled in the plants.[82]

Slaves usually harvested tobacco in September. That meant that every available laborer, male and female, young and old, had to work long hours during some of the hottest weather of the year. One ex-slave remembered that during harvest they worked from before sunrise until late in the night and had to build bonfires to see what they were doing. They picked the mature leaves, strung them on sticks and hung them in tobacco barns for drying and curing for another several weeks. Slaves then packed the dried tobacco in wooden hogsheads for shipment to market.[83]

At the same time that slaves were "working" tobacco, they also were preparing other fields and cultivating different crops—mostly grains. They cleared fields for planting wheat in August and sowed it from September until the end of November; they harvested corn in October. Some planters continued to grow tobacco during the nineteenth century, but most gradually reduced tobacco reduction as they increased grain cultivation.[84]

While tobacco workers were busy with their crop from late December through the next fall, grain farmers were finished harvesting by August. William H. Gray, owner of "Locust Hill" plantation in Loudoun, divided his 430 acres into six fields of approximately 47 acres each, leaving the rest to woods, meadow land, and a nine-acre house lot. By mid-August of each year, his slaves had begun fallowing his fields for fertilizing and planting. They began sowing wheat in mid- to late September, planting timothy and clover in October and until November when thrashing started. December was hog killing time. January and February were "slack" times devoted to farm repair, spinning, weaving, and sewing. Slaves also began preparing a small tobacco crop during this time. They planted potatoes and peas in March, corn in April, started harvesting wheat in late June, and finished sometime in August.[85]

Many hired out slaves when their work schedule permitted it, usually in the winter and early spring. "Marser Fallons . . . would hire his slaves in slack times to cut timber an' build barns or fences," local ex-slave Frank Bell explained. Yet according to Bell, the work on a wheat plantation was hard, particularly during harvest time. His owner, John Fallons, made all of his slaves, men and women alike, work in the fields. But his slave women did perform less physically demanding agricultural tasks than his men. While both had to sow and care for the young grain crop, only the men had to clear the land and cut and cradle the wheat. During harvest at Fallons's, the women only raked and bound the cut grain. Others recalled a slightly different division of labor among the sexes. "I mem'ers so well when dey uster to cut wheat dar w'uld be sixty or seventy cradles jes a cuttin," ex-slave Bacchus White reminisced. "Dey didn't 'ave anythin' to rake de wheat up wid 'cepting de rakes dey use wid de 'ands. Dey w'uld rake de wheat jes as clean, an' den de 'omen w'uld bind it up in shocks."[86]

Slaves on Loudoun's grain farms also sometimes worked in family groups. Frank Bell noted that while many overseers frowned on this practice, his uncle was their driver and let them work together. The ex-slave went on to explain that he had four brothers, all of whom especially felt protective of their mother, "who warn't very strong." They regularly shared her assigned portion of the field work.[87]

Like their male peers, most female slaves were agricultural workers; and despite some differences, many usually did the same kind of field work as men. Austin Steward, for example, noted that on the local plantation on which he worked, "it was usual for men and women to work side by side . . . ; and in many kinds of work, the women were compelled to do as much as the men." Some males did perform more physically strenuous work, but women generally worked more—spinning, weaving, nursing, and cooking once their field work was over, to say nothing of the child care and domestic work they did in the quarters.[88] Gender, therefore, did impact the slave experience. Occupational differences outside the field, for instance, were substantial. A significant minority of females, but many fewer males, were domestics. Large holdings employed both, but antebellum women dominated these positions especially among smaller slaveholdings. Male slaves, on the other hand, had greater opportunity to hold skilled and supervisory positions and, therefore, had greater opportunity to earn extra cash and to hire themselves out. They also could have leadership positions as drivers, overseers, foremen, and head craftsman that women systematically were denied.[89]

Men not only could have jobs of higher status, but owners routinely gave them better material support. Slaveholders rarely gave female field workers as much meat or other food as males. Since slave women usually lived with their children and had to share some of their smaller portion with them, a mother's quota could be especially sparse. Evidence suggests that some fathers may have put aside part of their food allowance for their families, but owners did not compel them to do so. Similarly, the long pants, shirts, jackets, and other clothing that slave masters provided males were much more appropriate for bending, stooping, and repelling insects endemic to field labor than the skirts and dresses females had to wear. Many slave owners might have expected women to work as hard as men, but this expectation did not translate necessarily into equitable material support.[90]

Gender also affected the ways in which owners and slaves interacted at the workplace. Women, for example, were more easily excused from work, especially when they complained of gynecological problems. Masters, unable to discern fact from fiction, but protective of their investment in a woman's ability to "reproduce," often succumbed to complaints. John Fitzgerald, for example, reported in late 1858 that his "servant woman" Mobrina had recently suffered gynecological problems. "During the month of January '57," he recalled, "she was sick for a day or two, I think, as she said from too great a flow of Her menses." A year later, the man who rented Mobrina from Fitzgerald informed him that she had been ill and he feared she was pregnant. Mobrina was then "indisposed more or less from that time [April 1858] till the 5th of May [1858]." One physician from the Loudoun area asserted that slave women generally lost from four to eight work days per month on account of such problems. Even if his assessment was an exaggeration, it is certain that a slave woman's childbearing years were difficult ones, both physically and psychologically.[91]

Pregnant slave women clearly did not receive the same kind of emotional support, work reprieves, nutritional or medical attention that most white expectant mothers did. Instead, they were at the mercy of drivers, overseers, owners, and slaveholding women who often were ambivalent at best about the prospects of losing a woman's labor while she was pregnant. Most field women worked until their delivery time was near. Some became part of "trash" gangs charged with lighter agricultural and maintenance tasks. Regardless of the exact circumstances, pregnancy usually did mean less work. When Nelson Berkeley's overseer wrote to him in January 1828 to tell him about the general condition of the plantation and slave property, for example, he noted routinely: "The Negroes and stock are All well at present—2 or 3 of the Negroe women are pregnant which will throw me behind time in my crops." Domestics probably received less consideration since masters and mistresses believed their work was less strenuous. Of course ill or pregnant "pet" slaves got the most support.[92]

Slave men and boys hardly could claim such conditions, but they did complain of problems symptomatic of venereal diseases and other disorders. It was more difficult for them to get time off from work, but masters also provided males with medical attention. Slave artisans probably received the best because of their value and their "freedom" of movement, affording them the opportunity to get their own care. Slaveholding women routinely monitored slave health and administered medication. Some called in physicians when conditions seemed threatening. "Jackson's arm is mending and the Doctor says he will recover the use of it," Elizabeth Conrad was relieved to report. William Gray could not say the same about the condition of his slave man Daniel, who died five days after breaking his leg.[93]

Gender also impacted the slave's work environment. Ex-slave testimony and the personal papers of slaveholding whites both indicate that the psychological and social distance, as well as the physical and cultural differences, between white men and their black female laborers created an extremely abusive work environment for the latter. In a society where one derived status, power, and control largely from gender, race, and class, slaveholders perceived slave women as especially threatening to their authority.

Rape of female slaves was perhaps the most potent example of the combined influence of misogyny and racism. In a county such as Loudoun where almost one-third of the slave population and more than half of free people of color were "mulatto," sexual coercion and rape were not unusual. Slave masters also devised other violent measures to dehumanize females. Isaac Williams was a black driver who remembered his owner's treatment of one "yellow girl": "He tied her across the fence, naked, and whipped her severely with a paddle bored with holes, and with a switch. Then he shaved the hair off of one side of her head, and daubed cow-filth on the shaved part." He did this, Williams insisted, "to disgrace her—[to] keep her down." As Williams realized, masters meant to accomplish much more through this kind of public, sadistic maltreatment than just to chastise an unproductive or disobedient slave. They meant to shame them, to strip black women, both privately and publicly, of their humanity, femininity, and power (sexual, emotional, and moral) that they held within their families and communities.[94]

"Beat women! Why sure he beat women," ex-slave Elizabeth Sparks exclaimed. "Beat women jes' lak men." Stripped of their clothing, faced against a tree or wall, tied down or made to hang from a beam, their legs roped together with a rail or board between them, beating provided owners and overseers with the vehicle to strip blacks symbolically of their pride while invoking terrifying images of white male power. Silas Jackson testified that on the local plantation where he grew up there not only was a two-room, stone building with iron bars that his owner used as a jail but that his master "always carried a cowhide with him." "If he [Master Ashbie] saw anyone doing something that did not suit his taste, he would have the slave tied to a tree, man or woman, and then would beat his victim until he got tired, or sometimes, the slave would faint." "I have seen men beaten until they dropped in their tracks or knocked over by clubs, women stripped down to their waist and cowhided," Jackson added. Local slaves Austin Steward and Christopher Nichols described the tools of torture: "a whip about nine feet long, made of the toughest kind of cowhide, the but[t]-end . . . loaded with lead, . . . about four or five inches in circumference;" and a "cobbing-board full of auger holes" combined with "cutting switches." Whips made of hard cowhide or whipcords, cat-o'-nine-tails, leather straps, and wooden paddles detailed with small holes were typical.[95]

Jackson's, Steward's and Nichols's autobiographical statements indicate that Loudoun slave masters and overseers made no distinction in the ways they punished male and female field slaves. It was a brutal, disfiguring, health-threatening attack. "The whip," medical historian Todd Savitt concludes of its use in Virginia, "was an integral part of slave life . . . which inflicted cruel and often permanent injuries upon its victims." According to Savitt, the typical whipping "caused indescribable pain," "multiple lacerations of the skin, . . . loss of blood, injury to muscles, and shock," and even the "possibility of death." Muscle damage also sometimes left the slave permanently deformed or crippled, causing inexorable physical and emotional pain, but also threatening the slave's potential as a worker.[96]

Both slave men and women strove to complete work quotas and took pride in their labor. Still they had some sense of what were "reasonable" and "fair" labor practices, and many refused to be overworked. Most understood that they contributed to their master's financial support and they expected some reward for their efforts. Others insisted that labor supervisors and owners respect the slave's sense of what were acceptable work conditions and assignments. Time and time again, they demanded material support, acceptable treatment, and some control of their intimate relations in exchange for their toil and a cursory allegiance. While slave men believed that it was their right as men not to be driven "like mules" or treated like brute animals, slave women believed that they had a right, as childbearers, to protect their bodies from the harm that harsh prenatal treatment or physical abuse might bring to them or their offspring. One Virginia slave woman, speaking to a missionary in a contraband camp in 1861, voiced a typical concern for one of her children whom she believed had suffered developmentally because of her unrelenting work routine while pregnant. "Marster worked me so hard," she explained, "he [her son] warn't quite bright, so I feel I ought to do more for him than anybody else.[97]

Women, like men, who felt these silent labor agreements between themselves and masters (or mistresses, overseers, and drivers) violated, acted to protect themselves, often rebelling against the demands that they be obedient, efficient workers under all circumstances. They ran away, usually for short periods of time, refused to work, talked back, pouted, stole food, held secret meetings, plotted against whites, and sometimes even physically harmed them. Remembering her mother's account of her own personal revolt, Virginia Shepherd explained:

> One day she had worked and worked and worked until she just couldn't go any faster. The overseer told her to work faster or he'd beat her. She said she simply stopped and told them, "Go ahead, kill me if you want. I'm working as fast as I can and I just can't do more." They saw she was at the place where she didn't care whether she died or not; so they left her alone.[98]

Realizing that overwork was tantamount to physical punishment in itself, Shepherd's mother, like others, was willing to assert that the work quota was too harsh. She was willing to trade the work for a whipping, at least this one time.

The personal histories of slave women provide a rich source of information about the day-to-day physical and psychological challenges that slavery imposed on the slave and the master. So too do the experiences of slave men. Like women, they experienced sexual, physical, and psychological abuse. Perhaps because they were men, slave masters especially were determined that they recognize white, patriarchal authority. "The young master—this one I ran from," one slave recalled, "used to say, 'a man must be whipped, else he wouldn't know he was a *nigger*.'" Another slave remembered that one of the worst beatings his owner ever gave him was because he refused to call his young masters "masters." His master threatened to sell him and his brother "because they was too proud and couldn't be managed." Slave men also were affected by their families' pain. Not a few felt emasculated because they were unable to prevent it.[99]

Some men risked everything to do just that. Madison Jefferson recalled an incident from Loudoun in which six brothers physically prevented an overseer from whipping their mother. Their master retaliated by selling the men to the Deep South. Determined not to leave, at least not on his master's terms, one chopped off his right hand with an ax when his master told him to go with the slave trader. Tom Lewis, another Loudoun slave, warned his overseer never to whip him. But, as the slave's biographer recalled: "One day Tom did something wrong. The overseer ordered him to de barn. Tom took his shirt off to get ready fer de whippin' and when de overseer raised de whip Tom gave him one lick wid his fist and brake de overseer's neck." The owner sold Tom to a neighbor. Violent slave resistance was such a problem in Loudoun that many overseers carried weapons. When a slave man belonging to Leesburg's Asa Rogers attacked his overseer with a butcher's knife, for example, the armed overseer shot him. A slave man belonging to local planter Sanford Ramey also found cause to assault his overseer; he responded by shooting the slave in his leg.[100]

The work world of field, domestic, and skilled slaves also profoundly differentiated the slave experience. An earlier discussion of skilled slaves introduced their unique status. Not surprisingly, gender again played a significant role since most antebellum domestics were slave women supervised by slaveholding women.

While some slaves did not like the constant close contact with whites, most agreed that there were at least three substantial benefits to house service: most domestics had less strenuous work conditions than field slaves; they received better clothing, food, housing, and medical attention; and punishments usually were private affairs and perhaps less severe. This is not to say that slaveholding women could not be cruel, or sometimes devise perverse punishments for recalcitrant or insolent slaves. But few insisted on the public humiliation of slaves that their husbands and overseers demanded. For them to do so would have meant that they would have had to move outside the private boundary of their domestic sphere and into the public domain of men. Faced with a particularly disruptive or disobedient slave, most felt compelled to ask some man to resolve the matter, especially if the slave was a male. "When I was taken to the house, my mistress used to find fault with me before him [her husband]," Leesburg slave Charles Lucas noted. "[H]e would give me a kick or two in the house, then take me to the barn-yard, and finish it off with the cowskin."[101]

Domestic service, even given its benefits, still was difficult for some to withstand. It meant working long hours, sometimes being accessible twenty-four hours a day. Many lived in a segregated portion of their owner's home, above the outdoor kitchen, the carriage house, or in slave housing located near the main house for easy availability. Some even had to spend every night sleeping on pallets in their owners' rooms. They also did physically hard work.

Since most Loudoun masters had only one or two house slaves, if that many, domestics performed a wide variety of skilled and unskilled house and yard work. Female responsibilities could encompass everything from the care and nurture of several children to cleaning, gardening, butchering, cooking, serving meals, sewing, carding, weaving, midwifery, and nursing. Male domestics were dining room servants, tended fireplaces, took care of the livestock, cultivated the vegetable and flower gardens, ran errands, and were carriage men, hostelers, and butlers. Others were personal servants, accompanying their charges on business trips and vacations, to boarding academies and sometimes to college and even war.[102]

Some domestic slaves also had to contend with the orders of a domestic overseer. Although it was not commonplace, the practice of hiring experienced white servant women to supervise slave domestics seemed to be a growing one. Slaveholders employed them for an obvious reason—to relieve their wives of some of their supervisory tasks. Like male overseers of field slaves, these white women established work quotas for domestics, inspected their work, maintained discipline, and punished or at least recommended their punishments.[103]

House servants could suffer from an overwhelming emotional strain. They soon discovered that the mistress could be just as difficult and demanding as the master, and cruel as well. Slaveholding women's first priority was to create comfortable homes for their families. They often were relentless in their efforts to get slaves to work accordingly. Many entered intense apprenticeships with the slave girls and boys they selected for their domestic staff, hoping to create efficient, well-mannered "servants," even if it meant scolding, beating, and forcing their assimilation. Many domestics undoubtedly found that the cultural, social, and political compromises that they had to make in order to be acceptable domestics were a high price to pay.[104]

Soon after her marriage to Robert Conrad, for example, Elizabeth Powell decided that she would train as a house servant one of the slaves that her parents had given her as a wedding gift. She chose Henry, an adolescent who had been a field worker at her father's estate. Mrs. Conrad commandeered Bob, a mannerly, skilled domestic, to help her train the new recruit. "Henry is right awkward as you may imagine but I think he will do very well," she reported to her doubting father some time later. "He seems to be very willing to learn and if his limbs were about half their present length I think he would be much more graceful—but he seems to be very much at a loss to know what to do with his hands."[105]

A few days afterward, Betty had occasion to write to her father again. While discussing Henry's slow progress in some detail, her tone suggested the pressure that the slave adolescent must have felt while trying to perform under her constant critical eye. Describing a small dinner party she had hosted, Mrs. Conrad noted that they had "got through pretty well—at least Henry did [not break] his neck nor any of the dishes"—a decided accomplishment, she concluded. Sometime later, the young mistress assured her mother that Henry's training still was proceeding well. "You would be quite pleased to see how well Henry performs his part as dining room servant," she beamed. "He seems to be very anxious to learn and really does very well considering from whence he came and the training he has had." Jack, another slave teen Mrs. Conrad hoped to train as a domestic, was a different matter altogether, proving to be "rather too free and easy" for the job.[106]

Although Mrs. Conrad was determined to shape Henry into a fine servant, her husband and father were more than a little skeptical. Despite Betty's compliments, her father concluded that he "deplore[d]" the young slave's "depravity" and suggested to Mr. Conrad that he sell him at the earliest opportunity. Henry apparently had escaped, temporarily, from the pressures of his new job to indulge in a night of frivolity in town—without permission.[107]

The uncertainty of the success of domestic apprenticeships often caused misunderstandings and mistrust between slaveholding women and their charges. Loyal "servants" often were dismayed by what they believed were acts of deliberate cruelty. Cordelia Long, for example, believed she was a devoted slave and, therefore, felt compelled to confront her mistress after she had beaten her. Long demanded to know how her owner could do so after so many years of dedicated service. Her appeal to her mistress's conscience, however, "was of no avail." Documentation of this kind of cruelty is not meant to imply that slaveholding women did not act kindly toward their slaves or provide them with a variety of services. Yet there also is significant proof that slaveholding women frequently did not treat their slaves well.[108] Both opinions hold some validity. But if one is to credit the plantation mistress with having significant impact on the lives of slaves, then one also must credit her with her contributing to a system that was oppressive and harsh. Isolated incidences of slaveholding women's kindness, care, and even manumission did little to challenge or change the institution. In fact, their "propensity" for such, if indeed it was a propensity, only strengthened proslavery arguments of benevolence and, thus, legitimacy.[109]

Race, class, and gender shaped slaveholding women's perceptions of slavery, the slave, and their roles as mistress. Few were willing to risk their husbands' disapproval, or worse, in order to protect even their favorite slaves. As women, even wealthy women, they did not have the power to challenge the profoundly entrenched institution. Bound by the precepts of their roles as obedient, submissive wives, slaveholding women acted principally as their husbands' representatives in the lives of slaves, not as independent, rebellious agents out to reconstruct or even to refine the system.

Slaveholding men both designed and perpetuated chattel slavery. Loudoun slave masters might have pressured their wives to provide certain services to their "black family," but they did not expect or sanction any undermining of the system, not even by their beloved female kin. Moreover, as members of the white slaveholding elite, many of these women closely identified with their husbands', fathers,' and brothers' socioeconomic priorities. They too felt that they had an investment in perpetuating planter hegemony and a racial hierarchy.[110]

Virginia women who held slaves as property in their own right employed them as laborers and hired them out to work for others with the same eye to making a profit as their men. Loudoun slave mistress Sarah Ellzey rented many of her slaves each year. Jane Swann Hunter, a female slaveholder of more than 100 slaves, did likewise during the 1840s and 1850s. So too did Catherine McCall, whose receipts and deeds from the years 1816 to 1829 indicate that she hired out the majority of her slaves for more than $1000 per year. The remainder, other than her domestic staff, McCall employed on her tobacco plantations under the direction of overseers. Anne Nalle, another Virginia slaveholder, annually rented three of her slave blacksmiths for more than $500 per year. Had she, or the others, not been able to derive some financial reward from their slave ownership, they probably would have acted again like their male peers, and sold their property.[111]

Elizabeth Jones, for example, was a Loudouner whose deceased husband had left her and their daughter a small lot of land and thirteen slaves. The widow was unable to find lucrative use of her slaves because of a number of unforeseen circumstances: two had died since her husband's death; another had obtained her freedom; two of the women had small children; one was expecting a child; and one of the older children was an "idiot." Petitioning the state legislature in 1817, Jones asked that the terms of her husband's will, which stipulated that she could not sell his slaves, be put aside. She hoped to sell her less productive slave property and rent out the three men.[112]

Most slaveholding female entrepreneurs like Catherine McCall all but withdrew from the system, absenting themselves from the day-to-day business of agriculture and slave labor and leaving these details in the capable hands of male kin, attorneys, and overseers. Some may have remained at the "seat" of their business, but usually still deferred control to males. Sarah Ellzey depended on her nephews Burr Harrison and Thomas Ellzey, for example, to handle all of the business aspects of her plantation, including her slaves. George Carter pleaded with his sister Julia to either sell or rent out her slave property. The spirited widow relied on her overseer instead. After George Carter's death in 1842, his wife Elizabeth also kept his many operations going, relying on able overseers and business advisors to supervise Loudoun's largest slaveholding.[113]

Although slave ownership did guarantee some women financial security, it was not a position that southern society sanctioned as appropriate for them. Men and women alike typically believed that white women, particularly elite white women, were ill-suited for leadership or business management, and that it was unseemly for them to expose themselves to the "indelicacies" of black labor and control. Confronted with this widespread sense of inability, self-imposed and derived from the attitudes of kin and society in general, coupled with the resistance of slaves, many female slave owners felt compelled (and relieved) to place much of the power that slave ownership might have afforded them in the hands of white men.

It also was not just that slaveholding women wanted to turn a profit and felt incapable of doing so on their own. They, like their husbands, held profoundly racist views of their slaves. Class biases and priorities combined with their racism and lack of sophistication to create an ethnocentric view which effectively denied slaveholding women acknowledgment of their slaves' humanity.[114]

The testimony of slaves as well as the letters and private papers of slaveholding women document that slave mistresses rarely viewed slaves' emotional and material needs or their characters as similar to their own. They made few exceptions in their judgments, only sometimes affording individual, favorite slaves such positive traits as "loving," "kind," "devoted," "loyal," and "industrious". Yet even while giving praise to their closest slave associates, mistresses refused to, or could not, perceive the slave as a total person whose needs and desires as a human (as a husband, wife, or child, for example) should be afforded the same consideration as their own.[115] Consider, for example, some of the kinds of relationships that slaveholding women established with those slaves with whom they had the most consistent contact—their domestic servants.

One would expect that because most domestics were children and women, the most benevolent and thoughtful exchanges would occur. Yet, time and time again, the data descriptive of slaveholding women's feelings about and interactions with these slaves document consistent acts of physical and psychological brutality, as well as a stunning disregard for their personal relationships. Indeed, sometimes white females who were in charge of domestics did grow attached to their charges and allowed them certain "favors." They sometimes gave them secondhand clothing, nursed them when they were ill, and offered advice, moral supervision, and guidance, for example, when choosing a marriage partner. Catherine Powell and her daughter Betty Conrad often discussed the various activities or behavior of their favorite domestics. "You dont [sic] say how your ward Nelly is," Mrs. Powell wrote in 1830, "I hope she is better than Celia who has got to be such a rogue [th]ere is no living with her." "Eliza relieves me from so much manual labor . . . that I think that she has contributed to my better estate," the aging mistress complimented her slave in 1843. Even Mrs. Powell's much more reserved daughter, Sarah Harrison, had to admit that Eliza was "really a good girl as servants are."[116]

Mrs. Powell expressed positive feelings about her "servants" in other ways as well. When she was away visiting her children or friends, for example, she concerned herself with her domestics' health. She was particularly fond of her slave Eliza, whom she had known most of her life. Indeed, all of the Powell women seem to have been taken with Eliza. Regardless of their expressions of superficial concern and interest, however, they fundamentally perceived Eliza as a laborer whose primary purpose was to serve them. They did not view her as another woman with the same hopes, feelings, and concerns as theirs. She did not form part of that wonderful network of southern rural women bound together by race, class, gender, culture, and locale. Southern society placed her squarely outside of these womanly circles.

Men in the Powell family typically revealed much less interest in their slave property. Gender prescription, of course, sanctioned a female's emotional display of affection for one's "black family," but hardly allowed males to act similarly; some even criticized women for acting overtly so. Writing to his sister-in-law in 1840, for example, Robert Conrad reported in typical fashion that Mrs. Powell was in good health but "she cannot lay aside her anxieties about the housekeeping on The Hill, [and] laments as much over a lost turkey or a laying-up servant as if they were yet matters of personal concern to her."[117]

All in all, however, slaveholding women rarely considered black women to be their equals on any level. Just as slavemasters considered black men "boys," their wives perceived black women, regardless of their age, as "girls" who always would need their guidance and discipline. Writing to her sister in 1843, for example, Sarah Powell Harrison reported that she believed that her mother's maid had congestive fever, a "dreadful disease" that she hoped the "girl" did not have. Fortunately, Eliza survived congestive fever and went on to serve the Powell family devotedly for several more years. Emily, another domestic in the family, fared much worse.[118]

Margaret Harrison, sister-in-law to Sarah Powell Harrison, found her domestic Emily to be a most devoted, kind, and loyal servant. So much so, that Margaret could never think of parting with Emily even if it meant separating the aged and ailing slave woman permanently from her family. Accordingly, when Margaret migrated from Loudoun to Alabama in the late 1830s, she carried Emily with her. Once there, Emily became very ill. Although Margaret was willing to spend her time and energy trying to nurse Emily back to health, she would not oblige the sick woman's desire to see her family again. Writing back to her Loudoun relations, she described Emily's poor health and her concern for her. Margaret admitted that she was determined to help Emily and would have to postpone her scheduled vacation to Loudoun until the slave woman's condition was resolved.[119]

Undoubtedly, Emily would have fared much more peaceably if she could have returned to Virginia to spend her last days with her family and her "friends." Miss Harrison's sympathy for her maid came too late to comfort her. It was only after Margaret witnessed the pain that the dying Emily endured that she was even moved to consider what she had cost the slave woman by forcibly separating her from her family. It seems as if at no time during the many years Emily had served Margaret Harrison's family so faithfully had the slaveholding woman considered the importance of this black woman's emotional ties to her own people.

Often slaveholding women had favorite male domestics who usually were very young or very old, for few plantation mistresses could appear to be emotionally attached to a mature, virile male slave. Oscar Ball of Alexandria, for example, recalled that when he was a house boy of seven or eight years, his "maiden" mistress, Elizabeth Gordon, "made it a practice" to have him sleep with her. Betty Powell Conrad was particularly fond of her adolescent domestic Henry. Decades after the Civil War had ended, Mrs. Conrad's daughter wrote a touching account of the role of another dining room assistant and carriage man, Stephen. Recalling the kindness that the elderly slave had paid her and her siblings while they were young, she made note of her mother's attachment to him, the only slave she would let drive her. She also seemed to like her cook Silvia very much. "We have a delightful cook, one too who is perfectly honest or is thought to be so," she reported to her father soon after her marriage. Silvia was a favorite of Betty Conrad's mother-in-law as well, so much so that the elderly Mrs. Conrad left instructions in her will that Silvia was not to be sold, could choose either of her sons to be her future master, and was to receive an annual $50 allowance from her estate.[120]

It is clear that slave masters and mistresses recognized some of their slaves' human qualities, even if they usually did not respect them. Time and time again, slaveholding men and women attested to their slaves' humanness, even if to curse it. Just a casual survey of advertisements for fugitive slaves, for example, provides an array of characteristics of slave personality type or character that slaveholders perceived. Bill Lazenbury's owner, for example, described her runaway as a "smart and cunning fellow." Bob Mead could be "quite polite" and of "smiling countenance." Vincent Warner, his owner asserted, sometimes had a "contemptuous smile." The sense that slaves were untrustworthy was particularly vivid in the slaveholder's mind. "If Mason would behave himself," Burr Harrison explained to his son, "it wd be better to retain him[,] but I have no confidence in him or his promises." Their mistrust was not ill-founded. Despite pretense to the otherwise, most slaveholding men and women fundamentally understood that the slave detested his or her position and, given the opportunity, would do almost anything to subvert white authority. It was during this acknowledgment of the slave's rejection of his or her status that slaveholders could be most eloquent when attesting to the slave's humanity.[121]

Cultural difference, historical experiences, gender convention, and racial bias also informed slaves' views of owners and their wives. Female slaves, for example, generally were very critical of both slaveholding men and women, but particularly their mistresses. Male slaves, on the other hand, seemed to be more fond of and willing to act respectfully toward slaveholding women than men. The autobiographical narratives and accounts of ex-slaves who resided in the Loudoun vicinity as well as throughout Virginia detail these attitudes and how they influenced the ways in which male and female slaves responded to white authority.

Regardless of the number of years that female commentators were slaves, for example, they generally held derogatory views of the whites for whom they worked. Slave women particularly resented slaveholding women, usually describing them as both cruel and selfish. Some even drew discerning contrasts between the behavior of male slaveholders and their wives, noting the relative benevolence of the former compared with the harsh treatment they received at the hands of the latter. Slave women gave several reasons for their dislike of slaveholding women, but generally focused on personal ill-treatment, such as frequent scoldings and beatings, or their mishandling of slave children. Others insisted that slaveholding women exerted a considerable influence over their husbands' treatment of slaves and often used their power to goad these men on to be more abusive than they would have been otherwise.[122]

Calling planter women "hell cats" and "devils," slave girls and women implicated the "unholy" behavior of slaveholding women whom they believed abandoned their promise of moral female behavior when they forced black women to steal food, lie about slave activities, feign illness, and generally participate in all kinds of resistance behavior. While black women believed that their political, social, and economic oppression as slaves and their physical and moral victimization as women were valid excuses for their behavior, many assumed that the socially and economically elite status of slaveholding women left them much less justification for misconduct. Clearly, female slaves surmised that slaveholding women often had the wherewithal to act "good," that is to be kind, generous, understanding, protective, loyal, and honest, when slave women, more often than not, did not.[123]

Male slaves perceived slaveholding women very differently. Most did not blame them for the harsh treatment they received, asserting instead that they were powerless to help in the face of their husbands' control. Many men insisted that slaveholding women were kind, nurturing, and thoughtful and assumed that they would have been even more solicitous and responsive to the needs and humanity of their slaves if slaveholding men had not demanded otherwise. "In fact she was an angel," one ex-slave added to his glowing description of his former mistress. Male slaves not only believed slaveholding women to be kind and considerate, but some also noted her need for physical protection and voiced their willingness to provide it. They also found these women physically attractive. Female slaves, on the other hand, rarely commented on the appearance of slaveholding men or women but, when prompted to do so, they usually described their mistresses as "old" or ugly.[124]

Slave men, like slave women, reserved their most denigrating descriptions for those of their own gender. It was slaveholding men, not women, who were their villains and held the worst characteristics their gender could exhibit— they could be brutal, cowardly, dishonest, and abusive of those dependent on them. Time and time again slave men included in their autobiographical accounts what they believed was the despicable behavior of their male owners and overseers. They used the emasculating experiences slave masters imposed on them—rape and physical abuse of their wives, lovers, and daughters; attempts to gain complete control of slaves' lives; destruction of families; refusal to reward them for their labor; and barbarous public whippings—to point to the perversion of white masculinity.[125]

Both slave men and women were most critical of slaveholding whites of either sex when they believed that they had interfered with or hurt their kin or family relations in any significant way. Slave marriages, kin networks, and communities formed in Loudoun in the context of, and in spite of, an oppressive system that was driven by the prerogatives of an elite, white patriarchy. These prerogatives shaped the contours of slave domesticity in unmistakable ways. The slave trade, both international and domestic, for example, produced a group that for many years was male-dominant. Even after the presence of native-born and African women allowed conjugal relations among slaves, labor demands insured that many husbands and wives did not reside together. The incidences of abroad slave marriages, matrifocal families, and extended kin networks were disproportionately high and remained so.

As the domestic slave trade grew more intense and lucrative, new threats to the slave family emerged. Men not only had to leave in large number, but so too did women. During the early antebellum era, owners sometimes sold mothers with their small children, but this practice too waned with time. Men, women, and children who were wives, husbands, and offspring increasingly entered the domestic market as individuals—sold and bought independent of any marriage or familial ties. Few slaves did not feel the impact of the slave trade or local slave labor needs on their families and communities. It is little wonder then that in George Johnson's descriptive summary of slavery in Loudoun, quoted at the beginning of this chapter, he centered his remarks on the domestic slave trade, for "slaves were always afraid of being sold South."[126]

7

Slave Family Structure

A most tragic occurence [sic] had lately taken place . . . , occasioned by
those monsters who traffic in HUMAN FLESH. A man by the name of
Crooks, living near Hillsborough in this county, lately sold this
FAMILY OF BLACKS to some of those inhuman traders. . . . They were
secured in a room that night, and in the morning when they went to
awaken them, Lo! a middle aged woman had laid down to rise no
more! ! ! IT WAS SUPPOSED SHE HAD TAKEN SOMETHING BY
WHICH SHE PUT A PERIOD TO HER EXISTENCE: choosing death
rather than be dragged off by these tyrants.
  Loudoun County Resident, Genius of Universal Emancipation,
                                                  March 29, 1829

Those county residents who knew about the Crooks slave incident may
have been shocked at the suggestion that a slave woman would kill herself
rather than leave her family or community, but few sincerely could be surprised
by the general scenario. It was, after all, during the years between 1800 and 1860
that more than 7000 slaves left Loudoun under similar auspices. Local newspapers persistently documented much of this trade—not in the form of moral-
izing editorials such as the excerpt from the *Genius of Universal Emancipation*,
but rather in numerous advertisements for slave sales. Just as the international
slave trade of the colonial years had destroyed families and communities in
western Africa and other parts of the continent, the interstate slave trade of the
nineteenth century wreaked havoc on generations-old Loudoun slave networks
as mothers and fathers, sons and daughters, aunts and uncles left on their forced
treks to New Orleans and other points south and southwest, most traveling
without their kin. To be sold in such a manner was the most frightening aspect
of slave life, and one which blacks wholeheartedly resisted, even if it meant
leaving their families on their own terms.

  "'I have always lived in Loudoun County, Virginia," Charles began his description of his early life as a slave. "My mother was the cook, and I worked
about the house, and sometimes traveled with master—went to Washington,

Baltimore, Cumberland, and once to Wheeling, on horseback." But Charles's life was irreparably changed when, one day while serving him dinner, his mother replied anxiously, "Charley, all my children gone but you, and Massa's done gone and sold you, and I'll never see you 'gin." Charles escaped the next morning without disclosing his plan to anyone. Overnight, the Loudoun black had decided to end his enslavement even if it also meant ending his physical ties with his family.[1]

While the domestic slave trade was one of the defining characteristics of Loudoun black life, there were other important events and circumstances which had significant impact on slave individuals, families, and communities. The size of the farm or plantation on which slaves lived had immense importance; so too did the nature of the work they performed, and where they performed it. That is, whether a slave lived in Loudoun's plantation district or in the largely nonslaveholding Quaker and German locales affected their domesticity, as did a slave's generation since a slave's life often was shaped by the life cycles of his or her owners, their business pursuits and economic priorities. And, as ever, a slave's gender, age, and cultural makeup had longlasting effect.[2]

Yet it still is difficult to ascertain what "family" must have meant to those first African and creole blacks who arrived in Loudoun during the eighteenth century. Although the conditions under which they lived and worked were determined by numerous circumstances, it is certain that the harshness of slave life—psychologically, physically, and materially—the slaves' cultural and linguistic diversity, and the lack of females in their population were early deterrents to the creation of childbearing families. Still the examples of cooperation and miscegenation between white servants and black slaves document close, kin-like relationships. Family for many of the first African and creole blacks forced to migrate to the Loudoun frontier, therefore, undoubtedly existed in the memories of those they had to leave behind when they traveled to Virginia and in the relationships found with fellow servants and slaves in the colonies.[3]

While blacks began to arrive in Loudoun during the 1720s and 1730s, there is no real count of their numbers until 1749, and this first enumeration, in the form of a tithable list, does not give sound evidence of their family life. What these lists do document, however, is that their numbers increased almost sevenfold between 1750 and 1760, prompting a gradual decline in their adult sex ratio, and allowing some physical basis for the creation of heterosexual slave marriages. One can imagine that by 1760, for example, a minority of slave men and women had the opportunity to create marital ties, if not with someone on their particular farm or plantation, then perhaps at a neighbor's or maybe even further away.[4]

It still was difficult, though, even under the best circumstances for some midcentury slaves to find permanent spouses.[5] And Loudoun's colonial slaves hardly lived under the best circumstances. Mortality remained high and African women had low fertility rates. Slave natural increase became important only during the 1760s and 1770s, after native-born slave women began to marry and bear children.[6]

Many of these early couples undoubtedly lived away from one another and did not comprise co-residential (both spouses living together) nuclear households. Instead, there was an array of household types—a few nuclear and nuclear extended types, but also single-parent (mother) groupings, same-sex single adolescents living together, and single or widowed elderly folk who lived in their owners' homes or alone. Many slaves married abroad even after the numbers of men and women in the general slave population moved toward equality, since there continued to be uneven numbers within individual slave holdings. Abroad marriages, in turn, contributed to the apparent variety of slave household membership.

Because the size of a slaveholding had many implications for slave domestic life, it is important to note that Loudoun slaves remained almost equally divided on small (five and fewer persons) and moderately sized (15 and fewer) holdings. By 1760, for example, just a little more than one-half[7] were part of holdings of ten or fewer slaves. Over the years, this changed little,[8] although an important minority usually were part of larger holdings.[9]

While both colonial and antebellum slavery scholars have argued that the size of a holding determined much about the potential for a slave to marry within that holding and, therefore, form the basis for a nuclear, co-residential family, that often was not the case in Loudoun. There, women dominated small holdings, living on farms and in households where there were few, if any, adult men. Men, on the other hand, tended to dominate moderate and large groups. It was only among the largest slaveholdings that men and women of marriageable ages were close to being even in number.[10] So that even when the general sex ratio of county slaves was virtually 1.0,[11] and within adult age cohorts specifically,[12] most Loudoun slaveholdings, whether large or small, did not have nearly equal numbers of both sexes. Loudoun slaves who were part of small holdings, therefore, were not the only ones who had a large incidence of "abroad" marriage. So too did those who were part of larger holdings, especially men. [13] Despite scholarly speculation to the contrary, even the largest local slaveholdings often did not translate into monogamous couples or nuclear core families who resided together on a daily basis. To understand fully that the domestic experiences of slaves in small holdings also were shared by those in larger groups is to know more about the nature of occupational stratification and labor division on large plantations.

A slave's domestic life was wedded not only to the life cycles of his or her owner, but also to their business interests. Wealthy planters usually owned hundreds and sometimes thousands of acres of land that they divided into various agricultural production sites. Since neither tobacco nor grain, the two most

important Virginia commodities, necessitated large labor forces, they traditionally did not employ all of their slaves at the same locale. During the colonial
years, their farms and slave property might be spread throughout tidewater and
piedmont Virginia, as well as in the Caribbean. In the antebellum years, they
had developed properties in Virginia's piedmont, but also in the Deep South.
John Mercer, for one, owned colonial plantations not only in Virginia's Loudoun, Stafford, and Spottsylvania counties, but also on the Caribbean island of
Antigua. William Fitzhugh had two quarters in Loudoun and numerous
working farms in Fairfax County. Various members of the Carter clan, the
Lees, and Tayloes had plantations spread throughout six or seven Virginia
counties and in Maryland. Antebellum planter Thomas Ellzey owned "Mount
Middleton" in Loudoun and cotton plantations in Alabama and Louisiana. His
peer George Rust had agricultural investments and slaves in both Loudoun and
Maryland; so too did William Lewis, Joseph Beard, and others.[14]

To own many slaves, therefore, typically meant that one employed them at
several farms or plantations that could be as close as adjoining properties or as
far apart as the Upper South and the Southwest or even the Caribbean. Production priorities, not slave marriages or families, determined slave residence and,
therefore, had great impact on slave domesticity. Co-residential, nuclear households were particularly difficult for slaves to achieve. Large slaveholders with
several farms in production at one time were not any more likely to shift a slave's
living arrangement in order to keep a black couple or family physically together
than smaller slaveholders were willing to unite a slave couple by buying a slave's
spouse. Smaller slaveholders, in fact, may have been more willing to do so because a co-residential slave couple could substantially increase an owner's property through consistent childbearing, while large slaveholders could afford to
buy the additional slaves they needed. They also could afford to sell or rent out
those they could not employ. Both the small and large slaveholder acted out of
like-minded economic concerns. Yet the consequences of their actions could
have very different results for the private lives of their slave property.

A slave master's decision about the living arrangements of his black property
helped to create a variety of slave marital and familial relationships and structures. Especially prevalent were abroad marriages, matri- focality,[15] and all-
male households. Extended kin networks usually were of greatest importance,
despite what other familial or marital structures also might be in place. The
various domestic patterns of slaves probably can best be viewed through surveys of the residential and marriage patterns of area blacks.

George Washington, for example, was one of the largest slaveholders in the
Loudoun vicinity at the end of the eighteenth century. The details of the
physical distribution of his slave property and those that his wife held are illuminating because of the size of their slaveholding and the meticulous description Washington left of the slaves themselves—their marriages, ages, familial

composition, and residential and occupational designations. According to his own compilations, Washington controlled 188 slaves in 1783, 216 in 1786, and 316 in 1799, whom he distributed among the five farms which comprised his Mount Vernon estate. The overall adult ratio for his slave   population was excellent for a holding as large as his—1.03 in 1786 and 0.90 in 1799, representing a slight shift from a male to a female majority (87 men, 96 women) as the eighteenth century came to a close.[16]

It is clear from his diaries, correspondence, and last will and testament that George Washington was aware of slave family ties and sympathetic to them, perhaps more so than most of his peers. Yet while it is certain that Washington was opposed to destroying slave families through sale, it also is obvious that he routinely determined the residences of his slaves based on his labor and production needs, not his concern that slave couples or families share the same homes. His priorities, in turn, helped create an expansive slave community across his property—a slave community characterized by a diversity of marriage styles and family and household structures. Particularly prevalent were examples of abroad marriage, structural and functional matrifocality, and significant numbers of single parents and single adults. The patterns of family life among the Washington slaves deny that there was a preponderance of residentially nuclear families and questioned the functional importance of monogamy even when it did exist, since most "monogamous" couples did not live together. (See Table 6.)

Among George Washington's five farms, the "Mount Vernon," or "home" plantation, had the largest slaveholding. Its size and the nature of the work of the house, yard, and skilled slaves, which would have brought them physically and perhaps emotionally "close" to their master, might have provided a conducive atmosphere for the maintenance of residential nuclear families among the slaves. To some extent it did—there were six families which comprised at least a father, a mother, and their children living together at his Mansion House property in 1799. But these six families characterized the familial experiences of only a minority, or 27 percent, of the 96 slaves in residence at the time. The remaining persons lived quite differently. Altogether, 10 couples were abroad, 11 husbands did not live with their wives and children, and at least one, but probably three, married mothers did not live with their husbands. There also was one single mother. Consequently, most fathers did not live in the homes where their children were present.[17]

There are two obvious reasons why Washington's slaves did not form more co-spousal residential, nuclear households. First of all, the adult men at the Mansion House outnumbered the women by almost 2 to 1 (44 men, 23 women), allowing few of the men to marry the women who worked and resided on this part of the Washington estate. More than one-third of the Mansion House slave men were not married. Likewise, 10 of the women were

Table 6 Slave Family Household Types: Mount Vernon, 1799[a]

Household type	Mansion House	Muddy Hole	Dogue Run	Union Farm	River Farm
Nuclear	6	1	3	0	1
Couple	2	1	1	0	5
Abroad couple	10	3	2	2	3
Wife, children, abroad husband	1–4	4	4	3	6
Husband, abroad wife and children	11	0	0	1	0
Single mother, children	1	3	2	4	2
Single father, children	0	0	0	0	0
Single women	9	2	2	3	1
Single men	16	1	1	4	4
Adolescents	0	2	1	0	1
Siblings	1	0	0	0	1
Children	0	0	0	1	0

[a] Compilations derived from: "Negroes Belonging to George Washington in His Own Right and by Marriage, 1799," MVL.

single and 81 percent of the married men had abroad wives. They usually lived with extended family members, their families of birth, or in gender-segregated housing. Clearly, it was not unusual for Washington to disperse members of slave families he owned over quite a distance, some as far as seventeen miles away and across the Potomac River on his River Farm. Others lived at the homes of friends, kin, and business acquaintances such as Washington's secretary Tobias Lear, Major West of "Bellhaven," south of Alexandria, and Captain Thomas Marshall of "Marshall Hall" in Maryland, and at Daniel McCarty's Loudoun "Cedar Grove."

Collectively, the other four farms which Washington owned offer even more exaggerated conditions of structural and functional matrifocality, abroad marriages, and single adults. "Union Farm," Washington's latest acquisition, whose slaveholding included many blacks that Washington hired from Mrs. Daniel French, had the largest incidence of non-nuclear families and abroad marriages. The slave household composition on this farm is important because it exemplifies slave domesticity on newly established farms—a low incidence of coresidential married couples and nuclear families. Of the 36 slaves who resided at Union Farm in 1799, none lived together as a married couple or within a nuclear-structured family: there were three married mothers residing with their children but with abroad husbands; only one married man, and his wife lived elsewhere; four single mothers; four single men; three single women; and one orphan child named Jesse.

Thus, of the 183 men and women who resided on all of Washington's five farms in 1799, only 40 lived together as married couples, while as many as 104, or 72 percent of all those who were identified as married, had abroad spouses. Many of Washington's slaves who were married, therefore, may have had "monogamous" relationships, but they routinely did not live with their spouses and could not provide each other with regular emotional or sociosexual support. Moreover, a large minority of adult slaves were not married at all— 61 percent of the slave men and women who resided on "Union Farm," for example, were "single." Significantly, as many as 74 percent of those slave families with children did not have fathers present on a daily basis—46 percent of the slave mothers had abroad husbands, while 28 percent were "single" or had no identifiable spouses. Slave mothers, therefore, usually raised their children in functionally or structurally matrifocal households, without the daily support and input of fathers. Two-parent dwellings were more myth than reality on Washington's Mount Vernon estate in 1799. (See Appendix A.)

The residential patterns of George Washington's slaves provide a compelling example of the physical context in which slaves who were part of large holdings in the Loudoun vicinity (even those who had favorable sex ratios) developed their marital and familial relations. So too do those of the slaves belonging to William Fitzhugh, a planter with farms in both Loudoun and neighboring Fairfax. According to Fitzhugh's estate inventory for 1801, he quartered 224 slaves on the four farms which comprised his "Ravensworth" estate that year.[18] Although the majority (70 percent) lived in discernible kin groups, 71 percent of his slave mothers lived with their children, but had no husband present. While adult women and their children usually lived together, Fitzhugh's slave men, like those of Washington, were much more likely to live outside kin groups. Fully 69 percent of the 68 slaves belonging to Fitzhugh who did not live in family groups, for example, were adult males, many of whom were either single or had abroad wives or families who belonged to someone else.[19]

The next generations of Fitzhugh slaves, represented by the 1830 estate inventory of William Henry Fitzhugh, who inherited "Ravensworth" and many of its slaves, lived somewhat differently. The smaller size of the younger William Fitzhugh's slaveholding, due to the limitations of his inheritance, and possible slave death, sale, gifts, and transfer to other properties, suggests serious consequences for this slave community which are obvious when one reviews the changes in slave family composition and household membership. There were only 83 slaves residing on the Ravensworth estate in 1830, 63 percent fewer than in 1801. Within the context of this greatly diminished slave community, the toll to slave family life is clear: while a slight majority still lived in family groups, fully 46 percent did not. Moreover, less than half of those who lived with at least one family member lived in residential nuclear households. The majority lived instead in a variety of household types, including units with just mothers and children present or only grandparent(s) and grandchildren present; or with other kinds of extended family groups. Thus, while the representation of residential nuclear families among the Fitzhugh slaves increased slightly from 1801 to 1830, the numbers of persons who lived with blood or marital kin decreased by 24 percent during these years, a haunting indictment of what could and did happen to slave marriages, families, and communities over time.[20]

The various kinds of living arrangements and marriage and family styles apparent in the Loudoun vicinity resulted from a number of countervailing forces. Examples of gender imbalance among slave adults on individual farms and plantations abound even after an equal ratio was established generally within their population. Other conditions, many of them part of the natural cycle of life for slaves and slaveholders—their deaths, births, marriages, and migrations, for example—also periodically destroyed or at least mandated a reconfiguring of slave kin networks and communities which, up until that time, often had persisted over generations.

When General George Rust, one of Loudoun's largest slaveholders, married Maria Marlow of Maryland in 1810, for example, he received as part of her dowry 29 slaves that he removed to his Loudoun property. Edward Marlow, perhaps a relative of Maria Marlow Rust, also moved to the county that year, bringing only part of his slave property with him. When John Harding of Leesburg married Dorcas Davis, of Montgomery County, Maryland, the couple moved her house slaves to Loudoun—Jenny and her five children, Nancy and her child Sarah, and a slave man James. The slave communities that the Marlow and Harding slaves left when they came to Loudoun certainly suffered from their loss. Some, particularly those from nearby Montgomery, probably retained some, but less significant, ties with the kin they left behind while at the same time broadening the communities they helped to establish or joined when they moved to Loudoun.[21]

Slave families and marriages underwent similar changes in the wake of destructive crises within the slave master's family. A slave master's death could be particularly undermining to a slave's domestic world because oftentimes executors sold some of the slaves to pay off debts or to make an equitable distribution of capital to heirs. Amanda Edmonds, for example, recalled the horror of watching her deceased father's slaves sold off for debts. Even the domestics— Ligga, Turner, Rufus, Marshall, Shirley, and Mary Jane were sold. "I know servants are very aggravating sometimes and [you] wish they were in Georgia," Amanda confided to her diary. "[B]ut when I see the poor ignorant, and sometimes faithful, ones torn away so, I cannot help feeling for them."[22] Others did not sell all of their property, but did divide slaves among heirs who lived in different households and sometimes in different locations. Consider two Loudoun examples, one from the late colonial period and the other from the early nineteenth century.

William West was a man of means and well respected in his community. He had been one of Loudoun's first settlers and, by 1769, owned several tracts of land in Loudoun and in nearby Prince William County and fifteen slaves. He also had sat on Loudoun's first court, was part of the local vestry, and was one of the original trustees of the town of Leesburg. When he died in 1769, there was much property to be divided among his wife Mary, their four adult children, and several grandchildren. All of the family connections in his two-generational slave community are not certain, but it is clear that some of these ties were severed when they went to their new owners. The domestic slaves, Hannah, Tom, Nace, and James, may have represented two couples. If so, they were fortunate enough to remain together, the bequest of West to his wife. He gave his son Charles four slaves who also may have represented couples in their own right or his making—Jack, Congo, Leah, and Mariah. His son Thomas received Dick and Melford. He gave his daughter Ann a slave woman named Sarah. A grandson, Francis Peyton, inherited the "negro girl Phebe"; his brother, Craven, received Delilah; their sister Margaret got an unnamed "negro girl"; and another unnamed "negro girl" went jointly to his daughter-in-law Anne West and her daughter Elizabeth. All or some of these "girls" or women may have been the children of some of the other adult slaves distributed elsewhere. It is probable, therefore, that West kept slave couples united (how better to insure that his heirs would continue to benefit from his bequests), but scattered their children through his relatives' households in the larger Loudoun vicinity.[23]

When Adam Shover of the German community of Lovettsville died in 1817, the county court ordered his executors to sell all eighteen of his slaves, "it appearing to the Court that the slaves . . . c[ould] not be distributed in kind among his legal representatives." Although various family members bought most of them, the executors sold two men, Isaac and Just, and two women, Sally and Hitt, outside of the family. Yet the fourteen slaves Shover family members purchased still were not safe from further dispersal. Part of the family soon moved to Ohio and probably sold their slaves before leaving. Another relative, George Shover, bought four of his Uncle Adam's slaves—a woman and her three children—only to sell them, along with a slave man he inherited from his father, a few years later when facing bankruptcy. Loudoun slaves like those of the Shovers, therefore, not only lost their spouses, but also their children, extended kin, and close associates when a master died. Slave communities, marriages, and families traditionally had life cycles that were inextricably bound to and, in large measure, determined by the cyclical quality of their masters' lives, families, and communities.[24]

Consider again what can be gleaned from the records regarding the slave property of some of Loudoun's most prominent citizens and slaveholders—Burr Powell of Middleburg, his brother George of "Llangollen," and their cousin Sarah Ellzey of Leesburg.[25] In comparison with the slave property of Washington and Fitzhugh, those of the Powell-Ellzey clan were only moderately sized, but they were respectfully large slaveholdings for most Loudouners. As such, a review of some of the aspects of their slaveholdings affords an opportunity to view some of the domestic structures and realities of slaves who lived on holdings of fifteen to thirty slaves, as did a great minority in colonial and antebellum Loudoun. It also allows one to consider some of the aspects of slave family life in both urban and rural Loudoun households—Ellzey's slaves mostly were confined to her Leesburg home, while the Powell brothers divided their slaves among the domestic and agricultural staffs at their more rural estates.

In 1820, Burr Powell, retired state assemblyman, prominent attorney, and planter, was one of Loudoun's most prestigious residents. He and his family lived at "The Hill," a large estate located just outside of Middleburg, the town that his father, a Revolutionary War hero, politician, and planter had founded. Powell truly was a member of Loudoun's gentry. His two-story brick mansion accommodated his large family, several house slaves, and their children. Altogether approximately twenty-nine persons lived in and around the Powell mansion—nine white and twenty black. Burr Powell employed most of his slave property (13) in field labor and quartered them in small stone buildings located at some distance from his house. The others worked in his home in one domestic capacity or another.[26]

Because Powell was one of Loudoun's largest slaveholders during the first three decades of the nineteenth century, one might expect that his holding might boast the demographic conditions necessary for stable, long-term slave marriages and nuclear slave families with residential spouses. Instead, unequal numbers of males and females consistently characterized his slaveholding and prevented these kinds of developments. The ratio of males to females at "The Hill" in 1820, for example, was 1.75 to 1, and males outnumbered females in every age cohort. What is even more significant is that within the marriageable age groups (fourteen years and older), there was even more disparity between the number of men and women: the Powell slave men outnumbered the women two to one. While certainly some married slave couples existed among Burr Powell's slave property in 1820, the acute gender imbalance minimally compelled several of his men to seek "abroad" wives.[27]

Major Powell owned 32 slaves in 1830. While the number in his possession was about the same as it had been ten years earlier, the ratio between his male and female slaves had shifted dramatically—females now outnumbered males 1.33 to 1. Despite the obvious increase in female representation among his quarters, however, there still were few women available to marry Powell's slave men. The increase in his female property was largely confined to his slave children—Powell's male slaves still had superior representation in every age cohort except children aged ten years or younger. Among the adult slaves, the men continued to outnumber the women almost two to one (1.86 to 1.0). This statistic is even more dramatic when one considers that Powell gave away several of his adolescent male slaves to his two daughters as part of their dowries sometime between 1820 and 1830. Both Sarah Harrison and Betty Conrad received from their father three to five male slaves each when they married in 1823 and 1829 respectively, thus markedly lowering the male/female slave ratio on their father's plantation. If these males had remained in Burr Powell's household, the number of adolescent and adult males without possible marriage partners would have been even more impressive. Powell's removal of these males from Middleburg to Leesburg (home of Sarah) and Winchester (home of Betty) undoubtedly broadened the slave kin network centered on his plantation. Yet it also weakened the bonds between these young men and their families of birth.[28]

The large number of female children (8 compared with only 4 males) within Burr Powell's 1830 holding not only suggested that there were there few married couples on his plantation. It also suggested that within the next ten years a more equitable gender balance between the adults might emerge. Their master's death in 1838, however, permanently prevented this development. Since he made no stipulations to his heirs which would have protected the integrity of slave family life, his death meant the end to what little security many of his slaves had during his life. Given his economic priorities, commitment to protect and provide for his own family, and his general distrust and dislike of his slave property, it is little surprise that Powell did not act to protect the domestic relations of his blacks. Accordingly, the executors of Burr Powell's estate sold the bulk of his slave property to both local and long-distance buyers. In so doing, they destroyed in part a slave community that had persisted for three, possibly four, generations.[29]

Like his brother, George Cuthbert Powell was a wealthy and valued member of Loudoun's gentry—a planter and businessman who served in the Virginia state legislature and as a member of the United States Congress. For many years, Powell also owned a lucrative dry goods business in Alexandria, and sat on the Loudoun County Court. Although Powell obviously enjoyed the retail business and politics, he retained a love for the land and farming. The five farms which comprised his "Llangollen" estate were some of the best-kept and prosperous in the region.[30]

George Powell owned 21 slaves in 1820. While the overall sex ratio of his slave property (1.3 males for every 1 female) during that year was more impressive than his brother's, the statistic descriptive of the number of adult males to females in his holding was not: 2.5 adult male slaves for each adult female. Indeed, there was a preponderance of males in every age cohort among the slaves at "Llangollen" except those aged under fourteen years. Like the slave men on Burr Powell's plantation, those of George Powell sought spouses on other farms and plantations. Some evidence suggests, for example, that one of them married Emily, a favorite domestic among Burr Powell's slave property. Marriages between slaves whose owners were related by blood or marriage were not uncommon. The joint social activities of kin-connected slave owner households often included not only the white members, but black household members as well. Furthermore, both slaves and their masters realized that interplantation slave marriages might be more convenient for all involved if the owners of slave couples were related or friends. Emily's residence at Burr Powell's estate during the 1820s was only a few miles north of her husband's home at George Powell's plantation, and his owner may have allowed him to visit her as frequently as once a week.[31]

By 1830, the composition of George Powell's slaveholdings, which now only numbered 18, had changed significantly. While Powell's male slaves still outnumbered his female slaves 1.57 to 1, the ratio of adult males to females had declined to 1.33 to 1. This statistic represented the most balanced adult gender slaveholding for George Powell for the period 1820 to 1840, and certainly provided his men with greater access to potential marriage partners among those women living in their quarters. This important decline in the number of men to women was due in part to the coming of age of Powell's female slave children (five girls versus two boys in 1820) during the previous decade and the loss (through sale, gift, or death) of three male slaves. The "loss" of these males, however, also may indicate an assault on pre-existing slave marriages or male-inclusive families.[32]

The change in the gender composition of George Powell's slave property, however, undoubtedly did little to aid the marital relationship of the slave Emily and her husband. In 1829, Burr Powell's daughter Betty married and moved to Winchester, some fifty miles northeast of her home in Middleburg. Some time later, Emily supposedly went to live in the Conrad household, undoubtedly limiting her contact with her husband, still a slave on George Powell's plantation near Upperville.[33]

George Powell's slave property increased by ten between 1830 and 1840 to reach 28 altogether. The almost even adult male/female ratio apparent from his 1830 census listings (1.33 to 1) obviously increased Powell's chances of increasing his slave property through procreation: his slave women gave birth to nine children during that decade. The increase in the number of slaves, however, did not guarantee a balanced gender composition within his overall holdings. By 1840, Powell's male slaves again outnumbered his females 2.5 to 1. Among the adults the trend was even more definitive: there were almost three (2.8) men for every woman. There also was little hope that this statistic would improve over the next several years unless Powell intended to buy more slaves, for the next generation, embodied in those nine children born during the previous decade, also boasted a male numerical superiority of three to one.[34] Clearly the slaveholdings of Burr and George Powell during the 1820s, '30s, and '40s strongly suggest again an adult male domination of Loudoun slaveholdings of ten or more slaves.

Unfortunately, George Powell's death in 1849 put an effective end to much of the slave community centered on his estate. His death, like that of his brother, meant a virtual destruction of many of the marriages, families, and kinship networks of his slaves as well as of those in the vicinity whom they had married. Powell had determined that, upon his death, the administrators of his estate should sell all of his slaves and distribute the proceeds among his heirs. He made no specific stipulations regarding the maintenance of slave marriages or family groups. Nor did he ask that the executors seek local buyers when they sold his slaves. No status of slave was to be spared, not even longtime family domestics. "Among the Negroes, a first rate cook, Seamstresses, house servants and field hands," read an advertisement for the liquidation of George Powell's estate in the October 19, 1849, edition of the Leesburg *Washingtonian*.[35]

Certainly, Emily and her husband were not the only slave couple threatened by George Powell's death and the subsequent sale of his property. While no information remains descriptive of the fate of others, however, information strongly suggests that this couple tried desperately to find someone in the Loudoun vicinity to purchase him or both of them. With the date of the dreaded sale of her husband approaching, Emily, who had worked in several Powell homes, finally appealed to Powell Conrad, one of the young men she had helped to raise. Sixteen-year-old Powell was moved by Emily's desperate situation, but, as a student at the University of Virginia with no funds of his own, he was not certain how he could assist her. He eventually referred the matter to his father, asking him to buy the man and unite the slave couple.[36]

"This trouble of Emilys gives me a good deal of concern, and I would do much to relieve her from it," the elder Conrad responded. "But I fear it will not be in my power to buy her husband" for he had "not the least use for him." "I do not have the funds to buy him," he explained, "without borrowing," particularly given the family's current financial commitments. Although he promised to give the matter more thought, Robert Conrad eventually decided not to purchase the slave man. There is no other indication of the couple's fate.[37]

Burr and George Powell's cousin, Sarah Ellzey, was one of Loudoun's largest female slaveholders. In 1830, she owned 23 slaves when the average number Loudoun slaveholding women owned was six.[38] Unlike her male cousins, Ellzey prided herself in her efforts to support and sustain her slave families, particularly those of her favorite domestics. Concern for the welfare of her white family and black household members, she no doubt believed, was her

Christian duty as a woman and slaveholder. The ratio of male to female slaves in her holding that year (1.33 to 1), particularly that of adults (1.29 to 1), appears to reflect, in some measure, her sensitivity to the issue of slave marriage. Yet a closer look at the composition of Ellzey's holdings indicates that there was a definite lack of compatibility between the age groups of her male and female slaves.

Although the number of those aged between 10 and 23 was almost even, for example, there were five males but only one female aged 24 to 54 years. Between the ages of 10 and 54, her male slaves outnumbered her females 2.25 to 1. Even Ellzey's older slaves, due to low life expectancy rates or indiscriminate sales and gifts, could not look forward to residing with their spouses. While she owned no men older than 55 years in 1830, for example, she did have three slave women who exceeded that age.[39]

Clearly, moderate to large slaveholdings in Loudoun, such as those among the Powell and Ellzey families, therefore, did not guarantee the slaves who comprised them that marriage partners would be available among those who shared their places of residence. In each generation of slaves belonging to these large slaveholders, the adult sex ratio greatly favored men and suggested there were few women within their holding with whom they could establish co-residential, nuclear households.

Over the next ten years, Sarah Ellzey's slave property shrank considerably. By 1840, she only had 10 slaves, and her slave community, having sustained a loss of more than one half of its members, must have suffered tremendously. The year 1840 also was when Ellzey made out her will. It is in that document that she made clear her thoughts about the black and white families that comprised her household.[40]

Sarah Ellzey's last will and testament, dated October 8, 1840, clearly demonstrated some concern for her slaves, but her final wishes still wreaked havoc on their domestic relations. Among the bequests of her church pew, land, and household items, following the instructions regarding the disposal of her debts and her requests to have her sister Ann's grave "properly enclosed," she designated the fate of her slave property. Ellzey held three slaves in joint custody and they were to be returned to their co-owner. She directed her executors to give away and sell to local buyers all other slaves whom she owned outright and to use the proceeds to settle her estate equitably among her heirs. One of her first requests was that they immediately sell the slave man "Stephen" and invest the money for her favorite nephew. "Hannah and her children," Ellzey decided, "were to go to the use of two of her nieces" and, at their death, "to be sold" and the proceeds distributed among other family members.[41]

Another niece, Emily Russell, was to "select one of Cynthia's children" for herself. Ellzey further ordered that the slave woman Cynthia and the remainder of her youngsters be divided among two female kin living in Alabama. She treated more kindly her favorite male domestics. Although she ordered that they be sold, she made it clear that her executors should make an effort to find them local owners so that they might be kept near their "abroad" wives and children. "I expect that Alfred Lee and John Milton Lee will both wish to be sold or hired near where their wives and children live," she conjectured. "[I]f they do I hope my Nephews Burr Wm Harrison and Thomas L. Ellzey will attend to it and try to get them comfortable and permanent homes in the County where I live."[42]

When Sarah Ellzey finally died in 1853, the three-generational slave community among her holding was dispersed, many remaining in the homes of her Loudoun kin, others hired out locally, some sold, and others sent to Ellzey kin in Alabama. The end of this slaveholding woman's life, the migration of her kin to the Deep South and elsewhere, the marriage of her nieces, the continued financial well-being of her heirs—these were the kinds of "external" events and priorities which contextualized and helped to define, create, and destroy slave marriage, family, and community.[43]

The types of phenomena which characterized slave family structure in the Loudoun vicinity were not limited to the colonial and early antebellum decades, but persisted through the pre-Civil War years as well. The composition of the slaveholdings of Burr and George Powell as well as of Sarah Ellzey make this conclusion clear. Furthermore, slave lists from Virginia counties as geographically diverse as Sussex and Gloucester in the southeast, Nottoway and Charlotte in the southern piedmont, Essex in the central tidewater region, Frederick in the north, Madison in the mountainous west, and the city of Richmond provide extensive documentation of these kinds of domestic situations for slaves throughout the state.[44]

Slave registers retained in the family papers of Colonel Claiborne William Gooch of Richmond, for example, provide an opportunity to view the changes that occurred in a moderate-sized slaveholding in urban tidewater Virginia. Three Gooch family slave registers have survived: one from 1830 which lists 29 slaves; another from 1839 with 27 slaves included; and the last, dated 1850, which named 40 slaves. The slave list from 1830 does not designate family groups; those dated 1839 and 1850 do. When one analyzes the Gooch documents, general patterns of matrifocal family structures in children-inclusive, non-nuclear households reappear. While 70 percent of the Gooch slaves lived in blood-related kin groups in 1839, for example, three of the five residential family units among these slaves were comprised only of a mother and her children. Remarkably, the numbers of Gooch slaves living with family members, that is, blood relations or spouses, increased by the next generation (represented by the 1852 list) to include virtually everyone. Yet, out of the nine discernible family households, only one-third were two-parent inclusive or residentially nuclear. Six, or the remaining two-thirds, were composed of households that included only one parent and his or her children—five of the six were mother-present, again indicating the prevalence of matrifocal families.[45]

What perhaps is even more indicative of challenges to and changes in family life among these slaves, however, is evidence of slave community dispersal and possible destruction, akin to what eventually occurred among the Powell and Ellzey slaves in Loudoun. The Gooch list of 1830, for example, when compared with those of 1839 and 1852, suggests just such a pattern: 21 of the 35 Gooch slaves (or 60 percent) listed in 1830 did not reappear on the slave registers of 1839 or 1852. Nine males and eleven females, or over half of the Gooch slave community, disappeared from 1830 to 1839. Sale and high mortality rates undoubtedly produced this extreme loss over this brief interim. A note written on the 1830 list provides details of the fate of some of these slaves: "Sell Juliet and child and Milly and put two boys in their places[.] Sell William and replace him with a likely Tractable boy for the house—hire some of the young females out—and put out others for their victuals and clothes—."[46] (See Appendix B.)

It is clear that such monumental losses over a relatively short period of time (22 years) not only created tremendous strain on slave marriages and families as well as the general slave community, but continually forced slaves to reconstruct their families and communities in order to respond to these losses and additions through sales and rentals. Although the Gooch slaves continued to form single-parent, primarily matrifocal households, they had to do so without the aid of numerous extended and fictive kin who no longer were a part of their community. As they braced themselves to cope with these inevitable losses, they also had to find ways to envelop incoming slaves who would be new community members. Clearly, the realities of family life for Virginia slaves not only could be unpredictable and harsh, but also routinely denied the predominance of cohabitative spouses and two-parent households with slave children.

Slave lists from the Loudoun vicinity and the state in general document that structural and functional matrifocality were extremely prominent in slave domestic life. The matrifocal households and families that Virginia slaves attest to, however, were not merely a result of skewed adult gender distribution in large and small holdings, the separation of married couples on various plantations owned by the same person, or even the domestic slave trade. The reality of a functional slave matrifocality also was rooted in early colonial law and custom. There also were African cultural mandates for such families.

Colonial slave masters quickly established the right to define and structure the most intimate connections and activities of their slaves and servants, electing to control various aspects of their sexual behavior and family life through their power as lawmakers.[47] Legislation, which in part defined "family" for these blacks, both paralleled and contributed to the African's decline in status from that of indentured servant to that of slave. This declining status, in turn, had great impact on black marriage, family, and community. An act passed in

1662 which mandated that the children of a black female, regardless of the color or condition of their father, had to take the status of their mother, had a profound effect on slave families for the following two centuries.[48] It not only placed a brand of perpetual servitude on the next several generations of Virginia blacks, but also provided the legal context for matrifocal kinship groups among succeeding generations of slaves. As such, slaveholders not only identified a slave child's status with that of his or her mother, but routinely identified the child's parentage solely with the mother, often denying any acknowledgment of the father's role—biological, emotional, social, or material.

The legal association between slave mother and child reinforced, within the owner's perception of an ordered domestic world, some of the cultural dictates of their society with regard to gender-differentiated responsibility. Owners believed that slave women, as childbearers, had a natural bond with their children and that it was their responsibility, more so than that of the children's fathers, to attend to the daily care for their offspring. Many masters, for example, frowned upon separating mothers from their young children, but refused to act similarly for fathers. Slave owners' preferential treatment of slave mothers made it difficult for slave men to have equal influence in the day-to-day activities of their families, particularly since many of them did not live with their children. It is not surprising, therefore, that among a compilation of reminiscences of Virginia ex-slaves, only 18 percent lived in a core nuclear household, and only 11 percent lived in strictly nuclear households. Moreover, the large majority spoke of the importance of their mothers while they were growing up, but only half referred to their fathers and less than one-third actually lived with their male parent. Taken altogether, the evidence overwhelmingly supports the conclusion that matrifocality was a fundamental characteristic of most slave families, even when fathers lived locally.[49]

Matrifocal slave families were not inherently problematic, structurally or functionally. The day-to-day absence of a father from a slave family did not necessarily mean that there were not other males available to take on some, if not all, of the socializing responsibilities, nurture, discipline, emotional commitment, and even protective stances that slave fathers ideally provided. Stepfathers, older brothers, uncles, grandfathers, and male cousins often were active in the lives of slave children whose natural father was not (or was not often) present. Of course these "surrogate" fathers were much more available within larger communities than smaller ones, especially since those holdings with ten or fewer slaves had a decided absence of males in their population. Children being raised under these conditions had much fewer options for daily, familial-like contact with adult male slaves than those who lived among larger numbers of men generally found in more populous quarters.

There also were other reasons why matrifocality could be a positive familial experience. Functionally matrifocal homes were prevalent throughout precolo-

nial western Africa and certainly an increased incidence of structural matrifocality occurred in colonial Africa as a result of the influence of intercontinental
slave traders. The reappearance of black matrifocal households in the colonial
and antebellum South suggest an important relationship between the slave's indigenous cultural and historical past in Africa and his or her southern familial
relations and structures, albeit within profoundly different social contexts. It is
reasonable to surmise, for example, that the African's past familiarity with matrifocal households allowed African American slaves to make useful, or perhaps
even to prefer, this kind of domestic structure. It made it possible for those persons who were part of matrifocal families to have a stable, functional, successful family life despite the "difference" in household structure and organization
they experienced in relation to other southerners.

It was not, therefore, matrifocality which implied instability in slave marriages and families. Rather, the varying conditions, generated by racist and
sexist customs, under which matrifocal slave families had to operate in the
American South were the undermining forces. The lack of control that slave
mothers, for example, had of their domestic affairs as a result of discriminatory
legislation and customs did much to destabilize matrifocal slave families. Designation of a child's status as a slave, based on the legal disposition of a mother
who had no protective rights over her sexual being, her reproductive organs, or
her offspring, effectively relieved the matrifocal slave family's head of much of
her power within her houshehold.

Unfortunately, slave owners often benefited from, and thus were willing to
instigate or ignore, the tragedies which crippled a slave family's emotional and
physical well-being. Even the sexual abuse of slave mothers and daughters, for
example, often meant a financial gain for owners who could claim as their
property and sell or use as labor the children who might result. The law of 1662
which ascribed the connection between slave child and mother and an 1691 act
which instructed the courts to "banish forever" those whites, free or bound,
who intermarried with a Negro, mulatto, or Indian landed a triple assault on
slave families: they institutionalized the sexual degradation of Virginia slave
women; they made possible the commodification of slave children; and they
bastardized biracial offspring. These kinds of conditions clearly provided the
groundwork for much slave familial instability regardless of the slave's household membership or leadership.[50]

Likewise, the domestic slave trade presented the slave family with problems
that sometimes even defied the resilience of a vibrant slave community. As the
antebellum era progressed and increasingly more slaves left Loudoun and Virginia as part of the interstate trade, the incidence of marital destruction, matrifocality and family dispersal became very great. Few Loudoun slave families,
kin networks, and communities remained untouched.[51] Indeed, the loss of
slave spouses and family members came to be so great that there is evidence

that the last generations of slave families even were threatened with loss of their most resilient familial characteristics—matrifocal structures and supportive extended family and community networks. A small, but substantial, population of slave orphans emerged, orphans who rarely had the benefit of a family when they were growing up. In fact, about 18 percent of Virginia's ex-slaves represented in the Purdue compilation did not speak of any consistent contact with either of their parents during much of their childhood.[52]

Henry Johnson, for example, was separated from his family at such an early age that he did not even realize he had living parents until he was eighteen. Finally spotted by his father after general emancipation, Johnson had to admit that while his kin were so happy to see him that they "shouted and cried and carried on," he was frightened of the strangers and tried to run away from them. "My fathers and brothers would go to work every day and leave me at home with my mother for over a year. They wouldn't trust me to work, feared I would run off 'cause I didn't know nothin' about them. Hadn't ever heard of a mother and father."[53] "Dar was a great crying and carrying on 'mongst the slaves who had been sold," Fannie Berry described a scene whose rate of incidence is difficult to estimate. "Two or three of dem gals had young babies taking with 'em. Poor little things. As soon as dey got on de train dis ol' new master had [the] train stopped an' made dem poor gal mothers take babies off and laid dem precious things on de groun' and left dem behind to live or die." The children were left, Berry asserted, to be claimed by anyone who found them. "[M]aster who bought de mothers didn't want gals to be bothered wid dese chillun 'cause he had his cotton fields fer new slaves to work."[54]

It was not the case that all slave masters were like those Berry described and cared little about the fate of slave families and children. Once a slave master or mistress committed to maintaining their own financial well-being by selling some of their slaves, however, slave families were bound to suffer. Even slaveholders like Sarah Ellzey, who wanted to keep at least some of her slave couples and families united, had little control over their future once someone else actually purchased them. Donald Sweig's survey of the familial histories of slaves in Loudoun and neighboring Fairfax County, for example, indicates that as many as 74 percent of those slaves who traders exported from this area left without accompanying family members. One also can reasonably surmise that since the majority of these slaves were between the ages of twenty and forty-nine years, many were married and/or had children at the time of their departure. Moreover, given the preponderance of female slaves found among those leaving the Upper South for the Lower South and Southwest during the last pre-Civil War decade, it is certain that this trade undermined many matrifocal slave households.[55]

A Loudoun Quaker, while petitioning the United States Congress in support of the discontinuation of slavery in the nation's capital, documented the destruction of slave marriages and families in his own home county due to the interstate slave trade, noting: "These people are without their consent torn from their homes, husband and wife are frequently separated and sold into distant parts, children are taken from their parents without regard to the ties of nature, and the most endearing bonds of affection are broken forever."[56]

This kind of separation had extreme impact on slaves of all generations and was expressed in a number of ways, both physically and emotionally, that often even a functional slave community or extended family could not alleviate. Henry Watson recalled that his mother was sold away from him as a small child. Although an elderly woman tried to console him and perhaps provide him with some maternal care, Watson could not be comforted. "Every exertion was made on my part to find her, or hear some tidings of her," he explained, "but all my efforts were unsuccessful; and from that day I have never seen or heard from her. This cruel separation brought on a fit of sickness, from which they did not expect I would recover."[57]

8

Slave Marriage and Family Relations

Arican American romance and marriage within the context of the institu-tion of slavery could be the most challenging and devastating of slave ex-periences. From the initiation of a romance, black men and women had to confront and compromise with their masters about control of their intimate lives, aware that their owner typically had the final say about if and when they could marry, and even who. Even after a slave's marriage, his or her master still commonly decided when slave husbands and wives could see each other, if and when they could live or work together, the fate of their children, and some-times even the number of children they had.[1]

Slaves nonetheless had their own way of doing things, refusing to concede too much, sometimes refusing to concede at all. If the slave master's interfer-ence in the slave's personal life was interminable, so too was the slave's resist-ance to this kind of intervention. Like their owners, slave attitudes and decisions about courtship and marriage were shaped by gender convention and community concerns, but not necessarily the same conventions or concerns. The matrifocality of many slave families, for example, meant that the realities of slave manhood and womanhood differed substantially within the context of family life from those whose familial experiences were nuclear and patriarchal. Likewise, extended families and slave communities were important, not just because they monitored slave behavior and maintained slave values, thereby protecting the integrity of the community. Members of slave communities also actually played substantial physical, material, and emotional roles in the lives of slaves. To a large extent, they were the slave's family. The presence of meaningful kinship ties embodied in the extended family or community, therefore, allowed slaves to take on a variety of marital arrangements and familial structures. One's master might have had the final authority, but there also were other slaves and slave institutions that exerted influence, perhaps more influence than masters realized. Within the broad contours of slave life that masters insisted on designing, slaves found spaces of their own, choosing what lines to and not to cross as they constructed their own domestic terrain.

It was a terrain structured by diverse, yet nonetheless respected rules and standards. Those who wanted to marry, for example, had to consult their parents or other black authority figures first. The man usually initiated the process, asking for permission from the would-be bride, her kin, and their owners. "First you picks out de gal you wants, den ax her to marry up with you," Levi Pollard explained. "[D]en go to Mars en ax him ifen you ken have her. If Mars like dat couple den he says yes."[2] Pollard's recollection suggests that male slaves and owners controlled much of this process, but mothers and elderly women also held power in certain slave quarters, particularly in relation to younger slave women. They could control vital aspects of a woman's courtship and marriage, sometimes even to the exclusion of owners or slave men.

The predominance of matrifocality and the large percentages of slave women in smaller holdings, therefore, had significant impact on slaves' domestic lives, giving slave women great influence in their families and communities. It was an influence not recognized in the larger society's hierarchy, but nonetheless functional in the slave's world view. Elderly slave women who had lived in the quarters for years, particularly where adult females were in the majority, were accorded great respect. Their long lives and the wisdom assumed derived from it, their years of service to their families, and their knowledge of their community's history were the basis for their authority. Likewise, mothers who raised their children without paternal input commanded their children's obedience and deference.

Female power in slave families and communities was not power that they took lightly or used sparingly. Ex-slave Philip Coleman, for example, admitted that "there was a likely girl" that he "took a great fancy to" and wanted to marry. According to Coleman, his owner approved of the match and the young woman did too, but the girl's mother "put up so strong [an] objection that the wedding . . . was called off." Caroline Johnson Harris explained of her courtship and marriage that "Ant Sue," and not her master, had to give permission to the slave couples in her quarters before they could marry. As an elder and a holy woman, "Ant Sue" especially compelled communal respect.

Harris recalled that when she and her prospective husband approached the powerful woman for her blessing, "She tell us to think 'bout it hard fo' two days, 'cause marryin' was sacred in de eyes of Jesus." Having followed her directions carefully, Caroline and Mose (the would-be-fiancé), returned to "Ant Sue" and told her that, after much consideration, they still wanted to marry. The elderly woman then assembled the other members of the slave community and asked them to "pray fo' de union dat God was gonna make. Pray we stay together an' have lots of chillun an' none of 'em git sol' way from de parents." A broomstick ceremony followed her prayer, but not before "Ant Sue" queried the couple again about the certainty of their decision.[3]

"Ant Sue's" and the discriminating mother's control carried considerable weight in their slave communities. Masters who where unaware of or disinterested in slaves' distribution of social power within their world claimed that their authority as owner took priority. If the couple had the same master, there usually was no problem in gaining his or her permission, although sometimes an owner would question each about their feelings before giving consent. If the couple had different owners, both masters had to give their permission and usually the husband and wife continued to live separately after their marriage. "My father was owned by John Butler and my [mother] was owned by Tommy Humphries," Loudoun slave George Jackson explained. "When my father wanted to cum he had to get a permit from his massa. He would only cum home on Saturday. He worked on the next plantation joinin' us." A few owners bought a favorite slave's spouse. William Gray of "Locust Hill" just outside of Leesburg, for example, purchased Emily, the wife of his male slave George, after their first child was born in 1839. The couple had five more children during the next eight years. Gray later sold the slave family to a local farmer in 1853, "all at their own request" for $3200.[4]

Emily and George, as most slaves, probably had a brief, "informal" wedding. Despite its brevity and seeming informality, however, slave weddings and the commitments they symbolized were extremely important events for black families and communities. William Grose, for example, was appalled when a new master insisted that he marry again simply because he had been sold far away from his first wife. He was equally distressed when the owner presented him with a new wife without any "ceremony."[5] Slave marriage rituals varied considerably. "Jumping the broom" was popular among some. Georgianna Gibbs remembered that when the slaves on her farm married they had to "jump over a broom three times" before they actually were considered married.[6]

The act of "jumping the broom" as part of slave marriage ritual is important to consider, not only because it was a popular practice, but also because of its cultural and sociopolitical implications. Although many contend that "jumping the broom" had African origins, evidence suggests otherwise. "Jumping the broom," in fact, was a popular practice in early Anglo-Saxon villages where a couple jumped together across a broom placed at their family's threshold in order to signify that they entered the residence as husband and wife. Jumping backward across the broom to the other side of the threshold meant the end to a marriage. Since "jumping the broom" was a pre-Christian ritual in much of western Europe, it probably passed down to later generations as an amusing, perhaps quaint, relic of their "pagan" past. By imposing this cultural albatross on slaves, southern whites suggested the lack of respect and honor that they held for their blacks' attempts to create meaningful marital relationships. The slave's acceptance of this practice, on the other hand, demonstrated the ability of slave culture to absorb, reconfigure, and legitimize new ritual forms, even those masters imposed out of jest or ridicule.[7]

Those slaves who did not "jump the broom" solemnized their marriages in other ways. Slave masters sometimes participated, reading a few words from the Bible or giving their own extemporaneous text. Tom Epps recalled that he had heard of "jumping the broomstick," but "us never did nothin' like dat in our place." Instead, the slaves participated in a ceremony whereby the "Marsa would hol' a light, read a lil' bit an' den tell 'em dey was married."[8]

On very rare occasions, local ministers actually officiated. Ex-slave Fannie Berry remembered with delight her wedding to a free black man named John Taylor. Because she was a favorite of her owners, she was able to have the ceremony in her mistress's front parlor, a minister perform the service, and many slaves and local free blacks attend. A festive reception followed with "ev'ything to eat you could call for."[9] Berry's husband worked on the railroad, and she saw him only occasionally until after general emancipation. Her abroad marriage was typical even if her lavish nuptials were not.

Fannie's owner let her marry the man she chose. Yet inevitably some masters refused to respect the choices that their slaves made about their private lives. Despite family or community support, those slaves who defied their masters paid a high price. Still slaves willingly, and sometimes willfully, chose to marry in spite of their owner's wishes. Martha and David Bennett, for example, married without her master's permission. David belonged to Captain James Taylor and Martha was a slave of George Carter. Taylor seemed not to resent the union, but evidence suggests that Carter felt otherwise—Martha reported that Carter had had her stripped naked and "flogged" "after her marriage."[10]

Whether or not Carter rejected the marriage, however, is only part of this puzzle. What is perhaps more intriguing is why Martha married David in the first place. Why would Martha, a member of a slaveholding that boasted a large and equal number of men and women, choose a man with whom she could not live and whose children she would have to raise without their father's daily input? Why would she commit to an abroad marriage and a functionally matrifocal family style when she did not have to do so? Why didn't she choose instead one of the men on Carter's plantation? Certainly for her to do so would have added some measure of security to her marriage and family. It also would have pleased her owner. Martha's marriage begs a number of important questions not only about the reasons why slaves married who they married, but also about the kinds of marriage and family styles they deemed acceptable.

Slaves so frequently married persons belonging to other masters that Martha's behavior does not seem odd. But Martha was not confronted with the kinds of conditions that usually are attributed to abroad marriage. Neither the demographic conditions nor residential patterns of Carter's plantation mandated that Martha marry abroad. Neither did the domestic slave trade nor slave rental business, for Carter did not routinely sell or rent out his slaves. Martha's marriage to George Bennett, therefore, suggests that there may have been other reasons why so many slaves had abroad marriages and matrifocal households.

While this question may never be completely answered, there are some partial explanations. Complex rules of exogamy, notions of slave manhood and womanhood, and a desire to extend one's social world beyond one's residential community were significant considerations. So too was the slave's psychological need to establish some "emotional distance" between oneself and one's loved ones, to say nothing of the slave's cultural heritage. All these factors contributed to what "choices" slaves made about their domestic lives within the context of the rigid constraints that masters imposed.

The slaves' great concern about marriage to a close blood relation, for example, could have influenced greatly the numbers of abroad marriages that existed even among quarters like those of George Washington, William Fitzhugh, or George Carter where there were many men and women from which to choose a spouse. In generations-old quarters such as these, long years of intermarriage and procreation created intricate and complex kinship ties, ties that may have been discernible only to slave community members. While older quarters housed particularly stable communities because of extended family networks, they also contained closely connected kin (first cousins, for example) whom slaves would consider ineligible as marriage partners. Unfortunately, this kind of avoidance is practically undetectable by scholars who have to rely on slave lists produced by owners or overseers who had different rules of exogamy. Even so, many masters seemed to have realized that their slaves were upholding stringent rules of exclusion. Georgia Gibb's recollection that her master "never sell none of his slaves, but he'd always buy more . . . dat keeps de slaves from marrying in dere famblies" suggests her owner's knowledge of operative rules of exogamy.[11]

Martha Bennett, therefore, may have looked for a husband outside of Carter's slaveholding because his quarters presented her with a preponderance of male kin. There also may have been other reasons why she agreed to marry abroad. Growing up in communities filled with matrifocal slave families, it is not surprising that slave women like Martha were socialized to function in such. Slave women may have foreseen other benefits as well. Having abroad husbands and matrifocal households, for example, allowed them a kind of management of their children and day-to-day domestic life that live-in husbands may not have. As such, matrifocality had the potential to define effectively slave womanhood in ways that were quite distinct from free womanhood. Likewise, abroad marriages could give women greater domestic power, ideally affording them the moral sanctity of marriage, but also lessening some of their responsibilities—physical and emotional—to their husbands.

Slave men like David Bennett would have had other motives for choosing an abroad wife, some linked to African American conventions of manhood and leisure. Nineteenth-century black men, as white, often viewed travel and "adventure" as a "natural" desire and activity of a "man." "In the year 1827, a spirit of adventure, natural to most young men, took possession of me, and I concluded to leave Virginia and go to Ohio," John Malvin, a free black reared in the Loudoun vicinity, confessed.[12] Abroad marriage also had other implications for slave men. The slave husband's sense that his "manhood" in part hinged on his ability to protect his wife and children inspired some to marry abroad—at least he did not have to witness his family's daily abuse. When local slave Dan Lockhart's wife was sold to a man who lived eight miles away from him, he believed it was "too far" and he managed to get his owner to sell him to someone who lived closer. He stayed with his new master for more than three years before he decided to run away to avoid seeing his wife and children being whipped. He explained that he "could not stand this abuse of them, and so I made up my mind to leave." [13]

Abroad marriage also meant an extended social world for slave men. "Slaves always wanted to marry a gal on 'nother plantation cause dey could git a pass to go visit 'em on Saddy nights," ex-slave Tom Epps recalled. These descriptions and others not only suggest the delight slave men gained from "travel" to their wives' homes and the opportunity those excursions afforded them to broaden their community. It also allowed slave husbands a "break" from their daily physical and psychological routines, a "break" which enhanced their leisure time.

Love and romance were as important reasons as any that slaves insisted on choosing their spouses even if it meant a long-distance marriage. The story of Loudoun slave William Grose and his free black wife is instructive. Grose's owner never approved of his abroad marriage to the free woman, for he feared that she would find some means to help William escape. Eventually he decided that the best way to protect his investment was to sell William to a long-distance trader. Sent to New Orleans, he was sold again, this time as a domestic to a creole widower. Grose's new owner, who seemed to have several slave wives himself, insisted that William marry another woman. "He sent for a woman, who came in, and said he to me, 'That is your wife,'" William explained. "I was scared half to death, for I had one wife whom I liked, and didn't want another. . . . There was no ceremony about it—he said Cynthia is your wife."[14]

It is not certain from Grose's autobiographical account whether or not he and Cynthia ever lived as husband and wife, but he continued to care deeply for the Loudoun free black woman he had married. Remarkably, the two managed to remain in contact. A year later, Grose's Virginia wife arrived in New Orleans and managed to get a position as a domestic in the same family in which he worked (an American family he had been hired out to serve), and the two secretly carried on their marriage. Grose's master eventually found out about their relationship and she was forced to leave New Orleans. But this was not the end of their story. "After my wife was gone," William confessed, "I felt very uneasy. At length, I picked up spunk, and said I would start." William finally managed to escape to Canada where he, his Loudoun wife, and their children finally were reunited.[15]

The history of William Grose, his free black wife, and their struggle to remain married in spite of his owners' opposition is an incredible and rare one. Yet the kind of determination they demonstrated was more common than one might imagine. Unfortunately, few were able to triumph, but many made admirable attempts. Willis Garland, for example, requested permission to marry Martha Brown even though she lived some forty miles away, and he would be able to see her and any children they had only a few times a year. His master agreed, but clearly laid out his restrictions. "He will be allowed to visit . . . as often as can be spared—at least three times annually," Garland's owner informed Scott's mistress.[16]

The kinds of decisions about their intimate lives that slaves made, even given the many restrictions which encumbered them, were very important to their sense of individuality, control, and self-esteem. For those slaves like the Groses, Willis Garland, Martha Brown, and even the Bennetts, therefore, it obviously was just as important, if not more so, to marry the person whom they "chose," even when they knew they would have to live apart, as to marry someone simply to please their master or because they could expect to share a home with that person on a daily basis.

"Marsa used to sometimes pick our wives fo' us," Charles Grandy complained. "Wasn't no use tryin' to pick one," he added resentfully, "cause Marsa wasn't gonna pay but so much for her. All he wanted was a young healthy one who looked like she could have children, whether she was purty or ugly as sin." Most slaves knew that their owners preferred that they marry within their own holding. To do so allowed masters to claim as property all children born to these cohabitative couples, usually considerably more in number than those born of abroad marriages. Slaveholders also believed that couples who resided together reduced security problems, eliminating the need to give passes for conjugal visits and providing masters with the potent threat of selling or hurting slave family members in order to insure obedience.[17]

The large numbers of abroad marriages, the substantial incidence of serial marriages, even the rare examples of polygamy, therefore, can be linked both to the slave's lack of control over his or her domestic life and to his or her resilient assertion of control. Jo Ann Manfra and Robert Dykstra's survey of late antebellum slave couples who resided in the southside of Virginia indicates that serial marriages often resulted from the 10.1 percent of slave marriages that ended with mutual consent and another 10.8 percent that ended because of spousal desertion. John Blassingame's analysis of slave couple breakage in Mississippi, Tennessee, and Louisiana suggests similar conclusions. One of the most compelling examples of slave choice and its impact on slave marital structures and relations is that offered by ex-slave Israel Massie. Massie insisted that slave men and women not only "understood" polygynous marital relations, but some sought them out. His insistence helps to further establish the premise that slaves adopted a variety of marriage and family styles and that they were comfortable with that variety. According to Massie, slaves sometimes made a conscious choice to create certain marital arrangements and family structures which were not monogamous and nuclear.[18]

"Naw, slaves didn't have wives like dey do now," he began his explanation. "Ef I liked ya, I jes go an' tell marster I wanted ya an' he give his consent." "Ef I see another gal over dar on another plantation, I'd go an' say to de gal's marster, 'I want Jinny fer a wife.' . . . Hit may be still another gal I want an' I'll go an' git her. Allright now, dars three wives an' slaves had as many wives as dey wanted." Massie insisted that the multiple wives of one slave man "didn't think hard of each other" but "got 'long fine together." He illustrated antebellum slave polygyny with an example from his own farm. "When Tom died," he continued, "dar wuz Ginny, Sarah, Nancy, an' Patience." According to Massie, all of Tom's wives came to his funeral and publicly mourned for him. "Do ya kno' . . . dem women never fou't, fuss, an' quarrel over dem men folks? Dey seemed to understood each other."[19]

Polygyny, or something akin to it in which a slave man had longstanding, contiguous intimate relationships with more than one woman, probably was a much more popular alternative among slaves than heretofore has been realized. The unavailability of marriageable slave men in smaller holdings and the scarce number of men in those slave communities hit particularly hard by the domestic slave trade provided the physical conditions for polygamy, particularly when coupled with pressures (internal and external) on women to "breed." Moreover, at least scarce knowledge of ancestral domestic arrangements (in Islamic or many traditional African religious groups) and a continual tradition of matrifocality among slaves provided cultural sanction for polygamy. Still few actual accounts of slave polygyny remain. This probably is because polygynous marriages could not be legalized after general emancipation. Given the general predilection of local churches, northern missionaries, teachers, and the Freedmen's Bureau to establish monogamy among freed slaves, polygynous or polygamous relationships after emancipation may have been largely ignored, or given some kind of culturally bound, misleading label such as "promiscuous couplings," "immoral" behavior, or adultery that have hidden from view the practice of polygamy among freed slaves.

Federal, state, and private agencies coerced freedmen and women to change this aspect of their lives, or at least to camouflage it from public scrutiny. Massie again is instructive, alluding to the reasons why polygyny ended with emancipation: "Now, out of all dem wives, when Lee surrendered, ya choose from dem one 'oman an' go an' git a license an' marry her. Some turned all dey wives loose an' got a new wife from some t'other place." Massie, and probably many other ex-slaves, was aware that it was illegal for "free" people to have more than one spouse. Former slaves, hoping to legitimize their domestic world through acquisition of the marriage "license," had to publicly abandon polygyny. Regardless of the reason for this postbellum change, however, it is clear that Massie, and the slaves he referred to, acted as if monogamy, even serial monogamy, was not the only marriage alternative or ideal they had as slaves.[20]

It is not unreasonable to assume, therefore, that even when demographic conditions theoretically could provide a high incidence of monogamy and nuclear families among the slaves of a particular holding, black men and women sometimes made other choices based on a complex combination of reasons; choices that, on occasion, resulted especially in abroad marriages and functionally matrifocal families, sometimes serial marriages, or even polygamy. Operative extended kin networks of various description undoubtedly allowed slaves some assurance that these kinds of decisions would not result in dysfunctional marriages or families.

Slave marriages, like those of any group, varied in terms of their internal dynamics, longevity, and the ways in which the couple acted out their roles as husband and wife. Given the variety of conditions under which slaves married and the numerous forms of marriage and family households they formed, it is difficult to discuss conclusively the various ideals which guided their domestic behavior. Yet one can begin to comprehend these roles if one has an understanding of operative adult sex roles among them.[21]

The emphasis on gender-specific behavior became an important part of child socialization as slave youth grew older. Slave females, who were more likely than males to remain in their families of birth through adolescence, received most of their gendered socialization from their mothers, other female kin, or community women. Usually by the time slave girls reached their teens, these women already had prepared them to take on the most important commitments of their adult lives—motherhood and marriage. Slave women taught their girls that as adults it would be their responsibility to cook, clean, bear, and rear children for their families, all this despite the labor demands of masters. They were supposed to take pride in their "womanly" skills and service they rendered their families.[22]

Clara Allen, for one, placed great esteem on the domestic arts that her mother taught her and her service to her family. Contrasting the skilled talent and familiar commitment of slave women with the carefree, unsolicitous attitudes of early twentieth-century black women, Allen openly disapproved of the abandonment of domestic skills that had been so important to Virginia slave women; that had, in fact, helped to define them as women. "Nowadays, do you think any dese girls w'd set still long enuf to WEAVE?" she asked rhetorically: "No sir, dey cyan't set still long 'nuff to thread a darnin' needle . . . dey cyan't weave, nor cook, nor do up a silk mull dress, nor flute de curtain ruffles, nor make pickle an' p'serbs, nor tend a baby liken it oughter be tended. Dey doan know nuttin'!" Allen added coolly, with a sense of female pride and purpose, "I could take the wool offen the sheep's back an' kerry it thru ter CLAWTH. Wash it, card it, spin it, weave it, sew it inter clothes—an' (with a laugh) wear it, when I gotter chance."[23] This sphere of domestic labor that Allen specified—taught, supervised, and performed almost exclusively by females—reinforced within slave girls and women a sense of their "femaleness" while helping them to maintain strong bonds across generational, cultural and occupational boundaries.

A woman's role as head of a matrifocal family mandated that she make some of her family's most vital decisions and suffer the consequences if her master or her abroad husband disagreed. It meant that she had to act protectively and aggressively for the sake of her dependents, often in open conflict with her owner. Slave mothers, for example, routinely rebelled against the poor material support owners provided, especially the amount and quality of their food. Few hesitated to steal, lie, and cheat in order to guarantee their physical survival or that of their children. Marrinda Jane Singleton, for example, remembered that as a single mother she stole food—vegetables and meat—in order to feed herself and her children. Speaking of one particular incident, she explained: "Dis pig was now divided equally and I went on to my cabin wid equal share. All de chillun was warned not to say nothin' 'bout dis. If dey did, I tole 'em I would skin 'em alive, 'cause dis pig was stole to fill their bellies as well as mine." "Negro Bet," a Loudoun slave woman belonging to Leannah Jenkins, who was accused of hogstealing, probably felt the same. Fortunately, she was acquitted; many others were not.[24]

The challenges of slave matrifocality, therefore, inspired idealized behavioral traits of self-protection, self-reliance, and self-determination among many black women. It was these ideals, in turn, which contextualized their physical and psychological resistance to white authority and shaped their roles within their families.[25]

Slave women across age, cultural, and occupational lines were forthright in their appreciation of self-reliant, determined black females who had the wherewithal to protect themselves and theirs, confrontationally if need be. Of course, most women were not able to act in any openly confrontational manner for fear of severe retaliation. But it is clear that slave women held great pride and esteem for those who did so. These were the women whom other slave females spoke most often about in "heroic" terms, attributing to them what seem like (and may have been) fantastical deeds and attitudes. Thus, while white southern society believed that this kind of female conduct was unfeminine, if not outright masculine, slave women utilized aggressive, independent behavior to protect their most fundamental claims to womanhood; that is, their female sexuality and physicality, and their roles as mothers and wives.

True stories about slave female rape and physical abuse, for example, abound in the records produced by slaves. Most slave women found no way to fight back (and win). Those women who found some manner to resist emerged in the lore and mythology of slave women as both heroic and ideal. Slave mothers, in fact, often told stories of these women to their daughters as part of their socialization. Virginia Hayes Shepherd, for one, spoke in glowing terms of three heroic slave women she had known personally or through her mother's stories—one successfully avoided the sexual pursuit of her owner, while the other two refused to be treated in the fields like men, that is, to be worked beyond their physical endurance as childbearing women.[26]

Seventy years after her emancipation, Minnie Folkes still felt the pain of witnessing her mother being whipped by her overseer. Yet her explanation of the older woman's suffering (that she had refused "to be wife to dis man") and her description of how her mother had taught her to protect herself from sexual abuse ("muma had sed 'Don't let nobody bother yo principle; 'cause dat wuz all yo' had'") are tinged with pride and respect. The elder Folkes was determined to have control of the physical attributes of her womanhood even if it meant routinely withstanding brutal beatings. Her resistance was a powerful lesson to Minnie.[27]

Fannie Berry told many accounts of female slave resistance to sexual abuse, including her own. But she was most proud of Sukie Abbott's daring rebuff of both her owner's sexual overtures and the slave trader's physical violation. Both Berry and Abbott rightfully linked the two as equally dehumanizing.

Sukie was the Abbott house slave who, according to Berry, had been the target of her master's unwarranted sexual advances. One day while Sukie was in the kitchen making soap, Mr. Abbott tried to force her to have sex with him. He pulled down her dress and tried to push her onto the floor. Then, according to Berry, "dat black gal got mad. She took an' punch ole Marsa an' made him break loose an' den she gave him a shove an' push his hindparts down in de hot pot o' soap. . . . He got up holdin' his hindparts an' ran from de kitchen, not darin' to yell, 'cause he didn't want Miss Sarah Ann [his wife] to know 'bout it." A few days later, Abbott took Sukie to the slave market to sell. The defiant woman again faced sexual abuse and physical invasion as potential buyers stared, poked, and pinched her. According to Fannie, Sukie got mad again. "She pult her dress up an' tole those ole nigger traders to look an' see if dey could fin' any teef down dere. . . . Marsa never did bother slave gals no mo," Berry concluded with relish.[28]

Many witnesses at the slave market that day no doubt thought Sukie vulgar and promiscuous, a perfect picture of black "womanhood." Fannie Berry concluded something altogether different. In Berry's estimation, Sukie had exacted a high price from the men who tried to abuse her. It was true that the slave woman had lost her community when Mr. Abbott sold her in retaliation for her resistance; but she still managed to deny her owner his supposed right to claim her "female principle." She also demanded that her new buyer see her for what she was, a woman, not an animal, by insisting that he acknowledge her female sexual organs. Perhaps most important, Sukie's response to Mr. Abbott's attempted rape deterred him from violently pursuing other slave women on his plantation. The moral of Berry's story of Sukie Abbott lies, therefore, not only in Sukie's ability to sacrifice her "privilege" as a domestic and her permanence in a nurturing community in order to protect her female body and her humanity, but also in the good that sacrifice did for others. Fannie Berry's rendition of the Sukie Abbott biography, whether true or embellished, is an important example of the kinds of stories of female heroism and humanity that slave women told and retold as a kind of inspirational socialization and legitimizing process.[29]

Thus the story had to be told within a certain context to give the desired effect. Neither Fannie nor Sukie probably would have approved of a woman baring her sexual organs publicly if the circumstances had been different. Slave women usually frowned on blatant female sexual exhibition or promiscuity. This is not to say that they were ashamed of their sexuality. Nor were they shy about the promise of sexual pleasure and human procreation that they as women embodied. There were rules, however, which guided their sexual expression, rules which many of them respected and tried to incorporate in their social lives.

Sex in the female slave world, for example, was part of the culture of adults. As girls grew older, it was acceptable for them to become more aware of the significance and value of their sexual power, to realize that women, through their sexuality, provided great service to their families and communities.[30] A woman's body in the world of slaves was an important, complex symbol. Her body, therefore, was a sign, in the face of heart-wrenching tragedy and oppression, of human pleasure, immortality and future security. Many expected that much about a young woman should suggest the sensuality and immortality that she (as a sexual, procreative being) held. A single women's dress, hair, walk, dance, and language could and sometimes were supposed to be sexually suggestive. Yet girls and adolescents still were not supposed to yield to the temptation of sexual intercourse out of a sheer desire for sexual pleasure. That right and responsibility was reserved for married women, those who were soon to be married, or those who wanted to bear children.[31]

The diverse cultures of slaves produced varying guidelines about a woman's sexual behavior and responsibility. Some mothers, for example, went to great lengths to shield their daughters from sex until after they were married. Others acted differently, expecting young women to marry after they became pregnant or gave birth to their first child. Usually, however, sex was communally sanctioned only for those women who were ready to marry, to have children, or both. Matrifocality was such a widespread phenomenon among slaves that many slave elders did not always demand marriage before intercourse or even before the birth of a first child. Extended families and operative slave communities were good support networks for single mothers and children. A woman with a child, regardless of her marital state, however, had to be willing to take that responsibility seriously. If her family and community came to her aid, the community expected that she, and later the child, would give back in kind.

Of course the conditions of life for slave females often made any social rules difficult to maintain. Moreover, rules of sexual expression differed for slave men and women. To complicate the matter even further, black men often were not the only ones that slave women had to respond to and negotiate sexual contact. When assumptions of male sexual prerogative and female submission shared by both black and white men influenced their relationships with slave women, men of either race might have used whatever advantage they had to seduce or even to exploit and sometimes abuse these women.

Of course terms like sexual seduction, exploitation, and abuse are relative to one's time and place. Slave women probably would not have chosen contemporary language or their definitions to describe their sexual relationships with slave men, particularly their husbands. Slave wives, even abroad wives, were expected to submit to their husband's will, particularly those who had regular contact. A woman's submission to her man went hand in hand with her service to her family and community. Minnie Folkes's mother, for example, taught her that a woman should not only "cook, clean up, wash, an' iron" for her husband, but "please" him because it was her "duty as a wife." William Grose's free black wife routinely traveled on foot twelve miles to bring her slave husband clean clothes. Nancy Williams affirmed that her father had ultimate control in their family even when her mother thought he was being abusive to their children.[32]

Colonel Leven Powell. Portrait by Charles Balthazar Julien
Fevret de Saint-Memin. *Courtesy of the Art Museum of Western
Virginia.*

Major Burr Powell. *From* The Powells of Virginia *by Rosalie Noland Powell, 1938.*

Catherine Brooke Powell. *From* The Powells of Virginia *by Rosalie Noland Powell, 1938.*

(*Above*) "Chestnut Hill," home of Burr and Catherine Powell. Photograph by John G. Lewis. *Courtesy of the Virginia Department of Historic Resources.* (*Below*) Interior of slave cabin at "Chestnut Hill." *From* The Powells of Virginia *by Rosalie Noland Powell, 1938.*

Elizabeth Whiting Powell Conrad.
*Courtesy of the Winchester-Frederick
County Historical Society.*

Robert Young Conrad. *Courtesy of the
Winchester-Frederick County
Historical Society.*

Home of Robert and Elizabeth Conrad. *Courtesy of the Winchester-Frederick County Histori-cal Society.*

"Oak Hill," Loudoun home of President James Monroe. *Courtesy of the Loudoun County Museum.*

George Carter. *Courtesy of the Loudoun County Museum.*

Elizabeth Osborn Lewis Carter. *Courtesy of the Loudoun County Museum.*

"Oatlands," home of George and Elizabeth Carter. Photograph by Beverly J. S. Harris. *Author's collection.*

(*Above, left*) Fannie Berry, Virginia slave woman. *Courtesy of Hampton University Archives.*
(*Above, right*) Frank Bell, Loudoun area slave man. *Courtesy of Hampton University Archives.*

Lucy Edwards, Virginia domestic slave woman. *Courtesy of the Eleanor S. Brockenbrough Library, The Museum of the Confederacy, Richmond, Virginia.*

Slave auction. *Courtesy of The Library of Virginia.*

(*Above*) Free Negro cabin in Virginia. *Courtesy of The Library of Virginia.* (*Below*) Log cabin, Loudoun County. Photograph by James H. Cones, III. *Author's collection.*

(*Above*) "Belmont," Ludwell Lee family home and later school of Margaret Mercer. Photograph by James H. Cones, III. *Author's collection.* (*Below*) Quaker meeting house and school, Lincoln, Virginia. Photograph by James H. Cones, III. *Author's collection.*

Lovettsville estate. Photograph by Beverly J. S. Harris. *Author's collection.*

"Morrisworth," home of Burr and Sarah Powell Harrison. Photograph by John G. Lewis shows twentieth-century addition of a south wing. *Courtesy of the Virginia Department of Historic Resources.*

(*Above*) "Llangollen," home of Cuthbert Powell. Photograph by D. A. Edwards shows home after twentieth-century enlargement. *Courtesy of the Virginia Department of Historic Resources.* (*Below*) "Springwood," Loudoun home of George Washington Ball. Photograph by John G. Lewis. *Courtesy of the Virginia Department of Historic Resources.*

Domestic slave quarters at "Springwood." Photograph by John G. Lewis. *Courtesy of the Virginia Department of Historic Resources.*

And while many slave couples did not live together on a daily basis and many abroad wives believed they had to take on an aggressive, protective, somewhat independent stance with regard to family matters, many slave husbands still wanted to be their families' protectors and supporters. Thomas Harper, for example, was a local blacksmith who decided to escape to Canada because he "thought that it was hard to see . . . [his family] in want and abused when he was not at liberty to aid or protect them." Dan Lockhart also decided to escape because he could not stand to see his wife and children whipped without being able to do anything to prevent it. Numerous Loudoun black men, such as Samuel Anderson, Peter Warrick, Joseph Cartwright and Cupid Robinson, managed to secure the freedom of their wives and/or children in order to insure that they could protect them. Dangerfield Newby, a local mulatto ex-slave who had been freed by his father, lost his life trying to rescue his wife and their children from a local slaveholder. Harriet Newby's letters entreating her husband to "do all you can for me, with I have no doubt you will," were found on his body after he was killed as part of John Brown's contingent during the raid on Harpers Ferry in 1859.[33]

A wife's submission and service to her husband, therefore, was supposed to be rewarded by his efforts to aid and protect her and her children. Sex complicated this brokered balance because it virtually was impossible for some slave women to submit to their husband's desire for sexual exclusivity. Loudoun slave masters who believed that they held sexual rights to their female slave property continued to be an enormous problem for couples. Some masters actually reserved the most attractive slave women for themselves, regardless of the woman's marital status or even their age. Loudoun planter George Carter, for example, was known to purchase female adolescents for his sexual pleasure. Writing to the wealthy bachelor in 1805, William Forbes was explicit about Carter's preferences: "Girls are more frequently for sale than boys—would you object to a very likely one—*a virgin*—of about 14 or 15." Several years later, Carter's sister Sophia sternly criticized her brother's infamous behavior. Writing in response to her accusations, Carter admitted his history but added by way of an explanation: "My habits like most men are vicious & corrupt," "a Sin" that he was "only answerable for" to his God.[34]

Indeed, George Carter's declaration that he was only one of many was well founded. Loudoun county census takers in 1860 described 27 percent of resident slaves and 51 percent of local free blacks as mulatto. Miscegenation was frequent, but not spoken about openly. Slaves, threatened with whippings and sale, typically had the most to lose from exposing slave/master sexual liaisons. Once the threat of public exposure surfaced, slaveholding families did not hesitate to blame and punish the slave women. Liz McCoy painted a not unusual scenario: "Aunt Charlotte . . . was sold to Georgia away from her baby when de Chile won't no more 3 months. . . . [She] had a white baby by her young master. Dats why dey sold her south." A slaveholder reacted typically to an incident of miscegenation within his family that had become public knowledge. "She had offended in my family," he explained of his son's concubine, "and I can only restore confidence by sending her out of hearing [to Georgia]."[35]

Miscegenation is a sterile, emotionless term that often shrouds acts of sexual submission characterized by violence and degradation. The women and their biracial children clearly were the true victims in these situations; but slave men also could faced grave consequences. Many often found themselves in the precarious, if not dangerous, position of competing with slaveholding men for the same slave women.[36] Slave beaus and husbands could suffer brutal physical and emotional consequences if a slaveholding man wanted his woman. Undoubtedly when white men raped black women they did so not only to subject these females to a violent and dehumanizing experience, but also to emasculate husbands and male kin. The various reactions of male slaves, therefore, were equally responses to their own sense of powerlessness as they were a recognition of the physical and psychological pain that these females experienced. "Marsters an' overseers use to make slaves dat wuz wid deir husbands git up, [and] do as they say," one ex-slave man noted. "Send husbands out on de farm, milkin' cows or cuttin' wood. Den he gits in bed wid slave himself. Some women would fight an' tussel. Others would be [h]umble—feared of dat beatin'. What we saw, couldn't do nothing 'bout it. My blood is b[o]ilin' now [at the] thoughts of dem times. Ef dey told dey husbands he wuz powerless."[37]

When slave husbands did intervene, they suffered awful retaliatory actions—sometimes permanent separation from their families, severe beatings, or murder. Many probably felt as did Charles Grandy, who concluded of the fatal shooting of a male slave who tried to protect his wife from the advances of their overseer: "Nigger ain't got no chance." Some slave husbands targeted the female victims of rape rather than the powerful white males who attacked them. Regardless of whomever they struck out at, however, their responses usually had little effect on the abusive white men involved.[38]

But not all sexual relations between slave women and white men were physically coerced, just as not all sex between slave women and men was voluntary. Masters and slave men had many ways to gain control of and manipulate black women's sexuality. Some slave women responded to material incentives like food, clothing, and better housing that white men offered in exchange for sexual favors. Certainly they were much more able than slave suitors to "romance" slave women with gifts and promises of a better life. Others promised, and sometimes granted, emancipation. The unavailability of marriageable slave men, particularly for those women who lived in small holdings, also could have been something of a coercive factor. It is not inconceivable that some of these women established sexual/marital relations with available white men, just as these kinds of demographic conditions may have enjoined some to commit to polygynous relations with whatever black men were available.[39]

One also cannot discount the impact on biracial sexual relations of a combination of factors endemic to life in a racialist constructed society, including internalized racism and a desire to identify with and be accepted by the "superior" race. Under these circumstances, some slave women may have agreed to become concubines to, or may have even desired, white men. Racially mixed slave women who were socialized to be more culturally akin to whites than blacks could be particularly vulnerable to the sexual overtures of white men. Ary, for example, was an quadroon slave woman raised, as the favored domestic, in the home of her father's brother. By the time she reached young womanhood, she had become the concubine of her young master, her paternal first cousin. Convinced that she was her father's favorite child, Ary often boasted of her elite white parentage and her young master's love for her. Remembering her lover's pronouncement that she was to have nothing to do with "colored men" because they "wern't good enough" for her, Ary was determined not to associate too closely with any blacks.[40]

Despite Ary's belief that white men were superior to black, men of both races lived by a double and privileged sexual standard. Tales of male sexual prowess were applauded in the slave community, while female promiscuity was frowned on. Masters followed the same sexual code in their white communities and, therefore, understood only too well the importance of sexual conquest to the male ego. Some undoubtedly used the masculine esteem derived from sexual triumph to help convince slave men to act as "breeders." West Turner was born in about 1842 and remembered well the tales of breeding men: "Joe was 'bout seven feet tall an' was de breedinges' nigger in Virginia," he began one story. "'Member once ole Marsa hired him out to a white man what lived down in Suffolk. Dey come an' got him on a Friday. Dey brung him back Monday mo'nin'. Dey say de next year dere was sebenteen little black babies bo'n at dat place in Suffolk, all on de same day."[41]

Clearly, Mr. Turner's story expanded the limits of Joe's sexual prowess to that of the legendary. But this does not diminish the evidential significance of Turner's story with regard to the importance of male sexual veracity as a tenet of slave manhood. On the contrary, his exaggeration underscores the point. Moreover, Turner's master's willingness to recognize and reward Joe for such a demonstration of sexual vigor created an even deeper appreciation among slave men—the legendary Joe "[d]idn't have no work to do, jus' stay round de quarters sunnin' hisself 'till a [breeding] call come fo' him."[42]

Slave men traditionally applauded their sexual potency, celebrating it in song, dance, jokes, and heroic tales. Unlike slave women, men did not have to restrict their sexual activity to marital or procreative duties. A man could derive great status from having sexual relations with as many women as possible, or as many times as possible with one woman, without marriage or children being at issue. Even elderly men like Cornelius Garner still spoke proudly of their youthful sexual verve and refused to accept that the possibility of infertility diminished their record of sexual performance or their status as men. Speaking of his three wives, Garner boasted: "Pretty good ole man to wear out two wives, but de third one, ha, ha may wear me out." When asked if he had any children, Garner was quick to answer that he had never had any children, but that that was not his fault : "I did what God tole me. 'Wuk and multiply,' ha ha. I wuked but 'twon't no multiplying after de wuk."[43]

The emphasis that slave men placed on their sexual prowess had profound impact on slave courtship and marriage, particularly when they treated their women as sexual objects to pursue and dominate, often without a hint of marriage or longstanding commitment. The impact of slavery on the relationships that slave males had with their families, especially the women in their families, may have helped to exaggerate female sexual objectification. Recall from the previous chapter the discussion of slave residence patterns. It was typical for slave boys to be raised in matrifocal households. It also was typical for them to leave these households as they reached puberty. They did so, temporarily, as part of the redistribution of prime males to their owners' more labor-intensive units. They also endured more permanent leave as part of the domestic slave trade or slave rental process, or to take up residence in all-male households in the quarters. This abrupt withdrawal from a social and socializing world of women to one of men was a difficult transition. Unfortunately, this separation experience was only the first of what could be two or three more for slave men. This constant experience and fear of separation, along with the need to be able to adjust, physically and emotionally, to it, may have inhibited some slave men from allowing themselves to construct complex relationships with the women with whom they came in contact, resulting instead in their sexual objectification.[44]

A song that ex-slave Levi Pollard sang proudly when interviewed summarizes some aspects of slave sexual relations. From the first stanza on, it is a celebration of slave male eroticism, sexual casualness, and female slave objectification.

> Black gal sweet,
> Some like goodies dat de white folks eat;
> Don't you take'n tell her name,
> En den if sompin' happen you won't ketch de blame.
>
> Yaller gal fine,
> She may be yo'ne [yours] but she oughter be mine,
> Lemme git by
> En see what she mean by de cut er dat eye.

Better shet dat door,
Fo' de white folks'll believe we er t[e]arin' up de flo'.

When a feller comes a-knockin',
Dey holler Oh, sho,
Hop light ladies,
Oh, Miss Loo. . . .

. . . De boys ain't a gwine,
When you cry boo hoo,
Hop light, ladies,
Oh, Miss Loo. . . . [45]

Pollard's song not only is about sexual relations in the quarters, but specifies the kind of sexual control that slave and white men joked about or perhaps hoped to have over slave women. The significance of this text is that it documents, in the words of slave men themselves, many of the popularized perspectives they held about sex and the female slave. It is replete with allusions to vital issues of slave sexuality, including: competition for slave women across and within racial lines ("Some like goodies dat de white folks eat;" "She may be yo'ne but she oughter be mine"); questions of paternity and sexual responsibility ("Don't you take'n tell her name,/ En den if sompin' happen you won't ketch de blame"); the voyeuristic essence of slaveholders' interest in slaves' private lives ("Better shet dat door/ Fo' de white folks'll believe we er t'arin' up de flo'"); female promiscuity ("When a feller comes a-knockin',/Dey holler Oh, sho"); and the ways in which slave women used their sexual attractiveness and femininity to manipulate slave men ("De boys ain't a gwine, /When you cry boo hoo/ Hop light, ladies").

Particularly interesting, in relation to the continuing discussion of matrifocality, is the text's suggestion that some slave men avoided taking responsibility for children born of casual sexual liaisons ("Don't you take'n tell her name,/ En den if sompin' happen you won't ketch de blame"). If this is true, then the impact on the lives of those slave women involved, their children and their communities could have been significant. Did single and married slave men in fact contribute significantly to the numbers of matrifocal slave families by refusing to acknowledge their children by women to whom they were not publicly tied? This song suggests that a woman's family or community might hold a man accountable if his identity could be documented.

The contours of slave society, however, diminished the opportunity for a woman, or her family, to authenticate such paternity claims. Since most slaveholders were much more likely to give their slave men, rather than their women, passes to travel from one farm to the next, it was not difficult for these men to avoid sexual accountability. Recall, for example, Israel Massie's description of polygynous practices in which slave men had the opportunity to "marry" several women who resided at different places in their neighborhood. Certainly these slave men had just as much, if not more, opportunity to pursue casual sexual relations with a variety of women who did not live in their quarters. This kind of behavior, in turn, might have led to the creation of numerous matrifocal households.

Slave girls and women recently separated from the "protection" and advice of their kin as pawns in the domestic slave trade must have been especially vulnerable to the sexual and romantic advances of local dandies. For those females whose families and communities demanded that they remain sexually inactive until after marriage, or at least marry once they became pregnant, the decision of a slave man not to admit paternity could mean a lowering of a woman's esteem within her kin network.[46]

Casual sex in the quarters, therefore, rarely had casual consequences. When casual sex translated into adultery, stakes were very high. Slave men were jealous not only of the sexual attention that white men paid their wives, but also of the flirtations and seductions of other black men. Slave women were equally intolerant. Records from the era, however, indicate that both slave men and women would stray. As early as May 1774, for example, records of the local Broad Run Baptist Church documented that the church excommunicated the "Negro Dick" for "having lived in Adultery." Several years later, they excommunicated "Negro Grace belonging to Mr. Colbert for adultery." Over the next fifty years, the church ousted several other slave worshippers, the majority for adultery.[47]

Few Loudoun slave masters held great concern for the complex and diverse conventions of gendered behavior, beauty, marriage, or family that slaves respected and tried to maintain within their families and communities. Even if they had wanted to know, and do, more about these aspects of black life, slaves were quick to shelter the less obvious details of their personal lives and choices from their masters' control. Records indicate, therefore, that only sometimes did slave owners betray a curiosity about a slave child's paternity or the ways in which slave men and women might have manipulated each other sexually. This was not likely to happen unless some event threatened their slave property's economic potential or behavior or, if as fellow church members, their slave property's actions violated established religious mores. Broad Run Baptist Church, for example, excluded the slave woman Polly from membership in September 1840 for "fornication"; ousted the slave man Joe for complaints given by the slave woman Sally in February 1843; and turned away the slave Gabriel, who was charged with "immoral" conduct in July 1850. Overall, however, slaveholders usually did not promote slave marriages, families, or related values unless they believed it would benefit themselves in one way or another. For the slave master the slave family had two important roles: it gave an owner the opportunity to manipulate for the owner's benefit a slave's concern for his or her family; and it was the center of slave procreation.[48]

Some masters undoubtedly promoted long-term slave marriages if the couple proved to be amply fertile. Betsy and Henry Jackson, for example, had fifteen children. Although they lived on neighboring farms in Loudoun, Mrs. Jackson's owner seemed to have had no objection to Henry's conjugal visits every Saturday and Sunday. Loudoun planter William H. Gray bought his slave woman Emily in 1839 along with her small child Lizzie. At that time Emily, who was married to Gray's slave George, was pregnant with another child. By 1853, Emily and George had increased Gray's slave property by another four children. Although there is no evidence to suggest that the Jacksons' owner or William H. Gray pressured their slaves to have children, there are testimonies from other slaves as well as documentation within planters' papers which indicate that slave breeding was a concern of many slaveholders. "The masters were very careful about a good breedin' woman. If she had five or six children she was rarely sold," one ex-slave explained, as did several others. Likewise, owners and traders did not hesitate to advertise young female slaves as "good breeding wenches" and buyers interested in purchasing female adolescents and adults routinely inquired of their general health and specifically their ability to bear children.[49]

Sometimes slave owners promised female slaves material rewards such as larger food allowances, better clothing, or more spacious cabins if they would consent to have many children. Some undoubtedly accepted these incentives, while others resented their masters' attempts to control their bodies. A slave woman's sexuality and her reproductive organs were key to her identity as a woman and she claimed a right to have power over that identity. "Muma had sed 'Don't let nobody bother yo' principle'; 'cause dat was all yo' had," Minnie Folkes explained of her reticence to have sexual relations even after she married. Some female slaves in fact may have taken the matter of reproduction into their own hands, secretly using contraceptive methods in order to maintain control over their procreation. One slave woman, for example, indicated that she was able to regulate her childbearing when she explained that she used to have a child every Christmas, "'but when I had six, I put a stop to it, and only had one every other year.'"[50]

Masters often suspected slave females of using contraceptives and inducing miscarriage, but rarely were able to prove it. Eliza Little, for example, spoke of her owner's attempts to discover information about "a slave girl who had put her child aside." He beat several of the slaves and inquired of the incident, but was unable to get the details of this carefully guarded secret of the female slave community. A few slave mothers went so far as to commit infanticide. The Loudoun *Democratic Mirror* reported on November 11, 1858, for example, that the court had found a slave woman named Marietta guilty of infanticide and ordered her deportation to the lower South.[51]

Sometimes what slaveholders might have construed as a slave woman's resistance to bearing children, however, was a result of temporary or permanent female infertility. Given their overall poor physical condition due to heavy work loads, regular harsh treatment, nutritionally deficient diets, and limited access to proper medical attention, it is not difficult to understand why many black women were unable to reproduce as quickly as some of their owners might have wanted. Even though slave women usually began having children earlier than white women, they eventually had fewer, and the space between their live births was lengthier and more erratic. The average age at first birth of Loudoun area female slaves was 19.98 years, while the spacing of their children was approximately two and a half years.[52]

Local white women, on the other hand, usually married between the ages of twenty and twenty-two and gave birth to their first child during the next twenty-four months. Moreover, the spacing of white children, approximately two years, was shorter and more regular compared with those born to slave women. It was not unusual, therefore, for white Loudoun females to give birth to eight or ten live children during their lifetimes. Loudoun slave women, however, generally only had between five and six, and only then when they had a history of long-term marital relations. The same was true for most slave women in Virginia. A review of slave lists from across the state inclusive of birthing patterns from the 1760s through 1860 verify that the average age of first birth for these women was 19.71 years; the average number of live births was 4.94; and the average spacing between live children was 2.4 years. [53]

Certainly these statistics reveal much, in a general sense, about the domestic lives, marital relations, health, and labor of adult female slaves. A "typical" slave woman might begin to have occasional sexual relations during her mid- to late teens. She usually conceived her first child when she was almost nineteen; her second when she was almost twenty-one. If by then she had settled into a marital relationship that allowed her to have conjugal sexual relations at least once a week, she might have four other children who would be born alive; and perhaps four to five miscarriages or still births before she reached menopause.

Keep in mind, however, that there were many slave women who did not fit this pattern at all, and for several reasons. The availability of men—a condition which varied greatly for women who lived in large or small holdings—could be an important deterrent. So too could be the impact of sale and displacement of slave women and their spouses as a result of the "natural" cycle of slaveholdings, an owner's financial concerns, or retaliation for slave resistance. Important as well was a woman's work load and its seasonal quality. Other influences included a woman's living conditions and diet and her overall health—if she, for example, suffered from some common illnesses such as hypertension and anemia, was a victim of one of a number of epidemics that swept the county and state, or had permanent gynecological problems or suffered from a venereal disease. One also must consider the medical resources that were available to slave women, her knowledge of contraception and her attitude about using this knowledge, and, of course, the owner's attitude toward a pregnant woman and her potential offspring. Thus, while generalities and "averages" tell us much about female fertility and something about the slave's domestic life, there is much more to uncover and consider.

The overall disparities between the fertility of white and slave women, for example, occurred against a backdrop of important demographic changes. As the era progressed, evidence suggests that slave women had more children, while the number of children white women had began to decline. Using information available from manuscript census records, one can establish child/woman ratios for both white and slave women in Virginia during the period 1800 to 1860. This data, as well as slave registers, confirm that slave women did begin to have children at an earlier age than white women, but eventually had fewer. A comparison of fertility ratios, however, also suggests that the gap between white and black female fertility diminished somewhat over time. (See Table 7.) Likewise, slave lists document that the numbers of children born to slave women increased over time as a result of earlier ages at first birth and shorter average spacing between births. Yet these gains in female slave fertility may have been only academic. There are also indications that child mortality rates increased almost proportionately with the decline in child spacing. In the end, therefore, slave women during the later decades of the pre-Civil War period probably bore about the same number of offspring to reach adulthood as those in the 1790s and early nineteenth century.[54]

Consider, for example, the birthing patterns of the slave females who resided on the plantations of Samuel Vance Gatewood between the years 1772 and 1863. The Gatewood slave register is a particularly important document because of the length of time it covers and the large numbers of slaves in the Gatewood holdings: it records the birth of 124 children to 26 mothers over a 91-year period beginning with the late colonial era. Gatewood's list provides a great amount of information about slave families, but particularly about slave fertility and breeding. This register documents a steady decline in the age at first birth of slave females from 17.4 years between 1834 and 1854, for example, to 17.26 years between 1855 and 1863. Although the age at first birth of the Gatewood female slaves is inconclusive for earlier generations, the data that it does offer suggests a much older age at first birth, about 19 years for the earlier generations of Gatewood slave women. More convincing, however, is the data from the slave list which indicate a significant decline in the average gap between live births. The spacing of live births recorded for the Gatewood slave

Table 7 Child/Women Ratios for Slave and White Women in Virginia, 1820–1860

Census Year	Ratio of children (0–14 yrs.) to women (14/15–49)		Ratio of children (0–9) to women (10–49)	
	Slave	White	Slave	White
1820[a]	1.92	2.50	—	1.24
1830[b]	1.82	1.14	1.31	0.95
1840[c]	1.96	2.17	1.35	1.23
1850[d]	2.06	2.16	1.08	1.13
1860[e]	2.01	2.19	1.05	1.02

[a] *Census for 1820* (Washington, D.C.: G504, 512, 518, Gales and Seaton, 1821), pp. 23–26.

[b] The unusually low ratio produced from census information available for 1830 is probably indicative of a substantial undercount of white children aged 0–14 years old. The error also is reflected in the white child/woman ratio for 1830 descriptive of the age cohorts 0–9 years (children) and 10–49 years (women), and to a lesser extent for blacks during this census year in both categories of compilation. *Fifth Census or Enumeration of the Inhabitants of the United States, 1830* (Washington, D.C.: Duff, Green, 1832), pp. 87, 89.

[c] *Compendium of the Enumeration of the Inhabitants and Statistics of the United States* (Washington, D.C. 1841), pp. 32–33, 36–38.

[d] J. D. B. Debow, *Statistical View of the United States . . . Being a Compendium of the Seventh Census . . .* (Washington, D.C.: A.O.P. Nicholson, 1854), pp. 215, 253–255, 257.

[e] Joseph G. Kennedy, *Population of the United States in 1860; Compiled from the Original Returns of the Eighth Census* (Washington, D.C.: Government Printing Office, 1864), pp. 507–508, 512.

women decreased from 38.12 months during the years 1773 to 1793, to 31.81 months between 1794 and 1813, and finally to 19.71 months from 1834 to 1854. Clearly the average spacing between live slave births on the Gatewood plantations had been cut in half over an eighty-year period (1773-1854).[55]

The decline in average spacing, however, occurred against a backdrop of increased child mortality rates that probably was not coincidental. The numbers of slave children belonging to the Gatewood family who died before reaching adolescence increased from 20 percent of their population during the years 1773 to 1793 to one-third during the next twenty-year period. By the 1830s, the mortality rate of slave children on these plantations had increased again to nearly 40 percent. Between the years 1834 and 1854, there was an overall slave child mortality rate among the Gatewood slaves of almost 47 percent. Thus, while the spacing between live slave births for Gatewood women declined by almost 50 percent during the years 1834 to 1854, the mortality rate of these children increased almost proportionately, to slightly more than 50 percent during the same time period.[56]

The statistics which define natural slave increase document the impact of their harsh lifestyles on childbearing women and on the health of their children. While it is uncertain the number of times slave women conceived, had spontaneous abortions, ectopic pregnancies, or miscarried, it is known that the number of live slave births was much smaller than for white women. Moreover, the number of slave children who survived the first decade of their lives was fewer than those of white women. Demographer Richard Steckel, for example, calculates that, throughout the South, more than one-half of slave infants died before they were one year old, a mortality rate that was almost double that of whites. Although the survival rate for slave children improved after they reached the age of one, their mortality rate was still twice that of white children until they became fourteen years old. Among many slaveholdings, infant and small children had mortality rates of almost 50 percent.[57]

Not only did slave parents have to contend with a devastating number of child deaths, they also had the difficult task of socializing those who survived. The most important barrier they faced was a legal one. Put simply, slave kin were not the legal guardians of their children, slaveholders were.

Masters took seriously their ownership of slave youth and often pre-empted parental authority. Not only did slave masters sell and give away slave youngsters, but they also assigned them tasks when their parents felt that they were either too young, ill, or otherwise indisposed to perform them; punished them without parental knowledge or consent; and sometimes offered "favorites" protection from parental disciplinary measures. It was difficult for slave parents to wrestle control from their masters, particularly when owners believed that all slaves, young and old, were psychologically and cognitively like "children" and insisted on publicly treating adult slaves like they were.[58]

"During slavery it seemed lak yo' chillun b'long to ev'ybody but you," one ex-slave recalled of her mother's painful struggle to maintain some control over her children and some status in their eyes. Not only did the woman have to watch her owner cruelly beat her sons and daughter, but she also suffered the humiliation of witnessing her children in an audience collected for her own beating. "Dey didn' only beat us, but dey useta strap my mama to a bench or box an' beat her wid a wooden paddle while she was naked." Stripped naked and beaten before her daughter, other family members, and her slave community, Mrs. Hunter must have feared that this example of her powerlessness in the face of white control would jeopardize the authority she deigned to hold in her family and that she needed in order to rear her children properly. Her fears were not in vain. While Caroline seemed to respect her mother's position, Mrs. Hunter's sons refused to follow convention and accept parental or white authority. Hunter's master first beat them severely because they refused to work; he then sold them south.[59]

Sometimes slave parents tried to challenge an owner's control of their children, but with little tangible success. One slave woman recalled an argument that she had with her mistress: "I said to my Missis if folks owns folks, then folks owns their own children." "'No, they don't . . .' [her mistress responded] 'white folks own niggers.'" "Well," the slave mother replied with a note of superiority, "the Government owns you and everything." "Aunt Crissy was a smart talkin' woman, an' when Master sold [her daughters] Lucy an' Polly, she went to him an' tole him he was a mean dirty slave-trader," Beverly Jones recounted. Some time after her owner sold her two daughters, her son Hendley died. "Aunt Crissy ain' sorrored much," her unofficial biographer added. "She went straight up to ole Master an' shouted in his face 'Praise gawd, praise gawd, my little chile is gone to Jesus. That's one chile of mine you never gonna sell.'"[60]

White owners balked at overt attempts by kin or any other potential authority figure to gain control of slave children without their permission. Slaveholders understood that such challenges to their rights as owners by black parents were potent signs of rebellion; that slaves were teaching their children, through example, to resist their oppression. Not surprisingly, most slave masters met this kind of resistance with extreme hostility and brutality, often punishing the would-be usurper and slave child.[61]

Loudoun slave owners typically did not allow parents to reduce their labor quotas in order to care for their children. New mothers usually spent about two weeks with their infants before they had to return to their hectic work schedules. Given the work loads of slaves, one or two persons, even the child's parents, rarely were able to attend to all of the components of the childrearing task. Parents, therefore, had to share childcare and -rearing with others. While they relied on other members of their families, nuclear and extended, for aid, owners assigned temporary caregivers of their own—usually infirm, elderly, or very young female slaves. Slaveholders, therefore, not only claimed a large role in the lives of slave children, but they also shared their authority with others who were not slave parents or kin. In addition to a slave child's kin, slaveholding women, white overseers, black drivers, and slave nurses especially were important authority figures at various stages of a slave youngster's development.

Within the auspices of the slave family and extended kin network, the importance of one's contribution to the rearing of slave children was determined by a number of conditions. Parents, grandparents, step parents, older siblings, aunts, uncles, and sometimes cousins and community associates contributed to the upbringing of slave children if circumstances of the slave family made it necessary to do so.[62] The closeness of the consanguineous tie and one's gender generally implied differential responsibility. The size of the family and the slaveholding, as well as the birth order, also were determinants. So too were the ages and health of possible rearers; their availability and willingness to do so; and certainly the opinions of kin and owners. Clearly there were a number of operative variables. Yet slave masters generally made the final decision as to who took care of slave children and under what conditions.

Loudoun slave masters routinely assigned and protected slave mothers as the primary "in house" caretakers for their young. The day-to-day domestic responsibilities performed within slave families, therefore, remained divided along gender lines. Later generations of slave children adopted this gender-differentiated behavior which, in turn, further promoted gender-segregated activities and bonding. While mothers usually assumed the most significant long-term obligation to their offspring, substitute childrearers, drawn from nuclear and extended kin groups, also were female—usually older daughters, grandmothers, and single aunts. Among those Virginia slaves whose biographies are compiled in *Weevils in the Wheat*, for example, 14 percent attested to the importance of their grandmothers during their childhoods and 10 percent identified their aunts as persons of consequence. Local slaves like Silas Jackson typically described older sisters as caring for young children, cooking for the family, or helping their mothers with other domestic tasks.[63]

Many slave families were not only matrifocal, but also matrilocal. Those fathers who lived locally had the privilege of seeing their families on weekends and holidays. George Jackson, who lived near Bloomfield in Loudoun, recalled that his father lived on the next plantation, but could visit only on Saturdays and Sundays. John Fallons allowed his slave Moses to visit his wife, who lived some twelve miles away, each Sunday. Fallons even supplied Moses with transportation. "Every Sunday Marster let Uncle Moses take a horse an' ride down to see his wife an' their two chillun, an' Sunday night he come riding back; sometimes early Monday morning just in time to start de slaves working in de field," the slave's nephew recalled. While Moses Bell was a vital part of his extended family (his sister, her husband, and sons) on the Fallons plantation—supervising their labor, protecting them from punishment, exemplifying the importance of kin and freedom—it was more difficult for him to act as protector for his own wife and children because he lived away from them.[64]

Most slave fathers who had an opportunity to do so served their families in a number of capacities. Ideally, they provided emotional support and affection, moral instruction, discipline, and physical protection. Some also were able to give material support, particularly food. Many taught their boys how to hunt, trap, and fish. Those with lucrative skills did likewise, passing down their knowledge of metal and wood working, carpentry, and blacksmithing along with a host of other traditional skills such as folk medicine. George White, for one, recalled: "Papa was a kinda doctor . . . an' . . . knowed all de roots. I know all de roots too. . . . My daddy . . . showed dem to me."[65]

In their absence, other available male kin, such as uncles and grandfathers, assumed some of these duties. Looking back at their lives as children, ex-slaves often vividly recalled the emotional support and survival skills that their grandparents, as indispensable members of their extended families, provided. "'Son, I sho' hope you never have to go through the things your ole grandpa done bin through,'" Frank Bell remembered his grandfather telling him when he "wus a little tot dat ain't nobody paid no 'tention to." Amanda Harris recalled that her grandmother told her that smoking a pipe helped her to ease the pain of slavery. "'Tain't no fun, chile,'" the elder explained to the adolescent. "'But it's a pow'ful lot o' easement. Smoke away trouble, darter. Blow ole trouble an' worry way in smoke.'"[66]

The manner in which slave kin and owners perceived slave children in relation to themselves directly influenced the ways in which they treated these youngsters and tried to shape their development. Slave children were potentially important resources for family members and their masters. Slaves viewed their young as extensions of themselves and kinship lines, often naming them for favorite family members. Slave children also were providers of future security for their parents and kin, persons whom they could depend on for love, comfort, and service once they became old and infirm.[67]

Slave masters, on the other hand, regarded slave children as a financial resource who were valuable only as obedient, submissive, efficient workers. Many also anticipated a kind of loyalty, respect, and affection from their slave property which did not differ greatly from the expectations of parents. These different perceptions were the source of great internal and external conflict. Slaves responded in a variety of ways, from overt resistance to passive acceptance of an owner's will.[68]

Slave parents and kin, for example, clandestinely challenged brutal lessons of owners about obedience, docility, submission, and hard work with words and acts of kindness and care that reassured slave youth of their self-worth and humanity. They also taught slave youngsters through stories and example that it was possible to outmaneuver and manipulate whites. Loudoun slave George Jackson, for example, grew up knowing that his grandfather had successfully escaped from slavery with the help of Harriet Tubman. After escaping, the elder slave eventually was able to purchase and emancipate his wife. The attempts of Verlinda Perry's literate male slave to distribute abolitionist literature to other Loudoun slaves certainly had some lasting effect on local black youth. Obviously many others learned that it was possible to leave Loudoun and its oppressive environment through careful planning and with the assistance of family members and friends. Escape became the inevitable fantasy of the young and old.[69]

Persistent pressure on marital relations and family life was a primary reason that many Loudoun slaves initiated escape plans. David Bennet and his wife Martha, who were both from Loudoun, readily admitted that they decided to escape with their two children, a little boy and a month-old infant, because of the cruelty of Martha's owner, George Carter. Although the Bennets gave no details of how they managed to leave Loudoun without detection, there was a county Underground Railroad station run by local Quakers and free black ferryman. "It afterwards came to be known that the ferryman at Edward's Ferry, on the Potomac was the underground agent of these organized thieves . . . and the Chesapeake and Ohio Canal was a part of the route which received, on certain boats, fugitives brought over by the ferryman," one Loudoun planter recalled in his autobiography.[70]

Some of the most successful slave escapes from Loudoun were group affairs comprising family members and friends. On Christmas Eve, 1855, for example, six county slaves began their journey to Canada. The group included one married couple, Barnaby Grigby and his wife Elizabeth, Elizabeth's sister Emily, her fiancé Frank Wanzer, and two other male friends from neighboring Fauquier County. The slaves traveled both by carriage and horseback, "courtesy" of their unsuspecting masters. The owners, William Rogers and Townsend McVeigh of Middleburg, Lutheran Sullivan of Aldie, and Charles Simpson of Fauquier, did not initially believe that their missing slaves had run away. As was the custom, they had extended their slaves the right to travel short distances in order to visit friends and loved ones during the Christmas holidays. It was not until the next day, when the slaves were approximately forty miles from Loudoun, that whites discovered that these slaves, connected by blood, marriage, and friendship, were fugitives.[71]

Traveling through Maryland on the way to Pennsylvania, Grigby and company met a group of white men who insisted on seeing their passes. When they refused to comply, the suspicious whites demanded that they surrender to a search and seizure. The fugitives, who had concealed guns, opened fire. The four slaves traveling in the carriage (the two couples) escaped, one of the men riding on horseback at the rear of the carriage was killed, and the other was captured.

Grigby and his wife, along with the other couple, finally reached Pennsylvania. There they came into contact with a local vigilance committee that helped them to reach Syracuse. It was there that the Reverend Jermain W. Loguen married Frank Wanzer and Emily Foster. Shortly thereafter, the group settled in Toronto. Wanzer, however, could not console himself with the thought that he had left some of his family behind in Loudoun. Several months later, he left Toronto determined to return to Aldie to help them escape. The official records of the Pennsylvania Vigilance Committee document his successful rescue of his sister, her husband, and a family friend. It read: "August 18, 1856. Frank Wanzer, Robert Stewart, alias Gasberry Robinson, Vincent Smith, alias John Jackson, Betsey Smith, wife of Vincent Smith, alias Fanny Jackson. They all came from Alder [*sic*], Loudoun county, Virginia."[72]

Unfortunately, not everyone was able to escape with family members in tow. Even those who left with one or a few still faced the pain of leaving others behind. Women with small children, the elderly, those who were physically weak or lacked the psychological resolve to succeed were not allowed to go along. Considerations of group size, and the related issue of safety, also determined who was included. The larger the group, the greater chance of discovery and failure. Vincent Smith, for example, successfully escaped with his wife, but felt compelled to leave his mother and several siblings behind if he hoped to avoid detection. Robert Stewart's mother, four brothers, and two sisters remained in Loudoun when he journeyed to Canada. Thomas Harper, a slave blacksmith from nearby Alexandria, did not believe that he could escape successfully with his wife and children and eventually went alone.[73]

Loudoun slaves not only "ran away" from the pain, humiliation, and material deprivation that slave masters imposed, but also "ran to" family members. Many resisted the separations that slave owners engineered, clandestinely returning to their homes and families. The November 12, 1836, edition of the *Washingtonian*, for example, carried an advertisement by William Schaffer describing a "Dark Mulatto Woman, 25 years old" who had escaped from his custody. Schaffer presumed that the woman was on her way to visit some of her relatives who were the property of George Carter at "Oatlands." Carter recently had sold her to one of his cousins, Fitzhugh Carter of Fairfax. "I think it is likely she is in that settlement, or about Mr. George Carter's Oatlands, as she has connexions there," Schaffer explained in the notice. Relatives worked hard to maintain the safety of these fugitives, sometimes successfully shielding them from detection for months or even longer. When this particular advertisement appeared in the Leesburg newspaper with a $100 reward attached, for example, the "dark mulatto woman" already had been missing for more than a year.[74]

Of course, the large majority of Loudoun slaves never escaped. Several other couples and families, however, were successful in gaining their freedom through individual acts of emancipation that owners implemented for various reasons. Albert and Townsend Heaton, of "Exedra" in Loudoun, for example, eventually freed several slaves that comprised much of the Lucas slave family network. While some remained in Loudoun, others settled in Liberia. Wilson Selden of "Exeter" freed the slave woman Nannie and her two children Anne and Harlow. Charles Binns, a Loudoun county clerk, emancipated all of his slaves upon his death, as did others. Some Loudoun bondsmen and women, like Cyrus Tripplett, Samuel Anderson, and John Watson also found ways to purchase themselves as well as their family members.[75]

Many who remained as slaves in Loudoun learned to take solace in their families and friends whom they were spared to live near. The development of a strong sense of identity and community ethos was one of the most important ways slaves coped with and resisted the stress on their domestic relations. Slave kin, for example, hoped to teach their children not only how to survive as individuals, but also the importance of the slave community and their responsibility to help others. They emphasized the value of demonstrating respect for other slaves and, in complete opposition to the lessons of owners, instructed their youngsters in a code of morality that paid homage to blacks rather than to whites. They preached against lying to and stealing from one another, the importance of keeping slave secrets, protecting fugitive slaves, and sharing work loads. Teachers working among contraband slaves in Virginia noted the affection that slaves held for one another and the many polite courtesies they extended among themselves. One ex-slave eloquently explained the basis for such relations. "The respect that the slaves had for their owners might have been from fear," she admitted, "but the real character of a slave was brought out by the respect that they had for each other. "Most of the time there was no force back of the respect the slaves had for each other. [T]hey were for the most part truthful, loving and respectful to one another."[76]

But slaves, like other Loudouners, were not always successful in their attempts to withstand long-term pressures on their domestic or social relations. As individuals with the same range of emotions and capable of the same moral triumphs and failures as free persons, many acted inappropriately toward their loved ones. Adultery was not the only internal problem which occasionally plagued Loudoun slave marriages and rocked slave families or communities. The slave quarters often was a place of smoldering emotions and anger. Disagreements and frustrations could erupt into violence, while verbal and physical abuse were sometimes responses to complicated issues of discord within slave marriages and families. Spousal abuse was not uncommon, prompting one slave woman, for example, to comment that "some good masters would punish slaves who mistreated womenfolk and some didn't." Child abuse and neglect also were well-documented phenomena.[77]

Alcoholism seemed to have been a problem which often interfered with smooth slave marital and familial relations. Drinking was as popular a pastime for slaves as for free people. Those who habitually consumed large quantities typically were less responsive to their families' needs. Drinking also enhanced other disruptive behavior, sometimes triggering arguments and abuse. Divisive attitudes within slave families and communities, such as social status based on color or occupation, also proved to be problematic. So too were the cynicism and alienation of some who came to accept prevailing societal attitudes about the legitimacy of slavery and the "natural" degradation of slaves. The continual demands of the domestic slave trade, coupled with the other devastating conditions slave owners imposed, sometimes effectively eroded slave communities and family networks that had been functional for generations. Those who witnessed and were part of this destruction could not escape its physical or emotional impact.[78]

Faced with overwhelming problems, as well as their own individual pressures and priorities, some slave couples responded in ways that further damaged rather than protected their marriages and families. More than a few voluntarily separated. Manfra and Dykstra's survey of the fate of late antebellum slave couples in southside Virginia has much broader applicability.

They concluded that of those slave marriages terminated before general emancipation, at least 20 percent did so because of the desire of at least one spouse.[79]

The slave's family and community, therefore, often faced profound conflicts and problems which they responded to in a variety of ways, sometimes successfully, sometimes not. Slave masters and their representatives involved themselves in and tried to influence many vital aspects of their slave property's private lives. Slaveholders' economic and social priorities, in particular, often were in direct opposition to the needs of slaves trying to organize and function as family groups. Consequently, slave marital relationships, family structure, composition, and performance differed significantly from those who were not slaves, particularly whites.

Clearly many, if not most, Loudoun slaves lived in family groups that were matrifocal and matrilocal. But there also was a diversity of structure, membership, and relations that cannot be denied. This diversity was due not only to the pressures of slave life, but also to the cultural and situational choices of the slaves themselves. The question as to whether slaves preferred a nuclear family structure still looms large and undoubtedly will shape future historiography. What is clear, however, is that throughout, extended family membership and flexibility were at the foundation of most functional slave families, not monogamous marital relationships. Indeed, the high volume of slaves exported as part of the domestic slave trade meant an ever-increasing number of husband or father-absent slave families.

Moreover, slave husbands were not patriarchs. To establish this reality of the role of the slave father and husband in the slave family does not characterize him as "inadequate," but rather testifies to the harshness of slave life. It also challenges traditional, western-centered, ideals of fathers and husbands. Much the same can be said for the slave mother whose labor for her owner had to come before her duty to her family.

Neither "fathering" nor "mothering," therefore, were embodied in one person in a slave family. But there were some similarities between slave and free "domesticity." Gender-differentiated expectations and behaviors at home, for example, were not so different. Females, for example, performed most of the tasks associated with the day-to-day care of children, their families' clothing, and food preparation. Yet by the last decade of the antebellum era, the group being hardest hit by this trade were not young men, but rather young women—many of whom were mothers.[80] This reality certainly had a devastating impact on the large number of Loudoun slaves whose families were decidedly matrifocal. Had the institution of slavery continued to exist as it had for Loudoun slaves during the years 1850 to 1860, undoubtedly the definition, function, and composition of the slave family would have undergone great change to accommodate the absence of young mothers and females from kin groups. The withering away of functional slave extended families and communities in some areas that were hardest hit by the domestic slave trade meant much suffering for those slave children, and adults, who became virtual orphans.

Despite all this, the Loudoun slave family survived and served many of its constituents well. It did not necessarily exist or function in the ways of other southerners. Slaves drew on rich African, European, and American cultural heritages, but also were forced by oppressive socioeconomic and political conditions and diverse domestic climates to construct domestic ideals and functional families that were different from the "norm." Given the difference that their status and cultures made in all other aspects of their lives, certainly it is not surprising that enslaved blacks in the American South also defined family life differently.

9

Free Blacks

*You have felt and witnessed the degradation of your colour in this
country . . . few indeed of the free black have done well here &
Never Can—*

Albert Heaton, 1830
Loudoun County Slaveholder and Colonizationist

I t is uncertain when free people of color first came to live in Loudoun. A few
families, like the Robinsons and the Lanes of Waterford, took up permanent
residence and had begun to build their communities by the 1750s.[1] But unlike
slaves, little reference is made to colonial free blacks except in some early court
records and indentures. Only three, for example, are clearly discernible on the
county's 1771 tithable list—John and Joan Grant, who had their own household, and Levy, a resident at Henry Oladacre's home. A few free black men
probably came as hunters and trappers in the early eighteenth century. Others
no doubt arrived with the first settlers looking for frontier land. Some followed
slave family members. Certainly many arrived as slaves themselves, later earning their ambiguous status as "free blacks."[2]

Once black slavery legally was established in Virginia, the question as to
how persons who were born enslaved could become free became relevant.[3]
Most free people of color inherited their status from free mothers. But for those
born to single, free white or black women who could not afford to suppport a
child, their "freedom" came only after years of mandatory apprenticeship. As
such, Margaret Mulligan, a white Loudouner, came forth on October 5, 1810,
and gave oath that she had living with her, "a mulattoe girl named Mariah
Martin aged 18 years." Mariah was the impoverished, illegitimate daughter of

a white woman and a black man. As she had turned eighteen, she was eligible to leave Mrs. Mulligan's service. A few years earlier, a mulatto woman named Jenny Ball went before a Loudoun county justice in order to testify that she was the child of a white woman, Susanna Ball, and a black father. Indentured as a small child, it was time for her to receive her freedom.[4]

Financially unstable and socially marginalized, most of these mulatto ex-servants began their "free" adulthood with precious few resources—not a particuarly auspicious building block for any community. Often severed from their black or white mothers as small children, and not given the legal right of attachment to fathers who could not marry their mothers because of prohibitive interracial marriage laws, or would not do so for other reasons, many of these early free blacks emerged from their indentured lives without even the rudiments of a family.

The lives of some must have seemed part of a vicious cycle, spinning painfully out of their control. Although they had the right to withdraw from their indentures when they reached adulthood, some already had committed a new generation of free people of color to mandatory apprenticeships by that time. Children born to these women while they still were indentured had to serve similar terms. Prominent Loudoun citizen Francis Peyton, for example, took an oath on April 21, 1801, that his "negroe" servant Betty Davis, then twenty-three years old, had completed her stint of service. Betty's mulatto mother, Ann Ward, had been bound to Mr. Peyton. Betty had been born during Ann's period of service and, consequently, was compelled to serve Peyton until she became an adult. Jane Robinson, a mulatto servant of George Ward, faced a similar problem. While bound out to Ward, Robinson met and married George Watson, a local free black. The Watsons had five children before Jane could gain her "freedom."[5] Virginia law demanded that they too serve George Ward, or someone of his choosing, until they reached adulthood.

Involuntary apprenticeship was a difficult experience for both the adults and children involved since often the circumstances of mulatto and black servants' lives in rural southern communities were painfully harsh. A December 30, 1800, ad in the local *True American* suggests some of the difficulties: "For Sale. A likely NEGRO GIRL who has to serve for the term of nineteen or twenty years. She is now about twelve years of age, and very well grown and will have to serve one year for every child which she may have during the term of her servitude."[6] Like slaveholders, masters could sell or hire out indentured servants. There were other similarities to slave life as well. Single mothers and fathers of free children of color often faced the same kind of heartbreak as slave parents when they lost their children to the domestic slave trade. Like slave females as well, servant women and girls were subject to their masters' sexual abuse or manipulation and breeding schemes. It certainly was no coincidence, for example, that the author of the *True American* ad included a flattering physical description of the "Negro girl" and alerted any potential buyer of the benefit he or she might derive if the "girl" had a child while in service. The language of the advertisement was more eloquent than those of slave notices, but it still translated like the "breeding wench" sale pitches of slave traders. Stigmatized because of the conditions of their birth, race, and status, most of these youth lived under the same conditions, did the same kinds of labor, received comparable material support, and were subject to similar punishments as slave youngsters.

Over the years, fewer and fewer free people of color were born into servitude, but there remained connections and a commonality between free blacks and slaves. The legacy of interracial matings, for example, continued to influence both communities. Over half of Loudoun free "blacks" were light-skinned enough to be considered "mulatto" by 1860 census enumerators, as was more than a quarter of the local slave population. There also were few free black Loudoun families that did not have intimate ties with slaves, particularly during the early decades of the nineteenth century. Wilson Anderson, Fanny Smith, and Peter Warrick, for example, were just a few who remained married to county slaves even after they became emancipated. But while they were able to establish independent households, a significant minority of county free blacks were not. They lived instead on the property of slaveholders who were their employers or owned some of their kin.[7]

One can only imagine the frustration of a free person of color who wanted to buy a slave family member, but was unable to do so. Nancy Cartwright's tragedy was a familiar one. She was a free black woman reared near Loudoun but who moved to New York after acquiring her freedom. In so doing, she left behind a family of slaves—her mother, a daughter, two sisters, and a host of nieces, nephews, and other kin—who meant everything to her. Sometime after Cartwright arrived in New York, she received a desperate letter from her daughter explaining the details of her sale to a long-distance trader. "I take this opportunity of writing you a few lines," Emily's letter read, "to inform you that I am in Bruin's jail and Aunt Sally and all of her children, and Aunt Hagar and all her children, and grandmother is almost crazy." She pleaded with her mother to intercede and buy her before Joseph Bruin moved her to New Orleans for resale.[8]

Cartwright acted immediately. She asked a local abolitionist named William Harned to contact Bruin to arrange a possible purchase of Emily and perhaps other kin. "Will you tell me, by return mail, at what price you will sell Emily Russell to her mother," Mr. Harned queried, "and how long you will give her to make up the amount? [A]lso," he added, "at what price you hold her [Nancy Cartwright's] sisters and their children? I shall confidently expect a reply from you immediately; and in the mean time, that you will not dispose of them." Bruin had a reputation for selling slaves to abolitionists or kin at inflated prices, usually allowing them eight days to raise the purchase price. Not surprisingly, it was impossible for Cartwright to accumulate the large sum he required. Emily's selling point was her beauty. Bruin had decided to sell the young mulatto in New Orleans as a prostitute for $1200, she being, in his estimate, "the finest-looking woman in this country." He asked an additional $5300 for her relatives. Refusing to lower his prices so that Nancy Cartwright might be able to afford even one family member, Bruin placed Emily Russell, her aunts, and cousins in a slave coffle that he was shipping South.[9] Emily died in route.

Unlike Nancy Cartwright, some free blacks did succeed in buying and later emancipating loved ones. Every pre-Civil War census listing indicates that there were some Loudoun free blacks with slaves in their households. Most were family members they had managed to purchase, but not yet manumit. Inflated slave prices and a growing hostility to free blacks, however, increasingly curtailed this kind of family venture. In 1820, for example, almost 14 percent of Loudoun's free black-headed households had slave members. Just ten years later, only 5 percent did. By 1860, just 4 percent of free black-headed households were slave-inclusive.[10]

Although scant records descriptive of the fate of those slaves living in free black households survive, some information is available. Tracing the composition of these households over time, it becomes clear that many free blacks eventually did manage to secure the emancipation of the slave kin they purchased. Of those nineteen free black households that had slave members in 1820, only eight reappear in the 1830 census. Of these eight, however, six, headed by free black farmers and laborers James Bigsby, Clement Watson, Peter Mars, Henry Hopkins, Joseph Cartwright, and Cupid Robinson, had emancipated household members who had been slaves in 1820.[11]

The few remaining deeds of manumission and registration slips for Loudoun also provide documentation of free blacks who purchased and freed kin. On September 11, 1802, for example, Cyrus Triplett, who gained his freedom only in 1795, filed a deed of manumission for his wife Lucy. He managed to not only purchase his wife but also James Mahoney, and completed the legal process of emancipation for both. Sixteen years later, the widowed Lucy Triplett continued this family tradition, filing deeds of manumission for the two children whom she had had while enslaved. Likewise, when the free black John Watson married the slave woman Cate, he wanted to make certain that he obtained her freedom before they had any children who would inherit her status. Luckily he was able to borrow $200 from Loudoun County Clerk Charles Binns to purchase his wife.[12]

Free blacks usually placed great emphasis on following through the procedure of legal manumission, understanding only too well their precarious status and its implications for the loved ones they held as slaves. Often in debt and threatened with mandatory removal laws, they feared what might become of their "precious" property if they were sued for some payment, forced to leave the state, or died before they had an opportunity to settle their affairs. Their uneasiness often prompted them to act quickly and decisively. Samuel Anderson eloquently expressed such feelings in a deed of emancipation that he filed in a Loudoun court in 1818:

> Know all men by these present that I Samuel Anderson . . . a free man of Colour, do hereby manumit and set free my daughter Charity aged twenty one years so that neither I my executors or administrators nor any other person or persons Whomsoever shall have any claim to the said girl named Charity, but that she shall be absolutely free from all manner of Servitude from this date forever. . . .[13]

Peter Warrick's explanation was more succinct but no less passionate on the occasion of his purchase and manumission of his wife, their daughter, and his two grandchildren—he did so, he explained, "'in consideration of . . . [his] Natural love and affection'" for them. Lucy Triplett tried to make certain that her two children would be able to maintain their freedom regardless of her eventual fate. As such, she stipulated in their emancipation deeds that they were not to obtain their free status until adulthood and that two local Quakers, Daniel Janney and Amos Gibson, should serve as their guardians if she should die before they reached maturity. In so doing, Mrs. Triplett could assume that should Lemmon and Peggy become orphans, the county court would not arbitrarily place them in servitude, but that two Friends, known for their sympathy and aid to the free black population, would decide their future.[14]

The men and women who purchased their freedom and that of their loved ones worked long and hard to do so. The difficulty of their task, the nature of the institution of slavery, and the economic structure of the Loudoun economy all helped to shape the trends of this phenomenon. These trends, in turn, tell much about free black families. What is most obvious when viewing self- or familial emancipation, for example, is that most of the Loudoun families that were able to succeed had adult male heads. In 1810, two out of the three; in 1820, 17 of the 19; and in 1830, seven out of the nine slave-inclusive, free black households had male heads. By 1860, the trend had not changed—seven out of the eight free black households with slaves listed as members were male-headed.[15]

This trait comes as no surprise since free black women lacked a kind of economic viability that more men enjoyed. Their strategies for survival and gaining access to resources that they could use to buy an enslaved family member, therefore, sometimes differed significantly from those of their male peers. Men, for example, could borrow money and use long-term labor contracts as collateral. Women, on the other hand, had to rely more on close, personal ties with employers and patrons in their time of need. When the slave woman Fanny Smith faced the threat of being forced to leave Loudoun permanently, for example, she asked her longtime employer to help her raise enough money so that she could buy herself and her daughter. Chapel, her hirer, had taken a liking to Fanny and did not mind interceding on her behalf. Even before her request, he had tried to secure her future in his family as the wife of one of his slave men by buying her outright. When his first attempt to buy Fanny failed, he returned her to her owners. With word that Fanny's owners were leaving the area permanently, he was determined to try again. This time Chapel succeeded, helping Fanny to purchase herself and her two children and also using his political clout to gain permission for her to remain despite the expulsion law of 1806 which mandated manumitted slaves leave the state within twelve months of their emancipation. He did so, he explained, because of Fanny's years of dedicated service and her "extraordinary character."[16]

Amy Grayson and Harriet Cook also were able to evoke "benevolent" feelings in their ex-owners and employers when they needed their help. Because so many domestic slaves and servants were female, women of color had a greater opportunity to develop emotional ties and a beneficient client-patron relationship than the men in their communities. The aid of whites, especially that of white men of importance, bought these women some security and tolerance, important resources in a society where one's place was insidiously tied to one's race, class, and gender.

Free blacks who had several slave family members they wanted to purchase not only honed their resources carefully, but systematically planned who to buy and when. The law provided some guidelines—an 1832 statute, for example, dictated that free people of color could not hold slave property, other than a spouse, parents, or children, except by inheritance.[17] These restrictions, combined with the natural pull of marital ties and close consanguineous bonds, persuaded most to purchase spouses first and then children and parents. Rarely could someone afford to buy other kin such as their siblings, aunts, or uncles. Women of childbearing age often got top priority because the longer they remained enslaved, the greater the possibility they would have children who bore their status. Other considerations also shaped these decisions, especially the potential buyer's perception of each family member's unique situation—their master's treatment, the threat of abuse or sale, the slave's emotional and physical health, the response of owners to a request to purchase, and whether or not a woman of childbearing age might become pregnant. Able-bodied, income-producing adults also were a priority, since the proceeds from their labor could help to buy other kin. Most men also tried to buy their wives and small children together so as not to have them separated. The next priority was to buy any remaining offspring before they became old enough to command lucrative prices in the domestic market. Parents were particularly careful to purchase their daughters before or during early adolescence, perhaps to avoid possible sexual abuse or breeding plots.[18]

Free people of color clearly faced immense odds when they set out to buy and emancipate slave kin. It virtually was impossible for them to do so, for example, if a slave owner objected. Even if they did not, it was a very difficult legal procedure. The last years of the eighteenth and the beginning of the nineteenth century, however, provided a unique window of opportunity. Responding to the egalitarian sentiments of the American Revolution, patriot slave efforts, and especially the perception of a "surplus" of slaves in the upper South, state assemblymen acted to ease the burden of emancipation. Accordingly, they passed a bill in 1782 which allowed any master to manumit his or her slaves by last will and testament or by some other written document that was witnessed and sealed. This law, along with the conditions which influenced its passage, precipitated a substantial increase in slave purchase and emancipation by free black family members and some masters.[19]

Slave owners, like black kin, had certain criteria which guided their choices for emancipation. Some acted out of a sense of moral obligation. Others had financial concerns in mind when they freed slave property. More than a few freed illegitimate, biracial kin. But perhaps these were not the most significant reasons. Most Loudoun slave masters did not want to free all of their slaves. Rather, they typically freed one or a few slaves who they believed deserved special compensation for long years of loyal service or outstanding behavior. Presley Cordell, for example, manumitted his slave Amy Grayson in 1832 for "her good conduct and meritorious service." Sarah E. Chichester stipulated in her will that the first priority of her executors should be to emancipate her father's slave, Richard Barnes, "as a reward for [his] faithfulness and good conduct." James Saunders explained that his father had asked him to liberate his favorite slave "Leenzy" as a "reward for fidelity and good conduct."[20]

Private manumission had its heyday between 1790 and 1806.[21] The sharp decline in the number of emancipations after 1806 was a direct response to new state legislation which stipulated that all slaves "hereafter emancipated" must permanently leave Virginia within twelve months of their emancipation or risk re-enslavement. The new law placed an additional burden on the ex-slave and his or her emancipator to arrange for residence outside the state or to petition to remain. Between 1806 and 1818, county residents filed only nine acts of manumission—one-seventh of those filed in the previous period. Perhaps in response to the dwindling number of emancipations by owners after 1806, free blacks intensified their effort to purchase slave kin. In 1810, for example, only three free black households had slave residents. By 1820, however, 19 did. But despite these attempts by black kin, the 1806 law, growing white hostility, and the increasing profitability of the domestic slave trade[22] effectively curtailed the flow of emancipations by either slave master or free black kin.[23]

Some of the most important conditions which influenced white attitudes about black emancipation were economic ones such as the value of free black labor, particularly in relation to the profitability of slave labor, and the domestic slave trade. Economic concerns and racialist reasoning which posited black well-being secondary to that of whites unfortunately created situations in which whites cheated free blacks out of their status and slaves out of an opportunity to gain freedom.

Some slaveholding families argued bitterly over the future of slaves who had been emancipated by deed or will. Likewise, some owners did not trust their kin to carry out their last wishes concerning the disposition of their human property. When Loudoun's famous agricultural reformer and the owner of "Clover Hill" plantation, John Alexander Binns, died in 1813, for example, his will stipulated that all of his slaves were to be freed when they became twenty-five years old and then relocated outside the state. Although Binns left a handsome estate to be generously divided among his white heirs, he still feared that they would not comply with his wishes regarding his blacks. As a matter of insurance, he bequeathed $500 to his brother Thomas with the proviso that he would be "at the trouble of taking to Maryland or any other state all [his] negroes . . . so that they obtain their freedom at the time prescribed." Binns further stipulated that if Thomas failed to act accordingly, "any other . . . relations stepping forward for that purpose shall be entitled" to the $500. Should all of his kin refuse to cooperate, Binns dictated that the money was to go to anyone who carried out his request.[24]

Several years earlier in 1791, Robert Carter recorded a deed of gradual emancipation of more than 500 slaves who resided on his plantations scattered throughout several counties of the Northern Neck, including the 48 who lived in Loudoun. His reasons for so doing are vague, but seem to have derived from both moral and economic concerns. Accordingly, each of Carter's heirs was to receive the temporary services of a "parcel" of his slaves, but were to free on January 2 of each year every slave who had reached adulthood (21 years for males, 18 years for females) during the past year. His kin generally responded angrily to what they believed was an incredibly irresponsible act, financially and socially, on the part of the aging patriarch. And in the end, the family's hostility to the emancipations had dire consequences for Carter's slaves—some never received their freedom.[25]

Loudoun's John Tasker Carter especially opposed his father's plan to dispose of this huge fortune in slaves. He openly "'declared that the Negroes who became his property would be sold and taken to a place where they would never hear talk of freedom again.'" John threatened to do everything possible to "'overturn and frustrate'" Robert Carter's deed of manumission. His younger brother George, also of Loudoun, seemed to have complied with his father's wishes. Yet it is certain that some of the other heirs did not honor the will. Ann Maund, granddaughter to Robert Carter, wrote to her Uncle George in 1808, for example, that three of the slaves in her household had run away before their set date for emancipation. She reasoned that the three young women feared that they too would be sold before their emancipation as had their sister.[26]

James Saunders was not nearly as opposed to his father's desire to emancipate one slave as were Carter's heirs at the prospect of losing several hundred thousand dollars' worth of slave property. Yet Saunders still refused, at least initially, to carry out what he knew was his father's intention to free the slave man Leenzy. In a petition to the state legislature in 1815, James admitted that he had waited several years to act on his father's wish, but finally had acquiesced and freed the slave man. Saunders arbitrarily decided not to emancipate Leenzy after his father died, choosing instead to hire him out and use the proceeds to support his younger siblings. Presumably, the family's financial status improved by 1815 (or Leenzy's earning potential dwindled) when Saunders finally manumitted the slave. While his refusal to give Leenzy his due may have helped his own family, it undoubtedly wreaked havoc in the slave man's life for he remained a slave for more than ten years after he should have been emancipated. Saunders's petition in 1815 was not just to free Leenzy, but also to ask permission for him to remain in Virginia. While Leenzy was being held in bondage illegally, state laws changed dramatically regarding a free black's permanent residence privileges. Leenzy lost his "place" in Loudoun while he waited to be freed.[27]

More than a few slaves who were unaware of the contents of their owners' wills must have suffered villainy at the hands of unscrupulous heirs. Even most of those who suspected wrongdoing lacked the resources or legal savvy to pursue justice. A few Loudoun slaves, however, did fight for and win their freedom. Samuel Jackson, for example, appeared before the county court in November 1818 where he accused James W. Rumolds and Jeremiah Burton of holding him in slavery illegally. The court heard the slave's petition on December 4, 1818 and ordered prominent Leesburg attorney Richard Jackson to serve as his counsel. Meanwhile, the county sheriff took the plaintiff into temporary custody in order to protect him from possible sale or abuse by his alleged owners. The court "further ordered that [Jackson's] said Master do not presume to beat or misuse him upon his account," but allow him to appear at the Clerk's office in order to give his statement and to attend the examination and trial of the defendants. Samuel Jackson's persistence and patience paid off—he eventually won his case and the court released him from bondage.[28]

The problem of free blacks being held illegally as slaves was one that continuously plagued their community, even after local authorities established a county-wide registration of free people of color in 1793. This law was a response to the federal fugitive slave legislation enacted that year and was meant to help local law enforcement officials recover escaped slaves. Still, it also provided free people of color, who had to register before the county clerk every three years, some documentation of their status. The clerk's report included a detailed physical description of everyone who registered, including his or her age, color, height, size, any visible scars or marks, as well as the means by which they claimed their freedom. "The Bearer hereof Peyton Watkins who was bound by the overseers of the poor of Loudoun County on the 13th day of February 1810 to Armstead Long," began a typical slip of registration. "[He] is a dark Mulatto man about twenty nine years of age[,] five feet and one fourth inches high[,] a small scar on the left arm, a scar on the great toe of the left foot[,] two small scars on the wrist of the right hand is a free man of Color as . . . granted by the County court of Loudoun. . . ." Free African Americans could buy copies of their certificates for 25 cents each, and the state required that they carry this proof of their status with them at all times. State law further mandated that no one employ a black claiming to be free without such a certificate in possession. The county sheriff held in jail those arrested without their "freedom slips" and eventually sold or rented out those who were unable to prove that they were not slaves.[29]

A growing antagonism toward free people of color proved to be their greatest threat. Antebellum county slaveholders feared, and rightfully so, the influence that free blacks had on local slave property. Many believed that the reality of black freedom, evident in the status of free people of color who were often the friends, family members, and "business associates" of slaves, caused slave discontent and resistance. After Robert Carter initiated the emancipation of his slaves, for example, he received a number of letters from irate and frightened neighbors. Littlebury Apperson, for one, complained that his slaves had been terribly excited by the news of Carter's actions. Some, believing that Robert Carter had the power and inclination to free all slaves, left Apperson's plantation in search of the retired planter. Mr. Apperson suggested that Carter act decisively to quell the "notions of freedom" that his emancipated brood was spreading. Another neighbor wrote anonymously about the manumissions, complaining of the crimes that Carter's freed slaves committed in the vicinity. Yet, he emphasized, the "'worse effects'" of Carter's act of "liberality" was brought about "'by [free blacks] mixing with those [still] in bondage [for] they disquiet their minds—aid them in procuring false & stupid certificates of which they seek their fortunes, as they call it, [and] some escape. . . .'"[30]

"Once in a while they was free nigguhs come from somewhere. They could come see yer if yer was their folks," a Virginia ex-slave recalled. But the kinds of restrictions on their movements and interactions with slaves, regardless of their kinship ties to them, caused immeasurable strain on these familial relationships. Caroline Hunter's father's experiences were typical—he eventually left his slave wife and four children because their owner insisted on treating him as if he were slave property. He allowed Hunter no more privileges or control of his family or himself than residential slave men. "Papa was free, an' he didn' think massa had no business beatin' him, so he left . . . ," Caroline explained.[31]

Whites' anxiousness over the connections between their slaves and local free blacks caused consistent strain between the two black communities. "Free Negroes had to be very careful of mixing with slaves or white folks in those days," James Bowser, for one, noted. "Some white folks watched all the time, to keep them from mixing with the slaves." Bowser felt so much pressure to stay away from local slaves that he refused to let any of the neighboring bondsmen court his daughters. "Who are you? Are you your own man?" were questions he routinely asked when he found a man he did not know in his home. If the man was a slave, Bowser demanded that he leave. Unfortunately he had good reason to act cautiously. Mr. Bowser believed that the whites in his community wanted to seize his property, and would have used any excuse, including his meeting with slaves, to do so. Eventually, they did just that.[32]

Prominent whites like Littlebury Apperson, who was outraged at Robert Carter's emancipation deed, did not limit their protest to writing heated letters or trying to keep free people of color away from slaves. Over the years, their efforts to be rid of free blacks became increasingly structured and militant, particularly after the Nat Turner rebellion in 1831. Loudoun's first organized efforts to repulse free blacks came that following December, bringing about a curious union of of both conservatives and liberals. Several county slaveholders, along with a tiny antislavery element, joined forces to author a petition to the state legislature pleading for the gradual emancipation of slaves and the removal of the "entire colored population" from the state. When the General Assembly decided not to act on their petition, the more conservative element refocused their attention on ridding their communities of those blacks who already were free. Again, they sought the help of the state assembly, authoring several petitions to the legislature.[33]

In January 1836, for example, nineteen leading male citizens from Loudoun and Fauquier counties, among whom were representatives of the powerful Powell, McCarty, Rogers, and Adams families, informed the General Assembly of their concern for the "great and growing evil arising from the residence of the Free Black population" in their counties. They explained that they perceived an "obvious evil growing out of that state of Society in which an unrestricted communication is permitted to exist between Free Blacks and [the] Slave Population." They documented the validity of their concern with a reminder of the constant exchange of stolen goods that went on between free people of color and slaves. Accordingly, they offered their support of any law "that might grow out of this petition," particularly one which might expedite the permanent removal of all free blacks.[34]

Loudoun slaves and free people of color did give white residents some cause for concern. There were many incidences of joint, "underground," financial endeavors and plots of black resistance. Some free blacks even actively aided slave escapes. Thomas, a slave from the northern part of the county, for example, told the story of a free black man in his neighborhood who intercepted his master's note and was able to warn him that he was about to be sold. Thomas managed to escape while the "friends" of the free black intervened on his behalf and arranged his release from jail. The inability of whites to put an end to this kind of cooperative resistance not only was a source of continual frustration, but also was further evidence that there was an operative black community which embraced both slaves and free people of color.[35]

The petition of 1836 came to little fruition but, six years later, white Loudouners, who by then had grown tired of what they believed were paltry concessions on the part of local and state authorities to settle the free black issue effectively, again petitioned the General Assembly. This time they were much more precise about acceptable solutions, even suggesting specific, remedial legislation. In their estimation, the mandatory removal law of 1806 was "at most useless." They proposed instead a simple informant/reward system whereby the General Assembly would pay informers to identify violators of the 1806 act out of monies generated from the proceeds earned when the guilty were sold back into slavery.[36]

Despite their obvious concern for the inefficacy of the removal statute, the state legislature still chose to reject the Loudoun petition rather than sanction what was tantamount to the creation of a squad of bounty hunters. But their rejection only fueled more petitions and protests. The 1842 petition, in fact, was neither the first nor the last attack on the 1806 law that Loudoun residents sponsored.

As early as 1836, Richard Henderson, the county's first Commonwealth Attorney, complained bitterly that, despite the removal law, it virtually was impossible for him to prosecute and effectively sentence free people of color on charges of illegal residency. According to Henderson, the county court consistently frustrated his efforts by granting indicted blacks continuances on their cases or extensions on their removal deadlines. In the meanwhile, guilty defendants had the opportunity to galvanize white community support and petition the state legislature for a review of their cases. Henderson documented his charge with a review of the court's record, proving that out of hundreds of possible prosecutions for violation of the 1806 law in Loudoun, only 27 had been successfully pursued between 1806 and 1836. Moreover, all of these convictions had taken place since he had become Commonwealth Attorney in 1833. Even more damning, however, was Henderson's evidence that the Loudoun county court had given at least two extensions for removal to each of those 27 persons found guilty. His records further proved that, on average, the court granted between seven and eight extensions for each person so prosecuted.[37]

Clearly the white community was at odds over their response to the free black presence. To their credit, free people of color often were able to manipulate this conflict to their benefit. Their ability to garner some white support, even in the face of mounting opposition from others, suggests an array of relationships that free blacks had with Loudoun's diverse European-American residents. Yet much of the white support came as an effort to aid one "exceptional" free black, not the entire community. Certainly most whites would have felt comfortable, and many relieved, if there were not any free people of color in their society. Still, some blacks were able to call on those who were long-term acquaintances, employers, or perhaps blood relations to help them protect themselves, their families, and, consequently, their communities by gaining the right to remain in Loudoun.

To be sure, many county free blacks worked long and hard to create mutually beneficial or cordially dependent associations with local elites. They also honed other survival strategies. Most believed, for example, that if they remained quiet, orderly, economically secure, and did nothing to attract the attention or the disapproval of powerful whites, they could stay in Loudoun indefinitely, despite the mandatory removal law. Certainly the county court's indulgence of many members of their community bolstered these hopes. Fearing the notice that they might draw if they petitioned the General Assembly for permission to remain Virginia residents, and sometimes uncertain of the legal procedure, most refused to act at all. Consider, for example, the circumstances surrounding Amy Grayson's plea to remain a resident.

Presley Cordell freed Amy Grayson "five or six years" before 1837, the year she first petitioned the state legislature for permission to remain in Virginia permanently. Grayson could have approached the Assembly much earlier, but according to her, she feared her request would be denied on "some technicality." A literate black woman who had managed to gain the amiable support of some of Loudoun's most prestigious citizens, Grayson was keenly aware of the state's laws regarding her residency status. The General Assembly allowed county courts to make such decisions, but only if the free black made his or her petition available for public notice at least two months prior to the court date, and three-quarters of the court justices had to be present on the day of the petition hearing. Grayson explained that she feared that if she appealed to the county court they would deny her petition because "it would be impossible to collect a majority of acting magistrates . . . at one time." By incidentally placing the blame for her failure to act on the inefficiency of the county court system, she hoped to avoid a punitive judgment.[38]

Grayson not only was aware of court procedure, but she also knew that she needed substantial white support for her petition to succeed. Accordingly, she had "always endeavored to be of good conduct and deportment; honest and desirous . . . to obtain the good will and the good opinion of her neighbors and the town [of Leesburg] in general." Grayson's sense of assurance that she would not be prosecuted for her violation of the 1806 statute obviously derived from her belief in an operative free black/elite white patronage system. When eventually forced to appeal to the Assembly to settle the matter once and for all, she could only hope that the white "friends" who endorsed her petition would impress the legislature favorably. Her former master, as well as six other prominent Leesburg citizens, wrote in her support.[39]

Despite her fears, the Assembly did grant her permanent residency. In fact, this state body rarely rejected these kinds of petitions from Loudoun's free people of color. Those who presented evidence of strong support from elite and "respectable whites" were most successful.

Still free black strategies for permanent residency did not go unnoticed by those local whites who resented their side-stepping the county court system through the aid of biracial support networks. Some, in fact, were so angered by the legislature's tendency to overturn local rulings that they counterpetitioned some requests. In 1850, for example, Thomas Saunders, Y. D. Nixon, and E. Hammat asked the Assembly to reject the petitions of Harriet Cook and William Watson, two local free blacks who requested the state's intervention after the county court already had prosecuted them for residency violations.[40] The free black response to these "attacks" is instructive, because their efforts suggest attempts not only to facilitate white patronage support, but also to manipulate deeply espoused societal norms, such as gender conventions, for their own purposes.

Although one can be certain that gender differentiated the experiences of free black males and females in numerous ways, it is difficult to ascertain just how so. While males certainly had the economic advantage for example, females experienced more social tolerance. Thus, it might have been easier for women to live in Loudoun without generating the same level of suspicion, hostility, and harassment as males. Relatedly, because free black women had limited financial resources and marketable skills, they did not pose a potential threat to white male laborers, farmers, and artisans. Gender, therefore, was an important differentiating measure, albeit a complex one whose impact was often immeasurable.

Harriet Cook had lived in Leesburg all of her life and, according to the numerous county whites who supported her petition, was exemplary, "sustaining a high character as a religious, honest, and valuable member of Society." Since her emancipation in about 1838, Cook had worked long and hard to build and impress her clientele as a washerwoman. Her employers wholeheartedly endorsed her efforts to gain permanent residence, noting in their deposition not only her strong moral character, but also their dependence on her services as a laundress. "It would be a serious inconvenience to a number of the citizens of Leesburg," they swore, "to be deprived of her services as a washerwoman and in other capacities in which in consequence of her gentility, trustworthiness, and skill she is exceedingly useful." "No possible injury," they concluded, could result from her presence "so long as she conducts herself honestly and properly," as they predicted she would do.[41]

An unprecedented number of Loudoun's citizens (93 white men) signed her petition. Included among the stellar list were seven justices of the peace, five members of the executive council, one postmaster, and six lawyers. Cook's patrons argued her case pragmatically, insisting on her usefulness as a laborer, her economic self-sufficiency, and her strong moral character, all the while trying to undermine commonly held fears of free black economic dependency, violence, dishonesty, and sexual promiscuity. Their statements assured legislators that Harriet Cook was in no way a threat, but rather an asset to their community.[42]

William Watson's petition to the Virginia state assembly preceded that of Harriet Cook's by three years, but was similar to hers in important ways. Watson too had many signatures of support from some of Loudoun's most prestigious citizens. They too asserted that he was of "good character," had "industrious habits," and served the county well as a dependable, hard-working day laborer. But his patrons also went a step further. Drawing on gender convention shared by free blacks and whites alike, they argued that a decision in favor of Watson was a decision in favor of patriarchal responsibility. Watson, they emphasized, was the head "of a large family" and wished to remain in the state to fulfill his obligation to them. Although Harriet Cook also was the head of her household, her advisors may have thought it inappropriate to portray her in this kind of "masculine" light. Their references to her ability as a washerwoman made note of her usefulness to members of Leesburg's white families through work traditionally relegated to impoverished women, but ignored what benefit her labor brought to her own family. Her role as primary breadwinner for her household (traditionally a male prerogative and duty) was not part of the defense she, or her white male supporters, forged.[43]

William Watson's gender, and the responsibilities associated with it, probably were not the most favorable factors operative in his behalf, but they may have had some impact on the outcome of his case. Unfortunately, the records of the General Assembly do not indicate whether or not they ever granted or denied Cook's or Watson's petition. Yet it is unlikely that either won their appeal since neither appear as Loudoun residents in the census of 1850 or 1860. Given the notoriety of their cases, it would have been difficult for Harriet or William to act as many others felt compelled to do—that is, to remain in Loudoun clandestinely. The Assembly's rejection may have forced them to leave; or, fed up with dwindling economic opportunities, the complexities of their cases, or growing white hostility, they finally may have "chosen" to leave.

These episodes of petition and counterpetition not only document local white factionalism on issues of race, but also suggest a larger conflict between county and state authority. In their 1850 petition to the General Assembly meant to thwart those of Cook and Watson, for example, Thomas Saunders and his associates openly criticized the limited power the state allowed local officials and bureaus of authority to settle issues of county interest. They were particularly angered that state authorities seemed to be turning a deaf ear to the concerns of local residents. "Your memoralists are of opinion," they charged, "that the law places the remedy in such cases where it ought to be[;] in the county and corporation courts, and therefore that the petitions in favor of said free negroes be not granted. . . ."[44] Yet it was not just a matter of presumption of authority by the Assembly that they objected to. It also was a matter of the elite versus the average man. Many resented prominent county whites using their influence with the state legislature to further the wishes of their "pet" blacks.

The degree of "leniency" with which some whites and the General Assembly dealt with the fate of those free blacks who had proven their strong "moral" character and general usefulness certainly was out of step with what other residents believed appropriate. Other than the controversial petitions of Cook and Watson, for example, the state legislature rejected only one such petition from a Loudoun free black, and then only because of extraordinary circumstances.

The General Assembly undoubtedly denied Clem Chaney's 1822 appeal because he had lived outside of the state for several years. His desire to live in the county again was founded on his family ties and those of his wife, a free woman of color who also was from Loudoun. Virginia law dated 1793, however, explicitly prohibited the migration of free blacks or mulattoes into the state. Having established a long history of exporting "troublesome" blacks to other locales, the General Assembly undoubtedly refused to accept the residence of free blacks whose character and industry could not be vouched for by local whites.[45]

Regardless of the fate of William Watson, Harriet Cook, Clem Chaney, or the others who faced similar residency crises, tension in the local white community centered on the issue of the free black presence continued to mount. While most whites believed blacks were naturally inferior to them and opposed their presence, some were willing to concede that there were a few exceptions to their general "degraded" condition. This small minority of exemplary blacks, their supporters asserted, should be allowed to remain, particularly if they provided an important service to whites. Some even petitioned the state legislature to curtail the creation of discriminatory and expulsory acts.

In response to the 1842 petition that Loudouners submitted to the General Assembly concerning stiffer enforcement of the 1806 statute, for example, another group of 38 county citizens, who were primarily Quaker and of German origin, counterpetitioned. In so doing, they not only dramatized the growing rift in the white community, but also summarized the remnants of liberal social ideology in this small, upper South county. Their statements to the General Assembly, for example, characterized the laws passed against free black residency as "unjust, oppressive and contrary to the moral sense of this community." They mounted a forceful economic argument for maintaining a free black presence, but it was their articulation of the threat to communal morality that was most compelling in the arguments of Janney, Shoemaker, Hogue, and others who signed the 1842 counterpetition. They argued eloquently that it was their "duty" and "privilege as citizens of the commonwealth to remonstrate against" these laws or any activity which threatened the moral well-being of their society. As such, they felt compelled to approach the assembly on this matter.[46]

They carefully laid the foundation for their moral argument. Drawing on language popularized during the era of the American Revolution (and frequently used by northern abolitionists of the time), the petitioners hoped to sway legislators with linguistic references to a time of purer political morality: "We hold it to be a self evident truth," they began, "that every man, *not convicted of a crime*, has a natural right, to reside in the community where he was born and that no law can expel him without violating the principles of justice and humanity." By asserting that free people of color had "natural rights" and, therefore, deserved to be included in the white community's compact of justice and humanity, these 38 petitioners produced an extraordinary, revolutionary document. They proposed startling moral consequences for those who, during the previous decade, had passed one bill after another to restrict free black activity and growth. To deny "natural rights" to free blacks, they implied, was to demonstrate the profound injustice and inhumanity of southern slave society.[47]

Although these petitioners asserted in the right of free persons of color to reside in Virginia and to function as other free people, they did not really believe that their testament to black humanity and incumbent rights would win their case. Thus, after having firmly established the moral tenets of their position, they went on to argue other benefits to the white community. In so doing, they mimicked proslavery advocates who opposed abolition on the grounds of supposed economic harm to the southern economy. In this one petition, therefore, they brilliantly managed to intertwine the two most important philosophical tenets white southerners embraced—"natural rights" and economic pragmatism. They openly admitted their resentment of the economic burden they shouldered as a result of forced free black emigration and suggested that others felt similarly. "There are many citizens of this state," they continued, "who from conscientious motives have a preference for the employment of free labor, but owing to the emigration of the whites,[48] and the expulsion of the free colored people,[49] this kind of labour has been scarce." "It is therefore a grievance and an impingement of their rights," the petitioners stressed, "to expel by arbitrary laws a class of people whose labour might be useful and whose conditions ought to be inspired by extending to them the protection of law and the rights of humanity."[50]

The General Assembly never officially responded to either petition. Loudoun's proslavery force remained dissatisfied, but persevered. Four years after the Janney-Hogue-Shoemaker petition, eight of the county's most powerful slave owners, including prominent members of the Powell-Noland political dynasty, asked the General Assembly to either remove all free people of color from the state or re-enslave them. The legislature refused to act on their recommendation.[51]

Loudouners were not the only Virginians who resented the presence of free people of color. Petitions concerning the "growing menace" streamed into the state legislature from across the Commonwealth. Particularly virulent were those from Virginia's Eastern Shore, although no region was silent on the question. The hostility only increased over time. With abolitionists attacks mounting, proslavery forces steadily focused their attention on the free African American. Their strategy was predictable. In order to document the relative "good" of slavery, they had to depict the free black condition as one of deprivation and degradation. Although some Loudouners obviously were displeased with the General Assembly's handling of the situation, there was an impressive accumulation of discriminatory legislation aimed at free people of color during the antebellum decades.[52]

Particularly significant was the mass of bills which emerged during the legislative sessions of 1831 and 1832 largely as a result of the Nat Turner slave rebellion. State lawmakers tried to reduce widespread hysteria by legalizing restrictions on black education, organization, residence, their relationships with slaves, and self-protective measures. These new laws denied free people of color the right to learn how to read and write within the state, or the right to return to Virginia once having acquired these skills elsewhere. No free black could serve as a minister, nor could they continue to meet for religious purposes or any other without written permission from local officials. As early as 1793, the General Assembly forbade "free Negroes or mulattoes from migrating into the Commonwealth" and made it a criminal offense for anyone to transport them into the state. A similar law came into effect in 1834, exempting only those who accompanied their employers. In 1841, additional laws restricted free black immigration to those who came as servants and would not be staying longer than five days.[53]

While an 1806 law prohibited free African Americans from owning unlicensed firearms, an 1832 statute denied them the right to own any weapons. A subsequent law dated 1839 authorized patrols to "force open" and search the homes of free people of color and slaves (when masters were absent) for "fire-arms or other weapons." Other legislation also curtailed free black business interests. An 1843 statute, for example, mandated that free people of color who sold agricultural products had to present certificates from "respectable" whites who could verify that the goods were not stolen. Ten years later, the Assembly enacted a law which denied free blacks the right to "sell or give away ardent or spirituous liquours near any public assembly," effectively curtailing their own-ership of ordinaries or other businesses where liquor would be sold. Finally, state legislators in 1856 offered free people of color the "privilege" of choosing their own master and volunteering to become slaves. Four years later, they made it legally possible for county courts to sentence free blacks convicted of felonies to "absolute slavery."[54]

Although all of this legislation frustrated, angered, and frightened Lou-doun's free people of color, they perhaps were most incensed by the antiliteracy acts. Clearly, the inability even to teach one's children the rudiments of reading and writing was a powerful symbol of their bleak futures. Prior to the prohibi-tive 1831 statute, some had attended local Quaker schools where they studied reading, spelling, mathematics, writing, geography, grammar, surveying, and algebra. Others learned from literate free blacks or white sympathizers. Even during the pre-1830 era, however, few were able to gain an education, and then only at extraordinary sacrifice. Families whose children attended Quaker schools, for example, not only had to provide proper clothing and school sup-plies, but also had to live in the vicinity of the school and be on good terms with the local Friends. It is no wonder then that the largest enclaves of Loudoun free blacks resided in the Quaker towns of Waterford and Hillsboro. Some also may have hired out their children to Friends, hoping that they could attend their schools. John Janney, who grew up in Loudoun and attended the Goose Creek Meeting School, for example, remembered that "Friends who had colored boys living with them sent them to school along with their own chil-dren. There were two mulatto and one negro boy who attended our school, and they were taught and treated just as the other children were by both teacher and pupils." Those free blacks who took advantage of educational op-portunities during the first decades of the nineteenth century undoubtedly were among the elite, economically and socially, within their communities.[55]

With the passing of the 1831 ordinance, however, the small number of free black children who received any kind of formal instruction dwindled drasti-cally. A very few managed to send their children to the Quaker schools in Alexandria, but this option disappeared when Virginia reannexed Alexandria in 1846. The only alternative was to send youngsters to live with relatives or friends in the District of Columbia, Pennsylvania, or other free states where there they could attend school, but after 1848 these persons could no longer re-enter the state. As the antebellum era came to a close, therefore, fewer and fewer resources for free black education remained available. The only safe avenue was teaching in the home, although there probably were secret school meetings. As late as 1860, a small but important group of literate free blacks, approximately 14 percent of the adult population, still lived in Loudoun.[56]

Most of Loudoun's free African Americans chose to remain in the county despite growing legal and customary hostility, and its negative impact on their family life. Facing rising white antagonism and fewer opportunities for economic stability and social expression, more and more considered emigration as a feasible option. Loudoun whites supported free black migration under the auspices of colonization societies which were both locally based and connected to the national movement. Founded in 1816, the American Colonization Society espoused state and federal support for the removal and relocation of free people of color to a black colony. By 1821, the organization had chosen Liberia, located on the west coast of Africa, as the site for resettlement. Members of the organization named its capital "Monrovia" for Loudoun's most illustrious resident at the time, President James Monroe.[57]

Administered and supported by some of the nation's and the state's most prominent citizens, many Virginians believed colonization was the most realistic answer to the question of a free black presence. Whites like Loudoun's Charles Fenton Mercer, who served as vice president of the national organization for several years, argued that free blacks were both a moral and economic blight to society. They pointed to their general poor economic status and concluded that most were either paupers or dishonest. Free people of color were, in Mercer's words, a growing force that "every day [was] polluting and corrupting public morals" for "more than half the females are prostitutes and [half] of the males rogues."[58] There also was a considerable slaveholder element among the colonizationist ranks who had strong reservations about the frequent contact between free people of color and enslaved blacks. While many did not consciously anticipate a violent free black/slave insurrection, they did believe that free people of color engendered some kind of "discontent" among slaves.

Some white colonizationists exhibited less selfish intentions, writing, for example, about the public good they hoped to do: "[our] principles will be purified and rendered consistent; our morals chastened; our apprehensions annihilated; our comforts improved; our national strength augmented; and our national character will cease to wear its most marring blemish."[59] More than a few hoped to provide a black Christian missionary force to the indigenous people of Liberia. They also wanted to assuage their own feelings of guilt for holding people in bondage. Colonizationists supplied, after all, not just travel expenses, but also substantial material and financial support for free blacks' first few years in Liberia. One local supporter was even moved to tell a group of free people of color who were about to depart: "Servants, hear me, we have been brothers and sisters, we have grown up together. We have done the best for you" and to explain that:

> Besides your freedom, we have spent $2,000 in procuring everything we could think of to make you comfortable—clothing, bedding, implements of husbandry, mechanics' tools, tools for the children, Bibles, . . . all these have been provided, and when you have been there some few months, we will send you out another supply of provisions and will continue to do so. . . .[60]

Some, clearly, wanted to give "their" blacks an opportunity to live decent, productive, "free" lives, not possible for them to have in Loudoun. "You have felt and witnessed the degradation of your colour in this country whether slaves or the free people of colour," county colonizationist Albert Heaton wrote to two of his slaves he helped to relocate as a free man in Liberia. "But you have gone to a Country where the No'blest feelings of Liberty will spring up, and knowing full well the prize you have won in going to Liberia, you will I hope secure it—the prize I mean is the prize of Liberty[,] the dearest right of man, the strongest passion of the soul."[61]

A few Loudouners, particularly among the ranks of Quaker supporters but others as well, believed that a successful colonization effort would promote the acceptance of a gradual end to slavery. Perhaps the most well-known county abolitionist was Samuel Janney, a local Quaker minister, teacher, and activist.

Born in Loudoun in 1801, the eldest child of Abijah and Jane Janney, Samuel was a well-educated businessman, teacher, and Quaker minister. He lived for a while in Alexandria, where he began to champion the cause of free blacks and slaves. In 1824, for example, he helped to establish a day school for free children of color. The following year he, along with other Quaker associates and some local Methodists, organized the Benevolent Society in order to "rescue" free people of color "illegally held in bondage" by slave traders and to "enlighten the public mind in regards to the evil of slavery." Janney rapidly became more and more involved in abolitionist activities. By 1827, he was busy writing a series of essays criticizing slavery and the slave trade that was published in the *Alexandria Gazette* and had been co-author of a petition to Congress requesting the end to slavery in the District of Columbia. He also had decided that "immediate and unconditional emancipation" was the most expedient answer to the African American question and shared his views with his coterie of abolitionist friends and associates. Likewise, he realized that the large majority of area whites were virulently opposed to such ideology; that it, in fact, stood in stark opposition to local custom and challenged the community's racial hierarchy. "But knowing the prejudice against it in the minds of the people, I only asked for gradual emancipation," he confessed.[62]

Janney moved back to Loudoun in 1839, opening a popular boarding school named "Springdale" for well-to-do girls while serving as an activist Quaker minister. "There is no part of our religious concerns in which these considerations are more important than in supporting our righteous testimony against slavery," he wrote in "An Epistle to the Members of the Society of Friends in the State of Ohio" in 1844. That same year he wrote another series of articles published in the *Alexandria Gazette*, this time "showing the disastrous effects of slaveholding" in his "native State" and the "superiority of free labor in promoting public prosperity and individual happiness."[63]

Janney's efforts were tireless, but he clearly was not an antislavery activist in the tradition of the Garrisonians or the Tappans. He criticized the national antislavery organizations for one's denunciation of the Constitution and the other's attempt to embody abolitionist activism in a political party. "The Constitution of the United States, so far as it upholds slavery, ought to be amended, but not destroyed," he concluded firmly. "[F]or if we let go our anchor . . . [a]narchy and confusion may ensue." "A calm, temperate, and yet decided bearing," such as that modeled by Woolman, Benezet, and other Quaker zealots, Samuel Janney maintained, "will have the most salutary influence in promoting the great cause of emancipation."[64]

Janney's efforts did not go unnoticed in Loudoun—many local whites thought him a radical. Some even believed he was dangerous. There were several attempts to undermine his influence. In 1849, for example, Loudoun's Grand Jury doubly accused Janney: first, of mounting a "calculated" effort to "incite persons of color to make insurrection or rebellion," and, second, of maintaining that slave owners "'had no right of property in their slaves.'" Janney was tried in June 1850 but was able to convince the court of his innocence. His court appearance gave him the opportunity to express his antislavery views directly to his accusers—the county's large proslavery element. "Our concern is not to meddle with the slave, but to appeal to the master," he reassured the court. "Our course is open and aboveboard; our aim is to accomplish a Christian object by Christian means." But certainly Samuel Janney's "Christian object" and "means" were not those of most county whites, even the colonizationists.[65]

Janney initially supported colonization. During the 1820s, he was a member of a local society, believing, at the time, that it "would be the means of promoting emancipation in the Southern States, and of planting a colony that would spread civilization and christianity" to West Africa. His opinion changed quickly. "Subsequently, I became convinced that the tendency of the scheme of colonization," he admitted, "was to quiet the conscience of the people, lead to false security, and put off, to a distant day the work of emancipation."[66]

Yet many prominent Loudoun whites—slaveholders, businessmen, and politicians—supported the county's colonization efforts. Local organizing officially began in the fall of 1817, and, by the end of December, George Carter had written to Bushrod Washington, president of the American Colonization Society requesting information about the national effort. "I have cut out of the

Lees[burg] *Washingtonian* . . . the proceeding of a meeting a few inhabitants of this county who are desirous of forming themselves into an Auxiliary Colonization Society had," Carter explained. Washington was happy to oblige the request, and within a few months, county residents had formed the Loudoun Auxiliary of the American Colonization Society. Six years later, a more radical faction of this organization created the Loudoun Manumission and Emigration Society.[67]

Like its mother organization, the primary objective of the Loudoun Auxiliary was to organize, support, and help sustain the migration of Loudoun free blacks to Liberia. While the auxiliary could boast that its constituents represented some of the county's most prominent citizens and largest slaveholders including Burr Powell, George Carter, William Noland, Charles Ball, Ludwell Lee, William Ellzey, and Asa Moore, important Quaker reformers like Israel Janney, Yardley Taylor, and Mahlon Taylor also were members.[68]

Carter, Powell, Lee, and the other members of the planter faction generally embraced the colonization effort in order to rid Loudoun of its free black population. They seemed to have little intention of emancipating any of their own slaves and county records indicate that they never did. Richard Henderson, who also was a member, for example, was the county official who twice petitioned the state assembly requesting that legislators fortify free black expulsion laws. Quakers Israel Janney and Mahlon Taylor, however, opposed slavery on moral grounds and hoped that widespread, gradual emancipation combined with colonization abroad eventually would end the southern institution. Other county colonizationists like James Heaton and Presley Cordell, slaveholders who eventually freed some of their slaves and supported their settlement in Liberia, fell somewhere between these two poles. Yet internal strife compromised the organization from its inception for, as one might imagine, the combination of conservative slaveholder and liberal Quaker did not inspire a congenial agreement among its members on key ideological issues. [69]

Much of their conflict centered on the issue of the domestic slave trade. Quaker members vehemently opposed this aspect of Loudoun slavery, while most of the slaveholding faction did not. No doubt information about participation of local members in this trade caused friction. Even more disturbing, however, were the stories about the participation of the national leadership in the trade. On July 3, 1821, for example, Loudoun's *The Genius of Liberty* carried an article which described the recent march of approximately 100 slaves through Leesburg on their way to the Deep South. The writer noted that more than fifty of these "'unhappy wretches had been sold by Judge Washington, of Mount Vernon, President of the Mother American Colonization Society.'"[70]

The article immediately drew heated debates among Loudoun's colonization sympathizers. Was Washington acting morally or not? Opinion was mixed, but most whites publicly supported Washington, demanding the news-paper's apology for insinuating that he had behaved wrongfully. Although the editorial board finally acquiesced and concluded that "'it does not appear Judge Washington, in the sale of his slaves, did violate any *prescribed* rule of the So-ciety,'" this debate underscored the irreconcilable differences among local co-lonizationists. As the conservatives held on to the view that colonization was a promising answer to the problem of the free black presence, the more liberal faction began to more clearly articulate an antislavery stance. On August 21, 1824, this group founded the Loudoun Manumission and Emigration Society, electing prominent Quaker activist Yardley Taylor as their first president.[71]

Unlike the Loudoun auxiliary, the Manumission and Emigration Society primarily was comprised of Quakers who regularly spoke out against slavery and the domestic slave trade. According to its guiding principles, its members were to "expose the evils . . . of African slavery," work toward gradual abolition, and "aid and encourage . . . emigration of [the] colored population to Hayti, Africa or elsewhere." Tapping into local and regional antislavery efforts which had existed in northern Virginia since the 1790s, they were able to attract mem-bers and support by publicly expressing their opinions in well-advertised forums and newspaper editorials which emphasized the negative moral and economic effects of slavery on both whites and blacks. Three years after its founding, the society sponsored a momentous event, the first annual Virginia Convention for the Abolition of Slavery. Twenty-one delegates from seven area societies met at the Goose Creek Quaker schoolhouse where they resolved, among other things, to continue to support the colonization effort; to advise the state constitution convention, which was to begin to draft a new constitution in 1829 to include a plan for gradual emancipation in the new document; and to ban the purchase of slave products sold locally.[72]

Strong interest in colonization among some Loudoun whites continued well into the 1830s, intensifying dramatically following the Nat Turner rebellion. Only a few months after that event shook the state, Loudouners submitted a petition to the state legislature supporting the gradual emancipation and re-moval of all blacks. Surprisingly, some of those who signed the document, in-cluding Dr. Wilson C. Selden, Fayette Ball, George Chichester, and H. Carter, were among Loudoun's largest slaveholders. Quaker activist John Janney also was a supporter. Like so many of those documents which poured into the capi-tal after the slave insurrection, theirs maintained that slavery generally was det-rimental to southern society. "The labor of slaves in a community like ours," they conceded, "is the most expensive that can be used; second . . . slavery tends to lay to waste the region in which it subsists[;] and third it fills with apprehen-sion and inquietude the bosom of those who employ it." It would be for the common good, the "love of peace," and "the sentiment of security for all that is near to the heart of social man" for southerners to rid their soil of the "evil" of slavery and the "race irreconcilably antagonistic to ours."[73]

Five years later, Richard Henderson, County Commonwealth Attorney for Loudoun, requested that the General Assembly act to remove all free blacks to the "new flourishing colonies on the Western coast of Africa." Henderson supported his petition with "evidence" of free black social and economic marginality, stating that those who were illegal residents had been "flying from neighborhood to neighborhood, and from County to County," and lived in a condition of "poverty, vagrancy, and crime." The most appropriate way to manage their growing presence, he surmised, was to order their deportation to Liberia.[74]

The Virginia legislature rejected Henderson's petition—not an unexpected response given the spotty history of the colonization movement in the state. Although there was a great deal of support within some influential circles, the cause never received the kind of endorsement or monetary support that its founders had anticipated. The General Assembly outright rejected the American Colonization Society's pleas for funding when it first was founded in 1816. But it did respond to post-Turner rebellion pressure by agreeing to support the voluntary emigration of the state's free people of color to Liberia with an annual donation of $18,000 for five years. They stipulated, however, that each adult emigrant was to receive only $30 of the fund, a miniscule sum considering relocation costs. Between 1850 and 1853, the legislature set aside additional funding for colonization—$30,000 annually for five years. That same year, they instituted an additional tax on free blacks—one dollar for each free black male between the ages of twenty-one and fifty-five years—supposedly to fund state colonization efforts. In the end, however, officials used most of it as general funds, leaving private donations to comprise the large bulk of colonization's financial backing.[75]

Most of Loudoun's free black population did not support colonization. Like free people of color across the state and the country, many were repulsed at the unflattering ways in which white colonizationists often depicted them. Equally damning was their racist exclusion from the organizations, and the founding premise of the movement that advocated the necessity of their removal from their life-long homes. Some particularly disliked the idea of moving to West Africa, a place that was so far away, that many knew very little about, and that seemed so different—physically and culturally—from Loudoun. Faced with mounting opposition at home, however, some had to reconsider. Those slaves whose owners gave them the choice of remaining in bondage or agreeing to leave for Liberia if freed must have felt as if they had very little choice whatsoever.[76]

For those Loudoun free blacks who did leave for Liberia, the venture was a family one. Few considered travelling to this distant and foreign country without the emotional support of their families. Indeed, family was one of the primary reasons for moving. At least in Liberia, they must have mused, one had a chance to really develop and protect one's family. Since so few knew anything at all about West Africa, and many were weary of false reports, most probably took a "wait and see" attitude, relying on the reports of other free blacks who went before them.

"Many have come to this country through the advice and persuasion of their friends living out here, when they have become so dissatisfied that they were no comfort to their friends nor themselves, until finally they would manage to get back to the United States," the ex-slave William Burke wrote back from Liberia. He, in fact, had "seen so much of this" that he refused to advise anyone to come. Although Burke was pleased with his situation and the prospect of a fine future for his family, he understood that Liberia's undeveloped "resources" and its general "inconvenience" discouraged those who had expected the same material "comforts" of the United States. Undoubtedly that part of the Lucas clan that remained in Loudoun while Mars and Jesse Lucas departed for Liberia also were waiting to be advised whether or not to join them. The Lucas brothers, however, were not as convinced as Mr. Burke that their choice had been the right one.[77]

Most of the Lucas family lived as slaves and free blacks at "Exedra," the Loudoun estate that Dr. James Heaton built when he migrated from Pennsylvania in the 1780s. Heaton was a founding member and vice president of the Loudoun Auxiliary of the American Colonization Society. His sons also were active in the organization. While some of the Lucas clan still belonged to Heaton when he died in 1824, others already had obtained their freedom. William Lucas, for example, was emancipated in 1799. He and his wife Nancy registered their nine children as free in 1828. Another relative, Thomas Lucas, was free by 1820. Mars and Jesse, however, still were Heaton's slaves.[78]

Much happened during the next decade. By 1829, the two brothers were not only free, but about to embark on a voyage for Liberia. When they finally left Loudoun for a Hampton Roads port in December of that year, they were traveling with several other family members who made up a distinct minority among the Loudoun contingency. Altogether, there were nine Lucases who sailed on January 15, 1830: Mars, his brother Jesse, Jesse's wife Amelia, their four children, and two other adult female family members, Mary and Hannah. Thirty Loudouners in all were among the 49 passengers, including members of the Cook, Bell, Oliver, Dennison, Dillard, and McPherson families.[79]

After a 43-day sea voyage, the Lucas clan reached their new home of Caldwell, Liberia in early March 1830. The two brothers, aided by their female kin, quickly established themselves in the colony, and set about to make their venture a lucrative one. On March 10, 1830, Jesse Lucas wrote to his family and the Heatons that he and his brother had arrived safely, were getting settled, and had begun some trading with the indigenous people. Lucas provided a careful description of the colony, its surrounding sites and vegetation, perhaps to convince other family members to migrate. He greeted them cheerfully and affectionately, then briskly went on to business, asking his brother Solomon to send him some beads and handkerchiefs that he could use to trade with the local people. His letter also included an additional incentive for his male kin to join them—the lure of "many purty girls."[80]

A few days later, a letter arrived at the Heaton home from Mars Lucas. Although he was somewhat disappointed in the indigenous people, referring to them as "lazy, stingy natives" who only cared for hunting, fishing, and rum, Mars believed that their venture would be a prosperous one for the land was fertile. A year passed and the Lucas clan struggled to get themselves settled— to clear and start planting on their land, to learn to communicate and trade with the "natives," and to survive the indigenous "fever." Yet, by 1831, Mars had become frustrated and disappointed. He conveyed his feelings and fears in a letter to Townsend Heaton dated June 19 of that year.[81]

The correspondence brought devastating news. Although Mars had recovered sufficiently from his "fever," Jesse's wife and two of his children had died that past year. So too had half of the other thirty free blacks who had traveled with them from Loudoun. The disease, death, and general difficulty of life in Liberia obviously had taken its toll. Disillusioned, he accused the Loudoun Manumission and Emigration Society of lying to free blacks in order to get them to agree to migrate, concluding bitterly: "Times is very Hard." Six months later, Jesse confirmed his brother's assessment, confessing to his ex-master that they were considering returning to the United States. He asked Heaton to please not send any more of his kin.[82]

Their desire to return home was not unusual. George McPherson, another free black who had arrived in Liberia with the Lucases, visited his Loudoun family at least once before returning permanently to the United States in 1834. Jesse and Mars, however, persevered. On April 24, 1836, Jesse again wrote to his friends and family at "Exedra," this time reporting that the remaining Lucas clan still lived in Caldwell, but that he had remarried and he and his new wife had had a son. He further explained that conditions still were hard, but that they planned to return to Loudoun within the next year for a visit. Addressing a separate letter to their mother, the two brothers complained bitterly that during the previous four years life had been so difficult that they had not had any flour for bread and only monkey and rodent for meat.[83]

It is not certain whether some of the Lucas family ever returned to Loudoun, but the fate of Jesse and Mars is known. They died in Liberia in 1839 and 1841 respectively. By 1843, the date of the Liberian census, only four of the thirty Loudoun emigrants still were in residence. Of the twenty-six others, two had returned to the United States, four had moved to other parts of West Africa, and everyone else had died. Their demise and the information that they were able to disseminate to their friends and relatives before they died certainly convinced others not to come. Still, those who chose to remain in Loudoun also faced increasingly harsh social and economic conditions which were a threat to every aspect of their lives, especially their families.[84]

Free Black Family
and Household Economy

In November 1839, several members of Philip and Minty Nelson's family moved from Leesburg to Philadelphia, becoming one of hundreds of free black families who left the South during the second half of the antebellum era. Nelson, a small farmer and tradesman who had managed to acquire some land, a house, livestock, and equipment in the ten years or so that he and his family had had their own household, finally had given up on Loudoun. Since the Nat Turner rebellion of 1831, the Nelsons had witnessed the swift loss of free black rights and opportunities, the drawing of a customary racial hard line that threatened their very existence. Discriminatory legislation was undermining their community's economy. They could no longer hope to educate their children or prepare them for a better life. Their small, but thriving, community groups were under constant scrutiny. Richard Henderson, the county's Commonwealth Attorney since 1833, had vowed to prosecute free people of color who violated the 1806 residency law and was doing it. The new legislation, Henderson's vigilance, and the unchecked threat of unscrupulous slave traders who stole free people of color and sold them South helped create an atmosphere rife with persecution and danger.

Meanwhile, more and more frequently free blacks found themselves caught in the middle as the slavery debate heated up in the white community. Local slaveholders routinely held them up as shining examples of black degradation and racial inferiority who should either be ousted or re-enslaved. Not so, the county's small antislavery contingent countered. Free people of color could be respectable, hardworking members of any community if educated and treated fairly. Given all this, like many of his friends and neighbors, Philip Nelson picked up and moved on to what he hoped would be more a welcome destination. Who could blame him?[1]

The "City of Brotherly Love" did provide relative economic opportunity for black men and women who had skills and some capital to get established. There also was the availability of public and private education for their children and a small but substantial black middle class with family names like Purvis, Forten, and Douglass who touted among their accomplishments impressive reform and self-help activism. Even the declining economic and social status of Philadelphia's free people of color did little to deter the growing tide of which the Nelsons were a part in 1839. For them, it was not just the hope of jobs and education that were so attractive. It also was the pull of other free black Loudouners who already had moved there and promised to help them get settled. When Philip Nelson arrived, for example, he stayed with the Wilmores, another ex-Loudoun free black family, until he could find a nearby home for his family. There also was the connection between Loudoun Friends and Pennsylvania Quakers—strong family and community ties that also might prove helpful to men and women like Philip and Minty Nelson.[2]

Free people of color left Loudoun often carrying only a few necessities and token symbols of their former domicile. "Tell them to Sell all they Can fore Cash with Acceptions [*sic*] of the Beads [beds] and Beading [bedding] fore we can get things here quite Reasonable," Nelson wrote to a Leesburg associate. He was afraid that his family would not have enough money to get re-established and was willing to sell most of their belongings. Yet it was difficult for him to leave too, and before the end of his letter he had relented a little, asking his friend to please tell his wife that "If they have not Made Sale of the decanters and Casters that I think So much of and a China pitcher I would like her to put them in the Beading [bedding] and bring them on and all the spoons[.]"[3] These small items, delicate symbols of their domestic life in Loudoun, would mean much to him and his family once they reached Philadelphia.

Philip Nelson's directions to his family via his long-term patron, Dr. Thomas Clagett, are instructive for several reasons. They not only document the phenomenon of migration, but also provide a partial inventory of the kinds of household items of "middling" southern free black households. Equally important, they remain as a record of permissible gender roles among them. So little is known about free black life that most information is welcomed, but in particular that which describes their day-to-day personal experiences and ideals. If the small body of extant correspondence that Philip Nelson wrote to Thomas

Clagett between 1839 and 1841 tells little else, it tells how Nelson defined himself as a husband and father.

Quite simply, he embraced the "traditional" values of his day. As head of his nuclear-core family, Philip Nelson was most concerned with fulfilling his duties as their breadwinner and protector. He worked hard and bought a home in Leesburg, all the while cultivating cordial relations with whites whom he could call on for aid. His correspondence, therefore, also suggests the kinds of patron-client relationships that some free people of color were able to negotiate with local whites.

Philip Nelson had a special relationship with members of the Clagett family, a well-off planter-professional clan centered in Leesburg. Dr. Clagett supervised all of Nelson's local financial interests after he moved to Philadelphia—trying to sell his property for him, collecting payments due for work that he had performed, and offering him business advice. In return, Nelson probably provided the Clagetts with some sort of service, possibly his labor or that of family members. Clagett also seemed to have benefited, perhaps even more than his client, from some of the financial deals he arranged for Nelson after he left Loudoun. But even if the free black suspected his "patron" was taking advantage of his increasingly desperate situation—and there is little evidence to suggest Clagett was doing this except his seeming inability to dispose of Nelson's property in a timely or profitable manner—there was little Philip could do to remedy the situation. He was a black man with little or no legal power to question the honesty or honor of a prestigious southern white patriarch.[4]

The familial responsibility that Nelson undertook was a heavy burden. So much of what he wanted to achieve for himself and his loved ones was beyond his grasp. Looking for some measure of control and contentment in Philadelphia, they found instead severe financial problems. Life was more expensive in the city; lucrative work was hard to find; and money that he had hoped to recoup from his property's sale did not come.

Mr. Nelson, therefore, struggled to fulfill his role as his family's principal breadwinner. It was a frustrating duty, but not one without its rewards. It was a responsibility, after all, that afforded him substantial domestic power. He alone had final say on all major decisions concerning the Nelson family—whether or not they should leave the South and, if so, when and under what circumstances; where they should move; what house they should buy; what would become of their old property; and even what furnishings they could keep.

Philip Nelson's patriarchal power was not unique, but it was somewhat unusual. The nature of the economic and social oppression southern free people of color faced, their ties to a slave past, and their distinct cultural heritage collectively meant that many did not live in patriarchally structured households. It also meant that a growing number did not have nuclear families. Free black domestic relationships were much more fluid and malleable—ones whose composition, structure, and leadership could change both within and between generations. Despite this diversity, however, patriarchal authority remained an underlying theme in the social world of free blacks, even if more ideal than real. It was apparent not only in their families and households, but also in their social and philanthropic organizations.

Loudoun's economy centered on agricultural production. One's land and labor resources, therefore, were the most important determinants of one's financial success or failure. Unfortunately, the majority of free blacks, even agriculturists, usually owned neither. They necessarily worked for white planters and farmers, rather than as independent farmers or for other free blacks. While kin and neighbors could have provided valuable labor to a free black farm family, free people of color were especially land-poor.

Loudoun's land market was a tight one by any measure, and had been so almost since a small corps of wealthy planters, many of whom were land speculators or doubled as land agents and surveyors, established a virtual monopoly of Loudoun property during the colonial era. If this kind of competition made it difficult for even the middling classes to buy land, it made it virtually impossible for the poor. The situation became even more aggravated after the American Revolution when large numbers of settlers, most of whom aspired to be independent farmers, began to arrive. Land prices tripled between 1780 and 1800 alone, and as early as 1782, one-third of Loudoun's residents were tenant farmers.[5]

The creeping infertility of local farmland, a noticeable problem by the second decade of the nineteenth century, caused even greater price inflation. By 1850, farmers' attempts to restore some land fertility had begun to pay off—much of Loudoun's land was valued at about $30 per acre, but many were buying at much higher prices. While most continued to romanticize the yeoman farmer experience and dream of working on their own farms one day, few were able to move from the ranks of the tenant farmer or hired laborer to property owner.[6]

The position of the large majority of free blacks in the southern agrarian economy simply made it impossible for more than a few to purchase a home, much less land. There were few job opportunities, except those with the least prestige and permanence, the worst working conditions, and the lowest pay. Only a small number of skilled free blacks, men like Adolphus Randolph, the shoemaker, and Richard Nickens, the cooper, worked in Loudoun and there were no certified professionals, although there certainly were some ministers, perhaps a few teachers, and medical experts of one kind or another. Even those who did have valuable skills often faced discrimination from a prospective employer who refused to hire free people of color or from white laborers who would not work alongside blacks. George Carter, for example, wrote to his contractor in 1808 that he preferred the builder employ only white labor while working on his plantation home. More than forty years later in 1850, Mr. L. W. Stewart of Aldie betrayed the same attitude, specifying in a local newspaper ad that he wished to "employ a first-rate Blacksmith (a white man would be preferred) to take charge of a shop. Good wages and constant employment will be given." While local free black men like Benjamin Smith, George Jackson, Enoch Mendley, Reuben Morton, and James Boyd sought work as accomplished blacksmiths, white men like Stewart sought to exclude them from "good wages and constant employment."[7]

If Stewart and others like him hoped to force skilled free people of color to leave the county by refusing to employ them, they were successful. None of the four free black blacksmiths who resided in Loudoun in 1850 lived there in 1860. Young and skilled, some with young children and elderly parents to provide for, others who wanted to earn a stable income on which they could marry and rear a family, undoubtedly decided it would be better if they moved to a place where they could work.[8]

White employers' discrimination derived from their racial bigotry, but also from their fear that free people of color were a threat to white security and welfare, particularly when they had some involvement with slaves. Their fears, in turn, influenced the Virginia legislature to gradually exclude blacks from many skilled and business occupations. Following the Nat Turner rebellion, state assemblymen targeted free black professionals, especially black teachers and ministers.[9] In 1834, for example, they struck at the heart of urban free black livelihood, social life, and culture, prohibiting free people of color from participating in public performances or exhibitions, selling goods, or working as barbers. Two years later, the General Assembly further restricted their occupational options while also trying to undermine free black assistance to fugitive slaves. They erected legislation which forced boatmen, long suspected of aiding runaways and shipping stolen goods, to obtain certificates from "respectable white persons" to verify that their shipping manifests were accurate. Sixty-two-year-old Basil Newman was only one of a few boatmen who still resided in Loudoun in 1840. Ten years later, the tenacious Newman was still working as a boatman and had successfully acquired $1000 worth of property, but he was the only "certified" black boatman in the county.[10]

The 1840s brought even more discriminatory employment statutes. As of 1843, for example, the state considered it a misdemeanor for any free black "to prepare or administer . . . any medicine of any kind," and it became a felony for any black to perform "chemical" abortions, punishable upon conviction of five to ten years in a penitentiary. These acts destroyed the livelihood of many free black and slave men and women who, since the colonial years, had served as doctors, midwives, and herbalists to blacks and whites alike. Fear that blacks would use the confidence whites had in their healing abilities to poison or harm them in some way, or were responsible for the low fertility rates of slave women, prompted many to support this legislation.[11]

Their fears were not without foundation. Slaves testified to both poisoning whites as well as providing contraception and abortions for slave women. There also was a thriving market in stolen goods among slaves, free blacks, and whites in Loudoun, the surrounding counties, and the District of Columbia. While many peddlers were legitimate dealers, others received, bought, and sold stolen goods. They were the target of the 1843 statute maintaining that they have certificates of ownership for the agricultural products they sold and an 1838 legislative petition which demanded that hawkers have court-authorized licenses. As with the boatmen, only "respectable" whites could validate such credentials. These acts also were meant, in part, to keep free blacks and slaves separated and from acting cooperatively. Loudoun petitioners, for example, also requested legislators to pass a law forbidding any contact between "free negroes" and slaves unless "specially authorized by their owners or masters."[12]

While their attempts to discourage free black/slave unity had uncertain results, their campaign against black economic independence was largely successful. In 1853, the General Assembly again struck a blow to black entrepreneurship and, not coincidentally, black social and cultural life as well when they curtailed free black ownership of ordinaries and small business where they sold alcoholic beverages.[13]

By the end of the era, therefore, it was illegal for free African Americans to own many kinds of businesses, to perform as medical practitioners, preachers, teachers, or entertainers. It even was difficult for them to do skilled and manual labor as boatmen, barbers, peddlers, or vendors. Not surprisingly, the numbers of skilled members of their community dwindled. An 1855 county-wide census indicates that only one free black ferryman, one merchant, and no barbers registered that year. (See Table 9.) The federal census of 1850 confirms that one boatman identified himself as such, but lists no barbers, peddlers, or vendors among the group; nor did the much more detailed federal census of 1860. (See Tables 8 and 10.)[14]

Still, free black men fared much better in the rural South labor market than free black women. White employers' sexism effectively combined with their racism to exclude black girls and women from either learning or using lucrative skills in the workplace. The only skilled jobs free black women performed outside of their own communities were those of seamstress, nurse, or midwife and, then, only when no white woman was available. Perhaps the best indication of free black occupations can be found in the 1860 federal census. Although census listings define the occupations of only a sample of those persons who did work, it is the most consistent source of information descriptive of the labor histories of free people of color. (See Table 10.) Of the 88 females whose occupations are listed, only one performed skilled labor—Nancy Turner of

Table 8   Occupations of Loudoun's Free African Americans, 1850[a]

Occupation	Total	Male	Female
Blacksmith	5	5	0
Boatman	1	1	0
Cooper	1	1	0
Farmer	2	2	0
Laborer	122	120	2
Shoemaker	1	1	0
Not specified	150	51	99

[a] Compiled from data in FedCenLC, Free Schedule, 1850, roll 957.

Pleasant Valley, a seamstress. Others were either day laborers (56 percent), washerwomen (28 percent), or house servants (6 percent), all occupations that routinely were temporary or part-time, and paid low wages. Their salaries suggest their financial vulnerability—most earned less than $25 per year. Many Loudoun employers gave women employees virtually nothing except some food and clothing.[15]

There were considerably more free black males than females with skilled jobs. Despite growing legal and customary antagonism, some men, albeit small numbers, still continued to ply their trades. In 1860, for example, there were three coopers, three blacksmiths, and at least one painter, wagoneer, boatman, shoemaker, miller, tanner, and stonemason among the hundreds of free black working men. The large majority of Loudoun's free black males, like black

Table 9   Occupations of Loudoun's Free African Americans, 1855[a]

Occupation	Number	Occupation	Number
Baker	1	House Servant	3
Blacksmith	4	Ironer	1
Brick Moulder	4	Laborer	128
Carpenter	1	Mason	2
Cook	6	Merchant	1
Farmer	3	Miller	1
Farm Hand	10	Tanner	1
Fence Maker	3	Washer	55
Ferryman	1	Wagoneer	3

[a] Donald M. Sweig, "Free Negroes in Northern Virginia: An Investigation of the Growth and Status of Free Negroes in the Counties of Alexandria, Fairfax and Loudoun, 1770–1860" (M.A. thesis, George Mason University, 1975), 42.

Table 10 Occupations of Loudoun's Free African Americans, 1860[a]

Title	Male	Female	Total	Title	Male	Female	Total
Blacksmith	3	0	3	Miller	1	0	1
Boatman	1	0	1	Pauper	0	1	1
Cook/washer	0	1	1	Seamstress	0	1	1
Cooper	3	0	3	Shoemaker	1	0	1
Farmer	4	2	6	Stonemason	1	0	1
Farm hand	19	0	19	Tanner	1	0	1
House painter	1	0	1	Wagoneer	1	0	1
House servant	0	4	4	Washerwoman	0	25	25
Laborer	105	49	154	Not specified	28	5	33

[a] Compiled from FedCenLC, Free Schedule, 1860, roll 1359.

females, however, were unskilled day laborers. Some 82 percent of those free black workers, male and female, included in the Loudoun's occupational census of 1855 had unskilled jobs. Given the growing mandate to ruin free African Americans economically, it is not surprising that those with skilled occupations gradually declined over time. In 1820, for example, 89 percent of those local free blacks who had occupations listed in the federal census were day (or unskilled) laborers. But by 1850, 96 percent of those with stated occupations worked as laborers or in some "nonspecified" (primarily unskilled) occupation. Among males, as many as 88 percent in 1850 performed unskilled day labor, usually some kind of agricultural work. The majority of the South's free black males performed the same kinds of labor, under similar conditions as black slaves; many worked alongside them. Free black females also worked as farm hands, although it was more difficult for them to get this kind of work than it was for males. [16] (See Table 8.)

The pay that unskilled free people of color, particularly women, earned was miniscule. Not only did employers pay women less, but females with unskilled jobs faced different standards than men. Skin color, for example, seemed to weigh heavily in the decision to hire female domestics. Full-time house servants like Hannah and Fannie Robinson, who had to help support their elderly mother and five children, or Eliza King, who was the sole support of her four young children, collected no more than $25 per year for their labor, and perhaps some in-kind payments of food, clothing, and shelter. But even this kind of work, relished by some because of the security it offered and the additional food and clothing benefits, was difficult to get on a permanent basis, particularly for dark-skinned women. Hannah, Fannie, and Eliza were all "mulattos," as were 75 percent of the women who had these kinds of jobs. A larger proportion of employed females, however, had to settle for the less prestigious, less secure, and less lucrative position of washerwoman, earning only a few cents a day. Washerwomen tended to be darker in color and slightly older, or, according to the standards of the day, less physically attractive.[17]

Agricultural workers, most of whom were men, earned more than domestics and washerwomen, but their pay still was meager. Wages could vary tremendously according to one's gender (women earned less than men), the type of labor performed, and, to a lesser extent, the employer. While Mrs. Samuel De-Butts paid a black man named Isaac 25 cents per day to plant corn for her in 1839, for example, General Edwards agreed to pay Philip Nelson $2.25 that same year for each acre of farm land that he "brok[e] up." Mr. Nelson earned more money because his job was much more physically challenging and he used his own team of horses. Free black males who did unskilled farm work usually earned between 25 and 50 cents per day; while farmers paid women only 15 to 30 cents. White male agricultural workers, on the other hand, routinely received between 50 cents and one dollar per day. Daily average pay rates for white males were approximately 50 cents for farm work, 63 cents for chopping wood, one dollar for plowing, $2.50 for hauling wood, and $3.00 for hauling ice.[18]

Many free people of color hired themselves out on an annual basis like slaves, meeting at the local courthouse or taverns on New Year's Day to find an employer. Describing one such "hiring day," a local reporter noted that at the first of every year places were "waked up" with "men, women and children, mechanics, field hands, dining room servants, cooks and house servants, of every color from the Octoroon . . . to the real wooly headed Congo" where they "commingled with the contractor seeking his complement of force, the small farmer [looking for] three of four able bodied fellows, the citizen of the town hunting his porter or house servants, and the spinster or childless widow looking for a girl 'tween ten and twelve to raise."[19] Their annual salaries varied substantially, but generally teenaged girls earned a minimum of $20; women usually received at least $50; and men could earn from $60 to $150 if they were skilled.[20]

Loudoun free blacks also worked along the Potomac River as boat and ferrymen during much of the year and as fishers and on the fish wharves during the late winter and early spring. Many temporarily removed to Alexandria, the center of the local fish industry, every March. There they lived in what was called "Fishtown"—a collection of crude shacks—where they salted, sold, and packed shad and herring. "For nearly a quarter of a mile the dock was lined with crowds of colored men and women, washing and cleaning fish," described one contemporary of the "Fishtown" era. "The women were especially worthy of observation, covered from head to heels with scales . . . ; and in the midst of songs and laughter they performed their tasks with wonderful alacrity and skill. Knife in hand, they clean and wash . . . with singular rapidity." They sold fish and fish spawn to local people, as well as to customers from Maryland and Pennsylvania.[21]

Because so much of their labor was either part-time or seasonal, most had several jobs and employers. Philip Nelson not only hired himself out to clear land, but also sold corn, livestock, wood, and straw, did construction work, and rented his horses out to local farmers. George Rivers characterized himself as a hireling, a good cradler, mower, and stone fence maker, and "faithful at all work that he may undertake." Joseph Hogan worked as a day laborer, but also raised livestock that he sold at Harper's Ferry. Hogan's moderate success provided his family with a home and the wherewithal to hire a young white man to drive his meat wagon while he was free to pursue other kinds of work. [22]

Women not only worked as washers and domestics, but also took on temporary nursing and midwifery jobs, accommodated boarders, and sold at local markets, social gatherings, and along the road homemade textiles, baskets, and brooms, vegetables, eggs, baked goods, and other foods. Twenty-four-year-old Catherine Allen was both cook and washerwoman, hiring herself out to several white families in addition to being the sole caretaker of her four-year-old daughter Ida. Harriet Cook was a successful washerwoman with an extensive clientele that, over the years, included more than 90 of the county's most important persons. She also earned money serving in "other capacities," probably as a midwife.[23] In a petition filed on her behalf, Cook's employer's described her as "gentile," "trustworthy," "skillful," and "useful." John Janney recalled that as a Loudoun youth the ginger cakes Betty Spence made to sell at neighborhood shooting matches were a special treat. According to Janney, Spence made two kinds: "one very large one which she sold for a quarter of a dollar . . . ; and a round one like a saucer for one cent."[24]

Family heads expected everyone to contribute to their household's support, young and old, men and women alike. Even when Sam Carter was ninety-two and Susan Byrnes was eighty-six, they were both working. Ten years later, Carter was still living with his wife Nelly in the Quaker village of Hamilton, and he was still working.[25] But the elderly's income was only one example of family survival strategies; the young did their part too. Adolescent and single women, for example, often took jobs as live-in domestics, while parents routinely hired out their sons as farm workers and day laborers. Fourteen-year-old Millie and her older sister Hester both helped their mother in her washer business; their brother George brought in money as a day laborer.[26]

Apprenticed children also earned family income, although sometimes it was difficult for free blacks to become apprentices given the dwindling number of artisans and craftsmen within their communities, and the reticence of whites to share such skills with blacks whom they did not own. There also were those parents who did not want to bound out their children because of the awful treatment they sometimes experienced. John Malvin, for example, was a free black born in nearby Dumfries in Prince William County in 1795, the son of a free woman and a slave man. At the age of seven, his mother bound him out to a Mr. Henderson, his father's master. Henderson not only took John a great distance from his family (some 300 miles west to Wood County), but allowed his white underlings to mistreat the boy. John served as attendant to one of Henderson's clerks, performing a variety of tasks from blackening his boots and taking care of his horse to field labor. For his work he received only a minimal amount of food ("one peck of corn meal a week") and clothing ("one pair of shoes, two pairs of tow linen pantallons, one pair of negro cotton pantaloons, and a negro cotton round jacket"). John not only experienced the material discomfort of slaves, but their brutal whippings too. Recalling one particularly harsh beating as a teen, Malvin wrote in his autobiography that

> my wrists were tied crosswise together, and my hands were then brought down and tied to my ankles; my shirt was taken off, and in that condition I was compelled to lie on the ground, and he began flogging me. He whipped me on one side till the flesh was all raw and bleeding; then he rolled me over like a log and whipped me on the other side in the same manner.[27]

When he put his shirt back on, his back was so badly cut by the whip that his blood and exposed flesh stuck to the shirt, which came off only after an elderly slave woman "applied grease to it." Finally released from his apprenticeship after Henderson's death, John had an opportunity to return to his family and learn carpentry from his father. Like so many young men of his generation, John eventually left Virginia in 1827 for Ohio.[28]

Yet despite joint economic ventures and contributions of family members, pitifully few free people of color could afford to buy land, initiate a business, or even own their family home. The lack of financial resources, however, was not their only obstacle. Many local whites actively prevented free people of color from acquiring land or skilled work, preferring instead to keep them as a cheap and easily manipulated source of day labor, rather than as competitive farmers and artisans.

When Robert Carter freed the first 30 of his 509 slaves (some in Loudoun and its vicinity) in 1791, for example, he not only employed some, but gave a few of them small parcels of land and rented to others. His watchful neighbors were full of resentment and protest. Those whites who also rented land from Carter were the most visibly upset, outraged by the audacity of the man who dared to "elevate" blacks to their status. Christopher Collins, for one, confronted the aging landlord, calling his actions "inexpedient" and lending "considerable dissatisfaction to the others [tenants], and neighbours around." Carter's sons, George and John, both Loudoun planters, would have heartily agreed. Recall, for example, that George refused to let a Baltimore builder employ free black labor to work on his home, and John altogether refused to free his father's slaves under his control.[29]

But there always were some free blacks who managed to acquire real estate, usually a family home, but sometimes a small farm or an urban lot. When Philip Nelson and his family left Leesburg in 1839, for example, he owned a small piece of forested land which he hoped to sell for no less than $250 and another lot, on which his house stood, that he priced at $1500. Forest Griffith of Hillsboro was born a slave, but eventually managed to purchase himself and his daughter as well as 15 acres of land valued at $500 in 1860. Sally Mercer's property was worth $200 in 1850, while fifty-year-old Mary Ashton, caretaker of three young grandchildren, owned $300 in real estate that year. These houses, barns, and lots of land were not only emblems of free black financial success, but also important assets that provided them and their families with a sense of security that most never experienced. They at least could rely on their land for food and shelter and a place to ply their trades. A few even had relatively substantial landholdings. Samuel Thompson, for example, owned property conservatively estimated to be worth $4500 in 1850. That same year, James Carr paid taxes on a local farm valued at $3500.[30]

Yet the number of free black property owners was tiny at best; so too was the value of their property. Indeed, the property holdings of Samuel Thompson and James Carr were enormous when compared with those of other local free people of color. In 1850, for example, only 34 free African Americans in the county owned property, seven of whom were women. While its value fluctuated from the meager $100 estate of eighty-year-old Nelly Minters to the $4500 farm of Samuel Thompson, the average holding was only worth one-tenth the value of Thompson's farm—about $473.[31] When compared with county-wide holdings, those of free people of color seem especially small. The average Loudoun farm, that is, the land and the buildings on it, in 1850, for example, was worth $6,648—almost one and a half times the value of the largest free black farm and 14 times the value of the average free black holding.[32]

It was not just that blacks barely managed to acquire any property over time; growing white hostility slowly eroded even their very limited access to the "propertied" classes. While records indicate a slow increase in free black population size and property holding for the first few decades of the nineteenth century, by 1840 the tide was beginning to turn. Free blacks fared better during the years between 1840 and 1850, for example, than during the next decade, which proved to be the most devastating. The losses experienced during those last ten years before the outbreak of the Civil War indicate not only a widening economic malaise but, relatedly, the emigration of free black property holders out of the county. By 1860, only 20 local free blacks, or 41 percent fewer than in 1850, owned real estate. The average value of their property also declined, by one-third, to $316.66 that decade. The total value of Loudoun free black real estate in 1860 was only $9,535, 42 percent less than the listed value of their property in 1850. Not surprisingly, while free blacks were losing the tiny amount of economic power they claimed through their real estate, white property values were increasing by an impressive 16 percent during the same decade. The average value of Loudoun County farms in 1860 was about $8700, almost equal to the value of all of Loudoun's free black real estate that year.[33]

Black women property holders were the most vulnerable—they experienced the slowest growth and sustained the heaviest losses over time. With little property to speak of during the first decades of the nineteenth century, the years between 1840 and 1850 registered the most substantial gains. Yet, in the course of the next ten years, the number of propertied females dwindled from seven to only three. Laundresses Nancy Robinson and Priscilla Lewis and an eighty-year-old laborer, Zilphia Davis, were the only women who still owned property in 1860, and that was worth only $950 collectively.[34]

These figures are even more daunting when one realizes that one woman—Nancy Robinson of Waterford—claimed $700 of that total amount. A survey of her household offers a quick explanation for Robinson's extraordinary financial circumstances. Although listed as head of her household, Robinson obviously received substantial financial support from another household member, her adult son Silas, a local miller who worked regularly. Besides their real estate, Nancy and Silas also owned four horses, no doubt useful in Silas's work. But even with two male boarders, Zilphia Davis barely was able to hold on to her status as a property owner. Priscilla Lewis, a washerwoman and caretaker of four children, also was struggling to maintain her real estate. Like Robinson, her household probably benefited from the earnings of her sixteen-year-old son John, a day laborer.[35]

Personal characteristics and family relations and structure were important determinants of a free black's ability to acquire and hold on to property. Gender was the most distinguishing factor—men who had real estate routinely outnumbered women five or more to one. It is not surprising that few women owned property given their limited occupational choices and general poverty. What is unusual is that, although Loudoun's free men of color had better access to skilled occupations and there was at least one tanner, fence maker, cooper, and boatman among the ranks of those who held property, few of the men who owned property did full-time skilled work. Instead, most black real estate owners, male and female, were "laborers," of one sort or another—68 percent in 1850 and 65 percent in 1860.[36]

Advanced age, residential longevity, and the cooperation of extended kin clearly were the most important advantages, after gender, of those who wanted to succeed financially. Almost everyone who owned property was an older adult who had resided in Loudoun for many years. The average age of free black landholders in 1850, for example, was almost fifty-six; ten years later, it was fifty-seven years. Like most free people of color, property holders had long histories of wage earning, beginning as youths and working until they were quite old. Many painstakingly saved money over the years, forcing themselves and their loved ones to accept long-term sacrifices while they did so.

The gender, age, and relative financial security of most free black owners no doubt helped to create a deep respect for patriarchal sentiment within black families and communities, a sentiment that patriarchs used to gain control over female and younger kin. In many ways, their roles within their families were similar to those of southern white men. Yet few free black men could have achieved economic stability, much less property, without the financial support that other family members continually provided. Their reliance on the financial contributions of their wives, children, and others as well as their uncertain legal status rendered their patriarchy much more tenuous and circumspect than that of most white men. Not even the moderate financial success of the wealthiest free black could protect him or his family from the blunt force of customary and legal discrimination. Still, some upwardly mobile free people of color found ways to succeed and sometimes even to prosper.[37]

Some drew strength from numbers, particularly those in large, extended families that were centrally located. It was not unusual, for example, for two or three separate free black households, located near each other and connected by close kin ties, to cooperate with one another in the purchase and upkeep of property. While the land might have been held in one person's name, usually the male "head" of the extended family, the entire group shared the profit and pride from its ownership and development. Still even these kinds of networks often were not strong enough to withstand hostile outside pressure. Some of the scant details of the family history of Loudoun's largest free black real estate holder, Samuel Thompson, provide an exemplary scenario.

In 1850, Samuel Thompson was a sixty-three-year-old, light-complected farmer whose property in Loudoun's rural "southern" district was valued at $4500. An elderly man by antebellum standards, Thompson was in his twilight years, but he probably was enjoying them. He was a prosperous farmer and the head of a large, tight-knit family. His household alone contained three generations—his wife, a son, and six grandchildren—as well as two adult boarders. Close by lived his brother Jonathan, who also resided with three generations of his own family—his wife Frances, daughter Louisa, and her five children. All of the members of Samuel Thompson's household, as well as his neighboring relatives, probably worked on the Thompson farm and thought of it as their own; therein lay Samuel Thompson's strength.[38]

The road to his obvious success had been a long one. Samuel Thompson was born in Loudoun during the 1780s, probably the son of John Thompson, a free black agricultural worker who lived during the late colonial era and early nineteenth century. Between 1820 and 1830, Samuel married Midey, another free black, and the two began to build a new generation for their families. Through hard work, careful planning, and good fortune, Samuel Thompson eventually bought a modest farm and home, producing marketable wheat and other grains as well as livestock. He and his son Landon, along with his grandsons David, Jonathan, and Samuel, also worked on neighboring farms, their wages providing an extra measure of financial security. A free mulatto couple, Delia and Charles Lucust (or Lucas), lived as boarders in the Thompson home, providing additional income and perhaps labor. With these collective monetary contributions, as well as the additional support that brother Jonathan and his family gave to the upkeep of the family farm, the Thompson clan was able not only to sustain their real estate holdings, but also to add to them. Curiously, the federal census of 1850 lists no occupation for Midey Thompson. This omission might indicate that the family finally had gained enough financial security to be able to allow the patriarch's wife to retire from the paid labor force. Although Mrs. Thompson surely worked on the family's farm and within her home, her retreat to the "domestic sphere" was a rare luxury and decided mark of financial security for a Loudoun free black woman, even at age sixty-two.[39]

Yet neither the Thompson family's good fortune, nor its cohesiveness, were secure. Between 1850 and 1860 all records indicate that the clan dispersed and, along with them, their property holdings. A number of variables could have affected their financial situation. A series of financial failures or white antagonism toward Samuel Thompson's success always were possibilities. Natural changes in the "life cycle" of the Thompson family, however, probably had the most impact. By 1850, at the "height" of their financial success, Samuel and Midey Thompson already were elderly and their son Landon was middle-aged with three sons of his own. The family was ripe for some change.[40]

Perhaps the death of Midey Thompson during the 1850s was an undeniable signal to them all. It is conceivable, for example, that Mr. Thompson may have chosen to liquidate some of his landed property in order to provide his son with capital with which to settle outside of Loudoun (Landon does not reappear in the county census for 1860). The elderly Samuel Thompson probably would not have consented to move himself given his age and the long personal struggle he had waged to obtain local status. Younger members of his family, however, may have believed that the time had come for them to pursue opportunities elsewhere, particularly in light of growing hostility. But Samuel Thompson's immediate family was not the only one which sustained changes. So too did his brother Jonathan's clan. Another possible scenario, for example, is that some of the members of Thompson's extended kin network, who also had a substantial investment in the farm, tired of the communal arrangement and requested that the "patriarch" sell the property and divide the proceeds.

Whatever the reasons, the Thompson family and their property holdings changed drastically over the decade. By 1860, Samuel Thompson was no longer the head of his own bustling household, but was himself a boarder along with his grandson Landon Jr. in the Philamont home of George Lewis, a local day laborer. At age seventy-three, Thompson still was working. His property, though dwindled probably through sale or familial division, still was valued at $1000, and continued to provide the aged farmer a great amount of financial security and status among his community. Only Thompson's grandsons, Samuel II and Landon Jr., still lived in Loudoun. His son Landon probably moved, taking his other children with him. There was no 1860 listing for brother Jonathan Thompson either, or any of his family members. They too perhaps had settled elsewhere.[41]

Clearly it was difficult for southern free blacks to sustain financial security for very many years. It was even more difficult for them to pass it on to future generations. Unlike his grandfather, the younger Samuel Thompson was not a farmer but a day laborer. By 1860, he had married a free black woman named Susan and they, along with their four children, lived in the small Loudoun village of Morrisonville. [42]

It seems that as a new generation of Thompson men pursued their own patriarchal status through establishing independent households away from the control of the elderly Samuel, they lost some of the security that their extended family of the past had provided. Yet the ability to create one's own household was in itself a significant accomplishment. As such, communal living and financial arrangements among free African American families may have been a temporary means of support for those trying to establish independence, rather than a permanent system of familial and fictive kin interaction.

Not all of Loudoun's few free black real estate owners, however, depended on extended families to help them; others relied solely on nuclear kin. Nathan (a.k.a. Wortham) Minor's property holdings in the Quaker town of Waterford, for example, increased substantially during the last decades before the Civil War, thanks to the contributions of his adult children. Like Samuel Thompson, Mr. Minor was the elderly head of his family by the time he had obtained a relatively large amount of real estate. His property acquisition was neither easy nor predictable. In 1850, he owned real estate worth about $500. Ten years later, his property had quadrupled in value. At age seventy, he finally had become the largest free black property owner in the county.[43]

Like the Thompson clan, everyone in Nathan Minor's family contributed their individual earnings to their household's budget. His wife Susan, a white woman seven years his junior, did not work; but their two eldest sons—Henry and Samuel—did. Unlike the Thompsons, however, the Minor men were skilled free blacks. Mr. Minor was a fence maker who had taught his sons the trade. Fencemaking was a lucrative occupation in a large, rural county like Loudoun. Their ability to earn more money as craftsmen, rather than as poorly paid day laborers, allowed this nuclear family to achieve financial success without the cooperative assistance of other extended kin, friends, or boarders, as had the Thompsons.[44]

Mrs. Minor may not have lived long enough to witness her husband's financial peak, for she died sometime between 1850 and 1860. Although she had been a central part of the family, the Minor clan remained intact and actually thrived despite the loss of the senior female member. Nathan Minor and his sons still were living and working together as fencemakers in 1860. His daughter Sarah also remained in the family home, but eventually joined the paid labor force, working as a washerwoman. As the only woman in the household after her mother's death, she undoubtedly performed most of her family's domestic work along with her regular duties as a laundress.[45]

It is obvious that neither Nathan Minor nor Samuel Thompson could have achieved financial success without the support of their families. They needed the income of every household member physically able to work (except Mrs. Minor) in order to provide them with the financial means to purchase and hold on to property. Their labor was important, for, given their limited financial resources, few could afford to hire workers or buy slaves. Free black women again fared worse than men in this situation, as documented by the comparatively few numbers of slaves they owned. Moreover, Virginia law dated 1832 prevented even those blacks who had the means from buying slaves unless they were purchasing a family member of direct descent.[46]

While most with some measure of financial stability were not able to pass it on to the next generation, patriarchs like Samuel Thompson and Nathan Minor were more successful in preparing their children to establish independent households. So too was Cupid Robinson, who, at the time of his death, was able to bequeath $200 worth of real estate to his wife Malinda.[47] Among Loudoun's free African Americans, Robinson uniquely was successful in providing protection and some security for his family. Moreover, he obviously believed these were his responsibilities as a father and a husband.

Born in about 1770, Cupid was first listed as head of his own household in 1810. Sometime after that date, he married a mulatto slave from neighboring Prince William County named Malinda. The couple struggled to obtain her freedom, and between 1828 and 1830, they were able to do so. But this was not before Malinda gave birth to a slave daughter that they named Fanny. The couple managed to buy the child soon after her birth and by 1830, Cupid and Malinda Robinson's household also included their daughter and two free sons born in 1829 and 1830. As usual, everyone in the Robinson clan held down a job as long as their health permitted. In 1850, for example, Cupid Robinson still was working steadily as a day laborer; his wife had some kind of unspecified wage-earning job; his sons, Henry and James, worked as farm hands; and his two daughters were domestics for local whites.[48]

Like so many other free black households, the Robinson's included several generations under one roof. By 1850, Cupid, his wife, and children, as well as two grandchildren, all lived in his home. Fanny Robinson's two children, Hannah and Joseph, were the youngest members of the clan. These kinds of intergenerational and/or extended free black households often remained together for several years, not only because of their deep emotional ties to one another, but also because it was economically expedient to do so for both the older and younger generations. Fanny, in particular, must have appreciated her parents' continual emotional and material support. Apparently unmarried, Fanny had her first child when she was nineteen years old. One year later, she gave birth to a second. Inclusion in her father's household guaranteed her and her young the kind of material support, sharing of childrearing duties, and an emotionally rich family life that she could not duplicate on her own.[49]

There also were other kinds of household structures and arrangements. A considerable minority of free people of color, for example, lived as part of white households, rather than in independent free black homes. In 1810, some 108 of Loudoun's white households accommodated 186 free blacks, or 31 percent of the county's total. Over the next twenty years, a substantial growth in the number of free blacks in the county was accompanied by a sizable decline in the percentage who lived in white households. In 1830, only 18 percent did. The following two decades, however, marred by increasing hostility reflected in free black economic, legal and social repression, witnessed a remarkable increase in the numbers who were inhabitants of white households. By 1850, 37 percent lived in the homes or on the property of local whites.[50]

Little is known about these free people of color. What information that is available indicates that most white-headed households that included free people of color only had one or two living with them. Some of these men, women, and children undoubtedly were related to slave property on the premises. John Malvin and his mother Dorcas, for example, lived with his slave father's master. Fanny Smith and her two children lived in Leesburg at the home of her slave husband's owner. Perhaps others were freed slaves who continued to reside in the homes of their ex-masters. Samuel Clapham, who owned 40 slaves, for example, also had one free person of color living on his estate. So too did Bayley Powell, the owner of 37 slaves. Sarah Powell, the largest female slaveholder in the county in 1810, had four free African Americans and 21 slaves living on her property that year. George Carter had 61 slaves and 35 free people of color, but only three whites (including himself) living on his "Oatlands" estate in 1830; his cousin Landon had 22 slaves and 11 free people of color on his Loudoun property in 1840. Certainly many were live-in domestics or some kind of servant. Most free blacks who lived in white households, for example, were female—55.6 percent in 1830. Others may have been the mulatto offspring of white men or women, indentured servants, apprentices, or permanent farm laborers who could not afford their own homes or to live with their kin.[51]

While little is known of the day-to-day lives of specific free people of color who lived in white homes, many persons in like situations often complained that when they stayed with slaveholders, they were treated as slaves. Certainly there was no guarantee that they, like John Malvin, would not be unexpectedly separated from their slave or impoverished free black families. The freedom to pursue secure marital and familial relations undoubtedly was more easily obtained within their own households. Many free people of color, in addition, probably felt more at ease in the home of local nonslaveholders, especially those who extended patronage or protection in one fashion or another. A number of Loudoun's Quakers, such as Isaac Nichols, Elisha Janney, and Mahlon Gregg, as well as persons living in or near the county's German community, like Susan Crim, Jonathan Kalb, and Thomas Heitner, for example, accommodated free blacks on their property. This is not surprising since few in the German community and even fewer Quakers owned slaves, but often relied on free black labor.[52]

Whites also lived in free black households as either family members, boarders, or laborers. Despite immense social pressure to do otherwise, local white women had romantic relationships and sometimes cohabited with free black men as their wives. Elizabeth Beach Fouch, for example, lost her white family and respectability when she had an affair with free black James Watt. Ignoring her husband's repeated advice concerning the "Wickedness of such a course, of the infamy and disgrace which must result from it, [and] that if persisted in [the] separation [that] would assuredly take place," Elizabeth finally ran away with her lover in 1808. Others stayed, married, and raised families. David Smallwood, for example, married a white woman. So too did the mulatto and propertied brothers Jesse, Henry, Nathan, and Thomas Newman. At least two descendants of the Newman interracial clan, Bassell and Ratt, also married European American women, as did their neighbor Robert Ambrose.[53] Nathan Minor, Loudoun's most propertied free black in 1860, also was married to a white woman.[54]

Local whites clearly were opposed to interracial marriages, but they continued to exist, some openly. Not surprisingly, there is little evidence of legal marriage or even marital-like relations between a white man and a black or mulatto woman. The persistence of large numbers of free black persons light enough to be considered "mulatto" in the Loudoun census (by 1860, mulattos comprised 51 percent of this population), however, provide adequate evidence of at least some kind of sexual activity between these women and white men.[55]

White women who married free black men faced the white community's rejection. Yet there remains little indication of how free people of color treated them or their families. It is clear that many of these interracial families, clustered together in small communities, provided both a society and protection for themselves. Moreover, the inordinate number of male property holders and skilled laborers among their black husbands had to assure these women some measure of respectability, perhaps not in the white community, but certainly among free people of color. Likewise, their husbands' property and skills guaranteed them a modicum of material comfort that most women of color never had. The large majority of the white women married to free black men, like Patsy Kemp, Percella Johnson, Susan Minor, and Fanny Griffith for example, did not work outside of their homes.[56]

Marriage, however, was not the basis for all of Loudoun's interracial households. There were several examples of whites of no apparent blood or marital relation to free blacks living in their homes or on their property. William Dixson, for instance, resided as an elderly laborer in the home of Laura Eastern of Goresville. Mary Frances, Washington Bradly, and Leven Posting all lived on Wyatt Allen's property. William and Sarah Batt and their three children, William Jr., Susan, and Jonathan, stayed with Nellie Thomas, a local mulatto woman and her two small children, along Broad Run. It is uncertain what relationships these whites had to their free black household heads. Perhaps some were related by blood, but given the social mores of the day, those relationships would not be specified in extant records. Perhaps more romantic or sexual relationships existed between some of the adults. They also could have been boarders or employed in one capacity or another on the property. John Mobberly, for example, worked for Joe Hogan.[57]

It also is possible, and in some instances probable, that some of the persons labeled "white" on census records may have been African Americans who were either "passing" or were mistaken as white because of their physical attributes. Virginia defined anyone with one-eighth "negro" blood as black, and several generations of miscegenation in one family could produce persons who had some black ancestry, but were no longer legally African American. Relatedly, there were numerous persons among the free people of color community who could, on physical appearance alone, pass for white. Ann Royall, a news reporter, noted of Alexandria in 1824, for example, that "the street and market-square presented groups of men, women and children, every shade of colour, from the fairest white, down to the deepest black. . . . Some of these were about half-white, some almost white, leaving it difficult to distinguish where the one ends, and the other begins."[58] Census enumerators, charged with making a distinction of race for every person in the county, undoubtedly found the task just as confusing. It especially must have been difficult when free people of color chose to "pass."[59]

Certainly there were persons within each free African American community who crossed over the color line in order to take advantage of the many privileges afforded whites. Lewis Lee and Cornelius Brooke, for example, were local slaves who were able to escape by posing as free white men. The secrecy incumbent in the act of passing necessarily has hidden many, and their acts of racial "redefinition," from the historical record. Yet some evidence has surfaced. Perhaps one example will serve to illustrate something of their lifestyles.

Daniel and David Bruce were born in neighboring Prince William County during the late eighteenth century. Both passed for white and were able to work as mail carriers between Alexandria, Washington, and Fairfax counties most of their adult lives. Their access to education and other advantages, routinely denied free black youth, persuaded the Bruce children not only to move in and out of the white world when necessary, but also guaranteed them a privileged position in the free black community.

Of David Bruce's children, little is known. Their genealogist assumes that they "disappeared forever into the white race." Daniel, however, had ten children with his wife Hannah, a free woman of color, and much is known about their fate. They had various occupations of status within the free black community—dressmakers, barbers, stevedores, and caterers. Hannah, named for her mother, married a Civil War veteran who went on to become a federal clerk, a trustee of "Colored Schools" in Washington, and a Reconstruction politician. Alexander married and raised sixteen children while successfully building a Washington catering service. Ellen migrated to Minnesota, where she married a farmer and Civil War veteran. Another son, Robert, became a barber and served in the U.S. Colored Infantry during the Civil War. Erma, one of the younger children, married Alston Burleigh, son of the famed composer Harry T. Burleigh.[60]

The structure and composition of this privileged family are the same as those of the most financially successful among other local free people of color. Perhaps the most striking differences are the large sizes of the families they produced (Hannah and Daniel had 10 children; one son had 16; one daughter, 9; and another son had 12) and the persistent nuclear core of their families over the generations, both indices of stability as well as cultural assimilation.[61]

The Bruces also adopted some strategies for family survival, most notably the operative extended family, that were quite similar to those of other free people of color. When Frances, the oldest daughter of Hannah and Daniel, died, for example, her sister Mary, who had married and moved to New York, raised and educated two of her children. Likewise, a number of older free black couples and individuals in Loudoun acted as the primary caretakers for their grandchildren—keeping them in their homes while the children's parents resided elsewhere. Some of children may have had mothers who were live-in servants. Others may have been orphans. Charles and Mary Ann Gant, for example, were free black laborers in Aldie who took care of their three young grandchildren—Sarah, Isabel, and John Gant. Eliza Grayson was another Aldie free black who lived alone with her grandchildren. They, in turn, helped

Grayson, an elderly domestic, by contributing to the upkeep of her home with some of the money they earned as day laborers.[62]

Clearly the financial vulnerability of free women of color distinguished their experiences from those of men tremendously. There were other differential experiences as well. Consider, for example, those who were heads of households. An unusually large number of free black females in Loudoun held that position and increasingly so over time. In 1810, for example, black women headed 17.5 percent of all independently established free black households. By 1820, their representation had increased to 27.1 percent. Although there was a slight decline between 1820 and 1830, the actual numbers of persons who lived within these households also increased noticeably during this decade. In 1820, for example, an average female-headed household in Loudoun's free black community had between three and four persons. Ten years later about five persons usually lived in these homes. By 1850, 28 percent of Loudoun's free black households had female heads. The numbers increased again over the next decade to represent 34 percent in 1860, with slightly more than five persons typically living in them. [63]

The presence of large numbers of female-headed households is not suggested by the actual numbers of male and female free people of color in the county. Throughout the first half of the nineteenth century, the ratio between the two sexes was almost even in every age cohort except among the elderly. There were, however, several societal conditions, especially free black economic repression, and cultural norms as well which may have precipitated this relatively exaggerated number of female-headed households.

Given the pressures many free black men felt to be their families' primary breadwinners, apparent, for example, in the behavior of Philip Nelson, Samuel Thompson, and Nathan Minor, their inability to do so may have kept some from making marital commitments even to those women with whom they were intimately involved or with whom they shared children. As economic conditions worsened over the era, fewer may have felt capable of sustaining a family, thereby contributing to the gradual increase in female-headed households. This does not mean that none of these men helped to support their offspring. But it does mean that some may have done so while living in other households or even outside of Loudoun. Other women and mothers undoubtedly had husbands and lovers who left the county as a consequence of mandatory removal laws, or relocated in order to find work. Philip Nelson, for example, temporarily left his wife and children in Leesburg while he sought work and a new home in Washington and then in Philadelphia. Large numbers of free blacks eventually left Loudoun, and men were more likely to be emigrants than women. It is certainly no coincidence, for example, that the number of female-headed households within the free black community increased by 6 percent during the same decade (1850–60) when, for the first time in their history, the number of free

Table 11   Distribution of Male and Female Heads of Households and
Average Household Size among Loudoun Free Blacks, 1810–60[a]

Year	Percent male-headed	Household size	Percent female	Household size
1810	82.50	4.74	17.50	3.79
1820	72.86	4.41	27.14	3.29
1830	76.44	5.10	23.56	4.63
1840	78.99	4.99	21.01	4.14
1850	72.05	4.97	27.95	4.64
1860	66.49	4.90	33.51	5.23

[a] Data compiled from: U.S. Department of Commerce, Bureau of the Census, Manuscript Federal Census, Loudoun County, Virginia, 1810, roll 69; 1820, roll 137; 1830, roll 1193; 1840, roll 564; 1850, Free Schedule, roll 957; 1860, Free Schedule, roll 1359, National Archives, Washington, D.C.

blacks in the county declined, (by almost 8 percent) and the value of their real estate dwindled to 42 percent of what it had been in 1850.[64]

There were other reasons as well for the persistence of this large minority of female-headed households. Some free black females who were married to slaves chose to live independently, rather than be part of the slaveholding households of their husbands' masters. Moreover, the shorter life span of free black males, as compared with females, may have meant that many middle-aged free black women who were heads of households were widows. The cultural legacy of slavery also was important, since the institution produced patterns of slave matrifocality and matrilocality that continued to be familiar and, for some free blacks, acceptable alternatives to the two-parent, nuclear-core households of the Thompsons, Minors, and others.

Clearly there was little material advantage for women to establish their own households, since they generally were much poorer and less stable than those

Table 12   Gender Distribution among Heads of Free Black,
Probable-Nuclear Core Households, 1820–60[a]

Year	Percent male	Percent female
1820	90.91	9.09
1830	75.40	24.60
1840	94.44	5.56
1850	93.16	6.84
1860	91.20	8.90

[a] Data compiled from U.S. Department of Commerce, Bureau of the Census, Manuscript Federal Census, Loudoun County, Virginia, 1820, roll 137; 1830, roll 1193; 1840, roll 564; 1850, Free Schedule, roll 957; 1860, Free Schedule, roll 1359, National Archives, Washington, D.C.

Table 13 Average Number of Children in Free Black-Headed Households
According to Gender of Household Head, 1820–60[a]

Year	Male	Female
1820	3.03	2.27
1830	2.57	3.19
1840	2.51	2.60
1850	2.59	4.33
1860	3.06	3.60

[a] Data compiled from U.S. Department of Commerce, Bureau of the Census, Manuscript Federal Census, Loudoun County, Virginia, 1820, roll 137; 1830, roll 1193; 1840, roll 564; 1850, Free Schedule, roll 957; 1860, Free Schedule, roll 1359, National Archives, Washington, D.C.

that males headed. By every measure of financial stability, they lagged behind, far behind. Free African American women earned less money, owned less property—landed, slave, and personal—and had fewer persons on whom they could rely to contribute to their households' financial support than male household heads. Many women like Eliza King, a domestic whose Goresville household was comprised of just herself and four young children, also had more dependent children and fewer working adults in their homes than male peers. While the incidence of child-inclusive households among those headed by women (66 percent in 1820, 62.5 percent in 1850, and 63.8 percent in 1860) was less than those which males headed (between 75 percent and 79 percent for the entire era), those women who had children in their homes during the last few decades of the era had, on an average, more children than those men with child-inclusive homes. (See Table 13.)

Still the overall size of female-headed households continued to be smaller than those of men. (See Table 11.) The additional persons in male-headed

Table 14 Child-Inclusive, Free Black-Headed Households, 1820–60[a]

Year	Percent of all free black households	Percent male-headed	Percent female-headed
1820	66.96	70.00	30.00
1830	73.14	72.66	27.34
1840	66.17	82.95	17.05
1850	74.29	76.92	23.08
1860	71.83	70.59	29.41

[a] Data compiled from: U.S. Department of Commerce, Bureau of the Census, Manuscript Federal Census, Loudoun County, Virginia, 1820, roll 137; 1830, roll 1193; 1840, roll 564; 1850, Free Schedule, roll 957; 1860, Free Schedule, roll 1359, National Archives, Washington, D.C.

Table 15 Probable-Nuclear Core Households among
All Free Black-Headed Households, 1820–60[a]

1820	*1830*	*1840*	*1850*	*1860*
71.00%	80.16%	52.17%	66.86%	67.93%

[a] Data compiled from: U.S. Department of Commerce, Bureau of the Census, Manuscript Federal Census, Loudoun County, Virginia, 1820, roll 137; 1830, roll 1193; 1840, roll 564; 1850, Free Schedule, roll 957; 1860, Free Schedule, roll 1359, National Archives, Washington, D.C.

households, however, were not youngsters. They usually were adult kin and boarders who made substantial financial contributions to household budgets. Samuel Murray, for example, had ten people living on his Snickersville property in 1860: his immediate family (his wife Betsy and three children aged sixteen to nine years old); his elderly, widowed father Francis; and another family— Charles and Sally Fields and their two young children. While the occupations of the women are unknown, all three of the adult men in Murray's household, worked and could contribute to the household's support.[65]

Few female-headed households that were child-inclusive, on the other hand, had adults present other than the household head. This meant that not only were these women the principal, and often the only breadwinners, but that they had little domestic help except that of their older children. There were very few men in their homes who could share the burden of their financial, physical, and emotional responsibilities. Male household heads, on the other hand, usually had wives who not only were wage earners, but who also routinely took on the housekeeping and childrearing responsibilities. The few adolescent and adult males in female-headed households usually were their sons, not husbands or lovers. Of the probable nuclear households among Loudoun's free blacks for 1820 (71 percent) and 1860 (67.9 percent), for example, 90.9 percent and 91.2 percent respectively had male heads. (See Tables 12 and 15.) Unlike the female heads of households that Suzanne Lebsock describes in her study of Petersburg, Virginia, those of Loudoun were the poorest and most vulnerable of their group.[66]

Despite the various forms of free black family structure and household composition in Loudoun, however, the majority contained a nuclear core. (See Table 15.) Moreover, most free black children lived in homes where at least one of their parents and an adult of the opposite sex was present. (See Table 14.) In these ways, independent free black households were similar to those of county whites and quite distinct from those of local slaves. Consider, for example, the households of Lucian and George Readman, two brothers who lived beside one another in Hillsborough. George and Lucian were the sons of a mulatto slave woman, Cassie, and a Cherokee man, "Indian Joe," a.k.a. Joe Redman.

Although Joe never legally emancipated Cassie after he bought her from her father/master, their four sons lived as free people of color. By the end of the antebellum era, Lucian and George had established their own thriving nuclear households. They still probably shared ownership with and worked in their father's stone quarry, as both appear in the county's 1860 census as property holders and "laborers." By that year, Lucian and Martha Readman were in their thirties and had six children twelve years old and younger. George and his wife Amanda were in their early forties and had only two of their children living with them, a son James, ten years old, and a daughter Mary, five. Elsy and Fannie Furr, neighbors to the Readmans, also lived in a nuclear household. Elsy, a laborer with $100 in property, and his wife resided alone with their six children, Robert, Henry, Harriett, Mary, Forrest and Permelia. Heuson and Lydia Smith lived similarly with their three children. Still, there were some substantial differences between the nuclear-core households of Loudoun free blacks and whites.[67]

Compared with white households, for example, those of free blacks with either a male or female head were substantially smaller. The average size of free black-headed households remained between four and five persons, while white male- and female-headed households averaged about eight to nine persons. These differences were largely due to the greater incidence of non-family-member inclusion, such as slaves, free black employees, and white servants in white households than in free black homes. But even white nonslaveholders, like Samuel Prill, who had ten household members in 1810; his neighbor Jasper Poulston, who had fifteen; Lilly Dennis, who had nine in 1830; or William Lanier, who had ten people living on his property in 1850, still had larger households than local free people of color. Altogether, Loudoun's white nonslaveholders had between one and three more persons living in their homes than free blacks.[68]

Whites also tended to have more children living with them (and possibly more children in general) than free blacks. While free black women began to bear children at about the same age as white women, that is, between the ages of twenty-one and twenty-two, the spacing between live births appears to have been considerably longer for free women of color (about 34 months) than white women (approximately 24 months). The longer and more fractured childbearing patterns of free women of color, higher child mortality rates, the involuntary removal of poor black children from their homes, and the voluntary apprenticeship of others, altogether meant smaller numbers of children in free black households.[69]

While free women of color married or established longstanding sociosexual relationships in their early twenties, free black men may have been among the oldest cohort of Loudoun men to begin to have legitimate children. The approximate average age of free black men at the time their wives gave birth to their first child was twenty-nine. White males usually married during their mid-twenties.[70]

This difference in the ages of first birth of children for which they were responsible, that is, "legitimate children," may help to explain some of the financial and structural differences in free black women's and men's households. Relatedly, the advanced age at which free black males entered marital commitments may account for some of the inordinate incidence of matrifocal families within their communities. Certainly free men of color may have had children with women before they were in their late twenties. Yet they might have waited until they had sufficient financial resources before they married and initiated nuclear-core families. Many women, like Hannah and Fannie Robinson of Bellmont, who had their children out of wedlock, continued to live in their parents' homes. Others, like the Robinsons' neighbor Catherine Allen, a mulatto washer and cook with a daughter named Ida, established independent households of their own.[71]

While it is clear then that most persons residing in free black independent households lived among some nuclear kin, it is much less certain how the members of this nuclear core interacted with one another. One realizes, for example, that most courting couples experienced the awe and delight of romance and sexual attraction. When Indian Joe first met the slave woman Cassie, for example, he immediately was "charmed" by her beauty and wasted little time before asking her owner for permission to court her. He spent the next several weeks visiting on Sundays and in the evenings trying to get to know Cassie better. It is also clear that many free black marriages were long-lasting, like that of Jesse and Jane Bigsby, who had been together at least 30 years by 1860. John Jackson, a cooper, and his wife Rebecca had been married for almost 20 years when they migrated from Augusta County to Loudoun with five of their children and two grandchildren. The tight-knit, intergenerational family did not move alone—their daughter Emilia and her husband William Francis came along, making a home right next to her parents.[72]

Free Loudoun African Americans, like the Readmans, Bigsbys, and Jacksons, left few written documents descriptive of their everyday lives. The correspondence and other private papers that did survive mostly came from a special group of free people of color—those who migrated elsewhere and wrote back to their friends, relatives, and white patrons. Although these letters offer information that must be approached with some caution, they do allow one to catch glimpses of what life might have been like within the southern homes of the writers. They certainly tell us much about the kinds of domestic lifestyles these persons wanted to have and desperately tried to affect.

One of the most striking aspects of free black family life, as detailed in these documents, is the seriousness with which husbands and fathers approached their roles as family breadwinner, protector, and leader. Although free black women, married and single alike, worked all of their lives, most male family heads believed that their single most important priority was to provide income and a measure of comfort and security for their families.

Writing back to his white patron and friend, Dr. Thomas Clagett of Leesburg, for example, Philip Nelson concerned himself almost completely with his financial affairs in Loudoun and his new home in Philadelphia. Nelson had left several accounts for Clagett and other associates to handle for him. He also charged the good doctor with selling his most valued possessions—his home, a lot of land, horses, hogs, and personal belongings such as beds and china cups. They all were financial resources that were bitterly hard for Philip Nelson to come by, and ones that he sorely needed to liquidate.[73]

As such, Nelson's letters to Clagett betray a desperate concern over his inability to support his family. Writing to Dr. Clagett on several occasions in November and December of 1839, for example, Nelson continuously articulated his worries about his lack of money and the opportunity to earn it. On December 5, 1839, he informed Clagett that "the times are dull and I am Scarce of money," and asked him for his advice as how to remedy his predicament. Four weeks later, Nelson wrote again, this time complaining that he still was "in want of money." He also requested a loan of $50 and letters of recommendation for his children so that they also might find work.[74]

Over the next two years, Philip and his family struggled to survive in Philadelphia, but life remained difficult. Nelson and his son, as well as the other members of his household, took whatever jobs became available. But it seemed almost impossible for them to acquire the kind of lifestyle and financial security that Mr. Nelson wanted. Under these circumstances, his sense of responsibility as a breadwinner and protector was a constant source of frustration. Although Philip expected, and appreciated, the income that his wife and children brought into his household, he profoundly believed that it was his duty to support them.

Philip Nelson's financial problems did not just spring from his underemployment in Philadelphia. He had acquired considerable property in Loudoun before he migrated, and had hoped to be able to draw on these resources until he found some steady work. But these funds seemed indefinitely stalled. Times were tough in Loudoun too, and there seemed few buyers for Nelson's property. Fourteen months after the Nelsons left, Dr. Clagett still had not managed to sell his house or horses. Nor had he found a suitable renter for Nelson's land. As time passed, and Nelson became more desperate for money, he was forced to lower his selling prices. In 1839, for example, he stated quite emphatically that he would not sell his house and the lot it stood on for less than $1500. Two years later, he accepted a purchase price of $1000. By January 1841, Nelson was ready to leave Philadelphia, confessing: "I shall be compelled to leave . . . and seek a place where I can do something as I am making nothing here."[75]

By April 1841, Philip had set his sights on Michigan as a possible place to re-locate. Again he conveyed his plans to Clagett, emphasizing that he had de-cided to migrate once again because he needed to be able to support and protect his family:

> I *wish* and *intend shortly* to leave here for Michigan on a visit to see the Country, as I wish to have a *house* and if I like *that Country* I shall return and take my family *with me* for I am not satisfied here for this *reason[:]* there is nothing to be made here, at least I am not making a living, and, therefore I think it incumbent upon me to *seek*, some place where I can make sufficient to support my family, and not be compelled to *sink*, what little I have, I would rather *increase*, than diminish my *means*[.][76]

Philip Nelson's "means," or rather, his financial assets, were the only tangible guarantees of stability that he could offer his family, and an important measure of his worth as male household head and, in his estimation, as a man.

While Minty Nelson, Philip's wife, obviously played an important role in her family, Mr. Nelson depicted her most essential duties as those of caregiver, housekeeper, and childrearer. He never mentioned to Clagett, for example, whether or not Minty had found employment in Philadelphia, although it is likely that she did perform some kind of labor for pay or took in some board-ers. Their children also worked. Still, it is clear that, even within their house-hold's domestic sphere, Philip Nelson retained ultimate control—choosing his family's housing, furniture, and even their clothing. He also managed his adult children's business and, perhaps, social affairs—actively soliciting jobs for them, paying off their debts, and demanding detailed accounts of their daily ac-tivities, even when they lived away from him. While Nelson obviously was proud of his family, he expected, as their patriarchal head, their respect, defer-ence, and loyalty to his priorities and ideals.[77]

Writing back to their families and friends at Arlington, William and Rosabella Burke also conveyed detailed accounts of their lifestyles which sug-gest much about their ideals of marriage and family life. An analysis of the the-matic content of William's and Rosabella's correspondence points to the distinct gender divisions toward which they at least aspired while living in the Lou-doun area. Mr. and Mrs. Burke and their four children sailed to Liberia aboard the *Banshee* in November 1853. Arriving safely, they immediately concerned themselves with finding a proper location for their homestead. Although Rosa-bella may have participated in the decision not to live in the capital city of Mon-rovia, which she described in a letter as "too gay and fashionable" for her taste, her husband had the final say. After all, it was he who would have to find work in their new home, he who would have to find a way to support his family.[78]

Like Philip Nelson, William Burke wrote almost completely about financial issues, conveying his great concern for his family's economic security. His cor-respondence back to Virginia essentially was a chronicle of the economic development of the colony at Liberia and his potential or real role in it. Writing to William McClain, Secretary of the American Colonization Society, soon after his arrival, Burke eagerly thanked "Almighty God" for his safe trip and the society for "the comfortable support" that he and his family had "received so far." He especially was excited about the possibility of economic gain and emphasized his belief that he would be able to create a better lifestyle for his family in Liberia than in America, explaining: "This certainly is a fine place for anyone that has money or goods to sell, to get along very fast[.] At the same time, I am happy to say that the poor man may also live if he has health and will be industrious."[79]

Although William Burke believed that he eventually would become a teacher, he had settled comfortably into his old trade of shoemaking by the summer of his first year at Clay-Ashland. He also had seen to the construction of his family's home, which he boasted was 22′ by 13′ and "though very rough," was "very comfortable." Having been able to establish himself firmly as his family's breadwinner and provide them with a modicum of material support few free blacks in his Virginia birthplace could hope to obtain, Burke was pleased all around. "[M]y opinion is that it is a glorious country, and that God has blessed its inhabitants," he concluded.[80]

Rosabella Burke also was pleased with their new home, the progress that her husband had made, and her comfortable status in her family. "Remember me kindly to Aunt Elleanor; tell her that I love Africa, and would not exchange it for America," she wrote in February 1859 to a former mistress who still owned some of her relatives. Mrs. Burke's letters do not focus on financial issues, as do those of her husband. As a wife and mother, with some guarantee of financial support, she had other pressing interests. The themes in her correspondence indicate, for example, her notions of appropriate female behavior, notions that were quite similar to those of most white Loudouners and many slave women as well.

Mrs. Burke wrote, for example, almost exclusively about aspects of "women's sphere": her children's health, activities, and educational advances; the state of the colony's moral environment; social activities; and her concern for her extended family, particularly the females. As such, Rosabella Burke defined her "place," or her role within her household and society, as one of the loving, affectionate mother and wife who held up a moral standard for her family and concerned herself with their general well-being, intellectual development, and future prospects. She clearly was pleased to finally claim domesticity as her primary occupation.[81]

Unfortunately, these kinds of marital and familial experiences rarely existed among Loudoun's free people of color, and when they did, they often were temporary. Denied the privilege of a formal education, customarily and then legally, while routinely discriminated against occupationally, southern free blacks had very limited financial opportunities to acquire a measure of security or comfort for themselves or their kin.[82]

Many lived below acceptable levels of southern poverty. Their poverty, in turn, threatened their families structurally and functionally. County officials were much more willing to destroy impoverished free black families by parceling out their children to strangers than to provide them with some temporary financial support or, better still, some chance to bolster their family income permanently. Records of Loudoun's Overseers of the Poor, for example, document that the county's welfare agency rarely aided free blacks, providing relief only to a few who found themselves among the 40 to 60 who routinely lived in the Poor House or worked on the county farm.[83]

Local churches were much more responsive, routinely sponsoring their own charities and relief funds for needy members. A number of free people of color who lived in Loudoun's southern region, for example, attended the Broad Run Baptist Church. Although custom segregated their seating and did not allow them to participate actively in church business, black members still could receive the aid offered the poor and dispossessed. Members collected food and clothing, sought medical attention for the very ill, provided some with temporary housing and others with jobs, and sometimes even gave small sums of money. They helped people like Agga, a "free coloured woman" who joined on October 9, 1834, and to whom, a few months later, the church had committed itself to giving an undisclosed amount of temporary "support." Other religious institutions acted in like fashion.[84]

Relief from interracial church memberships and the county's Overseers of the Poor suggest the limited and somewhat strained connections among the South's interracial community. Some free people of color responded by creating their own regional-wide charities such as the "Mutual Relief and Friendly Society," founded in 1824. The all-male, multifaceted organization drew its membership from the middling and well-to-do blacks of Alexandria, Loudoun, and Fairfax, making it one of the most prominent in the area. The society, and others like it, provided a number of services to its members and their families, including financial and emotional support to the ill, honorific burial services for the dead, and aid to widows and children. Wives of deceased members, for example, could depend on the organization to take care of them and their children until they remarried. Free blacks also united in local Masonic organizations which performed similar philanthropic deeds. Although a Virginia law of 1832 forbade the existence of these kinds of groups within the black community, a report in the local *Alexandria Gazette and Virginia Advertiser* confirmed the "regular meetings" of "negro (so called) Masonic Lodges" in the Loudoun vicinity as late as 1856.[85]

The efforts of local or regional black philanthropic associations were commendable, although their impact was extremely limited. Most were short-lived and necessarily secretive. Moreover, they provided services only for their members and their families. Since the large majority of free people of color were too poor to afford membership dues, most remained unaffected by their philanthropy. When one considers, for example, the financial obligation of members of the Mutual Relief and Friendly Society, the dilemma is apparent. Each member had to pay fifty cents to join and monthly dues of twelve and a half cents. While these demands were not substantial, there were other real and implied expenses—three dollars to withdraw one's membership, hefty donations for funerals, proper clothing for various social events, and fines for being absent from meetings or funerals. Altogether, these financial obligations were unreasonable for those who usually earned less than $100 per year.

Dues and other required monies, however, were not the only bars to the organization's community effectiveness. Some promised benefits were not always reliable. If a member found himself in want, for example, the society did not "give" him money but only allowed him to "borrow," at "bank interest," a maximum of ten dollars. Likewise, if a member became sick, the society had to "decide" whether or not he was unable to "pay" his expenses before they would do so.[86]

What is perhaps most telling, however, is the ways in which the Mutual Relief and Friendly Society responded to the needs of women in their community, a substantial portion of whom were household heads with children. Women could not join the organization outright and, therefore, could derive benefits only indirectly as the wives or daughters of male members. The organization did, however, extend a protective, patriarchal arm to widows, noting in their official rules that "when a member dies his wife must be taken care of by the Society." Yet their guidelines further stipulated that they would support a widow only "as long as she conducts herself with prudence, and no longer." Any woman who ceased to live up to their standards of appropriate female behavior, or remarry, was denied support despite the continual needs of her children.[87]

There also was a certain elitism associated with those groups, no matter their purpose, that were comprised principally of the community's "upper crust." Divisions were derived not just from one's vocational or financial status, but also from one's color and, relatedly, often the kinds of social and financial associations one had with prominent members of the white community. But even if the black Masons or relief societies had extended a helping hand to those outside of their membership, their financial resources were not extensive. They still would have been able to do little to alter the appalling poverty of many within their communities.

Most free blacks responded to adverse economic conditions in a number of other ways which affected their domestic relations and community life. Not a few turned to criminal activities for money. "Negro John residing near

Waterford," for example, was indicted on March 14, 1808, for "keeping a disorderly house." John and many others were part of an "underground" economy that local free blacks fashioned with slaves as well as some whites; an economy that allowed many of Loudoun's poor and dispossessed to find lucrative work. The criminal records from the era are rife with Commonwealth cases against local free people of color accused of "petty larceny" and selling stolen goods, anything from harvested crops and livestock to clothing and kitchen utensils. Sometimes these crimes ended in tragedy for all concerned. Leah Henderson's slave man Tom, for example, was convicted of killing Ruben Hurley, a free black man, near Aldie one Friday night. Apparently Hurley owed Tom some money, presumably for stolen goods, which he refused to pay. A fight ensued, Hurley threatened Tom with a scythe, and Tom retaliated with a stone that killed Hurley. The Loudoun county court convicted him of second-degree murder and he was sold to the lower South.[88]

Everyone seemed aware of this kind of "business." Residents from Loudoun and Fauquier counties even petitioned the state assembly in 1838 to pass legislation to curtail such illegal trading. "It consists in the purchase by persons of bad character from slaves and runners of stolen property, usually free negroes and mulattos, but not infrequently a depraved class of white persons without any visible means of subsistence," the petitioners explained. If caught and found guilty, free blacks faced some kind of penalty, usually a public whipping. Others were imprisoned, thereby absenting themselves from their families and perhaps heightening their vulnerability. Elijah, a Loudoun free male laborer, for example, was found guilty in August 1817 for petty larceny and sentenced to 18 months at hard labor, three of which were to be spent in solitary confinement.[89]

The marital, blood, cultural, and even criminal connections that Loudoun's free people of color had with the slave community bound the two groups tightly to one another. Yet Loudoun's free blacks also formed a community that was in several ways distinct from that of local slaves. Their legal right to marry and their ability to claim ownership of their own person and their children were the basis for substantial marital commitments and nuclear families. Although there was a significant minority of matrifocal families among county free blacks, the majority of their households had male heads. Consequently, most children grew up in male-headed households with their parents. While these familial arrangements certainly were similar to those of most whites in the county, free black households were considerably smaller in size, had fewer economic resources, and fewer children than those of local whites.

Although it is difficult to assess the familial ideals or actual behavior of a group of persons who left behind so few written documents descriptive of their personal lives, it is clear that many within nuclear-core families embraced gender conventions much like those of their ex-masters and white neighbors. It is true that most free black women worked and helped to provide income for their families, but, it also is obvious that many believed that the principal role of the husband and father was to provide material support and, in that fashion, protection for his family. The wages that free black washerwomen, domestics, and day laborers brought to their families were important, but did not seem to diminish, in many male-headed families, the patriarchal status that resident husbands claimed.

Free black female heads of households struggled to survive against the most tremendous of odds. They earned less income, had less financial support from the other household members, and had more dependents than free black males. They also owned less property—real estate, slave, or personal. Still, their numbers continued to increase. Indeed, their growing presence was a powerful symbol of the losses—economic, legislative, and social—that free blacks suffered over the era, a constant reminder of their history as slaves, and their uncertain future as free people.

Conclusion

While we move in the bright, beautiful world, unsuspicious of the
enemies prowling around, just waiting for our lives! what a blow!
—Amanda Edmonds, November 11, 1859

Amanda Edmonds, the flirtatious beauty of Belle Grove, was shaken to the
core that extraordinary fall of 1859. The "bright, beautiful world" that
she had known all of her life was coming to an abrupt end, and she knew it. Inextricably intertwined as southern society was with the institution of slavery,
any real challenge to the one certainly meant a profound change in the other.
The news of John Brown's raid on Harpers Ferry, located across a narrow expanse of the Potomac and just a few hundred feet away from Loudoun's northwestern boundary, had awakened her and others to an inevitable finality. Life
would hardly be the same again.[1]

The story has been told over and over again. On or about July 3 of that year,
John Brown and two of his sons, Oliver and Watson, going by the assumed
name of Smith, came to live in the countryside near Harpers Ferry. Renting a
farm on the Maryland side of the Potomac, Brown, his men, and some of their
female relations spent the next three months finalizing plans, collecting ammu-
nition, and trying to recruit supporters. One of his co-conspirators, John Cook,
supposedly had been in the area for a year on an intelligence assignment,
gathering valuable information about local folk and the arsenal. Another, John
Kagi, had been born in Virginia and still had kin living in the area. So too did
Dangerfield Newby, one of the three black men who initially were recruits.

Newby was a Virginia ex-slave who joined Brown's forces for very personal reasons—his slave wife and seven children still lived in nearby Warrenton and he hoped the raid would give him the opportunity to liberate them. The over-arching agenda of virtually everyone else in the camp was straightforward enough—end slavery in Virginia and throughout the South by military inter-vention, or die as martyrs trying to do so. Either way, they would strike an un-forgettable blow against the institution and the southern way of life which embraced it.[2]

On the night of October 16, 1859, John Brown and 19 men (14 white, 5 black) mounted their attack. They managed to overpower the watchmen at the armory, the arsenal, a rifle factory, and one of the bridges leading into town, seizing control of those locations. They abducted several prominent citizens, along with some of their slaves, and took them as hostages. As day broke, they took others from the town, some forty persons altogether. But by that time, ex-aggerated accounts of Brown's offensive were spreading quickly and volunteer companies were beginning to form a defense. They soon managed to push Brown back away from the town and the bridge into the armory. State and federal troops continued their buildup during the day and throughout the eve-ning. Colonel Robert E. Lee arrived that night, commanding a unit of marines. The next morning Lee sent his staff officer, Lieutenant J. E. B. Stewart, to Brown with a written demand that he surrender. When he refused to do so, Lee's forces stormed the armory's doors.[3]

The fighting lasted only a few minutes. John Brown was wounded and cap-tured. Altogether, twelve of his men were killed, including his two sons; five others were taken prisoner. Five local people also lost their lives. Tried and con-victed of treason, John Brown was hanged in Charlestown, Virginia, on De-cember 2, 1859.[4]

Despite the brevity of the events and the small loss of human life and prop-erty, the raid on Harpers Ferry had a profound and lasting effect on Loudoun, as it did on much of the South. It erased forever the illusion southern optimists might have had that their community could continue to exist as it had for the past century, while confirming the worst fears of cynics that they could not remain a slave society in a nation whose embrace of abolition was tightening quickly. The question of slavery had finally forced the chaos it had threatened for decades. Rebellious local slaves, supposedly emboldened by Brown's actions, were reported acting in irreverent, dangerous ways—drinking and gambling in churches, burning recently harvested wheat stacks, running away in record numbers, and threatening even more. Free blacks and local white "abolition-ists" were suspected of encouraging the rebellion and even of being a part of Brown's plot.[5]

Underlying Amanda Edmonds's response to the "raid" was a vindictive spirit, suggesting how deeply much of her community felt threatened by

Brown's actions. Of those local slaves found guilty of burning harvested wheat and participating in related resistance tactics, her solution was brutal retaliation: "What ought to be done with them?" she queried in her diary. "I would see the fire kindled and those who did it singed and burnt until the last drop of blood was dried within them and every bone smolder to ashes." Referring to a local "abolitionist," she could offer little better. "Three or four men were there after him," she explained of the "hunt" for "Old Smith—a celebrated abolitionist. "I would have rejoiced," she added, if they had caught him and made him pay dearly for his troublemaking. "They had the right spirit and I am glad they have."[6]

Fear and panic were the order of the day as folk questioned the strength of the very glue which held their society together. Could slaveholders trust their lives to their slaves? Could nonslaveholders trust slaveowners to control their property or to fend off the threat of outside attacks? Were those local whites who had openly espoused moderate abolitionist views really so radical and violent as to risk the utter destruction of their society to aid their cause? If so, how could the community defend itself against this kind of "internal" menace? Their society, its integrity, unity, and security, were, as ever, important underlying concerns. If their fears were at all justified, how could they ever function as a communal unit again? If some of the most basic premises of their society, and those who swore to uphold them, were effectively challenged, militarily or morally, from within or without, what would become of their community's power to impose its will? These were questions that re-emerged, in one form or another, not just in the aftermath of Harpers Ferry, but throughout the eighteenth-century and pre-Civil War slave South.

Community values and directives defined southern life in ways that would be difficult for contemporary readers to reconcile given the lack of importance many ascribe to "a" or "any" community today. "Community," its collective will and value system, however, was the linchpin of southern morality and the southerner's sociocultural ideology. It had tremendous worth and a defining presence for everyone, whether free or slave, man or woman, planter or pauper.

The larger southern society was of hierarchical structure, a phenomenon in which race, ethnicity or culture, class, and gender defined one's place in relation to others. These differentiating traits also were the basis for the formation of other smaller, internal "communities"—the Quaker communities of Waterford and Hillsboro, for example; the German community of Lovettsville; the communities shared by the landed gentry and those of their wives; the community of domestic and skilled slaves; free blacks; and others. These smaller communal units existed within the "boundaries" of the larger society, sometimes complementing it, and at other times resisting its influence or prerogatives, even acting oppositionally on occasion. They too had binding customs, designated status to form something of an internal hierarchy, determined who were "outsiders" and "insiders," and controlled vital resources. The southern "community," therefore, operated on several levels, each requiring the allegiance, support, and resources of its members. One's "place" in southern society or any of its communities, and the conditions which prescribed that place, had substantial influence on one's private life, particularly the nature and expression of one's marriage and family. While these institutions were vitally important to everyone, therefore, they differed, structurally and functionally, for southerners of various communities. Most of these differences can be linked both to the cultural differences manifest between persons of African and European descent as well as to the problematic logistics that race, and to a lesser extent class and gender, imposed.

Marriage and family clearly were the cornerstones of Loudoun's white communities, and had been so since the first few families of Quakers, Germans, Scotch-Irish, Welsh, British, and creole whites began to settle there. Many arrived in groups of families, bringing their individual hopes and dreams along with their community ties and values. German and Quaker immigrants, in particular, came with the determination to establish distinct communities of family farms and businesses which would allow them to retain their cultures. Others were less discriminating in their social interactions, but no less determined to pursue the kind and quality of life which placed family and community values at the center of their moral strivings and personal ambitions.

Their principal ideals about family were not unlike those of other white southerners with monogamous marriage and a strong patriarchy as their foundation. Their commonality of beliefs in this regard, in fact, suggested a tight bond between southern whites that often withstood what otherwise could be divisive class, ethnic, or cultural differences. Family values were not as binding as race or "whiteness," but the family values whites shared did come to represent, in part, these very concepts. This was possible because of the clear differences between "white" familial and marital experiences and those of slaves and to a lesser extent free blacks. Family, therefore, may not have drawn the line between white and black life in the South, but it did help to hold it in place.

Virtually everyone in white communities married and stayed married. Of course the availability of spouses, particularly husbands, varied over time in response to sweeping societal forces such as war, epidemic, economic depression, and especially emigration. But the consequences for someone not marrying, despite the reasons, remained constant. Both confirmed bachelors and spinsters lost the possibility of legitimate heirs of direct descent and lifelong intimate companionship. But, and not surprisingly, single men fared better than single women. Unmarried men still earned income, for example, and could exercise public power. As such, they still had access to patriarchal status in their kin groups. Moreover, the double sexual standard of the day meant that bachelors had much more access to intimate relationships than unmarried women.

Prolonged bachelorhood could, at times, even inspire some envy by married men since it, ostensibly, held the elusive promise of male "freedom." Still it was a man's duty to marry, procreate, and head his family. These duties, in many ways, defined manhood as did a loving wife and comfortable home. In the end, they usually were more alluring than the "spoils" of lifelong bachelorhood.

The consequences of permanent spinsterhood, on the other hand, were much more practically problematic than the "shame" of never fulfilling their potential as wives and mothers. Since women rarely had the means to support themselves or a household without the financial aid of a man, single white women usually were something of a "burden" on their families, despite the domestic labor they routinely performed for them. And there was no possibility of an acceptable romantic encounter outside the confines of appropriate courtship ritual. Anything else meant a permanent scandal that could erase the last vestiges of her self-esteem and respectability, to say nothing of her family's "kind" tolerance. But life in the South hardly was so simple as to guarantee lifelong happiness merely from marrying, or even from marrying the "right" person. Both spouses had difficult roles to maintain and often grappled with their seeming inability to do so, or the limited rewards that resulted. Since divorce was difficult, and even sometimes impossible to obtain, one could not just give up on a relationship even after years of trying, and start over with someone else. Only when a relationship clearly defied the sanctity of the institution or threatened to undermine other important social mores was a community likely to approve of a permanent end to a marriage.

Marriage and the exercise of duty, honor, and affection within that marriage was every white southerner's responsibility. The greatest duty of every man and woman within their marriage, however, was to his or her children, that is, to prepare them to grow up to be responsible adults who one day would marry, begin their own families, and continue the cultural and kin traditions they inherited. Parents painstakingly invested much of their time and energy instilling ideals of appropriate adult behavior. Faced with what they believed was mounting hostility from "outside" in the form of northern abolitionism, and black cultural corruption from "within," they hoped that strict adherence to and acceptance of their prescribed rules of behavior would convince the world of the South's moral superiority.

Free blacks and slaves also were determined to maintain the integrity of their families and communities despite often overwhelming pressures to the otherwise. The combination of their cultural heritage and the pressures their status imposed helped to create and sustain substantial differences between southern black and white domesticity.

The slave family was not a static, imitative institution that necessarily favored one form of family organization over another. Rather, it was a diverse phenomenon, sometimes assuming several forms even among the slaves of one community. But this diversity cannot in itself be equated with a weak or flawed institution. The diversity of slave marriage and family norms, as a measure of the slave family's enormous adaptive potential, often was instrumental in allowing the slave and the slave family's survival.

The black family under slavery differed profoundly from that of European American southerners structurally and in the ways in which family members functioned as contributors, administrators, and recipients of family resources. Virginia slave families, after all, essentially were not nuclear and did not derive from long-term monogamous marriages. Their most discernible ideal for kinship organization was a malleable extended family that, potentially, provided its members with nurture, education, socialization, material support, and recreation in the face of the social chaos that the slaveholders' power imposed. Matrifocality, polygamy, single parents, abroad spouses, one-, two-, and three-generational households, all-male domestic residences of both blood, marriage, and fictive kin, single- and mixed-gender sibling dwellings—these, along with monogamous marriages and co-residential nuclear families, all comprised the slave's familial experiences. Beneath this overwhelming record of diversity, the extended slave family remained the most consistent norm and the most clearly identifiable ideal.

Even when the physical basis for a nuclear family among slaves—the presence of a husband, wife, and their children—existed, as it did for a significant minority, this type of family did not function as it did for blacks in precolonial Africa or whites in the colonial and antebellum South. Gender-differentiated roles that were so prevalent in white families and also lauded in many free black, nuclear-core families, for example, often did not hold forth in slave kinship groups.

Gender, to be sure, was an important differentiating trait in the lives of slaves. Yet slave husbands never provided the sole or most significant means of financial support for their wives and children. Moreover, these husbands had no legal claim to their families and, accordingly, could not legitimately demand their economic resources or offer them protection from abuse or exploitation. Likewise the primary role of the slave mother, if compared with "mainstream" American gender convention, also was deeply compromised—she never was able to give the needs of her husband and children great priority. Even though most slave children were part of matrifocal families, the slave woman's most important daily activities encompassed the labor that she performed for her owner, not her family. This responsibility claimed so much of her time and energy that childbearing was limited, while childrearing necessarily was a task she shared with a number of females, within and outside of her blood- and marriage-related family.

Monogamy also was expressed differently. Slave couples committed in monogamous marriages may have been devoted to one another and able to sustain mutual feelings of love and respect, but many did not have the opportunity to express such sentiment for more than a few years while enslaved. Across time and space, the frequent and indiscriminate separation of slave spouses, temporarily and permanently, denied them the opportunity to live together, to share the responsibilities of their households and children, and to provide each other with sociosexual outlets.

Slave importation records hardly allow one to determine the exact ethnic or cultural heritage of the slaves who came to reside in Loudoun or its environs, but ethnographic studies of western and central African groups do suggest the plausibility that there was some connection between the domestic arrangements and institutions of marriage and family among precolonial western and central Africans and those of county blacks. Extended kinship, matrifocality, and polygamy, for example, may have arrived from Africa and remained as culturally sanctioned alternatives for slaves across the generations.

Thus, while the issue of master "force" versus slave "choice," and all the sociopolitical and cultural variables which affected it, obscures an unimpeachable decision as to the slaves' marriage and familial ideals, three conclusions have been substantiated. First, neither monogamous marriages nor nuclear families dominated slave family forms. Matrifocal families, abroad spouses, and extended families were much more significant. Second, slave marriages and families exhibited a diversity of form and relationship that marked them substantially different from those of European Americans. Third, the slaves' ideals of marriage and family were not imitative or necessarily sanctioned by European Americans.

Race, culture, class, gender, and legal status shaped the similarities and differences between the domesticity of free blacks and that of slaves and whites. While the law protected free black marriage and family in ways that it did not do for slaves, their families still were subject to injustices, pressures, and assaults that most white families did not experience. Because most free black families were working-class or poorer, for example, they often had material and medical support that was no better than that of slaves. The majority of free black households were smaller in size than those of county whites. The difference in household size also was linked to class difference—it was due not only to the greater number of children that white women had, but also because white households were much more likely to include slaves, servants, and employees. Free people of color, on the other hand, routinely "lost" family members when they went to live with their white employers. Relatedly, those free black children and adolescents forced into indentureship because of their families' poverty often suffered the same kind of long-term separation from loved ones as many slaves since their "masters" also had the right to sell their contracts or rent them out at will.[7]

Free black cultural antecedents and poverty also bolstered the importance of matrifocality and extended kin networks within their communities. As in the slave community, extended kin networks, intergenerational, and multi-surnamed member households were important survival mechanisms because they provided much needed supplemental support. They were particularly vital to the growing number of free black women household heads, since their families and households were much poorer than those of their male peers. As in other families, therefore, gender was a powerful factor which shaped the day-to-day lives of free women of color. Free black female household heads in Loudoun were the poorest and least powerful of their clan.

Despite the growing number of matrifocal families among free blacks, however, most free people of color, like whites, had male family and household heads. Likewise, most free black children in independent, free black households lived with both their parents. While husbands and wives, as well as all other able-bodied household members, helped to support free black families and households financially, resident men usually controlled these collective funds. Moreover, the legal right to marry and "own" one's children meant that free African American men could claim their families' labor and resources. Free black husbands, therefore, could and did take on some of the patriarchal rights and responsibilities that were customary among white southerners. Unlike slaves, many free people of color were part of patriarchally governed, nuclear-core families.

Financial difficulties and white hostility however, still could have a paralyzing effect on free black patriarchy, indiscriminately stripping men of power within their communities and sometimes within their homes. The evidence descriptive of Loudoun's free black life documents widespread financial instability and economic decline as a direct result of growing restrictions on their occupations, land ownership, and wage levels. While some families managed to survive, most just barely did. Many felt forced to leave and, in so doing, contributed even more to the drain on their communities' economic resources. It was not, after all, just the poor and unskilled who left; few of them could afford to relocate even if they wanted to do so. Instead it was members of the propertied class who took the opportunity to emigrate in increasing numbers.

Free black families and communities in Loudoun, as throughout the state and the region, therefore, presented a curious amalgam of lifestyles, living conditions, and cultural traits. Intricately bound to both whites and slaves, they struggled to maintain a separate identity that neither denied their past nor jeopardized their future. It was an uphill battle, and all along the way they lost ground, legally, economically, and socially. Like their neighbors, they clung to their families and communities as they negotiated their lives in black and white.

Appendix A

Location of Slaves and Their Family Members Belonging to George Washington, 1799[a]

A. Mansion House (Craftspeople and Domestic Servants)

1. Nat (blacksmith)

   Family at Dogue Run Farm
   Lucy (wife, 50), Ned (son, 14), Teney (daughter, 10)

2. George (blacksmith)

   Family at River Farm
   Lydia (wife, 50), Lydia (daughter, 11)

3. Isaac (carpenter)
   Kitty (milk maid, wife)
   Barbara (daughter, 10)
   Lenna (daughter, 6)

4. James (carpenter, 40)

   Family at Muddy Hole Farm
   Darcus (wife, 36), Moses (son, 19)
   Townshend (son, 14), Alce (daughter, 8),
   Nancy (daughter, 2)

   Nathan (brother-in-law, cook, Mansion)

   Peg (sister-in-law?, 34), Lucy (niece, 11), Diana (niece, 8), Alexander (nephew, 3), Darcus (niece, 1)

5. Sambo (carpenter)

   Family at River Farm
   Agnes (wife, 36), Henky (son, 17), Cecelia (daughter, 14)

6. Davy (carpenter)

   Family at Union Farm
   Edy (wife, 26), Sarah (daughter, 6), Nancy (daughter, 1)

[a] This chart identifies the general location of George Washington's slaves on his five farms probably in the year 1799. Also includes his dower slaves. Based on Washington's own compilation, it enumerates each person, as he does, followed by identifiable family members and their locations. Each adult in the families is numbered separately with his or her kin (children and adults) listed afterwards. Compiled from "List of Negroes Belonging to George Washington in His Own Right and By Marriage, June 1799," Mount Vernon Library, Fairfax, Va.

7. Joe (carpenter)
   Dolshy (spinner, wife)
   Sucky (daughter, 5)
   Dennis (son, 2 months)

8. Tom (cooper)

Family at Muddy Hole Farm
Nanny (wife, old)

9. Moses (cooper)

No wife

10. Jacob (cooper)

No wife

11. George (gardener)

Family at Dogue Run Farm
Sall Twine (wife, 38), Barbary
(daughter, 11), Abbay (daughter, 10),
Hannah (daughter, 4), George (son, 1)

12. Harry (gardener)

No wife

13. Boatswain (ditcher)   ·
    Matilda/Myrtilla (spinner)

Family at Dogue Run
Lawrence (son, 14)

14. Dundee (ditcher)

Wife at Mr. Tobias Lear's

15. Charles (ditcher)

Family at Union Farm
Fanny (wife, 36), Jamie (son, 11),
Daphne (daughter, 5), Charles (son, 1)

16. Ben[a] (ditcher)

Family at River Farm
Penny (20)

17. Ben (miller)
    Dinah (wife)
    Nancy (daughter)

18. Forrester (miller)

No wife

19. Nathan (cook, 31)

Family at Muddy Hole Farm
Peg (wife, 34), Lucy (daughter, 11),
Diana (daughter, 8), Alexander (son, 3),
Darcus (daughter, 1)

   James (brother-in-law,
   carpenter, Mansion)

Darcus (sister-in-law?, 36), Moses
(nephew, 19), Townshend (nephew, 14),
Alce (niece, 8), Nancy (niece, 2)

20. W. Muculus (bricklayer)

Wife at Captain Thomas Marshall's

21. Juba (carter)

No wife

22. Frank (houseservant)
    Lucy (wife, cook)
    Phil (son)
    Patty (son)

[a] The slave Ben is listed both as a resident of the Mansion and River Farm. His wife Penny is listed only as a resident of River Farm. This double listing may suggest he divided his time between both places and, therefore, would have been able to reside with his wife at least half of the year.

Burwell (son)

Mike (also listed separately at Mansion House as an adult worker, see no. 53 below)

23. Will (shoemaker, lame)   No wife

24. Frank (80, passed labor)   No wife

25. Gunner (90, passed labor)   *Family at River Farm*
    Judy (wife, 55)

26. Sam (cook, 40)   *Family at Muddy Hole Farm*
    Alce (wife, 38), Kate (daughter, 18), George (son, 8), Adam (son, 7), Cecelia (daughter, 2)

27. Tom Davis (bricklayer)   *Wife at Mr. Tobias Lear's*

28. Simms (carpenter)   *Wife at French's*

29. Cyrus (postillion)   *Family at River Farm*
    Lucy (wife, 18)

30. Wilson (postillion)   No wife

31. Godfrey (carter)
    Mima (wife)
    John (son)
    Randolph (son)

32. James (waggoneer)
    Alla (wife)

33. Hanson (ditcher)   No wife

34. Peter (ditcher)   No wife

35. Nat (ditcher)   No wife

36. Daniel (ditcher)   No wife

37. Timothy (ditcher)   No wife

38. Slammin Joe (ditcher)   *Family at Dogue Run Farm*
    Sylla/Priscilla (wife, 36), Sophia (daughter, 14), Savary (daughter, 13), Penny (daughter, 11), Israel (son, 10), Isrias (son, 3), Christopher (son, 1)

39. Chriss (house servant)   *Wife at Major West's*

40. Marcus (house servant)   No wife

41. Molly   No husband or children

42. Charlotte (seamstress)
    Elvey (daughter)
    Jenny (daughter)
    Eliza (daughter)   No husband

43. Sall (house maid)   No husband or children

44. Caroline (house maid)
    Rachel (daughter, 12)
    Jemima (daughter, 9)
    Leanthe (daughter, 8)
    Polly (daughter, 6)
    Peter B (son, 4)

        Peter Hardman (husband)
        Location uncertain

45. Alce (spinner)
    Emery (son)
    Tom (son)
    Charles (son)
    Henriette (daughter)

        Charles (husband, *Freeman*)
        Location uncertain

46. Betty Davis (Spinner)
    Nancy (daughter, 9)
    Oney (daughter, 6)
    Lucinda (daughter, 2)

        Mrs. Washington's Dick (husband)
        Location uncertain[b]

47. Ana
    Daniel (son, 6)
    Anna (daughter, 4)
    Sandy (daughter, 1 1/2)

        Husband living at Georgetown

48. Judy (21)
        No husband or children

49. Delphy
        No husband or children

50. Peter (lame knitter)
        No wife

51. Will
        Family at Dogue Run Farm
        Agnes (wife, 25), Guy (son, 2)

52. Joe (postillion)
        Family at River Farm
        Sall (wife, 30), Henry (son, 11), Ralph
        (son, 9), Elijah (son, 7), Dennis (son, 5),
        Guthridge (son, 3), Charity (daughter,
        2), Polly (daughter, 1), Charles (son, 1)

53. Mike
    (Family of origin, see no. 22 above)
    Frank (houseservant, father)
    Lucy (wife, cook, mother)
    Phil (brother)
    Patty (brother)
    Burwell (brother)

        No wife

54. Lucy (knitter)
        Husband at Daniel McCarty's

55. Grace
        Husband at Mr. Tobias Lear's
        Juba (husband)

56. Letty
        No husband or children

57. Nancy
        No husband or children

[b] Not listed as among dower slaves.

58. Viner   No husband or children

59. Eve (17, dwarf)   No husband or children
    Delia (sister, 14)

60. Delia (14)   No husband or children
    Eve (sister, 17)

61. Doll (passed labor)   No husband or children

62. Jenny (passed labor)   No husband or children

B. Dogue Run Farm

1. Ben (57)
    Peg (wife, 30)
    Billy (son, 6)
    Fendall (son, 2)
    Peg (daughter, 8 mos.)

2. Long Jack (60)
    Molly (wife, cook, 45)

3. Dick (46)
    Charity (wife, 42)
    Fomison (daughter, 11)
    Dick (son, 3)

4. Carter Jack (40)
    Grace (wife, 35)
    Roger (son, 10)
    Molly (daughter, 6)
    Jenny (daughter, 3)

5. Simon (20)   No wife

6. Lawrence   *Family at Mansion House*
                       Boatswain (father, ditcher),
                       Matilda/Myrtilla (mother, spinner)

7. Judy (50, blind)   *Family at Muddy Hole Farm*
                       Gabriel (husband, 30)

8. Priscilla (36)   *Husband at Mansion House*
    Sophia (daughter, 14)   Slammin Joe (husband, ditcher)
    Savary (daughter, 13)
    Penny (daughter, 11)
    Israel (son, 10)
    Isrias (son, 3)
    Christopher (son, 1)

9. Linney (27)   No husband
    Bartley (son, 6)
    Matilda (daughter, 1)

10. Agnes (25)   *Husband at Mansion House*

Guy (son, 2)   Will (husband)

11. Sarah (20)   No husband
    Lucy (daughter, 2)

12. Betty (16)   No husband or children

13. Hannah (60, passed labor, partly an idiot)   No husband or children

14. Lucy (50)   *Husband at Mansion House*
    Ned (son, 14)   Natt (husband, blacksmith)
    Teney (daughter, 10)

15. Sall Twine (38)   *Husband at Mansion House*
    Barbary (daughter, 11)   George (husband, gardener)
    Abbay (daughter, 10)
    Hannah (daughter, 4)
    George (son, 1)

16. Kate (18)   *Husband a Negro of Moreton's*

17. Sue (70, passed labor)   No husband or children

18. Sophia (14)   *Father at Mansion House*
    Priscilla (mother , 36)   Slammin' Joe (father, ditcher)
    Savary (sister, 13)
    Penny (sister, 11)
    Israel (brother, 10)
    Isrias (brother, 3)
    Christopher (brother, 1)

19. Savary (13)   *Father at Mansion House*
    Priscilla (mother , 36)   Slammin' Joe (father, ditcher)
    Sophia (sister, 14)
    Penny (sister, 11)
    Israel (brother, 10)
    Isrias (brother, 3)
    Christopher (brother, 1)

20. Ned (14)   *Father at Mansion House*
    Lucy (mother, 50)   Natt (father, blacksmith)
    Teney (sister, 10)

C. River Farm

1. Robin (80, nearly passed labor)   No wife listed

2. Nald (55)
   Doll (58)
   Doll (daughter, 16)
   Jack (son, 12)
   Peter (son, 9)

3. Ned (56)
   Hannah (wife, old, cook)

4. Ben (22, Carter)
   Penny (wife, 20)

5. Peg (56)
   Old Ben (husband, "nearly done")

6. Judy (55)   *Husband at Mansion House*
                                     Gunner (husband, 90, passed labor)

7. Cloe (55)   No husband or children

8. Suckey (50)   No husband
   Daniel (son, 15)

9. Suckey Bay (46)   *Husband belongs to Adams*
   Nancy (daughter, 11)
   Nancy (daughter, 4)[b]

10. Sall (30)   *Husband at Mansion House*
    Henry (son, 11)   Joe (husband, postillion)
    Ralph (son, 9)
    Dennis (son, 5)
    Guthridge (son, 3)
    Charity (daughter, 2)
    Polly (daughter, 1)
    Charles (son, 1)

11. Rose (28)   No husband
    Harper (son, 6)
    Simon (son, 4)
    Tom (son, 2)
    Joe (son, 1)

12. Lucy (18)   *Husband at Mansion House*
                                     Cyrus (husband, postillion)

13. Hannah (12)   No husband or children
    Hannah (mother, deceased)

14. Ruth (70, passed labor)
    Breechy (husband, 60, "not better than nearly done")

15. Johnny (39)
    Esther (wife, 40)

16. Richmond (20)   No wife

17. Ned (20)   No wife listed

18. Henky (17)   *Family at Mansion House*
    Agnes (mother, 36)   Sambo (father, carpenter)
    Cecelia (sister, 14)

19. Jack (22)   No wife listed

[b] Both daughters to Suckey Bay specified as named Nancy.

20. Lydia
   Lydia (daughter, 11)

Husband at Mansion House
George (husband, blacksmith)

21. Agnes (36)
   Henky (son, 17)

Husband at Mansion House
Sambo (husband, carpenter)

22. Lydia (11)
   Lydia (mother, 50)

Family at Mansion House
George (father, blacksmith)

23. Cecelia (14)
   Agnes (mother, 36)
   Henky (brother, 17)

Family at Mansion House
Sambo (father, carpenter)

24. Alce (26)
   Suckey (daughter, 4)
   Jude (son, 1)

Husband is Mr. Tobias Lear's John

25. Fanny (30)

Husband at Alexander's

26. Betty (20)
   Milley (daughter, 1)

Husband is Mr. Tobias Lear's Reuben

27. Doll (16)
   Nald (father, 55)
   Doll (mother, 58)
   Jack (brother, 12)
   Peter (brother, 9)

28. Jack (12)
   Nald (father, 55)
   Doll (mother, 58)
   Doll (sister, 16)
   Peter (brother, 9)

D. Muddy Hole Farm

1. Gabriel (30)

Family at Dogue Run Farm
Judy (wife, 50, blind)

2. Uriah (24)

No wife listed

3. Moses (19)
   Darcus (mother, 36)
   Alce (sister, 8)
   Nancy (sister, 2)
   Townshend (brother, 14)

Family at Mansion House
James (father, carpenter)

Peg (aunt?, 34)
Lucy (cousin, 11)
Diana (cousin, 8)
Alexander (cousin, 3)
Darcus (cousin, 1)

Nathan (uncle, cook, Mansion)

4. Townshend (14)
   Darcus (mother, 36)

Family at Mansion House
James (father, carpenter)

Alce (sister, 8)
Nancy (sister, 2)
Moses (brother, 19)

Peg (aunt?, 34)   Nathan (uncle, cook, Mansion)
Lucy (cousin, 11)
Diana (cousin, 8)
Alexander (cousin, 3)
Darcus (cousin, 1)

5. Darcus (36)   *Husband at Mansion House*
   Moses (son, 19)   James (husband, carpenter)
   Townshend (son, 14)
   Alce (daughter, 8)
   Nancy (daughter, 2)

Peg (sister?, 34)   Nathan (brother-in-law, cook,
Lucy (daughter, 11)   Mansion)
Diana (daughter, 8)
Alexander (son, 3)
Darcus (daughter, 1)

6. Kate (old)
   Will (husband, mintr., 60)
   Kate (daughter, Long, 18)

7. Nanny (old)   *Husband at Mansion House*
                                 Tom (husband, cooper)

8. Sacky (40)   No husband or children

9. Peg (34)   *Husband at Mansion House*
   Lucy (daughter, 11)   Nathan (husband, cook)
   Diana (daughter, 8)
   Alexander (son, 3)
   Darcus (daughter, 1)

Darcus (sister?)   James (brother-in-law, carpenter,
Townshend (nephew, 14)   Mansion)
Alce (niece, 8)
Nancy (niece, 2)

10. Alce (38)   *Husband at Mansion House*
    Kate (daughter,18)   Sam (husband, cook)
    George (son, 8)
    Adam (son, 7)
    Cecelia (daughter, 2)

11. Kate   *Family at Mansion House*
    Alce (mother, 38)   Sam (father, cook)
    George (brother, 8)
    Adam (brother, 7)
    Cecelia (daughter, 2)

12. Amie (30)   No husband
    Rainey (daughter, 8)
    Urinah (daughter, 2)

13. Nancy (28)   *Husband Abram at French's*
    Oliver (son, 11)
    Siss (daughter, 8)
    Martin (son, 1)

14. Molly (26)   No husband
    Sylvia (daughter, 10)
    James (son, 7)

15. Virgin (24)   *Husband Gabe [at] Mr. Tobias Lear's*

16. Letty   No husband
    Billy (son, 2)
    Henry (son, 1)

17. Isbel   No husband or children
    Sarah (mother, deceased)

18. Davy (overseer, 56)
    Molly (wife, 76)

19. Patience (14)   *Family at Union Farm*
                                        Doll (mother, 52, passed labor, "lame or
                                        pretends to be so")

20. Mary (11)   *Family at Union Farm*
                                        Betty (mother, 62, cooks), John
                                        (brother, 16), Gideon (brother, 15)

E. Union Farm

1. London (64)   No wife

2. Joe (24)   No wife listed

3. Edy (26)   *Husband at Mansion House*
   Sarah (daughter, 6)   Davy (husband, carpenter)
   Nancy (daughter, 1)

4. Flora (64, passed labor)   No husband

5. Sam Kitt (78)   *Wife at Daniel Stoses*

6. Caesar (50)   No wife

7. Paul (36)   No wife

8. John (16)   *Family at Muddy Hole*
   Betty (mother, 62, cooks)   Mary (sister, 11)
   Gideon (brother, 15)

9. Betty (62, cooks)   No husband; *Family at Muddy Hole*
   John (son, 16)   Mary (daughter, 11)

Gideon (son, 15)

10. Gideon (15)   *Family at Muddy Hole*
    Betty (mother, 62, cooks)   Mary (sister, 11)
    John (brother, 16)

11. Lucy (50)   *Husband at Cap. [sic] Marshalls*

12. Fanny (36)   *Husband at Mansion House*
    Jamie (son, 11)   Charles (husband, ditcher)
    Daphne (daughter, 5)
    Charles (son, 1)

13. Jamie   *Family at Mansion House*
    Fanny (mother, 36)   Charles (father, ditcher)
    Daphne (sister, 5)
    Charles (brother, 1)

14. Jenny (34)   *Husband is Mrs. Lund Washington's*
    Felicia (daughter, 7)   *George*
    Jonathan (son, 3)
    Hellam (son, 1)

15. Rachell (34)   No husband
    Ephraim (son, 11)
    Davy (son, 8)
    Beck (daughter, 4)
    Guss (son, 3)
    Eneas (son, 1)

16. Ephraim (11)
    Rachell (mother, 34)
    Davy (brother, 8)
    Beck (sister, 4)
    Guss (brother, 3)
    Eneas (brother, 1)

17. Milly (22)   No husband
    Diana (daughter, 1)

18. Lucretia (20)   No husband

19. Daphne (70, passed labor)   No husband

20. Doll (52, passed labor, "lame or   No husband; *Family at Muddy Hole*
    pretends to be so")   Patience (daughter, 14), Suckey
    Elizabeth (daughter, 9)   (daughter, 11) at Mrs. L. W[ashington]'s,
        Elias (son, 2 mos.) at Mrs. L.
        W[ashington]'s

21. Jesse (6)
    Son to Patt (deceased)

Appendix B

Slave Families, Unattached Adults, Adolescents, and Children Belonging to
Colonel Claiborne Gooch of Richmond, Virginia[a]

A. Gooch Slave Community, 1830 (Family Ties Generally Not Available)

Females
Old Eve (about 62)
Jane (59)
Nelly (30)
Sarah (30)
Aggy (26)
Aggy's two [children]
Juliet (21)
Lydia (19)
Lydia's one [child]
Anna (14)
Patty (?)
[?]bira (12)
Lavinia (12)
Milly (11)
Harriet (8)
Apphia (daughter to Sarah, 7)
Patsy (6)
Betsy (5)
Georgianna (daughter to Sarah, 4)
Sophia (daughter to Nelly, 1)

Males
Prince (49)
William (30)
Turner (25)
Tom (21)
Nelson (18)
Dick (17)
Patrick(14)
William (11)
Lewis (?)
Dixon (?)
Davy (1)
Solomon (3)
Hunter (3)
Henry (1)

B. Gooch Slave Community, 1839 (Family Groups Indicated)

John (32) and Polly (30)
Vinny (daughter, 7)
Caroline (daughter, 6)

Patrick (23) and Anna (22)
George (son, few days old)

[a] Compiled from Slave lists of Col. Claiborne Gooch, 1830, 1839, 1852, Gooch Family Papers, Virginia Historical Society.

Sarah (about 39)
Apphia (daughter, 15)
Georgiana (daughter, 13)
Mary (daughter, 8)
Matilda (daughter, 3)

Lydia (28)
Hardenia (daughter, 6)
Mahala (daughter, 1)

Nelly (38)
Sophia (daughter, 9)
Margaret (daughter, 6)
Ellen (daughter, 1)

Children and Adolescents Without Designated Family Ties, 1839
Emanuel (12)
Solomon (12)

Horace (10)
Peter (?)

Adults Without Designated Family Ties, 1839
Turner (about 32)
Nelson (27)

Anthony (36)
Tom (30)

C. Gooch Slave Community, 1852 (Family Groups Indicated)

Patrick (37) and Anna (35)
Mary Jane (12)
Tom Princer (10)
Charles (6)
Beverly (4)
Adeline (2)
Edward (4 mos.)

Nelson (43) and Judy (33)
Jim (son, 2)

Mary (44)
Sarah (20)
Solomon (18)
Joe (16)
Fanny Ellen (16)
Mary Ann (14)
Linsy (12)
Elisabeth (9)
Jane (6)

Matilda (36)
Henry (15)
Laura (12)

Aaron (62) and Sukey (56)
Julia (15)
Richard (12)
Lavinia
Lavinia's child (19 or 20 mos.)

Turner (45)
Evelyn (7)

Sarah (50)
George (27)
Big Solomon (23)

Milly (33)
William (12)

Sophy (20)
Molly (10)

Robert (10)
Alice (7)

NOTES

PREFACE

1. Robert Conrad to Powell Conrad, 28 May 1851, Conrad Family Papers (hereafter referred to as ConFP), Virginia Historical Society, Richmond (hereafter referred to as VHS).

2. Biographical information on Burr Powell and his family located in Powell Family Genealogical Notes, n.p., Gray Family Papers; miscellaneous correspondence in the Powell, Harrison and Conrad Family Papers, VHS; "A Brief History of the First Harrisons of Virginia: Descendants of Cuthbert Harrison, Esquire of Ancaster, England From A.D. 1600 to A.D. 1915," pamphlet, n.p., n.d., Harrison Family Papers (hereafter referred to as HarFP), VHS; "Notes on Brooke-Powell Family," *Virginia Magazine of History and Biography* 15, no. 2 (June 1908): 201–3.

3. Marie McGraw-Tyler, ed., "'The Prize I Mean is the Prize of Liberty': A Loudoun County Family in Liberia," *Virginia Magazine of History and Biography* 97, no. 3 (July 1989): 355–74.

4. Miscellaneous Accounts, Receipts and Correspondence of George and Susannah Shover, 1816–39, Shover Family Papers, Virginia State Library, Richmond.

5. Donald Sweig, "Northern Virginia Slavery: A Statistical and Demographic Investigation" (Ph.D. dissertation, College of William and Mary, 1982), 238–39; 240nn7–8; *Genius of Universal Emancipation*, 29 March 1829.

6. Most non-Loudouners included in the study, many of whom had Loudoun familial or financial ties, resided in those counties which bordered Loudoun and collectively comprise the northern piedmont region of Virginia—Fairfax and Prince William to the southeast, Fauquier and Culpeper to the south, and Clarke and Frederick to the west and southwest respectively.

7. Harrison Williams, *Legends of Loudoun: An Account of the History and Homes of a Border County of Virginia's Northern Neck* (Richmond: Garrett and Massie, 1938), 178–81.

8. Charles Poland, Jr., *From Frontier to Suburbia* (Macelines, Mo.: Walsworth Publishing, 1976), 163–67, 178–79; Elizabeth Powell Conrad to Holmes Conrad, 7 Nov. 1859, ConFP, VHS.

9. Ann Patton Malone, *Sweet Chariot: Slave Family and Household Structure in Nineteenth Century Louisiana* (Chapel Hill: Univ. of North Carolina Press, 1992); Her-

bert Gutman, *The Black Family in Slavery and Freedom, 1750–1925* (New York: Pantheon, 1976); John Blassingame, *The Slave Community: Plantation Life in the Old South*, rev. ed. (New York: Oxford Univ. Press, 1980); Deborah Gray White, *Ar'n't I a Woman?: Female Slaves in the Plantation South* (New York: W.W. Norton, 1985); Suzanne Lebsock, *The Free Women of Petersburg: Status and Culture in a Southern Town, 1784–1860* (New York: W. W. Norton, 1984); Michael Johnson and James Roark, *Black Masters: A Free Family of Color in the Old South* (New York: W. W. Norton, 1984); Catherine Clinton, *The Plantation Mistress: Woman's World in the Old South* (New York: Pantheon,1982); Anne Firor Scott, *The Southern Lady: From Pedestal to Politics, 1830–1930* (Chicago: Univ. of Chicago Press, 1970); Elizabeth Fox-Genovese, *Within the Plantation Household: Black and White Women of the Old South* (Chapel Hill: Univ. of North Carolina Press); Daniel Blake Smith, *Inside the Great House: Planter Life in Eighteenth-Century Chesapeake Society* (Ithaca, N.Y.: Cornell Univ. Press, 1980); Jane Turner Censer, *North Carolina Planters and Their Children, 1800–1860* (Baton Rouge: Louisiana State Univ. Press, 1984); Bertram Wyatt-Brown, *Southern Honor: Ethics and Behavior in the Old South* (New York: Oxford Univ. Press, 1982); Allan Kulikoff, *Tobacco and Slaves: The Development of Southern Cultures in the Chesapeake, 1680–1800* (Chapel Hill: Univ. of North Carolina Press, 1986); Orville Vernon Burton, *In My Father's House Are Many Mansions: Family and Community in Edgefield, South Carolina* (Chapel Hill: Univ. of North Carolina Press, 1985).

PART I. INTRODUCTION

1. Loudoun Legislative Petitions, 31 Jan. 1848 (hereafter referred to as LouLP), Virginia State Library, Richmond (hereafter referred to as VSL).

2. Virginia outlawed dueling in 1810. Harrison Williams, *Legends of Loudoun: An Account of the History and Homes of a Border County of Virginia's Northern Neck* (Richmond, Va.: Garrett and Massie, 1938), 190.

3. LouLP, 31 Jan. 1848, VSL.

4. Ibid. Regarding gender convention and marriage in the antebellum South, see: Elizabeth Fox-Genovese, *Within the Plantation Household: Black and White Women of the Old South* (Chapel Hill: Univ. of North Carolina Press, 1988), 192–241; Anne Scott, *The Southern Lady from Pedestal to Politics, 1830–1930* (Chicago: Univ. of Chicago Press, 1970), passim; Anne Scott, "Women's Perspective on the Patriarchy," *Journal of American History* 61, no. 2 (June 1974): 52–64; Suzanne Lebsock, *The Free Women of Petersburg: Status and Culture in a Southern Town, 1784–1860* (W. W. Norton, 1984), 15–86; Jean E. Friedman, *The Enclosed Garden: Women and Community in the Evangelical South, 1830–1900* (Chapel Hill: Univ. of North Carolina Press, 1985); Bertram Wyatt-Brown, *Southern Honor: Ethics and Behavior in the Old South* (New York: Oxford Univ. Press, 1982), 117–324; and Catherine Clinton, *The Plantation Mistress: Women's World in the Old South* (New York: Pantheon, 1982).

5. "The Origin and Formation of an Old Bachelor," *American Gleaner and Virginia Magazine* 1, no. 1 (14 Jan., 1807): 2, Virginia Historical Society, Richmond (hereafter referred to as VHS); "Old Maids," *American Ladies Magazine* 9, no.2 (Feb. 1837): 98, VSL.

6. Williams, *Legends of Loudoun*, 165–66.

CHAPTER 1. THE WHITE COMMUNITY:
PATTERNS OF SETTLEMENT, DEVELOPMENT, AND CONFLICT

1. John Smith, in his exploratory travels throughout Virginia during the early seventeenth century, was the first Englishman to record the presence of these Native Americans in 1608. Because the Manahoacs resided in the piedmont region of Virginia south of the Potomac River, they also were known as the Piedmonts. The Algonquins were referred to as the Nacotchtanks or Anacostans. Also present in the area were the Dogues. The Algonquins and the Dogues were part of the Powhatan Confederacy. David I. Bushnell, *The Manahoac Tribes of Virginia, 1608* (Washington, D.C.: Smithsonian Institution, 1935); Keith Egloff and Deborah Woodward, *First People: The Early Indians of Virginia* (Richmond: Va. Dept. of Historic Resources, 1992); Bernard Sheehan, *Savagism and Civility: Indians and Englishmen in Colonial Virginia (Cambridge: Cambridge Univ. Press, 1980)*, passim; Harrison Williams, *Legends of Loudoun: An Account of the History and Homes of a Border County of Virginia's Northern Neck* (Richmond: Garrett and Massie, 1938), 1–9, 15–16, 20–26; Nan Netherton et al., *Fairfax County, Virginia, a History* (Fairfax: Fairfax County Board of Supervisors, 1978), 2–3; Fairfax Harrison, "Parson Waugh's Tumult, *Virginia Magazine of History and Biography* 30 (1922): 31–37.

2. Alexander Spottswood served as lieutenant governor of Virginia from 23 June 1710 to 27 Sept. 1722. George Hamilton, Earl of Orkney, was Virginia's governor from 18 Feb. 1710 to 29 Jan. 1737, but never went to Virginia. Spotswood was the first and most celebrated representative of Orkney in the governor's post.

3. Regarding stories descriptive of the colonial and antebellum Indian presence in Loudoun, see "A Memorial of John Janney," n.p., Janney Family Papers, Virginia State Library, Richmond (hereafter referred to as VSL); and Joseph V. Nichols, *Legends of Loudoun Valley: True Stories from the Lives and Times of the People of Loudoun County, Virginia* (Leesburg, Va.: Potomac Press, 1961), 39–41. Regarding Native American artifacts, including arrowheads, spearpoints, and pottery see: Collection in the Loudoun County Museum, Leesburg, Va.

4. Williams, *Legends of Loudoun*, 12–13. The best general history of Loudoun is Charles Poland, Jr., *From Frontier to Suburbia* (Maceline, Mo.: Walsworth Publishing, 1976). Also see Yetive Weatherly, *Lovettsville: The German Settlement* (Lovettsville, Va.: Lovettsville Bicentennial Committee, 1976); Eugene M. Scheel, *The History of Middleburg and Vicinity* (Warrenton, Va.: Piedmont Press, 1987); Penelope M. Osburn, *The Story of Middleburg, Virginia, 1787–1958* (Middleburg, Va.: Middleburg National Bank, 1958); James V. Head, *History and Comprehensive Description of Loudoun County, Virginia* (Leesburg, Va.: Park View Press, 1908); and Williams, *Legends of Loudoun*.

5. Christopher Falkus, *The Life and Times of Charles II* (Garden City, N.Y.: Doubleday, 1972); Heskety Pearson, *Charles II: His Life and Likeness* (London: Heinemann, 1960).

6. At the time he issued the original patent, Charles II was a refugee in France, but was the acknowledged sovereign of Scotland, Ireland, Virginia, and other overseas lands. The following year Cromwell's victory at Worcester ended Charles's dominion for ten years. In 1662, a restored Charles II ordered Governor Berkeley and his Council to respect his patent of 1649. Faukus, *Life and Times of Charles II*, passim; Williams, *Legends of Loudoun*, 13–15.

During the time between the original patent and Charles II's restoration, Ralph Lord Hopton, John Lord Culpeper, Sir Dudley Wyatt, and Thomas Culpeper died before ever seeing their land. Williams, *Legends of Loudoun*, 13–15.

7. Williams, *Legends of Loudoun*, 13–15; Edmund Morgan, *American Slavery, American Freedom: The Ordeal of Colonial Virginia* (New York: W. W. Norton, 1975), 244; Matthew Page Andrews, *Virginia: The Old Dominion*, vol. 1 (Richmond: Dietz Press, 1949), 139–40; *Fauquier County, Virginia Historical Notes* (Warrenton, Va.: Warrenton Printing, 1914), 21–22.

8. Charles II issued a new patent on 8 May 1669, which not only recognized the ownership of lands settled during Cromwell's rule, but also stipulated that the remaining land granted to the Proprietors had to be "inhabited or planted" by 1690. He later rescinded this provision. This new "Arlington Charter" granted Arlington and Culpeper, an heir to part of the Northern Neck through his father, the power to assign land patents, receive quit rents and taxes, establish local governments, and assign municipal officers until 1704. If forcefully undertaken, these rights would have challenged the authority of the colonial government already in place, its financial support, and possibly old land patents. Williams, *Legends of Loudoun*, 14–15.

9. Lord Culpeper's cousin, Alexander Culpeper, who also had inherited a 1/6th interest in the Northern Neck, did not sell his land. He did, however, will his property to Lord Culpeper's widow, Margaret, who passed it on to her daughter, Catherine and then to Thomas, fifth Lord, Baron of Cameron in Scotland.

Lord Culpeper was part heir to the Northern Neck grant and co-owner of the "Arlington Charter." Culpeper also succeeded Berkely as governor of Virginia in 1677, although he did not arrive on Virginia soil until 1680. He served until 1682. Culpeper sold his rights to the Arlington Charter back to the Crown in 1684.

Thomas, Sixth Lord Fairfax, came to Virginia in the early eighteenth century and established a home, "Greenway Court," in Frederick County. The Virginia Commonwealth then usurped the family's inheritance rights to the proprietary upon his death in 1781. John Wilson, *Fairfax: A Life of Thomas, Lord Fairfax, Captain General of All the Parliament Forces in the English Civil War, Creator and Commander of the New Model Army* (London: J. Murray, 1985); Stuart E. Brown, *Virginia Baron; The Story of Thomas, Sixth Lord Fairfax* (Berryville, Va.: Chesapeake Book, 1965); Williams, *Legends of Loudoun*, 13–18, 32–33. Andrews, *Virginia: The Old Dominion*, 1: 139–40.

10. The settlers named their new county for John Campbell, Fourth Earl of Loudoun who in 1756 became the appointed commander-in-chief of British forces in America and governor-in-chief of Virginia. Campbell never took the position of governor because of his military duties; he probably never even visited Virginia. He did, however, have relations who came to reside in Loudoun. Colonel William Douglass was a descendant. Owner of the estates of Garalland and Montressor, he was a Loudoun justice in 1770 and sheriff in 1782. Loudoun Legislative Petitions, Dec. 5, 1781, 1520P, 1520 A-P to G-P, 1521–P, and June 4, 1782, 1655–P, 1655 A-P, VS; Emily Salmon, ed., *Hornbook of Virginia History*, 3rd. ed. (Richmond: Virginia State Library, 1983), 109, 113, 117, 119, Williams, *Legends of Loudoun*, 77–78, 100.

11. Williams, *Legends of Loudoun*, 77–78, 100.

12. Lord (Sixth) Fairfax retained permanent management of his land office from

1745 until 1781. Land agents for the Fairfax families included Robert Carter (1702–10, 1722–32), Thomas Lee (1710–17), Edmund Jennings (1717–22), and William Fairfax (1734–36, 1739–45). Surveyors of the property included George Washington, John Hough, John Warner, and Amos Janney.

It was not unusual for land agents (and surveyors) to purchase huge tracts of some of the most valuable property available and to resell it at inflated prices. Robert "King" Carter acquired more than 5300 acres of Loudoun land this way. His successor, Thomas Lee, purchased 16,000 acres locally. George Washington, Hough, and Janney also owned land in Loudoun. Ann Stephens Thomson Mason, the widow of George Mason and mother to George Mason IV, author of the Bill of Rights, purchased approximately 10,000 acres of Loudoun land during the 1730s and 1740s. Penelope M. Osburn, "Exeter: Its History and Architecture," *Bulletin of the Loudoun County Historical Society* 2 (1960): 17–19. Williams, *Legends of Loudoun*, 32–46, 170, 176–77; Scheel, *History of Middleburg*, 5–8; Poland, *From Frontier to Suburbia*, 8n; Douglas R. Egerton, *Charles Fenton Mercer and the Trial of National Conservatism* (Jackson: Univ. Press of Mississippi, 1989), passim; Louis Morton, *Robert Carter of Nomini Hall: A Virginia Tobacco Planter of the Eighteenth Century* (Charlottesville, Va.: Univ. Press of Virginia, 1964), passim, esp. app. tables 5, 9, 15; W. E. Trout, "The Goose Creek and Little River Navigation," *Virginia Cavalcade* 16, no.1 (Winter 1967): 31–32; Head, *History and Comprehensive Description*, 7n. 2; "Coton," *Bulletin of the Loudoun County Historical Society* 5 (1975): 14–15; Robert Carter Land Book, Carter Family Papers (hereafter referred to as CarFP), Virginia Historical Society, Richmond (hereafter referred to as VHS).

13. Because the tithable list for Fairfax County in 1749 does not give complete information regarding its upper parish (Loudoun), it is difficult to ascertain if, in fact, McCarty was the largest holder or the exact number of slaves he quartered on property that became Loudoun. He may have had almost 20 living there. McCarthy's holding may have been second to Thomas Lee's, who had a quarter in Fairfax (which might have been partially on his upper parish property). Netherton et al., *Fairfax County, Virginia*, 32; Williams, *Legends of Loudoun*, 37–38; Scheel, *History of Middleburg*, 6; Elizabeth Donnan, ed., *Documents Illustrative of the History of the Slave Trade to America,* vol. 4, *The Border Colonies and the Southern Colonies* (Washington, D.C.: Carnegie Institution of Washington, 1935), 175.

14. Daniel did so for his boy Dennis who did the same for his son Thaddeus, bequeathing him 1,220 acres of Loudoun land and the slaves to work it. This legacy meant eventual accomplishments as a planter and businessman. Williams, *Legends of Loudoun*, 37–38; Scheel, *History of Middleburg*, 6, 26, 48.

15. His son James became one of Loudoun's largest landholders, acquiring almost 11,000 acres by the end of the eighteenth century. *Hillsboro: Memories of a Mill Town* (Hillsboro: Bicentennial Committee, 1976), 7–8.

16. *They Knew the Washingtons: Letters from a French Soldier with Lafayette and from His Family in Virginia.* Princess Radziwill, ed. (Indianapolis: Bobbs-Merrill, 1926), passim, esp. 193–234, 254–56.

17. Carter rented more than 3000 acres alone on Goose Creek to 105 tenants for an annual sum of 5300 pounds of tobacco and 325 pounds sterling. His Loudoun plantation was called "Leo" and was only one of 13 that he owned throughout the colony.

Robert Carter Landbook, CarFP, VHS; Morton, *Robert Carter of Nomini*, 11, 13–17, 75–78, tables 2–9, 15, 16.

18. Robert Carter Landbook, CarFP, VHS; Morton, *Robert Carter of Nomini*, 11, 13–17, 75–78, tables 2–9, 15, 16.

19. Loudoun's first county court in 1757 comprised Anthony Russell, Fielding Turner, James Hamilton, Aeneas Campbell, Nicholas Minor, William West; and of the Quorum: Richard Coleman, Josias Clapham, George West, Charles Tyler, John Moss, Francis Peyton, and John Mucklehany. The first county clerk was Charles Binns and the first sheriff was Aeneas Campbell. Loudoun's first county lieutenant was Francis Lightfoot Lee, who, along with James Hamilton, represented Loudoun in the House of Burgesses. George West was the county's initial surveyor. Most of these men were large landholders. Harrison, *Legends of Loudoun*, 101–4.

20. Nicholas Cresswell, *The Journals of Nicholas Cresswell, 1774–1777* (London: Jonathan Cape, 1925), 48.

21. The system typically worked like this. Francis Awbrey of Westmoreland county began to acquire Loudoun land in in 1725. A few years later he moved to Loudoun. Once settled on his own plantation, he began to sell some of his other property, perhaps to raise the funds to further develop his farms or his ferry service across the Potomac. Over the next few years he divided one section of his Loudoun holdings, called the "Kittocktin Land" tract, into lots which ranged in size from 150 to 300 acres. He leased this property, totaling almost 1500 acres, to local folk who paid him an annual rent of 40 shillings per 100 acres. Williams, *Legends of Loudoun*, 38–42; Poland, *From Frontier to Suburbia*, 8; Lizzie Worsley, "History of the 'Chapel Above Goose Creek': The First Episcopal Church, Loudoun County, Near Leesburg and the Ancestor of St. James Church," Miscellaneous Files, Loudoun Church Records, VHS; C. O. Vandevanter, "Goose Creek Chappell," Miscellaneous Files, Loudoun Church Records, VHS.

22. Timber was an important source of local revenue, as well as the basis for much of the fuel and building in the area. The original trees also suggested the age of the forest and the quality of its soil.

23. Champe also had to guarantee that he would keep the orchards "well trimed and pruned." He leased the land for "three lives." Erecting housing was a stipulation of land ownership that landholders passed on to their renters, at the renters' expense.

Scheel reveals that the designation "farmer" in the Loudoun vicinity meant anyone who owned less than 400 acres of land; planters owned greater amounts. Scheel, *History of Middleburg*, 13.

24. The average size Loudoun farm was 235 acres in 1850 and 245 acres in 1860. Colonial leases often were for 99 years or 3 lives. Head, *History of Loudoun County*, 92, 110; Morton, *Robert Carter of Nomini*, 76; Poland, *From Frontier to Suburbia*, 8; Williams, *Legends of Loudoun*, 38–42.

25. Ulster Scotch-Irish initially settled in the Virginia tidewater. One local historian estimates that the Scotch-Irish represented almost half of the county's earliest residents. They congregated especially near what became the south-central town of Middleburg. Nichols, *Legends of Loudoun Valley*, 10; Poland, *From Frontier to Suburbia*, 26 n.77. Regarding the ethnic heritage of white southerners, see Grady McWhiney, *Cracker Cul-*

ture: Celtic Ways in the Old South (Tuscaloosa: Univ. of Alabama Press, 1988), 2–50 passim; Carl Bridenbaugh, *Myths & Realities: Societies of the Colonial South* (New York: Atheneum, 1966), 7–8, 122–24; and Bertram Wyatt-Brown, *Southern Honor: Ethics and Behavior in the Old South* (New York: Oxford Univ. Press, 1982), 36–38.

26. Loudoun Quakers began to arrive during the 1730s, mostly from Pennsylvania but a few from Maryland and England. By 1749, they represented almost three-fourths of the households in northern and central Cameron parish. They dominated several small towns including Waterford, Hillsboro, Hamilton, Lincoln, and Purcelville. Marian Marsh Sale, "Old Waterford: Amos Janney's Town Has Changed Little in Two Hundred Years," *Virginia Cavalcade* 18, no.2 (Spring 1969): 13–14; Scheel, *History of Middleburg*, 7–8; Poland, *From Frontier to Suburbia*, 41; Nichols, *Legends of Loudoun Valley*, 30–31; Werner L. Janney and Asa Moore Janney, eds., *John Jay Janney's Virginia: An American Farm Lad's Life in the Early 19th Century* (McLean, Va.: EPM Publications, 1978), 3–5.

27. Samuel M. Janney, *Memoirs of Samuel M. Janney, Late of Lincoln, Loudoun County, Va., a Minister in the Religious Society of Friends,* 3rd ed. (Philadelphia: Friends' Book Association, 1882), 4; Nichols, *Legends of Loudoun Valley*, 30–31; Julia Spruill, *Women's Life and Work in the Southern Colonies* (1938; rpt., New York: W. W. Norton, 1972), 248–54.

28. Gap Friends met at the home of David Potts, Hillsboro's earliest settler, from 1755 until 1768. They built a temporary meeting house in 1770, and then a a permanent meeting house, school, and burial ground on the Beaver Dam fork of Goose Creek. Loudoun Friends also established a Goose Creek Meeting in Lincoln. *Hillsboro: Memories of a Mill Town,* 7–8; Nichols, *Legends of Loudoun Valley*, 30–31, 80; quote from Janney and Janney, eds., *John Janney's Virginia*, 4.

29. During the American Revolution, for example, patriot neighbors expressed outright hostility because many Friends refused to bear arms or pay muster fines and "substitution" taxes. Not a few Friends lost their property as a result. Williams, *Legends of Loudoun*, 137.

30. Scheel, *History of Middleburg*, 9.

31. "Epistle" in Janney, *Memoirs of Samuel M. Janney*, 73, 96; Patricia Hickin, "Antislavery in Virginia, 1832–1860" (Ph.D. dissertation, University of Virginia, 1968), passim.

32. Many first settled in Pennsylvania. A few families settled in the Loudoun vicinity during the 1720s, but it was only during the next decade that substantial numbers began to arrive. In 1732, approximately 65 German families joined the small group who had arrived a few years earlier. The DeKalbs represented German nobility, but most others had a more modest ancestry. The "German Settlement" that they established eventually became the town of Lovettsville.

Evidence suggests that most did not begin to intermarry with those who were not of German descent and culture until just before the American Revolution. Weatherly, *Lovettsville*, 8–10.

33. They depended on men like William Wenner, one of the original settlers who served as a minister in their first Reformed Church and as a community-wide teacher, to provide early guidance. Wenner's family actually may have been from Sweden and

not Germany. Extant records describe Wenner as a man of "ability" and "charm" who married three times, had over twenty children and was believed to have lived past the age of one hundred. The first wave of Germans brought members of the German Reformed Church. Substantial numbers of German Lutherans did not arrive until 1765. Weatherly, *Lovettsville*, 8–9, 15–18, 25–30; Nichols, *Legends of Loudoun Valley*, 57. Also see: Klaus Wust, *The Virginia Germans* (Charlottesville: Univ. Press of Virginia, 1969), passim; Samuel Kercheval, *A History of the Valley of Virginia* (Strasburg, Va.: Valley Press, 1925), passim; and Briscoe Goodhart, "The Pennsylvania Germans in Loudoun County, Virginia," *Pennsylvania German* 9 (1908): 123–25.

34. Chastenay Maussion was a French immigrant who resisted. See, for example, her story in Radziwill, ed., *They Knew the Washingtons,* 199–200.

35. Weatherly, *Lovettsville,* 8–10.

36. Wust, *Virginia Germans* , 69–70, 121–28; Weatherly, *Lovettsville,* 13.

37. Very small numbers of Virginia Germans, usually only members of the Mennonites, Dunkers, and United Brethren, were openly opposed to slaveholding. Wust, *Virginia Germans*, 121–28; Weatherly, *Lovettsville,* 8, 13, 75.

38. According to Lovettsville historians, almost every man of military age fought on the patriots' side, participating in Colonel Charles Armand's legion because he could speak German. Weatherly, *Lovettsville,* 17–18.

39. Scheel, *History of Middleburg,* 8.

40. Cresswell, *Journal,* 47–48.

41. By 1749, for example, the only representatives of the wealthy Blackburn, Mercer, Peyton, Bronaugh, and Chinn households in the Middleburg section of the county still were overseers and slaves. The Carters, Lees, Tayloes, and Fitzhughs also still lived outside of Loudoun. Scheel, *History of Middleburg and Vicinity*, 10.

42. Janney and Janney, eds., *John Janney's Virginia,* 17.

43. Boys also helped women to make the soap and candles, wash clothing, tend livestock, clean the barnyards, care for young children, and do a number of other "female" jobs if there were no young females in the household to do so. Spruill, *Women's Life and Work in the Southern Colonies,* 23–59; Catherine Clinton, *The Plantation Mistress: Woman's World in the Old South* (New York: Pantheon, 1982), 18–29. Regarding German female domestic and field work, see Wust, *Virginia Germans,* 69–70. Regarding Quaker female labor, see Janney and Janney, eds., *John Janney's Virginia,* 59, 67, 80, 84–86, 101–3, 110–11.

44. Poland, *From Frontier to Suburbia,* 25–49; Williams, *Legends of Loudoun,* 31.

45. Loudoun County Will Book A, 169, VSL.

46. Williams, *Legends of Loudoun,* 168–81.

47. "Springwood," the home of Colonel Burgess Ball; the Mason family estates of "Raspberry Plain," "Selma," and "Exeter"; "Belmont," the home of Thomas Lee; and magnificent "Oatlands," belonging to George Carter, dazzled ordinary folk with their size, elegance, imported tapestries and furniture, their ornate gardens, and stunning self-sufficiency. "Coton," 14–15; Williams, *Legends of Loudoun,* 168–81. Also see Marguerite DuPont Lee, *Virginia Ghosts* (Berryville, Va.: Virginia Book, 1966), passim; Eleanor Lee Templeman and Nan Netherton, *Northern Virginia Heritage: A Pictorial*

Compilation of the Historic Sites and Homes in the Counties of Arlington, Fairfax, Loudoun, Fauquier, Prince William and Stafford and in the Cities of Alexandria and Fredricksburg (Arlington: Eleanor Templeman, 1966), 112–155; and Osburn, "Exeter," 17–28.

48. John Janney's family were middling farmers in the Quaker town of Lincoln. They owned approximately 263 acres of land and usually employed 2–3 indentured servants (white and black). Simon Shover was a farmer in the German community of Lovettsville, owner of several hundred acres of land and, at the time of his death, four slaves. Janney and Janney, eds., *John Janney's Virginia*, 84; Inventory of the Property to the Estate of Simon Shover, Sept. 1821, Shover Family Papers, VSL.

49. Janney and Janney, eds., *John Janney's Virginia*, 2–5, 16.

50. Quoted in Weatherly, *Lovettsville*, 23.

51. Poland, *From Frontier to Suburbia*, 34–38. Twelve men and one woman applied for and received an ordinary license in seven months in 1807 and 1808. Loudoun County Order Book, v.1–2, 4, 105, 107, 127, 132, 133, 136, 264–66, 269, 273, 276.

52. Wust, *Virginia Germans*, 178.

53. Janney and Janney, eds., *John Janney's Virginia*, 4.

54. Quakers who lived in and around Hillsboro organized the "Gap Meeting" in 1755. Friends in the Waterford district began to worship regularly at private homes and then at a regular place in South Fork about 1745. Williams, *Legends of Loudoun*, 78. Sale,"Old Waterford," 13–14; Scheel, *History of Middleburg*, 7–8; Poland, *From Frontier to Suburbia*, 41; Nichols, *Legends of Loudoun Valley*, 30–31; Spruill, *Women's Life and Work in the Southern Colonies* 248–54; Janney and Janney, eds., *John Janney's Virginia*, 3–5.

55. Official records of Presbyterian gatherings date from 1765, but they undoubtedly began with the arrival of large numbers of Scotch Irish during the 1730s. In 1804 the Presbyterian Society built a permanent church structure in Leesburg. Penelope M. Osborn, "Tory's Remarks in Diary Point Up Patriotism of Early Presbyterians," n. p., Miscellaneous Files, Loudoun County Church Records, VHS.

56. The Reverend Charles Green's early tithable list recorded an inauspicious beginning in Loudoun—23 persons, many of whom were Irish, identified as "papists" in 1749. Among the Catholics there were such illustrious county names as Awbrey, Binns, and Noland. Others included local Irish families. Local historians estimate that there were approximately 150 known Catholics in the county by the mid-eighteenth century.

On Jan. 16, 1786, the Virginia General Assembly adopted the Statute of Religious Freedom. Afterward Loudoun Catholics began to benefit from the occasional visits of Catholic priests from Maryland. Saint Peter's at Harper's Ferry was completed in 1830. Eugene M. Scheel, *A History of Saint John the Apostle Church, Leesburg, and the Catholic Faith in Loudoun County, Virginia* (Leesburg, Va.: Saint John the Apostle Church), 5–8.

57. Weatherley, *Lovettsville,* 4–15 passim, 75–77; Wust, *Virginia Germans*, 43–49, 139.

58. Local civic activist and vestryman Francis Awbrey invited his neighbors to use his 1720s house as an Episcopalian meeting place. Later, he built the area's first church—a small log building that had pews according to "several ranks and degrees." *Legends of Loudoun*, 38–42; Scheel, *History of Middleburg*, 9; Worsley, "History of the

'Chapel Above Goose Creek,'" Miscellaneous Files, Loudoun Church Records, VHS; C. O. Vandevanter, "Goose Creek Chappell," Miscellaneous Files, Loudoun Church Records, VHS.

59. The Baptists began to have formalized meetings as early as Oct. 1751, with the creation of their Ketoctin Church. There also were several other Baptist churches in the area, enough so that by 1766, they could organize the Ketoctin Baptist Association.

By the last decade of the century, local Baptists were attracting well over 2000 persons to their revivals. Membership included large numbers of blacks, free and slave, but neither could hold offices nor sit with white worshippers.

The Methodists first purchased a building in Leesburg to serve as their church in 1766. Four years later, they erected their own place of worship, the first Methodist Church built in Virginia. By 1851, there were at least 15 Methodist churches in Loudoun. Broad Run Baptist Church Records, 1762–1872, VHS; *Hillsboro: Memories of a Mill Town*, 7–8; William Ford, ed., *Ketoctin Chronicle* (Leesburg, Va.: Potomac Press, 1965), 3–4, 10, passim; Poland, *From Frontier to Suburbia*, 46.

60. There were approximately 1,555 whites and 636 blacks, mostly slaves, in Cameron Parish (Loudoun County) in 1749. By 1800, there were 15,210 whites, 6,078 slaves, and 333 free blacks. Note that both white and especially black populations in Loudoun declined between 1790 and 1800 because of the reannexation of the southeastern portion of Loudoun to Fairfax County in 1798. This region had been part of Loudoun's richest slaveholding district. Fairfax County historians estimate that Loudoun lost 4,034 residents with the annexation (2,376 whites and 1,658 slaves). Donald M. Sweig, "Free Negroes in Northern Virginia: An Investigation of the Growth and Status of Free Negroes in the Counties of Alexandria, Fairfax and Loudoun, 1770–1860" (M.A. thesis, George Mason Univ., 1975), app. C, 66; Netherton et al., *Fairfax County, Virginia*, 29.

61. Residents established Leesburg in 1758 on Nicholas Minor's land. After the Revolution, the politically astute Minor changed the name of the town from Georgetown to Leesburg in honor of Francis Lightfoot Lee, Loudoun resident, Revolutionary War hero, and a signer, along with his brother Richard Henry Lee, of the Declaration of Independence. Williams, *Legends of Loudoun,* 183–88; Head, *History of Loudoun*, 71–74.

62. Williams, *Legends of Loudoun,* 183–88; Head, *History of Loudoun*, 71–79; Poland, *From Frontier to Suburbia*, 67–72; Weatherly, *Lovettsville*, passim; Scheel, *History of Middleburg*, 21–44; Scheel, *Story of Purcellville*, 3–8; *Hillsboro*, 10–20.

63. U.S. Department of Commerce, Bureau of the Census, Manuscript Federal Census, Loudoun County, Virginia (hereafter referred to as FedCenLC), 1810, roll 69; 1820, roll 137; 1830, roll 193; Free Schedule, 1850, roll 957; Free Schedule, 1860, roll 1359; J. D. B. Debow, *Statistical View of the United States . . . Being a Compendium of the Seventh Census . . . 1850* (Washington, D.C.: A. O. P. Nicholson, 1854), 62–63, 320–27; Joseph G. Kennedy, *Population of the United States in 1860; Compiled from the Original Returns of the Eighth Census* (Washington, D.C.: Government Printing Office, 1864), 517; Sweig, "Free Negroes in Northern Virginia," app. C, 66.

64. Significantly, 77% of Loudoun's farm land in 1850 was improved. Poland, *From Frontier to Suburbia*, 77.

65. Cresswell, *Journal*, 197; Williams, *Legends of Loudoun*, 159; Poland, *From Frontier to Suburbia*, 74–81; Head, *History of Loudoun*, 49–71.

66. Binns also experimented with new sanitation measures in his stables, stockyards, and livestock pens, claiming that these practices resulted in a decline in the incidence of disease among his animals and family.

Loudouners initially did not trust his findings. Yet Binns continued to buy what was known to be worn-out land and drastically turn around its crop yields. His neighbors eventually began to take his experiments seriously. He provided a full explanation of his techniques in an 1803 booklet entitled *A Treatise on Practical Farming, embracing particularly the following subjects, viz. The Use of Plaster of Paris with Directions for Using it: and the General Observations on the Use of Other Manures. On Deep Ploughing; Thick Sowing of Grain; Method of Preventing Fruit Trees from Decaying and Farming in General.* Binns freed his slaves upon his death in 1813. Williams, *Legends of Loudoun*, 160–64; Poland, *From Frontier to Suburbia*, 90–91; Richard Beale Davis, *Intellectual Life in Jefferson's Virginia, 1790–1830* (Chapel Hill: Univ. of North Carolina Press, 1964), 153–67.

67. Local dry goods shops were still advertising lime-based fertilizers in 1849. Iron plows became very popular after 1820. Williams, *Legends of Loudoun*, 160–62; Poland, *From Frontier to Suburbia*, 90–91; *Washingtonian*, 26 Oct. 1849; Davis, *Intellectual Life in Jefferson's Virginia*, 152–53; Janney and Janney, eds., *John Janney's Virginia*, 82.

68. Students at the Loudoun County Agricultural Academy and Chemical Institute took a basic classical curriculum but also learned contemporary theories of agriculture including soil properties, plant refinement, topography, mineral composition, the use of fertilizers, how to survey farms, prepare chemicals and analyze soils and minerals. Poland, *From Frontier to Suburbia*, 92, 93, 93n.96; Loudoun Legislative Petitions (hereafter referred to as LouLP), 4 Dec. 1855, VSL.

69. Not all of Loudoun's inventors, however, turned their talents to assisting "men's work." Robert Robinson, David Dungan, and Andrew Glendening all received patents for their "washing machines" between 1809 and 1824. Glendening also patented an apple cutter, fly killer, and sausage machine. Poland, *From Frontier to Suburbia*, 89n.78; *Washingtonian*, 25 May 1844.

70. Some time after 1840, county residents began to pay differing amounts of tax, depending on whether they lived in Shelburne or Cameron parish. The Overseers taxed according to the assessed need and the number of tithables in each parish. In 1849, for example, they taxed Shelburne residents 40.5 cents per tithable, while those in Cameron only paid 30 cents for each taxable resident. Records of the Overseers of the Poor, Loudoun County, Virginia, 1800–1833, 1836–40, 1843, 1851 passim, VSL.

71. Ibid.

72. Loudoun County Minute Book, County Court Records, 10 May 1813, VSL.

73. It was only in 1846 that the Loudoun county court established school districts and made provision for the regular instruction of "indigent" white male and female children. Annual Report of the Board of School Commissioners for Indigent Children, Loudoun County, Virginia, 13 Oct. 1851, VSL.

74. *Loudoun Chronicle*, 16 Nov. 1849, VSL; Wade Hinshaw, ed., *Encyclopedia of American Quaker Genealogy*, 10 vols. (Ann Arbor: Edwards Bros., 1950), 6: 640.

75. Agnes Davisson to Rose Davisson, 26 Nov. 1852, in Jane W. Poulton, ed., *A Loudoun Love Story* (Durham, N.C. by the editor, 1988) (hereafter referred to as PouFP); Janney and Janney, eds., *John Janney's Virginia*, 91.

76. Janney and Janney, eds., *John Janney's Virginia*, 91.

77. The grave that Edmund Carter's neighbors placed him in that night actually was one that the offender had had dug for himself during a previous night of debauchery. Janney recalled of that particular event: "He finally said he was to die, and had his grave dug . . . and a coffin made, and at the time fixed he laid himself out in a neat shroud with a cent . . . on each eye. He laid nearly twenty four hours but finally concluded he was not dead." Carter then tried to commit suicide by getting into a "large tub of warm water" where he "opened a vein in his arm, and when found was nearly exhausted." Ibid., 91–92.

78. Ibid. A notice for a meeting of the Sons of Temperance is found in the *Loudoun Chronicle,* 10 July 1840. LouLP, 25 Feb. 1848, VSL.

79. Loudoun Order Book, vols. 1–2, 9 Nov. 1807, 14 March 1808, 15 Sept. 1807, pp. 87, 138, 270.

80. LouLP, 5 Dec. 1781: 1520-P, 1520 A-P to G-P, 1521-P; and 4 June 1782: 1655-P, 1655 A-P, VSL.

81. Prior to 1852, the state restricted the right to vote to "every male citizen (other than free negroes or mulattoes) aged twenty-one years . . . [who was] . . . possessed of twenty-five acres of [improved] land . . . or . . . fifty acres of unimproved land, or a lot . . . in a city or town . . . with a house thereon. . . ." LouLP, 11 Jan. 1845, VSL; Charles Fenton Mercer, "Controversy between Armistead Thompson Mason and Charles Fenton Mercer" (Washington, D.C.: Charles Fenton Mercer, 1818), 8–9, Mercer Family Papers, VHS.

82. Charles Fenton Mercer of Aldie was the Federalist incumbent. The other, General Armistead Thompson Mason, was the leader of the Democratic-Republican party in Loudoun. In the end, Charles Mercer won the election, but a family quarrel that erupted on polling day between General Mason and his cousin John McCarty ended tragically several months later in a duel that left Armistead Mason dead on 5 Feb. 1819. Nichols, *Legends of Loudoun Valley*, 82–87; Mercer, "Controversy Between Armistead Thompson Mason and Charles Fenton Mercer," 8–9, Mercer Family Papers, VHS; Egerton, *Charles Fenton Mercer*, 132–37, 148–49, 156–57; Williams, *Legends of Loudoun*, 142,167, 170–71, 177, 179,183–85,188–95.

83. Scheel, *History of Middleburg*, 51; Poland, *From Frontier to Suburbia*, 96–103.

84. Loudouners gave little support to the Free Soil Party of the 1840s and 1850s, or the Republican party created in 1854. *Washingtonian*, 16 March 1844; Scheel, *History of Middleburg*, 51.

85. Matthew Harrison served as a member of the General Assembly during the 1862–63 session and was re-elected during the fall of 1875. "Death of Matthew Harrison," *Loudoun Mirror*, 28 Jan. 1875, VHS; Miscellaneous correspondences of Matthew Harrison, Walter Jones Collection, Leesburg Family Papers, Manuscript Division, Alderman Library, Univ. of Virginia. Biographical information on Burr Powell and his family located in Powell Family Genealogical Notes, n. p., Gray Family Papers, VHS. Miscellaneous correspondence in the Powell, Harrison and Conrad Family Papers, VHS; "A Brief History of the First Harrisons of Virginia: Descendants of Cuthbert Harrison, Esquire of Ancaster, England From A.D. 1600 to A.D. 1915," pamphlet, n.d., n., Harrison Family Papers, VHS; "Notes on Brooke-Powell Family," *Virginia Magazine of History and Biography* 15, no.2 (June 1908): 201–3; Scheel, *History of Middleburg*, 51.

86. Williams, *Legends of Loudoun*, 198–99; Poland, *From Frontier to Suburbia*, 65, 170–81; Mason Ellzey, "The Cause We Lost and the Land We Love," 27, Mason Family Papers, VHS.

87. In Lovettsville, 325 voted against secession, 46 voted for it; in Waterford, 220 persons voted against it and 31 for secession. Poland, *From Frontier to Suburbia*, 65.

88. Williams, *Legends of Loudoun*, 198–99, 218–21; Poland, *From Frontier to Suburbia*, 170–81.

CHAPTER 2. GENDER CONVENTION AND COURTSHIP

1. Burr Harrison to Matthew Harrison, 15 Feb. 1849?, Harrison Family Papers (hereafter referred to as HarFP), Virginia Historical Society, Richmond (hereafter referred to as VHS).

2. See, for example, Nancy Cott, *The Bonds of Womanhood: Woman's Sphere in New England* (New Haven: Yale Univ. Press, 1970), 63–100; Christopher Lasch, *Haven in a Heartless World* (New York: Oxford Univ. Press, 1977); Michael Gordon, "The Husband as Depicted in the Nineteenth-Century Marriage Manual," in *The American Man*, Elizabeth Pleck and Joseph Pleck, eds. (Englewood Cliffs, N.J.: Prentice-Hall, 1980), 147–57; and Elizabeth Pleck, "Two Worlds in One," *Journal of Social History* 10, no. 2 (Spring 1976): 178–95.

3. "Woman's Sphere," *American Ladies Magazine* 8, no. 5 (May 1836): 286, Virginia State Library, Richmond (hereafter referred to as VSL); Julia Spruill, *Women's Life and Work in the Southern Colonies* (1938; rpt., New York: W. W. Norton, 1972), 221.

4. "To a Young Bride," *American Ladies Magazine* 7, no. 11 (Nov. 1835): 487, VSL; "A Chapter from the 'Book of Marriage,'"*American Ladies Magazine* 6, no. 6 (June 1833): 262–64; "Female Influence," *Ladies Magazine and Literary Gazette* 1, no. 6 (June 1828): 268, all VSL.

5. "Female Piety, *Ladies Magazine and Literary Gazette* 1, no. 4 (April 1828): 177, VSL.

6. "A Good Wife," *American Ladies Magazine* 8, no. 4 (April 1835): 228–30; "On Domestic Industry: An Address to Young Ladies," *Ladies Magazine and Literary Gazette* 6, no. 7 (July 1833): 327; "A Good Wife," *American Ladies Magazine* 8, no. 4 (April 1835): 228–30. The Reverend Dr. Bishop's sermon originally appeared in *The National Preacher*. Writers continuously offered advice similar to Bishop's. "Temperance, Order, Activity, Industry, and Self-command . . . [are] essential to the health, happiness, and usefulness of woman," one offered. "Formation of Domestic Habits," *Ladies Magazine and Literary Gazette* 8, no. 11 (Nov. 1835): 465; Also see "What Women Should Do," *Ladies Magazine and Literary Gazette* 8, no. 5 (May 1835): 241–44; and "Woman's Piety," *Ladies Magazine and Literary Gazette* 6, no. 5 (May 1833): 245, all VSL.

7. There were several sources of information on proper gender role behavior available to Loudouners. Book-length works such as Margaret Coxe's *Young Lady's Companion: In a Series of Letters* (Philadelphia: Lindsay and Blakiston, 1839) and especially Virginia Cary's *Letters on Female Character, Addressed to a Young Lady on the Death of Her Mother* (Richmond: A. Works, 1830), for example, were important guides. Lou-

douners also purchased the writings of a local author, Margaret Mercer, whose *Popular Lectures on Ethics or Moral Obligation* (Petersburg, Va.: Edmund & Julien C. Ruffin, 1841), was a collection of essays on social and moral responsibility for youth. Literate county residents also relied on articles, sermons, short stories, poems, and aphorisms in locally produced journals.

8. The *Literary Messenger* ran from 1834 to 1864, while the *Southern Planter* began publication in 1841 and continued into the 20th century. Both were published in Richmond. Shorter-lived journals included: the *Virginia Literary and Evangelical Magazine* (1818 to 1820), the *American Gleaner and Virginia Magazine* (1807), and the *National Magazine* (1799 to 1800). Selections from Maryland included: the *National Magazine or Lady's Emporium*, (1830–31), the *Emerald* (Baltimore, (1810–11), and the *Ladies Literary Bouquet* (Baltimore, 1823–24). Others of regional importance were: the *Masonic Miscellany and Ladies Literary Magazine* (Lexington, 1821–23), the *Southern Ladies Companion* (Nashville, 1847–54), the *Southern Ladies Book*, *DeBow's Review*, and the *Southern Literary Gazette*. Sam G. Riley, *Magazines of the American South* (New York: Greenwood Press, 1972), passim, esp. 6–7, 101–4, 122–24, 136–41, 253–55, and passim; *Loudoun Chronicle*, 16 Jan. 1859, VSL.

9. "Domestic Sketches from a Southern Pen," *Ladies Magazine and Literary Gazette* 7, no. 2 (Feb. 1834): 62–64; "Woman's Sphere," *American Ladies Magazine* 8, no. 5 (May 1836): 262–67, all VSL.

10. "Domestic Sketches from a Southern Pen," 59.

11. After analyzing agricultural journals such as the *Agriculturalist*, *American Cotton Planter*, *American Farmer*, *Farmer and Planter*, *Southern Planter*, and *Southern Cultivator*, for example, D. Harland Hagler admitted that "there can be no doubt that the ideal of the southern lady exerted a strong emotional appeal to the minds of many people in both the antebellum and the postbellum south." Yet Hagler asserts that southerners generally preferred the "farmwife ideal"—an industrious, hardworking wife and mother who was more interested in her domestic productivity than her social charms and accomplishments. In reality, however, the agricultural press of the antebellum South dedicated little of its energy or space to the issue of gender convention, especially for women. Far more information on ideals of adult behavior, marriage, and family life was available in the literary journals, or even in local newspapers, than in agricultural journals. D. Harland Hagler, "The Ideal Woman in the Antebellum South: Lady or Farmwife," *Journal of Southern History* 46, no. 3 (Aug. 1980): 404n.2, 405. See, for example, the *Southern Planter*, 1845–60 passim, VHS. For examples of prescriptive journal literature available to Loudouners which addressed the roles of females, see *Washingtonian*, 25 Oct. 1849, 11 June 1852.

12. Fox-Genovese argues similarly in her discussion of the gender conventions of slaveholding women. She does not clearly label slaveholding women as the property of men, but rather emphasizes their perceived inferiority and, thus, dependence. Slaveholding men, she asserts, were the common master of women, black and white, and children. Elizabeth Fox-Genovese, *Within the Plantation Household: Black and White Women of the Old South* (Chapel Hill: Univ. of North Carolina Press, 1988), 194–203. Quote from 195.

13. W. J. Cash explained in *The Mind of the South*:

> She was the South's palladium, this Southern woman—the standard for all its rallying, the mystic symbol of its nationality in the face of the foe. At the last, I verily believe, the ranks of the Confederacy went rolling into battle in the misty conviction that it was wholly or her that they fought.

Perhaps the "ranks" believed so, but the leadership knew better. See, for example, Anne Scott's discussion of the importance of the idealized image of slaveholding women to the white patriarchy. Wilbur J. Cash, *The Mind of the South* (New York: Alfred A. Knopf, 1941), 86; Anne Scott, "Women's Perspective on the Patriarchy in the 1850s," *Journal of American History* 61, no. 1 (July 1974): 52–53, and *The Southern Lady: From Pedestal to Politics,* 1830–1930 (Chicago: Univ. of Chicago Press), 4.

14. George Fitzhugh, "Sociology for the South," in *Slavery Defended: The Voices of the Old South*, Eric McKitrick, ed. (Englewood Cliffs, N.J.: Prentice-Hall, 1963), 37–38.

15. Ibid., 45.

16. Scott, *The Southern Lady*, 4.

17. Quote from Rollin G. Osterweis, *Romanticism and Nationalism in the Old South*, (Gloucester, Mass: L. Peter Smith, 1964), 68. Also see Thomas Dew, "Influence of Slavery on the Condition of the Female Sex," in *Review of the Debate in the Virginia Legislature of 1831 and 1832* (Richmond: T. W. White, 1832; Westport, Conn.: Greenwood Press, 1970), 35–38; Thomas R. Dew, "Dissertation on the Characteristic Differences between the Sexes, and on the Position and Influence of Woman in Society," *Southern Literary Messenger* 1, nos. 11, 12 (July, Aug. 1835): 621–32, 672–91.

18. Quote from Ernest R. Groves, *The American Woman: The Feminine Side of a Masculine Civilization* (New York: Greenberg, 1937), 162. Also see Evelyn L. Pugh, "Women and Slavery: Julia Gardiner Tyler and the Duchess of Sutherland," *Virginia Magazine of History and Biography* 88, no. 4 (April 1980): 186–202.

19. As early as 1691, the Virginia colonial government demanded racial compatibility, banishing forever" those whites, free and bond, who married a Negro, mulatto or Indian. Anti-miscegenation legislation became even more restrictive during the antebellum era. Yet numerous intimate relationships continued to exist. By 1850, for example, 35% of the Loudoun slave population was "mulatto," and more than 50% of the county's free people of color. June Guild, ed., *Black Laws of Virginia: A Summary of the Legislative Acts of Virginia Concerning Negroes from the Earliest Times to the Present* (Richmond: Whittsett and Shepperson, 1936; New York: Negro Universities Press, 1969), 21, 23, 30; U.S. Department of Commerce, Bureau of the Census, Manuscript Federal Census, Loudoun County, Virginia (hereafter referred to as FedCenLC), 1830, roll 193; Charles Poland, *From Frontier to Suburbia* (Maceline, Mo.: Walsworth, 1976), 132 n.14.

20. Biographical information on Powell family located in Powell Family Genealogical Notes, n.p., Gray Family Papers; "A Brief History of the First Harrisons of Virginia: Descendants of Cuthbert Harrison, Esquire of Ancaster, England from A.D. 1600 to A.D. 1915," n.d., n.p., HarFP, VHS; and "Notes on Brooke-Powell Family," *Virginia Magazine of History and Biography* 15, no. 2 (June 1908): 201–3.

Regarding cousin marriage in Loudoun and throughout the South see: Nancy Conrad to Elizabeth Powell Conrad, Jan. 24, 1835, Conrad Family Papers (hereafter referred to as ConFP); Werner L. Janney and Asa Moore Janney, eds., *John Jay Janney's Virginia: An American Farm Lad's Life in the Early 19th Century* (McLean, Va.: EPM, 1978), 7; "Autobiography of St. George Tucker Brooke," Brooke Family Papers, VHS; Weatherly, *Lovettsville,* 12–13, 15–18, 74–77; Catherine Clinton, *The Plantation Mistress: Women's World in the Old South* (New York: Pantheon Books, 1982), 57–60; Steven Stowe, *Intimacy and Power in the Old South: Ritual in the Lives of Planters* (Baltimore: Johns Hopkins Univ. Press, 1987), 96–106; Bertram Wyatt-Brown, *Southern Honor: Ethics and Behavior in the Old South* (New York: Oxford Univ. Press, 1982), 197–225; and Suzanne Lebsock, *The Free Women of Petersburg: Status and Culture in a Southern Town,* 1784–1860 (New York: W.W. Norton, 1984), 15–86 passim.

21. Ages of first marriage compiled from data available in: FedCenLC, 1830, Roll 193; Free Schedule, 1850, Roll 957; Free Schedule, 1860, Roll 1359.

22. Quote taken from Robert Conrad to Powell Conrad, 18 March 1853, ConFP, VHS. Regarding the lands, slaves, and stock Robert Carter gave to John and George Carter, see Robert Carter Landbook, Carter Family Papers (hereafter referred to as CarFP), VHS.

23. Additional information on Burr Powell and his family in Eugene M. Scheel, *The History of Middleburg and Vicinity* (Warrenton, Va.: Piedmont Press, 1987), 14–17, 20–28, 35–39, 44–45, 50–51; Burr Powell to Elizabeth Powell, 29 June 1828, ConFP, VHS.

24. Burr Powell to Elizabeth Powell, 29 June 1828, ConFP, VHS.

25. The Conrad family home and family are described in Marguerite DuPont Lee, *Virginia Ghosts* (Berryville, Va.: Virginia Book, 1966), 193–95; and Virginus Hall, Jr., *Portraits in the Collection of the Virginia Historical Society: A Catalogue* (Charlottesville: Univ. Press of Virginia, 1981), 52–53; Burr Powell to Elizabeth Powell, 29 June 1828, ConFP, VHS.

26. Robert Conrad to Elizabeth Powell Conrad, 27 May 1850; Robert Conrad to Powell Conrad, 13 June 1851, ConFP, VHS.

27. Nancy Chappelear Baird, ed., *Journals of Amanda Virginia Edmonds: Lass of the Mosby Confederacy* (Stephens City, Va.: Commercial Press, 1950), viii–ix (hereafter referred to as Edmonds Diary with entry dates noted); Burr Harrison to Matthew Harrison, 15 Feb. 1849?, HarFP: Burr Powell to Robert Conrad, Jan. 1830, 13 Dec.1830; and Elizabeth Powell Conrad to Burr Powell, 25 Dec. 1830, ConFP, VHS.

28. Quote in Burr Harrison to Matthew Harrison, 15 Feb. 1849?, "A Brief History of the First Harrisons," n.p., HarFP, VHS; Harrison Family Genealogical Notes, Gray Family Papers, VHS; Also see "Death of Matthew Harrison," *Loudoun Mirror,* 28 Jan. 1875, VHS; and Walter Jones Family Genealogical Notes, Leesburg Family Papers, Manuscript Division, Alderman Library, Univ. of Virginia (hereafter referred to as UVA).

29. Hortensia Hay Rogers to Mary Randolph Custis Lee, 1829?, George Bolling Lee Papers, VHS.

30. Quakers married at a slightly older age than did other Loudoun whites. Mean age at marriage for Quaker females was 23.82 for females and 27.45 for males. This difference probably is attributable to the difficulty of finding a suitable Quaker to marry. Ages compiled from data provided in Wade Hinshaw, ed., *Encyclopedia of American*

Quaker Genealogy, 10 vols. (Ann Arbor: Edwards Bros., 1950), 6: 609–924 passim. Also see Eva Kaufmann, ed., ". . . *Our Loves to You All* . . .": *White Family Letters, 1804–1830* (Gaithersburg, Md.: by the editor, 1986), 9.

31. Goose Creek Quaker women were slightly more likely than men (1.125 to 1.0) to marry out of unity. Information descriptive of the marriage patterns of the Goose Creek Monthly Meeting of the Society of Friends, Loudoun County, Virginia, compiled from records in Hinshaw, ed., *Encyclopedia of American Quaker Genealogy*, 6: 609–724 passim. Also see Janney and Janney, eds., *John Janney's Virginia*, 5, 98–99; Joseph V. Nichols, *Legends of Loudoun Valley: True Stories from the Lives and Times of the People of Loudoun County, Virginia* (Leesburg, Va.: Potomac Press, 1961), 7–8.

32. Robert Conrad to Catherine Conrad, 27 May 1850, ConFP, VHS.

33. Burr Powell to Elizabeth Powell, 16 June 1828, ConFP; Burr Harrison to Matthew Harrison, 15 Feb. 1848?, HarFP, VHS.

34. Burr Harrison to Matthew Harrison, 1848?, HarFP; Robert Conrad to Kate Conrad, 22 Sept. 1851, ConFP; Alfred H. Powell to John Leven Powell, 24 Dec. 182?, PowFP; Louise Love to Sarah Harrison, 26 Jan. 1835, HarFP, VHS. Also see Elizabeth Powell to Catherine Powell, 3 May 1829; Elizabeth Conrad to Catherine Conrad, 30 June 1856, ConFP, VHS.; and Wyatt-Brown, *Southern Honor*, 256.

35. This is not to say that Loudouners did not believe that women could not be dishonest, or did not attack the reputation of one who proved to be. See, for example, Rose Davisson's critique of "Miss Hawkins" in Rose Davisson to John Poulton, 2 Oct. 1857, in Jane W. Poulton, ed., *A Loudoun Love Story* (Durham, N.C.: by the editor, 1988); Edmonds Diary, 11 March 1859, 22.

36. Burr Powell to Elizabeth Powell, 29 June 1829; Robert Conrad to Powell Conrad, 10 April 1859, ConFP, VHS. Also see Hortensia Hay Rogers to Mary Randolph Custis Lee, 1829?, George Bolling Lee Papers, VHS. Paul Henkel's poetry collected in part in F. V. N. Painter, *Poets of Virginia* (Atlanta: B. F. Johnson, 1907), 53–55, quote from 54. "Heathenish Housekeeping" originially appeared in Henkel's *Kurzer Zeitvertreib* in 1810 and was later translated into English.

37. Painter, *Poets of Virginia*, 55. Quotes from Rose Davisson found in Rose Davisson to John Poulton, 25 Sept., 2 Oct. 1857, in Poulton, ed., *Loudoun Love Story*, 66–67, 71. Clearly Ms. Davisson was distressed at her aunt's misfortune in choosing a dishonest man. Her diatribe against Dr. Turner, however, may also have been a warning to her own fiancé (to whom she was writing) since they were involved in a long distance, long term engagement.

38. William Gray of "Locust Hill" farm, for example, noted in his diary no fewer than 42 episodes of illness that his wife suffered between 1853 and 1856. More than two-thirds of these entries indicated that a physician had come to their home, and there were several accounts of trips that they had taken to Washington, D.C. and Philadelphia in order to consult with medical specialists about Mrs. Gray's health. In contrast to Mrs. Gray's history of persistent, debilitating illness, her husband only recorded 10 episodes of illness that he experienced during the same time period and only two occasions when he required the services of a physician. William H. Gray Farm Book, 1853–56 passim, Gray Family Papers, VHS; Rose Davisson to John Poulton, 25 Sept. 1857, in Poulton, ed., *Loudoun Love Story*, 66–67; Burr Harrison to Matthew Harrison, 15 Feb. 1848?, HarFP, VHS.

39. Elizabeth Powell to Burr and Catherine Powell, 18 May 1827?, ConFP. Also see Louise Love to Sarah Harrison, 26 Jan. 1835, HarFP, VHS.

40. Elizabeth Powell to Catherine Powell, 18 May 1828?, 31 May 1829; Robert Conrad to Robert Conrad II, 23 Feb. 1856, ConFP; Ann Maund to George Carter, 1 May 1805, Carter Family Papers, VHS.

41. Robert Conrad to Elizabeth Conrad, 26 Feb. 1830, ConFP, VHS.

42. *Loudoun Chronicle*, 10 Aug. 1849, VSL.

43. Louise Love to Sarah Harrison, 26 Jan. 1825, HarFP; Hortensia Hay Rogers to Mary Randolph Custis Lee, 24 Aug. 1829?, George Bolling Lee Papers, VHS.

44. See, for example, Sarah Powell Harrison to Elizabeth Powell Conrad, 9 Nov. 1843, HarFP, VHS. Also see Jean Friedman, *The Enclosed Garden: Women and Community in the Evangelical South* (Chapel Hill: Univ. of North Carolina Press, 1985), 22–31; Clinton, *Plantation Mistress*, 18–33.

45. Robert Conrad to Betty Conrad, 26 Feb. 1830, ConFP; Ann Maria Harrison to Harrision Family, n.d., 1850s, HarFP, VHS.

46. Robert Conrad to Elizabeth Powell Conrad, 28 Jan. 1844, ConFP. Also see George F. Harrison to Ann Harrison Byrd, 11 Sept. 1828, Byrd Family Papers, VHS.

47. See, for example, Thomas Peake to Sally Adams, 13 April 1802, Peake Family Papers, VHS; Agnes Davisson to Rose Davisson, 8 June 1853, in Poulton, ed., *Loudoun Love Story*, 23.

48. See, for example, Burr Powell to Sarah Harrison, 9 Nov. 1816; Burr Harrison to Catherine Harrison, 28 Feb. 1855, HarFP; Robert Conrad to Kate Conrad, 3 Nov. 1854, ConFP, VHS.

49. Robert Conrad to Betty Conrad, 26 Feb. 1830, ConFP, VHS.

50. Robert Conrad to Elizabeth Powell Conrad, 4 March 1830, ConFP, VHS.

51. Levi White to Joseph White, 8 Dec. 1804 in Kaufman, ed., "*. . . Our Loves to You All,*" 2.

52. John S. Peyton to Cadet Richard Peyton, 4 March 1829, Peyton Family Papers. Also see George Harrison to Ann Harrison Byrd, 11 Sept. 1821, Byrd Family Papers, VHS.

53. Edmonds Diary, 3 July 1857, 13 Jan. 1859, 20 July 1860.

54. A cursory view of the marriage records of part of Kate Conrad's family is instructive. Kate's mother and both of her mother's sisters married young—at ages 15, 18 and 19 years, and to men who were upper class. Predictably, one of the three married a first cousin. The following generation of Powell women, however, had a much more difficult time finding suitable partners. Kate's younger sister Sarah married a first cousin, but Kate never married. All five of Kate's adult brothers married, however, and within their class. Although little is known of the marriage patterns of the children of one of Kate's maternal aunts, a complete genealogical record of her Aunt Sarah and Uncle Burr Harrison's children sheds further light. While all of the women in the family during Sarah Powell Harrison's generation married "successfully," only one of Sarah Powell and Burr Harrison's four daughters ever married. Their third daughter married a maternal first cousin. On the other hand, all three of Sarah and Burr Harrisons' sons married women of equal or higher status. It is difficult to be more precise about this trend. The marriage records from Loudoun available in

Jewell's compilation do not indicate the age at marriage of the men and women. Aurelia Jewell, ed., "Loudoun Marriage Bonds, 1790–1860," Loudoun County Records, VSL. Regarding Harrison family genealogy see: Harrison. "A Brief History of the First Harrisons of Virginia, n.p., HarFP. For Powell family genealogy, see: Powell Family Genealogical Notes, Gray Family Papers, VHS.; Edmonds Diary, 15 Feb. 1859.

55. Rose Davisson to John Poulton, 18 Feb. 1857; 29 May 1858, in Poulton, ed., *Loudoun Love Story*, 128, 142; FedCenLC, 1830, roll 193, 2; 1840, roll 564, 221; Will of Sarah Ellzey, 8 Oct. 1840, HarFP, VHS.

56. Burr Powell to Elizabeth Powell, 7. June 1827; Robert Conrad to Elizabeth Powell, July 1827, ConFP, VHS.

57. Robert Conrad to Catherine Conrad, 14 July 1852, ConFP, VHS.

58. Edmonds Diary, 9 April 1859, 14 March 1861.

59. Dr. J.W. Taylor to Rose Davisson, 24 Feb. 1856, in Poulton, ed., *Loudoun Love Story*, 25.

60. Robert Conrad to Elizabeth Powell, 22 June 1829, ConFP, VHS.

61. Robert Taylor Scott to Fanny Carter, 26 Sept. 1856, 7 Nov. 1856, Keith Family Papers, VHS.

62. Robert Taylor Scott to Fanny Carter, 15 Oct. 1856, Keith Family Papers, VHS.

63. Rose Davisson to John Poulton, 22 Feb., 1857, 25 Sept. 1857, in Poulton, ed., *Loudoun Love Story*, 31, 68.

64. See, for example, Steve Stowe's description of didactic literature on letter-writing and its impact on courtship among the southern elite. Stowe, *Intimacy and Power*, 58–67.

65. Rose Davisson to John Poulton, 2 Oct. 1857, in Poulton, ed., *Loudoun Love Story*, 70.

66. See, for example, the many accounts of premarital pregnancies and illegitimacy found in the records of Loudoun Friends. Hinshaw, ed., *Encyclopedia of American Quaker*, 6: 609–724 passim; Poland, *From Frontier to Suburbia*, 24.

67. Nichols, *Legends of Loudoun Valley*, 7–8. Nichols's romanticized version of this love story completely excludes any mention of Hannah Nichols's premarital pregnancy but is corrected by the Quaker records. Hinshaw, ed., *Encyclopedia of American Quaker Genealogy*, 6: 600.

68. Burr Powell initially disinherited Ann Powell Noland but reinstated her in his will before his death. "Brooke Family," 203; "First Harrisons of Virginia," HarFP, VHS.

69. Hortensia Hay to Mary Randolph Custis Lee, 24 Aug. 1829, George Bolling Lee Papers, VHS.

70. Burr Powell to Elizabeth Powell, 29 June 1828, ConFP, VHS.

71. Rose Davisson to John Poulton, 17 Sept. 1857, in Poulton, ed., *Loudoun Love Story*, 62–63.

72. Elizabeth Powell to Burr Powell, 19 July 1828, ConFP; Thomas Peake to Sally Adams, 13 April 1802, Peake Family Papers, VHS; Ann Sidwell, "Life of Hugh Sidwell," Loudoun Genealogical File, Thomas Balch Library, Leesburg, Va., 2.

73. Janney and Janney, eds., *John Janney's Virginia*, 98.

74. See, for example, the letters of Elizabeth Davisson to John Poulton, 19 Feb. 1857, 3, 25 Feb. 1870, 4, 24 April 1870, 16 Sept. 1870, and 31 Dec. 1872, in Poulton, ed., *Loudoun Love Story*, 28–31, 200–205, 210–15.

75. Burr Powell to Rebecca Conrad, 11 Oct. 1829, ConFP, VHS.

76. Rose Davisson to John Poulton, 29 May 1858, in Poulton, ed., *Loudoun Love Story*, 142–43.

CHAPTER 3. MARRIAGE, FOR BETTER OR FOR WORSE

1. For the most important discussions of the marital experience for southern white women, see Elizabeth Fox-Genovese, *Within the Plantation Household: Black and White Women of the Old South* (Chapel Hill: Univ. of North Carolina Press, 1988); Catherine Clinton, *The Plantation Mistress: Women's World in the Old South* (New York: Pantheon, 1982); Anne Scott, *The Southern Lady from Pedestal to Politics, 1830–1930* (Chicago: Univ. of Chicago Press, 1970); Bertram Wyatt-Brown, *Southern Honor: Ethics and Behavior in the Old South* (New York: Oxford Univ. Press, 1982), 226–71; Suzanne Lebsock, *The Free Women of Petersburg: Status and Culture in a Southern Town, 1784–1860* (New York: W. W. Norton, 1984); Daniel Blake Smith, *Inside the Great House: Planter Family Life in Eighteenth Century Chesapeake Society* (Ithaca: Cornell Univ. Press, 1980), 55–81, 126–74; and Jean E. Friedman, *The Enclosed Garden: Women and Community in the Evangelical South, 1830–1900* (Chapel Hill: Univ. of North Carolina Press, 1985), 21–38.

2. Quote from William Fulton to John F. Poulton, Feb. 4 1857, in Jane W. Poulton, ed., *A Loudoun Love Story* (Durham, N.C.: by the editor, 1988). Regarding roles of the European American husband and father in southern families, see Wyatt-Brown, *Southern Honor*, passim, particularly 147–98, 254–324; and Smith, *Inside the Great House*, 82–174.

3. Robert Conrad to Elizabeth Conrad, 17 Feb. 1830, Conrad Family Papers (hereafter referred to as ConFP), Virginia Historical Society, Richmond (hereafter referred to as VHS).

4. Among literate circles, it was mandatory for those who could not attend to send a note of regret and explanation. Rose Davisson to John Poulton, 29 May 1858, in Poulton, ed., *Loudoun Love Story*, 142.

5. Werner L. Janney and Asa Moore Janney, eds., *John Jay Janney's Virginia: An American Farm Lad's Life in the Early 19th Century* (McLean, Va.: EPM Publications, 1978), 98.

6. Ibid., 98–100.

7. Agnes Davisson to Rose Davisson, 26 Nov. 1852, in Poulton, ed., *Loudoun Love Story*, 15.

8 Penelope M. Osburn, "Exeter: Its History and Architecture," *Bulletin of the Loudoun County Historical Society* 2 (1960): 24.

9. *Loudoun Chronicle,* 10 July 1846, Virginia State Library, Richmond (hereafter referred to as VSL); Yetive Weatherly, *Lovettsville: The German Settlement* (Lovettsville, Va: Lovettsville Bicentennial Committee, 1976), 106; Samuel M. Janney, *Memoirs of Samuel M. Janney, Late of Lincoln, Loudoun County, Va.*, 3rd ed. (Philadelphia: Friends' Book Association, 1882), 26–28. Lines of poetry taken from Janney's "Lake George" poem.

10. Rose Davisson to John Poulton, 29 May 1858, in Poulton, ed., *Loudoun Love Story*, 142–43.

11. W. E. Trout, "The Goose Creek and Little River Navigation," *Virginia Cavalcade* 16, no. 1 (Winter 1967): 31–32; Harrison Williams, *Legends of Loudoun: An Account of the History and Homes of a Border County of Virginia's Northern Neck* (Richmond: Garrett and Massie, 1938), 172.

12. *First Harrisons of Virginia*, n. p., VHS.

13. Carl Degler asserts that nuclear families generally were the most prevalent form of household and family structure for persons residing in North America. The southern family, white and black, however, moved more slowly toward a nuclear structure. Carl Degler, *At Odds: Women and the Family in America from the Revolution to the Present* (New York: Oxford Univ. Press, 1980), 5; Smith, *Inside the Great House,* 5; Joan E. Cashin, "The Structure of Antebellum Planter Families: 'The Ties that bound us Was Strong,'" *Journal of Southern History* 56, no. 1 (Feb. 1990): 55–70; "Agreement Concerning the Construction of a House for Matthew Harrison by John Morris, 1858," "Certificate of Election to the Virginia House of Delegates, 1861," Harrison Family Papers (hereafter referred to as HarFP), VHS.

14. Burr Powell to Robert Conrad, Jan. 1830, ConFP; Mary Lee Fitzhugh Custis to Mary Ann Randolph Custis Lee, 6 Oct. 1831, George Bolling Lee Papers, VHS.

15. Burr Powell to Burr Harrison, 26 Dec. 1824, HarFP, VHS.

16. Thomas Jefferson Harrison to Burr Harrison, 26 July 1827, HarFP, VHS; Miscellaneous Receipts and Slips, Shover Family Papers (hereafter referred to as ShovFP), VSL.

17. Elizabeth Powell Conrad to Burr Powell, 25 Dec. 1829, ConFP, VHS.

18. Elizabeth Powell Conrad to Catherine Powell, Jan. 1830, ConFP, VHS.

19. Burr Powell to Rebecca Conrad, 11 Oct. 1829, ConFP, VHS.

20. Elizabeth Powell Conrad to Rebecca Conrad, n.d. Jan. 1830, ConFP, VHS.

21. Elizabeth Powell Conrad to Rebecca Conrad, n.d. Jan. 1830, ConFP, VHS.

22. Elizabeth Powell Conrad to Catherine Powell, n.d. Jan. 1830, ConFP, VHS.

23. Elizabeth Powell Conrad to Catherine Powell, n.d. Jan. 1830, ConFP, VHS.

24. Ibid.

25. Catherine Powell to Elizabeth Powell Conrad, 1 July 1830, ConFP, VHS.

26. *First Harrisons of Virginia*, n.p., VHS; Nancy Conrad to Elizabeth Powell Conrad, 24 Jan. 1835, ConFP, VHS.

27. Sarah Harrison to Elizabeth Conrad, 9 Nov. 1843, HarFP, VHS.

28. Loudoun Legislative Petition (hereafter referred to as LouLP), 4 Dec. 1817, 31 Jan. 1849, VSL.

29. See, for example, the discussion of elite southern women in Clinton, *Plantation Mistress*, 16–35, 68–86, 140–79; Friedman, *Enclosed Garden*, 21–53; and Fox-Genovese, *Within the Plantation Household*, 100–192.

30. Alfred Harrison Powell to John Leven Powell, 24 Dec. 1825?, Powell Family Papers (hereafter referred to as PowFP), VHS.

31. *First Harrisons of Virginia*, n.p., VHS. Also see Burr Powell to Rebecca Conrad, 11 Oct. 1829; Elizabeth Powell Conrad to Rebecca Conrad, Jan. 1830; and Memorandum of an Agreement between David Holmes Conrad and Robert Conrad, 7 Jan. 1833, ConFP, VHS.

32. Robert Conrad to Elizabeth Powell Conrad, 10 June 1831, ConFP, VHS.

33. Robert Conrad to Elizabeth Powell Conrad, 5 Sept. 1831, 1, 28 Feb. 1841, ConFP, VHS.

34. Robert Conrad to Elizabeth Powell Conrad, 21 Feb. 1841, ConFP, VHS.

35. Robert Conrad to Elizabeth Powell Conrad, 8 March 1841, ConFP, VHS.

36. Robert Conrad to Elizabeth Powell Conrad, 1 Feb. 1841, ConFP, VHS.

37. Robert Conrad to Elizabeth Powell Conrad, 28 Jan. 1844, ConFP, VHS.

38. Robert Conrad to Elizabeth Powell Conrad, 14 March 1831, ConFP, VHS.

39. Catherine Powell to Elizabeth Powell Conrad, March, April 1831, ConFP, VHS.

40. For further discussion, see Clinton, *Plantation Mistress*, 20–29, 37–39, 68; Friedman, *Enclosed Garden*, 23–31; Fox-Genovese, *Within the Plantation Household*, 109–29.

41. Robert Conrad to Elizabeth Powell Conrad, 28 Jan. 1844, ConFP, VHS.

42. Robert Conrad to Elizabeth Powell Conrad, 12 April 1840, 1 Feb. 1841, ConFP, VHS.

43. For further discussion, see Smith, *Inside the Great House*, 159–64; and Wyatt-Brown, *Southern Honor*, 226–23, 254–59. Also of interest are proslavery advocate and Virginia scholar George Fitzhugh's ideas about the relationship of white women to their husbands. George Fitzhugh, "Sociology for the South," in Eric McKitrick, ed., *Slavery Defended: The Voices of the Old South* (Englewood Cliffs, N.J.: Prentice-Hall, 1963), 37–38.

44. Robert Conrad to Elizabeth Powell Conrad, 18 Aug. 1832, ConFP, VHS.

45. Loudoun Legislative Petition, 5 Jan. 1850, VSL.

46. Louis Morton, *Robert Carter of Nomini Hall: A Virginia Tobacco Planter of the Eighteenth Century* (Charlottesville: Univ. Press of Virginia, 1964), 229n.73; Land Book of Robert Carter, 1802, n.p., Carter Family Papers (hereafter referred to as CarFP), VHS.

47. Lebsock, *Free Women of Petersburg*, 54–86. Also see Marylynn Salmon, "Women and Property in South Carolina: The Evidence from Marriage Settlements, 1730 to 1830," *William and Mary Quarterly*, 3rd ser., 39, no. 3 (Oct. 1982): 655–85; and Carol Elizabeth Jenson, "The Equity Jurisdiction and Married Women's Property in Antebellum America: A Revisionist View," *International Journal of Women's Studies* 2, no. 2 (March-April 1979): 144–54; and especially Bertram Wyatt-Brown's general discussion of married women's property in the antebellum South in *Southern Honor*, 254–71.

48. George Carter to Sophia Carter, 26 June 1818, George Carter Letter Book (hereafter referred to as CarLB), VHS. Also see M. P. Burks, *Notes on the Property Rights of Married Women in Virginia* (Lynchburg: J. P. Bell, 1894).

49. George Carter to Sophia Carter, 26 June 1818, CarLB, VHS.

50. Susannah Sanbower Shover to Joseph Waltman, 19 Feb. 1829, ShovFP, VSL; Lebsock, *Free Women of Petersburg*, 54–86; George Carter to Sophia Carter, 26 June 1818; George Carter to Julia Carter Berkeley, 30 Aug. 1818, CarLB, VHS.

51. U.S. Department of Commerce, Bureau of the Census, Manuscript Federal Census, Loudoun County, Virginia (hereafter referred to as FedCenLC), 1810, 1830, 1850 Free and Slave Schedules, Reels 69, 193, 957, 989.

52. LouLP, 5 Jan. 1850, VSL; Susannah Sanbower Shover to Joseph Waltman, 19 Feb. 1829, ShovFP, VSL; Janney and Janney, eds., *John Janney's Virginia*, 62; William Stabler to Samuel Janney, 7 Sept. 1842; Samuel Janney to Elizabeth Janney, 2 May 1836,

30 May 1839; Samuel Janney to Phineas Janney, 17 Sept. 1842, Janney Family Papers (hereafter referred to as JanFP), VSL.

53. Sarah Powell Harrison to Elizabeth Powell Conrad, 9 Nov. 1843, HarFP, VHS.

54. Elizabeth Davisson to John Poulton, 19 Feb. 1857, in Poulton, ed., *Loudoun Love Story*, 30.

55. Robert Conrad to Elizabeth Powell Conrad, 16 Feb. 1832, July 1834, 13 March 1836, ConFP; Mary Lee Fitzhugh Custis to Mary Ann Randolph Custis Lee, 6 Oct. 1831, George Bolling Lee Papers; Marietta Powell to Sarah Harrison, 1844, HarFP, VHS.

56. Sarah Powell Harrison to Elizabeth Powell Conrad, 9 Nov. 1843, HarFP, VHS.

57. Robert Conrad to Elizabeth Conrad, 17 Feb., 4 March 1830, ConFP; Thomas Jefferson Harrison to Burr W. Harrison, 26 July 1827, HarFP, VHS.

58. Thomas Jefferson Harrison to Burr W. Harrison, 26 July 1827, HarFP; Matthew Harrison to Burr Harrison, 4 April 1826, HarFP, VHS.

59. Robert Conrad to Elizabeth Powell Conrad, 13 May 1835, Jan. 30, 1842, ConFP, VHS.

60. Robert Conrad to Elizabeth Powell Conrad, 30 Jan. 1842, ConFP, VHS.

61. Robert Conrad to Elizabeth Powell Conrad, 27 June 1839, ConFP, VHS.

62. Burr Powell to Catherine Powell, 9 Feb. 1814. Also see Burr Powell to Catherine Powell, 14 Jan., 7 Dec. 1814, PowFP, VHS.

63. Powell Family Genealogical Notes, n.p., Gray Family Papers, VHS. Also see "Letters of Leven Powell" in William E. Dodd, ed., *The John P. Branch Historical Papers of Randolph-Macon College,* vol. 1, nos. 1–3 (June 1901, June 1902, June 1903): 22–63, 111–38, 217–56.

64. Leven Powell to Sarah Powell, 5 Dec. 1775, PowFP, VHS.

65. Burr Powell to Catherine Powell, 7 Dec. 1814, PowFP; Robert Conrad to Elizabeth Conrad, 26 Feb. 1830, ConFP, VHS.

66. See, for example, the divorce petitions of Isaac Fouch and William Yonson, LouLP, 28 Dec. 1808, 31 Jan. 1848, VSL; Brenda E. Stevenson, "Black Family Structure in Colonial and Antebellum Virginia. A Revisionist Perspective," in *The Decline in Marriage Among African-Americans: Causes, Consequences and Policy Implications*, M. Belinda Tucker and Claudia Kernan Mitchell, eds. (New York: Sage, 1995), 27–53.

67. See, for example, Philip Nelson to Thomas Clagett, 16, 18 Nov., 5, 31 Dec. 1839, 14 Jan., 15 Feb., 26 March, 28 April, 26 July 1841, Clagett Family Papers, Manuscript Division, Alderman Library, Univ. of Virginia, Charlottesville (hereafter referred to as UVA).

68. Information on the property and business interests of Simon Shover are found in Miscellaneous Receipts and Accounts of Shover Family, 1818–40, and the Inventory of Estate of Simon Shover, 1819, ShovFP, VSL. Susannah Shover's maiden name of Sanbower is listed among those of the first German families to migrate to Loudoun. Weatherly, *Lovettsville,* 9.

69. Miscellaneous Receipts and Accounts of Shover Family, ShovFP, VSL. Robert Braden was a member of the Virginia General Assembly and one of the most prominent businessmen and politicians in Loudoun during the 1810s and 1820s. Braden helped to establish the first bank in Loudoun. See the correspondence of George Carter

to Robert Braden, 2 Jan. 1818, 26 Jan. 1819, CarFP, VHS. Also see Helen Hirst Marsh, "The Loudoun Company," *Bulletin of the Loudoun County Historical Society* 3 (1962): 43–44; and Poland, Jr., *From Frontier to Suburbia*, 113n70.

70. Miscellaneous Receipts and Accounts of Shover Family, ShovFP, VSL.

71. Ibid.

72. See, for example, the description of various businesses and artisan shops in antebellum Lovettsville found in Weatherly, *Lovettsville*, 20–21.

73. Miscellaneous Receipts and Accounts of Shover Family, ShovFP, VSL.

74. Ibid.

75. Susannah Sanbower Shover to Joseph Waltman, 19 Feb. 1829, ShovFP, VSL.

76. Miscellaneous Receipts and Accounts of Shover Family, ShovFP, VSL.

77. William Stabler to Samuel Janney, 7 Sept. 1842; Samuel Janney to Elizabeth Janney, 2 May 1836, 30 May 1839; Samuel Janney to Phineas Janney, 17 Sept. 1842, JanFP, VSL. Also see Samuel Janney, *Memoir of Samuel M. Janney, Late of Lincoln County, Virginia: A Minister in the Religious Society of Friends* (Philadelphia: Friends Book Association, 1881).

78. Janney, *Memoir of Samuel M. Janney*.

79. Samuel Janney to Phineas Janney, 17 Sept. 1842; Samuel Janney to Elizabeth Janney, 27 Oct. 1834, JanFP, VSL, 35.

80. LouLP, 4 Dec. 1817; 4 Dec. 1844, VSL; Joseph White to Sarah White, 11 Dec. 1810, in Eva E. Kaufmann, ed., *". . . our Loves to you all. . . :" White Family Letters, 1804–1830* (Gaithersburg, Md.: by the author, 1986), 70.

81. Joseph Franklin Caldwell, "Autobiography of Joseph F. Caldwell," 2, Caldwell Family Papers, VHS.

82. Ibid., 2–6.

83. E. P. Buck to William Buck, 14 Oct. 1848, Buck Family Papers, UVA; Caldwell, "Autobiography," 2–6, Caldwell Family Papers, VHS.

84. LouLP, 28 Dec. 1802, VSL; Hortensia Hay Rogers to Mary Randolph Custis Lee, n.d., George Bolling Lee Papers, VHS; Rose Davisson Poulton to John Poulton, 9 July 1862, in Poulton, ed., *Loudoun Love Story*, 143.

85. Elizabeth Janney to Samuel Janney, 5 Nov. 1825, Samuel Janney to Elizabeth Janney, 4 Oct. 1825, JanFP, VSL.

86. Robert Conrad to Elizabeth Conrad, 1 Aug. 1835, 4 Feb. 1844, ConFP, VHS.

87. Robert Conrad to Elizabeth Conrad, 15 Dec. 1851, ConFP, VHS.

CHAPTER 4. PARENTING

1. Regarding children in eighteenth-century and antebellum Virginia, see Jan Lewis, *The Pursuit of Happiness: Family and Values in Jefferson's Virginia* (Cambridge: Cambridge Univ. Press, 1983), and her article "Domestic Tranquillity and the Management of Emotion Among the Gentry of Pre-Revolutionary Virginia," *William and Mary Quarterly* 39 (Jan. 1982): 135–49; Bertram Wyatt-Brown, *Southern Honor: Ethics and Behavior in the Old South* (New York: Oxford Univ. Press, 1982), 117–74; Daniel Blake Smith, *Inside the Great House: Planter Family Life in Eighteenth Century Chesapeake Society* (Ithaca, N.Y.: Cornell Univ. Press, 1980); Sally McMillen, "Women's Sacred Occu-

pation: Pregnancy, Childbirth, and Early Infant Rearing in the Antebellum South" (Ph.D. dissertation, Duke University, 1985).

2. Daniel Smith, for one, convincingly traces the development of the privatized, nuclear family among the Virginia gentry as the antebellum era unfolded, helping to establish the intellectual trend perhaps best articulated by Carl Degler in *At Odds: Women and Family in America from the Revolution to the Present* (New York: Oxford Univ. Press, 1980).

Jan Lewis concluded that during the pre-Revolutionary era, there existed parental/child contracts of reciprocal duty. This study asserts that such "contracts" remained operative throughout the antebellum era.

3. John Robinson, "Of Children and Their Education (1628)," in Philip J. Greven, Jr., ed., *Child-Rearing Concepts, 1728–1861: Historical Sources* (Itasca, Ill.: F. E. Peacock, 1973), 11–12, 13.

4. For a detailed discussion of society's perception of children and adolescents in the nineteenth century, see Joseph Kett, *Rites of Passage: Adolescence in America, 1790 to the Present* (New York: Basic Books, 1977), 11–143; and "Children, Childhood, and Change in America, 1820–1920," in *Century of Childhood, 1820–1920* (Rochester: Margaret Woodbury Strong Museum, 1984), 32; Philip Aries, *Centuries of Childhood: A Social History of Family Life* (New York: Alfred A. Knopf, 1962), passim; and Greven ed., *Child-Rearing Concepts, 1728–1861*, passim. Quote from Horace Bushnell, *Christian Nature* (1847; New York: Charles Scribner, 1867), 9.

5. Literate, well-to-do Loudoun mothers often subscribed to this kind of specialty journal. Sarah Powell Harrison to Elizabeth Powell Conrad, 13 April 1836, Conrad Family Papers (hereafter referred as ConFP), Virginia Historical Society, Richmond, (hereafter referred to as VHS).

6. For a brief descriptive analysis of antebellum childrearing literature, see Robert Sunley, "Early Nineteenth Century Literature on Child Rearing," in *Childhood in Contemporary Cultures*, Margaret Mead and Martha Wolfenstein, eds. (Chicago: Univ. of Chicago Press, 1955), 151–67; and Catherine Scholten, *Childbearing in American Society*, 1650–1850. (New York: New York University Press, 1985), 67–97. Also see "A Mother's Journal," *Ladies Magazine and Literary Gazette* 8, no. 8 (Aug. 1835): 441–49; "To a Young Mother, *American Ladies Magazine* 9, no. 7 (July 1837): 390; and "Hints to a Young Mother," *Ladies Magazine and Literary Gazette* 7, no. 2 (Feb. 1834): 52, Virginia State Library (hereafter referred to as VSL).

7. John S. C. Abbott, *The Mother at Home; or the Principles of Maternal Duty Familiarly Illustrated* (New York: American Tract Society, 1833), 5; "A Plea for Children," *Ladies Magazine and Literary Gazette* 8, no. 2 (Feb. 1835): 94, VSL; Kett, *Rites of Passage*, 79.

8. During the colonial era, it was not unusual for fathers to mete out punishments, give moral instruction, and make decisions about their youngsters' education, recreational activities, career, and marital choices. Some even purchased children's clothes, chose their libraries, and led the family in daily prayers and religious instruction. "Sunley, "Early Nineteenth Century Literature on Child Rearing," 150–67; Julia Spruill, *Women's Life and Work in the Southern Colonies*, (1938; New York: W.W. Norton, 1972), 44. For a discussion of the transition in the role of the mother from the

colonial to the antebellum era, also see Ruth H. Bloch, "American Feminine Ideals in Transition: The Rise of the Moral Mother, 1785–1815," *Feminist Studies* 4, no. 2 (June 1978): 100–126; "A Mother's Journal," *Ladies Magazine and Literary Gazette* 8, no. 8 (Aug. 1835): 441–49, VSL. A typical discussion on the parental role of child discipline is found in: "Government of Young Children," reprinted from Phelps's *Progressive Education* in *American Ladies Magazine* 8, no. 6 (June 1836): 335–59, VSL. Also see John Demos, *Past, Present, and Personal: The Family and the Life Course in American History* (New York: Oxford Univ. Press, 1986), 43–60.

9. Spruill, *Women's Life and Work in the Southern Colonies*, 44; "A Father's Influence in the Domestic Circle," *Mother's Magazine* 3, no. 8 (Aug. 1835): 116–19; "The Father's Position and Influence," *Mother's Magazine* 2, no. 12 (Dec. 1853): 346–47.

10. See, for example, "Woman's Sphere," *American Ladies Magazine* 8, no. 5 (May 1836): 262, VSL.

11. "Letters from a Mother," *Ladies Magazine and Literary Gazette* 1, no. 4 (April 1828): 167; Female Education," *Ladies Magazine and Literary Gazette* 1, no. 1 (Jan. 1828): 24, VSL.

12. Some specialists suggested using clean, pious nurses who resembled the mother both in appearance and nature, but only if it was impossible for the natural mother to fulfill this duty. Sally McMillen, "Mother's Sacred Duty: Breast Feeding Patterns Among Middle- and Upper-Class Women in the Antebellum South," *Journal of Southern History* 51, no. 3 (Aug. 1985): 333–56; Scholten, *Childbearing in American Society*, 61–63.

13. The conclusions of historians regarding breast feeding trends among southern women remain at odds. See Spruill, *Women's Life and Work*, 555–57; Catherine Clinton, *The Plantation Mistress: Women's World in the Old South* (New York: Pantheon, 1982), 155–56; McMillen, "Mother's Sacred Duty, 333–56; Elizabeth Fox-Genovese, *Within the Plantation Household: Black and White Women of the Old South* (Chapel Hill: Univ. of North Carolina Press, 1988), 136–37, 147–48; Charles Perdue, Thomas Barden, and Robert K. Phillips, eds., *Weevils in the Wheat: Interviews with Virginia Ex-Slaves* (Charlottesville: Univ. Press of Virginia, 1976), 288. Quote from Dorothy Sterling, ed., *We Are Your Sisters: Black Women in the Nineteenth Century* (New York: W. W. Norton, 1984), 45.

There is a clear indication that increasingly more white women of the upper class were beginning to nurse their own children during the antebellum era. The distinction must be made, however, between suckling and actual care of the child. Slaveholding women did not hesitate to employ slaves to care for their older children and white women to care for the younger ones. On weaning, see Sunley, "Early American Literature on Child Rearing," 153–54.

14. June Guild, ed., *Black Laws of Virginia: A Summary of the Legislative Acts of Virginia Concerning Negroes from Earliest Times to the Present* (Richmond: Whittet and Shepperson, 1936; New York: Negro Universities Press, 1969), 23–24, 27, 30; Loudoun County Order Book, vols. 1–2, 1807–9; Loudoun County Records of the Overseers of the Poor, VSL.

15. Leesburg *Washingtonian*, 25 July 1846, VSL.

16. Robert Conrad to Catherine Powell, 28 Feb., 1831; Robert Conrad to Powell Conrad, 19 March 1852, ConFP, VHS.

17. Nan Netherton et al., *Fairfax County, Virginia: A History* (Fairfax: Fairfax County Board of Supervisors, 1978), 241.

18. Perdue et al., eds., *Weevils*, 120–21.

19. Klaus Wust writes, for example, asserts that German women worked alongside men folk as mowers and reapers. Klaus Wust, *The Virginia Germans* (Charlottesville: Univ. Press of Virginia, 1969), 69–70. Elizabeth Powell Conrad to Catherine Conrad, 1855, ConFP, VHS.

20. Harrison Williams, *Legends of Loudoun: An Account of the History and Homes of a Border County of Virginia's Northern Neck* (Richmond: Garrett and Massie, 1938), 173.

21. Burr Powell to Robert Conrad, 13 Dec. 1830, ConFP, VHS.

22. Burr Powell to Elizabeth Powell Conrad, 16 April 1830, ConFP, VHS.

23. Biographical information on Burr Powell and the local Powell clan located in Powell Family Genealogical Notes, Gray Family Papers, VHS; and "A Brief History of the First Harrisons of Virginia: Descendants of Cuthbert Harrison, Esquire of Ancaster, England from A.D. 1600 to A.D. 1915," pamphlet, n.d., n.p., Harrison Family Papers (hereafter referred to as HarFP), VHS; and "Notes on Brooke-Powell Family," *Virginia Magazine of History and Biography* 15, no. 2 (June 1908): 201–3.

24. Marietta Powell to Sarah Powell Harrison, ? 1840, HarFP; Burr Powell to Elizabeth Powell Conrad, 16 April 1830, ConFP, VHS.

25. Robert Conrad to Catherine Conrad, 6 May 1852, ConFP, VHS.

26. Samuel Janney to Elizabeth Janney, n.d. [1830s], Janney Family Papers (hereafter referred to as JanFP), VSL; Nancy Conrad to Elizabeth Powell Conrad, 6 June 1838, ConFP, VHS.

27. Joseph and Elizabeth White to Sarah White, 1 Nov., 1806, in *". . . Our Loves to You All . . . ": White Family Letters, 1804–1830* Eva Kaufmann, ed. (Gaithersburg, Md.: by the editor, 1986), 1, 46.

28. Donald Sweig, for example, claims that the child mortality rates for white children under the age of 16 was 61% in Loudoun and its vicinity. Poor children, a growing minority, greatly influenced this statistic. Donald Sweig, "Northern Virginia Slavery: A Statistical and Demographic Investigation," (Ph.D. dissertation, College of William and Mary, 1982), 107; Levi White to Joseph and Samuel White, 8 Dec. 1804, in ibid., 1.

29. The nearby city of Alexandria provided through its dispensary medical attention for poor families, especially women and children. Some local officials also provided for the cleaning of town gutters, alleys, and privies and the dispensing of lime to residents. Netherton et al., *Fairfax County, Virginia*, 241–42. Todd Savitt asserts that the leading known causes for deaths among whites of all ages, ethnicities and socioeconomic status for 1853–60 were tuberculosis, diarrhea, respiratory disease, nervous system diseases, digestive system diseases, typhoid, scarlet fever, diphtheria, old age, dropsy, accidents, maternity (2.2%), whooping cough, heart diseases, "neoplasms," measles, intemperance, teething, worms, and cholera. Todd L. Savitt, *Medicine and Slavery: The Diseases and Health Care of Blacks in Antebellum Virginia* (Urbana: Univ. of Illinois Press, 1978), 136–46.

30. Robert Conrad to Powell Conrad, 14 Feb. 1852, ConFP, VHS.

31. Robert Conrad to Holmes Conrad, 9 May 1857, ConFP, VHS.

32. Robert Conrad to Powell Conrad, 28 Sept. 1851; Robert Conrad to Robert Conrad II, 17 Oct. 1855, ConFP, VHS.

33. Robert Conrad to Powell Conrad 30 Sept. 1851; Robert Conrad to Holmes Conrad, 9 May 1857, ConFP, VHS. Regarding parent's emphasis on adolescent physical and mental health, see Robert Conrad to Robert Conrad II, Dec. 1855; Elizabeth Conrad to Robert Conrad II, 29 Dec. 1857; Robert Conrad to Elizabeth Conrad, 11 April 1848; Robert Conrad to Powell Conrad, Sept. 1851, 31 Oct. 1851, ConFP; Burr Harrison to H. M. Cotton, Sept. 1852; Burr Harrison to Edward Harrison, 4 Dec. 1847, HarFP, VHS. Regarding parent's emphasis on their children's dental health and adolescent acne, see: Burr Harrison to Catherine Cornelia Harrison, 28 Feb. 1855; William Harrison to Burr Harrison, 19 Dec. 1853, HarFP; Robert Conrad to Powell Conrad, 1 Dec. 1851, ConFP, VHS.

34. Louise Harrison Love to Sally Powell Harrison, 26 Jan. 1825, HarFP, VHS. Also see Elizabeth Powell Conrad to Catherine Powell, 20 March 1832; Nancy Conrad to Elizabeth Powell Conrad, 24 Jan. 1835, ConFP, VHS.

35. Elizabeth Powell Conrad to Sarah Powell Harrison, 30 Aug. 1846, HarFP, VHS.

36. Thomas Peake to Sarah M. Peake, 1 May 1820, Peake Family Papers; Elizabeth Powell Conrad to Catherine Powell, 20 March 1832; Nancy Conrad to Elizabeth Powell Conrad, 24 Jan. 1835, ConFP, VHS.

37. Robert Conrad to Rebecca Conrad, 18 July 1831; Robert Conrad to Elizabeth Conrad, 31 Oct. 1831, 5 Sept. 1831, 23 April 1837, 28 Aug. 1838, 30 Nov., 1840, ConFP, VHS.

38. William Ellzey to Burr Harrison, 4 Jan. 1828, HarFP, VHS.

39. Charles Poland, Jr., *From Frontier to Suburbia* (Maceline, Mo.: Walsworth Publishing, 1976), 24; Loudoun Legislative Petition (hereafter referred to as LouLP), 4 Dec. 1817; Samuel Janney to Elizabeth Janney, 10 Nov. 1833, JanFP, VSL; Joseph White to Sarah White, 11 Dec. 1810, in Kaufmann, ed., *". . . our Loves to You all. . . ,"* 70.

40. Samuel Janney to Elizabeth Janney, 10 Nov. 1833, JanFP, VSL; Werner Janney and Asa Moore Janney, eds., *John Jay Janney's Virginia: An American Farm Lad's Life in the Early 19th Century* (McLean, Va.: EPM Publications, 1978), 91.

41. Janney and Janney, eds., *John Janney's Virginia*, 93.

42. Sunley, "Early American Literature on Child Rearing," 155; Alfred Donne, *Mothers and Infants, Nurses and Nursing* (Boston: Phillips, Sampson, 1859), 170; Perdue et al., eds., *Weevils*, 318.

43. Janney and Janney, eds., *John Janney's Virginia*, 155.

44. Sunley, "Early American Literature on Child Rearing," 155; Donne, *Mothers and Infants*, 154; Andrew Combe, *Treatise on the Physical and Medical Treatment of Children* (Philadelphia: Carey and Hart, 1826), 43.

45. Samuel M. Janney, *Memoirs of Samuel M. Janney, Late of Lincoln, Loudoun County, Va.*, 3rd ed. (Philadelphia: Friends' Book Association, 1882), 4. Regarding Quaker childrearing, see Walter Homan, *Children and Quakerism: A Study of the Place of Children in the Theory and Practice of Friends, Commonly Called Quakers* (Berkeley: Gillick Press, 1939). Regarding early child governance, see Degler, *At Odds*, 88–89; Sunley, "Early American Literature on Child Rearing," 162–63.

46. Janney, *Memoirs of Samuel M. Janney*, 4; Sunley, "Early American Literature on Child Rearing," 162–63; Abbott, *Mother at Home*, 29, 38–39.

47. Perdue et al., eds. *Weevils*, 48–49; Janney and Janney, eds., *John Janney's Virginia*, 52–53. Also see Kett, *Rites of Passage*, 46–47.

48. Samuel Janney, "Memoir of Julia Rebecca Headley," n.d., 1–2, JanFP, VSL.

49. Janney, *Memoirs of Samuel M. Janney*, 4.

50. Sarah Harrison to Elizabeth Conrad, 9 May 1834, ConFP, VHS.

51. See, for example, Janney, "Memoir of Julia Headley," JanFP, VHS.

52. Joseph Nichols, *Legends of Loudoun Valley: True Stories from the Lives and Times of the People of Loudoun County, Virginia*, (Leesburg, Va. Potomac Press, 1961), 59–61; LouLP, 4 Dec. 1844, 4 Dec. 1817, VSL.

53. Henrietta G. Dangerfield, "Our Mammy," *Southern Workman* 30 (1901): 599–600; and Kate B. Conrad, "Uncle Stephen," *Southern Workman* 30 (1901): 153–56. Loudouner Mason Ellzey also recorded a similar relationship between an elderly slave man and his younger sister. "The Cause Lost and the Land We Love," 19–20, Ellzey Family Papers, VHS.

54. Dangerfield, "Our Mammy," 599–600.

55. Perdue et al., eds., *Weevils*, 190–91.

56. Ibid., 47–48.

57. Ibid., 85.

58. For a discussion of nineteenth-century adolescence in the United States see: Kett, *Rites of Passage*, passim, but esp. 11–16, 134–37. Kett distinguishes some general qualities that society associated with adolescence, especially, "semi-dependency." For farm youth, this "semi-dependency" meant their ability to contribute to their family's support through farm or paid labor. Kett also notes that by the late antebellum era, society also was beginning to view adolescence as a "dangerous" stage in a youth's development because "desires before tame now become almost resistless" and male youth was overwhelmed with new emotions, feelings and goals. Experts also argued that girls too felt change, "producing a maiden coyness, a modest bashfulness, a sweet smile, a sentimental reverie," etc.

59. Robert Conrad to Powell Conrad, 18 March 1853, ConFP, VHS; *Washingtonian*, 48, no.6, 6 Aug. 1852, VSL.

60. It is not certain exactly when Loudoun area parents believed that childhood ended and adolescence began. As Kett asserts, farm and artisan youth began to take on some of the duties and liberties of adolescence once they began to work—anywhere between ages eight and eleven. Males from wealthy families had less pressure to work, but they still took on the duty of doing well in school. Females, regardless of class, remained overwhelmingly dependent (and, in this sense, like children). Poor girls and orphans who worked, however, could experience the beginning of a kind of "adolescence" as early as age ten. Joseph Kett, "Adolescence and Youth in Nineteenth-Century America," *Journal of Interdisciplinary History* 2 (Autumn 1971): 284–298, especially 293–296.

61. John Brown's infamous raid on the federal arsenal at Harpers Ferry, Virginia, on 16 Oct. 1859, took place just north of the Loudoun County northern border. He was hanged on 2 Dec. 1859.

62. Mason Ellzey's second cousin George Turner, a Loudoun resident, was the first person killed during the raid on Harpers Ferry. Mason and his friends rallied more than 300 Virginia students studying at various schools in Philadelphia, chartered a train and traveled to Richmond, some stopping in Baltimore. Mason Ellzey, "The Cause We Lost and the Land We Love," 23–26, Mason Family Papers, VHS.

63. *The Idea of a Southern Nation, or Idea of Southern Nationalism*, as quoted in Clement Eaton, *The Growth of Southern Civilization, 1790–1860* (New York: Atheneum, 1969), 204.

64. Eric L. McKitrick, ed., *Slavery Defended: The Views of the Old South* (Englewood Cliffs, N.J.: Prentice-Hall, 1963), 20–21; *Idea of a Southern Nation*, as recounted in Eaton, *Growth of Southern Civilization*, 207–8.

65. Burr Harrison to Matthew Harrison, 30 Jan. 1854, HarFP, VHS.

66. Robert Conrad to Catherine Conrad, 14 July 1851, ConFP, VHS.

67. Ibid.; Kett, "Adolescence and Youth in Nineteenth-Century America," 287, 295–96.

68. Wade Hinshaw, ed., *Encyclopedia of American Quaker Genealogy*, vol. 6 (Ann Arbor: Edwards Bros., 1950), 609–724 passim; Also see Loudoun County Order Book, vols. 1–2, 1807–9; Loudoun County Records of the Overseers of the Poor, VSL; Leesburg *Washingtonian*, 25 July 1846, VSL; Hortensia Hay to Mary Randolph Custis Lee, 24 Aug. 1829, George Bolling Lee Papers, VHS; Nichols, *Legends of Loudoun Valley*, 7–8; Rose Davisson to John Poulton, 2 Oct. 1857, in Jane W. Poulton, ed., *Loudoun Love Story*, (Durham: By the author, 1988), 70.

69. Nichols, *Legends of Loudoun Valley*, 31–32.

70. Catherine Powell to Elizabeth Conrad, 20 Jan. 1830s?, ConFP; "Notes on Brooke-Powell Family," 201–3; Burr Harrison to Matthew Harrison, 1849?; "Brief History of the First Harrisons," n.p., HarFP, VHS.

71. Young ladies studying at these institutions had to attend church services regularly, follow strict rules, and had only limited contact with outsiders, even through correspondence. See, for example, Robert Conrad to Kate Conrad, 7 Sept. 1851, 15 Feb. 1853, ConFP, VHS.

72. For further discussion, see Kett, *Rites of Passage*, 2–4; Robinson, "Of Children and Their Education," 242–48;

73. Ellzey, "The Cause We Lost and the Land We Love," 3–8, Ellzey Papers; Robert Conrad to Elizabeth Conrad, 13 June 1855, ConFP; William Harrison to Burr Harrison, 9 Dec. 1853, HarFP, VHS.

74. Robert Conrad to Elizabeth Conrad, 13 June 1855. Also see Robert Conrad to Holmes Conrad, 5 Dec. 1854, ConFP, VHS.

75. Robert Conrad to Elizabeth Conrad, 13 June 1855, ConFP, VHS.

76. Burr Harrison's concept of an ideal home life is similar to that Jan Lewis describes as characteristic of eighteenth-century Virginia gentry. Robert Conrad's concept is closer to that which Daniel Blake Smith suggests for the eighteenth-century Virginia planter class. Conrad probably thought that his brother-in-law was a little old-fashioned, perhaps more like the men in their father-in-law's early nineteenth-century generation than the more urbane planter-professional father of the 1840s and 1850s. Burr Harrison to Matthew Harrison, 4 Dec. 1849?, 5 Feb. 1849; Burr Harrison to H.M.

Cotton, 6 Sept. 1852, HarFP, VHS; Smith, *Inside the Great House*, passim; Lewis, "Domestic Tranquillity and the Management, 134–49 passim.

77. Francis Powell, needless to say, soon stopped complaining. He graduated from the College of William and Mary and, as his father advised, went on to medical school in Philadelphia. Burr Powell to Elizabeth Conrad, 13 April 1830, ConFP, VHS.

78. Robert Carter had decided not to divide his property according to the gender and age of his offspring as many others did, but rather to do so according to those "'who bid fairest to be useful to mankind.'" Louis Morton, *Robert Carter of Nomini Hall: A Virginia Planter of the Eighteenth Century* (Charlottesville: Univ. Press of Va., 1964), 210–30, 270–73.

79. William P. Tebbs to George Carter, 7 Nov. 1803, Carter Family Papers (hereafter referred to as CarFP); George Carter to Thomas Hope, 18 Sept. 1807; George Carter to John Scott, 25 Jan. 1810, George Carter Letterbook (hereafter referred to as GCLB), VHS.

80. George Carter to Thomas Hope, 18 Sept. 1807; George Carter to John Scott, 25 Jan. 1810; George Carter to John Scott, 15, 25 Jan. 1812, 29 Oct. 1810; George Carter to Thomas Hope, 18 Sept. 1809; George Carter to Robert Maund, 11 Sept. 1810; George Carter to John Scott, 29 Oct. 1810, GCLB, VHS.

81. Regarding the relationships of Robert Carter, George Carter's father, with his children, see Morton, *Robert Carter of Nomini*, 220–29, 270–72.

82. W. E. Harrison to Burr W. Harrison, 9 Dec. 1853, 2 Dec. 1854, HarFP, VHS; Eugene M. Scheel, *The History of Middleburg and Vicinity* (Warrenton, Va.: Piedmont Press, 1987), 39; Kett, *Rites of Passage*, 75–78.

83. Elizabeth Conrad to Holmes Conrad, 30 Jan., 11 Nov. 1858; Robert Conrad II to Elizabeth Conrad, 13 April 1857, ConFP, VHS.

84. Janney, *Memoir of Samuel M. Janney*, 4; Nichols, *Legends of Loudoun Valley*, 30–31; Kett, *Rites of Passage*, 76–78.

85. Hortensia H. Rogers to Mary R. Custis, 24 Aug. 1829, George Bolling Lee Papers, VHS; Janney, "Memoir of Julia Rebecca Headley," n.d., 2–3, JanFP, VSL.

86. Levi White to Richard White, 11 Aug. 1830; Kaufmann, ed., ". . . *our Loves to You All* . . . ," 90–91.

87. George E. Harrison to Ann Harrison (Byrd), 10 Aug. 1820, Byrd Family Papers; Robert Conrad to Dr. Daniel Conrad, 13 Aug. 1855, ConFP, VHS.

88. William E. Harrison to Ann Maria Harrison, 30 Jan. 1846; Burr Harrison to Ann Maria Harrison, 30 Jan. 1846, HarFP, VHS.

89. Janney, *Memoirs of Samuel M. Janney*, 6. Also see Morton, *Robert Carter of Nomini Hall*, 221–22, 226–27; and Harrison, *Legends of Loudoun*, 76.

90. Robert Conrad to Powell Conrad, 4 Dec. 1851. Also see Robert Conrad to Powell Conrad, 3 Oct. 1851, 14 Feb. 1852, ConFP, VHS.

91. In 1850, there were approximately 2000 such institutions in the region with more than 3200 teachers and 70,000 students. There also were growing numbers of adolescents and young adults who attended college. These "colleges" were in large measure comparable to most of the other institutions of higher learning found throughout the country at the time. Many scholars considered the Univ. of Virginia, for example, as "one of the most attractive and enlightened colleges in the nation." In 1856, 558 students

were enrolled at Thomas Jefferson's Univ. compared with Harvard's student population of 361. Eaton, *Growth of Southern Civilization,* 119. Regarding the founding of Virginia's colleges, see Emily J. Salmon, *A Hornbook of Virginia History*, 3rd ed. (Richmond: Virginia State Library, 1983), 194.

92. The cost of tuition, room and board, and laundry service was $200 for a ten-month session running from October through Aug. LouLP, 4 Dec. 1855, VSL; Poland, *From Frontier to Suburbia*, 93–94.

93. LouLP, 5 Dec. 1799, 5 April 1852, VSL; *Washingtonian*, 16 May 1851, VSL.

94. The annual cost of these academies varied substantially over the years. Middleburg Academy cost between $20 and $30 in 1803, exclusive of board. Boarding fees raised the cost to $100, but parents still had to provide their children's beds. The Loudoun Agricultural Institute was $200 in the 1850s. Poland, *From Frontier to Suburbia*, 93–94; LouLP 4 Dec. 1855, VSL; Scheel, *History of Middleburg*, 39–40.

95. In the English school, students learned the basics of the English language, writing, and arithmetic. Those enrolled in the mathematical program took English, writing, arithmetic "in all its various branches," bookkeeping, and other mathematics. The grammar school curriculum included English grammar, Latin, Greek, French, and geography. Scheel, *History of Middleburg*, 31–40.

96. There were other institutions of higher learning for males in the state, many affiliated with specific denominations: Washington College (Presbyterian), Randolph-Macon College (Methodist), Emory and Henry College (Methodist), Richmond College (Baptist), and Hampden-Sydney College (Presbyterian). Salmon, ed., *Hornbook of Virginia History*, 198–205; Horace Mann to Samuel Janney, 22 Aug. 1846; Samuel Janney to Elizabeth Janney, 7 Nov. 1845, JanFP, VSL; Mason Graham Ellzey, "The Cause We Lost and the Land We Love," 9, Ellzey Papers, VHS; Wust, *Virginia Germans*, 163–64.

97. Poland, *From Frontier to Suburbia*, 154.

98. Miss Mercer first opened "Belmont" in 1836; Janney's began operating "Springdale" in 1839. Mercer conducted a smaller female academy during the late 1820s and early 1830s before moving to more luxurious accommodations. Teaching was only one of Samuel Janney's vocations. A dedicated Friend, Janney was a Quaker minister and a leading supporter of public education, abolition, and other reform issues. Mercer usually enrolled about 30 girls; Janney no more than 20. "List 1849 of Students in Miss Margaret Mercer's Ethics Class at 'Belmont,' Loudoun, Co., Va.," Belmont School Papers, VHS; *Washingtonian*, 12 Nov. 1836, VSL; Poland, *From Frontier to Suburbia*, 72, 154; Margaret Mercer, *Popular Lectures on Ethics, or Moral Obligations for the Use of Schools* (Petersburg: Ruffin Brothers), 1841; Scheel, *History of Middleburg*, 40.

99. Carter offered English, writing, math, painting, and drawing for an annual fee, along with room (but not bed) for $100. Needlework classes were additional. Scheel, *History of Middleburg* 40.

100. Robert Conrad to Powell Conrad, 8 July 1851, ConFP; Elizabeth Conrad to Elizabeth Harrison, 12 Jan. 1853, HarFP, VHS.

101. Robert Conrad to Catherine Conrad, n.d., 1851; Elizabeth Conrad to Robert Conrad II, n.d., 1852, ConFP, VHS; Mercer, *Popular Lectures on Ethics, or Moral Obligations*, passim.

102. Mary Lee Fitzhugh Custis to Mary Ann Randolph Custis Lee, n.d., Lee Family Papers, VHS.

103. *Washingtonian*, 12 Nov. 1836, VSL.

104. Burr Harrison handled a similar situation with the same exactness. Burr Powell to Sarah Powell, 27 May 1813, HarFP; Burr Powell to Betty Powell, 7 July 1823, ConFP; Burr Harrison to Ann Maria Harrison, 30 Jan. 1846, HarFP; Robert Conrad to Catherine Conrad, 6 Aug. 1851, ConFP, VHS.

105. Rebecca Headley to Elizabeth Janney, 4 July 1842?, JanFP, VSL; Etta Davisson to Rose Davisson, 17, and 18 March 1853, Elizabeth Davisson to John Poulton, 19 Feb. 1857, in Poulton, ed., *Loudoun Love Story*. Also see Robert Conrad to Kate Conrad, 6 Aug. 1851, ConFP, VHS.

106. Robert Conrad to Powell Conrad, 28 May, 18 Nov. 1851; Robert Conrad to Robert Conrad II, 11 Oct. 1856, ConFP, VHS.

107. John Scott Peyton to Cadet Richard H. Peyton, 15 March 1829, Peyton Family Papers; Powell Conrad to Elizabeth Powell Conrad, 21 Dec. 1851, ConFP, VHS.

108. William Harrison to Burr Harrison, 11 July 1852, HarFP, VHS.

109. Francis Powell to Sarah Harrison, 15 Dec. 1833, HarFP, VHS.

110. Robert Conrad to Powell Conrad, 11, 20 March 1850, 14 Feb. 1852, ConFP, VHS.

111. George Carter to Henry Maund, 29 Dec. 1814, 8 Dec. 1817, GCLB, VHS.

112. Burr Powell to Elizabeth Powell, 4 Oct. 1825, Powell Family Papers (hereafter referred to as PowFP); Robert and Elizabeth Conrad to Robert Conrad II, 30 July 1854, ConFP, VHS.

113. Robert Conrad to Powell Conrad, 3 Oct. 1851, ConFP, VHS.

114. Robert Conrad to Kate Conrad, 10 Oct. 1852, ConFP, VHS.

115. Burr Harrison to Matthew Harrison, 23 Jan. 1847, 7 Feb. 1849, 28 Dec. 1849?, HarFP; Elizabeth Powell to Catherine Powell, 18 May 1828; Elizabeth Powell to Catherine Powell, n.d., ConFP, VHS.

116. William Harrison to Ann Maria Harrison, 30 Jan. 1846, HarFP, VHS.

117. Robert Conrad to Elizabeth Conrad, 8 Aug. 1828, ConFP; Ellzey, "The Cause We Lost and the Land We Love," 3–8, Ellzey Papers; Robert Conrad to Robert Conrad II, 9 May 1857, ConFP, VHS; Janney, *Memoirs of Samuel M. Janney*, 25–63; *Washingtonian*, 9 Feb. 1839; Burr Harrison to Matthew Harrison, 15 Feb. 1849?, HarFP, VHS; Williams, *Legends of Loudoun*, 183; Scheel, *History of Middleburg*, 21.

118. Will of Jonathan Carter, Loudoun County Will Book 2–D, 1847–50, p. 346, VSL.

119. Janney and Janney, eds., *John Janney's Virginia*, 93, 115.

120. Regarding the lack of teachers and educational facilities in Loudoun, see Ann Sidwell, "Life of Hugh Sidwell," n.d., 1, Loudoun Genealogical File, Thomas Balch Library, Leesburg, Virginia (hereafter referred to as TBL); George Carter to Dr. D. Mosman, 18 Jan. 1818, GCLB, VHS; Samuel Janney to Elizabeth Janney, 2, 7 May 1848, JanFP, VSL; *Washingtonian*, 19 Feb. 1837, VSL.

121. Local Quaker schools did allow children of different faiths to attend and were not sex- or race-segregated. A cousin to John Janney, Samuel Janney, disagreed somewhat with John's evaluation of the Quaker schools, conceding that he "had made but little progress" in his studies by age 14. Janney and Janney, eds. *John Janney's Virginia*, 50–53; Janney, *Memoirs of Samuel M. Janney*, 7–8.

122. John H. Sanbower to Henry Shover, n.d. [c. 1830s]; Miscellaneous Receipts of George Shover, 1825–29, Shover Family Papers, VSL.

123. Most German parochial schools closed in the area between 1825 and 1835 as parents began to demand that their children learn English. Wust, *Virginia Germans*, 159–62.

124. Schyler also founded the Woodstock Academy in Leesburg in 1812. He was a prominent member of the Lovettsville community. Ibid.

125. The bill would have established an educational system inclusive of county elementary schools that would provide three years of a boy's education, district schools which would allow promising scholars some college preparation, and a state-supported college where the most talented male students would matriculate. Salmon, ed., *Hornbook of Virginia History*, 193–94.

126. Annual Report of the Board of School Commissioners for Indigent Children, Loudoun County, Virginia, 13 Oct. 1851, VSL.

127. The county superintendent complained in 1851, for example, that due to the commissioners' inability to pay instructors more, they were "often compelled to avail themselves of teachers not so competent as they would desire." Ibid.

128. The system not only excluded large numbers of children for whom there was no funding available, but also some of those who were qualified. The entire school budget for 1851 was $1388. At the end of the year, a surplus of $301 remained—enough money to pay the educational costs of 107 additional children. Ibid.

129. Although few people spoke out or acted against Loudoun's mediocre free school system, there were some outstanding exceptions. Samuel Janney, for one, publicly denounced the system. He believed that the largely proslavery Loudoun electorate feared that a more expansive free school system, such as that in New England, might result in the spread of abolitionism. Janney, *Memoirs of Samuel M. Janney,* 93–95; Annual Report of the Board of School Commissioners for Indigent Children, Loudoun County, Virginia, 13 Oct. 1851, VSL; Janney and Janney, eds., *John Janney's Virginia*, 49–58; Burr Powell to Elizabeth Powell, 7 July 1823, ConFP; Burr Powell to Sarah Powell, 27 May 1813, HarFP, VHS.

130. Indenture dated March 1826, Shover Family Papers, VSL; Will of Alex McIntyre, Loudoun County Will Book D, 21 Oct. 1788, p. 25, VSL; Memoir of Joseph F. Caldwell, Caldwell Papers, VHS.

131. George Carter to John W. Scott, 29 Oct. 1810, 23 Jan., 8 Oct. 1811, 15 Jan. 1812, GCLB; Robert Conrad to Powell Conrad, 13 Dec. 1850, ConFP, VHS; Sidwell, "Life of Hugh Sidwell," 2–3, TBL.

132. George Carter to John W. Scott, 29 Oct. 1810, 23 Jan., 8 Oct. 1811, 15 Jan. 1812, GCLB; Robert Conrad to Powell Conrad, 13 Dec. 1850, ConFP, VHS. Also see Burr Harrison to Matthew Harrison, 15 Feb. 4 March 1849, HarFP; Robert Conrad to Dan Conrad, 24 June 1858; Robert Conrad to Powell Conrad, 2 April 1853, 25 June 1857, 20 Nov. 1858, ConFP, VHS; Morton, *Robert Carter of Nomini*, 227; Will of Jonathan Carter, 8 Oct. 1849, Loudoun County Will Book 2–D, 346, VSL; and Ellzey, "The Cause We Lost," 8, 21, Ellzey Family Papers, VHS.

133. Janney maintained that shooting matches were very popular throughout the area, but condemned in many Quaker neighborhoods. So too were gambling and horse racing. Janney and Janney, eds., *John Janney's Virginia*, 87–90.

134. Ibid., 89.

135. "Virginia's Hunt Country: Loudoun County" (Leesburg: Loudoun County Tourism Advisory Committee and the Office of Tourism, 1988), n.p., Loudoun County Museum, Leesburg; Robert Conrad to Kate Conrad, 4 Oct. 1851, ConFP, VHS.

136. Robert Conrad to Kate Conrad, 22 Sept., 4 Oct. 1851, ConFP, VHS.

137. Years after a man had grown old, for example, family and friends often reminisced about his skill as a hunter, with and without a gun. Robert Conrad to Kate Conrad, 4 Oct., 22 Sept. 1851, ConFP, VHS; Robert F. Bartlett, "Historical Sketch of the *Nickols-Thomas Family* in Ohio with Partial Ancestry, and Collateral Relatives in Virginia," 6, Loudoun Genealogical File, TBL.

138. Like most other events in farm country, there was a seasonal quality even to local recreation: swimming, fishing, playing ball, and running relays in the summer; horse sports, hunting, and trapping in the fall; ice skating and sleighing during the winter months; scouring the woods, picking berries, riding and flying kites in the spring, but only after the boys had finished their school lessons, farm work, and other chores. Janney and Janney, eds., *John Janney's Virginia*, 90; St. George Tucker Brooke, *Autobiography of St. George Tucker Brooke*, 12, Brooke Family Papers, VHS.

139. Robert Conrad to Powell Conrad, 28 Sept. 1851; Robert Conrad to Robert Conrad II, 21 Dec. 1855; Elizabeth Conrad to Robert Conrad II, n.d., 1855, ConFP, VHS.

140. Robert Conrad to Powell Conrad, 23 June 1852, ConFP, VHS.

141. Robert Conrad to Elizabeth Conrad, 21 June 1855; Elizabeth Conrad to Holmes Conrad, 7 Nov. 1859; Burr Powell to Elizabeth Powell, 4 Oct. 1825, ConFP; Molly Selden to Mary Anne Mason, 9 Jan. 1854, Mason Family Papers, VHS.

142. Elizabeth Conrad to Elizabeth Harrison, 12 Jan. 1853, HarFP; Elizabeth Conrad to Holmes Conrad, 5 Dec. 1854, ConFP, VHS. Also see Anne Martin Maund to George Carter, 1 May 1805, Carter Family Papers, VHS.

143. Burr Harrison to Matthew Harrison, n.d. 1850?, HarFP; Robert Conrad to Kate Conrad, n.d. 1851, ConFP, VHS.

144. Burr Powell to Elizabeth Powell, 4 Oct. 1825, PowFP, VHS.

145. Burr Harrison to Catherine Cornelia Harrison, 28 Feb. 1855, HarFP, VHS.

146. Robert Conrad II to Holmes Conrad, 24 Nov. 1856; Powell Conrad to Holmes Conrad, 22 Oct. 1859, ConFP, VHS.

147. Robert Conrad to Powell Conrad, 8 Jan. 1852; Janney and Janney, eds., *John Janney's Virginia*, 16. Also see Elizabeth Conrad to Holmes Conrad, n.d. 1859, ConFP; George Carter to John Scott, 8 Oct. 1811, GCLB, VHS.

148. Janney used that tactic in a petition he co-authored in 1827 to abolish slavery in the District of Columbia. He continued to do so during the next 30 years of his abolitionist crusade. Janney, *Memoirs of Samuel M. Janney*, 29–32, quote from 32; *Southern Cultivator* quoted in Frederick Law Olmstead, *The Cotton Kingdom: A Traveller's Observations on Cotton and Slavery in the American Slave States*, Arthur M. Schlesinger, ed. (New York, 1953), 172–73n. Olmstead quote on 475.

149. Perdue et al., eds., *Weevils*, 300–301.

150. Some fathers also tried to prevent their sons from having sexual involvements with slave females, but often without success. Perdue et al., eds., *Weevils*, 25, 91, 117,

199–200, 202; William Forbes to George Carter, 20 May 1805, Carter Family Papers, VHS; George Carter to Sophia Carter, 20 June 1816, GCLB, VHS.

151. W. Staber to Samuel Janney, 7 July 1842, JanFP, VSL.

CHAPTER 5. BROKEN VOWS AND "NOTORIOUS" ENDINGS: DIVORCE

1. Quote of Robert Conrad found in his correspondence to Elizabeth Powell Conrad, 17 Jan. 1841, Conrad Family Papers, Virginia Historical Society, Richmond (hereafter referred to as VHS). Regarding divorce laws in Virginia see: *Supplement to the Revised Code of the Laws of Virginia: Being a Collection of All the Acts of the General Assembly, of a Public and Permanent Nature, Passed Since the Year 1819, with a General Index* (Richmond: Samuel Shepherd, 1833), 222–23, 530–31. For the most important discussions of marital discord and divorce in the colonial and antebellum South, see Jane Turner Censer, "Smiling Through Her Tears: Antebellum Southern Women and Divorce," *American Journal of Legal History* 25, no. 1 (Jan. 1981): 24–47; Suzanne Lebsock, *The Free Women of Petersburg: Status and Culture in a Southern Town, 1784–1860* (New York: W. W. Norton, 1984), 68–72; Joan Gundersen and Gwen Victor Gampel, "Married Women's Legal Status in Eighteenth Century New York and Virginia," *William and Mary Quarterly,* 3rd ser., 39, no. 1 (Jan. 1982): 114–34; and Julia Spruill, *Women's Life and Work in the Southern Colonies* (1938; rpt., New York: W. W. Norton, 1972), 342–44. Also see Marylynn Salmon, *Women and the Law of Property in Early America* (Chapel Hill: Univ. of North Carolina Press, 1986). Loudoun Legislative Petitions, 5, 22 Dec. 1808, 4 Dec. 1817, 4 Dec. 1844, 31 Jan. 1848, and 31 Jan. 1849 (hereafter referred to as LouLP), Virginia State Library, Richmond (hereafter referred to as VSL).

2. *Supplement to the Revised Code of the Laws of Virginia,* 530–31; LouLP, 4 Dec. 1844, VSL.

3. LouLP, 31 Jan. 1848, VSL.

4. Ibid.

5. Ibid.

6. Ibid.

7. Ibid.

8. LouLP, 28 Dec. 1808, VSL.

9. Ibid. Although discussions of interracial sexual relationships in the antebellum South usually center on those between a black woman and a white man, the relationship of James Watt and Elizabeth Fouch was not unique in the divorce records of antebellum Virginia. See, for example, Samuel Shepherd, *The Statutes at Large of Virginia, from October Session 1792, to Dec. Session 1806, Inclusive, in Three Volumes (New Series), Being a Continuation of Hening* (Richmond: Samuel Shepherd, 1830–35; New York: AMS Press, 1970), 26, 321.

10. LouLP, 28 Dec. 1808, VSL.

11. Ibid.

12. Ibid.

13. Ibid.

14. Ibid.

15. LouLP, 4 Dec. 1844, VSL.

16. Ibid.

17. Ibid.

18. Ibid.

19. Ibid.

20. LouLP, 4 Dec. 1817, VSL.

21. Ibid.

22. Ibid.

23. Ibid.

24. Ibid.

25. Ibid. Although Mr. Turner had been absent for several years, Virginia law did not allow a divorce on the grounds of desertion until 1848.

26. LouLP, 5 Dec. 1808, VSL.

27. Ibid.

28. LouLP, 5 Jan. 1850, VSL.

29. Ibid.

30. Ibid. *Acts of the General Assembly of Virginia; Passed at the Session of 1850–51, in the Seventy-Fifty Year of the Commonwealth* (Richmond, Va.: William F. Ritchie, 1851), 197.

31. For the best discussion of issues of honor and gender in the antebellum South, see: Bertram Wyatt-Brown, *Southern Honor: Ethics and Behavior in the Old South* (New York: Oxford Univ. Press, 1984), passim.

32. *Supplement to the Revised Code of the Laws of Virginia,* 222–23; LouLP, 31 Jan. 1849, VSL.

33. LouLP, 31 Jan. 1849, VSL.

34. Ibid.

35. Ibid.

36. Ibid.; 28 Dec. 1808; 5 Jan. 1850, VSL.

37. LouLP, 28 Dec. 1808, VSL.

PART II. INTRODUCTION

1. Ian Elliot, ed., *James Monroe, 1758–1831: Chronology-Documents-Bibliographical Aids* (Dobbs Ferry, N.Y.: Oceana, 1969), 5–24; James Monroe, *The Autobiography of James Monroe,* Stuart Brown, ed. (Syracuse: Syracuse University Press, 1959), 15–17.

2. James Monroe owned 70 slaves in Loudoun in 1830. U.S. Department of Commerce, Bureau of the Census, Manuscript Federal Census, Loudoun County, Virginia (hereafter referred to as FedCenLC), 1830, roll 193, p. 4.

3. James Monroe to Samuel Lane, 17 Oct. 1819, Monroe Papers, Thomas Balch Library, Leesburg (hereafter referred to as TBL).

4. Writing in 1985, for example, Jacqueline Jones summarized what had become the general assertion of an entire generation of "revisionist" slavery scholars: "The two-parent, nuclear family was the typical form of slave cohabitation regardless of the location, size, or economy of a plantation, the nature of its ownership, or the age of its slave community." Jacqueline Jones, *Labor of Love, Labor of Sorrow: Black Women, Work and Family from Slavery to the Present* (New York: Basic Books, 1985), 32. See also John

Blassingame's discussion of the development of slave monogamous marriage in *The Slave Community: Plantation Life in the Antebellum South* (New York: Oxford Univ. Press, 1972), 77–78, 80–81, 87–88; ibid., rev. ed. (New York: Oxford Univ. Press, 1980), 149–91, esp. 157–91; Eugene Genovese, *Roll, Jordan, Roll: The World the Slaves Made* (New York: Vintage, 1974), 443–501; Herbert Gutman, *The Black Family in Slavery and Freedom, 1750–1925* (New York: Pantheon, 1976); Deborah White, *Ar'n't I a Woman?: Female Slaves in the Plantation South* (New York: W. W. Norton, 1985), 105–10, 146–50; Deborah White, "Female Slaves: Sex Roles and Status in the Antebellum Plantation South," *Journal of Family History* 3, no. 3 (Fall 1983): 248–61.

5. Colonialists were some of the first historians to take on the challenges for future scholarship that Gutman and other revisionists posed. For example, Allan Kulikoff in *Tobacco and Slaves: The Development of Southern Cultures in the Chesapeake, 1680–1800* (1986) discovered that on large plantations about half of the slaves lived in nuclear households, and on small plantations, about 18 percent did. He also documented substantial diversity in household membership, noting that the majority of slaves on either size plantation usually lived in single parent-child units, only with other siblings, in a number of versions of extended kin arrangements, or with no kin at all (18 to 41 percent) pp. 317, 370–72. Also see Jo Ann Manfra and Robert P. Dykstra, "Serial Marriage and the Origins of the Black Stepfamily: The Rowanty Evidence," *Journal of American History* 72, no.1 (June 1985): 18–44; Brenda Stevenson, "Distress and Discord in Virginia Slave Families, 1830–1860," *In Joy and In Sorrow: Women, Family and Marriage in the Victorian South,* Carol Bleser, ed. (New York: Oxford Univ. Press, 1990), 103–24, 293–97; and Ann Patton Malone, *Sweet Chariot: Slave Family and Household Structure in Nineteenth-Century Louisiana* (Chapel Hill: Univ. of North Carolina Press, 1992), 258–72.

6. Loudoun whites for example, submitted several petitions to the Virginia State Legislature requesting more stringent removal laws for free blacks. See, for example, Loudoun Legislative Petitions (hereafter referred to as LouLP), 7 Dec. 1842, 10 Dec. 1847, Virginia State Library, Richmond (hereafter referred to as VSL). Also see: Luther P. Jackson, *Free Negro Labor and Property Holding in Virginia, 1830–1860* (New York: American Historical Association,1942; New York: Atheneum, 1969), 6–32; Ira Berlin, *Slaves Without Masters: The Free Negro in the Antebellum South* (New York: Random House, 1974), 91–107.

7. In 1800, for example, the 333 Loudoun free people of color constituted only 1.5% of the total population and just 5% of the county's blacks. Slaves, on the other hand, numbered well over 6000 and represented 30% of Loudoun's residents. By 1810, the number of free blacks had almost doubled to 604 persons, and so too did their proportion in the county (2.8%) and overall black (10.8%) populations. In 1820, there were 829 free blacks, and by 1830, Loudoun's free people of color numbered 1,062 and, while they were only 5% of the general population, they then comprised 16.5% of the black community. Their numbers peaked at 1,357 persons in 1850. Yet county whites still outnumbered them almost 12 to one, and slaves more than four to one. By 1860, Loudoun's free people of color had declined to 1,252 persons. Yet similar losses among other groups of residents bolstered their total representation—they comprised 5.75% of the county population and 18.54% of its black inhabitants. FedCenLC, 1810, Roll 69; 1820,

Roll 137; 1830, Roll 193; Free Schedule, 1850, Roll 957; Free Schedule, 1860, Roll 1359; Donald M. Sweig, "Free Negroes in Northern Virginia: An Investigation of the Growth and Status of Free Negroes in the Counties of Alexandria, Fairfax and Loudoun, 1770–1869" (M.A. thesis, George Mason University, 1975), app. A, 63.

Although the proportion of free blacks in the general population of Loudoun was small, their representation was greater than the general proportion of free blacks in many other Virginia counties by 1830, and continued to exceed state levels until the end of the era. In 1830, for example, free blacks made up 5% of the total population in Loudoun, but only 3.91% of the total state population. In 1850, Loudoun free blacks comprised 6.45% of the county's population, but throughout the state, free blacks were only 3.82% of the total population. Debow, *Statistical View of the United States . . . 1790 to 1850*, 62–63, 246–59, 320–27, Kennedy, *Population of the United States in 1860*, 517; and Sweig, "Free Negroes," app. C, 66.

8. There were, for example, 35 free black households in the Quaker stronghold of Waterford in 1860 and 15 in Hillsboro, more than listed for any other Loudoun area. Locations of other free black-headed households: 1–3 households: Bollington, Broad Run, Guilford Station, Harpers Ferry, Lovettsville, Morrisonville, Mountsville, Nearsville, Pleasant Valley, Potomac Furnace, Round Hill, Union, Upperville, Whaley's Store; 4–9 households: Aldie, Arcola, Bellmont, Goresville, Hamilton, Mount Gilad, Philamont, Snickersville, Waterford Rural; 10–19: Hillsboro, Middleburg; 20 and above: Waterford. FedCenLC, Free Schedule, 1860, roll 1359. For a discussion of the role that Loudoun Quakers played in the colonization and antislavery movements in Loudoun, see LouLP, 24 Jan. 1843, VSL; Samuel Janney, *Memoir of Samuel M. Janney, Late of Lincoln, Loudoun County, Virginia: A Minister in the Religious Society of Friends* (Philadelphia: Friends Book Association, 1881), 28, 29, 93; Charles Poland, *From Frontier to Suburbia* (Maceline, Mo.: Walsworth Publishing, 1976), 143–50. Also see: Patricia Hickin, "Antislavery in Virginia, 1832–1860" (Ph.D. dissertation, Univ. of Virginia, 1968), passim.

9. While the greatest number of Loudoun slaves, 6,078 (28%), were in residence in 1800, their numbers surpassed 5000 during the entire era. See Table 1.

10. In 1810, for example, females headed 17.5% of the independently established Loudoun free black households. By 1820, they headed 27.49% of these households, 23.56% in 1830, 27.95% in 1850 and 33.59% in 1860. FedCenLC, 1810, roll 69; 1820, roll 137; 1830, roll 193; Free Schedule, 1850, roll 957; Free Schedule, 1860, roll 1357. Concerning the occupational structure of the Loudoun free black community, see the occupations, gender, and age of workers listed in the FedCenLC, Free Schedule, 1850, roll 957; FedCenLC, Free Schedule, 1860, roll 1359. Regarding household size, the average for Loudoun free blacks in 1820 was 4.11 persons compared with the average Loudoun white household size of 8.56 persons. By 1850, the average free black household size in the county had increased to 5.02 persons, while the average white household in the county had declined slightly to 8.05 persons. FedCenLC, 1820, roll 137; Free Schedule, 1850, roll 957.

11. Thomas R. Dew, "Review of the Debate in the Virginia Legislature of 1831 and 1832" (Richmond: T. W. White, 1832), reprinted in *Slavery Defended: The Views of the Old South,* Eric L. McKitrick, ed. (Englewood Cliffs, N. J.: Prentice-Hall, 1963), 22.

12. Harrison Williams, *Legends of Loudoun: An Account of the History and Homes of a*

Border County of Virginia's Northern Neck (Richmond: Garrett and Massie, 1938), 201; Poland, *From Plantation to Suburbia*, 129–220 passim. and 183–220; James W. Head, *History of Loudoun County, Virginia* (Leesburg, Va.: Park View Press, 1908), 145–57. Also see Eugene M. Scheel, *The History of Middleburg and Vicinity* (Warrenton, Va.: Piedmont Press, 1987), 59–84; and Yetive Weatherly, *Lovettsville: The German Settlement* (Lovettsville, Va.: Lovettsville Bicentennial Committee, 1976), 25–38.

13. Poland, *From Plantation to Suburbia*, 129–81, 138–208; Weatherly, *Lovettsville,* 25–27.

CHAPTER 6. THE NATURE OF LOUDOUN SLAVERY

1. Demographer Philip Curtin estimates that at least 86 percent of the approximately 53,500 slaves who arrived in Virginia between 1710 and 1769 came directly from Africa. Curtin, *The Atlantic Slave Trade: A Census* (Madison: Univ. of Wisconsin Press, 1969), 125, 157–58, 161, 245. Also see Herbert S. Klein, "Slaves and Shipping in Eighteenth Century Virginia," *Journal of Interdisciplinary History* 3, no. 4 (Fall 1975): 383–412; Mechal Sobel, *The World They Made Together: Black and White Values in Eighteenth-Century Virginia* (Princeton: Princeton Univ. Press, 1987), 5–6; Donald Sweig, "Northern Virginia Slavery: A Statistical and Demographic Investigation" (Ph.D. dissertation, College of William and Mary, 1982), 22–23, 86; Elizabeth Donnan, ed., *Documents Illustrative of the History of the Slave Trade to America*, vol. 4, *The Border Colonies and the Southern Colonies* (Washington, D.C.: Carnegie Institute of Washington, 1935), 55–56, 58; and Harrison Williams, *Legends of Loudoun: An Account of the History and Homes of a Border County of Virginia's Northern Neck* (Richmond: Garrett and Massie, 1938), 32–34.

2. Walther Michinton, Celia King, Peter Waite, eds., *Virginia Slave Trade Statistics, 1698–1775* (Richmond: Virginia State Library, 1984), 15–195 passim; Sobel, *The World They Made Together*, 5; Allan Kulikoff, *Tobacco and Slaves: The Development of Southern Cultures in the Chesapeake, 1680–1800* (Chapel Hill: Univ. of North Carolina Press, 1986), 320–23; Curtin, *Atlantic Slave Trade*, 156–57; Donald Sweig, "Northern Virginia Slavery: A Statistical and Demographic Investigation" (Ph. D. dissertation, College of William and Mary, 1982), 20–27; Donnan, ed., *Documents*, 4: 175–204; Ulrich B. Phillips, *American Negro Slavery: A Survey of the Supply, Employment and Control of Negro Labor as Determined by the Plantation Regime* (New York: D. Appleton, 1918; Baton Rouge: Louisiana State Univ. Press, 1966), 38–45; K. G. Davies, *The Royal African Company* (London: Longman Group, 1957; New York: Atheneum, 1970), 131–49 passim; Edmund S. Morgan, *American Slavery, American Freedom: The Ordeal of Colonial Virginia* (New York: W. W. Norton, 1975), 299–308.

3. Robert Carter, for example, mentions in 1726 that of the 119 slaves he sold from the *Snow Rose* only 38 were men. The ship had a total cargo of 125 slaves. During that same year he sold the 140 slaves on a ship owned by John Pemberton and Company; only 36 were men. Michinton et al., eds., *Virginia Slave Trade Statistics*, 61–70.

4. Regarding indigenous African slavery and/or its relationship to the Atlantic slave trade, see John Thornton, *Africa and Africans in the Making of the Atlantic World, 1400–1680* (Cambridge: Cambridge Univ. Press, 1992), 43–125; J. F. Ade Ajayi and

Michael Crowder, *History of West Africa*, vol. 1 (New York: Columbia Univ. Press, 1972), 242–63; Olaudah Equiano, "The Early Travels of Olaudah Equiano," in *Africa Remembered: Narratives by West Africans from the Era of the Slave Trade,* Philip Curtin, ed. (Madison: Univ. of Wisconsin Press, 1977), 76–78, 84; John Atkins, *A Voyage to Guinea, Brasil, and the West-Indies; in His Majesty's Ships, the Swallow and Weymouth . . .* , in Elizabeth Donnan, ed., *Documents*, vol. 2, *The Eighteenth Century* (Washington, D.C.: Carnegie Instutition of Washington, 1931), 280–82.

5. Thornton, *Africa and Africans*, 129–231.

6. Todd Savitt, *Medicine and Slavery: The Diseases and Health Care of Blacks in Antebellum Virginia* (Urbana; Univ. of Illinois Press, 1978), 18–47; and William D. Postell, *The Health of Slaves on Southern Plantations* (Baton Rouge: Louisiana State Univ. Press, 1951), 74–128 passim.

7. Nicholas Cresswell, *The Journals of Nicholas Cresswell* (London: Jonathan Cape, 1925), 18–19.

8. Regarding colonial slave life, see Lathan Windley, ed., *Runaway Slave Advertisements: A Documentary History from the 1730s to 1790*, vol. 1, *Virginia and North Carolina* (Westport, Conn: Greewood Press, 1983), passim; Ira Berlin, "The Slave Trade and the Development of Afro-American Society in English Mainland North America, 1619–1775," *Southern Studies* 20, no. 2 (Summer 1981): 122–36; Gerald Mullin, *Flight and Rebellion: Slave Resistance in Eighteenth-Century Virginia* (New York: Oxford Univ. Press, 1975), 34–83; Allan Kulikoff, "The Origins of Afro-American Society in Tidewater Maryland and Virginia, 1700 to 1790," *William and Mary Quarterly,* 3rd ser., 35, no. 2 (April 1978): 226–59; Sobel, *The World They Made Together*, 100–126; Sterling Stuckey, *Slave Culture: Nationalist Theory and the Foundations of Black America* (New York: Oxford Univ. Press, 1987), 17–26; Thornton, *Africa and Africans in the Making of the Atlantic World,* 162–77; John Blassingame, *The Slave Community: Plantation Life in the Antebellum South*, rev. ed. (New York: Oxford Univ. Press, 1979), 3–48. Regarding early slave housing and African antecedents, see George W. McDaniel, *Hearth and Homes: Preserving a People's Culture* (Philadelphia: Temple Univ. Press, 1982), passim; and Henry Swint, ed., *Dear Ones at Home: Letters from Contraband Camps* (Nashville: Vanderbilt Univ. Press, 1966), 107.

9. Thomas Bluett, *Some Memoirs of the Life of Job, the Son of Solomon the High Priest of Boonda in Africa; who was a Slave about two Years in Maryland . . .* in Donnan, ed., *Documents*, 2: 421–22.

10. African slave names found in "Loudoun County, Virginia 1771 Tithable List," transcribed by Miss Pollyanna Creekmore, *The Virginia Genealogist*, 16 (1972): 243–48; 17 (1973): 8–13, 107–13, 187–90, 270–76. The largest numbers of "outlandish" or unseasoned Africans arrived during the decades of the 1730s, 1740s, and 1750s. Regarding the volume of the African slave trade to the Rappahannock and Potomac rivers during these decades, see Michinton et al., eds., *Virginia Slave Trade Statistics, 1698–1775*, 68–189.

11. Slave advertisements from the *Virginia Gazette*, 16, 30 May 1745, compiled in Windley, ed., *Runaway Slave Advertisements*, 1: 12–13. Also see Kulikoff, *Tobacco and Slaves*, 327–28.

12. Mullin, *Flight and Rebellion*, 17–18. A growing body of scholarly literature concerning the development of creole languages in the New World is now available.

Among the most important texts are Lorenzo Turner, *Africanisms in the Gullah Dialect* (Chicago: Univ. of Chicago Press, 1949); Winifred Vass, *The Bantu Speaking Heritage of the United States* (Los Angeles: Center for Afro-American Studies, 1979), 23–31, 58–60; Ian Hancock, "The Domestic Hypothesis, Diffusion and Componentiality: An Account of Atlantic Anglophone Creole Origins," in *Substrata versus Universals in Creole Genesis*, Pieter Muysken and Norval Smith, eds. (Amsterdam: John Benjamin, 1986): 71–102; Ian Hancock, "Gullah and Barbadian-Origins and Relationships," *American Speech* 55, no.1 (Jan. 1980): 17–35; and Jeffrey P. Williams, "Women and Kinship in Creole Genesis," *International Journal of Social Language* 71 (1988): 81–89.

13. *Virginia Gazette*, 26 Oct. 1739, in Windley, ed., *Runaway Slave Advertisements*, I: 5, 7, 10; Olaudah Equiano, *The Interesting Life of Olaudah Equiano or Gustavus Vassa the African*, Paul Edwards, ed. (New York: Arno Press, 1966), 34.

14. Those few African women who did leave went with their husbands; those large numbers of "country" born women who escaped did so alone, as well as with husbands, female kin, and other female associates. Windley, ed., *Runaway Slave Advertisements*, I, passim.

15. The inability of African women to form companionate relationships with each other as well as a general indication of disorientation might be found in the small numbers who attempted to escape. Unlike creole slave women, African women rarely attempted to leave alone or with companions. Of the several hundred slave escape advertisements found in the colonial *Virginia Gazette*, for example, fewer than five were for outlandish African or new negro women. Windley, ed., *Runaway Slave Advertisements*, I, passim.

16. Regarding the varied traditional lifestyles of African women residing in those areas affected by the Atlantic slave trade, see, for example, Sylvia A. Boone, *Radiance from the Waters: Ideals of Feminine Beauty in Mende Art* (New Haven: Yale Univ. Press, 1986); G. Adaba et al., eds., *Marriage, Fertility and Parenthood in West Africa* (Canberra: Australian National Univ., 1978); C. Oppong, ed., "Fertility, Parenthood and Development: Yoruba Experiences," in *Sex Roles, Population and Development in West Africa* (London: International Labour Organization, 1987); Mary Smith, *Baba of Karo: A Woman of the Moslem Hausa* (New York: Frederick Praeger, 1964); John S. Mbiti, *African Religions and Philosophy*, 2nd ed. (Oxford: Heinemann International, 1990), passim; Denise Paulme, *Women of Tropical Africa* (Berkeley: Univ. of California Press, 1974), passim; Mary Douglas, "The Lele of Kasai," in Daryll Forde, ed., *African Worlds: Studies in the Cosmological Ideas and Social Values of African Peoples* (Oxford: Oxford Univ. Press, 1954), 2–7, 13–15; K. A. Busia, "The Ashanti," in ibid., 196–207; and P. Mercier, "The Fon of Dahomey," in ibid., 210–33.

17. Tom Hatless, "Tending Our Gardens," *Southern Changes* (Oct./Nov. 1984): 18–24; Martha Saxton, "Black Women's Moral Values in the Eighteenth Century Tidewater," unpublished manuscript presented at the Berkshire Conference on Women's History, Rutger's Univ., 1990; Suzanne Lebsock, *"A Share of Honor": Virginia Women, 1600–1945* (Richmond: Virginia Women's Cultural History Project, 1984), 36–41.

18. Evidence of the perpetuation of traditional African religions, including Islam, medicines, music, drumming, dance, textiles and sculpture indicate only some of the richness of African life that came to be part of the lifestyles of northern piedmont slaves.

See, for example, Mullin, *Flight and Rebellion*, 17–18, 34–52; Kulikoff, *Tobacco and Slaves*, 324–333; Loudoun County, Virginia 1771 Tithable List, *Virginia Genealogist*, 17, (1973): 11, 272; Lebsock, *"A Share of Honor,"* 40, 82,106; Thornton, *Africa and Africans in the Making of the Atlantic World* , 183–271; John Michael Vlach, "Afro-American Domestic Artifacts in Eighteenth Century Virginia," *Material Culture* 19 (1987): 3–23.

19. A number of scholars have contributed to the discussion and debates about the African element of African American culture during the colonial and antebellum eras. See, for, example, some of the most recent contributions: Roger Bastide, *African Civilization in the New World* (New York: Harper and Row, 1971); Blassingame, *Slave Community,* 3–104 passim; Peter Wood, *Black Majority: Negroes in Colonial South Carolina from 1670 through the Stono Rebellion* (New York: W. W. Norton, 1974); Lawrence Levine, *Black Culture and Black Consciousness: Afro-American Folk Thought from Slavery to Freedom* (New York: Oxford Univ. Press, 1977); Sterling Stuckey, *Slave Culture: Nationalist Theory and the Foundations of Black America* (New York: Oxford Univ. Press, 1987); Kulikoff, *Tobacco and Slaves*, 335–51; Mullin, *Flight and Rebellion*, 9–12; and Sobel, *The World They Made Together*, passim.

20. Some 11.5 percent of Loudoun slaveholders were absentee in 1771. They controlled 27.8 percent of county slaves. Absentee owners included William Fitzhugh, James Mercer, Mann Page, and Francis Lightfoot Lee. "Loudoun County 1771 Tithable List," *Virginia Genealogist* 16 (1972): 8–13; 17 (1973): 107–13, 187–90, 243–48, 270–76 passim; Sweig, "Northern Virginia Slavery," 28–44; Eugene M. Scheel, *The History of Middleburg and Vicinity* (Warrenton, Va.: Warrenton Printing, 1977), 9.

21. Mullin, for example, asserts the preferences that slaveholders had for native-born and acculturated slaves in positions of authority and status, almost, in comparison, shunning contact with Africans. Mullin, *Fight and Rebellion*, 8–12.

22. Some 57 percent of those slaves listed on the 1749 tithable list, for example, lived on agricultural units with slave populations ranging from ten to nineteen.

This is not to suggest that no owners of Loudoun slaves had large holdings. Absentee masters Robert and John Tayloe, for example, owned hundreds of slaves, as did William Fitzhugh, but distributed them on their various plantations. So too did Robert Carter. Carter's Loudoun plantation, "Leo," consisted of 1,809 acres and had an average labor force of 36 slaves. Louis Morton, *Robert Carter of Nomini Hall: A Virginia Tobacco Planter of the Eighteenth Century* (Charlottesville, Va.: Univ. Press of Virginia, 1964), app. tables 5, 9, 15; Richard S. Dunn, "A Tale of Two Plantations: Slave Life at Mesopotamia in Jamaica and Mount Airy in Virginia, 1799 to 1828," *William and Mary Quarterly,* 3rd ser., v. 34, no. 1 (Jan 1977): 32–65. Information on the 1749 population and slaveholding patterns in Upper Truro Parish found in Sweig, "Northern Virginia Slavery," 28–36.

23. Sobel, *The World They Made Together,* 4.

24. There were 992 slaves in Loudoun in 1760. Sweig, "Northern Virginia Slavery," 39–44.

25. Robert Carter, for example, owned 184 slaves in 1773 and 509 in 1791, which he distributed on 22 plantations in the counties of Westmoreland, Richmond, Prince William, Loudoun, and Frederick. The closest of his other plantations to "Leo" in Loudoun was "Cancer" in Prince William, but he did not transfer slaves to that location

until 1785. He had 29 slaves in Loudoun in 1773; 34 in 1782; 36 in 1784; 42 in 1788; and 48 in 1781, eight of whom he hired out that year. It probably was because of their wealth, power, and absence that they presumed to ignore local prejudice and elevate the status of some blacks to that of overseer. Morton, *Robert Carter of Nomini Hall*, app. table 9. Also see Jack Greene, ed., *The Diary of Colonel Landon Carter of Sabine Hall, 1752–1778*, vols. 1, 2 (Richmond: Virginia Historical Society, 1965, 1987), passim.

26. Windley, ed., *Runaway Slave Advertisements*, 1: 68; Poland, *From Frontier to Suburbia,* 29–30; Williams, *Legends of Loudoun*, 21.

27. Sweig, "Northern Virginia Slavery," 28–44; Kulikoff, "The Origins of Afro-American Society," 226–59. Diarist incident recorded in Charles Poland, *From Frontier to Suburbia*, (Maceline, Mo: Walsworth Publishing, 1976), 29–30, and Williams, *Legends of Loudoun*, 21.

28. Only nine out of 330 had slaves. Mann Page, for example, had 20 adult slaves and at least one Native American living on his Shelburne parish plantation in 1771. That same year, his brother-in-law Thompson Mason had at least 26 laboring slaves working on his neighboring estate. "Loudoun County 1771 Tithable List," *Virginia Genealogist* 17 (1973): 8–13, 107–13; Williams, *Legends of Loudoun*, 72–77, 170.

29. For information on the holdings of Thomson Mason and others in the area, see Sweig, "Northern Virginia Slavery," 47–53, 71–84, 115–33. Also see "Negroes Belonging to George Washington in His Own Right and by Marriage, 1799," Mount Vernon Library, Fairfax County, Virginia (hereafter referred to as MVL).

30. By 1771, the women on Mason's Loudoun estate outnumbered the men 1.27 to 1. The ratio of the number of men to the number of women in the county that year was 1.24 to 1. "Loudoun County 1771 Tithable List," *Virginia Genealogist*, 17 (1973): 11 and passim.

31. Ibid.

32. Although the number of slaves increased tremendously, they still comprised less than a third of the county's total population in 1800. Ibid. Loudoun Legislative Petitions (hereafter referred to as LouLP) (1520 P, A-G, 1521–P), 5 Dec. 1781, VSL. Williams, *Legends of Loudoun*, 43–59; Donald Sweig, "Free Negroes in Northern Virginia: An Investigation of the Growth and Status of Free Negroes in the Counties of Alexandria, Fairfax and Loudoun, 1770–1860" (M.A. thesis, George Mason Univ., 1975), app. C, 66.

33. U. B. Phillips, *American Negro Slavery*, 132–204 passim; Richard Sutch, "The Breeding of Slaves for Sale and the Westward Expansion of Slavery, 1850–1860," in *Race and Slavery in the Western Hemisphere: Quantitative Studies*, Stanley Engerman and Eugene Genovese, eds. (Princeton: Princeton Univ. Press, 1975), 173–210; Kenneth Stampp, *The Peculiar Institution: Slavery in the Antebellum South* (New York: Vintage Books, 1956), 237–78; Robert Fogel, *Without Consent or Contract: The Rise and Fall of American Slavery* (New York: W. W. Norton, 1989), 84–98; Poland, *From Frontier to Suburbia*, 84–90, 137–39; Williams, *Legends of Loudoun,* 159; Sweig, "Northern Virginia Slavery," 8, 191.

34. Robert Carter, for example, stopped cultivating tobacco for the market during the 1780s. Later his workers at his Loudoun plantation grew flax and hemp. The most important crops produced in antebellum Loudoun were wheat, corn, rye, oats, and barley. James W. Head, *History of Loudoun County, Virginia* (Leesburg, Va.: Park View Press,

1908), 91–93, 98–100; Morton, *Robert Carter of Nomini Hall*, 159; Poland, *From Frontier to Suburbia*, 27–28, 84–90; Williams, *Legends of Loudoun*, 159–62; Sweig, "Northern Virginia Slavery," 39; Sweig, "Free Negroes in Northern Virginia, app. C, 66.

35. From 1810 to 1820, traders removed approximately 1,870 county slaves, and about 29% of slave population between 1820 and 1830. Of these 1,402 blacks, only about 2% accompanied their owners. Another 1400 slaves were exported from 1830–40. U.S. Department of Commerce, Bureau of the Census, Manuscript Federal Census, Loudoun County, Virginia (hereafter referred to as FedCenLC), 1820, roll 137; 1830, roll 193; 1840, roll 564; 1850, Slave Schedule, roll 989; 1860, Slave Schedule, roll 1393. Sweig applies Michael Tadman's "survival rate method of demographic analysis" to approximate the rate of exportation of Loudoun slaves between 1820 and 1830. I have done so for 1830–40 and 1840–50. This method counts the numbers of slaves in specific age cohorts who survived over 10-year spans with some accounting for death rates, but does not consider entrance into these cohorts as a result of immigration and, therefore, are only approximations. Birth and death records for 1850–60 allow for a more accurate estimation. Michael Tadman, "Slave Trading in the Ante-bellum South: An Estimate of the Extent of the Inter-Regional Slave Trade," *Journal of American Studies* 13, no. 2 (Spring 1979): 195–220; Sweig, "Northern Virginia Slavery," 247–53.

36. Hundreds of slaves were exported from Loudoun during the 1840s. Most did not accompany family members and usually went with long-distance traders.

The census compilations for 1850 indicate that 183 slave children were born in Loudoun between 1 June 1849 and 1 June 1850, while 68 slaves died. If one accepts these annual figures as indicative of annual rates for both of these events, one can then multiply them by ten to establish a crude growth rate for the decade of 1,150 Loudoun slaves. Yet the population actually declined by 140 persons. One can crudely estimate, therefore, that approximately 1300 slaves left the county during this decade. J. B. D. Debow, *Statistical View of the United States . . . Being a Compendium of the Seventh Census . . . 1850* (Washington, D.C.: AOP Nicholson, 1854), 259.

37. Mr. Bell was a slave on Charles Fallons's plantation in Vienna, just east of the Loudoun county border. Charles L. Perdue, Thomas E. Barden, and Robert K. Phillips, eds., *Weevils in the Wheat: Interviews with Virginia Ex-Slaves* (Charlottesville: Univ. Press of Virginia, 1976), 27.

38. There only were 670 Loudoun slave-inclusive households in Loudoun in 1860, compared with 878 in 1810, 1,131 in 1820, and 785 in 1850. FedCenLC, 1810, roll 69; 1820, roll 137; 1850, Slave Schedule, roll 989; Sweig, "Northern Virginia Slavery," 103, 139, 143. Head, *History of Loudoun County*, 85; Poland, *From Frontier to Suburbia*, 132.

39. FedCenLC, 1820, roll 137; 1850, Slave Schedule, roll, 989; Sweig, "Northern Virginia Slavery," 139, 143; Head, *History of Loudoun County*, 85.

40. George Whitlock to George Carter, 27 April 1804, Carter Family Papers (hereafter referred to as CarFP), Virginia Historical Society, Richmond (hereafter referred to as VHS).

41. George Whitlock to George Carter, 18 Jan. 1805, CarFP, VHS.

42. Poland, *From Frontier to Suburbia*, 139–41; Perdue, et al., eds., *Weevils*, 23; Sweig, "Northern Virginia Slavery," 193; Nan Netherton, et al., *Fairfax County, Virginia: A History* (Fairfax: Fairfax County Board of Supervisors, 1978), 262.

43. *Loudoun Chronicle*, 1 March 1850; *Washingtonian*, 15 Dec. 1836, Virginia State Library, Richmond (hereafter referred to as VSL).

44. Burr Harrison to Matthew Harrison, 28 Dec. 1846?, Harrison Family Papers (hereafter referred to as HarFP), VHS; "Notice of Public Sale," 30 Oct. 1817, Shover Family Papers (hereafter referred to as ShovFP), VSL.

45. George P. Rawick, ed., *American Slave: A Composite Autobiography*, vol. 16, *Virginia* (Westport, Conn.: Greenwood Press, 1972), 33; Poland, *From Frontier to Suburbia*, 138–39; Robert Conrad to Elizabeth Conrad, 11 Dec. 1843; 11 Sept. 1831, Conrad Family Papers (hereafter referred to as ConFP), VHS.

46. Perdue et al., eds., *Weevils*, 67, 104; Rawick, ed., *American Slave*, 46; Catherine Powell to Elizabeth Powell Conrad, ?1830, ConFP, VHS; Burr Powell to Robert Conrad, 13 Dec. 1830, ConFP, VHS; George Whitlock to George Carter, 11 Nov. 1805, CarFP, VHS; Benjamin Drew, ed., *A North-Side View of Slavery, the Refugee; or the Narratives of Fugitive Slaves in Canada Related by Themselves with an Account of the History and Condition of the Colored Population of Upper Canada* (Boston: John P. Jewett, 1856), 52.

47. William Forbes to George Carter, 25 April, 20 May 1805, CarFP, VHS.

48. Inventory of Adam Shover's Estate, 13 Oct. 1817, ShovFP, VSL; Promissory note, Samuel DeButts, 29 Oct. 1838, DeButts Family Papers, VHS; Drew, ed., *North-Side View of Slavery*, 74; Poland, *From Frontier to Suburbia*, 139.

49. Dorothy Sterling includes in her discussion of Emily Russell a quote from a letter sent by Bruin and Hill in 1850 in which they request $1800 for Emily, whom they describe as "'the finest-looking woman in the country." Russell died on the overland trip to New Orleans. Dorothy Sterling, ed., *We Are Your Sisters: Black Women in the Nineteenth Century* (New York: W.W. Norton, 1984), 48.

The original owner of the Edmondson girls sold them in 1848 to the slave trading company as punishment for their attempted escape. According to Pennington, one of the negotiators for the two girls knew that Bruin and Hill intended their "destination [to be] prostitution." The father eventually raised the sum with the help of a northern branch of the Methodist Episcopal Church. James W. C. Pennington, *The Fugitive Blacksmith; on, Events in the History of James W.C. Pennington* 3d ed. (1850; Westport, Conn.: Negro Universities Press, 1971), v-x; Perdue et al., eds., *Weevils*, 236.

50. William Still, ed., *Underground Railroad: A Record of Facts, Authentic Narratives, Letters, etc.* (Philadelphia: Porter and Coates, 1872; New York: Arno Press, 1968), 122–23; Drew, ed., *North-Side View of Slavery*, 248;

51. Those males aged 14 to 26 years represented 53 percent of their cohort; men aged 26 to 45 years comprised 55 percent of their group. Sweig, "Northern Virginia Slavery," 106, 140.

52. The increase in the proportion of women also was due to a growing number of small slaveholders, like Betsy Sheppard, who owned only slave women, or John Newton, whose entire slaveholding was two women.

Female slaves comprised a very slight majority or 51 percent of those aged between 15 and 29 years, and 54 percent of those aged 30 to 49 years. Sutch, "The Breeding of Slaves for Sale," app. table 4, p. 208; FedCenLC, 1850, Slave Schedule, roll 989.

53. George Carter owned 61 slaves in 1830 and 75 in 1840. He died in 1846 with an

estate valued at about $500,000. FedCenLC, 1830, roll 193; 1840, roll 564; 1850, Slave Schedule, roll 989; W. E. Trout, "The Goose Creek and Little River Navigation Company," *Virginia Calvacade* 16, no.1 (Winter 1967): 31–32.

54. The percentages of Virginia slaves aged 0 to 14/15 years for the antebellum period, for example, were as follows: 1820: 44.67%; 1830: 45.92%; 1840: 46.47%; 1850: 45.02%; 1860: 44.74%. FedCenLC, 1820, roll 137, pp. 23, 25, 26; 1830, roll 193, pp. 87, 89; 1840, roll 564, p. 38; Debow, *Statistical View of the United States . . . 1850*, 253–55; Joseph G. Kennedy, *Population of the United States in 1860; Compiled from the Original Returns of the Eighth Census.* (Washington, D.C.: Government Printing Office, 1864), 512. Regarding Loudoun slave youth, see Sweig, "Northern Virginia Slavery," 140. Also see: Sutch, "The Breeding of Slaves for Sale," app. table 4, p. 208 regarding the age distribution of Virginia slaves exported to the lower South and Southwest.

55. *Washingtonian,* 3 June 1829, 19 Oct. 1848, VSL; *Genius of Liberty*, 26 Oct. 1818, VSL; *Loudoun Chronicle*, 1 March 1850, VSL; Sweig, "Northern Virginia Slavery," 107, 142; Rawick, ed., *American Slave*, 16: 45; Drew, *North-Side View of Slavery*, 74.

56. Burr Harrison to Matthew Harrison, 28 Dec. 1846?, HarFP, VHS; Drew, ed., *North-Side View of Slavery*, 30. A legal stipulation (1829) regarding the sale of young slaves in Louisiana, however, may have stemmed the tide there but not elsewhere in the Lower South and Southwest. Sweig, "Northern Virginia Slavery," 211.

57. Robert Conrad to Holmes Conrad, 8 Sept. 1831, ConFP, VHS; Pennington, *The Fugitive Blacksmith*, vi; Drew, ed., *North-Side View of Slavery*, 196–97.

58. Renters, like buyers, usually wanted young, healthy male laborers to do field work. There also was great demand for skilled and domestic slaves. Rarely did anyone want to rent children, but youngsters sometimes accompanied their mothers to their temporary workplace. *Loudoun Chronicle*, 10 March 1848, 6 Nov. 1849, VSL; Loudoun County Minute Book, 9 Dec. 1817, VSL; FedCenLC, 1860, Slave Schedule, roll 1393.

59. Robert Conrad to Elizabeth Powell Conrad, 2 Jan. 1843, ConFP; Receipt from Townsend McVeigh to Samuel Debutts, 2 Jan. 1839, Debutts Papers, VHS. Also see numerous agreements for hiring of slaves in the miscellaneous papers of Catherine McCall, 1816–29, Walter Jones Collection, Leesburg Family Papers, Manuscript Division, Alderman Library, Univ. of Virginia, Charlottesville (hereafter referred to as UVA).

60. Perdue et al., eds., *Weevils*, 27; Drew, ed., *North-Side View of Slavery*, 74.

61. Perdue et al., eds., *Weevils*, 318.

62. Robert McColley, *Slavery and Jeffersonian Virginia*, 2nd ed. (Urbana: Univ. of Illinois Press, 1978), 100–101. The article entitled "Hiring of Servants" first appeared in the *Warrenton Flag*, but was reprinted in the *Alexandria Gazette and Virginia Advertiser*, a paper with a much broader circulation. Southern Newspaper Collection, Univ. of Texas, Austin.

63. Anthony Burns was the slave of Colonel Charles Suttle, a shopkeeper and politician in Alexandria. The fugitive slave was arrested in Boston on 24 May 1854. His subsequent trial, and the attempt by prominent abolitionists to free him, stimulated one of the most virulent debates on the Fugitive Slave Law of 1850. The court found for Colonel Suttle. Jane and William Pease, *The Fugitive Slave Law and Anthony Burns: A Problem in Law Enforcement* (Philadelphia: J. B. Lippincott, 1975), passim, esp. 28–51.

64. Norman Yetman, ed., *Voices from Slavery* (New York: Holt, Rinehart and Winston, 1970), 176.

65. Diary of William H. Gray, 1852, passim, Gray Family Papers, VHS.

66. *Loudoun Chronicle*, 10 Aug. 1849, VSL. Jackson was a Loudoun slave who lived near Bloomfield. Rawick, ed., *American Slave*, 16: 45.

67. Thomas Harper was a resident of Alexandria before his successful escape via the Underground Railroad to Canada. Still, ed., *Underground Railroad*, 411.

68. Regarding urban slavery in the antebellum South, see Richard Wade, *Slavery in the Cities: The South, 1820–1860* (New York: Oxford Univ. Press, 1964); Phillips, *American Negro Slavery*, 402–24; Eugene Genovese, *Roll, Jordan, Roll: The World the Slaves Made* (New York: Pantheon, 1974), 388–95.

69. FedCenLC, 1850, Slave Schedule, roll 989. See, for example, the slave holdings of Henry Harrison, Burr Harrison, Sarah Russell, William Swann, and Lucy Ball.

70. Perdue et al., eds., *Weevils*, 332; Drew, ed., *North-Side View of Slavery*, 30.

71. For information regarding the kinds of labor that slave children performed, see Rawick, ed., *American Slave,* 16: 29–30; Yetman, ed., *Voices from Slavery*, 182; Perdue et al., eds., *Weevils*, 3–4, 78, 85, 149, 317; Swint, ed., *Dear Ones at Home*, 60; John W. Blassingame, ed., *Slave Testimony: Two Centuries of Letters, Speeches, Interviews, and Autobiographies* (Baton Rouge: Louisiana State Univ. Press), 217–18, 222; Drew, ed., *North-Side View of Slavery*, 38, 73.

72. Drew, ed., *North-Side View of Slavery*, 30, 50; Rawick, ed., *American Slave*, 16: 30.

73. Popular manuals, for example, stipulated that young slave children should receive a weekly food ration of one pound of bacon, a quart of corn meal with milk, buttermilk, or molasses added in; that older children should have more meat and meal; and that all should benefit from a vegetable garden. See, for example, *The Plantation and Farm Instruction Regulation Record, Inventory and Account Book* (Richmond: J. W. Randolph, 1852), 6, Baskerville Family Papers, VHS, passim.

74. Rawick, ed., *American Slave*, 16: 45, 46; Yetman, ed., *Voices from Slavery*, 176.

75. Burr Harrison to Matthew Harrison, 17 Feb. 1847?, HarFP, VHS; Still, ed., *Underground Railroad*, 477; Savitt, *Medicine and Slavery,* 91; Rawick, ed., *American Slave*, 16: 30.

76. The quality and quantity of slave clothing were determined by the attitude and wealth of their individual owners, the slave's proximity to owners, the ability of the slave to earn income, one's gender and social identity, and the slave's cultural choices. Burr Harrison to Matthew Harrison, 9 Dec. 1846, HarFP, VHS; Perdue et al., eds., *Weevils*, 6, 49.

77. Perdue et al., eds., *Weevils*, 210, 316–17.

78. Austin Steward, *Austin Steward: Twenty-two Years a Slave and Forty Years a Freeman* (Rochester: William Alling, 1857), 12–13.

79. James Mercer, for example, had 11 adult slaves and an overseer on his Loudoun tobacco farm in 1771. Edward Snickers had 9 prime slaves, as did William Bronaugh. Robert Carter had 12 on his "Leo" plantation in Loudoun. Mercer, Snickers, Bronaugh and Carter's numbers of prime slaves are from 1771. Phillips, *American Negro Slavery*, 82; Perdue et al., eds., *Weevils*, 309; Loudoun County, Virginia 1771 Tithable List, *Virginia Genealogist* 17 (1973): 112, 274. Moton, *Robert Carter of Nomini Hall*, app. tables 7, 9, 12, 15, 70, 73.

80. Williams, *Legends of Loudoun*, 160–63.

81. Rawick, ed., *American Slave*, 16: 45; Yetman, ed., *Voices from Slavery*, 176; Perdue et al., eds., *Weevils*, 316; Cresswell, *Journals of Nicholas Cresswell*, 17–18.

82. Perdue et al., eds., *Weevils*, 224; Drew, ed., *North-Side View of Slavery*, 196.

83. Perdue et al., eds., *Weevils*, 216; Phillips, *American Negro Slavery*, 82–83.

84. Perdue et al., eds., *Weevils*, 224; Phillips, *American Negro Slavery*, 232; Drew, ed., *North-Side View of Slavery*, 108.

85. William H. Gray Farm Book, 1846–80, Gray Family Papers, VHS.

86. Perdue et al., eds., *Weevils*, 26, 304.

87. Bell also noted that many overseers in the area refused to let family groups work together. Ibid., 26.

88. Steward, *Twenty-two Years a Slave*, 12.

89. *Genius of Liberty,* 21 Nov. 1820, 7 Jan. 1823, VSL; *Loudoun Chronicle*, 16 Aug. 1849, VSL; Poland, *From Frontier to Suburbia*, 138. For the best discussion of gender and slave labor in the antebellum South, see Jacqueline Jones, *Labor of Love, Labor of Sorrow: Black Women, Work and the Family from Slavery to the Present* (New York: Basic Books, 1985), 14–29; and Julie Matthei, *An Economic History of Women in America: Women's Work, the Sexual Division of Labor and the Development of Capitalism* (New York: Schocken Books, 1982), 74–97.

90. For information on the clothing of antebellum Loudoun and other Virginia slaves, see Burr Harrison to Matthew Harrison, 9 Dec. 1846, HarFP; Lists of Servants of Deephole Estate, Jan. 1830, Tayloe Family Papers, VHS; *Washingtonian,* 9 Feb. 1839, 27 Aug. 1842, 31 Aug. 1849, VSL; Yetman, ed., *Voices from Slavery*, 176; Perdue et al., eds., *Weevils*, 79–80, 97, 103, 107, 210, 229, 316–17. For differences in food allowances see: Diary of Richard Eppes, 12 Oct. 1851, Eppes Family Papers, VHS; Burr Harrison to Matthew Harrison, 17 Dec. 1847?, HarFP, VHS; Rawick, ed., *American Slave*, 16: 30, 45, 46; Perdue et al., eds., *Weevils*, 57, 63, 83, 100, 102–3, 124, 155, 301, 311, 333, 310; and Still, ed., *Underground Railroad*, 477.

91. Physician's account found in Savitt, *Medicine and Slavery*, 115; Affidavit of John Fitzgerald, ?, 1859, Fitzgerald Family Papers, VHS.

92. William Twisdale to Nelson Berkeley, 19 Jan. 1828, Berkeley Family Papers, UVA.

93. William H. Gray Farm Book, 11, 16 Oct. 1851, Gray Family Papers; Elizabeth Powell Conrad to Catherine Powell, n.d., ConFP, VHS.

94. Census takers recorded that 35% of Loudoun's slave population was mulatto in 1850 and 27% in 1860. Some 51% percent of the county's free black population was mulatto in 1860; 52% in 1850. Kennedy, *Population of the United States in 1860*, 517; Poland, *From Frontier to Suburbia*, 132n.14; Drew, ed., *North-Side View of Slavery*, 38. Female slaves also provided evidence which depicts black drivers as brutal in their treatment. See, for example, *Weevils*, 266. Yet many more females as well as the drivers themselves supplied evidence which denied this accusation. See, for example, ibid., 26; and Drew, ed., *A North-Side View of Slavery*, 38; Rawick, ed., *American Slave*, 16: 30; Brenda Stevenson, "Gender Convention, Ideals and Identity Among Antebellum Virginia Slave Women," forthcoming in *Black Women and Slavery in the Americas,* Darlene Clark Hine and D. Barry Gaspar, eds. (Bloomington: Indiana Univ. Press, 1996), passim.

95. Perdue et al., eds., *Weevils*, 274; Steward, *Twenty-two Years a Slave*, 12; Drew, ed., *North-Side View of Slavery*, 48. For a discussion of the medical implications of these kinds of whippings on slaves, see Savitt, *Medicine and Slavery*, 111–12. Owners often tried to awe slaves with their power through such brutal beatings. See, for example, the narrative of ex-slave Israel Massie in which he described his owner's affinity for sticking a hot pipe to a slave's skin while demanding that the slave call him "Lord." "Say 'Oh Lord. I'm your God.'" Perdue et al., eds., *Weevils*, 206–7.

96. "And yet, an overseer's instruction book published in Richmond advised whipping as punishment for a first offense," Savitt concluded. Savitt, *Medicine and Slavery*, 112–15.

97. Rawick, ed., *American Slave*, 16: 46; Poland, *From Frontier to Suburbia*, 140; Blassingame, ed., *Slave Testimony*, 222, 454–55; Perdue, et al. eds., *Weevils*, 120–21, 219, 293, 309, 316–17; Twisdale to Berkeley, 19 Jan. 1828, Berkeley Family Papers, UVA.; Swint, ed., *Dear Ones at Home*, 128.

98. Perdue et al., eds., *Weevils,* 257–59; quote taken from 259.

99. Drew, ed., *North-Side View of Slavery*, 31, 115; Perdue et al., eds., *Weevils*, 94; also see 206–7.

100. Rawick, ed., *American Slave*, 16: 46; Poland, *From Frontier to Suburbia*, 140; Blassingame, ed., *Slave Testimony*, 222; Drew, ed., *North-Side View of Slavery*, 31.

101. Some domestics also came under the direct supervision of male owners, rather than their wives. These primarily were male slaves used as personal servants. Most Loudoun slaveholders who had domestics owned only one or two. But many large slaveholders had several house servants among their labor force, such as George Carter, with almost twenty. FedCenLC, 1820, roll 137, pp. 135A, 136; 1830, roll 193, pp. 16, 105; 1840, roll 564, p. 138; Drew, *North-Side View of Slavery*, 73.

102. See, for example, Robert Conrad to Elizabeth Powell Conrad, 23 March 1831; Catherine Powell to Elizabeth Powell Conrad, 10 Jan. 1830; Elizabeth Powell Conrad to Burr Powell, 25 Dec. 1829?; Elizabeth Powell Conrad to Robert Conrad, 2 Jan. 1830, ConFP, VHS.

103. Many only held temporary positions, coming to work immediately preceding the birth of a mistress's child and staying through confinement. Others came during the vacation spring and summer months. See, for example, Robert Conrad to Elizabeth Powell Conrad, 23 March, 1831, 27 June 1837, 16 Oct. 1845, ConFP, VHS.

104. Their cultural assimilation often meant cultural alienation from other slaves. Perdue et al., eds., *Weevils*, 305.

105. Elizabeth Powell Conrad to Burr Powell, 25 Dec. 1829?, ConFP, VHS.

106. Ibid., Elizabeth Powell Conrad to Catherine Powell, ? 1830, VHS.

107. Elizabeth Powell Conrad to Robert Conrad, ? Jan. 1830; Burr Powell to Robert Conrad, 13 Dec. 1830, ConFP, VHS.

108. Blassingame, ed., *Slave Testimony*, 217–18; Perdue et al., eds., *Weevils*, 149; Drew, ed., *North-Side View of Slavery*, 38, 157–58; quote taken from Still, ed., *Underground Railroad*, 115.

109. Anne Firor Scott, "Women's Perspective on the Patriarchy in the 1850's," *Journal of American History* 61, no.1 (July 1974): 52–64. Suzanne Lebsock, *The Free Women of Petersburg: Status and Culture in a Southern Town, 1784–1860* (New York: W. W.

Norton, 1984), 136–41.

110. See, for example, Fox-Genovese's discussion of the relationships between slave-holding and slave women. Elizabeth Fox-Genovese, *Within the Plantation Household: Black and White Women of the Old South* (Chapel Hill: Univ. of North Carolina Press, 1988), 308–16, 334–67. Also see Brenda E. Stevenson, "Compassion and Powerlessness: Myths and Realities of the Plantation Mistress' Relationship with Slaves," paper presented at the Virginia Center for the Humanities Winter/Spring Colloquia, Charlottesville, June 5, 1990. For examples of slaves commenting on the propensity of slaveholding women to support the institution, see Perdue et al., eds., *Weevils*, 56, 297–298, 300; Blassingame, ed., *Slave Testimony*, 456.

111. Will of Sarah Ellzey, 8 Oct. 1840, HarFP; Miscellaneous Receipts of Jane Swann Hunter, 1843–44, Hunter Family Papers, VHS; and Miscellaneous Receipts and Deeds of Catherine McCall, 1816–29, Walter Jones Collection, Leesburg Family Papers, UVA; Receipt of Anne Nalle, 5 Jan. 1841, Nalle Family Papers, VHS.

112. LouLP, 4 Dec. 1817, VSL.

113. Catherine McCall relied almost solely on the advice of her lawyer and friend, Col. Walter Jones of Leesburg, who handled her immense estate. Jones hired several overseers to supervise the agricultural sector of McCall's business ventures. By 1850, Elizabeth Carter was Loudoun's largest slaveholder, with 85. Ten years later, she was still the county's largest slaveholder with 129. Miscellaneous Receipts and Deeds of Catherine McCall, 1816–29, Walter Jones Collection, Leesburg Family Papers, UVA; Will of Sarah Ellzey, 8 Oct. 1840, HarFP; George Carter to Julia Berkeley Carter, 26 June, 30 Aug. 1818, George Carter Letter Book, VHS.

114. See, for example, the discussion of the relationship between slaveholding women and female slaves in Fox-Genovese, *Within the Plantation Household*, 334–371 passim; Also see Stevenson, "Compassion and Powerlessness," passim. For examples of slave-holding women's assessment of their slaves, see, for example, Affidavits of Elizabeth Temple, Oct. 1850, 21 May 1859, HarFP, VHS; Mary E. P. Allen to John Allen, 27 April 1855, Allen Family Papers, UVA; Waverly Caperton to James Alexander, 8 June 1849, Caperton Family Papers, VHS.

115. See, for example, slave women's comments on slaveholding women in Perdue et al., eds., *Weevils*, 180, 297–98; and Still, ed., *Underground Railroad*, 112–14; Slaveholding women's comments about slave women in Margaret Harrison to Sarah Powell Harrison, 12 Nov. 1838?, HarFP; and Sarah Powell Harrison to Elizabeth Powell Conrad, 9 Nov. 1843, ConFP, VHS. Also see Suzanne Lebsock, *The Free Women of Petersburg: Status and Culture in a Southern Town, 1784–1860* (New York: W.W. Norton, 1984), 136–41; Fox-Genovese, *Within the Plantation Household*, 334–71 passim; and Stevenson, "Compassion and Powerlessness,"passim.

116. Catherine Powell to Elizabeth Powell Conrad, 20 Jan. 1830, 20 June 1843; Sarah Powell Harrison to Elizabeth Powell Conrad, 11 Nov. 1843, ConFP, VHS.

117. Robert Conrad to Sarah Powell Harrison, 31 Jan. 1840, HarFP, VHS. Also see Burr Powell to Robert Conrad, 13 Dec. 1830, ConFP, VHS.

118. Sarah Powell Harrison to Elizabeth Powell Conrad, 9 Nov. 1843, ConFP, VHS.

119. Margaret Lucinda Harrison to Sarah Powell Harrison, 12 Nov. 1838?, HarFP, VHS.

120. Oscar Ball's account is recorded in Still, ed., *Underground Railroad*, 399; Elizabeth Powell Conrad to Burr Powell, 25 Dec. 1829?, ConFP, VHS; Catherine B. Conrad, "Uncle Stephen," *Southern Workman* 30 (1901): 153–56; Indenture, 7 Jan. 1833, ConFP, VHS.

121. *Loudoun Chronicle*, 10 Aug. 1846, VSL; *Washingtonian*, 3 Aug. 1849, VSL; 27 Aug. 1842; Burr Harrison to Matthew Harrison, 4 Dec. 1856?, HarFP, VHS.

122. See, for example, slave women's accounts of slaveholding women in Perdue et al., eds., *Weevils*, 1, 55–56, 63, 72, 97–98, 180, 201, 257, 318, 332; Still, ed., *Underground Railroad*, 112–14; Yetman, ed., *Voices from Slavery*, 133.

123. Most slave women also associated the class status of Euro-American southerners with behavioral ideals and the ability to assume these standards. Perdue et al., eds., *Weevils*, 318.

124. See, for example, slave men's accounts of slaveholding women in ibid., 62, 78, 82, 85, 91, 167, 306; Still, ed., *Underground Railroad*, 112, 442, 447.

125. See, for example, Perdue et al., eds., *Weevils*, 25–26, 117, 206–7, 274; Drew, ed., *North-Side View of Slavery*, 38, 48, 115; Rawick, ed., *American Slave,* 16: 46.

126. Drew, ed., *North-Side View of Slavery*, 52.

CHAPTER 7. SLAVE FAMILY STRUCTURE

1. Eber M. Pettit, *Sketches in the History of the Underground Railroad* (Fredonia, N.Y.: McKinstry and Son, 1879), 17–23.

2. Several instructive discussions of the U.S. southern slave family are now available. See, for example, Ann Patton Malone, *Sweet Chariot: Slave Family and Household Structure in Nineteenth-Century Louisiana* (Chapel Hill: Univ. of North Carolina Press, 1992); Herbert Gutman, *The Black Family in Slavery and Freedom* (New York: Pantheon, 1976); John Blassingame, *The Slave Community: Plantation Life in the Old South*, rev. ed. (New York: Oxford Univ. Press, 1980); Eugene Genovese, *Roll, Jordan, Roll: The World the Slaves Made* (New York: Pantheon, 1974); Allan Kulikoff, *Tobacco and Slaves: The Development of Southern Cultures in the Chesapeake, 1680–1800* (Chapel Hill: Univ. of North Carolina Press, 1986); T. H. Breen and Stephen Innes, *"Myne Owne Ground": Race and Freedom on Virginia's Eastern Shore, 1640–1676* (New York: Oxford Univ. Press, 1980); Orville Vernon Burton, *In My Father's House Are Many Mansions: Family and Community in Edgefield, South Carolina* (Chapel Hill: Univ. of North Carolina Press, 1985); Deborah Gray White, "Female Slaves: Sex Roles and Status in the Antebellum Plantation South," *Journal of Family History* 3, no. 3 (Fall 1983): 248–61; Jo Ann Manfra and Robert Dykstra, "Serial Marriage and the Origins of the Black Stepfamily: The Rowanty Evidence," *Journal of American History* 72, no. 1 (June 1985): 18–44; and Brenda Stevenson, "Distress and Discord in Virginia Slave Families, 1830–1860," in *In Joy and In Sorrow: Women, Family and Marriage in the Victorian South, 1830–1900*, Carol Bleser, ed. (New York: Oxford Univ. Press, 1990), 103–24.

3. John Mbiti, *African Religions and Philosophy* (Garden City: Doubleday, 1970), 135–42, 174–94, Philip Curtin, ed., *Africa Remembered: Narratives by West Africans from the Era of the Slave Trade* (Madison: Univ. of Wisconsin Press, 1967), passim; Deborah White, *Ar'n't I a Woman?, Female Slaves in the Plantation South* (New York: W. W.

Norton, 1985), 63–69, 106–9; Kulikoff, *Tobacco and Slaves*, 326–34; Gutman, *Black Family in Slavery and Freedom*, 211–12, 328–55.

4. Donald M. Sweig, "Northern Virginia Slavery: A Statistical and Demographic Investigation" (Ph.D. dissertation, College of William and Mary, 1982), 23, 39, 54.

5. There was of course the possibility of biracial marriage, but colonial law as early as 1691 outlawed such relationships between blacks and whites, and few Native Americans still resided in the area to be available to be spouses. A growing mulatto class within the slave population and especially among the nascent group of free people of color in the county attest to continued sociosexual activity and perhaps family relationships. June Guild, ed., *Black Laws of Virginia: A Summary of the Legislative Acts of Virginia Concerning Negroes from Earliest Times to the Present* (Richmond: Whittet and Shepperson, 1936; New York: Negro Universities Press, 1969), 23–23; Loudoun Freedom Negro Slips, Loudoun County Court House, Leesburg, Virginia.

6. Native-born slave women, in contrast to those from Africa, usually began bearing children at an earlier age, could provide their infants with natural immunities to local illness, and generally had superior physical and emotional health. Consequently, they experienced more live births than their African peers and their children may have been healthier. Kulikoff, *Tobacco and Slaves*, 68–70; 326, 330–32, 334, 336–344.

7. 51.4% were part of holdings of 10 or fewer slaves. Sweig, "Northern Virginia Slavery," 113, 144.

8. By 1820, 54% were part of holdings of 10 or fewer slaves; by 1850, 54.5% were. U.S. Department of Commerce, Bureau of the Census, Manuscript Federal Census, Loudoun County, Virginia (hereafter referred to as FedCenLC), 1820, roll 137; 1850, Slave Schedule, roll 989.

9. 19% in 1760, 16% in 1820 and 21 % in 1850, for exmple, were part of holdings of more than 20. FedCenLC, 1820, roll 137; 1850, Slave Schedule, roll 989; Sweig, "Northern Virginia Slavery," 43.

10. The male/female ratio for those aged 15 to 45 years who were part of holdings of between two and ten slaves in 1850, for example, was 0.78. This relatively high number, however, accounts for less than two-thirds of those households. Fully 35% of small slaveholdings had at least one woman and sometimes two to three and no men present. Of those slaves between 15 and 45 years in Loudoun slaveholdings of 10 to 15 slaves slaves in 1850, however, there was a male/female ratio of 1.5 to 1.0 and men were present in virtually every holding. The ratio began to decline as the numbers of slaves in the holding increased to eventually become almost even in the largest holdings: 16–20 slaves, 1.352 to 1.0; 21–30 slaves, 1.198 to 1.0; and 31+ , 0.993 to 1.0. The statistics for 1860 are similar. The overall male/female adult ratio for holdings of ten and less in 1860 was 0.73. Yet 40% of the small holdings had no men present when women were present. The larger holdings suggest a larger male presence. In those holdings: 10–15, 1.2 to 1.0; 16–20, 1.27 to 1.0; 21–30, 2. 5 to 1, 31–40, 1.01 to 1, etc., FedCenLC, 1850, Slave Schedule, roll 989; 1860, Slave Schedule, roll 1393.

11. Males comprised 49% and females 51% of all county slaves aged 0 years and older in 1850, for example. Males comprised 52% in 1820 and 51% in 1830. FedCenLC, 1820, roll 137; 1830, roll 193; 1850, Slave Schedule, roll 989.

12. Males comprised 48.3% and females 51.7% in 1850 for example, of those slaves

aged 15 years and older, FedCenLC, 1850, Slave Schedule, roll 989.

13. FedCenLC, 1850, Slave Schedule, roll 989; Sweig, "Northern Virginia Slavery," 113, 144.

14. Miscellaneous Correspondence and Accounts of John Mercer and Charles Fenton Mercer, Mercer Family Papers, Virginia Historical Society, Richmond (hereafter referred to as VHS); Eugene Scheel, *The History of Middleburg and Vicinity* (Warrenton, Va.: Piedmont Press, 1987), 9–11; Douglas R. Egerton, *Charles Fenton Mercer and the Trial of National Conservatism* (Jackson: Univ. Press of Mississippi, 1989), 3; Mason Ellzey, "The Cause We Lost and the Land We Love," 16, Ellzey Papers, VHS. George Rust petitioned the Virginia Assembly in 1810 for permission to transfer 29 of his slaves usually held in Maryland to his plantation in Loudoun. Loudoun Legislative Petition (hereafter referred to as LouLP), 11 Dec. 1810, Virginia State Library, Richmond (hereafter referred to as VSL).

15. Nancy Tanner, "Matrifocality in Indonesia and Africa and Among Black Americans," in *Woman, Culture and Society,* Michelle Zimbalist Rosaldo and Louise Lamphere, eds. (Stanford: Stanford Univ. Press, 1974), 129–56, 131. Two simple types of matrifocality are discussed here: structural matrifocality which denotes the presence of a slave mother and her children in a single slave household with no identifiable father present; and functional matrifocality which indicates the presence of an identifiable, but "abroad," father who only occasionally (e.g. weekends and holidays) was in the household of a slave mother and her children.

16. George Washington owned several thousand acres of land in Fairfax, Frederick, Hampshire, and Loudoun counties. Like many of the other planters in the area, he divided his slave property among his various farms and business operations, hiring some out when possible, renting some himself when necessary. He also had white indentured laborers and hired several overseers and underoverseers to supervise his slaves. Washington also sometimes used black men as overseers of his Dogue Run, River, and Muddy Hole farms. "Negroes Belonging to George Washington in His Own Right and by Marriage, 1799," Mount Vernon Library, Fairfax County, Virginia (hereafter referred to as MVL); "Housing and Family Life of the Mount Vernon Negro," MVL; "A List of George Washington's Tithables in Fairfax County in June 4th 1761, 1762, 1763, . . . 1774, 1786–1789," MVL; "Black Mount Vernon," MVL; John C. Fitzpatrick, ed., *The Diaries of George Washington, 1748–1799,* vol. 3: 1786–1788 (Boston: Houghton Mifflin, 1925), 3:15–22; Donald Sweig, "African-American Families at Mount Vernon, 1799," MVL; Charles Cecil Wall, *George Washington: Citizen-Soldier* (Charlottesville: Univ. Press of Virginia, 1980), 55–61; Saul K. Padover, *The Washington Papers: Basic Sons from the Public and Private Writings of George Washington* (New York: Harper and Bros., 1955); Halsted L. Ritter, *Washington as a Business Man* (New York: Sears Publishing, 1931).

17. Compilations derived from: "Negroes Belonging to George Washington in His Own Right and by Marriage, 1799," MVL.

18. Regarding the ancestral line of William Fitzhugh and the family's lifestyle in seventeenth-century Virginia, see Richard B. Davis, ed., *William Fitzhugh and His Chesapeake World, 1676–1701: The Fitzhugh Letters and Other Documents* (Chapel Hill: Univ. of North Carolina Press, 1963), passim. The four farms which comprised the Ravensworth estate were Ravensworth, Centre, Backlick, and Pohick.

19. Lists of W. H. Fitzhugh's Ravensworth slaves dated 1801 and 1830 compiled in Sweig, "Northern Virginia Slavery," 116–31.

20. Ibid.

21. LouLP, 8, 11 Dec. 1810, VSL. Harrison Williams, *Legends of Loudoun: An Account of the History and Homes of a Border County of Virginia's Northern Neck* (Richmond: Garrett and Massie, 1938), 174–75.

22. Nancy Chappelear Baird, ed., *Journals of Amanda Virginia Edmonds: Lass of the Mosby Confederacy* (Stephens City, Va.: Commercial Press, 1950), 13, entry date 22 April 1858.

23. Will of William West, 26 June 1769, Will Book A, Loudoun County, Virginia, p. 226, VSL.

24. Loudoun County Court Order, 13 Oct. 1814; "Slave Inventory of Adam Shover," 2 Nov. 1817; "Notice," 2 Jan. 1822; Receipts of George Shover, 17 Jan., 20 June 1822, Shover Family Papers, VSL.

25. Powell Family Genealogical Notes, n.p., Gray Family Papers, VHS. Also see "A Brief History of the First Harrisons of Virginia: Descendants of Cuthbert Harrison, Esquire of Ancaster, England from A.D. 1600 to A.D. 1915," pamphlet, n.d., Harrison Family Papers (hereafter referred to as HarFP), VHS; "Notes on Brooke-Powell Family," *Virginia Magazine of History and Biography* 15, no. 2 (June 1908): 201–3; Scheel, *History of Middleburg*, 51; and "Death of Matthew Harrison," *Loudoun Mirror*, 28 Jan. 1875, VHS.

26. "A Brief History of the First Harrisons of Virginia," n.p.; FedCenLC, 1820, roll 137, pp. 135A, 136.

27. FedCenLC, 1820, roll 137, pp.135A, 136.

28. FedCenLC,1830, roll 193, p.16; 1820, roll 137, pp. 135A, 136; Burr Powell to Robert Conrad, 13 Dec. 1830, Conrad Family Papers (hereafter referred to as ConFP), VHS.

29. "Notes on Brooke-Powell Family," 201–3; "A Brief History of the First Harrisons of Virginia."

30. "A Brief History of the First Harrisons of Virginia"; Williams, *Legends of Loudoun*, 174; *Washingtonian,* 19 Oct. 1849, VSL.

31. FedCenLC, 1820, roll 137, p. 126A.

32. Ibid. 1830, roll 193, p. 105.

33. "A Brief History of the First Harrisons of Virginia"; Burr Powell to Robert Conrad, 13 Dec. 1830, ConFP, VHS.

34. FedCenLC, 1840, roll 564, p. 164.

35. *Washingtonian*, 19 Oct. 1849, VSL. The first sale of Powell's property was held on 7 Nov. 1849. Subsequent sales of all remaining property occurred in early December. *Loudoun Chronicle*, 7 Nov. 1849, VSL.

36. *Washingtonian*, 19 Oct. 1849, VSL; Robert Conrad to Powell Conrad, 26 Oct. 1849, ConFP, VHS.

37. Robert Conrad to Powell Conrad, 26 Oct. 1849, ConFP, VHS.

38. Fifty-six women in Loudoun owned 342 slaves in 1830 for an average of 6.11. Ellzey was the largest female slaveholder in the county that year. FedCenLC, 1830, roll 193, p. 2.

39. Ibid.

40. The fate of Ellzey's slaves who disappear from her household between 1830 and 1840 is uncertain. While she could have sold some or they could have died, it also is possible that, having completed her will in 1840, she began distributing her slave property to their future owners that year. These slaves would appear as living in other households when, legally, they still belonged to her. FedCenLC, 1830, roll 193, p. 2; 1840, roll 564, p. 221; Will of Sarah Ellzey, 8 Oct.1840, HarFP, VHS.

41. Will of Sarah Ellzey, 8 Oct., 1840, HarFP, VHS.

42. Ibid.

43. The final draft of Sarah Ellzey's will was written on 28 April 1852 and probated on 8 Aug. 1853. It is found in McDonald Papers, VHS.

44. Slave lists surveyed include: Fitzhugh List (Madison Co.), 1853, Ambrose Powell Hill Papers, VHS; Ledger of William and Samuel Vance Gatewood (Essex and Bath Cos.), 1772–1863, VHS; Robert and Charles Bruce Slave Lists (City of Richmond and Charlotte Co.), 1798–1859, Bruce Family Papers, VHS; William H. Gray List (Loudoun Co.), 1839–65, Joshua Skinner Slave List, 1785–1835, VHS; List of the Bryan Family Slaves (Gloucester Co.), 1845–65, Grinnan Family Papers, VHS; Slave Lists of Col. C.W. Gooch (Richmond), 1830, 1839, 1852, Gooch Family Papers, VHS; Slave List of Sarah Fitzgerald (Nottoway Co.), 1864, Fitzgerald Family Papers, VHS; Digges Slave List, 1770–1860 (Frederick Co.), Digges Family Papers, VHS.

The vast majority of ex-slaves from across Virginia who gave detailed information about their lives are represented in Charles L. Perdue, Thomas E. Barden, and Robert K. Phillips, eds., *Weevils in the Wheat: Interviews with Virginia Ex-Slaves* (Charlottesville: Univ. Press of Virginia, 1976). They overwhelmingly identified their mothers as the primary providers of care and socialization during their childhoods. Fully 82% of these ex-slaves, who represent the last generations of Virginia bondswomen and men from around the state, spoke of the physical presence of their mothers during most of their childhood years. Only 42%, however, recalled consistent contact with their fathers. Also, at least one-third of those who did make mention of the presence of their fathers during their childhood, noted that these men did not reside on the same farm or plantation with them, but lived elsewhere and only could visit on weekend days or holidays. Purdue et al., eds., *Weevils in the Wheat*, passim.

45. There also was a two-generational parent-inclusive household noted in the 1852 list: the elderly couple Aaron and Sukey, their three children—Louisa, Julia, and Richard, and the youngest generation of their family—Louisa's unnamed child of eighteen months. Slave Lists of Colonel C. W. Gooch, 1830, 1839, 1852, Gooch Family Papers, VHS.

46. Ibid., 1830.

47. See, for example, the numerous early laws established in Guild, ed., *Black Laws of Virginia*, 21–24.

48. The 1662 statute read: "Whereas some doubts have arisen whether children got by any Englishman upon a negro woman should be slave or free, *Be it therefore enacted and declared by this present grand assembly*, that all children borne in this country shall be held bound or free only according to the condition of the mother, *And* that if any Christian shall commit fornication with a negro man or woman, he or she offending shall pay

double the fines imposed by the former act." William Waller Hening, ed., *The Statutes at Large of Virginia (1619–1682)*, vol. 2 (New York: R. &. W. & G. Bartow, 1823), 170.

49. See note 44.

50. The law of 1662 also mandated that those "Christians" who had sexual relations with "negroes" were to be fined. The 1691 statute stipulated that the mulatto children born of free or servant white women and black males were to be "bound out" by church wardens until the age of thirty. The Virginia colonial legislation lowered the ages of release in 1765 to 21 years for males and 18 years for females. Further legislation passed in 1753 stipulated a six-month prison term and a fine of £10 for whites who intermarried with blacks or mulattoes. An additional law of 1792 set the fine for intermarriage at $30. Guild, ed., *Black Laws of Virginia*, 26–27.

51. Sweig estimates, for example, that 29% of the Loudoun slave population left the county during the decade 1820 to 1830, and 98% of those were part of the domestic slave trade. He asserts that throughout the area "family breakup of slaves transferred by the trade appears to have been especially high." Sweig, "Northern Virginia Slavery," 189–261, esp. 253–60. Quote from 259. I estimate from average rates of birth and death for the year 1849 to 1850 in order to establish a crude growth rate. Approximately 1300 Loudoun slaves, or about 19% of the total slave population, left the county between 1850 and 1860. The large majority of these slaves left with long distance slave traders. J. B. D. Debow, *Statistical View of the United States . . . Being a Compendium of the Seventh Census . . . 1850* (Washington, D.C.: AOP Nicholson, 1854), 259. Also see Blassingame, *Slave Community*, rev. ed. 175–77; Manfra and Dykstra, "Serial Marriage and the Origins of the Black Stepfamily," 32–34; Richard Sutch, "The Breeding of Slaves for Sale and the Westward Expansion of Slavery, 1830–1860," in *Race and Slavery in the Western Hemisphere: Quantitative Studies*, Stanley Engerman and Eugene Genovese, eds. (Princeton: Princeton Univ. Press, 1975), app. tables 4 and 5, pp. 207, 209; Robert Bruce Slave List, VHS; and Perdue et al., eds., *Weevils*, passim, esp. 1–5.

52. Of the 87 persons who discussed their childhood in Perdue et al., eds., *Weevils*, representing the last generations of Virginia's slaves, fully 18% suggested that neither their mothers nor their fathers contributed significantly to their rearing. Also see Stevenson, "Distress and Discord," 105–8.

53. Norman Yetman, ed., *Voices from Slavery* (New York: Holt, Rinehart and Winston, 1970), 181–84.

54. Perdue et al., eds., *Weevils*, 33.

55. Sweig, "Northern Virginia Slavery," 206; Sutch, "The Breeding of Slaves for Sale," app. tables 4 and 5, pp. 207, 209.

56. Samuel Janney, *Memoirs of Samuel M. Janney, Late of Lincoln, Loudoun County, Va.* (Philadelphia: Friend's Book Association, 1881), 30, Janney Papers, VSL.

57. Henry Watson, *Narrative of Henry Watson, a Fugitive Slave* (Boston: Bela Marsh, 1848), 5–6.

CHAPTER 8. SLAVE MARRIAGE AND FAMILY RELATIONS

1. Regarding slave marriage, see John Blassingame, ed., *Slave Testimony: Two Centuries of Letters, Speeches, Interviews, and Autobiographies* (Baton Rouge: Louisiana State

Univ. Press, 1977), 561–62; Charles L. Perdue, Thomas E. Barden, and Robert K. Phillips, eds. *Weevils in the Wheat: Interviews with Virginia Ex-Slaves* (Charlottesville: Univ. Press of Virginia, 1976), 129, 230.

2. Perdue et al., eds., *Weevils*, 230.

3. Ibid., 129; Blassingame, ed., *Slave Testimony*, 561–62; *The Negro in Virginia*, compiled by the Virginia Federal Writers' Project of the Work Projects Administration in the State of Virginia (New York: Hastings, 1940), 81.

4. George P. Rawick, ed., *The American Slave,* vol. 16, *Virginia* (Westport, Conn.: Greenwood Press, 1972), 45; Gray Family Bible; Gray Farm Book, 1 Jan. 1853, Gray Family Papers, Virginia Historical Society, Richmond (hereafter referred to as VHS).

5. Benjamin Drew, ed., *A North-Side View of Slavery, the Refugee; or the Narratives of Fugitive Slaves in Canada Related by Themselves with an Account of the History and Condition of the Colored Population of Upper Canada,* (Boston: John Jewett, 1856), 31.

6. John W. Blassingame, *The Slave Community: Plantation Life in the Old South* (New York: Oxford Univ. Press, 1972), 165–77; Deborah White, *Ar'n't I a Woman?: Female Slaves in the Plantation South* (New York: W. W. Norton, 1985), 144–58; Eugene Genovese, *Roll, Jordan, Roll: The World the Slaves Made* (New York: Pantheon, 1974), 443–523; Herbert Gutman, *The Black Family in Slavery and Freedom 1750–1925.* (New York: Pantheon 1976), passim; Randal D. Day and Daniel Hook, "A Short History of Divorce: Jumping the Broom—And Back Again," *Journal of Divorce* 10, no. 3/4 (Spring/Summer 1987): 57–58; quote from *Negro in Virginia*, 82.

7. Day and Hook, "A Short History of Divorce," 57–58.

8. *Negro in Virginia*, 84.

9. Quote from ibid., 83.

10. Several years later, Martha, David, and their children successfully escaped slavery in Loudoun. William Still, ed., *The Underground Railroad: A Record of Facts, Authentic Narratives, Letters, etc.* (Philadelphia: Porter and Coates, 1872; New York: Arno Press, 1968), 260.

11. Slaves often taught each other rules of exogamy through the stories they told of "mistaken" marriages between two persons too closely related by blood. Quote from: Perdue et al., eds., *Weevils*, 105; also see 89.

12. Masters allowed abroad husbands, but usually not wives, to visit their spouses, one day a week (Saturday evening through Sunday evening), if the woman did not live a great distance away. Ibid., 89, 209; Rawick, ed., *American Slave*, 16: 45; John Malvin, *The Autobiography of John Malvin, Free Negro, 1795–1880*, Allan Peskin, ed. (1879; Kent, Ohio: Kent State Univ. Press, 1988), 37.

13. Drew, ed., *North-Side View of Slavery*, 31.

14. William and two of his brothers were taken to Baltimore at the same time to be sold. William was sold with one to New Orleans; the other brother he believed was sold to Georgia. Ibid., 56–58.

15. Ibid., 58–59.

16. W. C. Scott to Mrs. Francis Cabell, 9 Jan. 1861, Scott Papers, Alderman Library, Univ. of Virginia, Charlottesville (hereafter referred to as UVA). Martha and David Bennett, slaves in Loudoun County, Virginia, eventually escaped to freedom with their two children. Still, ed., *Underground Railroad*, 260.

17. Perdue et al., eds., *Weevils*, 118, 104.

18. Ibid., 209. JoAnn Manfra and Robert Dykstra, "Serial Marriage and the Origins of the Black Stepfamily: The Rowanty Evidence," *Journal of American History* 72, no.1 (June 1985): 32; Blassingame, *Slave Community*, tables 1 and 2, p. 90.

19. Perdue et al., eds., *Weevils,* 209.

20. Ibid. As early as 1953, Miles Fisher identified one of the sources to the end of slave polygamy, writing with regard to the end of the Civil War that ". . . citizens did their utmost to bring the African cult to terms with American institutions. A host of missionaries sought to evangelize Negroes. The federal government put an end to its sanction of polygamous marital relations for Negroes in 1865 by decreeing that legal marriage, singling out Negroes, existed only when one man and one woman lived together under license." His statement, and the document from which it derived, also inadvertently suggests that polygamy was more than a rare act among slaves. Miles Mark Fisher, *Negro Slave Songs in the United States* (1953; New York: First Carol Publishing, 1990), 174–75. Also see various statements of contraband slave men and women in Virginia regarding marital structures in Henry Swint, ed., *Dear Ones at Home: Letters from Contraband Camps* (Nashville: Vanderbilt Univ. Press, 1966), passim.

21. White, *Ar'n't I a Woman?*, 145–48; John W. Blassingame, *The Slave Community: Plantation Life in the Old South*, rev. ed. (New York: Oxford Univ. Press, 1980), 171–73; Genovese, *Roll, Jordan, Roll*, 484–92, 500–501; Still, ed., *Underground Railroad*, 411. Also see "A Slave's Story," *Putnam Monthly Magazine* 9 (June 1857): 617; Blassingame, ed., *Slave Testimony*, 118.

22. See, for example, Blassingame, ed., *Slave Testimony*, 46–47, 96–97, 115–19, 491.

23. Perdue et al., eds., *Weevils*, 6.

24. Ibid., 201–2, 244–45, 266–67; Loudoun County Order Book, vols. 1–2, 16 Dec. 1807, pp. 216, 221.

25. For a discussion of text and ideas of gender convention available to colonial southerners, see Julia Cherry Spruill, *Women's Life and Work in the Southern Colonies* (1938; rpt., New York: W. W. Norton, 1972), 220–23; regarding antebellum conventions see, for example, "To a Young Bride," *American Ladies Magazine* 7, no. 11 (Nov. 1835): 487; "A Chapter from the 'Book of Marriage,'" American *Ladies Magazine* 6, no. 6 (June 1833): 262–64, VSL; "Female Influence," *Ladies Magazine and Literary Gazette* 1, no. 6 (June 1828): 268; "Female Piety," *Ladies Magazine and Literary Gazette* 1, no. 4 (April 1828): 177, VSL; "To a Young Mother," *American Ladies Magazine* 9, no. 7 (July 1837): 390, VSL; and George Fitzhugh, "Sociology for the South," in *Slavery Defended: The Voices of the Old South*, Eric McKitrick, ed. (Englewood Cliffs, N.J.: Prentice-Hall, 1963), 37–38, 45.

26. Perdue et al., eds., *Weevils*, 255–61.

27. Ironically, Folkes's account of her socialization stands in perverse contrast to those passed on by another group of antebellum Southerners. One Virginia ex-slave, for example, expressed the sorrow that he felt for a raped black female teen as he recounted a legacy of misogyny and violence that her owner perpetuated: "[Ethel Mae] told me 'bout Marsa bringing his son Levey . . . down to the cabin," the former bondsmen noted. "They both took her—the father showing the son what it was all about." Perdue et al., eds., *Weevils*, 36, 48–49, 93, 95–96, 257, 300–301.

28. Perdue et al., eds., *Weevils*, 257–59.

29. Ibid., 48–49.

30. Regarding the importance of children to ideas of immortality among slaves, see, for example, naming patterns indicated or discussed in: List of slaves of Ann Powell Burwell, VHS; Ledger of Cyrus and William Gatewood, Gatewood Family Papers, VHS. Also see Gutman, *The Black Family in Slavery and Freedom*, 197–201. Regarding slaves' view of children as future security, see, for example, Blassingame, ed., *Slave Testimony*, 10; Swint, ed., *Dear Ones at Home,* 61.

31. Minnie Folkes's mother married her as a young teenager and did not instruct Minnie in her sexual duties to her husband. She refused to have sexual intercourse with her husband until her mother told her that it was her duty as a wife to do so. Perdue et al., eds., *Weevils*, 238, 300–301.

32. Ibid., 95–96. See, for example, Still, ed., *Underground Railroad*, 41; Blassingame, ed., *Slave Testimony*, 118.

33. Still, ed., *Underground Railroad*, 41; Drew, ed., *North-Side View of Slavery*, 31; Dorothy Sterling, ed., *We Are Your Sisters Black Women in the Nineteenth Century* (New York: W.W. Norton, 1984), 45–46; U.S. Department of Commerce, Bureau of the Census, Manuscript Federal Census, Loudoun County, Virginia (hereafter referred to as FedCenLC), 1820, roll 137; 1830, roll 193; Loudoun County Deed Books, X, 407; 2–C, 5; 2–I, 344–45, Loudoun County Court House.

34. William Forbes to George Carter, 20 May 1805, Carter Family Papers (hereafter referred to as CarFP); George Carter to Sophia Carter, 20 June 1816, George Carter Letter Book (hereafter referred to as GCLB), VHS. Also see Perdue et al., eds., *Weevils*, 300–301.

35. Joseph G. Kennedy, *Population of the United States in 1860: Compiled from the Original Returns of the Eighth Census* (Washington, D.C.: Government Printing Office, 1864), 517; Perdue et al., eds., *Weevils*, 25, 199–200; James W. C. Pennington, *Fugitive Blacksmith; or, Events in the History of James W. C. Pennington, Pastor of a Presbyterian Church, New York* . . . (New York: G. P. Putnam's, 1903), v-vii.

36. Ironically, miscegenation elicited explosive issues of force, female purity, and sexual sanctity in both white and black families, all the while creating a class of women—biracial and multiracial—that both slave and slaveholding men found physically desirable. Color consciousness and stratification among blacks resulted from a combination of factors such as a consistently high rate of miscegenation and, relatedly, a large biracial population among slaves and free blacks, as well as the popularity of racist ideologies concerning color difference and racial hierarchy and their practical application in antebellum Virginia society. Unresolved feelings of "natural" black inferiority caused some slaves to treat racially mixed and generally light-skinned slaves as superior to their darker peers. Moreover, many biracial female slaves were domestics or skilled slaves who were afforded an elevated status in their masters' homes and their slave communities because of their occupational and cultural differences. See, for example, Perdue et al., eds., *Weevils*, 202; Austin Steward, *Twenty-two Years a Slave, and Forty Years a Freeman: Embracing a Correspondence of Several Years, While President of Wilberforce Colony, London, Canada, West* (Rochester, N.Y.: William Alling, 1857), 21.

37. Perdue et al., eds., *Weevils*, 117, 207.

38. Ibid.

39. Recall, for example, that Loudoun slave women aged 15 to 45 years dominated, by more than 1.5 to 1.0, their age cohorts in the slave population of those holdings of fewer than ten slaves. Ibid., 202; Kennedy, *Population of the United States in 1860*, 517; FedCenLC, 1850, Slave Schedule, Roll 989.

40. The slave's response to miscegenation differed widely and was complicated by a number of issues. Few felt comfortable embracing a slave woman who appeared to prefer the sexual attention of white rather than black men; and even those women who were forced to have sexual relations with slaveholding men (and most were forced) sometimes received a mixed reception in the slave community. Mothers and other kin, who were sensitive to the kinds of teasing, insults and rough treatment that their bi-racial children might receive at the hands of blacks and whites, often lied to their young about their paternity or taught them to avoid the issue when questioned about it. Swint, ed., *Dear Ones at Home* 39, 55–56, 73; Perdue et al., eds., *Weevils*, 108, 293.

41. Perdue, Barden, Phillips, eds., *Weevils*, 291.

42. Ibid.

43. Garner suggests that it was his wives' responsibility to have children, not his own. Indeed, slaves may have thought that infertility, when apparent, derived from a woman and not a man. Ibid., 101.

44. For further discussion, see Liam Hudson and Bernardine Jacot, *The Way Men Think: Intellect, Intimacy and the Erotic Imagination* (New Haven: Yale Univ. Press, 1991); Olga Silverstein and Beth Rashbaum, *The Courage to Raise Good Men* (New York: Viking, 1994); James H. Cones III and Joseph White, *The Social Psychology of the African American Male* (New York: Freeman Press, 1996, forthcoming).

45. Perdue et al., eds., *Weevils*, 232.

46. As slave girls grew older, issues of sexual and social morality gained great importance. Mothers and female kin stressed sexual purity and social accountability. Perdue et al., eds., *Weevils*, 92–95.

47. Broad Run Baptist Church Record, entries dated 18 May 1774, 22 March 1783, and passim. Other offenses warranting loss of attendance privileges included slandering and disobeying masters, fornication, bad temper, and drunkenness. Broad Run Baptist Church Record, 1782–1872, VHS.

48. Records of Broad Run Baptist Church, 1762–1872, VHS.

49. Three of the Jackson children died while very young. Rawick, ed., *American Slave*, 16: 45; William H. Gray Farm Book, 1839–65 passim, Gray Family Papers, VHS; Perdue et al., eds., *Weevils*, 204–5, 291; White, *Ar'n't I a Woman?*, 101–3; Norman Yetman, ed., *Voices from Slavery* (New York: Holt, Rinehart and Winston, 1970), 92.

50. Swint, ed., *Dear Ones at Home*, 61; Perdue et al., eds., *Weevils*, 96; Gutman, *Black Family in Slavery and Freedom*, 76–77; 80–83n.; White, *Ar'n't I a Woman?*, 84–86, 98–103.

51. Perdue et al., eds., *Weevils*, 277; Gutman, *Black Family in Slavery and Freedom*, 76–77; 80–83n.; White, *Ar'n't I a Woman?*, 84–86, 98–103; *Democratic Mirror*, 10 Nov. 1858.

52. See the discussion of ex-slave females of their prenatal treatment in Perdue et al., eds., *Weevils*, 63; Swint, ed., *Dear Ones at Home*, 128. For a more general discussion of

this issue, see Sterling, ed., *We Are Your Sisters*, 39–40; White, *Ar'n't I a Woman?*, 104. Data used to compile average age of first birth and spacing of births for Loudoun area slave women from: Slave List of Edward Digges, 1770–1860, Digges Family Papers, VHS; William H. Gray Slave List, 1846–63, Gray Family Papers, VHS; R. Stringfellow Family Bible, 1800–1860, London Family Papers, VHS; Fitzhugh Slave List, 1830, in Donald Sweig, "Northern Virginia Slavery: A Statistical and Demographic Investigation" (Ph.D. dissertation, College of William and Mary, 1982), 127–29.

53. Information for computation of the average age of Virginia slave mothers at first birth and their average spacing between live births was compiled from slave lists dated during the period, 1800–1865, located in the William H. Gray Farm Book, VHS; Ledger of George Saunders in Saunders Family Papers, Virginia State Library, Richmond (hereafter referred to as VSL); Ledger of William Gatewood and Samuel Vance Gatewood, William Gatewood Papers; Stringfellow Family Bible, Stringfellow Family Papers; Allen T. Caperton Family Bible, Caperton Family Papers; John Young Mason Papers (lists of slaves located at Richmond and Day's Neck Plantation); William Bolling Papers; and Slave List of James Alexander, Baskerville Family Papers, all VHS. Trussell and Steckel estimate that the mean age of first birth for slave mothers throughout the antebellum South was 20.6 years, "about two years earlier than Southern white women." James Trussell and Richard Steckel, "The Age of Slaves at Menarche and Their First Birth," *Journal of Interdisciplinary History* 8, no. 3 (Winter 1978): 492.

54. An analysis of the ages at first live birth of the slave mothers on William Fitzhugh's "Ravensworth" and his other three contiguous farms located in the Loudoun vicinity, for example, indicates that the average age at which slave women began to have children was 19.13 years in 1801 and 18.8 years in 1830. These lists also indicate that the average age of fathers at first live birth of an alive child with a long term spouse was 24.25 years in 1801, but only 20.8 years in 1830. Thus, the average age of first birth for both mothers and fathers declined from the beginning of the era to the midpoint. Looking at the numbers of live children born to women at least 40 years of age at Fitzhugh's Ravensworth farm in 1801, the average number is quite similar to that found throughout the state—4.8 or almost 5 live children per mother who reached the age of menopause. The numbers of children born to women seemed to have increased substantially by the middle of the century, however, and the Fitzhugh slave women were having about 6.5 children even when they were as young as 37. Conceivably, some could have borne at least 2 or perhaps 3 other children by the time they reached menopause. It is unclear if Fitzhugh was promoting slave procreation on Ravensworth, but his records do indicate that, by the middle of the antebellum era, some conditions on his farm had changed substantially (almost half of his slaves were living in double-headed households) and as such lowered the average age at first birth for slave mothers and fathers and increased the numbers of live children that slave women bore. In contrast, Robert Fogel calculates a "crude" birth rate for antebellum southern slave women of 6.2 children and a "total fertility rate" of 9.24 children. Sweig, "Northern Virginia Slavery," 127–29; Robert W. Fogel, *Without Consent or Contract: The Rise and Fall of American Slavery* (New York: W. W. Norton, 1989), 126, 149. White contends that the fertility rate of slave women "was usually similar to or slightly higher than that of Southern

white women," but does not provide any evidence for her conclusion. White, *Ar'n't I a Woman?*, 87. Gutman finds that slave women on the Good Hope plantation in South Carolina began having children at an earlier age than white women, usually only had between 4 and 7 children; and the numbers they had increased over time. Gutman, *Black Family in Slavery and Freedom*, 50–51.

55. Ledger of William Gatewood and Samuel Vance Gatewood, 1772–1863, VSL.

56. Ibid. Also see Brenda E. Stevenson, "Historical Dimensions of Black Family Structure: A Revisionist Perspective of the Black Family," in *The Decline in Marriage Among African-Americans: Causes, Consequences and Policy Implications*, Belinda Tucker and Claudia Kernan Mitchell, eds. (New York: Russell, 1995), 27–56; and Brenda Stevenson's analysis of similar demographic information for the William Bolling slave register in "Distress and Discord in Virginia Slave Families, 1830–1860" in Carol Bleser, ed., *In Joy and In Sorrow: Women, Family and Marriage in the Victorian South, 1830–1900* (New York: Oxford Univ. Press, 1991), 119.

57. Steckle's findings summarized in Michael Johnson, "Upward in Slavery," *New York Review of Books* 36, no. 20 (21 Nov. 1989): 53. Also see Richard Steckel, "Slave Mortality: Analysis of Evidence from Plantation Records," *Social Science History* 3, no. 3 (Oct. 1979): 86–114. For related information, see Kenneth F. and Virginia H. Kiple, "Slave Child Mortality: Some Nutritional Answers to a Perennial Puzzle," *Journal of Social History* 10, no. 3 (March 1977): 284–309.

58. For discussions of slave childrearing, see Thomas Webber, *Deep Like the Rivers: Education in the Slave Community, 1831–1865* (New York: W. W. Norton, 1978), passim. Also see Blassingame, *Slave Community*, rev. ed., 179–91; White, *Ar'n't I a Woman?*, 69–76, 95–98, 105–16; Genovese, *Roll, Jordan, Roll*, 486–519.

59. Perdue et al., eds., *Weevils*, 149–50.

60. Swint, ed., *Dear Ones at Home*, 127; Perdue et al., eds., *Weevils*, 150, 183.

61. Yetman, ed., *Voices from Slavery*, 176, 177; Perdue et al., eds., *Weevils*, 68.

62. For examples of extended family members providing childcare and socialization in slave families, see Perdue et al., eds., *Weevils*, 3, 26, 128, 246. Also see Chapter 7, note 56, of this text.

63. Masters compiling lists of their human property routinely identified slave children as offspring of their mothers, only sometimes identifying fathers. Also most slave children from infancy to preadolescence lived with their mothers and many did not have constant contact with their fathers. June E. Guild, ed., *Black Laws of Virginia: A Summary of the Legislative Acts of Virginia Concerning Negroes from Earliest Times to the Present* (Richmond: Whittsett and Shepperson, 1936), 128–29; Perdue et al., eds., *Weevils*, passim; Rawick, ed., *American Slave*, 16: 30. For examples of attempts of Loudoun masters to sell slave mothers and children as a unit, see *Genius of Liberty*, 26 Oct. 1818; *Washingtonian,* 19 Oct. 1848; *Loudoun Chronicle,* 1 March 1850.

64. Rawick, ed., *American Slave*, 16: 45; Perdue et al., eds., *Weevils*, 26.

65. Perdue et al., eds., *Weevils*, 310.

66. Ibid., 26, 128.

67. Gutman makes note of the repeated naming of slave boys for their father as an indication of the importance of fathers to slaves. Yet analysis of other slave lists, such as that of Ann Burwell, also indicates that many slave women named their daughters for

themselves and female members of the child's maternal kin. Gutman, *The Black Family*, 197–201; Slave List of Anne Burwell, Burwell Family Papers, VHS. For a detailed discussion of slave naming practices, see: Cheryll Ann Cody, "There was no 'Absalom' on the Ball Plantations: Slave-Naming Practices in the South Carolina Low Country, 1720–1865," *American Historical Review* 92, no. 2 (June 1987): 563–96. Regarding the ways in which slaves perceived children, see Swint, ed., *Dear Ones at Home*, 61; Perdue et al., eds., *Weevils*, 26; and Rawick, ed., *American Slave*, 16: 45; Webber, *Deep like the Rivers*, 27, 32–33, 37.

68. See, for example, Burr Powell to Robert Conrad, 13 Dec. 1830, Conrad Family Papers, VHS; Genovese, *Roll, Jordan, Roll*, 91.

69. Perdue et al., eds., *Weevils*, 67, 85; Loudoun Legislative Petitions, 11 Jan. 1840, VSL.

70. Still, ed., *Underground Railroad*, 260; Mason Ellzey, "The Cause We Lost and the Land We Love," 6, Ellzey Family Papers, VHS.

71. Still, ed., *Underground Railroad*, 124–29; Scheel, *History of Middleburg*, 24, 47.

72. Still, ed., *Underground Railroad*, 124–29.

73. Ibid., 129, 411.

74. *Washingtonian*, 12 Nov. 1836, VSL.

75. Marie Tyler-McGraw, ed., "'The Prize I Mean Is the Prize of Liberty': A Loudoun County Family in Liberia," *Virginia Magazine of History and Biography* 97, no. 3 (July 1989): 355–74; Loudoun County Deed Book, X, 407; 2–C, 5; 2–W, 334–45, VSL; FedCenLC, 1820, roll 137; 1830, roll 193.

76. See, for example, the lessons of slave parents and kin in Rawick, ed., *American Slave*, 16: 25, 29; Perdue et al., eds., *Weevils*, 67, 85, 91, 128, 211, 235, 265, 317, 332 (quote from p. 235); Swint, ed., *Dear Ones at Home*, 36, 55–56, 123; Yetman, ed., *Voices from Slavery*, 133.

77. Perdue et al., eds., *Weevils*, 16–17, 123, 161, 317; Swint, ed., *Dear Ones at Home*, 123.

78. Perdue et al., eds., *Weevils*, 15–17, 108–9, 119, 161; Swint, ed., *Dear Ones at Home*, 39, 55–56, 73.

79. Manfra and Dykstra, "Serial Marriage," 32. Comparatively, John Blassingame documents that 11.9% of broken slave couples in Mississippi; 9.4% in Tennessee; and 10.7% in Louisiana resulted from "personal choice." Blassingame, *Slave Community*, 1st ed., table 1, p. 90.

80. Sutch, "The Breeding of Slaves for Sale," app. tables 4 and 5, pp. 207, 209.

CHAPTER 9. FREE BLACKS

1. Robert O. Harrow, Jr., "Black Families Have Deep Roots in Waterford," *Washington Post*, 9 Aug. 1992; "Loudoun County, Virginia 1771 Tithable List," transcribed by Pollyanna Creekmore, *Virginia Genealogist*, (1973) 17: 10, 109.

2. Regarding the various ways free people of color in the area gained their freedom, see Donald Sweig, ed., *"Registrations of Free Negroes Commencing Sept. Court 1822, Book No. 2" and "Register of Free Blacks 1835 Book 3": Being the Full Test of the Two Extant Volumes, 1822–1861, of Registrations of Free Blacks Now in the County Courthouse, Fair-*

fax, Virginia (Fairfax, Va.: History Section, Office of Comprehensive Planning, 1977); Register of Free Negroes, Fauquier County, Virginia, 1817–65, Virginia Historical Society, Richmond (hereafter referred to as VHS); and especially Collection of Free Negro Registration Slips, Loudoun County, Virginia, Loudoun County Court House, Leesburg (hereafter referred to as LCCH). Concerning the movement of Europeans and Africans to Loudoun during the early eighteenth century and their activities once located there, see Eugene Scheel, *The History of Middleburg and Vicinity* (Warrenton, Va.: Piedmont Press, 1987), 3–27; Harrison Williams, *Legends of Loudoun: An Account of the History and Homes of a Border County of Virginia's Northern Neck* (Richmond: Garrett and Massie, 1938), 1–122; Charles Poland, *From Frontier to Suburbia* (Maceline, Mo.: Walsworth Publishing, 1976), 1–62; and Joseph V. Nichols, *Legends of Loudoun Valley: True Stories from the Lives and Times of the People of Loudoun County, Virginia* (Leesburg, Va.: Potomac Press, 1961), passim.

3. Yet before1691, legislators had not articulated a criteria for black emancipation. In that year, lawmakers enacted legislation which mandated the removal of all "Negroes set free" within 6 months after receiving their new status. In 1723, they passed a statute specifically meant to curb acts of black emancipation: "No Negro or Indian slave shall be set free upon any pretence whatsoever, except for some meritorious service to be adjudged by the governor."

These restrictive legal measures, however, could not curtail the rapidly growing free African-American population which largely inherited its status from free mothers. This 1662 statute is important not only because of its implications for children born of black and servant women, but also because it aptly demonstrates the ways in which early Virginia colonial authorities hoped to structure their racially plural society. In 1691, for example, they passed a law which allowed local courts to "banish" from the colony "forever" any English or other white man, "bond or free," who married a "Negro, mulatto or Indian." Similar legislation followed. It was not until the eighteenth century that Virginia lawmakers focused on the political rights of free blacks. In 1723, they denied free blacks the right to vote. In 1797, they excluded free blacks from testifying in court against whites or sitting on juries. William W. Hening, ed., *Statutes at Large, Being a Collection of All the Laws of Virginia,* 13 vols. (Richmond: Samuel Pleasants, 1819–23), 2: 170, 4: 132; June Guild, ed., *Black Laws of Virginia: A Summary of the Legislative Acts of Virginia Concerning Negroes from Earliest Times to the Present* (Richmond: Whittet and Shepperson, 1936; New York: Negro Universities Press, 1969), 21–32, 132.

4. County courts, operating through colonial parishes, bound out "free," but illegitimate, children until they were 31 years old. In 1765, the legislature shortened the mandatory period of indenture to 21 years for males and 18 years for females. Guild, ed., *Black Laws of Virginia,* 23–24, 27, 30.

5. Loudoun Freedom Negro Slips, LCCH; Sweig, "Free Negroes," 34.

6. *True American,* 39 Dec. 1800, Thomas Balch Library, Leesburg (hereafter referred to as TBL).

7. Joseph G. Kennedy, *Population of the United States in 1860: Compiled from the Original Returns of the Eighth Census* (Washington, D.C.: Government Printing Office, 1864), 517. For examples of free blacks living in white, slaveholding households with

their kin, see Loudoun Legislative Petitions (hereafter referred to as LouLP), 5 Dec. 1815; Loudoun County Deed Book, 2-O, 133, LCCH.

8. John W. Blassingame, ed., *Slave Testimony: Two Centuries of Letters, Speeches, Interviews and Autobiographies* (Baton Rouge: Louisiana State Univ. Press, 1977), 87; Dorothy Sterling, ed., *We Are Your Sisters: Black Women in the Nineteenth Century* (New York: W. W. Norton, 1984), 48.

9. Blassingame, ed., *Slave Testimony*, 87; Sterling, ed., *We Are Your Sisters*, 48.

10. In 1820, for example, 19 (13.6%) free black-headed households in Loudoun had slave members; in 1830, 9 (5.1%) of 175 included slaves. In 1860, 7 (4.2%) of the 166 free black-headed households were slave-inclusive. U.S. Department of Commerce, Bureau of the Census, Manuscript Federal Census, Loudoun County, Virginia, 1820, (hereafter referred to as FedCenLC), roll 137; 1830, roll 193; 1860, Free Schedule, roll 1359. Also see: Carter G. Woodson, *Free Negro Owners of Slaves in the United States in 1830, Together with Absentee Ownership of Slaves in the United States in 1830* (Washington: Association for the Study of Negro Life and History, 1924).

11. FedCenLC, 1820, roll 137; 1830, roll 193.

12. John Watson purchased his wife in 1799. Loudoun County Deed Books, X, 407; 2–C, 5; 2–W, 344–345, LCCH; Sweig, "Free Negroes," 34.

13. Quoted in Sweig, "Free Negroes," 32.

14. Loudoun County Deed Book, 2-O, 133, LCCH; Sweig, "Free Negroes," 33.

15. The prevalence of free black, slave-inclusive households with male heads is predictable given the comparative lack of occupational and economic opportunity that southern, rural society afforded free black women. Sweig, "Free Negroes," 31; FedCenLC, 1810, roll 69; 1820, roll 137; 1830, roll 193; 1850, Free Schedule, roll 957; 1860, Slave Schedule, roll 1393, Free Schedule, roll 1359.

16. Although Thomas Chapel may have hoped to keep Fanny Smith in his household by helping her to buy her freedom and that of her infant daughters, Smith later established her own household in Loudoun. LouLP, 5 Dec. 1818, 8 Dec. 1815, 25 Jan. 1850, VSL; FedCenLC, 1820, roll 137.

17. Virginia law first placed restrictions on whom blacks could buy as early as 1670. By the end of the antebellum era, they were not able to purchase anyone, regardless of their relationship to the person. Guild, ed., *Black Laws of Virginia*, 94; Luther P. Jackson, *Free Negro Labor and Property Holding in Virginia, 1830–1860* (New York: American Historical Association, 1942; New York: Atheneum, 1969), 23.

18. Sweig, "Free Negroes," 32–34; Blassingame, ed., *Slave Testimony*, 87; Loudoun County Deed Books, X, 407; 2–C, 5; 2–F, 168; 2–W, 344–45, LCCH.

19. This law also stipulated that slave owners who manumitted their slaves personally were responsible for the support of any such persons who were under the age of majority or over the age of 45 years, as well as those who were mentally and physically incapable of caring for themselves at the time of their emancipation. Hening, ed., *Statutes at Large*, 9: 39.

20. LouLP, 10 Feb. 1837, 8 Dec. 1815, VSL; Sarah Chichester to Burr Harrison, n.d., Harrison Family Papers (hereafter referred to as HarFP), VHS. Regarding the moral and financial motives of planters who freed their slaves, see Louis Morton, *Robert Carter of Nomini Hall: A Virginia Tobacco Planter of the Eighteenth Century* (Charlottes-

ville, Va.: Univ. Press of Virginia, 1964), 250–53.

21. Between 1790 and 1799, county residents filed 30 deeds of emancipation and another 33 between 1800 and 1806. They filed no deeds of emancipation between 1782 and 1790, perhaps responding more to financial priorities than moral or political ideals. It also is possible that county officials anticipated a large number of these transactions occurring as a result of the liberal legislation of 1782 and, consequently, may have kept them separate from other deeds during this time period. If so, this collection of deeds of emancipation may have been lost. See Sweig, "Free Negroes," 24–25. Concerning legislation restricting the permanent residence of free blacks in the state, see Guild, ed., *Black Laws of Virginia*, 72. For information regarding the numbers of free black households with slave members, see FedCenLC, 1810, roll 69; 1820, roll 137; 1830, roll 193; 1860, Slave Schedule, roll 1393.

22. The development of a high-volume domestic slave trade that served as a profitable depository for "surplus" slaves during the first decade of the nineteenth century reduced substantially the number of slaveholders willing to free their slaves. In Loudoun, where the number of excess slaves seemed to be substantial because of the county-wide shift in the agricultural sphere of the economy from widespread tobacco production to grain, more and more masters opted to sell their slaves at increasingly inflated prices rather than to set them free. Debow, *Statistical View of the United States . . . 1850*, 259; FedCenLC, 1860, Slave Schedule, roll 1393; Sweig, "Free Negroes in Northern Virginia," app. C, 66; Donald M. Sweig, "Northern Virginia Slavery: A Statistical and Demographic Investigation" (Ph. D. dissertation, College of William and Mary, 1982), 247–53; Michael Tadman, "Slave Trading in the Ante-bellum South: An Estimate of the Extent of the Inter-Regional Slave Trade," *Journal of American Studies* 13, no. 2 (Spring 1979): 195–220.

23. Consider, for example, the impact of slave renting as the era progressed. In 1860 alone, census records for Loudoun indicate that approximately 516 Loudoun residents hired the services of a minimum of 1,037 slaves, primarily from local slaveholders. Those slave represented at least 34% of the adult slave population in the county and almost one-fifth of the entire slave population in Loudoun. Slave hires not only helped provide labor for county residents who could not afford to buy slaves, but also were further incentives to prevent slaveholders from manumitting "excess" slaves. FedCenLC, 1860, Slave Schedule, roll 1393.

24. Will of John A. Binns, Loudoun County Wills, 11 Jan. 1813, VSL.

25. Morton, *Robert Carter of Nomini Hall*, 251, 264–72. For various references to slaves that Robert Carter freed and their descendants in the Loudoun vicinity, see Sweig, ed., *Registrations of Free Negroes*, Book II, nos. 37–55, 57, 58, 63, 67, 102, 111, 112, 120–22, 138–40, 150, 171–77 passim, 225, 228, 230; Book III, nos. 32, 66, 111, 165, 538.

26. Quote from John Carter and references to the slaves who ran away found in: Morton, *Robert Carter of Nomini*, 251, 269–72.

27. LouLP, 8 Dec. 1815, VSL.

28. Summations of Samuel Jackson's court case are found in Loudoun Minute Book, 10 Nov. 1818, 4 Dec. 1818, VSL.

29. The sale of undocumented blacks went to support the county poor. Samuel Shepherd, *The Statutes at Large of Virginia, from October Session 1792, to December 1806, In-*

clusive in Three Volumes, (New Series), Being a Continuation of Hening, vol. 1, *1792–1806* (Richmond: Samuel Shepherd, 1830; New York: AMS Press, 1970), 238–39; Guild, ed., *Black Laws of Virginia*, 95. Quote from: Sweig, ed., *Registration of Free Negroes*, Book II, no. 170.

30. Discussion of the local response to Carter's emancipation of his slaves and the quotes in this text found in: Morton, *Robert Carter of Nomini Hall*, 265–67.

31. Charles L. Perdue, Thomas E. Barden, and Robert K. Phillips, eds., *Weevils in the Wheat: Interviews with Virginia Ex-Slaves* (Charlottesville: Univ. Press of Virginia, 1976), 149; George P. Rawick, ed., *The American Slave*, vol. 16, *Virginia* (Westport, Conn.: Greenwood Press, 1972), 53.

32. Perdue et al., eds., *Weevils*, 259–60, 149.

33. LouLP, 28 Dec. 1831, VSL.

34. LouLP, 13 Jan. 1836, VSL.

35. Benjamin Drew, ed., *The Refugee: A North-Side View of Slavery* (Reading, Mass.: Addison-Wesley, 1969), 53.

36. LouLP, 7 Dec. 1842, VSL.

37. The question of free blacks in violation of the 1806 residency law was debated heatedly in the Virginia General Assembly in 1831, and members proposed a bill in Feb. 1832 which was meant to alleviate the problem. The measure mandated the removal from the state of all free African-Americans who were in violation of the 1806 statute and put aside an appropriation of $35,000 for 1832 and $90,000 for 1833 to colonize them outside of the United States. The bill passed in the House of Delegates, but was rejected in the Senate. Importantly, this proposed statute failed in the same session as that which determined not to abolish slavery. Jackson, *Free Negro Labor and Property Holding*, 14–15; LouLP, 15 Nov. 1836, VSL.

38. As a result of the numerous petitions from free blacks born after 1806 that the General Assembly received every year, they reaffirmed in 1837 an earlier law which allowed county courts to make such decisions. The determining criteria was "proof that the person is of good character, peaceable, orderly and industrious, and not addicted to drunkenness, gaming or other vice." They also insisted that the petition be placed on the county court house door for two months prior to the hearing and that 3/4 of the justices be present when deciding on the appeal. LouLP, 10 Feb. 1837, VSL; Guild, ed., *Black Laws of Virginia*, 111–12.

39. LouLP, 10 Feb. 1837, VSL.

40. LouLP, 19 Jan. 1850, VSL.

41. LouLP, 25 Jan., 1850, VSL.

42. Guild, ed., *Black Laws of Virginia*, 111–112; LouLP, 25 Jan. 1850, VSL.

43. LouLP, 7 Feb. 1848, 25 Jan. 1850, VSL.

44. LouLP, 19 Jan. 1850, VSL. Guild, ed., *Black Laws of Virginia*, 111–12, 118.

45. The Virginia state legislature did reject a few of the petitions that Loudoun free blacks submitted, but later reversed their decisions. See, for example, the petitions submitted by George Rivers dated 24 Feb. 1832 and 5 Sept. 1838. LouLP, 24 Feb. 1832, 5 Sept. 1838, VSL; and Clem Chaney's history compiled in LouLP, 7 Dec. 1822, VSL. The 1793 statute is summarized in Guild, ed., *Black Laws of Virginia*, 95.

46. LouLP, 24 Jan. 1843, VSL.

47. Ibid.

48. The census records indicate that there were only 272 more white persons in Loudoun in 1860 than there had been in 1790. From 1820–40, the numbers of whites declined by 14.27 percent. See Table 1.

49. The mounting hostility toward free people of color during the last decades of the antebellum era meant a steady decline in their numerical growth. Even with an equal sex ratio, the population of Loudoun free blacks declined by 105 persons between 1850 and 1860. See Table 1.

50. LouLP, 24 Jan. 1843, VSL. The General Assembly did not act on the petitioners' recommendation, but instead continued to establish discriminatory laws which circumscribed free black life. See, for example, Guild, *Black Laws of Virginia*, 95, 109, 111–12, 118; and Jackson, *Free Negro Labor and Property Holding*, 19–29, 31.

51. LouLP, 10 Dec. 1847, VSL.

52. Jackson, *Free Negro Labor and Property Holding*, 10–11; Robert McColley, *Slavery and Jeffersonian Virginia*, 2nd ed. (Urbana: Univ. of Illinois Press, 1978), 72–73; Ira Berlin, *Slaves Without Masters: The Free Negro in the Antebellum South* (New York: Random House, 1974), 79–107; John Hope Franklin, *The Free Negro in North Carolina, 1790–1860* (Chapel Hill: Univ. of North Carolina Press, 1943; New York: W. W. Norton, 1971), 58–120.

53. The law of 1834, unlike that of 1841, had not stipulated a maximum amount of time that workers could remain before the state expelled them. Guild, ed., *Black Laws of Virginia*, 95, 109, 113, 117; Jackson, *Free Negro Labor and Property Holding*, 19–29, 31.

54. Ibid.

55. Werner Janney and Asa Janney, eds., *John Jay Janney's Virginia: An American Farm Lad's Life in the Early 19th Century*. (McLean, Va.: EPM Publications, 1978), 50–56.

56. Guild, ed., *Black Laws of Virginia*, 117; FedCenLC, Free Schedule, 1860, roll 1359.

57. As early as 1777, Thomas Jefferson submitted a plan for the deportation of blacks to the Virginia state legislature. In 1800, the General Assembly passed a resolution which requested the governor to suggest to the President that the country purchase lands on which they could settle their free blacks. Five years later, the Assembly passed another resolution which requested Virginia's national congressmen request the federal government to act on colonization. In 1816, they again asked the United States government to grant land for the resettlement of free people of color, this time suggesting the northern Pacific Coast as a possible location. Beverley B. Munford, *Virginia's Attitude Toward Slavery and Secession* (New York: Longmans, Green, 1909), 60–61; McColley, *Slavery and Jeffersonian Virginia*, 130–31; Berlin, *Slaves Without Masters*, 199–205.

58. Charles Fenton Mercer to Andrew Stevenson, 3 Nov. 1823, Benjamin Brand Papers, VHS.

59. *Address of the Colonization Society of Loudoun, Virginia*. (Annapolis: J. Green, 1819), n.p., VHS.

60. Quoted in *The Negro in Virginia*, compiled by the Workers of the Writers' Program of the Works Projects Administration in the State of Virginia (New York: Hastings, 1940), 119.

61. Albert Heaton to Jesse and Mars Lucas, 29 April 1830 in Marie Tyler-McGraw,

ed., "'The Prize I Means is the Prize of Liberty': A Loudoun County Family in Liberia," *Virginia Magazine of History and Biography* 97, no. 3 (July 1989): 367.

62. Samuel M. Janney, *Memoirs of Samuel M. Janney, Late of Lincoln, Loudoun County, Va.*, 3rd ed. (Philadephia: Friends' Book Association, 1882), 2–38, quotes from 28, 33.

63. Ibid., 50–91 passim, quotes from 73, 86.

64. Ibid., quotes from 75.

65. In Aug. 1849, William A. Smith, a Southern Methodist minister and president of Randolph Macon College, gave a lecture on education at the Loudoun court house in Leesburg in which he included several proslavery arguments. According to Janney, Smith "took the ground that slavery is right in itself and sanctioned by the Bible." Janney took offense at Smith's address and offered a published rebuttal. His statements in the rebuttal were the basis for his arrest and subsequent trial. "The Freedom of the Press Vindicated" in ibid., 97–106. Quotes from 103.

66. Ibid., 29.

67. George Carter to Hon. Mr. Bushrod Washington, 22 Dec. 1817, George Carter Letterbook, VHS; Poland, *From Frontier to Suburbia*, 143–45; Douglas R. Egerton, *Charles Fenton Mercer, and the Trial of National Conservatism* (Jackson: Univ. of Mississippi Press, 1989), 105–12.

68. Poland, *From Frontier to Suburbia*, 142n.60.

69. Ibid., 143–46; LouLP, 23 Dec. 1831, 17 Dec. 1836, VSL.

70. Quoted in Poland, *From Frontier to Suburbia*, 143–144n.66.

71. Ibid.

72. *Genius of Universal Emancipation*, 4 July, 5 Nov. 1825 quoted in ibid., 143–45.

73. LouLP, 23 Dec. 1831, VSL.

74. LouLP, 17 Dec. 1836, VSL.

75. Jackson, *Free Negro Labor and Property Holding*, 28–31; Berlin, *Slaves Without Masters,* 200–203.

76. Berlin, *Slaves Without Masters*, 204–7.

77. Blassingame, ed., *Slave Testimony*, 105; Tyler-McGraw, ed., "'The Prize I Mean is the Prize of Liberty,'" 355–74; Nichols, *Legends of Loudoun Valley*, 59–61.

78. Register of Free Blacks, Loudoun County, n.p., LCCH; Nichols, *Legends of Loudoun Valley*, 59; Tyler-McGraw, ed., "'The Prize I Mean is the Prize of Liberty,'" 355–58.

79. Tyler-McGraw suggests that the Heatons compelled Mars and Jesse Lucas to relocate in Liberia or remain slaves. Among the other Loudoun free blacks who travelled with them were: Samuel and Susan Cook; John, Catharine, Francis and Amey Bell; John, John Jr., Maria, Helen, Samuel, Harrison, Addison, and Charles Oliver; Ally, Susan, and Athenia Edmonds; and Abraham, Amelia, Martha, Frances, Hannah and John Dennison. Tyler-McGraw, ed., "'The Prize I Mean is the Prize of Liberty,'" 355, 361, 364n.24, 368n.27.

80. Ibid., 363.

81. Ibid.

82. Ibid., 364, 368, 370–71.

83. Ibid., 362.

84. Ibid., 362, 372–74.

CHAPTER 10. THE FREE BLACK FAMILY AND HOUSEHOLD ECONOMY

1. Philip Nelson to Dr. Thomas Clagett, 16 Nov. 1839, Clagett Family Papers (hereafter referred to as ClagFP), Manuscript Division, Alderman Library, Univ. of Virginia, Charlottesville (hereafter referred to as UVA). The 1820 U.S. Department of Commerce's Manuscript Federal Census for Loudoun County (hereafter referred to as FedCenLC) does not list Philip Nelson as a household head, and he still may have been a slave on that date. He also may have been the free black male listed in Henry Clagett's household for the year. In 1830, however, Nelson is listed as a resident of Shelbourne Parish, the head of a household composed of 5 free people of color—himself, an adult woman, two adolescent to young adult-aged persons, and a male child. He does not appear in the 1840 census. FedCenLC, 1820, roll 137; 1830, roll 193; 1840, roll 564.

2. See, for example, Theodore Hershberg, "Free Blacks in Antebellum Philadelphia: A Study of Ex-Slaves, Freeborn, and Socio-economic Decline," *Journal of Social History* 5, no. 2 (Spring 1972): 183–209.

3. Philip Nelson to Dr. Thomas Clagett, 16 Nov. 1839, ClagFP, UVA.

4. See, for example, ibid., and 5, 31 Dec. 1839, 26 March 1841, ClagFP, UVA.

5. Harrison Williams, *Legends of Loudoun: An Account of the History and Homes of a Border County of Virginia's Northern Neck* (Richmond: Garrett and Massie, 1938), 32–34; Eugene Scheel, *History of Middleburg and Vicinity* (Warrenton, Va.,: Piedmont Press, 1987), 5–8; Douglas R. Egerton, *Charles Fenton Mercer and the Trial of National Conservatism* (Jackson: Univ. Press of Mississippi, 1989), passim; Louis Morton, *Robert Carter of Nomini Hall: A Virginia Tobacco Planter of the Eighteenth Century* (Charlottesville, Va.: Univ. Press of Virginia, 1964), app. tables 5, 9, 15; Charles Poland, *From Frontier to Suburbia* (Maceline, Mo.: Walsworth Publishing, 1976), 8n. Also see Allan Kulikoff, *Tobacco and Slaves: The Development of Southern Cultures in the Chesapeake, 1680–1800* (Chapel Hill: Univ. of North Carolina Press, 1986), 132–139; Robert Carter Land Book, Carter Family Papers (hereafter referred to as CarFP), Virginia Historical Society, Richmond (hereafter referred to as VHS).

6. Census data from 1850 placed the average value of Loudoun farm land at $28.33 per acre. James W. Head, *History of Loudoun County* (Leesburg, Va.: Park View Press, 1908), 92.

7. George Carter to William Day, 7 May 1808, George Carter Letterbook, (hereafter referred to as GCLB), VHS; *Loudoun Chronicle*, 8 March 1850, Virginia State Library, Richmond (hereafter referred to as VSL).

8. The federal census for Loudoun County in 1850 and 1860 list six free black blacksmiths, four of whom were married with growing families. FedCenLC, Free Schedule (hereafter referred to as FreSch), 1850, roll 957; FreSch, 1860, roll 1359.

9. Nat Turner was a literate slave who also was a preacher. Although there was no direct evidence that free people of color were involved in the Southampton County rebellion of August 1831, three were indicted, but not found guilty. Still the suspicion of free black/slave collusion remained keen. Regarding the insurrection in which 60 whites were killed and more than 100 blacks in the aftermath, see Thomas R. Gray, ed., *The Confessions of Nat Turner, the Leader of the Late Insurrection in Southampton, Va.* . . . (Baltimore: Lucas and Deafer, 1831); John Duff and Peter Mitchell, eds., *The Nat Turner Re-*

bellion: The Historical Event and the Modern Controversy (New York: Harper and Row, 1971); and Henry Tragle, ed., *The Southampton Slave Revolt of 1831: A Compilation of Source Material* (Amherst: Univ. of Massachusetts Press, 1971).

10. FedCenLC, FreSch, 1850, roll 957. Regarding local agitation about free black boatmen and fugitive slaves, see Loudoun Legislative Petition (hereafter referred to as LouLP), 11 Jan. 1840, VSL.

11. June E. Guild, ed., *Black Laws of Virginia: A Summary of the Legislative Acts of Virginia Concerning Negroes from Earliest Times to the Present* (Richmond: Whittet and Shepperson, 1936; New York: Negro Universities Press, 1969), 95, 102, 109, 113, 114, 115, 117; Jackson, *Free Negro Labor and Property Holding*, 19–29, 31; LouLP, 19 Jan. 1838, VSL.

12. Ibid.

13. Ibid.

14. Ibid., FedCenLC, FreSch, 1850, roll 957; FreSch, 1860, roll 1359.

15. FedCenLC, 1860, FreSch, roll 1359; William Gray Day Book, 1855–59, n.p., Gray Family Papers, VHS. Loudoun's free black females' occupations did not differ from those free women of color who lived in the North or elsewhere in the South. Jean Collier Brown, "The Economic Status of Negro Women," *Southern Workman* 60, no. 10 (Oct. 1931): 430–31; Lorenzo Green and Carter Woodson, *The Negro Wage Earner* (Washington, D.C.: Association for the Study of Negro Life and History, 1930); and Philip Foner and Ronald Lewis, eds., *The Black Worker: A Documentary History from Colonial Times to the Present*, vol. 1, *The Black Worker to 1869* (Philadelphia: Temple Univ. Press, 1978), 6–134 passim, but esp. 56–62, 117, 120–23, 125–26.

16. FedCenLC, 1820, roll 137; FreSch, 1850, roll 957; FreSch, 1860, roll 1359. With regard to the occupations of free black men who lived elsewhere in the country, see Foner and Lewis, eds., *The Black Worker*, 1: 56–62, 117, 120–23, 125–26; Charles H. Wesley, *Negro Labor in the United States, 1850–1925; A Study in American Economic History* (New York: Vanguard Press, 1927); Bayly Marks, "Skilled Blacks in Antebellum St. Mary's County, Maryland," *Journal of Southern History* 53, no. 4 (Nov. 1987) 537–66; and Shane White, "'We Dwell in Safety and Pursue Our Honest Callings'": Free Blacks in New York City, 1783–1810," *Journal of American History* 75, no. 2 (Sept. 1988): 445–70.

17. Although washerwomen did comparable levels of work, and sometimes earned as much as 20 cents per day, they had little guarantee that they would be hired from one week to the next and did not receive the same level of material support as full-time or live-in domestics.

A survey of female free black laborers in Loudoun County in 1860, for example, reveals that 72% of those reported as washerwomen were described as black; 28% as mulatto. 75% of domestics, on the other hand, were mulatto; while only 25% were darker in color. Washerwomen also tended to be slightly older than domestics. The average age of washerwomen was about 32 years (31.90); it was 27 years for domestics. FedCenLC, FreSch, 1860, roll 1359.

18. William Gray Day Book, 1854–56, Gray Family Papers, VHS; Bill Submitted by Jacob Sorbaugh Against the Estate of Simon Shover, 16 April 1822, Shover Family Papers, VSL; Philip Nelson to Dr. Thomas Clagett, 16 Nov. 1839, ClagFP, UVA; Ac-

counts of Samuel W. DeButts, 1838–39, DeButts Family Papers; Accounts of Samuel Updike, 1830–50, Updike Family Papers, VHS.

A few whites paid their female laborers on an equitable basis with black males who performed the same type of work. Robert Carter, for example, hired his adult female laborers at the same rate as he did unskilled male grain workers. He did not, however, pay free black parents for the work that their small children, aged 5 to 10 years, performed. Carter also stipulated in his labor contracts with his free black workers, all of whom were his ex-slaves, that they were to perform some jobs grati. Still he refused to continue to provide them with any kind of material support, noting in their labor contracts that they were to provide their own food, clothing, and beds as well as pay their county and state taxes. See, for example, Ex-Slave and Slave Labor Inventory, 1792, CarFP, VHS.

19. Nan Netherton, Donald Sweig, Janice Artemel, et al., *Fairfax County, Virginia: A History* (Fairfax: Fairfax County Board of Supervisors, 1978), 274–75.

20. Ibid., 275.

21. Ibid., 275–76, quoted in the *Alexandria Gazette*, 24 April 1844.

22. Philip Nelson to Dr. Thomas Clagett, 16 Nov. 1839, 31 Dec. 1839, ClagFP, UVA; LouLP, 5 Sept. 1832, VSL; Joseph V. Nichols, *Legends of Loudoun Valley: True Stories from the Lives and Times of the People of Loudoun County, Virginia* (Leesburg, Va.: Potomac Press, 1961), 59–61.

23. FedCenLC, FreSch, 1860, roll 1359; LouLP, 25 Jan. 1850, VSL.

24. Werner Janney and Asa Janney, eds., *John Jay Janney's Virginia: An American Farm Lad's Life in the Early 19th Century* (McLean, Va.: EPM Publications, 1978), 89–90.

25. FedCenLC, FreSch, 1850, roll 957; FreSch, 1860, roll 1359.

26. See, for example, Philip Nelson to Dr. Thomas Clagett, 31 Dec. 1839, ClagFP, UVA. Regarding the Jackson clan's occupations, see FedCenLC, FreSch, 1860, roll 1359.

27. John Malvin, *North into Freedom: The Autobiography of John Malvin, Free Negro, 1795–1880*, Allan Peskin, ed. (Cleveland, 1879; Kent, Ohio: Kent State Univ. Press, 1988), 29–33, quote from 32–33.

An 1839 state law stipulated that "when any free person of color shall be bound out by court order as an apprentice, the court shall consider what the reasonable value of his services for each year of the apprenticeship; [and] . . . the master shall pay . . . [the mother or father] the value of his services." The law also mandated that the earnings of those children who did not have parents were to be paid to the county Overseers of the Poor. A subsequent law of 1848 excluded the Overseers and mandated that the masters of these orphaned children were to give their earning to the apprentices at the time of their release. It still allowed parents to receive their children's income, but the last year's earnings were to go to the apprentices. Guild, ed., *Black Laws of Virginia*, 112–16.

28. Malvin, *North into Freedom*, 37.

29. Carter rented small plots of a few acres of land to those free blacks and their families whom he felt most reliable. Collins, and others, argued that his actions were inexpedient because blacks lacked the tools and work animals needed to succeed as independent farmers. Ex-Slave and Slave Labor Inventory, 1792, CarFP, VHS. Regarding

the response of his neighbors and other renters, see Louis Morton, *Robert Carter of Nomini Hall: A Virginia Tobacco Planter of the Eighteenth Century* (Charlottesville, Va.: Univ. Press of Virginia, 1964), 265–66.

30. FedCenLC, FreSch, 1850, roll 957; FreSch, 1860, roll 1359; LouLP, 29 Jan. 1849, VSL; Philip Nelson to Dr. Thomas Clagett, 18 Nov., 31 Dec. 1839, ClagFP, UVA.

31. FedCenLC, FreSch, 1850, roll 957.

32. FedCenLC, FreSch, 1850, roll 957; FreSch, 1860, roll 1359; Head, *History of Loudoun County*, 92–93.

33. Ibid.

34. FedCenLC, FreSch, 1850, roll 957; FreSch, 1860, roll 1359.

35. The term "laborer" used throughout the manuscript census may be misleading. Although most free people of color were unskilled workers, "laborer" also was a catch-all term which masked some skilled occupations. Ibid.

36. Ibid.

37. Ibid.

38. FedCenLC, 1820, roll 137; 1830, roll 193.

39. FedCenLC, FreSch, 1850, roll 957.

40. Ibid.

41. FedCenLC, FreSch, 1860, roll 1359.

42. Ibid.

43. The difference between Thompson's extended family and Minor's nuclear seen here may be a mere technicality of the families' life cycles. One has children who have married and begun their own families; the other has unmarried children. But this does not obscure the fact that Minor's skilled status placed him in better financial stead than Thompson's unskilled vocation. FedCenLC, FreSch, 1850, roll 957; FreSch, 1860, roll 1359.

44. FedCenLC, FreSch, 1850, roll 957; FreSch, 1860, roll 1359.

45. FedCenLC, FreSch, 1860, roll 1359.

46. Guild, ed., *Black Laws of Virginia*, 107.

47. FedCenLC, FreSch, 1850, roll 957.

48. FedCenLC, 1810, roll 69; 1820, roll 137; 1830, roll 193; FreSch, 1850, roll 957.

49. FedCenLC, FreSch, 1850, roll 957; FreSch, 1860, roll 1359. There were several other examples of three-generational family households among Loudoun's free blacks, although this form was not dominant within the population.

50. FedCenLC, 1810, roll 69; 1830, roll 193, FreSch, 1850, roll 957.

51. Ibid.; FedCenLC, 1840, roll 564; LouLP, 5 Dec. 1818; Malvin, *North into Freedom*, 29, 33.

52. FedCenLC, FreSch, 1850, roll 957; LouLP, 5 Dec. 1818; Malvin, *North Into Freedom*, 29, 33.

53. Census records list these couples as married, but state law outlawed marriages between whites and nonwhites. These women also may have been "technically" African American, but physically resembled Caucasians. "Passing" certainly was an issue in most communities of free people of color. LouLP, 5 Dec.1808, VSL; FedCenLC, 1830, roll 193; 1840, roll 564; FreSch, 1850, roll 957; FreSch, 1860, roll 1359.

54. Nathan Minor's wife is listed as white in the 1850 manuscript federal census. The

only adult woman listed in his household in 1830, however, is described as a free person of color. It is conceivable that the woman listed as his wife in the 1850 census is not the same woman he was married to in 1830. FedCenLC, 1830, roll 193; FedCenLC, FreSch, 1850, roll 957; FedCenLC, FreSch, 1860, roll 1359.

55. Census enumerators for 1860 designated 50 percent of free black males as "mulatto" and 52.27 percent of free black women as mulatto in Loudoun County. Only 27.01 percent of Loudoun slaves received the same designation. FedCenLC, FreSch, 1860, roll 1359, p. 517.

56. FedCenLC, FreSch, 1850, roll 957; FreSch, 1860, roll 1359.

57. Ibid.

58. Netherton et al., *Fairfax County, a History*, 272–73.

59. FedCenLC, FreSch, 1850, roll 957; FreSch, 1860, roll 1359.

60. William Still, ed., *The Underground Railroad: A Record of Facts, Authentic Narratives, Letters, etc.* (Philadelphia: Porter and Coates, 1872; New York: Arno Press, 1968), 122–23, 514–15; Henry S. Robinson, "Descendants of Daniel and Hannah Bruce," *Negro History Bulletin* 24 (Nov. 1960): 37–41. Also see Carter G. Woodson, *Negro History Bulletin* 11 (Feb. 1948): 99–107; and T. O. Madden, Jr., *We Were Always Free: The Maddens of Culpeper County, Virginia, a 200 Year Family History* (Chapel Hill: Univ. of North Carolina Press, 1992).

61. Robinson, "Descendants of Daniel and Hannah Bruce," 37.

62. Ibid. FedCenLC, FreSch, 1860, roll 1359. Eliza Grayson may have migrated from Fredricksburg to Fauquier County and then to Loudoun. The register of free blacks for Fauquier County indicates that one Eliza Grayson, a mulatto free woman of color, migrated from Fredricksburg, where she was born free, and was registered in Fauquier County in 1831 at the age of 22. Grayson may have had other relations in Fauquier, for the register also lists Hannah, Nancy, and Richard Grayson as residents in 1835. Register of Free Negroes, Fauquier County, Virginia, VHS.

63. According to the federal census, there was an average of 3.3 persons in free black female households in 1820. By 1830, the number had increased by 28% to 4.6 persons. By 1850, they headed 27.95% of these households, and in 1860, 33.59%. FedCenLC, 1810, roll 69; 1820, roll 137; 1830, roll 193; FreSch, 1850, roll 957; FreSch, 1860, roll 1359.

64. Their numbers declined by 7.7%. For a recount of the numbers of Loudoun free blacks during the era see Table 1. FedCenLC, FreSch, 1850, roll 957; FreSch, 1860, roll 1359.

65. FedCenLC, 1820, roll 137; FreSch, 1850, roll 957; FreSch, 1860, roll 1359.

66. Ibid.

67. The name appears as both Redman and Readman in county records, on the federal census and in local histories. Nichols, *Legends of Loudoun Valley*, 27–28; FedCenLC, FreSch, 1850, roll 957; FreSch, 1860, roll 1359.

68. There were, for example, an average of 4.57 persons in free black headed households in 1810; 4.11 in 1820; 4.99 in 1830; 4.02 in 1850; and 5.0 in 1860. Among white-headed households in Loudoun, there was an average of 8.56 persons in 1820 and 8.02 in 1850. Among white nonslaveholders, there was an average of 7.49 persons in their households in 1810; 5.69 persons in 1830; and 7.12 persons in 1850. FedCenLC, 1810,

roll 69; 1820, roll 137; 1830, roll 193; FreSch, 1850, roll 957; FreSch, 1860, roll 1359.

69. FedCenLC, 1820, roll 137; 1830, roll 193; FreSch, 1850, roll 957. Data used to compile average age of first birth and spacing of births for Loudoun area slave women from: Slave List of Edward Digges, 1770–1860, Digges Family Papers; William H. Gray Slave List, 1846–63, Gray Family Papers; R. Stringfellow Family Bible, 1800–1860, London Family Papers, all VHS; Fitzhugh Slave List, 1830, in Donald Sweig, "Northern Virginia Slavery: A Statistical and Demographic Investigation" (Ph. D. dissertation, College of William and Mary, 1982), 127–29. Also see Todd L. Savitt, *Medicine and Slavery: The Diseases and Health Care of Blacks in Antebellum Virginia* (Urbana: Univ. of Illinois Press), 135–45.

70. Quaker males and females, who had the additional burden of marrying another Quaker, wed somewhat later—the men usually were at least 27 years old, while the women married at about 24. Professional white males, bound to years of formal education and training, also married relatively late, at about 27 or older. Ages for Loudoun Quakers compiled from data in Wade Hinshaw, ed., *Encyclopedia of American Quaker Genealogy*, 10 vols. (Ann Arbor: Edward Bros., 1950), 6 (Virginia): 609–924 passim.

71. FedCenLC, FreSch, 1860, roll 1359.

72. Nichols, *Legends of Loudoun Valley*, 25–27; FedCenLC, FreSch, 1860, roll 1359.

73. Philip Nelson to Dr. Thomas Clagett, 18 Nov., 5, 31 Dec. 1839, 14 Jan. 1841, ClagFP, UVA.

74. Ibid.

75. Ibid.; also 26 March 1841.

76. Philip Nelson to Dr. Thomas Clagett, 28 April 1841, ClagFP, UVA.

77. Philip Nelson to Dr. Thomas Clagett, 18 Nov., 5 Dec, 31 Dec. 1839, 14 Jan., 26 March 1841, ClagFP, UVA.

78. Correspondence of the Burkes compiled in: John W. Blassingame, ed., *Slave Testimony: Two Centuries of Letters, Speeches, Interviews, and Autobiographies* (Baton Rouge: Louisiana State Univ. Press, 1977), 98–108.

79. Ibid., 99–100.

80. Ibid., 113.

81. Ibid., 102, 106–7.

82. For information on the economic status of southern free blacks, see, for example, James H. Brewer, "Negro Property Owners in Seventeenth-Century Virginia," in *The Making of Black America: Essays in Negro Life and History*, vol. 1, *The Origins of Black Americans*, August Meier and Elliott Rudwick, eds. (New York: Atheneum, 1974), 206–15; T. H. Breen and Stephen Innes, *"Myne Owne Ground": Race and Freedom on Virginia's Eastern Shore, 1640–1676* (New York: Oxford Univ. Press, 1980), 68–114; Berlin, *Slaves Without Masters*, 217–49; Franklin, *The Free Negro in North Carolina*, 121–62.

83. Loudoun County Minute Book, 9 Feb. 1818, VSL; Records of the Overseers of the Poor, Loudoun County, 1800–1833, 1836–40, 1843, 1851 passim, VSL.

84. Records of the Broad Run Baptist Church, Fauquier County, 1762–1872, VHS.

85. "Rules and Regulations for the Government of a Society of the Free People of Color in the Town of Alexandria, To Be Called the Mutual Relief and Friendly So-

ciety," Broadside, March 1824, VHS; *Alexandria Gazette and Virginia Advertiser*, 20 Dec. 1856, Southern Newspaper Collection, Univ. of Texas, Austin. For further information on free black self-help and improvement organizations, see Dorothy Porter, ed., *Early Negro Writing, 1760–1837* (Boston: Beacon Press, 1971), 5–166; Dorothy Porter, "The Organized Educational Activities of Negro Literary Societies," in *The Making of Black America*, 1: 276–88; Berlin, *Slaves Without Masters*, 284–315.

86. "Rules and Regulations for the Government of a Society of the Free People of Color," VHS.

87. Ibid.

88. Loudoun County Order Book, vol. 1, 14 March 1808, p. 270, VSL; Poland, *From Frontier to Suburbia*, 139–40.

89. *Alexandria Gazette and Virginia Advertiser* 12 May 1813, 13 Aug. 1817, 20 Dec. 1856, VSL.

CONCLUSION

1. Amanda Edmonds Diary, 11 Nov. 1859, Virginia Historical Society, Richmond (hereafter referred to as VHS).

2. There are numerous accounts of John Brown and the Harpers Ferry raid of 1859. See, for example, Elijah Avey, *The Capture and Execution of John Brown: A Tale of Martyrdom* (Chicago: Afro-Am Press, 1969); Richard O. Boyer, *The Legend of John Brown: A Biography and a History* (New York: Alfred A. Knopf, 1973); and "The John Brown Letters," *Virginia Magazine of History and Biography* 9 (July–April 1901–2): 385–95; 10 (July–April 1902–3): 17–32, 161–76.

3. "Col. R. E. Lee's Report, 19 October 1859," *Virginia Magazine of History and Biography* 10 (July 1902–April 1903): 18–25.

4. Ibid.

5. Amanda Edmonds Diary, 11, 17 Nov. 1859, VHS; Truman Nelson, *The Old Man: John Brown at Harper's Ferry* (New York: Holt, Rinehart and Winston, 1973), 106–7.

6. Amanda Edmonds Diary, 17 Nov. 1859, VHS.

7. Virginia law as early as 1691 stipulated the servitude of free, but illegitimate, children until they reached adulthood. Another law mandated that any children born of an indentured servant woman while she still was bound to her master would inherit her indentured status. June E. Guild, ed., *Black Laws of Virginia: A Summary of the Legislative Acts of Virginia Concerning Negroes from the Earliest Times to the Present* (Richmond: Whittet and Shepperson, 1936; New York; Negro Universities Press, 1969), 23–24, 27, 30.

One of the most compelling examples of a free black family losing members while indentured is in T. O. Madden, Jr., *We Were Always Free: The Maddens of Culpeper County, Virginia: A 200-Year Family History* (New York: W. W. Norton, 1992), 13–24. Regarding examples from Loudoun specifically, see Loudoun County Freedom Slips, Loudoun County Court House, Leesburg.

Bibliography

PRIMARY SOURCES

Unpublished Manuscripts

Alderman Library, University of Virginia, Charlottesville
Allen Family Papers
Berkeley Family Papers
Buck Family Papers
Thomas Clagett Papers
Leesburg Family Papers
Lupton Family Papers
Asa Rogers Papers

Thomas Balch Library, Leesburg
Janney Family Papers
Loudoun County Genealogical Collection
James Monroe Papers

Loudoun County Court House, Leesburg
Loudoun County Deed Books
Loudoun County Free Negro Registration Slips

Loudoun County Museum, Leesburg
Loudoun County Material Culture Collection

Mount Vernon Library, Fairfax County, Virginia
Annual List of Negro Tithables of George Washington, 1761–74, 1786–89
List of Negroes Belonging to George Washington in His Own Right and By Marriage, June 1799
Donald Sweig, Chart of African-American Families at Mount Vernon, 1799

"Black Mount Vernon"
"Housing and Family Life of the Mount Vernon Negro"

National Archives, Washington, D.C
U.S. Department of Commerce, Bureau of the Census, Federal Manuscript Census,
    Loudoun County, Virginia, 1800–1860 (microfilm)

Virginia Historical Society, Richmond
James T. Alexander Diary
American Colonization Society Papers
Archer Family Papers
Armistead-Blanton-Wallace Family Papers
George Bagby Papers
George Washington Ball Papers
William and James Baskerville Papers
Belmont School Papers
William Benton Papers
Carter Berkeley Family Papers
Binns Family Papers
Blanton Family Papers
William Bolling Family Papers
Benjamin Brand Papers
Broad Run Baptist Church Papers
Brooke Family Papers
Francis Byrd Papers
Joseph Caldwell Papers
Allen Caperton Papers
Carrington Family Papers
George Carter Letter Book
Robert Carter Family Papers
Samuel Clendining Papers
Conrad Family Papers
Custis Family Papers
Davie Papers
DeButts Family Papers
Digges Family Papers
Ebenezer Baptist Church Records
Ellzey Family Papers
Richard Eppes Diary
William Fairfax Papers

Fauquier County Free Negro Register

William and Samuel Vance Gatewood Papers

Gooch Family Papers

William Hill Gray Papers

Grinnan Family Papers

Harrison Family Papers

Ambrose Hill Family Papers

William Hite Commonplace Book

James M. Howell Papers

Hunter Family Papers

Philip DeCatsby Jones Papers

George Bolling Lee Papers

Loudoun County Church Records

Mary Walker Lupton (Irish) Family Papers

McDonald Papers

John Young Mason Papers

Mason Family Papers

Mercer Family Papers

Nalle Family Papers

Thomas Peake Papers

Peyton Family Papers

Powell Family Papers

Stringfellow Family Papers

Updike Family Papers

Absalom Wolliscraft Diary

Virginia State Library, Richmond

Annual Report of the Board of School Commissioners
      for Indigent Children, Loudoun County

Carter Family Papers

Janney Family Papers

Loudoun County Church Records

Loudoun County Court Records

Loudoun County Deed Books

Loudoun County Guardian Accounts

Loudoun County Land Records

Loudoun County Legislative Petitions

Loudoun County Marriage Bonds

Loudoun County Marriage Records

Loudoun County Personal Property Tax Records

Loudoun County Records of the Overseers of the Poor

Loudoun County Will Books

Miscellaneous Genealogical Records

Powell Family Bible Records

Truro Parish Records

George Saunders Papers

Shover Family Papers

Periodicals

Alexandria Gazette and Virginia Advertiser (Alexandria), 1831–60, Southern Newspaper
    Collection, University of Texas, Austin

American Gleaner and Virginia Magazine, 1807, Virginia Historical Society

American Ladies Magazine, 1834–36, Virginia State Library

American Missionary Magazine, 1861–70, University of Texas, Austin

DeBow's Review, 1848–60, University of Texas, Austin

Genius of Liberty (Leesburg), 1818–21, Virginia State Library

Ladies Magazine and Literary Gazette, 1828–33, Virginia State Library

Loudoun Chronicle (Leesburg), 1846–51, Virginia State Library

Loudoun Mirror (Leesburg), 1857–61, Virginia Historical Society

Southern Planter, 1845–60, Virginia Historical Society

The True American (Leesburg), 1800, Thomas Balch Library

Washingtonian (Leesburg), 1836–44, Virginia State Library

Printed Diaries, Correspondence, Autobiographical and Biographical Accounts

Adams, Nehemiah. *A South-Side View of Slavery; or, Three Months at the South, in 1854.*
    3rd ed. Richmond: T. R. Marvin, 1855.

Avey, Elijah. *The Capture and Execution of John Brown, A Tale of Martyrdom by [an] Eye
    Witness.* 1906. Chicago: Afro-Am Press, 1969.

Ball, Charles. *Slavery in the United States: A Narrative of the Life and Adventures of
    Charles Ball, A Black Man.* Indianapolis: Dayton and Archer, 1859; Detroit:
    Negro History Press, 1970.

Baird, Nancy Chappelear, ed. *Journals of Amanda Virginia Edmonds: Lass of the Mosby
    Confederacy.* Stephens City, Va.: Commercial Press, 1950.

Beverley, Robert. *The History and Present State of Virginia.* Edited with an introduction
    by Louis B. Wright. Chapel Hill: University of North Carolina Press for the In-
    stitute of Early American History and Culture, 1947.

Blassingame, John, ed. *Slave Testimony: Two Centuries of Letters, Speeches, Interviews,
    and Autobiographies.* Baton Rouge: Louisiana State University Press, 1977.

Conrad, Kate B. "Uncle Stephen," *Southern Workman* 30 (1901):153–56.

Cresswell, Nicholas. *The Journal of Nicholas Cresswell, 1774–1777.* London: Jonathan

Cape, 1925.

Curtin, Philip, ed. *Africa Remembered: Narratives by West Africans from the Era of the Slave Trade*. Madison: University of Wisconsin Press, 1967.

Dangerfield, Henrietta G. "Our Mammy," *Southern Workman* 30 (1901): 599–601.

Dodd, William E., ed. "Letters of Leven Powell." *The John P. Branch Historical Papers of Randolph-Macon College* 1, nos. 1–3 (June 1901, June 1902, June 1903): 22–63, 111–38, 217–56.

Drew, Benjamin, ed. *A North-Side View of Slavery, the Refugee: or the Narratives of Fugitive Slaves in Canada Related by Themselves with an Account of the History and Condition of the Colored Population of Upper Canada*. Boston: John P. Jewett, 1856.

Elliot, Ian. *James Monroe, 1758–1831: Chronology—Documents—Bibliographical Aids*. Dobbs-Ferry, N.Y.: Oceana, Inc., 1969.

Fitzpatrick, John C., ed. *The Diaries of George Washington, 1748–1799*. Boston: Houghton Mifflin, 1925.

Frothingham, Octavius Brooks. *Gerrit Smith: A Biography*. New York: G. P. Putnam, 1878.

Greene, Jack P., ed. *The Diary of Colonel Landon Carter of Sabine Hall, 1752–1778*. 2 vols. Charlottesville, Va.: University Press of Virginia, 1965; Richmond: Virginia Historical Society, 1987.

Hayden, William. *Narrative of William Hayden, Containing A Faithful Account of His Travels for a Number of Years, Whilst a Slave, in the South*. Cincinnati: William Hayden, 1846.

Hinton, Richard J. *John Brown and His Men: With Some Account of the Roads They Traveled to Reach Harper's Ferry*. Rev. ed. New York: Funk and Wagnalls, 1894.

Janney, Samuel. *Memoir of Samuel M. Janney, Late of Lincoln, Loudoun County, Virginia: A Minister in the Religious Society of Friends*. Philadelphia: Friends Book Association, 1881.

Janney, Werner, and Asa Moore Janney, eds. *John Jay Janney's Virginia: An American Farm Lad's Life in the Early 19th Century*. McLean, Va.: EPM, 1978.

Kaufmann, Eva E., ed. *". . . our Loves to you all . . .": White Family Letters, 1804–1830*. Gaithersburg, Md.: Eva E. Kaufmann, 1986.

Lemay, J. A. Leo, ed. *Robert Bolling Woos Anne Miller: Love and Courtship in Colonial Virginia, 1760*. Charlottesville: University Press of Virginia, 1990.

The Life, Trial and Execution of Captain John Brown, Known as Old Brown of Ossawatomie, with a Full Account of the Attempted Insurrection at Harper's Ferry. Compiled from Official and Authentic Sources. New York: Robert M. DeWitt, 1859.

McGraw-Tyler, Marie, ed. "'The Prize I Mean is the Prize of Liberty': A Loudoun County Family in Liberia." *Virginia Magazine of History and Biography* 97, no. 3 (July 1989): 355–74.

Malvin, John. *North into Freedom: The Autobiography of John Malvin, Free Negro, 1795–1880*. Edited by Allan Peskin. 1879; Kent, Ohio: Kent State University Press, 1988.

Monroe, James. *The Autobiography of James Monroe*. Edited by Stuart Brown. Syracuse:

Syracuse University Press, 1959.

_____. *The Writings of James Monroe, Including a Collection of His Public and Private Papers and Correspondence Now for the First Time Printed*. Edited by Stanislaus Murray Hamilton. Vols. 1–7. New York: G. P. Putnam's Sons, 1903.

Padover, Saul K., ed. *The Washington Papers: Basic Selections from the Public and Private Writings of George Washington*. New York: Harper and Brothers, 1955.

Pennington, James W. C. *The Fugitive Blacksmith; or Events in the History of James W. C. Pennington, Pastor of a Presbyterian Church, New York, Formerly a Slave in the State of Maryland, United States*. 3rd ed. London: Charles Gilpin, 1849; Westport, Conn.: Negro Universities Press, 1971.

Perdue, Charles L., Thomas E. Barden, and Robert K. Phillips, eds. *Weevils in the Wheat: Interviews with Virginia Ex-Slaves*. Charlottesville: University Press of Virginia, 1976.

Peyton, J. Lewis, ed. *Memoir of John Howe Peyton, In Sketches by his Contemporaries, Together with Some of His Public and Private Letters, etc., Also a Sketch of Ann M. Peyton*. Staunton: A. B. Blackburn, 1894.

Poulton, Jane W., ed. *A Loudoun Love Story*. Durham: Jane W. Poulton, 1988.

Rawick, George P., ed. *The American Slave*. Vol. 16 (Virginia). Westport, Conn.: Greenwood Press, 1972.

"A Slave's Story," *Putman's Monthly Magazine* 9 (June 1857): 614–20.

Slaughter, Rev. P., *The Virginia History of African Colonization*. Richmond: Macfarlane & Ferguson, 1855.

Sterling, Dorothy, ed. *We Are Your Sisters: Black Women in the Nineteenth Century*. New York: W.W. Norton, 1984.

Steward, Austin, *Twenty-two Years a Slave, and Forty Years a Freeman: Embracing a Correspondence of Several Years, While President of Wilberforce Colony, London, Canada, West*. Rochester, N.Y.: William Alling, 1857.

Still, William, ed. *Underground Railroad: A Record of Facts, Authentic Narratives, Letters, etc.* Philadelphia: Porter and Coates, 1872; New York: Arno Press, 1968.

Swint, Henry, ed. *Dear Ones at Home: Letters from Contraband Camps*. Nashville: Vanderbilt University Press, 1966.

They Knew the Washingtons: Letters from a French Soldier with Lafayette and from His Family in Virginia. Translated by the Princess Radziwill. Indianapolis: Bobbs-Merrill, 1926.

Watson, Henry. *Narrative of Henry Watson, a Fugitive Slave*. Boston: Bela Marsh, 1848.

Yetman, Norman, ed. *Voices from Slavery*. New York: Holt, Rinehart and Winston, 1970.

Miscellaneous Printed Primary Sources

Abbott, John, S.C. *The Mother at Home; or the Principles of Maternal Duty Familiarly Illustrated*. New York: American Tract Society, 1833.

Abrahams, Roger D., ed. *Afro-American Folktales: Stories from Black Traditions in the New World*. New York: Pantheon, 1985.

An Account of the Treaty between His Excellency Benjamin Fletcher Captain General and

Govenour in Chief of the Province of New York, &c and the Indians of the Five Nations viz. the Mohagues, Oneydes, Onnondoges, Cojonges and Sennekes, at Albany Beginning the 15th of August 1694. New York: William Bradford, 1694.

Acts of the General Assembly of Virginia, Passed at the Session Commencing December 6, 1847, and Ending April 5, 1848, in the Seventy-second Year of the Commonwealth. Richmond: Samuel Shepherd, 1848.

Acts of the General Assembly of Virginia; Passed at the Session of 1850–1851, in the Seventy-fifth Year of the Commonwealth. Richmond: William F. Ritchie, 1851.

Address of the Colonization Society of Loudoun, Virginia [December 1819]. Annapolis: J. Green, 1819.

Bushnell, Horace. *Christian Nurture.* New York: Charles Scribner, 1847, 1861.

Cary, Virginia. *Letters on Female Character: Addressed to a Young Lady on the Death of Her Mother.* Richmond: A. Works, 1830.

Combe, Andrew. *Treatise on the Physical and Medical Treatment of Children.* Philadelphia: Carey and Hart, 1826.

Coxe, Margaret. *Young Lady's Companion: In a Series of Letters.* Philadelphia: Lindsay and Blakiston, 1839.

Debow, J. B. D. *Statistical View of the United States . . . Being a Compendium of the Seventh Census . . . 1850.* Washington, D.C.: A.O.P. Nicholson, 1854.

Dew, Thomas R. "Dissertation on the Characteristic Differences Between the Sexes, and on the Position and Influence of Woman in Society." *Southern Literary Messenger* 1, nos. 11, 12 (July, August 1835): 621–32, 672–91.

Donnan, Elizabeth, ed. *Documents Illustrative of the History of the Slave Trade to America.* Vol. 2, *The Eighteenth Century.* Vol. 4, *The Border Colonies and the Southern Colonies.* Washington: Carnegie Institute of Washington, 1931, 1935.

Donne, Alfred. *Mothers and Infants, Nurses and Nursing.* Boston: Phillips, Sampson, 1859.

Ford, William, ed. *Ketoctin Chronicle.* Leesburg, Va.: Potomac Press, 1965.

Greven, Philip J. Jr., ed. *Child-Rearing Concepts, 1628–1861: Historical Sources.* Itasca, Ill.: F. E. Peacock, 1973.

Guild, June E., ed. *Black Laws of Virginia: A Summary of the Legislative Acts of Virginia Concerning Negroes from Earliest Times to the Present.* Richmond: Whittet and Shepperson, 1936; New York: Negro Universities Press, 1969.

Hening, William W., ed. *Statutes at Large, Being a Collection of All the Laws of Virginia.* 13 vols. Richmond: Samuel Pleasants, 1819–23.

Hinshaw, Wade, ed. *Encyclopedia of American Quaker Genealogy.* 10 vols. Ann Arbor: Edwards Bros., 1950.

Ireland, W. M. *Advice to Mothers on the Management of Infants and Young Children.* New York: B. Young, 1820.

Jefferson, Thomas. *Notes on the State of Virginia.* Edited by William Peden. Chapel Hill: University of North Carolina Press, 1955.

Kennedy, Joseph G. *Population of the United States in 1860; Compiled from the Original Returns of the Eighth Census.* Washington, D.C.: Government Printing Office, 1864.

Loudoun County, "Virginia 1771 Tithable List." Translated by Pollyanna Creekmore.

Virginia Genealogist 16 (1972): 243–48; 17 (1973): 9–13, 187–90, 243–48, 270–76.

McKitrick, Eric, ed. *Slavery Defended: The Voices of the Old South*. Englewood Cliffs, N.J.: Prentice-Hall, 1963.

Martin, Lawrence, ed. *The George Washington Atlas*. Washington, D.C.: George Washington Bicentennial Commission, 1932.

Mercer, Charles Fenton. "Controversy between Armistead Thompson Mason and Charles Fenton Mercer. " Washington, D.C.: Charles Fenton Mercer, 1818.

Mercer, Margaret. *Popular Lectures on Ethics or Moral Obligation*. Petersburg, Va.: Edmund & Julien C. Ruffin, 1841.

Minutes of the Vestry: Truro Parish, Virginia, 1732–1785. Lorton, Va.: Pohick Church, 1974.

Olmstead, Frederick Law. *The Cotton Kingdom: A Traveller's Observations on Cotton and Slavery in the American Slave States*. Edited by Arthur M. Schlesinger. New York: Bobbs-Merrill, 1953.

Porter, Dorothy, ed. *Early Negro Writing, 1760–1837*. Boston: Beacon Press, 1971.

Review of the Debate in the Virginia Legislature of 1831 and 1832. Richmond: T.W. White, 1832; Westport, Conn.: Greenwood Press, 1970.

"Rules and Regulations for the Government of a Society of the Free People of Color in the Town of Alexandria, To Be Called the Mutual Relief and Friendly Society." Broadside. March 1824.

Shepherd, Samuel. *The Statutes at Large of Virginia, from October Session 1792 to December 1806, Inclusive in Three Volumes, (New Series,) Being a Continuation of Hening*. 3 vols. Richmond: Samuel Shepherd, 1830–35; New York: AMS Press, 1970.

Supplement to the Revised Code of the Laws of Virginia: Being a Collection of All the Acts of the General Assembly, of a Public and Permanent Nature, Passed since the Year 1819, with a General Index. Richmond: Samuel Shepherd, 1833.

Sweig, Donald, ed. *"Registrations of Free Negroes Commencing September Court 1822, Book No. 2" and "Register of Free Blacks 1835 Book 3": Being the Full Test of the Two Extant Volumes, 1822–1861, of Registrations of Free Blacks Now in the County Courthouse, Fairfax, Virginia*. Fairfax, Va.: History Section, Office of Comprehensive Planning, 1977.

Taylor, Yardley. *Loudoun County Virginia from Actual Surveys*. Philadelphia: Thomas Reynolds and Robert Pearsall Smith, 1853.

Woodson, Carter G. *Free Negro Owners of Slaves in the United States in 1830, Together with Absentee Ownership of Slaves in the United States in 1830*. Washington: Association for the Study of Negro Life and History, 1924.

SECONDARY SOURCES

Books

Abrahams, Roger D. *Singing the Master: The Emergence of African American Culture in the Plantation South*. New York: Pantheon Books, 1992.

Ahlstrom, Sydney E. *A Religious History of the American People*. New Haven: Yale University Press, 1972.

Ajayi, J. F. Ade, and Michael Crowder. *History of West Africa*, vol. 1. New York: Columbia University Press, 1972.

Alexander, Adele Logan. *Ambiguous Lives: Free Women of Color in Rural Georgia, 1789–1879*. Fayetteville: University of Arkansas Press, 1991.

Amadiume, Ifi. *Male Daughters, Female Husbands: Gender and Sex in an African Society*. London: Zed Books, 1987.

Andrews, Matthew Page. *Virginia: The Old Dominion*. 2 vols. Richmond: Dietz Press, 1949.

Aquila, Richard. *The Iroquois Restoration: Iroquois Diplomacy on the Colonial Frontier, 1701–1754*. Detroit: Wayne State University Press, 1983.

Aries, Philippe. *Centuries of Childhood: A Social History of Family Life*. New York: Alfred A. Knopf, 1962.

Avey, Elijah. *The Capture and Execution of John Brown: A Tale of Martyrdom*. Chicago: Afro-Am Press, 1969.

Basch, Norma. *In the Eyes of the Law: Women, Marriage and Property in Nineteenth Century New York*. Ithaca: Cornell University Press, 1982.

Bastide, Roger. *African Civilization in the New World*. New York: Harper and Row, 1971.

Blassingame, John W. *The Slave Community: Plantation Life in the Old South*. New York: Oxford University Press, 1972.

————. *The Slave Community: Plantation Life in the Old South*. Rev. ed. New York: Oxford University Press, 1980.

Bleser, Carol, ed. *In Joy and In Sorrow: Women, Family, and Marriage in the Victorian South, 1830–1990*. New York: Oxford University Press, 1991.

Boone, Sylvia Ardyn. *Radiance from the Waters: Ideals of Feminine Beauty in Mende Art*. New Haven: Yale University Press, 1986.

Boyer, Richard O. *The Legend of John Brown: A Biography and a History*. New York: Alfred A. Knopf, 1973.

Breen, T. H. *Tobacco Culture: The Mentality of the Great Tidewater Planters on the Eve of Revolution*. Princeton: Princeton University Press, 1985.

————, and Stephen Innes. *"Myne Owne Ground": Race and Freedom on Virginia's Eastern Shore, 1640–1676*. New York: Oxford University Press, 1980.

Bridenbaugh, Carl. *Myths and Realities: Societies of the Colonial South*. New York: Atheneum, 1966.

Brown, Letitia Woods. *Free Negroes in the District of Columbia, 1790–1846*. New York: Oxford University Press, 1972.

Brown, Stuart. *Virginia Baron: The Story of Thomas, Sixth Lord Fairfax*. Berryville, Va.: Chesapeake Book, 1965.

Burks, M. P. *Notes on the Property Rights of Married Women in Virginia*. Lynchburg: J. P. Bell, 1894.

Burton, Orville Vernon. *In My Father's House Are Many Mansions: Family and Community in Edgefield, South Carolina*. Chapel Hill: University of North Carolina Press, 1985.

Bushnell, David. *The Manahoac Tribes of Virginia, 1608*. Washington, D.C.: Smithsonian Institution, 1935.

Bynum, Victoria. *Unruly Women: The Politics of Social and Sexual Control in the Old South*. Chapel Hill: University of North Carolina Press, 1992.

Cash, Wilbur J. *The Mind of the South*. New York: Alfred A. Knopf, 1941.

Censer, Jane Turner. *North Carolina Planters and Their Children, 1800–1860*. Baton Rouge: Louisiana State University Press, 1984.

Clinton, Catherine. *The Plantation Mistress: Woman's World in the Old South*. New York: Pantheon Books,1982.

Cott, Nancy. *The Bonds of Womanhood: Woman's Sphere in New England*. New Haven: Yale University Press, 1978.

Cresson, W. P. *James Monroe*. Chapel Hill: University of North Carolina Press, 1964.

Curtin, Philip D. *The Atlantic Slave Trade: A Census*. Madison: University of Wisconsin Press, 1969.

Davies, K. G. *The Royal African Company*. London: Longman Group, 1957; New York: Atheneum, 1970.

Davis, Richard Beale. *Intellectual Life in Jefferson's Virginia, 1790–1830*. Chapel Hill: University of North Carolina Press, 1946.

Degler, Carl N. *At Odds: Women and the Family in America from the Revolution to the Present*. New York: Oxford University Press, 1980.

Demos, John. *Past, Present, and Personal: The Family and the Life Course in American History*. New York: Oxford University Press, 1986.

Dennis, Matthew. *Cultivating a Landscaped Peace: Iroquois-European Encounters in Seventeenth Century America*. Ithaca: Cornell University Press, 1993.

Dumond, Dwight Lowell. *Antislavery: The Crusade for Freedom in America*. New York: W. W. Norton, 1975.

Eaton, Clement. *The Growth of Southern Civilization*. New York: Atheneum, 1969.

Egerton, Douglas R. *Charles Fenton Mercer and the Trial of National Conservatism*. Jackson: University Press of Mississippi, 1989.

Elkins, Stanley. *Slavery: A Problem in American Institutional and Intellectual Life*. Chicago: University of Chicago Press, 1959.

Faderman, Lillian. *Surpassing the Love of Men: Romantic Friendship and Love between Women from the Renaissance to the Present*. New York: William Morrow, 1981.

Falkus, Christopher. *The Life and Times of Charles II*. Garden City, N.Y.: Doubleday, 1972.

Fauquier County, Virginia Historical Notes. Warrenton, Va.: Warrenton Printing, 1914.

Fisher, Miles Mark. *Negro Slave Songs in the United States*. New York: First Carol Publishing, 1990.

Fitzgerald, Ruth Coder. *A Different Story: A Black History of Fredericksburg, Stafford, and Spotsylvania, Virginia*. Fredericksburg, Va.: Unicorn Press, 1979.

Fogel, Robert. *Without Consent or Contract: The Rise and Fall of American Slavery*. New York: W.W. Norton, 1989.

Fox-Genovese, Elizabeth. *Within the Plantation Household: Black and White Women of the Old South*. Chapel Hill: University of North Carolina Press, 1988.

Franklin, John Hope. *The Free Negro in North Carolina, 1790–1860*. Chapel Hill: University of North Carolina Press, 1943; New York: W. W. Norton, 1971.

Friedman, Jean E. *The Enclosed Garden: Women and Community in the Evangelical*

South, 1830–1900. Chapel Hill: University of North Carolina Press, 1985.

Frothingham, Octavius B. *Gerrit Smith: A Biography.* New York: G. P. Putnam's Sons, 1878; New York: Negro Universities Press, 1969.

Genovese, Eugene. *Roll, Jordan, Roll: The World the Slaves Made.* New York: Pantheon, 1974.

Goldin, Claudia. *Urban Slavery in the American South, 1820–1860: A Quantitative History.* Chicago: University of Chicago Press, 1976.

Green, Lorenzo, and Carter Woodson, *The Negro Wage Earner.* Washington, D.C.: Association for the Study of Negro Life and History, 1930.

Greene, Jack P. *Landon Carter: An Inquiry into the Personal Values and Social Imperatives of the Eighteenth-Century Virginia Gentry.* Charlottesville, Va.: University Press of Virginia, 1967.

Gregg, Larry Dale. *Migration in Early America: The Virginia Quaker Experience.* Ann Arbor: University of Michigan Microfilm International, 1978.

Greven, Philip J., Jr. *Childrearing Concepts, 1728–1861: Historical Sources.* Itasco, Ill.: F.E. Peacock, 1973.

Groves, Ernest R. *The American Woman: The Feminine Side of a Masculine Civilization.* New York: Greenberg Publishers, 1937.

Gutman, Herbert. *The Black Family in Slavery and Freedom, 1750–1925.* New York: Pantheon, 1976.

Harlow, Ralph Volney. *Gerrit Smith: Philanthropist and Reformer.* New York: H. Holt, 1939.

Head, James V. *History and Comprehensive Description of Loudoun County, Virginia.* Leesburg, Va.: Park View Press, 1908.

Herskovits, Melville J. *The Myth of the Negro Past.* Boston: Beacon Press, 1941.

Hillsboro: Memories of a Mill Town. Hillsboro: Bicentennial Committee, 1976.

Hiner, Ray N., and Joseph Hawes, *Growing Up in America: Children in Historical Perspective.* Urbana: University of Illinois Press, 1985.

Jackson, Luther P. *Free Negro Labor and Property Holding in Virginia, 1830–1860.* 1942; New York: Atheneum, 1969.

Jones, Jacqueline. *Labor of Love, Labor of Sorrow: Black Women, Work and the Family from Slavery to the Present.* New York: Basic Books, 1985.

Kercheval, Samuel. *A History of the Valley of Virginia.* Strasburg, Va.: Valley Press, 1925.

Kett, Joseph F. *Rites of Passage: Adolescence in America, 1790 to the Present.* New York: Basic Books, 1977.

Kulikoff, Allan. *Tobacco and Slaves: The Development of Southern Cultures in the Chesapeake, 1680–1800.* Chapel Hill: University of North Carolina Press, 1986.

Lasch, Christopher. *Haven in a Heartless World.* New York: Oxford University Press, 1977.

Lebsock, Suzanne. *The Free Women of Petersburg: Status and Culture in a Southern Town, 1784–1860.* New York: W. W. Norton, 1984.

Lee, Marguerite DuPont. *Virginia Ghosts.* Berryville, Va.: Virginia Book Company, 1966.

Levine, Lawrence. *Black Culture and Black Consciousness: Afro-American Folk Thought from Slavery to Freedom.* New York: Oxford University Press, 1977.

Lewis, Jan. *The Pursuit of Happiness: Family and Values in Jefferson's Virginia*. Cambridge: Cambridge University Press, 1983.

Litwack, Leon. *North of Slavery: The Negro in the Free States, 1790–1860*. Chicago: University of Chicago Press, 1961.

McColley, Robert. *Slavery and Jeffersonian Virginia*. 2nd ed. Urbana: University of Illinois Press, 1978.

McWhiney, Grady. *Cracker Culture: Celtic Ways in the Old South*. Tuscaloosa: University of Alabama Press, 1988.

Malone, Ann Patton. *Sweet Chariot: Slave Family and Household Structure in Nineteenth Century Louisiana*. Chapel Hill: University of North Carolina Press, 1992.

Matthei, Julie. *An Economic History of Women in America: Women's Work, the Sexual Division of Labor and the Development of Capitalism*. New York: Schocken Books, 1982.

Mbiti, John S. *African Religions and Philosophy*. Garden City: Doubleday, 1970.

Morgan, Edmund. *American Slavery, American Freedom: The Ordeal of Colonial Virginia*. New York: W. W. Norton, 1975.

Morris, Caspar. *Memoir of Miss Margaret Mercer*. Philadelphia: Lindsay and Blakiston, 1848.

Morton, Louis. *Robert Carter of Nomini Hall: A Virginia Tobacco Planter of the Eighteenth Century*. Charlottesville, Va.: University Press of Virginia, 1964.

Moynihan, Daniel P. *The Negro Family: The Case for National Action*. Washington, D.C.: United States Department of Labor, Office of Policy Planning and Research, 1965.

Mullin, Gerald W. *Flight and Rebellion: Slave Resistance in Eighteenth-Century Virginia*. New York: Oxford University Press, 1975.

Munford, Beverley B. *Virginia's Attitude Toward Slavery and Secession*. New York: Longmans, Green, 1909.

The Negro in Virginia. Compiled by the Writer's Program of the Work Projects Administration in the State of Virginia. New York: Hastings Publishers, 1940.

Nelson, Truman. *The Old Man: John Brown at Harper's Ferry*. New York: Holt, Rinehart and Winston, 1973.

Netherton, Nan, Donald Sweig, Janice Artemel, Patricia Hickin, and Patrick Reed, *Fairfax County, Virginia: A History*. Fairfax: Fairfax County Board of Supervisors, 1978.

Nichols, Joseph V. *Legends of Loudoun Valley: True Stories from the Lives and Times of the People of Loudoun County, Virginia*. Leesburg, Va.: Potomac Press, 1961.

Osburn, Penelope M. *The Story of Middleburg, Virginia, 1787–1958*. Middleburg, Va.: Middleburg National Bank, 1958.

Osterweis, Rollin. *Romanticism and Nationalism in the Old South*. Gloucester, Mass.: L. Peter Smith, 1964.

Painter, F. V. N. *Poets of Virginia*. Atlanta: B. F. Johnson, 1907.

Paulme, Denise. *Women of Tropical Africa*. Translated H. M. Wright. Paris: Mouton, 1960; Berkeley: University of California Press, 1974.

Pearson, Heskety. *Charles II: His Life and Likeness*. London: Heinemann, 1960.

Pease, Jane H. and William H. *The Fugitive Slave Law and Anthony Burns: A Problem in*

Law Enforcement. Philadelphia: J. B. Lippincott, 1975.

Phillips, Ulrich B. *American Negro Slavery: A Survey of the Supply, Employment and Control of Negro Labor as Determined by the Plantation Regime.* New York: D. Appleton, 1918; Baton Rouge: Louisiana State University Press, 1966.

Poland, Charles Jr. *From Frontier to Suburbia.* Maceline, Mo.: Walsworth, 1976.

Postell, William D. *The Health of Slaves on Southern Plantations.* Baton Rouge: Louisiana University Press, 1951.

Raboteau, Albert. *Slave Religion: The "Invisible Institution" in the Antebellum South.* New York: Oxford University Press, 1978.

Riley, Sam G. *Magazines of the American South.* New York: Greenwood Press, 1972.

Ritter, Halsted L. *Washington as a Businessman.* New York: Sears, Inc., 1931.

Robins, Sally Nelson. *Love Stories of Famous Virginians.* Richmond: Dietz, 1925.

Rouse, Parke Jr. *Virginia: A Pictorial History.* New York: Charles Scribner's Sons, 1975.

Salmon, Emily J., ed. *Hornbook of Virginia History.* Richmond: Virginia State Library, 1983.

Salmon, Marylynn. *Women and the Law of Property in Early America.* Chapel Hill: University of North Carolina Press, 1986.

Savitt, Todd. *Medicine and Slavery in Virginia: The Diseases and Health Care of Blacks in Antebellum Virginia.* Urbana: University of Illinois Press, 1978.

Scheel, Eugene M. *L'Auberge in Middleburg, Virginia: A New and Accurate History of this House, Built for Noble Beveridge in 1824.* Warrenton, Va.: Warrenton Printing and Publishing, 1977.

_____. *The Guide to Loudoun: A Survey of the Architecture and History of a Virginia County.* Leesburg, Va.: Potomac Press, 1975.

_____. *The History of Middleburg and Vicinity.* Warrenton, Va.: Piedmont Press, 1987.

_____. *A History of Saint John the Apostle Church, Leesburg, and the Catholic Faith in Loudoun County, Virginia.* Leesburg, Va.: Saint John the Apostle Church, 1978.

_____. *The Story of Purcellville, Loudoun County, Virginia.* Warrenton, Va.: Warrenton Printing and Publishing, 1977.

Scholten, Catherine M. *Childrearing in American Society: 1650–1850.* New York: New York University Press, 1985.

Scott, Anne Firor. *The Southern Lady: From Pedestal to Politics, 1830–1930.* Chicago: University of Chicago Press, 1970.

Sheehan, Bernard. *Savagism and Civility: Indians and Englishmen in Colonial Virginia.* Cambridge: Cambridge University Press, 1980.

Siebert, Wilbur H. *The Underground Railraod from Slavery to Freedom.* New York: Russell and Russell, 1898.

Slaughter, Philip. *The History of Truro Parish in Virginia.* Philadelphia: George W. Jacobs, 1908.

Smith, Daniel Blake. *Inside the Great House: Planter Family Life in Eighteenth-Century Chesapeake Society.* Ithaca, N.Y.: Cornell University Press, 1980.

Sobel, Mechal. *The World They Made Together: Black and White Values in Eighteenth-Century Virginia.* Princeton: Princeton University Press, 1987.

Soderlund, Jean R. *Quakers and Slavery: A Divided Spirit.* Princeton: Princeton University Press, 1985.

Spruill, Julia. *Women's Life and Work in the Southern Colonies*. 1938. Reprint. New York: Vintage Books, 1956.

Stowe, Steven M. *Intimacy and Power in the Old South: Ritual in the Lives of Planters*. Baltimore: John Hopkins University Press, 1987.

Stuckey, Sterling. *Slave Culture: Nationalist Theory and the Foundations of Black America*. New York: Oxford University Press, 1987.

Styron, Arthur. *The Last of the Cocked Hats: James Monroe & the Virginia Dynasty*. Norman: University of Oklahoma Press, 1945.

Templeman, Eleanor Lee, and Nan Netherton. *Northern Virginia Heritage: A Pictorial Compilation of the Historic Sites and Homes in the Counties of Arlington, Fairfax, Loudoun, Fauquier, Prince William and Stafford and in the Cities of Alexandria and Fredricksburg*. Arlington: Eleanor Templeman, 1966.

Thornton, John. *Africa and Africans in the Making of the Atlantic World, 1400–1680*. Cambridge: Cambridge University Press, 1992.

Turner, Lorenzo. *Africanisms in the Gullah Dialect*. Chicago: University of Chicago Press, 1949.

Vass, Winifred. *The Bantu Speaking Heritage of the United States*. Los Angeles: Center for Afro-American Studies, 1979.

Vlach, John Michael. *By the Work of their Hands: Studies in Afro-American Folklife*. Charlottesville: University Press of Virginia, 1991.

Wall, Charles Cecil. *George Washington: Citizen-Soldier*. Charlottesville: University Press of Virginia, 1980.

Warbasse, Elizabeth. *The Changing Legal Rights of Married Women, 1800–1861*. New York: Oxford University Press, 1987.

Weatherly, Yetive. *Lovettsville: The German Settlement*. Lovettsville, Va.: Lovettsville Bicentennial Committee, 1976.

Webber, Thomas L. *Deep like the Rivers: Education in the Slave Quarter Community, 1831–1865*. New York: W. W. Norton, 1978.

Wesley, Charles H. *Negro Labor in the United States, 1850–1925; A Study in American Economic History*. New York: Vanguard Press, 1927.

White, Deborah Gray. *Ar'n't I a Woman?: Female Slaves in the Plantation South*. New York: W. W. Norton and Company,1985.

Williams, Harrison. *Legends of Loudoun: An Account of the History and Homes of a Border County of Virginia's Northern Neck*. Richmond: Garrett and Massie, 1938.

Williamson, Joel. *New People: Miscegenation and Mulattoes in the United States*. New York: Free Press, 1980.

Wilmerding, Lucius Jr. *James Monroe: Public Claimant*. New Brunswick: Rutgers University Press, 1960.

Wilson, John. *Fairfax: A Life of Thomas, Lord Fairfax, Captain General of all the Parliament Forces in the English Civil War, Creator and Commander of the New Model Army*. London: J. Murray, 1985.

Wust, Klaus. *The Virginia Germans*. Charlottesville: University Press of Virginia, 1969.

Wyatt-Brown, Bertram. *Southern Honor: Ethics and Behavior in the Old South*. New York: Oxford University Press, 1982.

Dissertations and Theses

Hickin, Patricia. "Antislavery in Virginia, 1832–1860." Ph.D. dissertation, University of Virginia, 1968.

McMillen, Sally G. "Women's Sacred Occupation: Pregnancy, Childbirth, and Early Infant Rearing in the Antebellum South." Ph.D. dissertation, Duke University, 1985.

Sweig, Donald. "Free Negroes in Northern Virginia: An Investigation of the Growth and Status of Free Negroes in the Counties of Alexandria, Fairfax and Loudoun, 1770–1860." M.A. thesis, George Mason University, 1975.

————. "Northern Virginia Slavery: A Statistical and Demographic Investigation." Ph.D. dissertation, College of William and Mary, 1982.

Articles, Book Chapters, Research Papers

Benson, T. Lloyd. "The Plain Folk of Orange: Land, Work, and Society on the Eve of the Civil War." In *The Edge of the South: Life in Nineteenth-Century Virginia*, edited by Edward L. Ayers and John C. Willis, 56–78. Charlottesville: University Press of Virginia, 1991.

Berlin, Ira. "The Slave Trade and the Development of Afro-American Society in English Mainland North America, 1619–1775." *Southern Studies* 20, no. 2 (Summer 1981): 122–36.

Bloch, Ruth H. "American Feminine Ideals in Transition: The Rise of the Moral Mother, 1785–1815." *Feminist Studies* 4, no. 2 (June 1978): 100–126.

Brown, Jean Collier. "The Economic Status of Negro Women." *Southern Workman* 60, no. 10 (Oct. 1931): 430–31.

Brown, Stuart E. "Manors on the Frontier: The Northern Neck Was a Feudal Grant in Virginia." *Virginia Cavalcade* 16, no. 1 (Winter 1967): 42–47.

Busia, K.A. "The Ashanti of the Gold Coast." In *African Worlds: Studies in the Cosmological Ideals and Social Values of African Peoples,* edited by Daryll Forde, 190–209. Oxford: Oxford University Press, 1954, 1991.

Campbell, John. "Work, Pregnancy, and Infant Mortality among Southern Slaves." *Journal of Interdisciplinary History* 14 (Spring 1984): 793–812.

Cashin, Joan E. "The Structure of Antebellum Planter Families: 'The Ties That Bound Us Was Strong.'" *Journal of Southern History* 56, no. 1 (Feb. 1990): 55–70.

Censer, Jane Turner. "Smiling Through Her Tears: Antebellum Southern Women and Divorce." *American Journal of Legal History* 25, no. 1(Jan. 1981): 24–47.

Cody, Cheryll Ann. "There Was No 'Absalom' on the Ball Plantations: Slave-Naming Practices in the South Carolina Low Country, 1720–1865." *American Historical Review* 92, no. 2 (June 1987): 563–96.

"Col. R. E. Lee's Report, 19 October 1859." *Virginia Magazine of History and Biography* 10 (July 1902–April 1903): 18–25.

Cook, Mercer. "The Cook Family in History." *Negro History Bulletin* 9, no. 6 (June 1946): 214–15.

"Coton." *Bulletin of the Loudoun County Historical Society* 5 (1975): 14–15.

Cott, Nancy. "Divorce and the Changing Status of Women in Eighteenth Century

Massachusetts." *William and Mary Quarterly* 3rd ser., 33, no. 4 (Oct. 1976): 586–614.

————. "Eighteenth-Century Family and Social Life Revealed in Massachusetts Divorce Records." *Journal of Social History* 10, no. 3 (Fall 1976): 20–43.

Craton, Michael. "Changing Patterns of Slave Families in the British West Indies." *Journal of Interdisciplinary History* 10 (Summer 1979): 1–35.

Day, Randal, and Daniel Hook, "A Short History of Divorce: Jumping the Broom— And Back Again." *Journal of Divorce* 10, no. 3/4 (Spring/Summer 1987): 57–63.

Diedrich, Maria. "'My Love Is as Black as Yours is Fair': Premarital Love and Sexuality in the Antebellum Slave Narrative." *Phylon* 47 (Sept. 1986): 238–47.

Douglass, Mary. "The Lele of Kasai." In *African Worlds: Studies in the Cosmological Ideals and Social Values of African Peoples,* edited by Daryll Forde, 1–26. Oxford: Oxford University Press, 1954, 1991.

Gordon, Michael. "The Husband as Depicted in the Nineteenth-Century Marriage Manual." In *The American Man*, edited by Elizabeth Pleck and Joseph Pleck, 147–57. Englewood Cliffs, N.J.: Prentice-Hall, 1980.

Griaule, Marcel. "The Dogon of the French Sudan" (translated). In *African Worlds: Studies in the Cosmological Ideals and Social Values of African Peoples,* edited by Daryll Forde, 83–110. Oxford: Oxford University Press, 1954, 1991.

Griswold, Robert L. "Sexual Cruelty and the Case for Divorce in Victorian America." *Signs* 11, no. 3 (Spring 1986): 529–41.

Gundersen, Joan, and Gwen Victor Gampel. "Married Women's Legal Status in Eighteenth Century New York and Virginia." *William and Mary Quarterly* 3rd ser., 39, no. 1 (Jan. 1982): 114–34.

Hagler, D. Harland. "The Ideal Woman in the Antebellum South: Lady or Farmwife." *Journal of Southern History* 46, no. 3 (Aug. 1980): 405–18.

Hancock, Ian. "The Domestic Hypothesis, Diffusion and Componentiality: An Account of Atlantic Anglophone Creole Origins." In *Substrata versus Universals in Creole Genesis*, edited by Pieter Muysken and Norval Smith, 71–107. Amsterdam: John Benjamins, 1986.

————. "Gullah and Barbadian-Origins and Relationships." *American Speech* 55, no. 1 (Jan. 1980): 17–35.

Harrison, Fairfax. "Parson Waugh's Tumult." *Virginia Magazine of History and Biography* 30 (1922): 31–37.

Hartgrove, W. B. "The Story of Maria Louise Moore and Fannie M. Richards." *Journal of Negro History* 1, no. 1 (Jan. 1916): 23–33.

Heininger, Mary Lynn Stevens. "Children, Childhood, and Change in America, 1820–1920." In *Century of Childhood, 1820–1920*. Rochester: Margaret Woodbury Strong Museum, 1984.

Hershberg, Theodore."Free Blacks in Antebellum Philadelphia: A Study of Ex-Slaves, Freeborn, and Socio-Economic Decline." *Journal of Social History* 5, no. 2 (Spring 1972): 183–209.

Horton, James O. "Freedom's Yoke: Gender Convention among Antebellum Free Blacks." *Feminist Studies* 12, no. 2 (Spring 1986): 51–76.

Jackson, Luther P. "The Daniel Family of Virginia." *Negro History Bulletin* 11, no. 12 (Dec. 1947): 51–58.

Jenson, Carol Elizabeth. "The Equity Jurisdiction and Married Women's Property in Ante-bellum America: A Revisionist View." *International Journal of Women's Studies* 2, no. 2 (March-April 1979): 144–54.

"The John Brown Letters." *Virginia Magazine of History and Biography* 9 (July 1901–April 1902): 285–95; 10 (July 1902–April 1903): 17–32, 161–76.

Johnson, Michael P. "Upward in Slavery." *New York Review of Books* 36, no. 20 (Nov. 21, 1989): 52–54.

Kett, Joseph F. "Adolescence and Youth in Nineteenth-Century America." *Journal of Interdisciplinary History* 2 (Autumn 1971): 283–98.

Kiple, Kenneth F. and Virginia H. "Slave Child Mortality: Some Nutritional Answers to a Perennial Puzzle." *Journal of Social History* 10, no. 3 (March 1977): 284–309.

Klein, Herbert S. "Slaves and Shipping in Eighteenth Century Virginia." *Journal of Interdisciplinary History* 3, no. 4 (Fall 1975): 383–412.

Kalikoff, Allan. "The Beginnings of the Afro-American Family in Maryland." In *Law, Society, and Politics in Early Maryland*, edited by Aubrey C. Land, Lois G. Carr, and Edward C. Paperfuse, 171–91. Baltimore: Maryland State Archives, 1977.

_____. "The Origins of Afro-American Society in Tidewater Maryland and Virginia, 1700 to 1790." *William and Mary Quarterly* 3rd ser., 35, no. 2 (April 1978): 226–59.

Lewis, Jan. "Domestic Tranquility and the Management of Emotion among the Gentry of Pre-Revolutionary Virginia." *William and Mary Quarterly*, 3rd ser., 39, no. 1 (Jan. 1982): 134–49.

Little, Kenneth. "The Mende in Sierra Leone." In *African Worlds: Studies in the Cosmological Ideals and Social Values of African Peoples,* edited by Daryll Forde, 111–37. Oxford: Oxford University Press, 1954, 1991.

McDaniel, Antonio. "Historical Racial Differences in Living Arrangements of Children." *Journal of Family History* 19, no. 1 (Winter 1994): 57–77.

McGlone, Robert G. "Rescripting a Troubled Past: John Brown's Family and the Harpers Ferry Conspiracy." *Journal of American History* 75, no. 4 (March 1989): 179–200.

McMillen, Sally. "Mother's Sacred Duty: Breast Feeding Patterns among Middle- and Upper-Class Women in the Antebellum South." *Journal of Southern History* 51, no. 3 (Aug. 1985): 333–56.

Manfra, Jo Ann, and Robert R. Dykstra, "Serial Marriage and the Origins of the Black Stepfamily: The Rowanty Evidence." *Journal of American History* 72, no. 1 (June 1985): 18–44.

Marks, Bayly. "Skilled Blacks in Antebellum St. Mary's County, Maryland." *Journal of Southern History* 53, no. 4 (Nov. 1987): 537–66.

Marsh, Helen Hirst. "The Loudoun Company." *Bulletin of the Loudoun County Historical Society* 3 (1962): 43–44.

Mercier, P. "The Fon of Dahomey" (translated). In *African Worlds: Studies in the Cosmological Ideals and Social Values of African Peoples,* edited by Daryll Forde, 210–34. Oxford: Oxford University Press, 1954, 1991.

Morgan, Philip. "Three Planters and Their Slaves: Perspectives on Slavery in Virginia, South Carolina, and Jamaica, 1750–1790. In *Race and Family in the Colonial South,* edited by Winthrop D. Jordan and Sheila Skemp, 37–80. Jackson: University Press of Mississippi, 1987.

Nicholls, Michael L. "Passing through This Troublesome World." *Virginia Magazine of History and Biography* 73, no. 4 (Oct. 1983): 50–70.

"Notes on Brooke-Powell Family." *Virginia Magazine of History and Biography* 15, no. 2 (June 1908): 201–3.

Okonjo, Kamene. "The Dual-Sex Political System in Operation: Igbo Women and Community Politics in Midwestern Nigeria." In *Women In Africa: Studies in Social and Economic Change*, edited by Nancy Hafkin and Edna Bay, 45–58. Stanford: Stanford University Press, 1976.

Pleck, Elizabeth. "Two Worlds in One." *Journal of Social History* 10, no. 2 (Spring 1976): 178–95.

Pogue, Dennis. "The Mount Vernon Blacksmith Shops." *Mount Vernon Ladies Association Annual Report, 1987*. Mount Vernon, Va.: Mount Vernon Ladies Association, 1988. N.p.

_____. "Slave Lifeways at Mount Vernon." In *Mount Vernon Ladies Association Annual Report, 1989*. Mount Vernon, Va.: Mount Vernon Ladies Association, 1990. N.p.

Porter, Dorothy. "The Organized Educational Activities of Negro Literary Societies." In *The Making of Black America: Essays in Negro Life and History*, vol. 1, *The Origins of Black Americans*, edited by August Meier and Elliott Rudwick, 276–88. New York: Atheneum, 1974.

Pugh, Evelyn. "Women and Slavery: Julia Gardiner Tyler and the Duchess of Sutherland." *Virginia Magazine of History and Biography* 88, no. 4 (April 1980): 186–202.

Robertson, Claire. "Ga Women and Socioeconomic Change in Accra, Ghana." In *Women in Africa: Studies in Social and Economic Change,* edited by Nancy J. Hafkin and Edna G. Bay, 111–34. Stanford: Stanford University Press, 1976.

Robinson, Henry S. "Descendants of Daniel and Hannah Bruce." *Negro History Bulletin* 24, no. 11 (Nov. 1960): 37–41.

Sale, Marian Marsh. "Old Waterford: Amos Janney's town has changed little in two hundred years." *Virginia Cavalcade* 18, no. 2 (Spring 1969): 13–14.

Salmon, Marylynn. "Women and Property in South Carolina: The Evidence from Marriage Settlements, 1730 to 1830." *William and Mary Quarterly,* 3rd ser., 39, no. 3 (Oct. 1982): 655–85.

Scott, Anne Firor. "Women's Perspective on the Patriarchy in the 1850's." *Journal of American History* 61, no.1 (July 1974): 52–64.

Settle, E. Ophelia. "Social Attitudes During the Slave Regime: Household Servants versus Field Hands." In *The Making of Black America: Essays in Negro Life and History,* vol. 1, *The Origins of Black Americans*, edited by August Meier and Elliott Rudwick, 148–52. New York: Atheneum, 1974.

Smith, Daniel Blake. "In Search of the Family in the Colonial South." In *Race and Family in the Colonial South,* edited by Winthrop D. Jordan and Sheila Skemp, 21–36. Jackson: University Press of Mississippi, 1987.

Smith, M. G. "The African Heritage in the Caribbean." *Caribbean Studies, a Symposium* (1961): 35–53.

Smith-Rosenberg, Carroll. "Beauty, the Beast, and the Militant Woman: A Case Study in Sex Roles and Social Stress in Jacksonian America." *American Quarterly* 23, no. 4 (Oct. 1971): 562–84.

Steckel, Richard. "Slave Mortality: Analysis of Evidence from Plantation Records." *Social Science History* 3, no. 3 (Oct. 1979): 86–114.

Stevenson, Brenda E. "Compassion and Powerlessness: Myths and Realities of the Plantation Mistress' Relationship with Slaves." Paper presented at the Virginia Center for the Humanities Winter/Spring Colloquia, Charlottesville, June 5, 1990.

————. "Distress and Discord in Virginia Slave Families, 1830–1860." In *In Joy and In Sorrow: Women, Family and Marriage in the Victorian South, 1830–1900*, edited by Carol Bleser, 103–24, 293–97. New York: Oxford University Press, 1990.

————. "Historical Dimension of Black Family Structure: A Revisionist Perspective of the Black Family." In *The Decline in Marriage Among African-Americans: Causes, Consequences and Policy Implications*, edited by Belinda Tucker and Claudia K. Mitchell, 27–56. New York: Russell Sage, 1995.

Stuckert, Robert P. "Free Black Populations of the Southern Appalachian Mountains: 1860." *Journal of Black Studies* 23, no. 3 (March 1993): 358–70.

Sunley, Robert. "Early Nineteenth Century Literature on Child Rearing." In *Childhood in Contemporary Cultures*, edited by Margaret Mead and Martha Wolfenstein. Chicago: University of Chicago Press, 1955.

Sutch, Richard "The Breeding of Slaves for Sale and the Westward Expansion of Slavery, 1850–1860." In *Race and Slavery in the Western Hemisphere: Quantitative Studies*, edited by Stanley Engerman and Eugene Genovese, 173–210. Princeton: Princeton University Press, 1975.

Tanner, Nancy. "Matrifocality in Indonesia and Africa and Among Black Americans." In *Woman, Culture and Society*, edited by Michelle Rosaldo and Louise Lamphere, 129–56. Stanford: Stanford University Press, 1974.

Thomson, Mary V. "Christmas at Mount Vernon." *Mount Vernon Ladies Association Annual Report, 1990*. Mount Vernon, Va.: Mount Vernon Ladies Association, 1991. N.p.

Trout, W. E. "The Goose Creek and Little River Navigation." *Virginia Cavalcade* 16, no.1 (Winter 1967): 31–32.

Trussel, James, and Richard Steckel, "The Age of Slaves at Menarche and Their First Birth." *Journal of Interdisciplinary History* 8, no. 4 (Winter 1978): 477–505.

Welter, Barbara. "The Cult of True Womanhood: 1800–1860." *American Quarterly* 18, no. 2 (March 1966): 151–74.

White, Deborah Gray. "Female Slaves: Sex Roles and Status in the Antebellum Plantation South." *Journal of Family History* 3, no. 3 (Fall 1983): 248–61.

White, Shane. "'We Dwell in Safety and Pursue Our Honest Callings': Free Blacks in New York City, 1783–1810." *Journal of American History* 75, no. 2 (Sept. 1988): 445–70.

Williams, Jeffrey P. "Women and Kinship in Creole Genesis." *International Journal of Social Language* 71, no. 2 (Spring 1988): 81–89.

Woodson, Carter G. "The Waring Family." *Negro History Bulletin* 11, no. 2 (Feb. 1948): 99–107.

INDEX